Elizabeth I

Elizabeth I

a study in power and intellect

Paul Johnson

Weidenfeld and Nicolson
London

First published in paperback in Great Britain in 1988 by
George Weidenfeld & Nicolson Limited
91 Clapham High Street, London SW4 7TA

British Library Cataloguing in Publication Data

Johnson, Paul, *1928–*
Elizabeth I: a study in power and
intellect.
1. England. Elizabeth I, Queen of
England, 1553–1603
I. Title
942.05′5′0924

ISBN 0–297–79488–4

Printed and bound in Great Britain by
Butler & Tanner Ltd, Frome and London

Contents

To My Mother

Her Father's Daughter
(1533–1547)

In 1535, when the future Queen Elizabeth was a child of two, Stephen Gardiner, Bishop of Winchester – a man who grew to hate her, and whom she feared until his death – published his *Sermon on True Obedience*, in which he spoke of the role of sovereigns in the divine providence:

> Indeed, God, according to his exceeding great and unspeakable goodness towards mankind . . . substituted men, who, being put in authority as his viceregents, should require obedience which we must do unto them with no less fruit for God's sake than we should do (what honour soever it were) immediately unto God himself. And in that place he hath set princes, whom, as representatives of his Image unto men, he would have to be reputed in the supreme and most high room, and to excell among all other creatures.[1]

Five years before, the great Renaissance scholar Erasmus, whom Elizabeth never met but who exercised an imponderable influence over her fortunes, reflected gloomily on the bitter religious dissents of his day, and the difficulty of knowing God's true will, even as transmitted through his princely viceregents. He accurately predicted: 'The long war of words and writings will terminate in blows.'[2]

Here, then, we have the two themes which, interlocking and reacting on one another, were to dominate the life and reign of Elizabeth. On the one hand was the theme of kingship, supreme in the secular world, but dispensing wide, if debatable, powers on the way in which men and women were organized spiritually, and thus on their eternal destinies. On the other hand was the theme of religious truth: if the monarch were to determine it, in an age when men were fiercely divided on what it was, how was the throne to be kept above the debate, in origins religious, but increasingly political in its implications? Must not the religious dispute thus degenerate into civil war? And, if one section triumphed in one state, and its rival in another, must not the conflict internationalize itself, and engulf the civilized world?

In truth, the arguments about religious and secular ideology could not be separated. This was the problem which confronted Elizabeth, a woman who, by temperament and conviction, sought peace above all other objects. In tackling it she became, and remained, a liberal conservative. The power of the throne, vested in her person, must be conserved, but buttressed by the judicious and timely acceptance of liberal ideas; the authority of religion, for which the throne was ultimately responsible, must be conserved too, but made acceptable by the liberality of its exercise. This was her alternative formula to chaos, which she pursued with a tenacity concealed by ambivalence and hesitation, but which sprang from a deep conviction that it was the only way.

Such a formula cannot be made to work by the mere use of force; it demands persuasion too. Elizabeth's reign is thus a story of how authority is preserved, and civil peace maintained, by the application of intellect. It is, in fact, the story of a royal intellectual – but of an intellectual fascinated not by the abstract powers of mind, but by its practical ability to influence persons and events. It is also a story of success. Human societies are always faced by crises, of greater or lesser magnitude. In dealing with them, the essence of statecraft is to win a breathing space, during which more permanent solutions can evolve through the interplay of many intellects. No more can fairly be asked of any single statesman, or stateswoman. If this is a true definition of the duties of a ruler, Elizabeth may be said to have fulfilled them.

The origins of Elizabeth's birth, on 7 September 1533, lay in the fragility of the Tudor claim to the throne, and the nature of the English monarchy. This monarchy, as it had evolved in the Middle Ages, was consultative. The king was in theory an unfettered chief executive, but in practice reigned by the advice and consent of his subjects. His ability to maintain himself in power was thus limited by the accident of events, and the success of his policies. With such an ambiguous constitution, vaguely defined at its core, but increasingly specified at its periphery by a mass of parliamentary statutes, the strength of the monarch's claim to the throne was an important factor. And the Tudor claim was weak. It rested, in all essentials, on victory in battle and confirmation by parliament.[3] The Tudors were an old north Welsh family which rose from obscurity in the fourteenth century.[4] Owen Tudor (c. 1400–61) became a page in, or near, the household of Henry v, subsequently a gentleman-attendant to his widow, Catherine of Valois, and finally her husband. The date of the marriage is not known; it was contracted secretly and, though almost certainly canonically valid, it was some time before it received the political sanction of the authorities, that is, the granting to Owen Tudor of English citizenship.[5] In any case, this marriage was constitutionally irrelevant, for neither Catherine nor her heirs could have any claim to the throne. What it did, however, was to bring the Tudors into political prominence, as members of the Lancastrian faction. The eldest son of the marriage, Edmund Tudor (*c*. 1430–56), was made Earl of Richmond in 1452, and, more significantly, granted custody of the Plantagenet heiress, Margaret Beaufort. He married her as soon as she was physically capable of the act of consummation, about six months before he died in November 1456. Three months later, aged thirteen, Margaret gave birth to a son, the future Henry VII.

Margaret's claim was distant, and marked by dubieties. She was the great-great-grandchild of Edward III. But then, so were many other people. Moreover, she claimed descent through Katherine Swynford, mistress and subsequently third wife of Edward's son John of Gaunt, a marriage which parliament thought it necessary to validate by statute under Richard II. There was also some doubt about her own marriage to Edmund Tudor, for as an infant she had been previously married, nominally, to John de la Pole.[6] This marriage had been dissolved, but it might subsequently be made the basis of a claim against Henry VII's legitimacy, and thus of his right to the throne. But swords spoke louder than genealogies in fifteenth-century England. Henry killed the incumbent king, Richard III, won the Battle of Bosworth, and parliament confirmed his accession. He strengthened his position by marrying Elizabeth of York, eldest surviving child and heiress of Edward IV. Her legitimacy, too, was in doubt, and the marriage required a dispensation; but parliament and papacy swiftly moved to clear away these obstacles, and thus the houses of York and Lancaster were united.[7] Eight children were born, one of the survivors to become Henry VIII.

The Tudor succession thus seemed reasonably secure, but it was never as solid as it looked. The confusion caused by the extraordinary philoprogenitive capacity of Edward III and his sons, compounded by the inability of the Church to define exactly how a legal marriage could be contracted, continued to plague Henry VII, his son and his grandchildren. There were always shadows on the Tudor title, which lengthened immediately domestic crisis threatened. This explains much of the legal butchery carried out by Tudor sovereigns against members of the ruling class. Not all those with claims even attempted to press them. Some, indeed, tried to conceal them, preferring the quiet life of an aristocrat to the risk of the Tower, or the block, or both. But others might be eager on their behalf, and a claim, however dormant, was always a threat. By the mid-century there were four groups: Yorkists, Lancastrians, Stuarts and the foreigners. Of the Yorkists, Henry VII had stopped one claim by executing the

Earl of Warwick in 1499. Henry VIII dealt with others by beheading the Earl of Suffolk in 1513, the Marquess of Exeter in 1539, and the Countess of Salisbury and her son, Lord Montague, in 1541. Montague's celibate brother, Cardinal Pole, of course died without issue, but their sister Ursula married Henry, Lord Stafford, and this was another line of claim. Against the Lancastrians, Henry VIII carried on the demolition work by beheading the Duke of Buckingham (who had a double claim) in 1521 – perhaps the most serious threat of all for Buckingham was the last of the great Welsh marcher lords. Henry killed the Lancastrian Earl of Surrey in 1546, and only the King's own death saved Surrey's father, the 3rd Duke of Norfolk, by a few hours; it was left to Elizabeth herself, with agonizing reluctance, to execute his grandson, the 4th Duke, in 1572.

Moreover, the Tudors, anxious as they were to consolidate their line, added to the confusion themselves by marrying and begetting. It was the marriage of Henry VII's daughter Margaret to James IV of Scotland which set up the Stuart claim, relentlessly upheld by their grand-daughter, Mary Queen of Scots. Moreover, Margaret married again, the marriage leading in time to two grandchild-claimants, Lord Darnley and the Earl of Lennox. Darnley doubled up his claim by marrying Mary Queen of Scots – thereby producing the eventual winner, James I – and Lennox sired a daughter, Arabella Stuart, who married into the dangerous Seymour family, mercifully without issue. There was a further group produced by Queen Elizabeth's aunt, Mary, who married as her second husband Charles Brandon, Duke of Suffolk. Their daughter, Frances, carried the claim to her husband, the Marquess of Dorset. He was executed in 1554, along with his daughter Lady Jane Grey, but Lady Jane's surviving sisters posed threats and spent long years in prison. One of them, Catherine, foolishly and secretly married the Earl of Hertford (another Seymour), and it was their grandson who married Arabella Stuart, thus producing a further double claim. More remote pretensions could also be proffered, if they chose, by the Earls of Huntingdon, Westmorland and Derby, and there was, finally, a foreign claim, springing from the marriage of John of Gaunt's daughter Philippa, into the Braganzas, the royal house of Portugal, which eventually devolved, in 1580, on no less a person than Philip II of Spain. These complex patterns of descents and marriages are tedious to describe,[8] but they fascinated contemporaries and disturbed the night-thoughts of successive Tudor monarchs.

Henry VIII was fortunate in that he succeeded to the throne as the sole remaining, and adult, son of a powerful and much respected king. He devoted a great deal of his life to creating a similar certitude for his own male successor (and eventually failed). By the mid-1520s it was evident that his wife, Catherine of Aragon, who had produced a live daughter, Mary, was no longer capable of giving him a son, or indeed any other child. She was five years his senior: in 1527, he was thirty-five, she was over forty and they had long ceased to cohabit. The incapacity was not his. In about 1514 he had taken a mistress, Elizabeth Blount, and in 1519 she had borne him a son, created Duke of Richmond.[9] Henry's health was reasonably normal. By this date he was probably already suffering from osteomylitis, a disease of the bone, induced in his case by frequent falls from jousting and leading to an open and painful ulcer in the leg. A further fall in 1536, at his last joust, may have produced some brain damage.[10] But he was not a victim of syphilis: there is not a scrap of contemporary evidence to this effect, nor the slightest rumour put about by his many and vociferous enemies. Indeed the suggestion was first made as recently as 1888.[11]

Henry's problem was quite different: he had a conscience. It was eccentric, even *sui generis*, but powerful and persistent. Despite his extra-marital affairs, of which we know at least three, Henry was not a monster of lust. In some ways he was a Puritan. He disliked smut and any kind of obscene talk.[12] His elder brother, Prince Arthur, the heir, lived to the age of fifteen. Until Arthur's death, Henry may have been intended by his father for the Archbishopric of Canterbury or some other high clerical post, and have thus been educated on ecclesiastical lines.[13] At all events, he displayed throughout his life a passionate interest in theology, and in particular in the minutiae of doctrinal and biblical controversy. His niggling interest in these problems, which by mid-century had become gruesome with the blood they had spilt, may help to explain Elizabeth's distaste for them. He was learned in his way, though it has been well observed, by Professor G.R.Elton, that 'curiosity rather than stamina ever marked his intellectual exercises'.[14] He was an annotator, a margin-scribbler, a nit-picker and glossator – all characteristics of the second-rate schoolman – as scores of ecclesiastical documents which came beneath his gaze survive to testify. His library of over one thousand books at the Palace of Westminster was crowded with theological tomes.[15] He knew a little about a vast range of subjects, but his learning was wide rather than deep, and he almost invariably lost sight of the principle in a maze of detail.

But one thing he did know: that the scriptures and the early patristic writings laid down unalterable lines of conduct, and that breaches of them exposed the offender to ferocious penalties, in this world no less than in the next. In the case of a monarch, such earthly visitations were self-evident, visible to all: the state met with calamity because the King, wittingly or no, had broken the moral law. Henry had no legitimate son and heir, and seemingly could have none by Catherine. This was a threat to the state plainly engineered by God's will. Why? What had Henry done? During the 1520s the theological lumber-room that was Henry's mind moved slowly, but with increasing conviction, towards the true cause: he had contracted an invalid marriage. Catherine had been the wife of his brother, Arthur, and by marrying her he had broken the injunctions strictly laid down in Leviticus 19: 16 and 21. It was true that a papal dispensation had been duly provided, but then money (a portion of Catherine's dowry) had been at stake.[16] Besides, the Pope's dispensing powers had been based on Deuteronomy 15: 5, in Henry's eyes an inferior text. It seems to provide for a particular case, implying a duty on the brother of a dead husband to look after his widow. Moreover it forbids her to marry anyone else *but* a brother, a manifest absurdity as a general proposition.[17] It might be true, as Catherine indignantly claimed, that she had never slept with Arthur. But she should have said so at the time. The Bull of dispensation took no account of this fact – if it was a fact – and there was therefore an *impedimentum publicae honestatis*, a further ground for doubting the Bull's validity.[18]

In any case, Leviticus was quite clear: it forbade without qualification a man to marry his brother's widow. It has recently been suggested that the text was cunningly drawn to Henry's attention, by those, led by Cardinal Wolsey, who wished to end the alliance between England and the Habsburg Emperor Charles v, who was Catherine's nephew.[19] But this was quite unnecessary. It was already familiar to Henry, was indeed one of the most popular books of religious instruction of the times. Moreover, it was a book which appealed strongly to Henry's unimaginative temperament, with his grim insistence that authority explain itself in meticulous detail. It is a long and specific list of instructions and prohibitions, governing ritual, sacrifice, social behaviour, sex, medicine, hygiene, diet, agriculture, public service and the calendar. It does not argue through general propositions, but by cumulative detail, and thus to Henry had the familiar flavour of many early sixteenth-century Acts of parliament. In Book 26, especially 15–39, it culminates in a series of terrifying threats, which God will carry out not merely against individuals but against society as a whole, and especially the government, if the statutes are disobeyed. It is a kind of Magna Carta of the Old Testament, not at all a document that could be argued with, and is presented throughout, in the most solemn manner, as the imperious instructions of the Lord himself, direct to Moses. By contrast, Deuteronomy is merely the work of Moses, acting as a vicarious, temporal, and therefore fallible, law-maker.

The complex canon law of the divorce, and the long debates in London, Paris and Rome which sought to resolve it, need not concern us.[20] In England, the majority of ecclesiastical opinion sided with Henry, as was natural. On the Continent, the majority sided with Charles v, and Clement vii, the Pope he dominated, as was, again, natural. Thus Henry failed to win the consensus of Christendom, but his resolve strengthened as the debate proceeded. The Pope offered a number of compromises: to validate a bigamous second marriage, to legitimize the Duke of Richmond and allow him to marry his half-sister Mary, and so forth.[21] But he would not, or could not, give Henry the only thing he wanted: a decision that his union with Catherine was null – thus defying Henry's growing abhorrence of the sin he knew he had committed, and stoking his fears of the retribution which would overwhelm himself and his state. The only way Henry could resolve the dilemma was to snap the chain of ecclesiastical authority which ultimately led to Rome. The breach with the papacy, and the English Reformation which followed, were thus the product of a king's troubled conscience.

Henry's lust was of secondary importance, possibly of no importance at all. He first came across the Boleyn ladies some years before 1520. The elder sister, Mary, became his mistress about this time, and he subsequently married her off to a courtier, William Carey, in 1521.[22] The offspring of this marriage, Henry, Lord Hunsdon, was to flourish mightily under Queen Elizabeth. Mary had gone to France as maid-of-honour to Henry's sister Mary, when she married King Louis XII in 1514. Her younger sister Anne, born in 1507, had joined her in France about five years later, when she was twelve, and had been attached to the household of Queen Claude, wife of Francis I, but she was back in England by 1522.[23] The Boleyns were not exactly newcomers to high society, but they were not old landed stock either, and this seems to have been held as a major grievance against them both by humble folk and by the old aristocracy when they came into startling prominence. The great-grandfather of the sisters, Geoffrey Boleyn, was a Norfolk man who made a successful career in London as a hatter and mercer. He became sheriff of London and Middlesex, married into the aristocracy, was Lord Mayor (1457), and by his death in 1463 had acquired Blickling Hall in Norfolk and Hever Castle in Kent. His son, William, was knighted by Richard III, and married the Anglo-Irish Margaret Butler, co-heiress of the 1st Earl of Ormonde. Their son, Thomas, Anne's father, came to court and married Elizabeth, daughter of the 2nd Duke of Norfolk. So far, so good, and it was planned to marry Anne to the rival Ormonde claimant, Sir James Butler, and thus heal an old family feud. But the marriage did not come off; nor did a further match for her with Henry Percy, son of the Earl of Northumberland – a plan scotched by Wolsey, which earned him Anne's lasting hostility.[24]

By the mid-1520s Henry had taken sufficient notice of Anne to be exhibiting jealousy at her ability to attract court admirers, such as Sir Thomas Wyatt.[25]

Contemporary estimates of her beauty vary, but there seems general agreement that she had fine dark hair, large lustrous eyes, and a long neck. She was an accomplished dancer and musician, the latter calculated to appeal strongly to Henry, who was a prolific composer (one of his songs is still widely performed[26]). The assumption, at the time and since, is that she resisted Henry until it was certain he could marry her. But this rests on no evidence, and it is inherently unlikely. Anne had a universally bad reputation; complaints that she was a 'strong whore' were made throughout the controversy, and were duly tracked down by Thomas Cromwell's agents.[27] While it is most improbable that she was unfaithful to Henry after their marriage,[28] there seems no reason why she should have demanded it as the price of surrender. Henry treated his mistresses generously, and saw they were well married after he had finished with them.[29] Her sister Mary was a case in point. It is much more likely, granted Henry's character, that he declined to sleep with Anne until it was reasonably certain that a canonical marriage could take place, valid in the eyes of God, and thus certain to be blessed with a male heir. As he put it himself: 'All such issue males as I have received of the Queen [Catherine] died immediately after they were born, so that I fear the punishment of God in that behalf.'[30] Once the road to marriage was open, he felt he could go ahead in clear conscience; and Anne immediately complied, being rewarded with a marquisate and £1,000 a year.[31]

This would explain the chronology which surrounds Queen Elizabeth's conception. By early 1532 it was apparent that an annulment of Henry's marriage with Catherine would not be provided by Rome, and that other methods must be pursued. The machinery of the breach was put into operation. In May 1532, Sir Thomas More, the Chancellor, resigned in protest. This cleared the way for the Henrician element to become dominant on the Council, and for Cromwell to emerge as the master-mind behind the King's tactics. In July or August, a propaganda treatise, *The Glass of Truth*, made its appearance, setting forth the King's case in popular form, and adumbrating the course to be followed. Henry himself took a prominent part in its composition.[32] Parliament, said *The Glass*, could find a way to resolve the deadlock, if it would use its 'wits and good will', and then the 'metropolitans of the realm (their unjust oath made to the Pope notwithstanding)' would tidy up the ecclesiastical side. This in fact is what happened. In August, the elderly Archbishop of Canterbury, William Warham, died, and, since the Pope was still prepared to oblige Henry in everything but essentials, the King's supporter Thomas Cranmer was, in due course, canonically appointed. This ensured that Henry would get a favourable verdict in an English ecclesiastical court, as indeed he did on 23 May 1533. Meanwhile, on a parallel course, parliament had passed the Act in Restraint of Appeals, which effectively cut the umbilical cord with Rome or which, to put it another way, was the keystone in the Reformation arch. Thereafter the English Church could proceed, at Henry's direction, to do whatever he and his conscience thought fit.

All this was in train by the autumn of 1532. Hence Anne's marquisate, registered on 1 September 1532, probably marks the point at which she and Henry first slept together, his desires and his sense of moral duty now being reconciled. Elizabeth was presumably conceived early in December, and when the fact of Anne's pregnancy became established, the pair were secretly married on 25 January 1533.[33] After the annulment came through, the marriage was publicized, and Anne, now heavily pregnant, was crowned on 1 June.

Granted this background, the birth of a girl to Henry's new queen must have filled him with consternation and dismay. What had he done wrong *now*? True, the birth had been normal, indeed easy. Anne herself, in a letter to Lord Cobham despatched the same day (Sunday, 7 September; the birth took place between three and four in the afternoon, at Greenwich Palace), refers to the 'good speed in the deliverance and bringing forth'.[34] But no girl-child can ever have been less welcome to her father than the infant Elizabeth. The Imperial ambassador, Eustace Chapuys, writing to his master, Charles v, refers to 'the great disappointment and sorrow of the King, of the Lady herself and of others of her party, and the great shame and confusion of physicians, astrologers, wizards and witches, all of whom affirmed it would be a boy'.[35] After the christening, which took place on Wednesday, 10th, Chapuys reported that it had been 'very cold and disagreeable both to the court and to the City, and there has been no thought of having the bonfires and rejoicings usual in such cases.'[36] Of course Chapuys was both an interested and a hostile observer. In fact, an appropriate ceremonial was observed. At one o'clock the Lord Mayor, Sir Stephen Peacock, plus forty leading citizens, got into their state barge and were rowed to Greenwich. The walls between the palace and the Franciscan church were hung with arras, and the path strewn with green rushes. The church, too, was hung with tapestry; the font was of silver, covered with fine cloth, 'and divers gentlemen, with aprons and towels about their necks, gave attendance about it, that no filth should come to the font'. A fire burned so that the baby should not catch cold. Lady Mary Howard carried the christening robe, or chrisom, 'very rich of pearl and stone', and Elizabeth herself was in the arms of the Dowager Duchess of Norfolk. Cranmer stood godfather, the Duchess and the Dowager Lady Dorset were godmothers. John Stokesley, Bishop of London, baptized the Princess, and she was immediately afterwards confirmed by

Cranmer. Her first gifts were presented: a cup of gold, one of fretted pearl, and six gilt bowls. Those present were then served with biscuits, sweets, and hippocras to drink. By this time it was now dark, and five hundred torches lighted the party back to the palace, where the Mayor and his aldermen were taken to the cellars for a drink, before re-embarking. What made the occasion lacklustre was not meagre pomp but the conspicuous and deliberate absence of the King.

The disappointment of Elizabeth's birth did not mark the final breach between the King and Anne. By the summer of the following year, 1534, he was already paying attention to Jane Seymour, but he continued to sleep with his wife, who gave stillbirth to a premature boy-child on 27 January 1536 – by a supreme irony on the same day that her old rival, Catherine of Aragon, was buried. This was the final proof, to Henry's superstitious mind, that he was once more in trouble with the Deity, and those around him promptly supplied him with the material to set the machinery of disentanglement in motion – thus clearing the way for a third marriage which not even the Pope could pronounce invalid. On 24 April Henry set up a high-powered Treason Commission: Cromwell, the Dukes of Norfolk and Suffolk, Lord Chancellor Audeley, and several earls. In the light of its preliminary report, he left Greenwich suddenly for Westminster on 1 May, Anne remaining at the palace. She was rowed up-river to the Tower the next day. Between 2 May and 5 May, Henry Norris, Gentleman of the Privy Chamber, Mark Smeaton, a lute player, Anne's brother Viscount Rochford, Sir Francis Weston, William Brereton, Sir Richard Page, and the poet Thomas Wyatt were severally accused of 'using fornication' with the Queen and conspiring to encompass the King's death. On 12 May the first four commoners were tried before a special commission of Oyer and Terminer in Westminster Hall. Only Smeaton pleaded guilty, but all were condemned to death. On 15 May Anne and her brother were tried before another commission, headed by her uncle Norfolk, in the Tower. Both defended themselves, but were likewise condemned. The charges against Page and Wyatt were dropped; the other five lovers were executed on 17 May. Anne's execution was postponed for two days, to allow the official executioner from Calais to arrive: he was the only man in the King's dominions who knew how to execute with a sword as opposed to an axe, a less painful method. This was the sole gesture of mercy Henry extended to the woman he had once, presumably, loved. In law, of course, he might have burned her alive. Her marriage had already been annulled on 15 May, and Elizabeth consequentially bastardized. On the 20th Henry married Jane Seymour.[37]

Whether Elizabeth ever believed in her mother's guilt it is impossible to say.

The charges seem to us incredible, coloured only by Anne's flirtatious nature, which sometimes screwed itself up to a high pitch of gaiety, dissolving in hysterical laughter. She laughed thus, observers noted, even on her way to the Tower. She professed her innocence to the end. Ambassador Chapuys reported: 'The lady who had charge of her has sent to tell me in great secrecy that the Concubine, before and after receiving the sacrament, affirmed to her, on the damnation of her soul, that she had never been unfaithful to the King.'[38] Elizabeth had strong practical grounds for publicly professing belief in her mother's innocence. It is true that the annulment that made Elizabeth illegitimate was based on the grounds that the marriage with Anne had been void from the start, since Henry had already committed adultery with Anne's sister Mary.[39] But this was just clerical lawyers' nonsense; it could be reversed, and was. The real danger was that people might believe that Smeaton, who had pleaded guilty, had been a lover of long standing, and was Elizabeth's father. Her sister Mary, when Queen, asserted on various occasions that she could see a likeness between Elizabeth and Smeaton.[40] In her last months, Mary told Philip II's confessor, De Fresnada, that 'she [Elizabeth] was neither her sister nor the daughter of . . . King Henry'.[41] Elizabeth had no good grounds for admiring or loving her father, or revering his memory, and she professed to do so frequently, at least in public, chiefly to underline the fact that she was not the daughter of a lute-player. But she never displayed any posthumous affection for her mother, whom she is recorded as mentioning only on two occasions. Anne's body had been placed in an old arrow-chest, and buried in St Peter Vincula, at the Tower. When Elizabeth got her hands on the levers of power, there was no grandiose ceremony of rehabilitation. The statute she passed through parliament to give legal certainty to her title to the throne was terse and matter-of-fact. It made no gesture on behalf of her mother, in notable contrast to a similar statute Queen Mary passed when she came to power.[42] Another short Act of Elizabeth's simply brought in her mother to establish legal title as her heiress.[43] Elizabeth was a practical woman: she had no wish to reopen old sores and re-fight the battles of the past purely to satisfy her personal feelings of self-esteem. It is the first evidence we possess of her almost total lack of dynastic enthusiasm, so very uncharacteristic of her age. But, being a practical woman, she was generous, within limits, to her Boleyn relations.

What sort of a child was Elizabeth, thus conceived by the machinery of a political and religious crisis, and deprived of a mother at the age of two years and eight months? Let us look, first, at her physical appearance, about which many have written confidently. There is surprisingly little contemporary evidence on this point, at any stage in her life, and what there is often seems contradictory. Innumerable portraits of her, or what are termed portraits, survive. But they come from an age of iconography, when the painting of a royal image was in some sense an act of state, to be controlled and supervised – and falsified – accordingly. Governments, regarding the image of the sovereign as an important item of public property, sought to establish a stereotyped and idealized version. This was particularly true in Elizabeth's case. She was a sole and virgin ruler in her own right, in a country where religious change had banished the Virgin Mary from the position of overwhelming prominence she had occupied in the visual devotions of multitudes for many centuries. To some extent Elizabeth, as queen, was made – she was not unwilling – to fill the emotional gap left in people's lives, and her image thus acquired quasi-religious importance, and was adjusted accordingly.

The demand for portraits of Elizabeth was enormous, especially after her excommunication by the Pope in 1570, when to display a picture of her in your house was a useful sign of loyalty, and for those suspected of papist leanings essential. But even before this date Elizabethan ikons were in great demand. A draft proclamation of 1563 states that the desire to obtain them was expressed 'by all sorts of subjects and people both noble and mean'.[44] The same proclamation commanded that portraits of her must not be produced until 'some special person, that shall be by her allowed, shall have first finished a portraiture thereof, after which finished, her Majesty will be content that all other painters, or gravers . . . shall and may at their pleasure follow the said pattern or first portraiture'. But there is no evidence that this proclamation was ever put into effect.[45] For the Queen was extraordinarily reluctant to sit to anyone, let alone to decide which particular version should become her matrix. So unauthorized portraits, copies of copies of copies, circulated and sold. In his preface to his *History of the World*, Sir Walter Ralegh says that at one period she had all such pictures of her by 'common painters' cast into the fire.[46] He was alluding to the action of the Privy Council in July 1596, which ordered all public officers to assist the Sergeant Painter to seek out and destroy portraits which gave 'great offence' to her. This action was ineffective, and there were more complaints four years later. Indeed, there had been complaints all along, the Painter Stainers' Company twice petitioning, in 1575 and 1578, for some kind of rules to be laid down. A Book of Ordinances was actually established in 1581, to no effect. Elizabeth had her official Sergeant Painters: thus, George Gower held the post 1581–96, and was succeeded in 1598 by Leonard Fryer.[47] John de Critz I was also her Sergeant for a time. The Sergeants should have controlled the issue, but in practice could not: too much money

was involved. At one time there was a plan for Gower and Nicholas Hilliard
to exercise a joint monopoly, but this never got beyond the draft stage. As a
result of the confusion and rivalry even the best portraits provide an uncertain
guide to what she actually looked like at any stage. She probably sat personally
to seven painters: Levina Teerlinc (in 1551), Hilliard (about 1572), Federico
Zuccaro (1575), an unknown French painter in 1581, and Cornelius Ketel: this
we know from documentary evidence.[48] Gower and de Critz must have got
sittings, and so too, very likely, did Marcus Gheeraerdts. But their productions
which have survived are finished and approved ikons, naturally. The only
untampered drawing from the life which we possess, by Zuccaro, is a slight
thing, and tells us practically nothing.

The written evidence is hardly more satisfactory. There is no real agreement
on the colour of her eyes and hair, or the structure of her face. In 1557 the
Venetian ambassador, Giovanni Michieli, reported to the Doge: 'Her face is
comely rather than handsome, but she is tall and well-formed, with a good skin,
though swarthy; she has fine eyes.'[49] But here 'swarthy', or olive-skinned, may
reflect the fact that Elizabeth was apparently suffering from jaundice. Further
eye-witness descriptions date mainly from her old age, or are otherwise suspect.
In 1596 Francesco Gradenigo called her 'short, and ruddy in complexion; very
strongly built'.[50] Henry IV's agent, de Maisse, writing in the 1590s, said her
face was long and thin, her teeth yellow and decayed, but 'her figure is fair and
tall and graceful in whatever she does.'[51] Paul Hentzner, a German, saw her at
Greenwich in 1598 and reported: 'her face oblong, fair but wrinkled; her eyes
small, yet black and pleasant; her nose a little hooked, her lips narrow . . . her
hair . . . an auburn colour, but false'.[52] (This last description harmonizes with
the near-contemporary 'Ditchley Portrait' in the National Portrait Gallery, and
the unfinished miniature by Isaac Oliver in the Victoria and Albert Museum.)
Writing many years afterwards, Sir James Melville, a Scotch ambassador who
had several private meetings with Elizabeth, described her hair as 'more reddish
than yellow, and curled, in appearance, naturally'. He says she told him: 'I
myself am neither too high nor too low' (this in contrast to the tall Mary
Queen of Scots).[53] Francis Bacon, however, said she was 'tall of stature',[54]
while Sir Richard Baker reported her (on traditional evidence) as 'indifferent
tall; fair of complexion; her hair inclining to pale yellow; her forehead large
and fair; her eyes lively and sweet, but short sighted; her nose somewhat rising
in the midst'.[55] What does all this amount to? My view, for what it is worth,
is that she was a little above average height for her time and class; that she was
slim and extremely active; that her skin was fair, white and probably slightly
freckled; that she had fine deep-grey eyes, and a long, slightly hooked nose;

and that her hair was reddish-gold and curly, though she wore a red wig in her later years to conceal her thinning grey locks. The assertion that she went prematurely bald is false.[56] On one point all authorities, written and visual, are agreed: she had beautiful hands, with long fine fingers, to which she loved to draw attention by repeatedly drawing off, and putting on, her gloves. There can be little doubt that, in her day, she was an attractive woman.

Nor is this surprising. Both her parents were good-looking, though it is curious she bore so little resemblance to her mother, her one forebear of whom we can be absolutely certain. We know little of her maternal grandparents, but Henry VII had distinction, and Elizabeth of York inherited the glamour of her Yorkist-Plantagenet father.[57] Elizabeth probably resembled Henry VII more than any other progenitor. She had the same long nose, which in the Torrigiano bust and effigy of Henry VII in Westminster Abbey has been straightened out for representational purposes.[58] He, too, had grey eyes, according to the National Portrait Gallery portrait by Sittow, and the same poor teeth.[59] Like Henry VII, Elizabeth had an undeserved reputation for financial rapacity, which in fact reflected a prudent and determined resolve to keep the state solvent.[60] She shared with him a taste for regal and opulent, but carefully calculated, display, though she lacked the resources to emulate his judicious patronage of the arts. From him she inherited her deep sense of national responsibility, strong nerves and persistency in purpose. But none of this makes her, in essence, a Welshwoman. Henry VII's grandfather was wholly Welsh, but he himself had French, Bavarian and a great deal of English blood. He took no interest in Wales, once it had served his purpose, and there is no evidence he spoke its language. Elizabeth had some Welsh or Border servants, but she showed indifference (or hostility) to her Principality, and never visited it. The truth is, she had as much English blood as the great majority of her subjects, and when she claimed, as she often did, to be 'mere English', she meant it.

We have only scraps of information about Elizabeth's childhood. For her first two years and nine months she was treated as a princess of the royal blood, and moved in some state, often accompanied by her half-sister Mary, on a circuit of the royal palaces and manor houses which surrounded London and dotted the Home Counties: Hatfield, Eltham, Hunsdon, Hertford, the More (at Rickmansworth), Richmond and Greenwich. She rarely saw her parents, except at public festivals. When he visited her, Henry showed her considerable favour, as he was anxious to publicize the fact that she, not Mary, was the heir presumptive. She was five months old when he called on her at Eltham, and one of his suite, Sir William Kingston, reported that she was 'as goodly a child as hath been seen. Her Grace is much in the King's favour, as goodly child should be, God save her!'[61] On 9 October 1535, Sir William Paulet, Comptroller of the King's Household, commanded Cromwell, by the desire of the King and Queen, that Elizabeth, then twenty-five months, should be weaned.[62] Mary reported to her father: 'My sister Elizabeth is in good health . . . and such a child toward, as I doubt not but your highness shall have cause to rejoice of in time coming.'[63]

But Elizabeth's status changed immediately after Anne's execution. In June 1536 parliament passed an Act declaring the child illegitimate, though it gave the King full powers, failing heirs by Jane Seymour, to appoint by Will or Letters Patent any heir or heiress he chose, at any time. Furthermore, it gave a free pardon to anyone who, under an earlier Act, had incurred a charge of treason by calling Anne a whore or Elizabeth a bastard.[64] The practical effect was a reduction in the child's household and the virtual cutting off of supplies. Her governess, Lady Bryan, a widowed cousin of Anne, complained bitterly to Cromwell in August that she did not now know what Elizabeth's status was, and that in any event the child was desperately short of clothes:

> . . . for she hath neither gown, nor kirtle [slip], nor petticoat, nor no manner of linen nor smocks, nor kerchiefs, nor rails [nightdresses], nor body-stitchets [corsets], nor handkerchiefs, nor sleeves, nor mufflers [caps], nor biggens [night caps]. . . . I have driven off as long as I can, that by my troth I can drive it off no longer: beseeching you, my Lord, that ye will see that her Grace may have that which is needful for her . . . My Lord, Mr Shelton [Sir John Shelton] saith he is master of this house . . . Mr Shelton would have my Lady Elizabeth to dine and sup every day at the board of estate [high table]. Alas! my Lord, it is not meet for a child of her age to keep such rule yet. I promise you, my Lord, I dare not take it upon me to keep her Grace in health an' she keep that rule. For there she shall see divers meats, and fruit, and wine, which it would be hard for me to restrain her Grace from . . . and she is yet too young to correct greatly. . . . God knoweth my Lady hath great pain with her great teeth, and they come very slowly forth, which causeth me to suffer her Grace to have her will more than I would . . . [yet] she is as toward a child and as gentle of conditions [amenable] as ever I knew any in my life.[65]

This letter was effective. Elizabeth's household was reorganized on a more seemly basis, and it was soon joined by Elizabeth's half-brother, Edward, the longed-for son, to whom Jane Seymour gave birth in October 1537, dying in the process. Elizabeth was allowed to carry the chrisom at Edward's baptism, though she was so small she had to be held in the arms of Lord Beauchamp, the future Protector Somerset. This marked the point at which her formal education began. Catherine Champernowne, whom Elizabeth called Kat, was appointed her governess. She was a well-educated lady from Devonshire, who later, in 1545, married John Ashley, Elizabeth's senior gentleman-attendant and first cousin of Anne Boleyn. The inner circle of the household was completed by Blanche Parry, a maiden lady from the Welsh borders, who served Elizabeth with devotion until she died, blind, in 1596, and by Blanche's brother Thomas, a short-tempered gentleman who acted as the child's cofferer, or financial comptroller – not very efficiently.

Right from the start, Elizabeth was exceptionally fortunate in her education. Kat Champernowne gave her her first lessons so effectively that, in December 1539, when Elizabeth was six, Sir Thomas Wriothesley, who had come to Hertford Castle to present the King's Christmas greetings, was able to report to his master:

> She gave humble thanks, enquiring again of his Majesty's welfare, and that with as great a gravity as she had been forty years old. If she be no worse educated than she now appeareth to me, she will prove of no less honour to womanhood than shall beseem her father's daughter.[66]

Elizabeth's rapid progress was no doubt due, in part at least, to Kat's gentle and persuasive methods. Mary Tudor had not been so lucky. At the request of her mother, Catherine of Aragon, the Spanish pedagogue Vives had written out a scheme of education for Princess Mary. He recommended harsh treatment: 'Never have the rod off a boy's back; specially the daughter should be handled without cherishing. For cherishing marreth sons, but it utterly destroyeth daughters.'[67] Kat's fault, if she had one, was that she tried to push her eager charge too fast. Her husband's friend, Roger Ascham, exhorted her:

> If you pour much drink at once into a goblet, the most part will dash out and run over; if ye pour it softly, you may fill it even to the top, and so her Grace, I doubt not, by little and little may be increased in learning, that at length greater cannot be required.[68]

In 1542, when Elizabeth was nine, more professional schooling began, under the supervision of Dr Richard Cox, Provost of Eton, whose tutorials Elizabeth shared with her brother. Early in 1544 the royal schoolroom was again reorganized, under Sir John Cheke, Regius Professor of Greek at Cambridge, later Master of St John's, and one of the key figures both in the English Reformation and the academic Renaissance. He brought with him his pupil

Ascham, the greatest and wisest pedagogue of the age, and Sir Anthony Cooke, another learned Cambridge gentleman, whose progeny were to play spectacular roles in the Elizabethan age. Later that year they were joined by William Grindal, a fourth leading Cambridge scholar, who became Elizabeth's personal tutor until his death two years later. Elizabeth was a Cambridge girl.

The members of this fine team were all innovators both in scholarship and religion. It was Cheke who led the battle against the conservative Bishop Gardiner on the correct pronunciation of Greek, which convulsed learned society and was a touchstone of a man's general intellectual ideas.[69] More important, all were reformers in religion, though none of them fanatics. Elizabeth had been baptized according to the full Roman Catholic rite. But her religious upbringing was Protestant, in the sense that it was based on a spirit of inquiry, a repudiation of ecclesiastical authority as the sole guide to truth, and the personal study and interpretation of the Bible. She was not, and never became, a religious woman. She doubtless believed in a Divine Providence, especially in moments of crisis. She made a *bona mors*, as we shall see. But she saw Christianity more as an outward and secular instrument to preserve society from disorder, than as a set of immutable truths to be inwardly believed. In this, as in many other ways, she was the opposite of 'her father's daughter'. Throughout her life she loathed what she called 'preciseness' on matters of religious belief and practice. The speculations of theologians, she said, were 'ropes of sand or sea-slime leading to the Moon', arguments about doctrine 'a dream of fools or enthusiasts'. But she was thoroughly familiar with the subject-matter of religious debate. As she told the Commons at the end of the 1584-5 parliament: 'I am supposed to have many studies, but most philosophical. I must yield this to be true: that I suppose few, that be no professors, have read more . . . And yet, amidst many volumes, I hope God's book hath not been my seldomest lectures.'[70]

Elizabeth's tutors, and especially Ascham, taught her to read Greek fluently, using a new method of translation and re-translation, and to speak it moderately well. Ascham said he had dealt with many learned ladies but 'among them all, the brightest star is my illustrious lady Elizabeth'. With him she read the Greek Testament, the orations of Isocrates and the tragedies of Sophocles. Until his death in 1568, she continued to read Greek with him daily, whenever he was at court. After that, her spoken Greek was neglected, though she continued to study Greek texts until the end.

By contrast, her Latin never grew rusty, though she often liked to pretend that it had, thereby astonishing her hearers when she burst forth in what appeared to be – and sometimes was – a spontaneous Latin oration. When she visited Oxford or Cambridge, the ceremonies and exchanges were invariably conducted in Latin. She prepared, and possibly memorized, her texts, often, with false modesty, apologizing in advance. But she also spoke Latin impromptu. Of her visit to Oxford, 22–8 September 1592, Anthony Wood records that, on all occasions, 'she answered very readily with great affability in the Latin tongue': and, on the same visit, she deliberately interrupted her Latin speech, instructing the attendants to give a stool to the aged Lord Burghley, to show that she could resume the thread without effort (this was a rebuke to a less competent bishop, who had become completely confused when the Queen twice ordered him to shorten his memorized text).[71] There was a good deal of vanity in such behaviour, but no one doubted that she could speak spontaneous, correct, fluent, and indeed magisterial, Latin when she wanted. Thus, on 25 July 1597, she answered a speech by a Polish ambassador, which she considered impudent, with a torrent of angry Latin. If that, she concluded, was the way he had been taught to address princes, he had better go home until he had learned better: *Interea vero valeas, et quiescas* – 'In the meantime, farewell, and be quiet.' When the chastened Pole had left, Elizabeth said: 'God's death, my Lords, I have been enforced this day to scour up my old Latin that hath been long a-rusting.' No one else noticed the rust. As Robert Cecil reported to the Earl of Essex: 'I swear by the living God her Majesty made one of the best answers extempore in Latin that ever I heard.'[72] The next year, says Camden, she was at work, aged sixty-five, translating Horace's *De Arte Poetica*.

She was well grounded in modern subjects. As Chancellor of the University, Lord Burghley warned the Cambridge dons, who were preparing for a royal visit, not to make the mistake of patronizing her, 'who hath knowledge to understand very well in all common sciences'.[73] She was unusually well versed in modern languages, speaking French and Italian fluently. Her Italian was particularly fine: she had probably used William Thomas's brilliant and innovatory *Principal Rules of the Italian Grammar*, which became available about 1550, and she doubtless read his *History of Italy*, published the year before.[74] Fluent Italian was of great importance to Elizabeth, when later she came to the throne. During her lifetime Latin was rapidly ceasing to be the principal language of international diplomacy (it lingered on chiefly in Eastern Europe), being replaced by Italian, which in the second half of the century became dominant. After the death of Charles v, French was little used among the Spanish, and as a general rule Italian was the only second language of ambassadors and special envoys.[75] By being able to speak to ambassadors in their own tongue (as a rule), in Italian, or if necessary in Latin, Elizabeth could dispense with intermediaries, could hold interviews without her ministers being present, and thus exercise, when she chose, a personal control over foreign policy which no other sovereign of her time possessed. Of her Italian accent we know nothing. Her French aroused some comment: one French ambassador, De Busenval, used to imitate her long, drawling 'a's: '*Paar Dieu, paar maa foi!*'[76]

The services Ascham rendered her were by no means purely academic. He helped to broaden her mind. He was a Yorkshireman of multifarious interests, ranging from Cicero (his hero) to cockfighting (on which he was planning to write a book when he died). He travelled widely under Edward VI, serving on a diplomatic mission to Charles V (in 1550), and had many friends and scholarly correspondents abroad, including John Sturm, the famous Rector of the Strasburg Gymnasium. His book on archery, *Toxophilus*, first printed in 1545,[77] became the immensely popular standard work on the subject, and to him Elizabeth owed her lifelong passion for hunting, though unlike Ascham she preferred the crossbow to the longbow. His trouble was that he was a gambler, especially at dice, and lost heavily. This may explain why Elizabeth felt unable to raise him to high preferment in the Church, though she gave him a prebend at York (5 October 1559) and sometimes paid his debts. When he died she said that she would rather cast £10,000 into the sea than have lost 'her Ascham'; she was not so improvident in his lifetime, knowing the way the money would go. His oscillation between bloodsports and books paralleled her own curious mixture of scholarship and heartiness: indeed, he might be called a sixteenth-century Charles Kingsley, and Elizabeth an apt pupil. But he certainly gave her the capacity to develop her internal resources, which were to be her strength and comfort throughout her anxious and often lonely career. Camden says that never a day went past without her reading or writing something, and there was always a book or two in the capacious pouch she carried at her waist.

Ascham also taught her writing in the literal sense. Elizabeth was no stylist, or rather, her efforts to become one turned what she wrote into affectation and mannerism. Some poems of hers survive: they are no more than competent. Her prose was at its best when it was dashed off in the heat of rapid thought, or anger (especially the latter), just as her speeches, delivered from rough notes, are far more impressive when recorded by those who heard them, than in the elaborately doctored texts she prepared for publication. Indeed they were finest of all when spoken extempore, sometimes rising to truly Shakespearean heights of rhetoric.

But if Elizabeth was a natural, rather than a trained, writer, her actual penmanship could be superb. In this field she was fortunate to be a woman. When she was a girl, the old 'secretary hand', which had dominated Western European handwriting since the age of Charlemagne, was slowly yielding place to italic (also known, confusingly, as the 'Roman hand'). Italic had first reached England around 1500, but secretary was still dominant, for official purposes, until the middle of her reign. Indeed, the professional penman, Martin Billingsley, in his *The Pens Excellence* (1618), stated: 'the secretary . . . is so termed . . . because it is the only usual hand of England, for dispatching of all manner of business for the most part, whatsoever.' But it was difficult to acquire and exceedingly hard to read, then as now. Moreover, there were many 'court hands', or sub-varieties of it, favoured by individual offices such as the Exchequer or Chancery, secret codes, as it were, practised in the vested interests of professional clerks. By contrast, italic was simple, and could be written at speed without losing clarity. According to Billingsley:

> It is conceived to be the easiest hand that is written with pen, and to be taught in the shortest time: therefore it is usually taught to women, for as much as they (having not the patience to take any great pains, besides fantastical and humoursome) must be taught that which they may instantly learn.

His condescending masculine tone conceals the real impact which Elizabeth had on the art. For Ascham was a passionate propagandist for the italic, as were other enlightened scholars, and Elizabeth was taught it from the start. Thanks to her influence, italic ceased to be the exclusive hand of scholars and women, and was gradually adopted by leading politicians, such as Burghley and Essex (Francis Bacon wrote in both hands, using the italic, like modern printers, for emphasis). Indeed, as her sight deteriorated, she grew to dislike the secretary hand intensely, and during her last decades the English upper classes were switching to the modern style. At its best, Elizabeth's italic hand was superb, and a joy to Ascham. But later, under the pressure of work, she developed her 'running hand', which few could read at all. On 24 November 1586, at the height of the Mary Queen of Scots crisis, Lord Chancellor Bromley received her instructions about what he was to say in announcing the proclamation of the death sentence. He confessed he 'could not read one half-line of it', and Burghley, almost alone in his ability to decipher her letters written in moments of agitation, had to copy it out for him.[78]

The earliest holograph letters of Elizabeth that survive show her penmanship at its best. The first, dated 31 July 1544, is addressed to Catherine Parr, Henry's last wife, whom he had married twelve months before. It is an exercise in Italian, which Elizabeth had been learning from Battisti Castiglioni, and is a remarkable effort for a child of ten. She followed this by a Christmas gift to the Queen, an English translation of Margaret of Navarre's *The Mirror of the Sinful Soul*, and the next year, at Christmas, her offering was a translation of Catherine's own prayers in French and Italian. All three are of visual rather than intrinsic interest, the careful schoolwork of a dutiful and gifted stepdaughter.[79] Only the first hints, bafflingly, at some misunderstanding with her father, and begs the Queen's intercession, 'for heretofore I have not dared to write to him'.

Whether in fact she ever wrote to her father we do not know. Very likely she did, but nothing has survived. She never commented on him or his actions, on the pitiful Jane Seymour, on Anne of Cleves, the 'Flanders mare', whom she knew quite well, on the tragic and promiscuous Catherine Howard, or on the successive statesmen Henry raised and broke. Near the end of her reign, Shakespeare was to speak, through the voice of Horatio,

> *Of carnal, bloody and unnatural acts,*
> *Of accidental judgments, casual slaughters,*
> *Of deaths put on by cunning and forced cause* . . .[80]

This was the background of Elizabeth's childhood, reflected later in her passionate concern for civil peace and the rule of law, in her contempt for fanatics of all shades, and in her abhorrence of capital punishment. At the time, she kept her head down, her nose in her books, and said nothing. Only once, it is recorded, did she ask a question about her own position in the state.

The question was difficult to answer. Henry treated her with rough affection on the rare occasions when he noticed her at all. She lived as a princess, but had no title to the name. She was legally illegitimate, but plans were occasionally discussed to marry her to Continental royalties. By the Second Succession Act of 1536 parliament had given Henry absolute power to determine her status by Will, and indeed virtually everything else that concerned the succession. By the end of 1546 he was visibly nearing the end. He celebrated his last weeks by a grim onslaught on Elizabeth's Howard relatives. There were bitter political and religious divisions in the Council, its members eyeing each other across the board as potential executioners or victims, once the King's death removed the sole force that held them together. At one meeting, John Dudley, the future Duke of Northumberland, struck Bishop Gardiner in the face.[81] On 26 December Henry finally settled his Will, and it was read out in his presence to a group of councillors. It provided for the succession in enormous detail, should his son die without issue. Mary, then Elizabeth, were to follow; then a string of distant claimants in order, but excluding the Stuart line. Nothing was said about legitimizing the two half-sisters. Henry went to eternity without finally making up his mind on the obsessive point of whether either, and if so which, of his daughters was born in wedlock. Presumably he thought it was too late now, and he would soon know the true answer. But each was given an income of £3,000 a year. As for his son's regency, he made elaborate provisions for that, too. Four days later, a fair copy of the Will was duly signed. Whether it was lawfully sealed soon became a matter of acute controversy, which was to reverberate long into Elizabeth's reign.[82] At the time it scarcely mattered, for the immediate provisions of the Will – the composition and powers of the Regency Council – were promptly overthrown. Henry died in the early hours of 28 January 1547, though his death was concealed for three days. Almost at once Edward Seymour, Earl of Hertford, the young King's uncle, seized supreme power and proclaimed himself governor of the boy-King and Lord Protector of the kingdom, assuming the title of Duke of Somerset.[83]

From this episode, Elizabeth acquired a lifelong contempt for elaborate testimentory plans, or constitutional devices to provide for the future should she die. She learned that it was not within the power of a dead monarch to shape events. Decades later, a copy of Henry's Will turned up in the effects of old Bishop Tunstall of Durham, and attracted little attention. As a matter of fact, she ignored her father's Will herself. It had directed that his body should be laid alongside Jane Seymour, in a costly tomb, already under construction, in the Lady Chapel at Windsor. Instead, it was simply placed in Jane's existing tomb. When she became queen, Elizabeth, 'her father's daughter' or no, did nothing to remedy this defiance of his express wishes. She had the matter discussed in the 1560s; but to finish the tomb would have cost money, and she had better things to do with it. In the meantime, her father's death opened for her a decade of mortal peril.

Chaste and Unexpressive She
(1547–1553)

The maturity and self-confidence with which Elizabeth took decisions, the moment she came to the throne at the age of twenty-five, reflect the fact that, as an adolescent and a young woman, she had been closely involved in high affairs of state. For nearly twelve years, during the minority rule of her brother Edward (1547–53), and the rule of her sister Mary (1553–8), she lived through a period of political, social, religious and international crisis. During this time all her acts and omissions were closely scrutinized, and severely judged, by the state authorities, whose own policies oscillated violently, and to which she was expected to conform. She learned circumspection, judgment, the need for strict self-control and the virtues of silence – but also the necessity to speak out for herself, with all her courage and eloquence, when the occasion demanded. She survived, and in the process of surviving acquired a popularity among the people, citizens and gentry of south-east England which was to remain the basis of her authority for the rest of her life.

Elizabeth was a little over thirteen when her father died, and she came under the care and supervision of his widow, Catherine Parr, living mainly in the Queen-Dowager's house in Chelsea. Catherine had been well provided for by Henry and she was also a wealthy woman in her own right, having survived two earlier husbands, Sir Edward Burough and Lord Latimer. She had had a first-class education on Renaissance-humanist lines, acquiring a good knowledge of Latin, French and Greek.[1] Her religion was pietistic and contemplative, rather than stridently doctrinal, but there was no doubt that she inclined to the Protestant faction. Reformers like Miles Coverdale and Hugh Latimer were often at her house,[2] and her personal chaplain, John Parkhurst, was a keen propagandist of the new teaching.[3] Between 1545 and 1547 Catherine had published three devotional tracts, remarkable for their dignified language and distaste for sectarian zeal.[4] Henry had sometimes resented her theological knowledge ('A good hearing it is when women become such clerks; and nothing much to my comfort in mine old days to be taught by my wife'[5]), but in his decline he

23

found her brand of religion increasingly to his taste. With her emphasis on charity, and her dislike for the ferocity of doctrinal argument, she may well have inspired his last great speech to parliament on 24 December 1545. Quoting St Paul on charity, he asked angrily what had happened when

> the one calleth the other heretic and Anabaptist, and he calleth him again Papist, hypocrite and Pharasee. . . . I see and hear daily that you of the clergy preach one against another . . . some be too still in their old Mumpsimus, other[s] be too busy and curious in their new Sumpsimus . . . I am very sorry to know and hear how unreverently that most precious jewel, the Word of God, is disputed, rhymed, sung and jangled in every alehouse and tavern, contrary to the true meaning and doctrine of the same.[6]

Thus Henry, in his old age, came to adopt an attitude towards religion which Elizabeth was to hold throughout her life. Certainly, his last dispositions, which excluded the conservative Bishop Gardiner from the regency council, suggest he was moving towards a moderate Protestantism, and possibly the replacement of the Mass by a communion service in English.[7] He had failed to secure anything but a nominal submission from his daughter Mary, who remained a devoted papalist throughout her life, but the educational arrangements he made for Edward and Elizabeth, and the influence he allowed Catherine to exercise over all his children, make it clear he realized that the future of England lay with some form of Protestantism.[8]

Catherine, in some ways, was an excellent choice for her role. Though childless, as yet, she had a good deal of experience in bringing up other men's offspring; she was gentle, affectionate and understanding. All three of Henry's children grew to like her, and in Elizabeth's case there was a special bond. Catherine's fault was that she was over-romantic. When a handsome and strong-willed man appeared, her classical learning and her religious piety alike flew out of her head. Shortly after her husband Lord Latimer died, and before Henry's eye fell upon her, she had thought of marrying Thomas Seymour, younger brother of the future Protector Somerset, but, as she put it, she had been 'overruled by a higher power'. When Henry died she was still only thirty-three, and almost immediately Seymour reappeared. He had been thinking of marrying himself to Anne of Cleves, the Princess Mary, or Elizabeth.[9] But these were vague and dangerous plans: Catherine was more accessible and, moreover, willing. Sometime in May 1547 they were secretly married.[10] Thus Elizabeth was brought into close contact with one of the most forceful and reckless personalities of the age.

Seymour was then thirty-eight. He had come into official prominence after

Henry VIII married his sister, and during the great invasion scare of the 1540s, when Henry feared a joint attack by France and the Habsburgs, he had commanded the fleet. When his elder brother seized supreme power immediately after the King's death, Seymour, like the other magnates, had received a generous slice of the share-out in lands and titles with which Somerset sought to pacify his colleagues. He was made a Privy Councillor, Baron Sudeley, and, once more, Lord High Admiral. In terms of lands, his portion of the spoils was exceeded only by those allotted to the Earl of Warwick (later Duke of Northumberland), Sir William Herbert and Somerset himself. From crown and appropriated Church lands he got, by gift or cheap sale, forty-eight manors, which made him a leading proprietor in Wiltshire and the Welsh Marches.[11] But he wanted more, and his actions throughout seem to have been coloured by a fierce jealousy of his brother, of the unappeasable kind sometimes found among younger sons.

He was, moreover, a ruthless womanizer, and regarded any woman, or young girl, as fair game. Elizabeth was by now nubile and attractive, and her presence in the house of Catherine and her husband brought about a curious triangular situation. What we know of it is derived from formal depositions made by Mrs Ashley, Thomas Parry (who got most of his information from Mrs Ashley) and Elizabeth herself.[12] These statements were made when Seymour's treason came to light in January 1549. They referred to events which had occurred between May 1547 and May 1548, mainly in the later part of this period when Elizabeth was fourteen. They are thus recollections, and they were extracted under strict cross-examination by ferocious state lawyers, including the notorious Sir Richard Rich. According to Tudor practice, each witness was examined separately, and the others were then confronted with portions of his, or her, testimony. The evidence must therefore be treated with caution, but it tells, in essence, a simple and plausible tale. Seymour had the run of Catherine's Chelsea house: one of his many unpleasant characteristics was the habit of having keys made to rooms to which he would not normally obtain access. Sometimes in his wife's presence, sometimes with her reluctant encouragement or assistance, and sometimes in her absence, he engaged in sexual romping with Elizabeth. Mrs Ashley deposed:

At Chelsea, after my Lord Thomas Seymour was married to the Queen, he would come many mornings into the said Lady Elizabeth's chamber before she was ready, and sometimes before she did rise; and if she were up he would bid her good morrow, and ask how she did, and strike her upon the back or on the buttocks familiarly . . . And if she were in her bed he would put open the curtains and bid her good morrow and make as though he would come at her, and she would go further into the bed so that he could not come at her.

At Hanworth, on two occasions, Catherine was with him, and they both 'tickled my Lady Elizabeth in her bed'. On another occasion, at Hanworth, they romped in the garden; according to Parry, Seymour 'cut her gown, being black cloth, into a hundred pieces; and when Mrs Ashley came up and chid Lady Elizabeth, she answered, "She could not strive with all, for the Queen held her while the Lord Admiral cut her dress." ' Once, at Seymour Place, Catherine rebuked her husband for going into Elizabeth's room in his nightgown, 'bare legged', but the girl had by now formed the prudent habit of getting up early, and had her nose in a book by the time the Admiral arrived. The week after Whitsun, 1548, Elizabeth left Catherine's household, apparently after a disagreement. This arose, according to some confused passages in the depositions, after Catherine had seen Elizabeth in the arms of a man, possibly her husband, possibly someone else.

These episodes, when they emerged, caused Elizabeth great embarrassment. But they do not amount to much. Elizabeth was placed in a difficult position by the Admiral's attentions, especially as they appeared to have, to some extent, Catherine's sanction. There is no evidence that the two women quarrelled, as they must surely have done if Elizabeth had deliberately set her cap at the Admiral. She left the household in May 1548 chiefly because Catherine was now heavily pregnant, 'undoubtful of health' (as Elizabeth put it), and facing the risks of a first birth at the age of thirty-five. A child was in fact born three months later, on 30 August, and five days afterwards Catherine was dead of puerperal fever. After Elizabeth left, the two women exchanged friendly letters. Two of Elizabeth's survive. The first, undated but no doubt written in June, states

> . . . truly I was replete with sorrow to depart from your Highness, especially seeing you undoubtful of health; and albeit I answered little, I weighed it more deeper when you said you would warn me of all evilnesses that you should hear of me; for if your Grace had no good opinion of me, you would not have offered friendship to me at all, meaning the contrary.[13]

In a second letter, dated 31 July, Elizabeth says: 'Your Highness were like to be cumbered, if I should not depart till I were weary of being with you; although it were the worst soil in the world, your presence would make it pleasant.'[14] She thought it imprudent, no doubt, to return to the household and assist at the birth. Catherine, indeed, complained during her last hours at the absence of friends; she evidently wanted Elizabeth back.

If the romping with Seymour, under Catherine's aegis, later caused Elizabeth embarrassment, what happened after Catherine's death might have got her into serious trouble. Fortunately she had now learned to be extremely guarded in her dealings with the Admiral. When he offered marriage, she firmly insisted that any such match must be arranged openly, with the full knowledge and consent of the Council, as she later explained in letters to the Protector Somerset.[15] Seymour also offered to be of practical service to her. Her settlement, under her father's will, had not yet been carried out. Durham Place, south of the Strand, assigned to her as a London residence, was being used as a mint. In mid-December 1548 the Admiral offered her the use of his own house, Seymour Place. He also asked to be allowed to help her in speeding up the issue of the patents for the £3,000-worth of lands provided for her maintenance, throwing out the suggestion of a complex property deal which would have rounded off his own territories in the West, and placed Elizabeth's possessions in proximity to them. Elizabeth's account of how she responded to these interested ploys is confused, but she clearly declined to have any financial and territorial dealings with the Admiral, and at no point did she seriously think of marrying him.[16] She had already made her first contact with Sir William Cecil, her future minister, on 2 August 1548,[17] and was thinking of employing his skill in any major financial deal. To mix up her revenues with Seymour's would have been plain folly. As for a secret contract of marriage, any teenage Tudor child of the royal blood knew that this was to cross the threshold of treason.

The storm broke on 6 January 1549, when Privy Council investigators visited Laycock Abbey, the home of Sir William Sharington, vice-treasurer, and effective master, of the Bristol mint. From early December Somerset and his colleagues had been aware that the Admiral was engaged in some kind of conspiracy; his actions, and rumours of his sayings, left no doubt on the point.[18] He had quarrelled violently with his elder brother over his secret marriage to Catherine and, after her death, over her jewels; he had totally neglected his duties as Lord Admiral; he had formed a parliamentary faction against the government, of which he was nominally a member, threatening to create 'the blackest parliament that ever was in England';[19] and he was reliably reported to be building up a stock of arms at Sudeley. But the search of Sharington's splendid Renaissance house revealed much more. To build and maintain this house, Sharington had used his position at the Bristol mint to operate one of the biggest state swindles in English history.[20] He had bought large quantities of church plate, which he had turned into coin about two-thirds alloy. The mint records had been carefully falsified. By his own admission he had defrauded the crown of at least £4,000. That his activities had escaped detection is remarkable; but it must be remembered that, during the 1540s, the crown itself had been engaged in a systematic debasement of the currency, in a period of raging inflation, which had sent the face-value of pound sterling (expressed in Flemish shillings) down from 25 to 15.[21] No doubt, in the general dissatisfaction with the state of the currency, Sharington had hoped his own false issues would attract little attention. But many servants of the mint knew of the fraud. Rumours had spread, had reached the Lord Admiral, and he promptly pounced on Sharington and blackmailed him. The frauds would continue, but they would be used to finance the Admiral's rebellion by paying the wages of mercenaries. The Imperial ambassador reported (27 January) that the Admiral, when seized, had silver to the value of 200,000 crowns in his house.[22] At all events, Sharington promptly turned King's evidence, confessed volubly, and in due course was pardoned, restored to his house, lands and the crown's financial service, ending his life as sheriff of Wiltshire!

When Laycock Abbey was searched, Somerset wrote urgently to his brother, summoning him to a private interview, but the Admiral refused, on the grounds that he was too busy. This, I think, was the source of Elizabeth's later assertion, to Queen Mary, that Somerset had told her the Admiral would never have been beheaded if the two brothers could have met face to face. Somerset, she said, had complained 'that if his brother had been suffered to speak with him, he had never suffered; but the persuasions were made to him so great, that he was brought in belief that he could not live safely if the Admiral lived; and that made him give his consent to his death'.[23] No doubt Elizabeth got slightly the wrong end of the stick. Once the investigations had got thoroughly under way – and they were more comprehensive than those conducted during any other Tudor treason trial – there was no possibility of Somerset saving his brother. As the Protector said, in a letter to his friend Sir Philip Hoby, ambassador to the Empire, it was a case of 'plain sedition'.[24] The Admiral had been in league with a series of pirates, whom it was his duty to bring to trial. He had paid the Duke of Suffolk £2,000 to get possession of his daughter, Lady Jane Grey, with a view to marrying her to the young King. Worse, since June 1547, he had been in treasonable contact with the King himself, through John Fowler, a gentleman-attendant who slept in the King's bedroom. Fowler, too, confessed at enormous length. Evidently the Protector had subjected his young charge to a strict régime (he was used to being thrashed by his tutors[25]), and in particular had kept him short of pocket-money. The Admiral had sent the boy cash (on one occasion, as he admitted himself, £40), and they had exchanged notes; they had discussed the possibility of Somerset's death, and of Edward becoming a real ruler, under the Admiral's guidance. In short, Seymour had tempted a gullible boy with the object of usurping the Protector's functions and marrying into the blood royal himself. When questioned, Edward admitted all this, and turned, as it were, King's evidence against himself. His account, for obvious reasons, was not made public, but it was damning to the Admiral. Also, since it raised the question of the Admiral's marriage plans, it brought in Elizabeth.

Seymour was sent to the Tower on 17 January 1549, and within a week was joined not only by Sharington and Fowler, but by three members of Elizabeth's household, including Mrs Ashley and Parry. The Princess herself was at Hatfield, and a special commissioner of the Council, Sir Robert Tyrwhit, was sent there to take charge of the household and get Elizabeth to confess all. He found her, as he reported to Somerset on 22 January, 'marvellously abashed, and did weep tenderly a long time'. But she was not forthcoming: 'in no way will she confess any practice by Mistress Ashley or the cofferer [Parry] concerning my Lord Admiral; and yet I do see it in her face that she is guilty and do perceive as yet she will abide more storms ere she accuse Mistress Ashley.'[26] Next day, after a further long interrogation, he added ruefully: 'I do assure your Grace she hath a very good wit and nothing is gotten of her but by great policy.'[27]

Tyrwhit's object was to persuade her to accuse the Admiral, and to lay her own responsibilities on her servants, so that, as he put it, 'all the evil and shame should be ascribed to them, and her youth considered both with the King's Majesty, your Grace, and the whole Council'. Elizabeth's object was quite different. She did not care what happened to the Admiral; she knew nothing of his treasonable actions; his dealings with her had been entirely innocuous, and immediately he raised the question of marriage she referred him to the Council. Her object was to secure the exoneration of herself, not on the grounds of youth, but on the more solid foundation of her complete innocence; and to do this she needed to exculpate her servants and secure not only their release but their reinstatement and vindication.

In this battle of wits, she was more than a match for Tyrwhit. His first mistake was to allow her to write to the Protector – her principal judge, as it were – a privilege denied to most Tudor suspects of treason. She promptly passed to the offensive. Having dealt with the question of Durham House and the proposed marriage, she added:

Master Tyrwhit and others have told me that there goeth rumour abroad, which be greatly both against my honour and honesty (which above all other things I esteem) which be these: that I am in the Tower, and with child by my

Lord Admiral. My Lord, these are shameful slanders, for the which, besides the great desire I have to see the King's Majesty, I shall most heartily desire your Lordship that I may come to the Court after your first determination, that I may show myself there as I am.[28]

Tyrwhit's next mistake was to show her Kat Ashley's and Parry's confessions. She read them through, as he said, 'half breathless', as well she might, but she immediately perceived – something which had eluded Tyrwhit – that their revelations about the sexual rompings, though embarrassing, were legally harmless. She promptly confirmed them, adding a few details of no consequence. Exasperated, Tyrwhit wrote to Somerset: 'they all sing one song, and so I think they would not, unless they had set the note before.' In fact, Elizabeth was merely exercising her intelligence. She, too, wrote again to the Protector: her four surviving letters, in which she argued the case with him, may be termed her first state papers, marked by shrewdness, insight into his character, a clear understanding of the political issues involved, and a determination to turn the whole episode to her advantage. First, she cleared herself in the Protector's own mind. Having secured this, she pressed further, and asked for her innocence to be publicly admitted. Let the Council, she said, 'send forth a proclamation into the counties, that they refrain their tongues, declaring how the tales be but lies . . .'.[29] Having extracted a promise of this (no such proclamation was in fact issued), she then demanded the restoration of her servants, especially Kat Ashley. Mrs Ashley, she said, was a faithful servant. She had always advised Elizabeth to act on serious matters only with the consent of the Council, and, most important of all, if Mrs Ashley were not released, 'it shall, and doth, make men think that I am not clear of the deed myself, but that it is pardoned to me because of my youth, because that she I loved so well is in such a place.'[30] Elizabeth was doubtless motivated by genuine affection for her servant, but what is so striking about this correspondence is her precocious concern for public opinion, not just at court but in 'the counties', and her determination to have it swayed in her favour. She did not want a grudging admission that there was no proof of treason against her; she wanted the nation to be clearly informed that she was a loyal subject. And, in effect, this is what she got. Kat Ashley was soon out of prison and back with her, and even Parry, whose muddling of her accounts Tyrwhit had immediately noticed, was back at his job within a year. But, being a practical woman, Elizabeth appointed another financial official to assist him, and supervised their joint accounts, initialling every line herself, as her grandfather, Henry VII, had done, half a century before.[31]

The Admiral was accused of treason under thirty-three heads, to only three of which he deigned to answer; in any case, he was not permitted to defend himself, since the government proceeded against him by Bill of Attainder, the usual Tudor method in such cases. The Bill passed the Lords unanimously, and the Commons, 'in a marvellous full' House, gave their assent on 4 March, 'not ten or twelve at most giving their nays'.[32] Seymour tried to smuggle out letters, written 'with the lachet of his hose' to Mary and Elizabeth, but they were intercepted. He died on 20 March, angry and unrepentant, or, as Bishop Latimer put it, in a sermon: 'He died very dangerously, irksomely, horribly . . . whether he be saved or no, I leave it to God, but surely he was a wicked man, and the realm is well rid of him.' To which most said Amen. Elizabeth's own reputed comment was: 'This day died a man with much wit, and very little judgment.' But her saying we owe to Leti, an Italian historical novelist of the seventeenth century, whose forged letters of Elizabeth (including an exchange with Seymour), still reappear in the more meretricious accounts of her life.[33] Certainly, Seymour had given her no cause to respect his judgment, but it is hard to see where she would have found evidence of his wit, either.

The Seymour episode is often alleged to have left permanent scars on Elizabeth, and in particular to have given her a lasting distaste for sex. But this is pure supposition. None of her contemporaries thought of it in such terms, though the well-informed knew all the facts, such as they were. John Clapham, one of Burghley's clerks, who wrote an account based on long conversations with the old man, reported, immediately after Elizabeth's death, that the cause of the trouble lay elsewhere: '. . . in the time of her brother, King Edward, she greatly affected Edward Courtenay, then Earl of Devonshire, whom she would have married; but her will, being crossed in that match, was ever after less inclinable to marriage'.[34] Maybe so, but Elizabeth herself never gave the slightest hint, by word or action, that she cared for Courtenay, at the time or later. As for Seymour, her behaviour, once she left Catherine's household, appears to have been ice-cold and carefully calculated. It was a case, I think, of 'chaste and unexpressive she'.[35]

For Protector Somerset, the execution of his brother was an important link in a chain of events which led to his own extinction. He was not suited to his job. By nature he was kind-hearted, but in manner overbearing. His friend Lord Paget warned him that at Council he 'snapped' and 'nipped' so fiercely that one member had left a meeting in tears and 'seemed almost out of his wits'.[36] His wife, Anne Stanhope, was a bully, who fought stridently for precedence over the ex-queens, quarrelled with her husband's colleagues and, perhaps worse, with their wives.[37] The lash of her tongue fell on most people, including Kat Ashley, who was bitterly scolded for allowing Elizabeth to be rowed on the Thames in the cold evening air. None of this might have mattered in itself. But Somerset was engaged in a series of radical policies which antagonized a variety of interests, each narrowly based, but formidable in aggregate.[38] His first parliament repealed a mass of repressive legislation, including the heresy laws, the Henrician treason statutes, and Henry's attempt to settle the state religion, the Six Articles, which were aimed mainly at Reformers. Somerset's object was to introduce an era of toleration after the Henrician terror, but the effect of his actions was to dismantle much of the machinery through which Tudor magistrates maintained any sort of order at all. Next, under the influence of left-wing clergymen and civil service idealists like John Hales, he began the rapid enforcement of existing statutes and proclamations against enclosures. This won him the support of the peasants, who called him 'the good Duke', but it infuriated not only powerful magnates, like the Earl of Warwick, whose own parkland was ploughed up, but innumerable lesser men, whose enclosed lands dated back three generations or more. Finally, in 1549, he introduced the first reformed Prayer Book, which all clergy were commanded by parliament to use. It was little more than an English translation of the Mass, but it was repugnant to the conservatives without appeasing the Reformers. These policy changes, affecting almost every aspect of daily life, were introduced against a background of uncontrolled inflation, a debased currency, and a revolution in the ownership of land which had begun with the fall of Cromwell in 1540 and had been gathering speed ever since.

Somerset, indeed, had appeared to give the sanction of authority to rapid change, indeed disorder; and the result was a series of rebellions. In Devon and Cornwall, the peasants rose against the new prayer book; in East Anglia, against the landlords, but under the aegis of Protestantism. Somerset the appeaser was thus driven to repression, but, anxious to maintain his personal popularity with the masses, he assigned the avenging armies (composed mainly of Continental mercenaries) to hard-faced magnates who had done well out of the Reformation: Herbert and Russell (later Earls of Pembroke and Bedford) in the West, Warwick in East Anglia. This was his final mistake. Once the peasants had been hanged or dispersed, the magnate generals used the backing of their armies to present Somerset with an ultimatum ending his protectorate. He retired to Windsor with the King and five hundred household troops; made a half-hearted effort to raise peasant levies; then, faced with the unthinkable alternative of civil war, in a country taught to remember the chaos of pre-Tudor times, he surrendered. By October 1549 he was in the Tower.

Thus ended a notable, if misguided, attempt at reform from above. Warwick, promptly created Duke of Northumberland, came to power ostensibly as the instrument of reaction, in reality as the leading member of a wide-ranging but uneasy coalition. He found it necessary to justify his actions to the Princesses Mary and Elizabeth by dispatching explanatory letters to them. He relaxed the King's regimen and gave him more pocket-money. He brought Catholics back on to the Council, from which Somerset had excluded them. But he found himself attempting to govern, without any real basis of personal or political support, a country which was moving slowly but surely into the Protestant camp. His personal religious views are obscure. Probably he had none, though he died, so he claimed, a Roman Catholic. But for purely political reasons he found it necessary not merely to endorse the religious reforms of his predecessor, but to give them a strong impetus in a Protestant direction, and to place himself at the head of the movement. The 1552 prayer book thus marked a radical change from its 1549 predecessor; in all essentials it is the document which Elizabeth's parliament finally endorsed in 1559, and which forms the basis of the modern Anglican religion. But the result was to commit Northumberland's future, and his head, wholly into the hands of an adolescent King, himself – to all appearances – a strong Reformer. If the King lived, well; if he died, Mary, an irreconcilable Catholic, stood next in line, by Henry's Will and Act of Parliament. This was the dilemma which Northumberland, spurred on by the young Edward, eventually tried to resolve by desperate methods.

Initially, Elizabeth gained by Northumberland's accession, however distasteful it must have seemed to her. Anxious to secure her good will, he rapidly passed the patents of her landed jointure, in the process arranging a transfer which was much to her taste. Edward VI had given him the Hatfield Palace and its estates in 1548; now, in return for compensating lands, he made it over to Elizabeth.[39] It became, and remained, one of her favourite residences, and until her accession it was her centre of operations. It was an old episcopal palace, rebuilt by Cardinal Morton in the 1480s, and used by Henry VIII as a royal nursery. Not much of the palace as Elizabeth knew it now remains, since it was radically altered as recently as 1830, and, of course, it is overshadowed by the sumptuous Jacobean house built by her last great minister, Sir Robert Cecil, after her death. By the standards of her time, it was comfortable if old-fashioned. Its glory was its great park, seven miles in circumference, crowded with deer. Surrounding the house was a middle park of 350 acres, and, within this in turn, an Innings Park, where the keepers raised colonies of conies, or black rabbits, delicious to eat.[40] With the settlement of her estate, Elizabeth acquired a Surveyor, at £20 a year, in the shape of Sir William Cecil, now Principal Secretary of State.[41] Naturally he appointed a deputy, but he supervised her accounts, and thus began a working partnership, based upon a mutual regard for sound finance and administration, which was to last until his death nearly half a century later. From this point Elizabeth began to save money, judging that legally-acquired chests of gold and silver are useful insurance in moments of peril.

She was now a woman of some consequence in Northumberland's Protestant state. To her young half-brother she behaved with all the formality Tudor protocol demanded, addressing him on her knees while he sat under the royal canopy. As children, there had evidently been some real affection between them; as both grew older, the relationship assumed the overtones of monarch and subject. They exchanged frequent letters, many of which survive, mere essays in epistolary skill which tell us nothing.[42] Not much flavour of Edward's personality emerges from the records, or from his own *Journal*.[43] He assented to the deaths of both his uncles without apparent emotion, and recorded their execution with unvarnished brevity. Until about 1551, he was a Tudor royal automaton, though he wrote some curious letters, blending friendship with regality, to Barnaby Fitzpatrick, the son of an Irish peer.[44] Elizabeth was frequently at his court, where she held great state. On 21 January 1551 the Imperial ambassador reported that she had been received in London with a numerous suite of ladies and gentlemen, escorted by a hundred of the King's horse: 'She was most honourably received by the Council ... to show the people how much glory belongs to her who has embraced the new religion and is become a very great lady.' On 17 March 1552, she entered St James's Palace with two hundred men on horseback.[45] At home, she lived the life of a wealthy woman, paying out wages and liveries to the value of over £400 a year, and hiring for her entertainment drummers and pipers, playing-children from 'Mr Haywood' and the King's household, 'Lord Russell's ministrels', lute-players and harpers.[46] Various marriages were proposed for her; none got beyond the paper stage.

During these years Elizabeth was building up her popularity in the south-east, and especially London, as a Protestant princess of striking appearance and notable accomplishments. But the political equilibrium rested entirely on the King's life. Henry VIII had taken extraordinary pains to protect Edward from any risk of infection. This kept him in good health until at least 1541, when he caught a fever. But in the long run such isolation, which could not be maintained once he became King, may have done more harm than good. He contracted first measles, then smallpox. He survived both, but his health was visibly weaker in 1552. Courts were infectious places, and the King was more exposed to contacts than most. Possibly he died of tuberculosis, but it may well be that a cold, or series of colds, caught in the winter of 1552–3, simply developed into pneumonia. Stow called his illness 'a consumption of the lights [lungs]'; to Edward's latest biographer it was 'a classical case of acute pulmonary tuberculosis'.[47] At all events, by April–May 1553, the King seems to have believed he was dying and began to take drastic steps to regulate the succession. From 1551 until the onset of his illness he had been steadily assuming the burdens of power, had ceased indeed to be a royal automaton and was emerging as a sovereign just as imperious as his father. He regarded Mary as wholly unsuited, on national as well as religious grounds, to succeed him. But he could not upset the succession statute, and his father's will, in Mary's case without eliminating Elizabeth also. His draft, in his own hand, of *My devise for the succession*, written before he became ill, provided that the crown should go – assuming he himself had no children – to the 'heirs male' of Lady Jane Grey, eldest of the Dorset claimants. He now changed it to pass the crown directly to Jane. On 12 June he summoned the Lord Chief Justice, Sir Edward Montague, to his bedside, and told him to draw up a will on the basis of the *Devise*. It has usually been assumed that Northumberland himself was the author of this attempt to alter the succession. Of course he stood to benefit by it. On Whit Sunday, 21 May, he had carried through a triple marriage scheme: his son, Guildford Dudley, to Jane, his daughter Catherine to Lord Hastings, and Jane's sister, Catherine, to his ally Pembroke. But the principal mover seems to have been the dying King himself. On 15 June he again called Montague to his room, and with 'sharp words and angry countenance' gave him a direct order to draw up the will. Montague reluctantly complied, and six days later Edward forced the Privy Counsellors, the magnates and other notables to endorse the document.[48] But neither of Edward's half-sisters was prepared to accept the alteration in the succession, which was plainly illegal.

Elizabeth resolutely refused any co-operation. As Camden, briefed by Burghley, later recorded, she told Northumberland and his junta 'that they must first make their agreement with her elder sister, during whose lifetime she had no claim, or title, to resign'. On 21 June, the dying King signed the 'Device' and the news got out. Mary immediately retired to the fortress-house of Framlingham in Suffolk, where she was surrounded by friends and adherents. Elizabeth, summoned to court, blandly replied that she was too ill to move, and sent a doctor's certificate to prove it.[49]

Edward lingered on until Thursday, 6 July, leaving Northumberland, with both Henry VIII's daughters beyond his control, to set in motion, without much conviction, the machinery of the *coup*. On the Sunday, the extremist section of the Protestant clergy performed their part: preaching at St Paul's Cross in London, Nicholas Ridley, Bishop of the metropolis, announced that both

Princesses were bastards, while the former Bishop Latimer of Worcester chorused that it were better both were taken away by God than that they should endanger 'religion' by marrying foreign princes. Jane was proclaimed Queen the next day at 7.00 a.m. On the Wednesday, Mary's own proclamation was published in Norwich. On Friday, Northumberland left with his troops to arrest her. But his fleet capitulated at Yarmouth the next day, a section of the Council deserted him on Sunday, the remainder on the following Wednesday, and the next morning, Thursday, 20 July, he surrendered in Cambridge. Three days later he was in the Tower. Once Northumberland was under lock and key, Elizabeth emerged from Hatfield and came to London. She was one of a great company who went out to greet the new Queen, and bring her back in triumph to London, on 3 August.

There were many lessons Elizabeth learned from this lamentable episode, indeed from the whole troubled reign of Edward. One was the strength of the Henrician claim. Many Protestant gentlemen, knowing full well Mary's views, came out for her simply because she was her father's elder daughter. The attitude of one of them, the fiery Sir Nicholas Throckmorton, was paraphrased by his contemporary biographer:

> *And though I liked not the religion*
> *Which all her life Queen Mary had professed,*
> *Yet in my mind that wicked notion*
> *Right heirs for to displace, I did detest.*[50]

The same sentiment was evidently felt by ordinary people, even the predominantly anti-Catholic Londoners: as Northumberland passed, captive, to Tower Wharf, 'all the streets [were] full of people, which cursed him, and calling him traitor without measure'.[51] Elizabeth must have faced the prospect of her sister's reign with considerable personal foreboding: but Mary's claim underwrote her own, in that both were based upon the same Will and statute. Moreover, the succession, thus ordered, was the sole guarantee of stability, and the best available safeguard against civil war. Religion, in this sense, was of secondary importance, and the opinions of religious experts contemptible. Had not men like Ridley and Latimer, who had fawned on her at Queen Catherine's house, who had only recently hailed her as a Protestant princess of the blood, promptly reversed their view at the behest of an adventurer, proclaimed her illegitimate and wished her death? The incident left her with an abiding distaste for bishops of any hue, especially in their capacity as advisers of state. She was to recall it bitterly during the 1566 parliament, in one of her finest speeches, delivered in the full flow of her anger. '*Domini Doctores*', she sneered at the bishops. Who were they to tell their sovereign what to do, 'since after my brother's death they openly preached and set forth that my sister and I were bastards'?[52]

More fundamental still, for her, were the purely political lessons of the reign. Social and economic reforms, however well intentioned, were intrinsically dangerous unless carried through on the basis of a conservationist philosophy, and within the strict framework of law and order. *Ceteris paribus*, caution must always take precedence over experiment. Above all, the magnates of the realm, however individually useful as servants, were confused and irresponsible as equals, and intolerable as masters. If she were called to rule as Queen, as Mary was now called, she must take all the real decisions herself.

In Trust I Have Found Treason
(1553–1558)

With the accession of Mary, England for the first time tried the experiment of
a Queen-Regnant. True, for a few brief years in the 1140s, Henry I's daughter,
the Empress Matilda, had tried to establish her claim to the throne by force of
arms, but her authority had never been generally acknowledged outside a few
counties in the West, and the period had been engraved on the national memory
as 'the Anarchy'. Since then, two Queen-Consorts, Isabella, wife of Edward II,
and Margaret of Anjou, wife of Henry VI – two 'she-wolves of France' – had
sought to play a major role in English politics, with disastrous consequences to
themselves and the nation. The English had never accepted the principles of the
Salic Law. On the other hand, their experience, such as it was, of women at the
helm had been daunting. It was for this reason that Henry VIII tried for so long,
and at such risk, to breed a male heir. Mary's success in establishing her claim
rested in large measure on the fact that the only active challenger was likewise
a woman, Lady Jane Grey. Thus, once Northumberland was beheaded,[1] Mary
did not find it necessary to proceed with Jane's execution, though she was kept
in the Tower.

Mary's problem was not just that she was a woman; she was also an
ideologue. Where her grandfather had been an empirical conservative in matters
of religion, where her father had been an experimentalist, and in the last resort
an Erastian, where her half-sister was to be a *politique* and a sceptic, Mary was a
convinced and inflexible papalist, prepared, indeed determined, to accept the
authority of Rome in all its plenitude. She was the only Tudor sovereign to set
herself a fixed and dramatic purpose – the reunion of England with Rome – and
to pursue it at all costs. Therein lay the failure of her reign, whose conclusive
note, as Pollard observed, was sterility.[2] Elizabeth was to learn, from Mary's
bitter experience, that England could be effectively governed only by the
fusion of ideas, and that there was no alternative but to search for the consensus,
and abide by its decisions.

Mary, to do her justice, sought to create as wide a consensus as possible for her policies, at any rate among the ruling class, and in doing so added to her practical difficulties. The law of England was made by the sovereign in parliament, but, for all practical purposes, the country was ruled and administered by the sovereign in Council. Henry VII had employed a Council of forty to fifty members, but in reality had governed through an inner ring of senior office holders. Henry VIII had allowed Wolsey to assume quasi-prime ministerial functions, but under Cromwell a small, working Council had emerged, consisting of heads of departments and operating Henry VII's system on a more formal basis. With the fall of Cromwell, faction re-emerged, and the Council became its battlefield. During Edward VI's minority, the Council had necessarily assumed the shape of a consultative body of the magnates, and had expanded accordingly.[3] At Mary's accession it consisted of thirty-one members, with a further nine 'called into commission'.[4] Some of these were now arrested, others later expelled, but Mary added her own personal group of advisers, most of whom had no administrative experience, and she recruited others with a wide range of views in order to secure the maximum support for her grand object. The result was a Council approaching fifty, three-fifths of whom had never served before. Bishop Gardiner was its outstanding member, but he disagreed with his Queen on key issues, and was unable to assume the role of first minister. The result was faction at all times, and at certain crucial points virtual paralysis. Mary often attended meetings, in an anguished attempt to compose differences, or impose her will; but, as she confided to Simon Renaud, the Habsburg ambassador, 'I spend my days shouting at the Council and it makes no difference at all.'[5] Renaud's dispatches home tell a dismal tale of disputes and sulks, of councillors boycotting business in dudgeon, and of Mary's futile efforts to reduce the numbers of her advisers without narrowing the base of her support.[6]

Mary's aim was to reverse the religious proceedings of the two previous reigns, and to restore England to full communion with Rome. The breach had been carried through by Acts of parliament. She believed, with all her strength, that parliament had acted *ultra vires*, overriding a moral and natural law which no earthly assembly could challenge. But in practice she found that she, too, had to turn to parliament to undo the damage; and parliament, moreover, was only willing to go half the way. Her first parliament, which met on 5 October 1553, repealed the religious legislation of Edward VI and gave her a new Treasons Act.[7] But it resolutely declined to hand back the Church property seized at the dissolution of the monasteries and chantries; nor was it yet prepared to countenance repressive legislation in religious matters. Moreover, by appealing to parliament at all, Mary had already tacitly conceded its overriding authority. Hence her determination to underpin her religious counter-revolution by allying herself, through marriage, to the power of the Habsburgs. As early as 20 September, the Emperor Charles v had offered her his son, Philip. On 29 October she decided to accept him. But this, in turn, raised fresh and more formidable difficulties. The bulk of the Council, and the overwhelming majority of the nation, were hotly opposed to 'the Spanish marriage'. Gardiner wished her to marry Edward Courtenay, Earl of Devon, who had a Plantagenet claim, and thus keep the throne firmly in English hands. Along with most of the Council, he was prepared to re-forge the links with Rome, but only in a manner compatible with English nationalism. Unable to obtain the Council's acquiescence, Mary tried to bypass it. On 8 November she told Renaud she accepted Philip's offer; the audience was secret, and only five of her personal friends were present.[8] But a royal marriage was not a matter for secrecy; the news got out, and a week later the Commons presented a petition begging the Queen not to marry outside the realm. Furious, she silenced the Speaker before he could finish reading it.

Other men were prepared to go much further than present petitions, and by 25 November 1553, conspirators were already holding meetings in London. This immediately raised the issue of Princess Elizabeth. She was now twenty, and with a wide acquaintance in political circles. She was popular with the masses and believed to be a staunch Protestant – certainly an English nationalist. Her relations with her half-sister were delicate. When Elizabeth was a child, Mary had treated her with intermittent affection: there are records of gifts – a silver-embroidered box, worth 20s., for instance, and a kirtle of yellow satin, at 7s. 6d. a yard.[9] They were never close; how could they be? But they were indissolubly linked by the similarity of their title to the throne, and on her accession Mary underlined this by granting Elizabeth equal precedence with Anne of Cleves. She followed this by sending a valuable brooch of diamonds and rubies, and by instructing the Wardrobe to issue her sister with regal quantities of material for her coronation robes.[10] But there was a barrier, both intellectual and visible. As Elizabeth was later to put it, without qualification: 'We differed on religion.' During these years Elizabeth affected the appearance which Reforming clergymen thought suitable for young maids. She dressed simply, in costly materials, but usually without colour. Her outfits were of white, or black and white (which remained her favourite until the end).[11] She wore no make-up and little jewellery; for a time she declined to use the brooch and other valuables Mary had presented to her.[12] Her style – at a time when dress and ornamentation contained an infinity of symbolism for all – was in marked contrast to the riot of colour and gold that Mary, as a conscientious Catholic sovereign, felt obliged to wear. Where rival clergymen fought with texts, the weapons of women of rank were needle and thread. Elizabeth was an ocular rebuke to the old religion.

Mary began to put pressure on her sister to conform, and in particular to attend Mass openly, during August 1553.[13] Early in September, the two women had a long and painful interview, at which Elizabeth shed tears, complained she had 'never been taught the doctrines of the ancient religion', asked for books and instruction, but added a qualifying clause about her conscience.[14] She promised to attend Mass, and indeed did so on occasions, but it became clear that she went, as Mary put it, 'only out of hypocrisy'. She believed, and with reason, that Elizabeth was intellectually and temperamentally incapable of becoming a sincere Catholic. She also believed, and with equal reason, that Elizabeth would never scruple to tell a lie to protect herself. Indeed, it was a salient difference between these ill-matched sisters. Mary usually told the truth to the best of her ability. Except in moments of anger, Elizabeth always subjected the truth to political convenience. At all events, in the autumn Mary downgraded Elizabeth's precedence, and on 6 December, after repeated requests, she allowed her sister to retire from court and go to her house at Ashridge.

The falling out of the sisters, on what was palpably a matter of religion, became instantly public, and therefore a political factor. It coincided with the revelation of Mary's plans to marry Philip. For Henri II of France, and his London ambassador, Noailles, it was imperative to prevent the consummation of the Anglo-Spanish alliance or, failing this, to foster in England a faction opposed to it, grouped round an alternative claimant to the throne. To Renaud, and the Spanish party, the best solution was to marry Elizabeth promptly to a foreign, and Catholic, grandee, and spirit her out of the kingdom. To Gardiner, and the English Catholic nationalists, the right alternative was to marry her to Courtenay, and thus ensure an English succession if Mary were to die childless. To the English Protestants, Elizabeth was the natural focus of rebellion.

The conspirators who first met on 26 November were not a homogeneous group. Only one, William Thomas, Clerk to the Privy Council under Edward VI, was a strong Protestant. Sir Peter Carew was a West Country maritime adventurer. Together with William Winter, a former Surveyor of the Navy, he represented the English seafaring interest which was violently opposed to the Spanish connection, and anti-Catholic for commercial reasons. Most of the rest had served under Northumberland: Sir James Croftes as Deputy in Ireland, Sir William Pickering as ambassador in Paris, Sir Edward Rogers as Gentleman of the Privy Chamber, Sir Edward Warner as Lieutenant of the Tower. Others, such as Sir Thomas Wyatt, came from fashionable courtly families.[15] All were known to Elizabeth; two, Croftes and Sir Nicholas

Throckmorton, had regular access to her.[16] In November they asked Noailles for naval support, with the qualification that no Frenchman was actually to land. (This was not in fact agreed until 22 January 1554, by which time it was too late.) On 22 December, in conjunction with the Duke of Suffolk (formerly the Marquess of Dorset), they settled on a fourfold rising: Croftes was to raise Herefordshire; Carey (with Edward Courtenay) Devon; Suffolk, Leicestershire; and Wyatt, Kent.[17] Operations were planned to begin simultaneously on Palm Sunday, 18 March 1554. Mary was to be deposed, and Elizabeth, married to Courtenay, proclaimed Queen.

By the standards of most Tudor conspiracies, the plot was by no means amateurish. It had some genuine ingredients for success. For one thing, the marriage treaty with Philip, now in course of negotiation (it was actually signed on 12 January) was universally unpopular: on 23 December Noailles reported that Plymouth was preparing to resist the arrival of Philip by force. To most of Mary's councillors, the match was so abhorrent that they insisted on inserting unprecedented safeguards which Philip found humiliating – so much so that when he received the final draft he added a secret clause, with clerical sanction, absolving himself from its provisions. All this was fertile ground on which to base a change of government. But the number of the conspirators was so large, and the scope of the rebellion so wide, that secrecy proved impossible. By 2 January the Council had got wind of it. By 17 January they had garrisoned Exeter, thus effectively putting paid to the Western rising. The next day Renaud, who had his own well-rewarded sources, gave all his information personally to Mary. Wyatt and his colleagues, who heard this immediately, then decided to scrap their timetable and raise their followers at once.

The rebellion and its suppression revealed the English people not so much as partisans of either side, as hostile to the violence the process of choice involved. Wherever possible, they closed their gates, bolted their shutters, and waited. Suffolk rode down to the Midlands, but after Coventry refused him admittance, his rising collapsed. Carew could collect only seventy men in Devon and fled to France. Wyatt held a council of war at Allington Castle in Kent on 19 January, but only thirty gentlemen joined him. The government, however, could raise less than half this number locally. When the Duke of Norfolk tried to attack Wyatt's forces at Rochester bridge, on 29 January, most of his white-coated men deserted, and he retreated to London. But Wyatt failed to arouse much enthusiasm either. By 3 February he was at Southwark, with no more than 3,000 men, including some who had joined him from the capital. He found the bridge defended, so turned west to Kingston, where he crossed the Thames, finally entering London through Knightsbridge. Most people, including the predominantly Protestant inhabitants of London, seem to have been torn between loyalty to Mary, and hatred of her policies.

Wyatt might have negotiated with Gardiner the obvious solution: the scrapping of the Spanish marriage, and the settlement of the succession on all-English lines. When Gardiner advised Mary to leave for Windsor, this was clearly what he had in mind. He had already interrogated Courtenay on 21 January, and found him a wholly pliable instrument: he would marry either Mary or Elizabeth or, if necessary, both in turn. But Mary adamantly refused to leave London. On 1 February she went to the Guildhall and addressed leading Londoners. She promised them she would not marry 'out of the realm', except by the advice and consent of the Council, and that she would call a parliament and act 'as they shall find'. For once she told a deliberate lie, since she had already informed Renaud that she considered herself to be, morally, Philip's wife. But her speech, and her continued presence in London, tipped a delicate balance slightly in her favour. When Wyatt finally approached London, on 7 February, he was confronted by some regulars, under the Earl of Pembroke. His own men were tired and hungry, and it was apparent that both sides were unwilling to fight and anxious to desert. By 5.00 p.m. he had reached Ludgate, which he found shut against him. The issue could still have been resolved either way, but Wyatt was discouraged at his reception by the Londoners. When Pembroke, pressing behind him, called on him to surrender, he did so, to avoid bloodshed. In fact, less than forty men had been killed, all told. The nation, in so far as it reacted at all, had signified its desire that the future of the realm should be settled by political discussion and compromise, not by arms.

Meanwhile, what of Elizabeth, the designated beneficiary of the plot? That she knew its general outline seems certain. She took no active step to forbid it. Croftes, confident of her acquiescence, was able to assure Noailles that the rising had what he termed 'a foundation'. On the other hand, she did nothing whatever to provide encouragement, and the necessity for premature action removed any chance that she would be forced to show her hand, either way. When Wyatt left to rouse his followers, he wrote to her 'that she should get herself as far from the City as she could, the rather for her safety from strangers'. To this, 'she sent him word again, but not in writing, by Sir William Saintlow, that she did thank him much for his goodwill, and she would do as she should see cause'.[18] She was now a woman of ultra-cautious spirit, and of much experience in such matters. I find it hard to believe that she committed herself, even by inference, in writing. Gardiner at the time, and innumerable historians ever since, have failed to trace such a letter. Any unavoidable verbal communications she made were guarded and ambiguous. Gardiner could not get a single witness to testify that at any time she used words which could be construed as treasonable. It may be that she disapproved of the whole enterprise. She knew far more about her sister's physical condition than any of the conspirators, and might well have calculated that the succession would come to her in any case, and probably quite soon. Certainly, within the next decade, she had convinced herself that the conspirators had acted recklessly, and in flagrant disregard for her own interests and safety: by their folly, she had nearly been killed. This is the meaning of a bitter passage in her speech to members of both Houses on 5 November 1566. No one present, she complained, 'ever was a Second Person, as I have been, and have tasted of the practices against my sister – who, I would to God, were alive again. I had great occasion to hearken to their motions, of whom some of them are of the Common House . . . were it not for my honour, their knavery should be known . . . I stood in danger of my life, my sister was so incensed against me . . .'.[19] Two at least of the former conspirators were, almost certainly, present during this speech: Elizabeth was challenging them to tell a different tale. Neither could, or dared, do so.

But even if Elizabeth were wholly innocent, nothing could prevent her from becoming a leading suspect. Even before Wyatt raised his standard, Mary had written to her sister summoning her to court. Elizabeth's reply pleaded illness – 'such a cold and headache that I have never felt their like'. On 26 January Mary sent a more peremptory summons: 'with all convenient speed to make your repair hither to us, which we pray you, fail not to do . . .'.[20] Elizabeth replied, verbally, that she was too ill to set out. Mary had received a report that Croftes had been urging her sister to move from Ashridge to her defensible house at Donnington. Moreover, Gardiner discovered a copy of Elizabeth's previous letter to the Queen in an intercepted diplomatic pouch of Ambassador Noailles – how, and why, had it got there? On 9 February, Mary sent Lord William Howard to Ashridge with explicit orders to bring Elizabeth to Whitehall, if necessary by easy stages. He brought doctors with him, who reported that, though ill, the Princess was fit to move.[21] She travelled by litter, taking nearly a week over the short journey. The Londoners who saw her arrive reported her deathly pale, dressed in pure white; hostile observers described her as 'proud, haughty and defiant'.[22]

Already, on Sunday, 11 February, in a court sermon, Gardiner had made it plain that, in the government's opinion, heresy lay at the root of the conspiracy and must be extirpated: 'Whereby all the audience did gather there should shortly follow sharp and cruel execution.'[23] Gardiner had, by now, abandoned any plans he may have had for marrying Elizabeth to Courtenay, and was determined on her trial. This was also Renaud's view. The attitude of the Spanish party was put by Bernadino de Mendoza in a letter to the Bishop of Arras: 'It is considered that she will have to be executed, as while she lives it will be very difficult to make the Prince's [Philip's] entry here safe.'[24] But Lord Paget, the senior Secretary of State, was strongly opposed to proceedings against Elizabeth. Along with most of the Council, he believed they would merely precipitate further rebellion, and this time with a more popular base. In any event, the evidence against her was purely circumstantial. One of her household, Saintlow, had been seen with the rebels at Tonbridge, but he resolutely refused to make any statement against her. Lord Russell admitted to carrying Wyatt's letters to her – but where were the replies? On 25 February Sir John Bourne reported to Gardiner that he had 'laboured to make Sir Thomas Wyatt confess concerning the Lady Elizabeth' – but unsuccessfully, though torture had been employed.[25] At his trial on 15 March Wyatt merely said that he had written to Elizabeth, but had received only a verbal and non-committal reply. On the scaffold, he reiterated that he had betrayed neither Elizabeth nor Courtenay: '. . . I assure you that neither they nor any other now in yonder hold of durance [the Tower] was privy to my rising.' At this point he was interrupted by one of Mary's clerical advisers, Dr Weston, who shouted: 'Mark this, my masters, he sayeth that that which he showed to the Council in writing of my Lady Elizabeth and Courtenay is true.' This attempt flatly to contradict Wyatt's last statement was hotly resented by the crowd. It was against the protocol of capital punishment, and moreover fitted in too neatly to rumours spread by Gardiner that Wyatt had confessed all in writing. Later, Lord Chandos testified in Star Chamber that Wyatt had made such a confession the morning of his execution, but no such document was produced at the time, or has been found since. It is true that Gardiner had in his possession one useful piece of evidence against Elizabeth: the copy of her letter to Mary found in Noailles's bag. But, while anxious to eliminate Elizabeth, he was still more anxious to save Courtenay for a rainy day; and the dispatch itself described a secret and compromising interview he himself had had with the Earl. He was thus unwilling to produce the contents of the bag, and claimed they had been 'lost' when the rebels sacked his library at Southwark.

While the investigations proceeded, Elizabeth was held incommunicado at Whitehall Palace. On 16 March, the day following Wyatt's trial and conviction, Gardiner forced through the Council a decision to send her to the Tower. But there was no agreement as to the charges to be preferred against her, and an evident unwillingness among many councillors to accept personal responsibility for ordering her committal. After all, how soon might she be Queen herself? The Marquess of Winchester and the Earl of Sussex were deputed to escort her by water: the mob might demonstrate if she travelled through the streets. When they reached her room, on the morning of Saturday, 17 March, and explained their business, she demanded to see the Queen. This was refused, and she then insisted on writing to her. Winchester was unwilling even to concede this, but Sussex was anxious to cause no needless offence. So the letter was written, and during its composition the tide was falling, and the moment passed for the state barge to navigate the piles of London Bridge with safety. The journey was put off until the next day, and the letter delivered. It was not one of Elizabeth's most impressive compositions. It betrays considerable agitation and something approaching terror. On the top side of the paper the writing is regular and almost assured; on the reverse, it begins to degenerate and uncharacteristic repetitions and grammatical errors appear. What could Elizabeth do but deny any evil intention and protest her loyalty? There were no specific charges to refute. The letter is verbose, dominated by her evident horror of the Tower. Even so, she ran out of matter a third of the way down the reverse side and, with an uncertain hand, drew a series of diagonal lines across the rest of the paper, to prevent the insertion of a forged addition, before subscribing a final plea and signature. Yet, even in this moment of fear and abjection, Elizabeth's concern for public opinion emerged. In the letter's most significant sentence, she begs for a personal interview with Mary, 'for that thus shamefully I may not be cried out on, as now I shall be, yea, and without cause. Let conscience move your Highness to take some better way with me, than to make me be condemned in all men's sight afore my desert known.'[26] On the brink of the grave, as Elizabeth imagined herself, she retained the instincts of a politician.

Her entry into the Tower the next day, Palm Sunday, was later described in detail by the *Chronicle of Queen Jane*, Holinshed and above all by Foxe in his *Acts and Monuments*. They were, no doubt, embellishing what they saw as a supremely poignant moment in Protestant history. But we may well believe that Elizabeth, who had a talent for drama, took the opportunity to throw out some memorable phrases, and it is just possible that Foxe received his version from her own lips. What does carry the authentic ring of truth is Sussex's advice to the Tower authorities that she be well treated: 'Therefore let us use such dealing that we may answer it thereafter, if it shall so happen; for just dealing is always answerable.' Here he spoke for the majority of the Council, and especially for Lord Paget, who was strongly opposed to Elizabeth's arrest. Her quarters were not particularly spacious, for the Tower was crowded with prisoners and strict security was in force. But she got the large room on the second floor of the Bell Tower, in the south-west inner curtain wall, immediately above the room once occupied by Sir Thomas More. Her chamber had earlier housed Bishop Fisher of Rochester, and was later to be the quarters of James, Duke of Monmouth. It had a small lavatory, or *garderobe*, attached. She was allowed to take exercise along the wall northwards as far as the Beauchamp Tower, provided she was attended by no less than five persons, and this gave her a daily view of Tower Green and the block, then in constant use. Guildford Dudley and his wife Lady Jane had already been executed, on 12 February, immediately after the collapse of the rebellion. Lady Jane's father, Suffolk, followed on the 23rd. During Elizabeth's sojourn, Wyatt was executed on 11 April, Lord Thomas Grey, Suffolk's brother, on 24 April, and William Thomas on 18 May, the day before her imprisonment ended. She evidently believed each day might be her last, inquired anxiously 'whether Lady Jane Grey's scaffold has been taken down yet', and when Sir John Gaze was replaced as Lieutenant by Sir Henry Bedingfield, a dour Catholic and faithful supporter of Mary, she deduced from the arrival of fresh troops in armour that the moment had come.[27]

In fact she was throughout safer than she could possibly have imagined. The government handled the repression of the revolt with a good deal of leniency, though it was often confused and inconsistent. Whether this was due to Mary's desire for clemency, or divisions in the Council, or fear that the Londoners would rise if the butchery became too blatant, or, more likely, a combination of all three, the sources do not reveal. But a study of the Controlment Rolls, which indicate which sentences were actually carried out, suggests that surprisingly few of the rebels died.[28] Of those who took part in the attack on London, 430 had been convicted by 22 February, but 250 were immediately pardoned and released. Henry Machyn, the London undertaker whose chronicle covers these years – and who took a professional interest in such matters – says that 45 were executed on 14 February, and a few more at Southwark the following day; during the next fortnight 30 were sent down to Kent to be hanged locally, but some at least of these were pardoned. We can count 71 certain executions in all. In other cases local authorities, who did not wish to risk unpopularity, simply 'forgot' until the panic died down. On Easter Sunday Lord Paget took advantage of Gardiner's absence from court to see Mary in her private chapel, and persuaded her to mark the holy day by releasing prisoners. When Renaud heard of this and upbraided her, she said it was an old English custom.[29]

The higher the social status of the rebels, the more lenient their treatment. Winter, Warner, Rogers and Arnold were never brought to trial at all, and received pardons in due course. Sir Gawain Carew and William Gibbs, prominent in the Devon rising, were brought to the Tower but no notice was taken of them, and they were later pardoned too. Croftes was tried and convicted, on 28 April, but he was not executed, and he got his pardon two years later. Even the execution of Thomas seems to have been carried out purely to appease Renaud. Throckmorton was brought before a London jury on 17 April, but defended himself with tremendous spirit, and after a trial lasting from 7.00 a.m. to 5.00 p.m., he was acquitted. This rare forensic defeat for the Crown made Mary physically sick. Two of the jury (the joint foremen) were sent to the Tower, the rest to the Fleet, but all were released after payment of fines, and Throckmorton himself was let out the following January.[30]

This being so, there could be no question of executing a popular Protestant princess. In the weeks following the rising, a number of incidents in London and elsewhere terrified the authorities. A talking wall prophesied, and other Protestant 'miracles' took place. Noailles reported that, after Wyatt's beheading, the London mob struggled to dip their handkerchiefs in his blood. Within ten days his head had been spirited away, and a threatening letter was flung into Mary's own chamber.[31] Elizabeth's death would unquestionably provoke a popular explosion. In any case, how could she be brought to trial? What would be the charges, and the evidence, against her? Who would be prepared to serve as her judges? The days when Henry VIII could conjure up a treason commission of pliant magnates were long since gone. If Mary proceeded by Attainder, how could either House of Parliament be induced to pass the Bill? By mid-March, Renaud was reporting that the Council were hopelessly divided on the question of Elizabeth's execution. The lawyers urged there was no case against her, and, even if there were, the Admiral, Lord William Howard, whom Renaud said effectively controlled all the forces, would not permit it (he was, of course, Elizabeth's great-uncle). On 3 April Renaud wrote to Charles V reporting that, under English law, there was insufficient evidence to convict her. He had by now evidently given up the struggle, for in the same letter he again raised the question of marrying her abroad.[32]

By the end of April the Council had reached a compromise: Elizabeth would be removed to the country, away from rescue attempts by the London mob, and kept under strict house arrest. Early in May Bedingfeld arrived at the Tower with a hundred men, to take charge of the prisoner; on the 19th they set off on the long journey to Woodstock, a dilapidated royal hunting lodge in Oxfordshire. Elizabeth may still have believed she was on her way to a secret death, or so Foxe later reported.[33] But nothing could have been further from Bedingfeld's thoughts, or indeed his instructions. He was under orders to keep his prisoner isolated but also to guard her from seizure by Protestants or assassination by ultra-Catholics. Through his lengthy and painstaking letters to the Council, we can trace the evolution of one of the most curious personal relationships in Elizabeth's life.[34] Indeed in some ways it was the kind of relationship she thoroughly enjoyed: a battle of wits against someone of wholly different character and assumptions. She was later to establish similar relationships with some of her greatest servants, notably Sir Francis Walsingham. Sir Henry Bedingfeld was the head of an old Norfolk family. He was austere, conscientious, courteous to a fault, and unimaginative. He regarded his present employment with repugnance. The custody of a state prisoner in Tudor times was always costly, since it was difficult, and sometimes impossible, to recover the expense in full, and Bedingfeld, though he had broad acres, was not rich. More important, he was a gentleman of the old school, who venerated royalty as much as the ancient religion. He indignantly rejected Elizabeth's assertion that he was her 'gaoler'; he saw himself in the role of protective custodian, and he insisted on addressing her, even while adamantly refusing her demands, on his knees.

Bedingfeld was impregnated with the old medieval tradition that a crown servant should do nothing 'without sufficient warrant'.[35] He was anxious not to oppress his charge; equally anxious to carry out the Council's instructions to the letter, but not a whit beyond it. He thus became the embattled intermediary between the Princess's haughty insistence on a degree of freedom and privilege, and access, and the government's desire for severity and strict security. The trouble began on the journey itself. The escort of the prisoner turned into a triumphal progress, as Buckinghamshire and Berkshire peasants turned out to call 'God Save Your Grace!' At High Wycombe the citizens threw cakes and biscuits into Elizabeth's litter in prodigious quantities. At Rycote, near Thame, where she spent the night, her host, Lord Williams (later, with his wife, among her closest friends), entertained her in a style which Bedingfeld thought most inappropriate, but which he felt unable to forbid. At Woodstock itself, Elizabeth protested long and loud at the accommodation: a mere four rooms, in the old gatehouse, were fit for her use. Bedingfeld was more concerned to discover that only three of them had locks.

Here at Woodstock, for over nine months, a portion of her household reassembled to look after her. Her servants were carefully screened and, despite her complaints, Kat Ashley was not allowed to return as Mistress of the Maids. But Parry set up his accounts department at the local inn, the Bull, which Bedingfeld thought 'a most colourable place to practise in', much frequented by messengers and strangers, and beyond his sphere of control. Bedingfeld spent a great deal of his time refusing Elizabeth's requests – or demands – and writing to the Council to discover if they were allowable. He was constantly asking for fresh, or more precise, instructions, sometimes, as it were, echoing her insistent voice: 'and her Grace saith she is sure your lordships will smile in your sleeves when you know this my scrupulousness.'[36] She wanted more, and different, maids; paper and ink in unlimited quantities; permission to write letters to the Council, and above all to Mary (the Queen replied she did not wish to receive 'colourable letters'); a public state trial to clear her name, or alternatively her release; the right to walk in the great park, as well as the gardens, and to send messengers to court – and so forth. She also complained constantly of illness, arising, she argued, from the lack of exercise produced by Bedingfeld's restrictions. She demanded that the court doctors be sent down to look after her, and crushingly rejected the proposal that a learned physician from Oxford would do as well: 'I am not minded to make a stranger privy to the state of my body, but commit it to God.' She won this point, for eventually Dr Owen was dispatched, discovered that 'Her Grace's body is replenished with many cold and waterish humours', and recommended bleeding in the autumn. This was done. How genuinely ill Elizabeth was at any time during these years it is impossible now to discover. She could certainly produce symptoms, though one suspects they were caused by nervous anxiety, the tension of her relationship with Bedingfeld, and sheer bad temper as much as by any physical source.[37]

But she could also see the comedy of her position. Wit was never far away where Elizabeth lived. Some curious tales, all apochryphal, are told about her Woodstock days. Holinshed claimed that she used a diamond ring to scratch on the window of her chamber the words: 'Much suspected, by me; Nothing proved can be. Quoth Elizabeth, prisoner.'[38] But it was unlike her to leave such indelible traces of her feelings. As for Bedingfeld, as the restrictions were slowly relaxed, her dealings with him took on a more teasing tone. She bore him no grudge later: according to Foxe, she told him, when Queen, that she would be delighted to send him any prisoner who needed to be 'sharply and straightly kept'. In her litany of nicknames – always a sign of her affection – he remained 'her gaoler', and she once stayed at his house in Norfolk. All the same, both of them must have been vastly relieved when, on 17 April 1555, Mary decided to end Elizabeth's house-arrest and summoned her to Hampton Court.

The problem of what to do with Elizabeth continued to plague Mary until the end of her life. Her first statute legally bastardized her sister again, but did not erase her title. Gardiner's proposal for a further Bill to do precisely this met with no favour, and was dropped. The obvious solution, as the Spaniards all along suggested, was to marry her abroad. Their favourite candidate was the Duke of Savoy, a Habsburg client and a thorn in the side of France. But how could Elizabeth be compelled to marry except by force? Now and later she refused all offers unequivocally, including an adventurous personal approach by Prince Erik, son of the Swedish King. Meanwhile, Mary's own political difficulties were deepening. In the short term, the Wyatt rebellion strengthened her hand, and persuaded her to go further on her chosen course of re-establishing the Catholic faith and forging the Habsburg connection. On 1 May 1554 – while Elizabeth was still in the Tower – Paget persuaded the Lords to reject Gardiner's Bill re-establishing the old heresy laws. The Queen promptly disgraced Paget and forced him to retire to his estates.[39] This altered the balance of power on the Council. With Elizabeth safely in Woodstock, and the leading Protestant conspirators dead, in the Tower, or abroad, the Spanish marriage went ahead. It was not a very glamorous proceeding. Philip arrived at Southampton on 19 July 1554, aboard *The Holy Ghost*, and disembarked next day in the pouring rain. By the time he got to St Cross, outside Winchester, where he and Mary were to be married, his black velvet and white satin clothes were soaked. When they met, he kissed Mary on the mouth, 'English fashion'. He spoke no English but she taught him one phrase: 'Good night my lords all.'[40] During the wedding, her eyes never moved from the sacrament. The young bucks of Philip's suite deplored her piety and her ugliness alike: 'She is a perfect saint and dresses badly . . . older than we had been told . . . old and flabby . . . Not beautiful, small, flabby rather than fat . . . white complexion and fair, no eyebrows . . . It would take God himself to drink this cup.' The searing phrases arouse pity even at this distance of time.[41]

By September 1554 there were rumours, no doubt eagerly circulated by Mary herself, that she was pregnant. Parliament met on 11 November; the government had made some efforts to pack it with 'the old, wise and Catholic sort', and up to a point the assembly did as it was bid. It passed legislation ending the schism with Rome and brought back all the ancient heresy laws into force. Cardinal Pole, as legate, arrived from Rome bringing with him papal absolution for the realm, and in due course was made Archbishop of Canterbury. The government hoped that heretics would flee the country, and many did so, but others remained, and the first execution took place on 4 February 1555, when John Rogers, prebendary of St Paul's, was burned at Smithfield. To underpin security, parliament had been persuaded to pass a Regency Act, which gave Philip the government of the realm during the minority of his children, should Mary predecease him. But there was no question of his being formally crowned, and during these months Charles V was advised to prepare an army to secure Philip's English interests if Mary should miscarry and die. The Habsburgs had acquired their empire by two centuries of shrewd marriages; England was merely the latest plum they expected to fall into their lap. In these circumstances, it was felt important to bring Elizabeth to court, to be under close surveillance during the period of Mary's confinement.

Elizabeth left Woodstock, still escorted by Bedingfeld, on 20 April 1555. Her last stop before reaching Hampton Court was at the George Inn (which still stands) at Colnbrook, where some sixty of her gentlemen and yeomen had come to glimpse her. At the palace, there was no immediate summons to see the Queen, but Philip, according to Noailles, could not restrain his desire to examine this remarkable princess, and insisted on calling on her after three days. Mary sent her a rich gown – a Catholic gown, no doubt – to wear for the occasion. Elizabeth was also visited by Gardiner, Secretary Petre, and the Earls of Arundel and Shrewsbury. She greeted them: 'My Lords, I am glad to see you: for methinks I have been kept a great while from you, desolately alone.' She had evidently devoted a good deal of time to thinking out her line of policy, and stuck to it resolutely, on this and later occasions. When Gardiner, on his knees, begged her to submit and make a free confession, she declined: 'but rather desired the worst, if ever she did offend her Majesty in thought, word or deed ... in yielding I would speak against myself and confess myself to be an offender.... And therefore I say, my Lords, it were better for me to lie in prison for the truth, than to be abroad and suspect of my prince.' When this was reported to Mary she 'marvelled that she should so stoutly stand by her innocence'. But after Elizabeth had been at Hampton Court two weeks, the Queen decided to see her. Her Mistress of the Robes, Lady Clarence, was sent to her at 10.00 p.m. Elizabeth was ordered to wear her new best gown, and proceed across the gardens, by torchlight, to Mary's privy chamber, which she entered by a back staircase. Elizabeth fell on her knees at the sight of her sister, and the following exchange, according to Foxe, took place:

'God preserve your Majesty. You will find me as true a subject of your Majesty as any; whatever has been reported of me, you shall not find it otherwise.'

'You will not confess. You stand to your truth. I pray God it may so fall out.'

'If it does not, I desire neither favour nor pardon at your hands.'

'Well, you persevere in your truth stiffly; belike you will not confess that you have been wrongly punished?'

'I must not say so, your Majesty.'

'Belike you will to others?'

'No, please your Majesty. I have borne the burden, and I must bear it.'

Mary concluded this remarkable conversation between sisters by muttering, in Spanish, *Sabe Dios* – which Foxe, who recorded (or invented) it, took to be directed at Philip, whom he supposed hiding behind an arras.[42]

Mary was now, as she believed, in an advanced state of pregnancy. She may have been suffering from cancer of the womb; she certainly had the symptoms of amenorrhea, or absence of menstrual discharge. Midwives and doctors were probably aware of her true state, but encouraged her in her belief, thinking this might induce conception. New-born triplets were shown to her, born, she was told, 'of a woman of low stature and great age like the Queen'.[43] Her breasts swelled, and there was an emission of milk. For hours on end, she sat on cushions on the floor, silent and staring, her knees drawn up to her chin.[44] May passed into June, and then July. Hampton Court, packed with English and Spanish courtiers, impatient and increasingly sceptical, grew filthy, and the risk of plague became serious. On 3 August, Mary broke up the court and went to the hunting lodge at Oatlands; it was an admission of defeat. On the 29th, Philip left her at Greenwich and returned to the Continent.

Elizabeth was now virtually free. Mary had believed in her guilt, to some degree, from start to finish. As she told Renaud at the outset of the investigations, 'She is what I have always thought her.'[45] The latter had constantly urged – a telling point – that so long as Elizabeth and Courtenay were alive, Philip would never be safe in England and would remain in his own territories.[46] But now Philip was gone anyway, and Courtenay was pushed out of the country to Padua (where he died on 18 September 1556). After Philip's departure, Elizabeth was allowed to leave court, and reconstruct her household on the old lines, with Kat Ashley in attendance. In October, aged twenty-two, she returned to Hatfield. She was now, in conformity with the new law of the land, attending Mass regularly and even going to confession.[47] At first, her chaplain read much of the liturgy in English; later, on Mary's instructions, Latin alone was used in the Princess's chapel. Cecil and Ascham, among many others, conformed too; both were again in regular communication with Elizabeth, and in October Ascham resumed his Greek readings with her.

Mary was now fully engaged in the religious repression which was to consolidate Elizabeth's future kingdom. The burnings of heretics had begun in February 1555; they were to continue virtually to the last day of Mary's life. If Mary was merciful in avenging civil rebellion, she felt she had not the same right to exercise clemency in dealing with those who had defied the Deity. On 9 February she burned her first bishop, the earnest Hooper of Gloucester; Nicholas Ferrar of St David's suffered the next month. Other famous prelates followed: Hugh Latimer and Nicholas Ridley at Oxford on 16 October; Thomas Cranmer on 21 March 1556. With them went nearly 300 others, the great majority clergymen, artisans, agricultural labourers and other folk of very modest means; they included nearly 60 women.[48] The Marian burnings are worth analysis because they had an important bearing on Elizabeth's reign, not only during her first years, when the memory was fresh, but especially after the publication of Foxe's great book in 1563. This achieved immense popularity, second only to the English Bible, was constantly revised and reprinted, and, despite its cost (more than £6) had sold over 10,000 copies before Elizabeth died.[49] The martyrs were overwhelmingly from the younger generation, thus underlining Mary's identification with the ancient world, and the Reformers – including Elizabeth herself – with the new. Equally important, they were concentrated very largely in the south-east of the country. Apart from Gloucestershire, where 10 were burned, very few suffered in the West and Wales, and there was only one burning in all the northern counties. By contrast, there were 67 in London, 11 in Middlesex, 39 in Essex and 59 in Kent.[50] These were the economically advanced areas of the country, the areas where political consciousness was most acute. The capital and its surrounding counties held the key to the throne. No régime could hope to survive long against their enmity or even without their acquiescence, and any government which had their support, and still more enthusiasm, was strongly based.

There can be no doubt that the burnings were unpopular, above all in the localities where they took place. Heretics had been burned in England since the early fifteenth century (there are a few isolated cases before), but never on such a scale and in such a systematic manner. The actual executions, which men and women were encouraged, in some cases forced, to witness, were hateful affairs. Unless the fires were huge and burnt fiercely, the agony of death was prolonged. Sometimes the executioners tied bags of gunpowder to the bodies of the victims, to bring instant release. But rain – and the spring, summer and autumn of 1555 were exceptionally wet – frequently doused down the flames and turned the burnings into slow torture. The horror was heightened by the manifest courage of many of the victims, including women and youths, and rumour, in turn, dramatized their last speeches. Nor was there much doubt, in the public mind, where the responsibility lay: with the clericalist party and the Spaniards. Thus English anti-clericalism and English xenophobia, two mighty engines of political change, were steadily fuelled. How far the public was justified in pointing the finger of blame is open to debate. The lay Spaniards at Court were not averse in principle to the burning of heretics, but they certainly questioned its wisdom, in the light of Mary's predicament. Philip constantly urged restraint. Renaud, almost in despair, pointed the contrast between Mary's leniency towards political rebels and her reckless persecution of religious offenders. He did not appreciate that her conscience, which allowed her latitude in her treatment of threats to her throne or life, gave her no such freedom of choice – as she saw it – when the immortal souls of men and women were at risk. Thus, when he advised that, at least, the executions should take place in secret, she refused. It was the very publicity given to the terror which, she thought, might deter multitudes from the snares of heresy.

Equally, some clerical figures received a disproportionate share of the odium. Among the bishops, Gardiner and Edmund Bonner were singled out as the prime movers. It is true that Gardiner gave the initial impetus to the heresy-hunt. But he soon sickened of the killings, and died, on 12 November 1555, discouraged and disillusioned. Bonner, as Bishop of London, controlled the most difficult see in England, the prime nest of religious disaffection, and the place where the Queen demanded the sternest example should be set. He was thus heavily involved in the persecution. But, on a number of occasions, he substituted public whippings for burning and, when rebuked for scourging an old man, replied: 'If thou hadst been in his case, thou wouldst have thought it a good commutation of penance to have thy bum beaten to save thy body from burning.'[51] On 24 May 1555 Mary felt herself obliged to write to Bonner, reproaching him for delay in dealing with heretics.[52] Once Cardinal Pole took the reins of ecclesiastical power in his hands, he seems to have been the leading clerical proponent of the persecution: Foxe called him '*carnifex et flagellum Ecclesiae Anglicanae*'. But the ultimate spring of action lay in Mary herself. At the time of the passing of the heresy laws, she sent a personal note of instruction to Pole as to how they were to be applied. It survives only in translation in a Venetian dispatch,[53] and there is doubt whether the operative phrase should be 'without too much cruelty and passion' or 'without rashness'. But in any event, there is no instance where she advised, much less commanded, clemency; the evidence goes all the other way. Very likely she was much influenced by her Spanish confessors and chaplains, Bartolome Carranza, Juan de Villagarcia and Pedro de Soto, all of whom were experienced in Inquisition work and who took an active part in the English hunt. Another malign influence was Alfonso y Castro, an expert on persecution, who was a leading clerical figure at her court.[54] At all events, as late as August 1558, on the eve of her death, we find her writing a letter of direction to the Sheriff of Hampshire, rebuking him for staying the execution of a heretic who had recanted at the first touch of the flames, and bidding him see the business carried out.[55] The English were not wholly unjustified in calling her 'Bloody Mary' and in drawing, as they did at the time, a devastating contrast between her and her sister. In political terms, Mary was the leading victim of her own persecution, and Elizabeth its principal beneficiary.

Indeed, the closing years of Mary's reign passed in what might be termed an atmosphere of permanent conspiracy. Elizabeth was necessarily the cynosure of such activities. Indeed, she could never be sure that any friend or acquaintance, however discreet, might not – perhaps inadvertently – involve her in mischief. As she put it later, 'In trust I have found treason.' Moreover, there was now a double threat, for she stood in danger of the resurrected heresy laws. Mary might be unwilling, perhaps unable, to indict her for treason. But it was much easier to frame, and prosecute, a charge of heresy. An ecclesiastical court, manned by Catholic bishops who feared Elizabeth's accession, might be far more resolute in pursuing her than a commission of secular magnates, some of whom would be her friends and relations. As for Mary, granted her beliefs and character, it was not inconceivable that she might steel herself to burn her sister. This would explain the apparent fervour with which Elizabeth practised the Catholic religion after the end of 1554. If she was cautious on the political front, she was ultra-cautious on matters of religious ceremonial and outward observance. She also found it advisable to write Mary a series of letters, fulsome in their protestations of loyalty, and exuding a religiosity which was wholly alien to Elizabeth's character. They make curious reading. Thus, on 2 August 1556, she wrote of her horror at the activities of Protestant discontents, at seeing 'the rebellious hearts and devilish intents of Christians in name but Jews in deed, towards their annointed King'. St Paul was right to call seditious men the sons of the Devil; as for herself, 'the more such mists render obfuscate the clear light of my soul, the more my tried thoughts should glisten to the dimming of their hid malice'.[56] The last turn of phrase was characteristic of Elizabeth when in the mood for elaborate Italianate composition. Perhaps the thought behind it was more genuine than it seems, since Elizabeth may have squared her conscience by equating heresy with a threat to royalty as such. No doubt the letter was read in the spirit in which it was written.

But protest as she might, Elizabeth was always in the potential ambit of treason. There was no lack of men anxious to involve her. There was a plan to assassinate Mary and Philip as early as 25 November 1554. On 13 March 1555 Renaud reported a conspiracy to place Elizabeth on the throne and end enclosures. Ambassador Michieli of Venice noted another plot, in November 1555, to kill Mary at the state opening of parliament.[57] In March 1556 Philip was told by astrologers that there would certainly be a major uprising against him in England that year, a reasonable prediction in the circumstances. There were rumours that Edward VI was still alive, and one man was hanged for impersonating him. Bad harvests and economic depression deepened the general discontent. Mary was blamed by peasants and gentry alike, and, by a supreme paradox, it was generally supposed that Elizabeth, once on the throne, would on the one hand end enclosures and, on the other, show herself 'a gentleman's Queen'.

The only plot with any substance was the so-called 'Dudley Conspiracy' hatched in November 1555, against the background of a difficult and, to Mary's eyes, subversive parliament.[58] Its object was to remove Mary by force and place Elizabeth on the throne, and for this purpose it was planned to steal £50,000 from the Exchequer and transport it to France to hire ships and men. Although its master-mind, Sir Henry Dudley, was a fairly obscure member of the family of the late Duke of Northumberland, its roots went deep into the gentry and aristocracy, and it had the support of a large number of secular exiles, gathered in Calais. Dudley also had contacts in the Exchequer, and it was from that department that the plot was leaked. On 18 March 1556, twenty of the conspirators were arrested and sent to the Tower. Elizabeth was not directly involved. But in May two of her household, Kat Ashley and her Italian tutor, Baptiste Castiglione, were arrested and examined.[59] Moreover, a number of threads led to her. One conspirator, Lord John Bray, confessed that Elizabeth, as Queen, would be ' . . . a liberal dame, and nothing so unthankful as her sister . . . then should men of service be regarded . . . If my neighbour of Hatfield might once reign then should I have my lands again'.[60] Another conspirator, Sir John Perrot, was reputed to be Elizabeth's half-brother, as well as a Protestant. And her contact and supporter, Ambassador Noailles, was deeply involved, since on 4 June he found it necessary to leave the country in some haste. Sir Peter Killigrew, another friend of Elizabeth's, actually attempted an invasion, but was captured at sea. Most serious of all, 'seditious' (i.e. Protestant) books and pamphlets were found in Mrs Ashley's quarters, though neither she nor Castiglione was persuaded to admit anything incriminating.[61] By July, eight men, mostly of no great status, had been executed. Evidently Mary felt herself too weak, politically, to proceed against bigger people. Such executions as did take place were made the occasion for popular demonstrations against the régime. Even the investigations had to be entrusted to Mary's personal friends on the council, 'because Council matters are not kept so secret as they should be.'[62]

Moreover, by this time, Elizabeth had come under the protection – distant, unobtrusive, but none the less formidable – of no less a person than Philip himself. He was thinking, as he fondly imagined, in longer and wider terms than his spouse. What occupied the centre of his mind was not the divisions of religion, but the paramount need to keep the English-Habsburg alliance intact, and, if possible, to involve England in active warfare against his French enemies, the house of Valois. Elizabeth was more useful to him alive than dead, and as a friend rather than an enemy. Indeed, since he was by now convinced that Mary would never give him an heir, and in all probability would soon be dead, he was already thinking of Elizabeth as a prospective wife. These considerations dominated his strategy up to, and in fact well beyond, Elizabeth's accession. He did not always play his hand openly: thus, he permitted his servants to promote other marriage plans for Elizabeth, not only with the Duke of Savoy but even with his own young heir, Don Carlos. All the same, it is notable that, in preparation for his second visit to England, Elizabeth was brought out into the sun again, and became once more the grand lady she had been in the time of Northumberland. In the aftermath of the Dudley conspiracy, Elizabeth had been placed under the tutelage of Sir Thomas Pope, an affluent and generous gentleman, much given to the pursuit of learning. He founded Trinity College, Oxford, and he and Elizabeth often discussed its management and curricula. No doubt at Philip's suggestion, the supervision of Sir Thomas was progressively relaxed, and he was soon entertaining his charge with sumptuous theatricals, at his own expense. Philip, as a prolegomenon to his second visit, persuaded Mary to have Elizabeth at Hampton Court for Christmas, 1556. Mary may well have appreciated the suggestion, for in the absence of her husband she was an increasingly solitary and pathetic figure, and Elizabeth, if uncongenial in some respects, was her closest living relative.

Philip arrived at Greenwich on 20 March 1557, and three days later he and Mary rode in state through the City. Elizabeth's evident popularity was an important factor in Philip's policies. Her presence, alongside Mary and himself, appeared to signify her acquiescence in, even support for, their joint rule, and in particular for an English declaration of war against France. In April Mary was induced to pay her sister a visit at Hatfield. They saw the boys of St Paul's perform a Latin play, and watched bear-baiting.[63] At this point Philip had a stroke of unexpected fortune. On Easter Sunday, 18 April, Thomas Stafford, who had a distant claim to the throne, set sail from France with two ships to attempt a landing on the Yorkshire coast.[64] He took Scarborough Castle and proclaimed himself Protector of the Realm. But no one came to join him. On 28 April the Earl of Westmorland retook the castle, and Stafford was executed a month later. The *coup* was insignificant, but it had the political result of tilting the balance, within the Council, in favour of war with France, for there could be no doubt that Stafford had received French encouragement and help. War was declared on 7 June, and less than a month later Philip, his object achieved, sailed from Dover to the Netherlands. He never saw his wife again.

The final phase of Mary's reign was marked by a multiplicity of disasters. The economic recession continued. In the winter of 1557 a devastating influenza epidemic broke out on the Continent, reaching England early in the new year. By the end of 1557 both Spain and France were obliged to declare themselves formally bankrupt. England was in little better state, and it became increasingly difficult to ship silver across the Channel to support the operations of English forces in Flanders, or indeed to supply the Calais garrison. In August 1557, Spanish and English forces had won an ephemeral victory at St Quentin. But the fighting died down during the winter, and it therefore came as a shock to government and people alike when the French, in a surprise attack, stormed the walls of Calais on 7 January 1558. The English had held this large and wealthy town, without difficulty, for over two hundred years. It was the last remnant of their Gallic empire and, though the expense of its garrison greatly outweighed its strategic and commercial value, that was not how Englishmen, of all degrees and irrespective of their religion, saw it. Mary's councillors attempted to blame its fall on treachery by the Protestant exiles within the walls, but this excuse was brushed aside by public opinion, which placed the responsibility where it squarely belonged, on the Spanish connection and the incompetence of Mary's government.

Indeed, by insisting on English participation in the war, Philip had effectively destroyed any chance of maintaining the Tudor-Habsburg alliance in an active form. Whatever illusions he may have entertained, they were not shared by Simon Renaud. Renaud had retired at his own request from the English court in August 1555, but in March 1558 he wrote a long memorandum on the state of England which came close to the true position. It was certain, he said, that Elizabeth would now succeed her sister; the only question was how long Mary would live. Once she died, the religious settlement would be overthrown. 'It must not be forgotten that all the plots and disorders that have troubled England during the past four years have aimed at placing its government in Elizabeth's hands sooner than the course of nature will permit . . .' Elizabeth, he continued, was held in the highest honour and regard. It was impossible to stand between her and the throne; it might no longer even be possible to marry her to a safe foreign prince, such as Savoy. From the beginning she had been supported by an organized and influential party, which had saved her life after Wyatt's rising and thwarted Gardiner's attempts to bar her from the succession. It had stood in the wings, safe, while minor agents had woven plots, but once Mary died it would win all, and take England out of the orbit of Spain and Catholicism.[65]

In these circumstances, what could Mary do to ensure her policies were continued after her death? Even living, she went in peril of her life. She had doubled her guards and had taken to wearing armour. Only five trusted ladies were permitted to attend her, and she slept less than four hours a night. After the fall of Calais, Elizabeth withdrew her countenance from the régime. She saw her sister in February 1558 for the last time. Thereafter, she remained in her country houses, and waited. Whatever lingering thoughts Mary may have had of solving the problem by persuading Elizabeth to marry were dispelled by a report from Sir Thomas Pope, which he sent the Queen on 26 April 1558. Elizabeth, he said, was firmly opposed not merely to marriage to a particular person, but to marriage as such. He quoted her desire as: 'to remain in that estate I was, which of all others best liked me, or pleased me . . . I so well like this estate, as I persuade myself there is not any kind of life comparable unto it.'[66] This seemed, indeed, it was, final enough.

Elizabeth later compared the last months of Mary's reign to the experience, as she termed it, of being 'buried alive, like my sister'. It left an indelible impression on her memory and made her resolve never to designate a successor who would likewise overshadow her own throne; a resolve she kept till her death. As the summer of 1558 merged into autumn, it became manifest to all that Mary would not live, and that Elizabeth must succeed. The ill-informed may have supposed that, even at this stage, Elizabeth's claim might still be assisted by force. A letter from Elizabeth, written from Brockett Hall, Hertfordshire, and dated 28 October 1558, survives, in which she acknowledges an offer of troops from an unnamed person, presumably a magnate: she thanks him for his readiness 'to do unto us all the pleasure you can' and assures him she will not forget 'whensover time and power may serve'.[67] Certainly, almost till the last, Mary delayed designating Elizabeth her successor. When she finally made the gesture it was scarcely worth having. On 8 November she sent the Master of the Rolls and her comptroller, John Boxall, to Hatfield, with a message that she now recognized Elizabeth as her heir by right and law, and with a modest request to carry out the provisions of her Will.[68] For weeks virtually everyone else in a position to know the facts had regarded it as settled. The activities of government had been dying down. Cardinal Pole, like Mary, was mortally sick; he outlived her only by a few hours. Meanwhile, the traffic to and from Hatfield increased daily. Elizabeth had many visitors; a growing volume of mail was dispatched and received. Three messages from Parry survive, conveying cryptic instructions to one of her supporters.[69] Although no one anticipated trouble, Parry and Cecil clearly thought it right to take precautions. Parry was in touch with Sir Thomas Markham, commander of the Berwick Garrison, the largest regular military force in the country outside London and Dover. Markham had only 300 men under arms, but he received written undertakings from northern magnates to produce 10,000 if necessary, and he travelled south to Brockett to present the documents to Elizabeth. By the beginning of

November, Elizabeth had moved to Hatfield. Parliament met on the 5th, in anticipation of the change of régime. The same week, the Count de Feria, Philip's special envoy, arrived in London, with instructions from his master to smooth the way for Elizabeth's accession. In the name of Philip (who was still nominally King of England), Feria presided over a Council meeting on 9 November, which confirmed Elizabeth's right of succession. Archbishop Heath of York, who had succeeded Gardiner as Chancellor, received Cecil at his house on the 13th, to discuss arrangements for handing over the great seal, and the transfer of government. Feria had already seen Elizabeth, and reported to Philip that there would be a wholesale change of government personnel, with Cecil as Principal Secretary.

Mary died in the early hours of 17 November, and by 12.00 a.m. the same day Elizabeth had already been informed and had been proclaimed Queen. Tradition has it that she knelt down on receiving the news, and gave thanks to Providence in exquisite Latin. She had a good deal to be thankful for: the change of régime, with all that it implied, had been accomplished with remarkable smoothness. It was a thoroughly English operation, with everyone, in the end, leaning over backwards to avoid awkwardness or disturbance. As such, it exactly fitted the country's mood, for after twelve years of uncertainty and the constant threat of violence, there was a universal demand for stable government. But if Philip entertained the illusion that nothing fundamental had changed, it was not for want of accurate advice. As early as 14 December, Feria was warning him: 'The kingdom is entirely in the hands of young folks, heretics and traitors . . . The old people and the Catholics are dissatisfied, but dare not open their lips. [Elizabeth] seems to me to be incomparably more feared than her sister, and has her way as absolutely as her father did.' The new Queen had already crisply informed Feria that she owed her accession not to any efforts on Philip's side, but entirely to the will of the people. Feria added: 'We have lost a kingdom, body and soul.'

4

The Deep Consent of All Great Men
(1558–1567)

The twin kingdoms of England and Ireland, to which Elizabeth succeeded on Thursday, 17 November 1558, had seldom been in greater or more urgent need of strong, purposeful government. With a population (including Wales) of barely four million, England was puny compared with the French colossus and the Habsburg empire, still, during these years, growing rapidly in size and apparent wealth. Both these Continental powers were, in fact, shortly to manufacture for themselves crippling and divisive problems, but that was not foreseen at the end of 1558. The confused last years of Henry VIII, the faction-ridden minority of his son, the painful follies of his elder daughter, had cumulatively undermined the authority of English government, both at home and abroad. It was not clear how England was to be governed at all; still less, what methods were to be used. Among public men, there was almost universal pessimism. Two years later, Sir Thomas Smith, the distinguished Cambridge scholar who served as Secretary of State under both Edward VI and Elizabeth, recalled the situation at her accession:

> I never saw ... England weaker in strength, men, money and riches. ... As much affectionate as you [know] me to be to my country and countrymen, I assure you I was then ashamed of both ... They went to the wars hanging down their looks. They came from thence as men dismayed and forlorn. They went about matters as men amazed, that wist not where to begin or end. And what marvel was it? ... Here was nothing but fining, heading, hanging, quartering and burning; taxing, levying and pulling down of bulwarks at home, and beggaring and losing our strongholds abroad. A few priests, men in white rochets, ruled all; who, with setting up of six-foot roods and rebuilding of rood-lofts, thought to make all cocksure.[1]

In a government memorandum, written at the time, Armagil Waad, formerly clerk to the Council under Edward VI, summarized the situation tersely:

The Queen poor, the realm exhausted, the nobility poor and decayed. Want of good captains and soldiers. The people out of order. Justice not executed. All things dear. Excess in meat, drink and apparel. Divisions amongst ourselves. Wars with France and Scotland. The French king bestriding the realm, having one foot in Calais and the other in Scotland. Steadfast enmity but no steadfast friendship abroad.[2]

The advice he offered was that, in the circumstances, Elizabeth must proceed with extreme caution: steps must be taken on a number of fronts simultaneously, but with the watchword 'little by little':

I wish that you would proceed to the reformation having respect to quiet at home, the affairs you have in hand with foreign princes, the greatness of the Pope, and how dangerous it is to make alternations in religion, especially at the beginning of a prince's reign.[3]

Similar advice was offered by Richard Goodrich, an expert on ecclesiastical law, and even the fiery Sir Nicholas Throckmorton, the red-haired hero of Mary's treason trial – not a man normally given to caution – urged strongly the need 'to succeed happily through a discreet beginning . . . to have a good eye that there be no innovations, no tumults or breach of orders.'[4] Such counsel fell on fertile ground: it coincided with all Elizabeth's instincts, and with her intellectual appreciation that what the realm needed, and indeed wanted, above all else, was stability and public order.

Nevertheless, a very large number of decisions had to be taken, and with all deliberate speed. Probably at no time in her life did Elizabeth work so hard, or involve herself so closely in the detailed routine of government, as during the first weeks of her reign. Moreover, she had to get through this business while at the same time performing the dual role of superintendent and chief performer in the elaborate ceremonial build-up to her coronation – a vital aspect of her relations with the public. Her first executive step, and it was a crucial one, was taken on the morning of her accession, when she formally appointed Cecil her Principal Secretary of State. He was then thirty-eight, almost exactly thirteen years older than his Queen, and a man of great experience in the law, finance and diplomacy. He already had a well-deserved reputation for hard work and sobriety; even Ambassador de Feria of Spain, no friend, called him 'a prudent and virtuous man, albeit a heretic'.[5] The Cecils had come to court from southwest Herefordshire two generations ago, and were now settled at Stamford in Lincolnshire.[6] William's grandfather, David, had fought at Bosworth under Henry VII, been a yeoman of his guard and in his chamber, sat as an MP, served as steward of royal manors and sheriff of Northamptonshire. Among other property, he had acquired an inn in Stamford, the Tabard; Cecil's enemies later sneered he had been born in it. His father, Richard, had not done so well: he never sat in parliament and rose no further than Yeoman of the Wardrobe.[7] Cecil himself went to grammar schools at Grantham and Stamford, and later to St John's, Cambridge, where he married Mary, sister of John Cheke, the Professor of Greek. Mary's mother had kept an alehouse – which added to the smear-stories about Cecil's background – and the marriage evidently angered his father; but the connection with Cheke, later tutor to Edward VI, was a valuable one; and after Mary died, in 1543, Cecil married again, this time Mildred, eldest of the five remarkably clever and ambitious daughters of Sir Anthony Cooke, an Essex gentleman, Reformer and scholar.

Cecil was thus twice allied by marriage to the group of Cambridge intellectuals who came to prominence under Edward VI and who supplied much of the administrative driving force behind the English Reformation. But he was never a radical. Aged twenty-three, he sat as an MP as soon as he graduated from Gray's Inn, became a member of Somerset's household, and held judicial posts in the military Court of the Marshalsea and later in the Court of Requests. Somerset promoted him Secretary in 1548, and with Sir Thomas Smith he formed the conservative wing of a reforming government. In religion he was a right-wing Protestant, closely following Cranmer. When Somerset fell, Cecil spent a few months in the Tower, but within a year of his release, Northumberland made him Principal Secretary of State, in September 1550. Cecil was one of the durable 'survivors' of these difficult years. During the last months of Northumberland's rule he carried the main burden of an increasingly distracted administration; but he declined to sit in Edward's last parliament, and though, under pressure, he signed the formal papers excluding Mary and Elizabeth from the succession, he quickly disassociated himself from the *coup*, and was one of the first to pay his respects to Mary. She gave him no office, nor did he sit in most of her parliaments: though he conformed outwardly in religion, there could be no question of his Protestantism. But she used him on at least three diplomatic missions, and he seems to have formed a friendship with Pole, who left him a silver inkwell shortly before his death. Cecil took no part in the conspiracies against Mary, and his relations with Elizabeth (no doubt by mutual agreement) were confined to business matters. He seems to have shared her view that the succession would come to her anyway, and that it was preferable to preserve a reputation for conformity and loyalty to the crown.

At all events, she had no hesitation in making him the anchor-man of her government. He shared with her a deep conservatism, a passion for order and hierarchy, and a respect for established procedures and institutions; but, and this is equally important, both had a rationalist approach to politics, unencumbered by passion or ideology, which allowed them to see the necessity, and devise the means, for cautious reform. She appointed him with the following words, remarkable, coming from a young woman of twenty-five on her first day of power, for their regality, self-confidence and prescience:

> I give you this charge that you shall be of my Privy Council and content to take pains for me and my realm. This judgment I have of you, that you will not be corrupted by any manner of gift and that you will be faithful to the state; and that without respect of my private will you will give me that counsel which you think best; and if you shall know anything necessary to be declared to me of secrecy you shall show it to myself only. And assure yourself I will not fail to keep taciturnity therein and therefore herewith I charge you.[8]

Although the Secretaryship was not necessarily the most powerful office in the government – nor the most coveted – it brought its holders (especially the senior member of the pair: there were usually two) into a unique personal relationship with the sovereign. As Cecil's son Robert, who was to hold the office from 1596, later pointed out, the Secretary was not bound by a formal definition of his duties like other public officials: 'All officers and councillors of princes have a prescribed authority by patent, custom or by oath, the Secretary only excepted.' But he saw and registered all incoming mail, and supervised the drafting and dispatch of replies; through the Postmaster-General he had charge of the forty messengers attached to the court; and security, which embraced both the control of counter-espionage at home, and of intelligence abroad, was his special preserve.[9] He had a general knowledge of, and competence in, all matters of state; as Robert Cecil put it:

> ... a liberty to negotiate at discretion at home and broad, with friends and enemies, all matters of speech and intelligence ... As long as any matter of what weight soever, is handled only between the prince and secretary, those counsels are compared to the mutual affections of two lovers, undiscovered to their friends.[10]

Cecil's power thus depended essentially on his personal relationship with Elizabeth. It became close from the start and, except for a few weeks in 1587, was never really shaken. Cecil shared most of the conformist prejudices of his time, and he certainly began his work with a rooted disbelief in the judgment of women-rulers and in their capacity to conduct business professionally. But this slowly disappeared, as his admiration for Elizabeth grew. Within nine years, he was calling her, in a private memorandum for his eyes alone, 'the only physician, without whom neither remedies can be ministered, nor perils avoided'.[11]

Cecil's first memo to Elizabeth was written on the day of his appointment, drawing her attention to the most urgent matters: her proclamation and its publication, the manning of the Tower, a ban on all ships leaving harbour and on all transfers of money from the realm; the need to strengthen the defences against Scotland and France; all judges and JPs to continue in office; the dispatch of ambassadors to announce her accession; most important, the careful selection of an official preacher for the Sunday service outside St Paul's. This took place in the courtyard, attracted up to 5,000 people, and was a salient means of conveying the government's intentions to Londoners. Cecil advised 'that no occasion be given by him to stir any dispute touching the government of the realm'.

These matters were dealt with at the first, informal, meeting of the Council the following day, when a number of appointments – including Lord Robert Dudley to be Master of the Horse – were made. There was a formal session two days later, on Sunday, 20 November, when Cecil introduced Elizabeth to Sir Thomas Gresham, England's leading financier, who was immediately given a general mandate to deal with debt and currency problems. On the 23rd she renewed the authority of the English peace commissioners, who had been meeting since 15 October at Cambrai with the French and Spanish to end a war which was bankrupting all three countries. Records show that Elizabeth attended Council meetings on 21, 22, 24, 25, 26, 27 and 28 November, and on 1, 2, 4, 5, 6, 8, 9, 10, 11, 12, 13, 16, 17, 18, 20, 21 and 22 December.[12] During these weeks, she and her household were constantly on the move, first to Lord North's residence at the Charterhouse in London, then to Somerset House, then to the Tower, and finally, on 23 December to Whitehall Palace.

She was in some difficulty about her coronation. All the bishops, most of them appointed by Mary, were Catholics. Many refugee Protestant clergy were already returning from the Continent; as Bishop White of Winchester angrily remarked, in the sermon he preached at Mary's funeral on 14 December, 'The wolves be coming out of Geneva.' Elizabeth had already settled on 14 January as the most auspicious day for her coronation, in accordance with a cast made by the brilliant young mathematician and astrologer John Dee.[13] Could she get a Marian bishop to crown her? The English hierarchy were not well disposed towards the Pope. Giovanni Caraffa, who had been elected as Paul IV in May 1555, was a Neapolitan patriot with a violent hatred for the Habsburgs and Spanish rule. He had added to Mary's distress by excommunicating her husband; he had withdrawn Pole's legatine commission in a rage, and at the time of

Pole's death he was under orders to return to Rome to be tried for heresy.[14] As Archbishop Heath put it, Pope Paul had been 'a very austere, stern father to us'.[15] Elizabeth hoped to swing over some at least of the bishops, especially such senior men as Heath, and Tunstall of Durham, one of her father's appointments. Heath, in fact, continued to attend Council meetings until 5 January 1559. But Elizabeth was under great pressure from the other direction. On Christmas Day, at Mass, she withdrew when the host was elevated, and two days later she issued a proclamation permitting English to be used in all services. This might not have been decisive. What lost her the bishops was the growing realization that she was going to ask parliament – the writs had already gone out for a meeting on 24 January – to restore her position as head of the Church. She saw this as the only way to compose national differences in religion and secure some kind of uniformity. But the bishops as a group felt they could not eat their words again, and only one eventually did so.[16] After much negotiation, Bishop Oglethorpe of Carlisle agreed to crown the Queen, doing so in robes borrowed, ironically enough, from the hated Bonner of London.

The Londoners were probably unaware of these behind-the-scenes manoeuvres. At any rate, they made no secret of their delight at the new régime, and their loyalty to the new Queen. During December and January, amid all her other preoccupations, she showed herself frequently, both on the streets and in her state barge on the river. The Tower guns were constantly at the salute: 'There was great shooting of guns, the like was never heard before', and the City companies, following suit, mounted cannon on their barges, firing continuously as the Queen passed up and down the river. On 12 January, in preparation for her coronation, she followed custom and took up residence in the Tower. The next day she made a solemn progress through the City to Whitehall. Vast sums had been spent on the pre-coronation pageants, and on the ceremony itself. The state provided £16,741 19s. 8¾d., not including the cost of the banquet.[17] Elizabeth had already recognized in Robert Dudley a born impresario and master of ceremonies, and he seems to have been in general charge of the arrangements. Timber was brought up from the Windsor forest for seating. Other materials were shipped over from Antwerp, the great luxury emporium of north-west Europe. The Yeomen of the Guard got new scarlet coats, with silver and gold spangles. All the household, down to the jesters, Will and Jane Somers, were measured for new clothes; the thirty-nine ladies who attended Elizabeth were each provided with sixteen yards of velvet, plus two yards of cloth of gold; the senior officers of the state had crimson velvet and the Privy Councillors crimson satin. Elizabeth herself had four state dresses made: one, for her procession through the City, of twenty-three yards of gold and silver, with ermine trimmings, and silver-and-gold lace coverings. Her coronation robes, with their great cloak of ermine and embroidered silk, can still be seen in her official portrait,[18] but she had two other state dresses, of crimson and violet velvet, and changed her outfit twice during the ceremony. She had a crimson velvet hat, decorated with gold and pearls, and silk-and-gold finely meshed stockings. She had a new travelling litter, decked in yellow cloth of gold, and lined with white satin, which also covered her eight huge cushions. Some 700 yards of blue cloth, costing £154, was laid as a carpet between the Palace and the Abbey.[19]

The pageants were the responsibility of the City, and are described in considerable detail in a tract written by Richard Tottill, and published ten days after the coronation.[20] There were five major tableaux, and many minor ones, which were presented at intervals along the royal route. Tottill makes the point repeatedly that Elizabeth always stopped to ask the symbolism of the tableaux – in theory this was announced by a child, but small voices could not always be heard above the hubbub – and to thank those responsible. One of Elizabeth's great merits, as a public person, was the ability to listen attentively, and in patience, to such entertainments. A professional pamphleteer, Richard Fenchurch, recorded, at one tableau: 'Here was noted in the Queen's Majesty's countenance during the time that the child spoke, besides a perpetual attentiveness in her face, a marvellous change in look, as the child's words touched either her person, or the people's tongues and hearts.' She was, already, a great actress, with an enviable gift for the happy impromptu phrase. Thus, at the Little Conduit in Cheapside, she asked the significance of the pageant, 'And it was told her Grace, that there was placed Time. "Time," quoth she, "and Time hath brought me hither." ' In Cheapside, too, she was presented by the Recorder, on behalf of the City, with a purse containing 1,000 marks (£666) in gold. She took it, and answered 'marvellous pithily, so pithily that the standers by, as they embraced entirely her gracious manner, so they marvelled at the couching thereof.' Fortunately her words are preserved:

I thank my Lord Mayor, his brethren, and you all. And whereas your request is that I should continue your Good Lady and Queen, be ye assured that I will be as good unto you as ever Queen was to her people. No will in me can lack, neither, do I trust, shall there lack any power. And persuade yourselves that for the safety and quietness of you all, I will not spare, if need be, to spend my blood. God thank you all.[21]

The coronation itself was a magnificent and lengthy ceremony, for Elizabeth was determined to have the full political and symbolic benefit of the sacring, and to be crowned in the sight of all the assembled authorities of the realm. Virtually all the nobility was present, and the knights of the senior orders; the entire government; the judicial profession and the sergeants and councillors at law; the barons of the Cinque Ports and other provincial dignitaries, as well as the London corporation; and, not least, the bench of bishops, with the one notable and deliberate exception of Bonner. But on Elizabeth's instructions, the bishops performed their homage after the temporal peers, thus indicating not only her anger at those who had refused to crown her, but her considered opinion of their true status in the realm. Moreover, although this was essentially a coronation of the *ancien régime*, there were significant departures from the rubrics. When Oglethorpe administered the coronation oath, he did so from an English bible, held up to him to read by Cecil. The Bishop, who felt he was stretching his conscience as far as he was able, had adamantly declined to conduct the ceremony in English throughout. Indeed, after the crowning and homage, he insisted on saying a Latin Mass. But both the epistle and gospel were read out in English as well as Latin, and after the Offertory, which the Queen performed, kissing the paten, she withdrew to a pew, concealed by a curtain, in St Edward's Chapel, while the bread and wine were being consecrated and the host elevated. Thus the service was in some respects a muddle – one might call it a characteristic English compromise – pending the resolution of England's liturgical problems, but it was carried out with great aplomb and spirit, and there could be no doubt of its validity in the eyes of all.[22] Afterwards, Elizabeth, now in violet velvet, sat down to a banquet in Westminster Hall, which lasted from 3.00 p.m. to 1.00 a.m. the next morning. Sir Edward Dymoke, her champion, rode in mounted and in full armour, to issue the traditional challenge. There was more meaningful play-acting, too: two gentlemen, dressed symbolically as the Dukes of Normandy and Guienne, appeared to maintain her claims to her French territories. A joust planned in the Whitehall tiltyard for the next day was postponed; evidently Elizabeth spent it in her private quarters, sleeping and then working on her papers. Meanwhile, the citizens of London and Westminster had pounced on the costly blue carpet, and hacked it into thousands of fragments, to keep as mementoes.

During these weeks, Elizabeth had been forming a government of exceptional strength and great durability. She knew she had shortly to take, and win acceptance for, a series of decisions which would determine the whole character of her reign. She thus had to assemble an administration which embraced the widest possible spectrum of opinion, but grouped around a Council which combined manageable size, a reasonable homogeneity, professional experience

and relentless efficiency. I doubt if more careful thought has gone into the creation of any English 'cabinet' and the results rapidly became apparent.[23] Elizabeth
had thought out the matter carefully weeks before her accession, and she made
her views plain almost immediately, probably at the first formal meeting of the
Council on 20 November:

> . . . I shall desire you all, my lords (chiefly you of the nobility, everyone in his
> degree and power) to be assistant to me that I with my ruling and you with
> your service may make a good account to Almighty God and leave some
> comfort to our posterity on earth . . . And therefore considering that divers
> of you be of the ancient nobility, having your beginning and estates in my
> progenitors, kings of this realm, thereby [such] ought in honour to have
> the more natural care for maintaining of my estate and this commonwealth.
> Some others have been of long experience in governance and enabled by my
> father of noble memory, my brother and my late sister to bear office, the
> rest of you being upon special trust lately called of her service only and trust,
> for your service considered and rewarded . . . And for counsel and advice
> I shall accept you of my nobility and such others of you the rest as in
> consultation I shall think meet and shortly appoint. To the which also
> with their advice I will join to their aid and for ease of their burden others,
> meet for my service. And they which I shall not appoint, let them not
> think the same for any disability in them but that I do consider a multitude
> doth rather make discord and confusion than good counsel, and of my good
> will you shall not doubt, using yourself as appertaineth to good and faithful
> subjects.[24]

This signified a much smaller Council, from which the specifically Marian
elements would be excluded, but whose membership would emphasize continuity and the support of the senior magnates. Throckmorton had supplied her
with a suggested list of councillors, with various permutations for offices; she
did not follow his advice in detail, but almost all the men he mentioned got
something. Cecil's advice probably carried more weight in the actual appointments.[25] Of Mary's old councillors, less than a third were retained, and, as
Elizabeth hinted in her speech, these were mainly peers. Lords Montague and
Hastings, both Catholics and Mary's creations, were dropped, so were the
vicious and unpopular lawyer, Lord Rich, and Paget, closely associated with the
disastrous war against France. Among the peers Elizabeth kept, the Earl of
Derby was pre-eminent in Lancashire and Cheshire, and an important factor
in retaining the loyalty of the north, which Elizabeth believed with reason to
be highly conservative and pro-Catholic. The same could be said of the Earl of

Shrewsbury, who had been President of the Council of the North since 1550, and was lord lieutenent of seven northern and Marcher counties, as well as being, next to the Duke of Norfolk (too young yet for the Council), the richest peer in England. She also kept a third member of the ancient nobility, Arundel, whose title went back to Norman times, and whom she made Lord Steward. Her great-uncle, Lord Howard of Effingham, who had protected her after the Wyatt rising, was made Lord Chamberlain. The Earl of Pembroke was given no job, because he was barely literate,[26] but by virtue of his military experience and vast estates in the West he was retained on the Council, which he attended assiduously. Lord Clinton, Lord Admiral since 1557, was confirmed in his post and on the Council; he too had a good military reputation and had, moreover, married the mother of Henry VIII's bastard, Richmond. Elizabeth also kept, as councillor and Lord Treasurer, William Paulet, Marquess of Winchester, and the oldest member of the administration (he was probably born in the 1480s). She had no grounds for liking him, but he was devoted to the Tudor line, was the biggest landowner in Hampshire and, more important, had been engaged since 1554 in reorganizing the Exchequer.[27] To watch him, she appointed a cousin on her mother's side, Sir Richard Sackville, an expert financial lawyer, as Under-Treasurer, and Sir Ambrose Cave, a Cecil follower and also a financial lawyer, as Chancellor of the Duchy of Lancaster. She added two peers: Francis, 2nd Earl of Bedford, a strong Protestant, and another Protestant, William Parr, brother of Queen Catherine, whom she restored as Marquess of Northampton.

Of the Marian commoners on the Council, only four were retained. But one of these, Sir Thomas Cheyney, Treasurer of the Household, died before the end of 1558, being promptly replaced by Parry; Sir Edward Rogers, a Wyatt conspirator, took over Parry's job as Comptroller and was made a Privy Councillor. Elizabeth made Sir Francis Knollys, a second cousin by marriage, a strong Protestant and leading parliamentarian, her Vice-Chamberlain; and, next in importance to Cecil's appointment, she made his brother-in-law, Sir Nicholas Bacon, her Lord Keeper. Clergymen of all tendencies were rigorously excluded, with the one marginal exception of the diplomat Nicholas Wotton, the absentee Dean of both York and Canterbury, who can scarcely be called a cleric at all. (Indeed, the only clergyman Elizabeth ever appointed to the Council was Archbishop Whitgift, in the 1580s.)

The characteristics of Elizabeth's government were age and experience. Cecil was the youngest. Only three (or at most four) others were under fifty. Cave alone was a newcomer to high politics, and he had been a senior MP, sheriff and JP. Elizabeth's relations, and old friends and servants, were favoured, but not unduly. Thus, when Sir Francis Englefield, the only member of Mary's government to choose exile, left behind him the Mastership of the Wards – the biggest financial plum in the Queen's gift – she gave it to Parry. Her Boleyn and Howard connections were well looked after, but mostly on merit. Lord Williams of Thame got the Presidency of the Welsh Marches. Both the Dudley brothers, her companions in the Tower, got office: Robert, as already noted, the Mastership of the Horse, his elder brother Ambrose the Ordinance. Their sister's husband, Sir Henry Sidney, went to the Presidency of Wales when Williams died in 1559; and his brother-in-law, Lord Sussex, was retained as Irish Deputy. Most of the more respectable conspirators of the Marian years got appointments of one kind or another. Sir Edward Werner became lieutenant of the Tower, Croftes Captain of Berwick, Throckmorton himself went as ambassador to Paris; various Carews and Killigrews received minor appointments. But all these were kept outside the mainstream of political decision-making. Elizabeth did not disdain the service of enthusiasts and 'swordsmen', but she preferred to keep them in subordinate positions or transform them, like Dudley, into creatures entirely under her control. For major affairs of state she used 'scribes' and men of broad acres (and, if possible, ancient title).

Elizabeth's reconstruction of the royal household shows the same judicious blend of continuity and change. Among those who could be classed as 'civil servants' – the men who did the detailed work, both in the household and in the public offices, such as the Exchequer and Chancery – there was virtually no change. But a comparison of the lists of those present at Mary's funeral and Elizabeth's coronation shows that there had been major replacements among the more ceremonial officers – those whose choice reflected political or personal favour. Some thirty-eight out of fifty were new appointments; at the top, only Sir John Mason, Treasurer of the Chamber, survived. And Elizabeth threw out all the Marian ladies: Protestants with names like Knollys, Ashley, Cary, Cecil, and Throckmorton replaced the Catholic Whartons, Waldegraves, Cornwallises, Babingtons, Dormers and Southwells.[28]

In forming her government Elizabeth's chief consideration was the creation of a consensus grouped around an inner framework of efficiency. In an age when the deepening gulf between Catholic and Protestant was driving public men to act increasingly along ideological lines rather than from simple loyalty to their sovereign (or country), she naturally based this inner framework on men who could be described as Protestants or Henricians. But she sought the approval of all who mattered: 'The deep consent of all great men'.[29] Elizabeth's approach to politics was astonishingly consistent throughout her reign. The search for a community of views might be described as her first, and overriding, principle of government, and the occasions when she failed to obtain it she judged as her failures. Her second principle was that government should express itself through, and seek always to maintain, the natural hierarchy of society. Thus, in 1580, when rebuking Sir Philip Sidney for failing to apologize after a quarrel with the Earl of Oxford (who, she conceded, was in the wrong), she enunciated a harsh but clear doctrine:

> She laid before him the difference in degree between earls and gentlemen; the respect inferiors owed to their superiors; and the necessity in princes to maintain their own creations, as degrees descending between the people's licentiousness and the anointed sovereignty of crowns; and how the gentleman's neglect of the nobility taught the peasant to insult both.[30]

Being a liberal, Elizabeth saw plainly the inequity of her teaching; being also a conservative intellectual she recognized its necessity in a volatile and violent society, when only respect for rank stood between order and chaos. From this sprang her third salient principle; the need to draw an absolute line between monarch and subject. However much she might use her ministers, however carefully she might erect and balance factions among them, she ensured that the source of policy lay in herself and no other. As Sir Robert Naunton put it:

> Her ministers and instruments of state ... were many and those memorable, but they were only favourites and not minions; such as acted more by her own princely rules and judgments, than by their own wills and appetites, which she observed to the last ... The principal note of her reign will be, that she ruled much by factions and parties, which herself both made, upheld and weakened, as her own great judgment advised ... she was absolute and sovereign mistress of her graces; and all those, to whom she distributed her favours, were never more than tenants-at-will, and stood on no better ground than her princely pleasure, and their own good behaviour.[31]

This principle, in turn, drove her to seek to preserve the omniscience of the sovereign. The credit for success must go to her; the responsibility for failure must be placed in quarters where the throne would not be damaged. Again, it was unfair; again, it was necessary. As her godson, Sir John Harington, put it:

> Her wisest men and best councillors were oft sore troubled to know her will in matters of state: so covertly did she pass her judgment, as seemed to leave all to their discreet management; and, when the business did turn to better advantage, she did most cunningly commit the good issue to her honour and understanding; but, when aught fell out contrary to her will and intent, the Council were in great strait to defend their own acting and not blemish the Queen's good judgment.[32]

In short, she regarded the reputation and authority of the crown as the nation's biggest single asset; and this view was based not on personal vanity but on a cold, intellectual calculation – one in which her ablest ministers wholeheartedly concurred.

I have described what may be termed the metaphysical resources of the crown. What of its actual ones? As Queen, Elizabeth came into possession of the noble ruin of a great inheritance. Its extent, and also its dilapidations, could be seen in the physical structures she owned. The number of her castles was enormous.[33] They had steadily accumulated for the past seventy years. In 1485 Henry VII, as King, had inherited Berwick, Carisbrooke, Carlisle, Dover, the Tower, Nottingham, Porchester, Queensborough, Scarborough and Windsor, and a group of Welsh castles, plus Chester. As Duke of Lancaster he had Bolingbroke, Clitheroe, Halton, Hertford, Kenilworth, Lancaster, Leicester, Pevensey, Pickering, Pontefract, Tickhill, Tutbury, and other smaller ones. He got the castles of the Duchy of York and the Earldom of March: Conisborough, Sandal, Denbigh, Ludlow and Wigmore. By forfeiture he got the Neville castles: Warwick, Middleham, Barnard Castle, Sheriff Hutton, plus his own Richmond in Yorkshire. Between 1492 and 1507 he added Berkeley, Wark-a-Tweed, Pembroke, Cardiff, Chirk, Donnington and Powderham. In 1521 the forfeiture of Buckingham brought Henry VIII twelve more, including Thornbury and Tonbridge, which he retained. After the Pilgrimage of Grace in 1536 Henry acquired the Earl of Northumberland's castles: Alnwick, Warkworth, Langley, Wressel, Prudhoe and Cockermouth (Mary gave them back, but they returned to the crown again in 1569). With the dissolution of the monasteries, three clerical castles came into the royal hands, joined, in 1559, by Norham castle, forfeited by the deprived Bishop Tunstall of Durham.

What on earth was Elizabeth to do with this gigantic collection of obsolescent masonry, scattered all over England and Wales? Military technology was advancing with some speed, the size and power of siege guns constantly increasing. To keep these castles up to date, let alone maintain and garrison them, was clearly beyond Elizabeth's resources. In any event, as the internal stability of the country prolonged itself, what was the purpose? On the other hand, while Elizabeth, as she frequently said, coveted no man's possessions, she was instinctively unwilling to relinquish any of her own. Almost from the start of the reign, a consistent policy fell between the horns of this dilemma. The government actively pondered the problem from time to time. In 1561 Winchester, as Treasurer, conducted a survey of superfluous buildings, 'which may well be spared and not needful for our access'.[34] But few were actually pulled down; others were simply not maintained, allowing nature and the locals to do the rest. In 1562 Cave made a tour of the Duchy of Lancaster property; Elizabeth referred his report to a committee of six ministers, who recommended that all except Donnington and the Peak Castle be kept up; even Tickhill was to be looked after, being, so they said, 'an ancient monument' – the first such classified in England. In practice, Elizabeth kept up to date the Tower, to maintain control of London, and for purposes of external defence Carisbrooke in the Isle of Wight, Wark, the castles on the Channel Isles, and Dover, Berwick and Carlisle, the last two fortified towns. All this was expensive enough, and by the end of her reign Elizabeth was maintaining only nine fortresses, including Windsor.[35] Some castles were leased or lent to friends – thus Robert Dudley got Kenilworth and his brother Ambrose Warwick – who bore the expense of maintaining them; others, like Hertford, Fotheringay and Tutbury were scaled down and used as residences or progress-houses. Some became seats of local government or estate administration. For the rest, Elizabeth characteristically declined to adopt a radical solution and allowed dilapidation to do its work. After her death, when the Exchequer surveyed sixty crown castles in 1609, all of them, with one or two exceptions, were declared 'very ruinous' or 'utterly decayed'. In Elizabeth's eyes it was a small price to pay for half a century of civil peace and good housekeeping.

The royal palaces were of much more importance to her. Leaving aside the innumerable crown manor houses and lesser houses – some of which, in the south-east, she occasionally visited and all of which were maintained by one means or another, chiefly leases – she inherited a plethora of magnificent homes. No royal house in Europe, except the Valois, had anything like it. Henry VII and, still more, Henry VIII had been constant and extravagant builders; and Henry VIII, in addition, had gratified his envy of other men's property. Then, too, mansions built by Edward's Protectors had fallen in to the crown, and Mary, though not a builder, was an extender and maintainer. Elizabeth seems to have grudged every penny spent on bricks and mortar. On the whole she kept her palaces in repair, but the only surviving royal work undertaken during the whole of her reign was the construction of the Long Terrace at Windsor – and this served the severely practical purpose of allowing her to take brisk walks in the morning, 'to get up a heat'.[36] The same might be said for the gallery she installed at the Castle; the chapel she built was destroyed by Wyattville.

If the point were made that it was the function of a sovereign to build, Elizabeth would reply that it was not; in any case, had she not so much already? This argument was difficult to answer. For all practical purposes, Elizabeth resided, and hunted, in and around London and the Home Counties (on longer progresses she stayed with friends), and in this area her personal accommodation was abundant. The royal palaces and hunting lodges were grouped round the axis of the Thames.[37] Many were actually on the river, for this ensured sanitation and drainage, as well as rapid access. Elizabeth often used her private roads out of London: the King's Road on the north bank through Chelsea, which led to Richmond and Hampton Court, the road from Lambeth Ferry, along the south bank to Greenwich and Eltham, and Theobald's Road, leading north to (among other places) Cecil's great palace. But the heavy stuff, and often the Queen herself, went by barge when her destination had a river frontage.[38] The Thames, in fact, was the royal artery of England.

Of the outlying houses, Elizabeth barely used Woodstock at all, though she spent a night there occasionally while travelling. Hatfield she liked, and kept up, but it was a 'progress house' rather than a 'house of abode' or 'standing house'. Newhall, near Chelmsford, had personal associations for her since it had once belonged to the Boleyns. Her father had bought it in 1517 and had it 'incomparably adorned and beautified'. With its eight courtyards and its 500-foot-long entrance front façade, it must have been enormous: all that now remains is its fine Perpendicular Oriel window, rebuilt in St Margaret's, Westminster. But Elizabeth did not like this house, or use it much, and in 1573 she lent it to Thomas Radcliffe, Earl of Sussex.[39] More important to her was the hunting lodge of Oatlands, upstream from Hampton Court, on the high ground that tops the Surrey bank near Weybridge. Henry VIII had built it in 1528. It has now vanished, but excavations show it covered nine acres. Despite its size, it could not accommodate the whole court, many having to live in tents in the grounds. Elizabeth probably stayed there once a year for the hunting, which was superb (twenty visits are recorded); she also liked its vast flocks of rooks, which were protected birds.

Of her major palaces, her undoubted favourite was Richmond, another instance of her affinity with her grandfather, for it was Henry VII's creation. He had built it, round the turn of the century, virtually from scratch, on the site of the burned palace of Sheen. Though little now remains, it was, in its day, undoubtedly the great masterpiece of late Perpendicular, covering ten acres, with intricate fan-vaulting, huge windows, and a prodigious quantity of towers and pinnacles, crowned by onion-domes. Each had a gold and silver vane, which sang in the wind like a harp. Indeed, it was a fairy place of sounds and odours. There were 223 trees in the orchards which surrounded it, producing magnificent peaches, pears, apples, filberts and damsons. The elaborate gardens supplied salads, herbs, rose-water and masses of flowers – frequently sent from

Richmond to other palaces – and they were traversed by a network of brightly-painted galleries and loggias to provide protection from the rain. Spaniards in the train of Philip II were astonished by its grandeur – 'more rooms and better than the Alcazar of Madrid' – and its eighteen kitchens – 'and such a hurly-burly in them that each one is a veritable hell.'[40] Elizabeth was more impressed by its excellent water-supply, which came from two pure springs, by its plumbing system, 'custom-built' by her grandfather, and not improvised, and most of all by the absence of draughts in its state and privy rooms: 'a warm nest for my old age' as she termed it. Many of her friends and senior officials had houses in the immediate neighbourhood: it was a jewel in a court setting.

Hampton Court, up the river, was even bigger. It was magnificent enough when Wolsey built it, but Henry VIII spent vast sums on it, sometimes as much as £400 a month. Outside Whitehall, it was the most elaborately and richly decorated of the 'standing houses', with a throne-room known as the Paradise Chamber, perhaps the best thing of its kind in England, and much used to impress ambassadors. The room was hung with Persian tapestry, and the throne decked in brown velvet set with jewels, including three huge diamonds. It had a twenty-eight-foot table, covered with pearl-set velvet, and another of Brazilian wood inlaid with silver; on this was displayed a gilt mirror, an ebony draughts-board, a chess-board of ivory and seven ivory flutes mounted with gold, which produced various animal calls.[41] There was also a backgammon board, equipped with dice of solid silver, and many fine musical instruments. Here Elizabeth played on a virginal made of glass (except for its strings), and another, less gimmicky, equipped with strings of gold and silver. When she was not there, the room was open to the well-dressed public, but they had to pay a special fee to see it. Hampton Court was used chiefly for elaborate out-of-town ceremonials and court festivities, especially on the great feasts of Christmas, Easter and Whitsun. It was a display house, and not much to the Queen's liking, or comfort—especially after she nearly died from smallpox there.

More to her taste was the fantasy-palace of Nonsuch in Surrey, though she did not actually own it until after the death of the Earl of Arundel, who had been granted it by her father. If Richmond was Henry VII's masterpiece, Nonsuch was the characteristic and spectacular creation of Henry VIII – a Renaissance château in the English vernacular, built to outshine the Chambord of his rival, Francis I. As at Oatlands, most of the court had to live in tents, but the state rooms were sumptuous, with fine views; and the inner courtyard, which had a white marble fountain and a clock tower, was walled with gilt on a white stucco background, modelled in deep relief often five inches thick. It had innumerable statues, dominated by Henry himself, larger than life and enthroned in glory, and surrounded by Roman emperors. But the purpose of the house was hunting. In the gardens was a grove of Diana, with a statue of Actaeon in the middle. When Elizabeth was not hunting herself, she could watch the sport from the twin towers, five storeys high, each with all-round visibility on the fourth floor, connected by an airy gallery. For rainy days there was a fine library, based on the collection assembled by Archbishop Cranmer. Not surprisingly, she went to Nonsuch often even when Arundel was its nominal tenant. If Richmond was her favourite place for repose and work, she came for exercise to Nonsuch, 'which of all places she likes best'.[42]

At the other end of the Thames axis was Elizabeth's birthplace, the vast palace of Greenwich. Ambassadors and state visitors were frequently received there, being rowed down-river in the Greenwich barge, an eight-oared vessel with a red satin awning and a cabin – decorated with coats of arms, with flowers strewn on the floor, and with a cloth-of-gold bolster on which the ambassador sat. There was an imposing river-gatehouse to the palace, at which visitors disembarked. Greenwich had strong military and naval associations. The royal ships carried out formal exercises on the river, watched by the Queen from the gatehouse, and military reviews were held in the park, with the Queen taking the salute from the gallery of the detached gatehouse which overlooked the huge stretch of turf. On her first visit after her coronation, 2 July 1559, Elizabeth saw the militia at work: 'Guns were discharged on one another, the morris pikes encountered together with Great alarm; each ran to their weapons again, and then they fell together as fast as they could in imitation of close fight.'[43] She usually came to Greenwich in her personal barge, which had twenty oarsmen and a captain, and could accommodate a large party; it was moored on the South Bank, opposite Whitehall, near her bear-pit at Paris Garden, and it could take her upstream as far as Windsor.

In London itself the Queen owned a vast collection of buildings.[44] Apart from her formal visit before her coronation, she never held court in the Tower, though a suite of rooms was kept ready for her. It was a fortress, a mint, an armoury where guns were cast as well as arms stored, and a prison (together with the Bridewell, on the South Bank, it was the only prison in England where instruments of torture were kept). Elizabeth did not like the place, not only because of its hideous associations for her, but because it housed the royal menagerie, including, at one time in her reign, a tiger, a lynx, a wolf, a porcupine, an eagle and an old lion called Edward VI. Their roarings disturbed the night hours (Elizabeth had a tendency towards insomnia, like her mother, who had complained of the squealing of the peacocks at Greenwich), and their smells impregnated the place (Elizabeth always hated smells).[45] Most of her London houses she leased or lent to courtiers, or kept as accommodation for state guests. Thus, the London Charterhouse was used first by Lord North, later by the 4th Duke of Norfolk, who transformed it into a sumptuous town palace, and, after his execution, by the Earl of Rutland.[46] Durham House, once an episcopal palace, accommodated at various times the Spanish ambassador, Princess Cecilia of Sweden, Sir Walter Ralegh and the Earl of Essex, each of whom had a suite.[47] Elizabeth stayed at Somerset House at least fourteen times, but it was chiefly used by foreign visitors, though the Earl of Hertford (Somerset's son) had lodgings there, as did her cousin, Lord Hunsdon, who held the keepership.[48] Barnards Castle, directly on the river, continued to be occupied, nominally as keepers, by the Earls of Pembroke. The Savoy Palace was used as a hospital, though it also had private lodgings for her friends.[49] Crosby Hall was used by wealthy merchants.[50] Other houses accommodated minor state departments – thus, the Revels were at St John's Priory, Clerkenwell; the Wardrobe, or part of it, at the Wardrobe on St Andrew's Hill, and so forth.

Of the main London residences, St James's Palace, which had been Mary's favourite, ranked almost as a country house, with its enclosed park and sheet of artificial water, known as Rosamund's Pool. Elizabeth moved into it when Whitehall was being cleaned, and she did not wish to travel further.[51] But Whitehall was always her main base, and she must have spent far more time there than at any other house. It was a huge place, sprawling over twenty-three acres, and probably remained the biggest palace in Europe until most of it was burnt down under William III in the 1690s. It had been built over many centuries, and was, architecturally, a complete muddle, but foreigners were invariably impressed by the splendour of its decorations. When the Queen was away, and visitors admitted, the valuable tapestry and carpet hangings were taken down, being stored, along with much other furniture, in the Tower; nor were the furnishings always in perfect repair – thus we find instructions for a carpet to be provided for the Council Chamber, 'to cover the table that the oldness of the board be not seen'.[52] But nothing could diminish the magic of its wall-paintings, some of which went back to the time of Henry III. The Privy Chamber, where ambassadors were normally received, was dominated by Holbein's masterpiece, of the entire Tudor ruling house, grouped around the giant figure of Henry VIII. It filled visitors with astonishment, even fear: 'The King as he stood there,' wrote Carel Van Mander, 'majestic in his splendour, was so lifelike that the spectator felt abashed, annihilated in his presence.'[53] Elizabeth like to pose against this background, reminding all whose daughter she was.[54]

More than any other palace, Whitehall was equipped with all the apparatus of royal ceremonial. It had a majestic tiltyard, linked to the main palace by a gallery which passed through the 'Holbein Gate' into the long Privy Gallery leading into the state apartments. Below it, on the Westminster side, were a tennis court and cockpit. Plays were performed in the Great Hall until, in 1581, a spacious, and supposedly temporary, Banqueting Hall was built on the open space north of the Privy Gallery. Alongside this was Sermon Court, where open-air preaching took place in fine weather: it could hold four times as many people as the Chapel Royal. The Privy Garden, to the south of the Gallery, had thirty-four tall painted columns, with animals on top, carrying the Queen's escutcheon, and heavily gilt; they were grouped round a sundial which could tell the time in thirty different ways, set in a multi-spray fountain. It was a favourite trick of the gardeners, and courtiers, suddenly to turn on the fountain when the unwary were studying the sundial (not much of a joke in a period when men and women alike were terrified of getting their expensive clothes wet). Londoners were familiar with the palace, for the main road between the City and Westminster went right through it under the Holbein Gate. But security was maintained by placing the Queen's own apartments within a complex and heavily guarded nest of ante-rooms, and Great, Privy and Withdrawing Chambers. Her own bedroom was on the far, or river, side, equipped with a silver-topped table, and her favourite chair, built up with cushions. Her bed was of multi-coloured wood, with quilts of silk, velvet, gold and silver embroidery, and hung with painted Indian silk. There was a bathroom next door, probably lined from wall to ceiling with looking-glass, like her two bathrooms at Windsor. The bedroom itself was said to be dark, but its one window at least overlooked the Thames. From there, on a May morning in 1559, she watched a mock battle between two pinnaces, which ended in tragedy, for a squib fell in the gunpowder, blew up a pinnace, and drowned one of its seamen.[55] From her room, Elizabeth could walk privately to the river gate-house, and go for an evening row on the Thames – something she delighted to do until the end of her life. It was an excellent way of showing herself to the people without the discomfort of horseback or her litter. In June 1559, Baron Breuner, emissary of the Archduke Charles, was taking a similar airing: 'The Queen came there too, recognized and summoned me. She spoke a long while with me, and invited me to leave my boat and take a seat in the Treasurer's barge. She then had her boat laid alongside and played the lute.'[56]

This immense and expensive collection of castles, manor houses, lodges and palaces – and the multitude of people who lived in and around them – were maintained, in theory at least, by the income from the crown and crown-owned estates, which were also supposed to provide the main source of revenue for all government activities. Elizabeth always took a close, and sometimes a fanatical interest in certain aspects of royal finance, and in particular she watched expenditure. But she did not, and probably could not, grasp all the complex procedures by which revenue was acquired. It was beyond the grasp of any one human being. Since 1554 Winchester had been subjecting various financial departments, which had proliferated under Cromwell and since, as a result of the seizures of Church property, to the central control of the Exchequer. As a result of his reforms, and the supervision exercised by Cecil and other experts, such as Cave and Sir Walter Mildmay,[57] Elizabethan public finance was probably more efficiently conducted than that of any other European nation. But in her early years Elizabeth was faced with grave problems. Under Henry VII, the estates of the crown and its appendages were probably more extensive than at any time since the years following the Conquest – they covered perhaps one-fifth of the country. Henry VIII greatly diminished this patrimony, despite his acquisitions from the Church; there was further spoliation under Edward VI, and Mary sold or gave away £49,000-worth of crown lands, chiefly in pious reparation to the Church. Elizabeth acted swiftly to repair the damage: her officers, for instance, seized on Pole's property within days of her accession. Mildmay immediately managed to get her back £24,429-worth of Mary's alienations. By authority of parliament, she also forced on the bishops arrangements under which she swopped spiritualities, such as advowsons, for chunks of their temporalities. It is an exaggeration to say that she plundered the episcopal estates: most of the damage had been done under her predecessors, chiefly by the bishops themselves. They, especially the Catholics under Mary, let off estates on long, nominal leases, in return for huge cash payments, which went to their dependants.[58] But Elizabeth's scaling down of episcopal revenues, in accordance with her political policy of reducing their status in the community, undoubtedly benefited the crown: in some counties by as much as 20 per cent of the total yield from crown lands.[59]

In general, however, Elizabeth found it necessary to adopt a conservative policy towards the exploitation of her landed resources. 'Improving' landlords were necessarily unpopular, and this was something she could never afford for political reasons. There was, too, massive public resistance to the exaction of feudal dues. Moreover, since the time of Edward I, the crown had found it increasingly difficult to determine exactly who its tenants-in-chief were, and what was due from them. Elizabeth rewarded informers who 'discovered' debts and obligations, but, no doubt on her instructions, Winchester and Cecil were slow to use information from this source, and from their own surveys.[60] As a result, Elizabeth and her government did not, in general, exploit the rising prices from agricultural produce and land. During the period 1550–90, when food prices doubled,[61] her revenue from land went up by barely 25 per cent; in 1602 the crown estates brought in £88,767, only £22,319 more than at her accession.[62] In the middle of her reign the Duchy of Lancaster estates were bringing in no more than under her grandfather. Revenue from the Court of Wards, about £20,000 a year at her accession, actually fell during her reign. This was deliberate policy, rather than inefficiency. Elizabeth needed, and was determined to retain, the enthusiastic loyalty of her tenants, who included (in one form or another) the bulk of the nobility. If she needed money, she preferred to turn to parliament. Those who write of her growing 'dependence' on parliamentary revenue are using the wrong word. Perhaps it should be 'exploitation of'. There was nothing particularly new in this. As long ago as the reign of Edward III, the crown had shown a preference for turning to parliament rather than exploit its feudal position.[63] This brought the risk that parliament, in return, would encroach on the royal prerogative. But Elizabeth chose to take it because she felt, like Edward III, that in the last resort she could always handle the Commons; and she was usually right. If she needed cash quickly, she sold lands. Altogether, during her reign, she disposed of lands to the value of £813,332, which had been bringing in an annual income of £24,808.[64] But this shows a return of less than 3 per cent, little more than half the national average. The actual income was doubtless very much smaller, for most of the land disposed of was in small parcels, with a high cost of collection. Elizabeth's land sales were thus less improvident than appears at first glance, or than some contemporaries thought. They also brought political dividends, for throughout her reign land was in constant demand, and the buyers could be expected to be grateful. Indeed, one of the marked characteristics of Elizabeth, as a consummate political strategist, was that she always saw the business of revenue-raising in its overall political context – in this respect she was a wiser sovereign than her grandfather. In immediate cash terms it might benefit the crown to push its rights in a given direction; but there would be a political price to pay, ultimately reflected in parliament, and the net result might be a loss in total revenue. In the long run, as Elizabeth realized, the popularity of the crown was its greatest financial asset – the direct road to the purses of her subjects.

Following the same line of reasoning, Elizabeth grasped from the outset the imperative and urgent need to restore the value of the currency. Bad money and rising prices were the two biggest causes of the general discontent which confronted her at her accession. There was not much, in practice, she could do about prices, although by statute and proclamation she continued to nag at the problem throughout her reign: inflation has baffled all governments, even to this day. But a debased currency was a remediable source of human misery, and the direct responsibility of the crown. Elizabeth gave this problem her first attention – it had a higher immediate priority even than the religious settlement – and she superintended its solution closely. She was extremely fortunate to have the services of Gresham, probably the ablest financier in Europe, and was shrewd enough to make the greatest possible use of them.[65] Within days of his first meeting with her, on 20 November 1558, he reported his recommendations in a memo:

> First, your Highness has none other ways but, when time and opportunity serveth, to bring your base money into fine, of 11 ounces fine. And so gold after the rate ... The enterprise is of great importance, and the sooner it is put into use, the more honour and profit it will be to the Queen's Majesty and the Realm, for doubtless this will raise the exchange to 26s. 8d. at the least ... As the exchange is the thing that eats out all princes to the whole destruction of their common weal, if it be not substantially looked into, so likewise the exchange is the chiefest and richest thing only above all others, to restore your Majesty and your Realm to fine gold and silver ... the means that makes all foreign commodities ... cheap, and likewise keeps your fine gold and silver within your realm.[66]

In a sense this was crude economic advice, for to revalue sterling raised the price of English exports, and might diminish their volume. But in Elizabeth's circumstances, it was unavoidable, for the first need was the defence of the realm, and this meant the royal credit had to be restored, to purchase arms from abroad and, if necessary, raise forces at home. In any case, she accepted Gresham's recommendations. During December and January 1559, he commuted between the court and Antwerp. On 4 February, on the basis of his findings, she set up a six-man royal commission to undertake the actual details of the currency reform. Its work, which spread over eighteen months, was shrouded in great secrecy – a secrecy that was new, and was to become a distinguished feature of Elizabethan government. The commission was finished by 18 September 1560, when Cecil completed the draft of a proclamation for the calling-in and reissue. But the actual date, originally 29 September, was picked by the Queen herself: according to Lord Shrewsbury's London agent she informed no one.[67] When rumours got about, she brought it forward two days to prevent speculation on the exchanges. She followed the proclamation by publishing a pamphlet, written by Cecil, giving her reasons. All in all, £700,000-worth of silver pennies, half-groats (2d.) and testons (6d.) were called in and reissued. It was one of the most successful state finance operations in history, and Gresham even contrived to make Elizabeth a direct profit of £45,000.[68]

Meanwhile, Gresham was working hard on both sides of the narrow seas to compound and eliminate the Queen's debts, and extend her lines of credit, both with the London merchants and the Antwerp bankers. His *carte blanche* from her was effective, combined with his own intelligence service, 'having the brokers, as I have, at my commandment, for there is never a bourse but I have a note what money is taken up by exchange, as well by the stranger as by Englishmen'. Another factor was the growing realization that a strong government was in power in England, enjoying the confidence of the London business community. Gresham was soon able to boast that 'it will not be a little spoken of that her Majesty, in all her wars, doth make payment of her debts, when neither King Philip, nor the French king, nor the King of Portugal, in peacetime, payeth nothing, who oweth no small sums of money'.[69] By contrast, as he pointed out in 1560, Philip II was broke: 'I cannot see which way King Philip can annoy her Highness this year, considering he hath neither money, ships, nor men; nor munitions, nor armour.' Gresham was busy remedying these defects in Elizabeth's case, buying and importing arms, using his inside knowledge of the trade – 'There is not one word spoken by the customers, and what they intend to do, but I have perfect intelligence.' He even managed to buy up cannon and armour from Philip's own depots in the Low Countries, and ship them direct to the Tower, before his activities were discovered.

Of course, in the long term what Gresham, Cecil and Elizabeth were anxious to do was to make England self-sufficient in war production. At Elizabeth's accession, England made no brass, and little gunpowder or copper. To push home industries, monopolies – in general disliked by Elizabeth and her advisers – were allowed to develop in sulphur, gunpowder, saltpetre and other commodities. Great efforts were made to gather the secrets of brass-making from the Germans, and in 1561 Germans, plus their equipment, were imported to start home manufacture. Surveys were carried out, in considerable secrecy, to find English deposits of calamine, or ore of zinc, for copper-making: they were discovered near Bristol, and a copper wire works set up, soon employing 100 men, near Tintern.[70] Long before the end of the reign, England had achieved self-sufficiency in all essential armaments, and was even exporting them – to the anger of military lobbyists, such as Sir Walter Ralegh. Efforts were also made, over the whole range of extractive raw-materials and manufactured goods, to reduce dependence on imports by promoting domestic enterprise. These date from very early in the reign: in late 1560, for instance, the creation of the Mines Royal and the Mineral and Battery Works put the mining industry on an official footing. It is not entirely clear, from the evidence, how effective state pressure and control were in pushing home industry and mining.[71] But certainly Cecil was obsessed by what we now call the balance of payments and the need for import-substitution. As he put it: 'It is manifest that nothing robbeth the realm of England but when more merchandise is brought into the realm than is carried forth . . . The remedy hereof is by all policies to abridge the use of such foreign commodities as be not necessary to us.'[72] To the best of his power, he promoted the development of the English tin and lead industry, inshore and deep-sea fishing (his special interest), the iron and metallurgical industries, salt-mining, and the clothing trade.[73] Elizabeth herself took a hand in expanding the coal industry, centred on the great Durham–Newcastle field. The Bishopric of Durham had held back mining and, with its palatine powers, had restricted the activities of the Newcastle merchants. Elizabeth encouraged them to ship coal to London, and by taking over lands from the see worth £1,000 a year, and letting them to colliers at low rents, she enabled the industry to expand fast: from the mid-1560s shipments from Newcastle were doubling every fifteen years, and one colliery alone produced 20,000 tons for shipment in a single year in the early 1580s.[74] It was her policy, and Cecil's, to encourage the settlement of skilled personnel from the Continent – made easier as the Wars of Religion got under way – and to protect the immigrants, always the sign of a strong English government, from local prejudice. Over 4,000 Flemish weavers came to Norwich, and Elizabeth took a personal interest in their activities. The foreigners also brought new techniques in potteries, glass-engraving, printing, silk-weaving, linen-making, needle- and parchment-making, and the manufacture of sail-cloth.[75] From the early 1560s industry in England began to expand in a perceptible manner, and to acquire its modern geographical structure in many cases – iron manufactures in Sheffield, textiles in south Lancashire and the West Riding, metal implements in the West Midlands, and so forth.

Naturally, all this was for the future. For the immediate present, Elizabeth's salient object was to extract England from her disastrous Continental entanglements, place the nation in a posture of defence, and win time by diplomacy to reach an independent settlement of religion. Though in domestic terms it was already clear by the end of 1558 that Elizabeth's throne was secure, it was potentially threatened from abroad. One claimant, Mary Stuart, now sixteen, had been Queen of Scotland from within a week of her birth. Her mother was French and, for all practical purposes, Mary was a Valois. She had long been affianced to Francis, son and heir of Henri II, and shortly before Elizabeth's accession she married him. On 16 January, the day after Elizabeth's coronation, Mary and her husband adopted the style of King and Queen of England, and Mary quartered her escutcheon with the English royal arms. The Valois threat to England necessarily brought Elizabeth the bonus of a degree of Habsburg friendship – which she encouraged by dangling the wholly baseless prospect of her marriage to the Habsburg Archduke Charles of Austria. But this in turn raised the risk that England might become the central battlefield of Valois-Habsburg rivalry, as Italy had been a generation before.[76] As Lord Paget had put it, 'a bone between two dogs'. Fortunately, France and Spain, after half a century of almost continuous conflict, were exhausted by war. It was common sense, therefore, for Elizabeth to take advantage of this hiatus in their ambitions, and get a peace as quickly as possible, based on the *status quo*. This meant writing off Calais, in practice if not formally. As early as 20 November 1558, Sir John Mason had advised her that England was not in a position to negotiate ambitious terms, and that she should be willing to accept a peace which made no mention of Calais. She was not happy at thus bowing to realities, and in the end got a face-saving formula which left the question of Calais open. But in general she saw there was no alternative but to accept the advice she was given, and left the management of the peace treaty to the veteran courtier Lord Thomas Howard, who was fluent in French and a friend of the Valois chief delegate, the Constable Montmorency. Even at this early stage, she insisted on seeing diplomatic correspondence and holding private conferences on foreign affairs. We find Cecil rebuking the bearer of an ambassador's letter for discussing with her 'a matter of such weight, being too much for a woman's knowledge' – an indication that he was not yet fully aware of the woman he was serving.[77] He would soon learn. She also reacted strongly to any suggestion that her title become an issue in the talks. When the English team referred to her a French diplomatic speculation as to her right to her title, she thundered back that she was amazed the English delegates would allow the French to challenge it, even in theory, 'without due reprehension and misliking'; how dare they ask her pleasure on a point 'which might have been performed by any of you, that we may not nor ever will permit any over whom we have rule, or may have, to doubt, question or treaty on this matter'.[78] But otherwise she did not interfere, and by 22 March 1559 she regarded the treaty as settled.

The peace had direct relevance to the English settlement of religion, for Christian ideologies transcended frontiers. It is true that, in the Empire, the principle was now being accepted that individual princes had the right to determine the religion of their subjects without interference from outside: *cuius regio, eius religio*. But this was acceptable to the Catholic powers only because the dominant brand of Protestantism in Germany was Lutheranism, which did not challenge the essentially hierarchical structure of secular society. Calvinism, which did, was rightly seen as a threat to thrones as well as popes. It had, moreover, a proselytizing international character; with the return of the 'wolves' from Geneva and Frankfurt it was already infecting England, and John Knox, who reached Scottish soil on 2 May 1559, was to carry the message farther north. So long as the war continued, Elizabeth's freedom of action in determining the religious practices of her subjects would be circumscribed – and this might mean, as she very well realized, civil war on a religious basis, of a type which was soon to engulf France and the Habsburg empire. Time was not on her side: the Counter-Reformation was organizing itself. As early as 16 February 1559, Pope Paul IV published his Bull, *Cum ex apostolatus*, advocating the deposition of all sovereigns who encouraged heresy.

As it was, even with peace, Elizabeth's freedom of action was much narrower than she at first supposed. By the end of the 1550s the initiative in religion was no longer fully within the grasp of the crown, as it had been in her father's day. Men were beginning to believe that doctrinal truth, and liturgical practice, were matters for individual consciences and, in political terms, issues to be settled for and by the nation as a whole. Almost unconsciously, they were organizing themselves to pursue their aims independently of the sovereign's wishes, even against them. It was the real beginning of party, as opposed to mere faction, and a momentous development in human history. Granted complete freedom, it is not too difficult to conceive what kind of settlement Elizabeth would have chosen. She never had any doubt that the monarch must be the effective head of the Church, whatever the precise phrasing of the title. There could be no question of her acknowledging the authority of Paul IV, who 'regarded princes not as his sons but as his pupils' and who was accustomed to tell ambassadors 'that the place of kings was at the feet of the Pope, from whom they should receive their laws . . .'.[79] Nor was it conceivable, after the experience of Mary's reign, that Elizabeth could have had dealings with the Counter-Reformation in any form. The horrors of Continental persecution were just beginning. In 1558 the Dominican Michel Ghislien was made Grand Inquisitor. Erasmus, Petrach and Boccaccio, plus a host of others, were placed on the Index. Jews were again forced to wear yellow squares on their backs. From the end of 1558 the witch-hunt spread all over southern Europe. In Calabria, 2,000 were to be executed. On 21 May 1559, Philip II, accompanied by his fourteen-year-old son (later a sadist), watched 31 apostates and heretics burned alive in Valladolid, in a ceremony which lasted eight hours; they were again present at Seville on 24 September, when 16 were burned, and back at Valladolid on 8 October, for 14 more burnings. These events filled Elizabeth with as much repugnance as any of her Protestant subjects. For her, religious conformity must never be carried beyond the point of outward observance. As Francis Bacon, in a shrewd and accurate analysis, was later to point out, she had two principles – 'that consciences are not to be forced', but that, equally, 'cases of conscience, when they exceed their bounds and grow to be matter of faction, lose their nature.' He added: 'Her Majesty not liking to make windows into men's hearts and secret thoughts, except the abundance of them did overflow into overt and express acts or affirmations, tempered her law so as it restraineth only manifest disobedience . . .'[80]

Ideally, Elizabeth would have liked to go back to the spirit of her father's Six Articles of 1539, a statute whose significant title was 'An Act Abolishing Diversity in Opinions'.[81] Let men conform outwardly to the state religion, and keep their beliefs, if any, to themselves. In his opening speech to Elizabeth's first parliament, the Lord Keeper, Sir Nicholas Bacon – working from a text carefully drafted under her supervision – told members to refrain from 'all contentious, contumelious or opprobrious words, as heretic, schismatic, papist, and such like names and nurses of seditions, factions and sects'.[82] This was a distinct, perhaps even a conscious, echo of her father's last great speech. But what was the state religion to be? A manuscript has survived, dating from her accession, entitled 'The device for alteration of religion in the first year of Queen Elizabeth'.[83] It adumbrates, with some accuracy, what parliament eventually enacted, and it used to be regarded as a statement of the government's official programme. In fact, it was no more than a series of suggestions, which Elizabeth did not want. What her actual views of faith were it is impossible to determine. On the crucial issue of the eucharist and the Real Presence, she is usually credited with the quatrain:

> *Christ was the word that spake it,*
> *He took the bread and brake it;*
> *And what his words did make it*
> *That I believe and take it.*

But these lines are first linked with her name as late as 1643, when Baker's *Chronicle* was published. They had been going the rounds for nearly a century, though in the form we have them were perhaps polished by Donne.[84] They represented her thought in so far as she was anxious to evade the issue.

As she was a woman concerned by the externals, rather than the inner beliefs, of religion, her interest focused very largely on liturgy. Here we can be a little more specific. There can be no doubt that she preferred services to be conducted mainly, if not exclusively, in English. That, at a stroke, set her apart from the Catholics, or at least the Romanists. Second, she was strongly opposed to the more superstitious aspects of Catholicism: the cult of the Virgin (her rival), miracles, saints, indulgences and so forth. To be sure, as a professional monarch, she was willing to exploit the spiritual apparatus of kingship. She revived the practice of touching for the King's Evil, and was robust enough actually to put her hands on the diseased places. Among ordinary folk this was a highly popular gesture; but it is significant that she made it only after the Pope excommunicated her in 1570 – as it were, to prove his impotence – and that she had the text of the ritual translated into English, omitting all references to the Virgin.[85] In general, she preferred compromise in ceremonial. She detested incense, as she detested all pungent smells. When she went to open her first parliament, she waved away the torches carried by the Abbot of Westminster and his monks. But she liked a modest candle or two, and a crucifix. These were occasionally whisked away, as necessity demanded, from her private chapels, but they invariably made their reappearance sooner or later.[86] She approved of a seemly use of vestments, and the music in her chapels was always elaborate and splendid – much praised by foreign visitors, and much deplored by Puritans. Right to the end of her life, descriptions of services in her private quarters suggest that her religious practices did not vary much over more than forty years. In all probability, she would have happily settled for the first Edwardian Prayer Book of 1549, virtually an English translation of the Mass – with the Consecration omitted. But this was not what happened. Indeed, in some ways the religious settlement of 1559 was a defeat for the Queen; or, to put it another way, an important stage in her political education.

So far as we know, no efforts were made to pack the 1559 parliament. Mary had sent out circular letters to sheriffs. Elizabeth did not do so: it was not necessary. County elections invariably reflected the colour of the régime, known to be Protestant. The boroughs, now electing gentlemen, as opposed to burgesses, in growing numbers, mirrored the upsurge of Protestantism among landowners. All the councillors not in the Lords found seats, as did fifty to sixty other royal officials and courtiers. With one or two exceptions, vocal Catholics were conspicuously absent, and vocal Protestants – Sir Anthony Cooke and Sir Francis Knollys, Paul Wentworth and William Strickland – conspicuously present.[87] Almost as important, scores of leading Protestant clergymen, many from Geneva and Frankfurt – and including such future bishops as Cox, Grindal, Horne, Jewel, Sandys and Scory – had gathered in London to lobby both Houses. Cox, indeed, preached the opening sermon in the Abbey (he had once been Dean of Westminster), a tendentious affair lasting one and a half hours, exhorting the Queen to purify the Church; she cannot have been pleased to hear it, for she hated sermons at all times, and especially long 'political' ones.[88]

To begin with, Elizabeth was more worried by the attitude of the Lords. Anxious to follow the advice given her (as well as her instincts) and proceed slowly in matters of religion, she still had hopes of carrying parliament as a whole, even the Marian bishops, with her. Her uncontentiously worded Title Bill passed without a vote. But the bishops voted solidly against her Bill restoring the First Fruits and Tenths to the crown (a reversal of Mary's pro-Church financial legislation), and it became clear they would oppose any religious bills, even at risk of deposition. Fortunately, 10 sees were vacant, and the maximum number the Catholic clergy could muster in the Lords was only 18 (their highest vote was actually 11). As against this, there were 61 peers, who showed themselves solidly Protestant or Henrician; the government could always depend on between 20 and 40, and thus had a firm majority. As De Feria reported: 'The Queen has entire disposal of the Upper Chamber in a way never seen before in previous parliaments' (he meant under Mary).[89] On the other hand, it became apparent that there would have to be a complete change of bishops, and this inevitably pushed religious policy in a more radical direction.

Moreover, it was from the Commons that the real challenge came. Elizabeth wished her first parliament to confine itself, in religious matters, to establishing her Supremacy, and to proceed more slowly – no doubt in a later parliament – to settle the question of Uniformity, and a Prayer Book. A Supremacy Bill, by forcing the Catholic clergy to take an oath to her, which they could not in conscience do, would enable her to make whatever replacements were necessary. That was what the Bill her ministers tabled set out to do. But when it reached the Commons on 9 February, the dominant Protestant block seized control of it, debated it at length, sent it to committee, drastically altered and enlarged it, and returned it to the Lords, on 25 February, as a completely different Bill – a Bill, indeed, combining Supremacy and Uniformity. That the Protestants objected to Elizabeth being called 'Head' of the Church, mainly on anti-feminist grounds (here they were at one with the Catholics) was of little importance; she eventually settled for 'Supreme Governor', caring more for realities than words. What mattered was that the enlarged Bill dealt with doctrine and liturgy: among other things it authorized a Protestant form of service – in effect, the 1552 Prayer Book – and clerical marriage. It was pre-empting the Queen's own strategy and programme. When the revised Bill got back to the Lords, they promptly put it in committee, eliminated the Commons' additions, and restored it to its original shape. The Commons retaliated by passing a new Bill, 'that no persons shall be punished for using the religion used in King Edward's last year'. This was a defensive move: if they could not have the 1552

Prayer Book, they would have a system which permitted non-conformity. Grudgingly, when the Lords returned them the original government Supremacy Bill, they passed it, and it was ready for the royal assent on 22 March. A proclamation publishing it had been drawn up. By now a money Bill had been passed, and it was assumed that parliament, its work done, would be dissolved in time for Easter, on 26 March.

But it was at this point that Elizabeth decided she had to give way. She had already lost the Catholic clergy, or at any rate the bishops. Now she faced the prospect of sending parliament away, having alienated the powerful Protestant element. That would leave her standing on a very narrow base indeed – possibly not a base at all – the reverse of the national consensus she had been seeking. It was not simply a matter of antagonizing a majority of the gentry in the Commons. Many of her own ministers favoured the enlarged Commons Bill. Cecil, in particular, was later to claim that he had master-minded the change in religion: when accused of such by the Spanish ambassador he replied: 'I must confess that I am thereby guilty, but not thereby at fault, and thereto I shall stand as long as I shall live.'[90] In other words the government Bill represented the Queen's view, rather than that of her leading ministers. External events now tipped the balance, and persuaded her she could take a less cautious course. By 19 March information reached her that the Treaty of Cateau-Cambrésis was as good as signed: the war was over, and her options were widening. The very next day she made a preliminary concession to the Protestants, allowing their divines to meet for a public disputation on matters of faith with the Catholic bishops, to take place on 31 March in Westminster, under the chairmanship of the Lord Keeper (as the Protestants had hoped, the Catholics could not agree to the rules of procedure, and the meeting broke up in disarray on 3 April).[91] Three days later, after pondering the issue through most of the night of 23–24 March – a frequent practice of hers during moments of acute indecision – she decided not to dissolve parliament, but simply to adjourn it until after the Easter holiday.

When parliament reassembled on 3 April, it was evident that Elizabeth had now committed herself to a Protestant solution, not in some distant future, but here and now. It is true she had driven a hard bargain. The Commons volunteered an important Bill which allowed Elizabeth (as already described) to acquire a hefty slice of episcopal revenues – this was objectionable to the extreme Protestants as smacking of Caesaro-Papalism, and they voted solidly against it. But the government itself produced a third version of the Supremacy Bill, which effectively gave the Commons what they wanted, and a Uniformity Bill, providing for, and describing, a new Prayer Book to be drawn up by

Protestant divines. Both Bills became law without much trouble, though the Uniformity Bill secured only a narrow majority in the Lords, the Treasurer, Winchester (possibly on Elizabeth's instructions) voting against it.[92] Thus Elizabeth found herself obliged to accept the 1552 Prayer Book. It is true that the new Prayer Book, as eventually issued in 1563, contained her own conservative amendments. It dealt, for instance, with the Real Presence in double sentences, which expressed both points of view. A proviso on vestments could also be interpreted either way, providing grounds for future controversy. In terms of ecclesiastical organization, the old structure was retained intact – bishops, archdeacons and all; and this, too, was to prove important later. Elizabeth defended the settlement to the Spanish ambassador, saying that 'she wished the Augustinian confession [that is, the 1549 Prayer Book] to be maintained in her realm . . . it would not be the Augustinean confession, but something else like it, and that she differed very little from us, as she believed that God was in the sacrament of the Eucharist and she only dissented from three or four things in the Mass'.[93] But this was a gloss. She had made a major concession, on a central issue of policy, against her better – or at least her original – judgment. The best she could do, as parliament finally dispersed, was to point out, through the mouth of the Lord Keeper, that an agreed consensus had now been reached, and all must abide by it and make it work: she would have no patience with 'those that be too swift, as those that be too slow'. As for religious factions of any kind, 'the very mothers and nurses to all seditions and tumults . . . founded for the most part upon will or upon the glory of men's wits', they would be ruthlessly bridled and suppressed.[94] The realm had chosen uniformity, and uniformity it would get.

As it happened, the settlement was not only judicious, it was probably the only one obtainable. Moreover, it came just in the nick of time. Month by month, the religious cleavage was widening. The Protestants, in particular, were beginning to organize themselves, and stiffen their demands. If the Queen had done as she wished, and delayed the issue, she would probably have got no settlement at all. No subsequent parliament would have agreed to the compromise of 1559, except with terrible and lasting divisions. The Puritan movement would have become separatist, with the Catholics and Henricians following suit, leaving the crown stranded in the middle. This, indeed, was what happened in France, and civil war was the inevitable result. As it was, the compromise was embedded in a legal framework, which a great many people of varying views were willing to accept and make workable, and whose provisions could later be skilfully used to eliminate or emasculate the extremists of both parties. The conservative Elizabeth stumbled on an act of statesmanship by a liberal acquiescence in the power of parliament. It was a great lesson to her – though she never acknowledged it.

The provisions of the settlement were carried out with remarkably little trouble. The Act of Supremacy empowered commissioners to administer an oath, acknowledging the Queen's powers, to all ecclesiastical persons, judges, JPs, mayors and officers of state. Those refusing would be deprived; charges of Praemunire and High Treason would apply to second or third offences, but the Queen was not obliged to press the matter after the first offence – this suited her very well. Of the sixteen bishops, all except Kitchen of Llandaff refused the oath, and were immediately deprived. Eight went to the Tower. Some were put under house arrest, under custody of the new bishops; others given liberty provided they reported to the Council periodically. Bonner went to the Marshalsea, but complaints by Protestants of the luxury in which he lived there suggest he was not harshly treated. Heath was allowed to retire to his estate in Surrey, where Elizabeth visited him on occasion. The overwhelming majority of the rest of the clergy – 8,000 to 9,400 – submitted. Estimates of non-jurors vary from 175 to 700, but only about 200 clergy had to be deprived of their livings during the first six years in which the Act was in force.[95] Resistance from secular Catholics was negligible, though it is probable the Act was only loosely applied in the North. So far as doctrine was concerned, the onus of imposing uniformity was removed from the crown – Elizabeth did not want it – and placed on the ecclesiastical High Commission. But its powers were carefully limited, and the definition of heresy severely narrowed. When the Thirty-Nine Articles made their appearance, together with the Prayer Book, they allowed for great latitude of interpretation. Thus Elizabeth got a broad-based settlement, within the context of which a specifically Anglican system of religion, with its own distinguished literature, began to emerge. Such unpopularity as was involved in enforcing it was squarely placed where Elizabeth wanted it – on the shoulders of the bishops. Of course such a system stored up trouble for the future, as did many of Elizabeth's policies, for it gave the bishops a sphere of activity independent of the crown. But under a strong-minded sovereign, like herself, it worked reasonably well.[96]

The last of the Marian bishops had been dispossessed by November 1559; Elizabeth took her time about filling the vacancies, and the process was not complete until 1562. The key appointment was Matthew Parker, to Canterbury, where he was consecrated on 17 December 1559. He had been a member of Anne Boleyn's household, and must have been well known to Elizabeth, as well as a close friend of Cecil. He had lain low under Mary, and had little sympathy with the returned exiles, whose 'Germanic natures' as he put it, were alien to his spirit of tolerance. By temperament he was a scholar and bibliophile, and he did not want a high-powered job: 'Yes, if I had not been so much bound to the mother, I would not so soon have granted to serve the daughter in this place.'[97] His chief grievance was that Elizabeth expected him to maintain good ecclesiastical order without giving him any overt assistance, and indeed while allowing powerful magnates to protect extreme Protestant offenders: 'I may not work against precisions and Puritans, though the law be against them.' On the other hand, he was under Puritan pressure (from Knollys and others) to act against neo-Catholic scandals in Elizabeth's own chapel – 'the enormities yet in the Queen's closet retained'. Her relations with Parker, indeed, paralleled the inequitable, but politically shrewd, use of her ministers: she was to take any credit, he any odium. She gave him her countenance by visiting, and dining with, him. Thus, after he was severely rebuked by her, privately, for the state of the Church, he records:

> I was well chidden at my prince's hand; but with one ear I heard her hard words, and with the other, and in my conscience and heart, I heard God. Yet her Highness being never so incensed to be offended with me, the next day coming by Lambeth Bridge into the fields, and I according to duty meeting her on the bridge, she gave me her very good looks, and spake secretly in mine ear, that she must needs countenance mine authority before the people, to the credit of my service. Whereat divers of my Arches then being with me marvelled.[98]

As well they might; but it was typical of her methods.

Whether Elizabeth ever addressed her notorious remarks to Parker's wife Margaret, after dining with them, I very much doubt. Mrs Parker was a docile woman, the daughter of a Norfolk gentleman, who kept very much in the background. It was not Elizabeth's way to be rude in cold blood, except for a definite purpose. The story is told by Harington, who may not have been born, and who cannot have been more than nine, when the episode is said to have occurred.[99] But she certainly gave Parker her mind privately on the subject of clerical marriage:

> I was in horror to hear such words to come from her mild nature and Christianly learned conscience, as she spake concerning God's holy ordinance and institution of matrimony ... Insomuch that the Queen's highness expressed to me a repentance that we were thus appointed in office, wishing it had been otherwise.[100]

She never formulated her objections to clerical marriage in a logical manner, perhaps because she could not. Indeed, in some cases she did not object at all. Thus, in October 1568, when the Cardinal de Chatillon – who was a married Protestant – came over to England, Leicester reported to Throckmorton: 'I know assuredly her Majesty has a marvellous liking for him, and one thing more than I looked for, which is her liking to hear of his wife, and is very desirous to see her.'[101] No doubt Frenchmen were different in her eyes. She particularly disliked clerical wives being seen in cathedral closes, and in 1561 actually tried to prohibit it. But the bishops, led by Cox of Ely – a heavily married man – protested. If wives were driven out, the clergy would cease to reside: 'There is but one prebendary continually dwelling with his family in Ely church. Turn him out, doves and owls may dwell there for any continual housekeeping.' Fuel was added to Elizabeth's anger by the fact that some bishops married badly. Thus, Cooper of Lincoln's wife had had an affair with his brother, but the bishop took no action. Freake of Norwich was chained to a bully, a real Mrs Proudie, who interviewed all visitors to the Palace, and, if a suppliant brought no gift for her, would 'look on him as the devil looks over Lincoln'. Some bishops got into trouble through sex: thus, Archbishop Sandys of York was made the victim of a frame-up with an innkeeper's wife, and secretly blackmailed until he was obliged to confess all. Others committed the final enormity of marrying twice. The argumentative Cox, who dared to tell Elizabeth to her face that marriage, including the marriage of clergy, had been 'blessed by Christ himself', entered *en deuxième noces* at the age of sixty-nine, with a pretty young widow, and defended himself to Cecil that, without her, he would have been driven to incontinence! No wonder Elizabeth harassed his episcopal estates. She was even more furious when Richard Fletcher of Worcester (father of the future playwright) also married a young widow. She had liked his good looks, taken an interest in the trimming of his beard, made him her almoner and promoted him; when she heard of his second marriage she dismissed him from court.[102] But he was soon brought back into favour; indeed, Elizabeth never did anything decisive to stop her clergy marrying. It was beyond her power, for the acceptance of clerical marriage was one principal reason why the overwhelming mass of the clergy supported the régime. In any case, her objections really sprang from her dislike of marriage as such. For her, as for Mr Woodhouse in *Emma*, marriage was identified with change in her personal circle; and that kind of change was always unwelcome to her.

By the end of 1559, then, England was for all practical purposes firmly in the Protestant camp. This inevitably raised the Scottish question in an acute form. In the long run it was not a workable proposition for these two countries, with their infinite series of contacts and interrelationships – even ignoring the Stuart claim to the English throne – to maintain mutually hostile religious establishments. Scotland, in alliance with France, had always given the English the phobia of encirclement. The country was now, in effect, a French protectorate; moreover, the Regent, Mary of Lorraine, was a Guise, and thus a member of the ultra-Catholic party in France. The young Mary Queen of Scots was a Guise too; and in July 1559, when Henri II was killed by a lance-splinter at a joust, her husband became King of France. The crowns were thus united. This was ominous for England; ominous, in particular, for Elizabeth, because of Mary's claim to her throne; and, most of all, for English Protestants, for the huge power of France still appeared to be committed, monolithically, to the Catholic cause.

But the French regency – it seemed more like an occupation – was unpopular with most Scots. There, too, the Reformation was at work; and on 2 May 1559, John Knox arrived from the Continent to ignite it. Nine days later he inspired a fury of iconoclasm at Perth and elsewhere. Almost overnight, Francophobia and Reformation linked hands; Scotland lost its Catholic colouring, and became stridently Calvinist.[103] The Protestant Lords of the Congregation took authority over virtually the whole country, and by the end of the month the Regent Mary was shut up with her garrison in the fortress of Leith. But there the matter rested. The Protestant Lords could not defeat the French in the field. They lacked the equipment to storm Leith. Worse, they had no navy to prevent the Valois reinforcing Leith by sea; it was expected that an army of 10,000 French professional troops would soon be landed, and set about reducing the country by force. Though John Knox preached that it was lawful to execute the Queen, 'being an idolatress', and though the Regent was actually deposed by parliament in Edinburgh in October, the means to carry these decisions into effect – or even to defend the Reformation – were conspicuously lacking.

What was Elizabeth to do? It was the first great crisis of her royal conscience, her first real test as an international stateswoman and, not least, her first experience of managing a divided government. The episode shows her behaving throughout in a thoroughly characteristic manner: that is, searching for a consensus, moving it in the direction she thought necessary, while at the same time protecting her flanks. Her problem can be briefly stated. If she did nothing, Scotland would not only revert to the French connection, but she would face a French army, and fleet, on her northern frontiers. On the other hand, if she assisted the Protestant Lords, she risked war with France, at a time, and in a religious context, which ruled out Habsburg assistance. Moreover, by acting, she would be assisting a rebellion of subjects against their legitimate sovereign –

something she found ideologically abhorrent and directly contrary to her own long-term interests.

What made such a course particularly repugnant to her was that she was asked to act in company with a man she detested, John Knox. She never met him, but she hated him as a violent sectarian and an anti-feminist of surpassing vehemence. His 1558 pamphlet, *The First Blast of the Trumpet Against the Monstrous Regiment of Women*, had come into her hands about the time of her accession. It was thus very ill-timed, as he now recognized. In a curious letter to Cecil, 11 April 1559, he tried to explain that his words were directed against Mary Tudor, Mary Queen of Scots, and Mary of Lorraine, not Elizabeth, 'nor of the regiment of her, whom God hath now promoted'. But he did not help his case by adding that Elizabeth was a unique exception, by virtue of divine intervention, to the proposition that women were unfit to rule. For this she should be grateful, and if she sought to ground her title not on divine intervention, but on 'consuetude, laws and ordinance of men . . . I greatly fear that her ingratitude shall not long lack punishment'.[104] This argument was supposed to supply grounds for Cecil getting Elizabeth's permission for Knox to preach in England on his way back to Scotland. Cecil did not even dare show the letter to his mistress.

Nevertheless, Cecil, with Elizabeth's knowledge, had been in touch with the spokesmen of the Protestant Lords, William Maitland of Lethington, even before Knox's return precipitated the crisis. A trickle of money and arms flowed north of the border. The Berwick garrison was reinforced. Throughout the spring and summer of 1559, Elizabeth and Cecil handled the matter in great secrecy: only Parry in London, Croftes in Berwick and Throckmorton in Paris were privy to their thoughts. On the one hand, appeals for help from the Scots were growing more urgent; on the other, complaints of English interference, by the Regent and the French government, were numerous and threatening. Elizabeth did not like to lay the matter openly before the whole Council because she was aware that many of its members objected strongly to open English intervention. These included most of the councillors she had inherited from Mary, her experienced generals and admirals, such as Clinton, Howard and Pembroke, the Treasurer Winchester, and even the Cecilian Lord Keeper, Bacon. The decisive moment seems to have come on 7 August 1559, when she digested a long memo by Cecil, setting out the pros and cons. He concluded that 'the best worldly felicity Scotland can have is either to continue in a perpetual peace with England or be made one monarch with it'; in the short term, she should back a pro-English faction which would expel the French and abolish 'idolatry'. Elizabeth seems to have accepted this in principle. The same day she wrote a dissimulating letter, drafted in Cecil's hand, to the Regent, promising her that English offenders would be punished if specific details of their acts were produced.[105] The day following she dispatched to Berwick Sir Ralph Sadler, loaded with sacks of silver, to take charge of operations to support the rebels. He had been a trusted servant of her father, had more experience of Scottish affairs than any other Englishman, and was reputed to be the richest commoner in the country.[106] Elizabeth hoped that the money being sent north would be attributed to his own personal capacity to raise loans. One first result of his arrival in Berwick was the replacement of the Earl of Northumberland and Lord Dacres, respectively Wardens of the East and Middle, and of the West Marches, 'being indeed rank papists'. Reliable Elizabethans, Grey de Wilton and Sir John Foster, took over.

But by September it was clear that money alone would not do the trick. The Scots were almost in despair. As Knox wrote to Cecil in October: '. . . if you join not with us in open assistance, we will both repent when the remedy shall be more difficult'. This was a powerful argument. Thus Elizabeth was persuaded by the march of events to embark on her first military adventure. But, as Cecil wrote to Sadler, at all costs Knox's name had to be kept out of it: 'Of all others, [his] name is most odious here, and therefore I wish no mention of him hither.' Early in November, Elizabeth began to consider using the navy, to blockade Leith and fend off French reinforcements. On the 10th, for the first time, she laid the whole matter before the Council. Four days later, the fleet, under the old seafaring conspirator William Winter, was ordered to prepare for sea, and the young Duke of Norfolk was ordered north, to take overall command, with Sadler as the effective co-ordinator of operations. Elizabeth's moves were still shrouded in great secrecy. When Maitland came to London in late November, he was smuggled into Whitehall and concealed there, while he held talks with Cecil and the Queen. Throughout December there were long Council meetings; as Cecil reported to Sadler, there was 'some contrariety of opinion'; the majority wanted 'speedy and effective impeachment', a few 'to defer hostility', but they were united in agreeing 'to make all things in readiness by land and sea'.[107] Some of the hostile councillors were swinging round. Clinton 'did not think a good Englishman can ever consent that France should have the upper hand in Scotland'. He, and other 'swordsmen' like Howard and Pembroke, seem to have been convinced by sheer Francophobia; on 24 December, the rest – with the one exception of Arundel – agreed to go ahead with intervention. Elizabeth pondered their joint memo over the Christmas holidays and marked it, on the 28th, 'not allowed by the Queen'. But she yielded when Cecil threatened to resign. In any case, the fleet had left on the

17th, and was beyond the reach of countermanding orders, or fresh instructions of any sort. Norfolk had received his orders on Christmas Day. The die, indeed, was cast, and Elizabeth, having acquiesced earlier in a forward policy – and knowing it in her bones to be advisable – wavered at the last moment more by instinct than as a result of any rational process.[108]

This instinct was deep-rooted in her, and it often made sense. Elizabeth was always conscious of the fragility and impotence of sixteenth-century governments, of their inability to carry theoretical schemes into practice. The more ambitious the scheme – especially if it involved military operations – the more likely things would go wrong. The state was hard put to maintain order even in peacetime, even on the basis of pure conservatism. Once it began to *do* things, its weakness emerged. War was the greatest adventure of all; she hated it not merely because it involved killing, but because it almost invariably taxed the state beyond its strength. I do not think that any of her ministers, even the ultra-cautious Cecil, ever quite appreciated the power of this feeling within her. It explains all her hesitations. Her father, Edward's ministers, her sister Mary – all had committed themselves to active policies. Where had it got them? If ever there were the smallest possibility of her government successfully maintaining a defensive and passive role, that was the course she would take.

Moreover, her instinct was often justified by events. The Scottish campaign of 1560 was a case in point. Throughout the winter of 1559–60, the English military build-up in the north gathered pace, with all the creaking inefficiency of which the Tudor state was capable. As usual, the navy played its part without difficulty. Winter arrived off the Forth on 23 January, captured two French ships of war, and from then on effectively sealed off French naval intervention – or reinforcements. At the same time, the international political situation began to move decisively in Elizabeth's favour. On 4 February, while she was exercising with the trained bands of London, she received news from Throckmorton in Paris that France was on the verge of religious civil war. He followed this with a dispatch two weeks later signalling complete disarray among the French, 'who are so troubled that they know not where to levy any force'. Maitland had meanwhile hurried north from London, and on 27 February, Norfolk concluded at Berwick an offensive and defensive alliance with the Scots Reformers. On 17 March, civil war actually broke out in France, at the 'Tumult of Amboise', when the Huguenots attempted to seize leading members of the Catholic Guise faction. Elizabeth was keeping a very close watch on these events in France, since they had a crucial bearing on her Scottish policy. Whether she did anything to hurry them on is improbable.[109] At any rate, there is no positive evidence that she intervened secretly in French internal politics. But she certainly reacted promptly to the news of France's weakness. On 23 March she issued a proclamation that she was moving her troops into Scotland: 360 copies were printed: 60 in French, 60 in Italian, for Continental distribution. She was careful to point out that she had no territorial aims, and was merely anxious to restore the Scots to their ancient liberties and so forth – a characteristic, and so far as it went truthful, line of argument, which she was later to use in the Netherlands. Grey, who had command of the troops, was ordered to cross the frontier from Berwick, with 6,500 men, on the 28th.

But it was at this point that the trouble began, as Elizabeth, in her bones, had always known it would. Indeed, she had already expressly ordered Norfolk, Grey's nominal commander, to avoid any fighting if possible. Cecil also hoped to avoid fighting, since he feared 'Leith impregnable, having such a number of old men of wars' [experienced troops]; but he trusted in 'good courage in a good quarrel, as this is, to deliver a realm from conquest and consequently to save our own . . .'.[110] On 10 April, Philip II's special envoy to Elizabeth, De Glajon, agreed, after long discussions with Cecil and the Queen, that the invasion could go forward with his master's approval. This, indeed, was a welcome bonus. But it was vital that the French be crushed quickly. Elizabeth, having squared the diplomatic front, needed decisive results from her generals. It was her first – by no means her last – experience of what fragile vessels they were. Grey was an experienced soldier, but old, stupid, incompetent and over-cautious. He had not enough fodder for his horses, as it had to be brought up north, and therefore cut down on his cavalry. For fear of offending his captains, he did not dare order a muster, and therefore had far fewer men than anyone realized – though Elizabeth had to pay in full for the nominal totals, an abuse which filled her with rage throughout her reign. Grey had a siege train of sorts, but was slow in getting it into positions round the fortress. Moreover, in common with most of his English contemporaries, he still believed in the long bow. It was an article of English military faith, shared, among others, by Cecil and Ascham (but not Elizabeth).

Leith was a fortress-town of great natural strength, reinforced by high walls and bastions, forming a defensive perimeter so long that the English staff calculated that, ideally, they would need 20,000 men to take it by storm. The assault, moreover, could only take place after a prolonged artillery bombardment requiring three full batteries of guns. Theoretically, Grey had 12,644 men (including Scots), of whom 9,448 were infantry. The actual numbers were very much less, but we do not know the exact discrepancy, since no muster books have been preserved. Grey's army was probably less than 9,000. This might not have mattered so much if the French garrison had been weaker; but Henri D'Oysel, their commander, had 4,000 men, including a strong force of cavalry, which he could, and did, use to cover sorties. He was a resourceful general, who used every device, legitimate or not, to disrupt the preparations for the siege. Sir John Hayward, who was born in this year, but whose *Annals of the First Four Years of the Reign of Elizabeth* contains much information from men present at the siege, relates that, on one occasion, a party of French emerged from the fortress dressed as women, and so fascinated one of the English scouts that he deserted his post to join them; they promptly cut off his head and displayed it on one of the church steeples. The steeples were used for other purposes: D'Oysel had some of his heavy guns hoisted on to the steeple-towers of the churches of St Anthony and St Nicholas, which soared above the walls, and there was an acrimonious and learned debate among the English commanders as to the propriety of turning their guns on the sacred edifices. Passages from the Bible, Euripides and Plutarch were cited and argued over, before it was agreed to blow the steeples to pieces.

In the event, the English artillery preparations for the assault were woefully inadequate. Grey commanded it for 3.00 a.m. on Tuesday, 7 May, just as it was growing light. Sir Ralph Sadler, Sir James Crofts and the Scotsman Kirkaldy of Grange inspected the damage done by the guns, and reported to Grey, on the evening of 6 May, that the breaches were insufficient to make a successful assault possible. He ignored their advice and they did not insist on it, no doubt aware of Elizabeth's anxiety – expressed in many urgent letters – to get the military operations over as quickly as could be. The dawn attack proved a fiasco. As Sadler and Co. had warned, the breaches were minimal and covered by crossfire from neighbouring bastions. Only a few English soldiers managed to scramble across the rubble and get into the town, where they were promptly killed. Elsewhere, where the walls were unbreached, the scaling-ladders were found to be six feet too short. The archers proved useless, and succeeded only in wounding one man, who died more as a result of French medical science than his injury. The English were particularly incensed by the activities of a large number of Scottish whores, who had attached themselves to the free-spending French garrison. According to John Knox, in his *History of the Reformation in Scotland*:

The Frenchmen's harlots, of whom the most part were Scottish whores, did no less cruelty than did the soldiers: for besides that they charged their pieces and ministered to them other weapons, some continually cast stones, some carried chimneys of burning fire, some brought timber and impediments of weight, which with great violence they threw over the wall upon our men, but especially when they began to turn their backs.

The English attacked with great gallantry, but the task was impossible, and at the end of the day they left behind (according to the French count) 448 bodies; total English losses were around 500. Elizabeth was furious when she got the news of the reverse, and gave Cecil a roasting: 'I have had such a torment with the Queen's Majesty as an ague hath not in five fits so much abated.' But, as always, she was resolute in defeat, and commanded that the war be prosecuted with redoubled vigour: 'Order is given to send both men, money and artillery with all possible speed.'[111]

However, English naval supremacy, and growing shortages among the garrison, were having an effect. On 21 May, a French special envoy, De Randan, arrived in London with a commission to negotiate. Elizabeth was now back on familiar territory: words. Cecil was sent north to Edinburgh to make terms. His orders gave him a good deal of latitude, the *sine qua non* being to secure Scottish liberties and freedom of conscience. After he had left, Elizabeth sent him a touching note of encouragement, by fast messenger: it was, as she realized, the first time he had left her side since her accession.[112] On 10 June, before Cecil had even reached Edinburgh, news came of the Regent's death in Leith Castle, and an armistice was concluded four days later. Cecil negotiated the terms of the French withdrawal with great skill and thoroughness, helped by the fact that he had cracked their secret code. He reported back the transactions to Elizabeth at enormous length in formal dispatches, accompanied by secret letters for her eyes alone. The French agreed to renounce any claim to the English and Irish thrones, and to obliterate their quartering of the English arms on the insignia of Mary Queen of Scots. They even acknowledged, in an ambiguous form of words to be sure, the existence of the Anglo-Scottish league. In return, they were allowed to withdraw with honour. The Treaty of Edinburgh was proclaimed on 6 July. It was a very substantial victory for Elizabeth's diplomacy (if not for her armed forces). At one stroke, it removed the military threat from Scotland, and consolidated a friendly Protestant régime on England's northern border. It ended the Franco-Scottish alliance, and was the first step – a long one – towards the eventual union of the kingdoms. Thus, in less than two years, the Queen and Cecil had successfully established the régime, imposed an acceptable religious settlement on England, and ensured the supremacy of Protestantism throughout the British Isles (the Irish parliament had accepted the Anglican statutes between 12 January–1 February 1560). These were considerable, and in most respects lasting, achievements.

All the same, the successful English intervention left some ragged edges in Anglo-Scottish relationships, and in her attempts to smooth them down, Elizabeth involved herself in a second military adventure, which was to end disastrously. The Scots parliament ratified the Treaty of Edinburgh in August 1560, but the French, though they withdrew according to its provisions, never did so. In particular, their protégé, Mary Queen of Scots, flatly declined, now or at any time in the future, to renounce her claim to the English throne – a claim not merely to the succession, but against Elizabeth's title itself. Moreover, on 6 December 1560, two days before her eighteenth birthday, her husband King Francis II died. In one sense this was welcome news to Elizabeth: the crowns of France and Scotland were no longer linked. In another sense it was ominous: for Mary would now try to carve out a career for herself in the British Isles.

Elizabeth's first response, on 20 January 1561, was to dispatch the Puritan Earl of Bedford to Paris, to convey her condolences to the widow. At this stage, she and Cecil believed, or at least hoped, that there would be insuperable obstacles to Mary's return to Scotland: she was not only a confirmed Catholic, but in all essentials French, speaking neither English nor the Scots dialect. But in any event, Elizabeth wanted to make her return conditional on her ratification of the Treaty. This Bedford was instructed to press, and he did so during two remarkable interviews with Mary at Fontainbleau on 16–17 February.[113] But he got nowhere. From Mary he heard a good deal of sweet talk: how charmed she would be to have a picture of her illustrious fellow-sovereign Elizabeth, how nice it would be for the two Queens to meet, and so forth. On the key point she was wholly evasive: she was all alone, she had no councillors with her. She could take no steps without consulting them. Nor could she act without the advice and consent of the Scottish parliament. In short, she could do nothing until she was back in Scotland. All this was disingenuous, since the Edinburgh parliament had already ratified, and the views of the Scots Council were perfectly well known. When the conversation was reported back to Elizabeth, she drew her own conclusions, which she never had cause to revise: Mary was deceitful, ambitious and thoroughly untrustworthy.

But Elizabeth did not hold all the cards. She could not, in practice, prevent Mary from returning to her throne, if that was what the Scots wanted. Late in March, she saw Mary's half-brother, Lord James Stewart, Earl of Moray, at Whitehall, on his way to France to negotiate with his sovereign. She told him that Mary would not be granted a passport to travel north through England unless she had previously ratified the treaty. But when Moray saw Mary at Rheims on 14 April, she told him she did not intend to go through England: she would take the risk of the sea-voyage and sail direct to the Forth. She had no wish to be an English dependant, and disliked the Anglo-Scottish alliance. As for religion, she was perfectly happy that Scotland should remain Protestant: all she required was the privilege of practising her own in private. Moray was hardly in a position to refuse such terms, though evidently he put no trust in Mary's words: a letter from Throckmorton to him reveals that he had been trying to persuade Elizabeth to intercept Mary's ships and hold her in custody until she gave guarantees in writing. By the end of July Mary was preparing to leave France. At her last interview with Throckmorton, of which we have a full account, she adopted an altogether more hostile tone to Elizabeth, and used expressions – they might be termed threats – which must have alerted all the Queen's deepest suspicions. She had, Mary said, offered friendship: the refusal of a passport showed it had been rejected. But she was not alone in the world:

... both in this realm and elsewhere, I have both friends and allies, and such as would be glad and willing to employ their forces and aid to stand me in stead ... your mistress doth give me cause to seek friendship where I did not mind to ask it ... it will be deemed very strange amongst all princes and countries, that she should first animate my subjects against me, and now, being a widow, impeach my going into my own country. ... I do not trouble her state, nor practise with her subjects. And yet, I know there be in her realm some that be inclined enough to hear offers. I also know, they be not of the same mind, that she is of, neither in religion, nor in other things.[114]

This menacing communication adumbrated, indeed, exactly the situation Mary would create once she was back in play, as Elizabeth no doubt perceived. On the other hand, it also appealed, in some ways, to Elizabeth's own deep instincts and inclinations. It was not her policy to 'practise' with any one's subjects. She always regarded herself, as it were, as a fully-paid-up member of the monarchs' trade union. She had no wish to deprive Mary of her legitimate rights. Still less did she wish to acquire an embarrassing royal prisoner. She knew perfectly well what it was that Mary wanted: a specific declaration, by Elizabeth, that she was to have the English succession – in return for ratifying the treaty. But the one thing Elizabeth was never prepared to do at any time in her life, even on her deathbed, was to nominate her successor. The Stuart claim was the best and closest to the Tudor line itself. Assuming she herself did not marry and have children, this was the claim she favoured. Indeed, she said so privately to Maitland, when she saw him in London that September. But she added:

So long as I live, I shall be Queen of England. When I am dead they shall succeed me who have the most right ... If I meant to do anything to hurt her right, they [the Scots] have occasion to desire me to reform it. But the desire is without an example, to require me in mine own life to set my winding sheet before mine eyes ... I know the inconstancy of the English people, how they ever mislike the present government and have their eyes fixed upon that person who is next to succeed. *Plures adorant solem orientalem quam occidentalem.*[115]

What Elizabeth did propose was to modify the Treaty so that Article Six (the renunciation clause) was limited to her own lifetime, leaving Mary to pursue her claim freely after Elizabeth's death. This was a possible compromise, and in the hope of getting it, Elizabeth allowed Mary's squadron of three ships to leave Calais on 14 August 1561 and proceed to Leith, which they reached five days later. The navy was ordered to shadow the squadron, and even briefly arrested one of the ships. But this was a deliberate demonstration of English naval power, rather than an attempt to prevent Mary's return. The next summer, long negotiations took place to arrange a meeting between the two Queens, so that they could thrash out the problem of the ratification and the succession in private conclave. But they came to nothing, no doubt at Elizabeth's wish, for even a secret understanding would involve the hateful commitment of a designated heir. So these two ladies, who caused such grief to each other, never met.[116]

With Mary back in Scotland, it automatically followed that Elizabeth must strive hard to keep France out of play: either by widening her religious divisions, or by ensuring that the French Protestant party remained strong enough to prevent the pursuit of a pro-Catholic policy in the British Isles. The opportunity soon presented itself. By the Edict of St Germains, on 17 January 1562, the Huguenots were granted religious toleration, and indeed virtual self-government in specified towns and districts. This compromise was bitterly resisted by the Guise faction. In the last week of February they seized control of Paris – a city as passionately pro-Catholic as London was pro-Protestant – and on 1 March 1,200 Huguenots were massacred at Vassy. In this tense situation, Elizabeth found it prudent to dispatch to Yorkshire the Duke of Norfolk, her cousin Lord Hunsdon, and the Earls of Northampton, Rutland and Huntingdon, ostensibly on a hunting party, in reality to cover any threat of a rising by the northern Catholic peers. In April, Throckmorton, warning Elizabeth that civil war was breaking out in France, strongly urged her to take advantage of the troubles to recover Calais, 'or some port of consequence on this side'. He was not alone in seeing the French situation in this aggressive light. As even the cautious Gresham put it: 'Now is the time to recover those pieces we have lost of late in France, or better pieces.'

Paradoxically, such an adventurous course was calculated to appeal to Elizabeth. As she often said, she coveted no other prince's territories. But she wanted her own, and Calais, in her eyes, was legally English. Moreover, if England had a fortified foothold on the French coast, the prospect of a French invasion became remote, and any danger from Mary of Scotland would consequently recede. Her first response was to send Sir Henry Sidney to Paris with offers of her mediation: there was an outside chance that, if this were accepted, she might obtain Calais peacefully, as in theory the Treaty of Cateau-Cambrésis allowed. But with the summer of 1562, more martial counsels prevailed. There was now widespread fighting in France, and a real prospect that the Protestant cause would be crushed for ever. On 17 July, she personally attended a meeting of the full Council – now a rare event – and it was decided to man the fleet and summon levies for possible dispatch to Normandy. Three days later, Cecil presented her with an extraordinarily gloomy memo on the French situation: if the Protestants lost, Spain would seize Navarre, the Guises would put Mary on the English throne, she would marry the son of Philip II, and Ireland would go to Spain as part of the bargain.[117] Whether Elizabeth believed in this lugubrious scenario is doubtful: but she was worried enough to permit a naval demonstration off the Normandy coast. On 1 August she had a secret meeting with a French Huguenot envoy, the Vidame de Chartres, who commanded the port of Le Havre (which the English called Newhaven) to discuss the terms of English military intervention. After six weeks of negotiations, the Vidame and representatives of the Prince de Condé, head of the French Protestant faction, signed with Elizabeth the secret Treaty of Richmond. Under this, Le Havre was to be handed over to an English garrison – eventually to be exchanged for Calais – in return for money and other support. On 1 October, the Earl of Warwick, Dudley's brother, was appointed Captain-General of the expedition, and four days later he took over Le Havre.

Even granted the temptation dangled by the chance to recover Calais, it is very curious that Elizabeth agreed so easily to this venture. There is no evidence of the hesitations and *arrière-pensées* which marked her handling of the Scottish intervention. Moreover, whereas her forward policy in Scotland had been organized through the normal channels of the crown's military forces, Warwick's expedition had a smack of the freebooter about it. All kinds of wild, freelance 'swordsmen' took part; many, like Sir Henry Killigrew, Sir Edward Horsey and Sir Thomas Leighton, were old Wyatt conspirators: men of the type Elizabeth had learned to distrust, and whom she would not normally employ on business which involved her good name and reputation for judgment. She seems at the time to have been very much under the influence of

Dudley, who strongly favoured military intervention (though she, character-istically, would not let him take part in it). In October, she was desperately ill with smallpox, and spent most of the next month recovering. It is also true that she had a great many other things on her mind, as we shall see. She was under enormous pressure to make her mind up about marriage and the succession – the two things about which she cared the most, and on which she was deter-mined not to yield. It may be that, by giving way to the activists over Le Havre, she felt she could more successfully resist them on the central issues. All the same, her support for the venture ran contrary to her nature.

If she had any qualms, they were soon abundantly justified. On 26 October, Rouen fell to the royalists. A second English garrison in Dieppe had to with-draw. On 1 November, after a long meeting of the Council, it was decided to send reinforcements to Le Havre. But next month the Huguenots were defeated in open battle at Dreux, and Condé was taken prisoner. This left the Protestant leadership in France to Admiral Coligny; and on 24 January 1563, Elizabeth – still, evidently, anxious to see the thing through – sent him a message pledging all reasonable support, and followed it with 300,000 crowns (the hole this, and other military expenditure, made in her reserves was filled by a massive sale of crown lands in May). Coligny pocketed the money, but after the head of the Catholic faction, Francis, Duke of Guise, was killed on 24 February, he saw his way clear to a compromise settlement. Next month he signed the Peace Treaty of Amboise, which restored to the Huguenots their religious liberties and cautionary towns – and he did this without reference to English interests, or indeed without consulting Elizabeth. What is more, French Huguenots and Catholics alike now linked hands to expel the English from French territory. Cecil got the news of Coligny's betrayal on 29 March, and it was decided both to hang on to Le Havre, and commence naval operations against French ship-ping. As a mark of her continuing support for the venture, Elizabeth made Warwick a Knight of the Garter on 22 April. Indeed, it was still possible at this stage that the English would be able to retain the port, and thus extract some recompense from the fiasco. But in the first week of June Warwick reported an outbreak of plague in his garrison. By 15 July his effective strength was down to 1,500 men, and nine days later he lost control of the harbour, thus ending any chance of reinforcements. Sir Thomas Smith, who had replaced the activist Throckmorton in Paris, sent an urgent message to negotiate peace immediately, and there was a bitter row in the Council, Cecil – for the first and only time – having a personal quarrel with his brother-in-law, Lord Keeper Bacon. In any event, the plague's attrition of Warwick's troops left the English government with no alternative. On 29 July, with Elizabeth's authorization, Warwick capitulated.

He told her that the terms, 'though they be not so honourable as one could wish, yet, our state everyway considered, they are better than we looked for' – and he was allowed to take his garrison home.[118] Elizabeth, to do her credit, blamed nobody for what was termed 'the Newhaven Adventure'. For the only time in her life, she plunged heavily and heedlessly – and lost. It was a painful but valuable experience and, being a realist, she consoled herself with its lessons.

5

The Best Match in Her Parish

The question of whom Elizabeth should marry had been discussed, at intervals, ever since her birth, and from the moment of her accession it became a central political topic in England, and a source of endless speculation throughout Europe. Even Pope Sixtus V, an ideological enemy, but a man whose admiration for her knew no bounds, allowed his mind to dwell on the fantasy of a papal union with the English crown: what a wife she would make for him, he joked, what brilliant children they would have! Until the early 1580s, by which time Elizabeth was nearly fifty, the subject continued to fascinate the public and preoccupy her ministers. They probably spent more time, and more mental anguish, pondering on this problem than any other aspect of state policy. It induced in them, eventually, a kind of mental paralysis, so that some of Cecil's later memoranda on wedding plans – at a time when any emotionally uncommitted observer must have known that the Queen would never marry – border on the ridiculous.

It has often been alleged, and is still widely believed, that Elizabeth declined to marry because she knew she could never have children. But there is no evidence for this assertion; indeed, such evidence as we possess points in the opposite direction. Elizabeth seems to have been a normal, and on the whole a very healthy woman. All her various illnesses and indispositions were minutely recorded at the time. In aggregate, they naturally make a formidable total.[1] But she was never sick for long. She ate and drank sparingly, and she took a great deal of exercise almost until the last. Indeed, the best testimony to her health is that she lived longer than any previous English sovereign, was active until three weeks before her death, and was in possession of her faculties until her last hours. There is no evidence of any inherited disease, let alone congenital syphilis, and nothing to suggest any physical incapacity.

Moreover, the question of whether Elizabeth could bear children or not was naturally a matter of intense political and diplomatic interest, and was investigated narrowly. Successive Spanish ambassadors, for instance, had paid spies in her household; these included a laundress, who gave information about the nature and regularity of her menstrual periods.[2] Since the Spanish continued to believe that she might marry and have children, we can assume the laundress's reports indicated normality. More conclusive, however, are the careful investigations Lord Burghley had made on this very point early in 1579, at the time of the Alençon courtship. Elizabeth was then forty-five, and since the whole point of the marriage was to produce an heir, Burghley was anxious to find out if this were likely, or indeed possible. He interviewed her doctors who, by the standards of Tudor medicine, were first-rate.[3] He also carried out even more delicate inquiries among her women. He summed up the results in a memo dated 27 March 1579:

> ... considering the proportion of her body, having no impediment of small-ness in stature, of largeness in body, nor no sickness, nor lack of natural functions in those things that properly belong to the procreation of children, but contrary wise, by judgment of physicians that know her estate in those things and by the opinion of women, being most acquainted with her Majesty's body in such things as properly appertain, to show probability of her aptness to have children, even at this day. So as for anything that can be gathered from argument [investigation], all other things, saving the number-ing of her years, do manifestly prove her Majesty to be very apt for the procreation of children ... it may be by good reasons maintained that by forebearing from marriage her Majesty's own person shall daily be subject to such dolours and infirmities as all physicians do usually impute to woman-kind for lack of marriage, and especially to such women as naturally have their bodies apt to conceive and procreate children.[4]

He concluded with the hope that, by bearing a child, Elizabeth would cure the neuralgia in her 'cheek and face'.

Naturally, in her own day, malicious tongues were ready to attribute her celibacy to her own certainty that she could not conceive. Ben Jonson, who delighted to smear her – and many other people – used to tell a story to this effect.[5] But he is a thoroughly unreliable witness. A similar interpretation has been placed on certain cryptic references in diplomatic dispatches.[6] The only one which can, or might, bear this construction is a reference to 'secret reasons' why Philip II did not wish to marry her.[7] But in fact Philip was anxious to make the match, until he saw her personal objections were insuperable. On every occasion that offered, Elizabeth made it plain that, in her view, she was perfectly capable of childbirth. Only one tale suggests otherwise. Sir James Melville, a diplomat who was sent by Mary Queen of Scots to Elizabeth to announce the birth of the future James I, related that, when Cecil whispered the news to the Queen, she exclaimed: 'that the Queen of Scots was mother to a fair son, while she was but a barren stock.' But this tale is suspect for a number of reasons – quite apart from the inherent implausibility that Elizabeth would reveal her feelings (and her secret) in so conspicuous a manner in front of witnesses. It occurs in Melville's memoirs, written in old age many years after the event.[8] They are not, in general, very reliable. Melville reached court to make his announcement on 22 June 1566, more than three whole days after the birth, by which time Cecil already knew of it, and had informed the Queen.[9] So Melville cannot have been present when Elizabeth got the news, which would, in any case, have been given to her in private. The only contemporary evidence of her reaction is provided by Da Silva, the Spanish ambassador, who reported to Philip II: 'the Queen seemed very glad of the birth of the infant' – as, indeed she would be, for it might solve the vexed question of the succession.[10] So Melville's anecdote must be treated sceptically.

If Elizabeth was capable of bearing children, or believed herself to be, why then did she not marry? This was something most of her contemporaries could not, or would not, understand. They blindly assumed, as indeed do many men today, that any healthy and right-thinking woman would naturally wish to marry at the earliest suitable opportunity; that matrimony was a woman's chief trade, destiny and satisfaction in life. It occurred to few of them that an intellectual like Elizabeth, of imperious temper and fixed opinions, might not be prepared, under any circumstances, to accept the subjective role which sixteenth-century marriage imposed even on a Queen-Regnant. Curiously enough, one of those who spotted the truth – as least according to his own account – was Ambassador Melville. He says that after Elizabeth and he discussed the prospect of marriage for Mary – the date is 1564 – the Queen told him

> that it was her own resolution at this moment to remain till her death a virgin queen, and that nothing would compel her to change her mind, except the undutiful behaviour of the Queen her sister [i.e. Mary].

At which Melville smiled increduously, shook his head, and replied:

> that he knew she would never marry, because let Mary do what she would, the Queen of England had 'too stately a stomach [pride] to suffer a commander . . . you think if you were married, you would only be Queen of England, and now ye are king and queen both.'

I doubt very much if Melville would have dared to make such a remark, at any rate in those terms. But the thought behind his words was perfectly correct. If Elizabeth had an enduring passion, it was the assertion of her dominion over men by the power of her position and the force of her intellect. Once married, as she knew very well, it would be a case of 'Othello's occupation's gone.'

Certainly, she never made any secret of her dislike of the married state. For political and diplomatic reasons, she did not, until the mid-1580s, entirely close her options on marriage. That would have been imprudent. Moreover, it would have robbed her of one of her chief pleasures: the contemplation of marriage in the abstract. Her interest in sex was verbal and vicarious. She loved to talk of her possible marriages, and to hear others discuss them. She enjoyed the pantomime of courtship. She admitted, on more than one occasion, that it was desirable in principle that a Queen-Regnant should marry and bear heirs; but she repeatedly made it plain that her private inclination was strongly opposed to matrimony. At the time of the Anjou marriage negotiations, the Earl of Leicester told the French ambassador that, over the past twenty years, she had always said: 'I will never marry.'[11] As he put it in a letter to Walsingham in 1572: 'Surely I am persuaded that her Majesty's heart is nothing inclined to marry at all, for the matter was ever brought to as many points as we could devise, and always she was bent to hold with the difficultest.'[12] She explained her attitude to parliament on several occasions, as we shall see; and she rarely let slip an opportunity to express her views to a wider public. Thus, in the summer of 1564, for instance, when she was thirty-one, she paid a visit to Cambridge University; when the public orator, in a Latin address given outside King's College Chapel, praised her many virtues, she 'shaked her head, bit her lips and fingers, and sometimes broke forth into passion and these words: "*Non est veritas, et utinam.*" On his praising virginity, she said to the Orator: "God's blessing on your heart, *there* continue." '[13]

Elizabeth's objection to marriage, as I have suggested, was emotional; it sprang from a dislike of change as such; but she did not pretend, even to herself, that it was based on reason or logic. The brunt of her dislike, of course, fell on the senior clergy. There can be no doubt that the favour she showed to Archbishop Whitgift, in other respects a man whose intellect did not appeal to her (though she recognized in him a formidable instrument), was largely due to his celibacy. In one respect the effect of her disapproval was lasting: it became impossible for the Anglican clergy to secure any formal recognition of their wives in the hierarchy of the state, and even today they are not mentioned in *Crockford's.*[14] But this was a detail: in England, clerical marriage became the norm, under her disdainful aegis.

She also hated court marriages, especially among the maids of her chamber. These score or so young ladies were placed at court by their parents for precisely this purpose (among others), and engagements and marriages among them were therefore inevitable. But to contract one, under Elizabeth, was always to ask for trouble. If she had laid down a clear rule that none of her maids was to marry, under any circumstances, while in her service, many rows might have been avoided. But it was against her nature to place so interesting a sphere of human activity on a straightforward basis. She liked areas of uncertainty in conduct. For the maids, this posed insuperable problems. If they asked her permission to marry, it might be flatly refused, as in the case of Mary Arundell. Indeed, if they were pretty, and thought to be foolish and impertinent, like Mary Shelton, they were even beaten: one of the unpleasant characteristics Elizabeth inherited from her father was her habit of striking those around her, though she rarely touched the men. Sometimes they married secretly – a common practice in sixteenth-century England, even when there was no discernible reason for it; but in that case their husbands might be imprisoned, as happened to Sir Robert Tyrwhit and Sir Walter Ralegh. If they refused to disclose a marriage until they were pregnant, they as well as their husbands might go to gaol. Thus, when Elizabeth Vernon was discovered with child by the 3rd Earl of Southampton, the Queen lashed out in all directions:

> She threats them all to the Tower, not only the parties but all that are partakers in the practice. It is confessed that the Earl was lately here and solemnized the act himself, and Sir Thomas German accompanied him on his return to Margate . . . I now understand that the Queen has commanded that there shall be provided for the new Countess the sweetest and best appointed Chamber in the Fleet [prison].[15]

The maids were also in serious trouble if, like Mary Fitton, they allowed themselves to be seduced without making sure of their marriage lines.[16]

Elizabeth's attitude was not wholly indefensible. English sovereigns had always exercised a justified supervision of marriages between tenants-in-chief, and other important persons in the state. Unlike James I, and still more Charles I, she did not engage in match-making for political purposes, except to some extent in the case of Mary of Scotland, where England's immediate national interests were involved. Even when James I consulted her about his marriage, and said he favoured Anne of Denmark, Elizabeth (who would have preferred a French match) declined to interfere: she told him that, as she had foreborn marriage herself, she was not qualified to advise others.[17] In the case of the maids, she quite properly felt she was in a position of trust towards them – *in loco parentis*, as it were – and had a positive duty to protect them from folly and imprudent unions. What is more, her objections towards particular matches were often proved abundantly justified by their later history. She was a good judge of compatability; and, as a realist, felt that marriages should normally take place between social equals, especially when large fortunes were involved. In the late sixteenth century more than one in ten upper-class marriages broke down, and Elizabeth was concerned to restrict the number as far as possible.[18] She knew she was dealing with hot-blooded people who would repent at leisure.

In fact court marriages constantly took place, often with no trouble at all. Under Elizabeth, thirteen earls or future earls, and five barons, found wives among the maids. A glimpse of her methods is given by a letter from Frances Howard to her lover the Earl of Hertford, in January 1585:

> Many persuasions she used against marriage ... and how little you would care for me ... how well I was here, and how much she cared for me. But, in the end, she said she would not be against my desire. Trust me, sweet lord, the worst is past, and I warrant she will not speak one angry word to you.[19]

Elizabeth's fears were well-founded: as she had predicted, this marriage proved an unhappy one. In other cases, a moderate display of firmness broke down the Queen's resistance. Thus, on 19 March 1583, Sir Francis Walsingham wrote crisply to Hatton, who was at court, asking him to let the Queen know that there could be no question of her preventing the marriage of his daughter, Frances, to Sir Philip Sidney:

> I pray you sir, therefore, if she enter into any further speech on the matter, let her understand that you learn generally that the match is held for concluded, and withal to let her know how just cause I shall have to find myself aggrieved if her Majesty still show her mislike thereof.[20]

Of course, Walsingham was a masterful and much-valued public servant, the only one of her ministers who occasionally filled her with awe; not everyone could take such a high line. But in general, pertinacity, reasoned argument and above all straightforwardness usually convinced the Queen. She knew very well she was irrational on the subject of marriage – especially where her male favourites were concerned – and sometimes her words and behaviour betrayed a degree of emotional muddle, of which she must have been painfully aware. On 18 June 1578, Sir Christopher Hatton, who himself renounced marriage for the sake of the affection she had for him, wrote a sad letter to Leicester:

> Since your Lordship's departure the Queen is found in continual and great melancholy: the cause thereof I can but guess at, notwithstanding that I bear and suffer the whole brunt of her mislike in generality. She dreameth of marriage that might seem injurious to her: making myself to be either the man or a pattern of the matter. I defend that no man can tie himself or be

tied to such inconvenience as not to marry by law of God or man, except by mutual consents on both parts the man and the woman vow to marry each to other, which I know she hath not done for any man, and therefore by any man's marriage she can receive no wrong. . . . But, my Lord, I am not the man that should thus suddenly marry, for God knoweth I never meant it.[21]

Clearly Elizabeth was worried that Hatton would marry; knew that her hostility to such a prospect was unreasonable and unfair to him; but could not help herself. But it was fear of losing friends, and the increased loneliness this would bring, rather than sexual jealousy, which was her half-understood motive.

We cannot, of course, determine how strong Elizabeth's own sexual urges were. As her father's daughter, she was sometimes portrayed by her enemies as a monster of lust, but this was propaganda. Henry's sexuality, as I have suggested, was grossly exaggerated; he was much more concerned with decorum, and much more conscientious than popular legend has it. Elizabeth, too, was a punctilious and very dignified lady, deeply and often angrily attached, throughout her life, to the proprieties. It is inconceivable that she could have been guilty of casual amours. She made no secret of her preference for handsome men, provided they had brains and abilities. Nor did she conceal her affection – and something deeper than that – in the case of Hatton and Leicester. Her relations with all the men who served her in high office were, to some extent, tinged with emotion. But this was sublimation, rather than evidence of sexual intimacy. There is absolutely no proof whatever of her unchastity. Malicious rumours were naturally spread about her, and believed by the simple-minded. Sometimes those who spread them were brought to book. Thus, in 1581 one Henry Hawkins was accused of saying that 'my Lord Robert [Leicester] hath five children by the Queen, and she never goeth on progress but to be delivered.'[22] Some very unpleasant stories about her were related by the notorious Bess of Hardwick, Countess of Shrewsbury. Bess repeated them to Mary Queen of Scots, when the latter was in the Earl of Shrewsbury's custody, and Mary was foolish enough to set them down in writing – in the form of accusations – in a letter she wrote to Elizabeth. Thus, Elizabeth was said to have been found lying in bed with Leicester on many occasions, and (in effect) to have seduced Hatton by force. Fortunately, this scurrilous letter was intercepted by Burghley, and Elizabeth never saw it (we would certainly have known if she had!). But there is no evidence that Mary believed the tales – her motive in telling them was to get Bess, with whom she had quarrelled, in trouble – and Bess subsequently admitted to the Council that they were baseless.[23] Other tendentious charges were laid by Catholic apologists like Cardinal Allen and Nicholas Sanders; they can be dismissed.

The only possible piece of evidence I have come across which suggests Elizabeth was not chaste is contained in a letter which the poet Edward Dyer wrote to Hatton in October 1572, at a time when the latter was supposed to be jealous of the favour the Queen was showing to the young Earl of Oxford:

> For though in the beginning when her Majesty sought you (after her good manner) she did bear with rugged dealing of yours, until she had what she fancied, yet now, after satiety and fullness, it will rather hurt than help you. [Instead Hatton should] never seem deeply to condemn her frailties, but rather joyfully to commend such things as should be in her, as though they were in her indeed.[24]

But I do not think the words 'what she fancied' and 'satiety and fullness' can, or were intended to, bear a directly sexual construction. Such a meaning is not corroborated by any of Hatton's own letters to the Queen, which are couched in the platonic terms of amorous hyperbole.[25] What Elizabeth got from Hatton was his company, his attentions, his ingenious and thoughtful presents, his display of court accomplishments, and above all the purely verbal love-making she enjoyed: this was 'what she fancied', and no doubt in time 'satiety and full-ness' was reached; by that stage Elizabeth had determined on making her handsome courtier into a reliable parliamentary statesman. Hatton, as we know, got his sexual pleasures elsewhere, though discreetly.

Against this ambiguous passage, there is a mass of evidence about Elizabeth's seemly behaviour from observant and interested contemporaries. Thus, on 4 April 1561, the Swedish chancellor, Nils Guilderstern, visiting court on behalf of King Erik (who was interested in marriage), reported: 'I saw no signs of an immodest life, but I did see many signs of chastity, virginity and true modesty; so that I would stake my life itself that she is most chaste.'[26] Most other ambassadors were asked similar questions by their masters, and reported in the same sense. Thus Adam Swetkowitz wrote to the Emperor on 4 June 1565 that Leicester was 'loved by the most serene Queen with sincere and most chaste and most honourable love as a true brother'.[27] Ambassador Fénelon reported to Marie de Medici, 31 January 1571, that Elizabeth was 'good and virtuous'; rumours circulated abroad, he added (6 March 1571), were quickly dissipated by the atmosphere of the court, where the respect she inspired and received ruled out any possibility of lack of virtue.[28] Another French ambassador, Mauvissière, who knew her over a quarter of a century, summed up: 'and if attempts were made falsely to accuse her of love-affairs, I can say with truth that these were sheer inventions of the malicious, and of the ambassadorial staffs, to put off those who would have found an alliance with her useful.'[29] Spanish ambassadors were particularly asked to inquire on this point. All drew a blank. De Silva said he was never able to find any truth in the rumours about her virtue, and in the enormous mass of Mendoza's correspondence there is no imputation on her sexual morals. Indeed, as she herself observed to De Silva: 'I do not live in a corner – a thousand eyes see all I do, and calumny will not fasten on me for ever.' On the English side, there was a universal assumption, among those who knew her well, that she was chaste. As Bacon put it, 'This queen was certainly good and moral; and as such she desired to appear.'

Of course, among the people at large, the Queen was – among many other things – a transcendental object of sexuality, as well as a surrogate Virgin Mary, the biblical Deborah, and other quasi-religious symbols. She deliberately encouraged this feeling: it was another aspect of the vicarious sex she appreciated, as well as sound policy. As she often said, flourishing the plain gold coronation ring she always wore, she was married to the English people. They came to regard her as such, and not just in a symbolic sense. They often dreamed about her, not always decorously. One such dream is described by the professional astrologer Simon Forman, in his diary for 23 January 1597, when Elizabeth was sixty-four!

I dreamt that I was with the Queen, and that she was a little elderly woman in a coarse white petticoat all unready; and she and I walked up and down through lanes and closes, talking and reasoning of many matters. At last we came over a great close where were many people, and there were two men at hard words. One of them was a weaver, a tall man with a reddish beard, distract of his wits. She talked to him and he spoke very merrily unto her, and at last did take her and kiss her. So I took her by the arm and put her away; and told her the fellow was frantic. And so we went from him and I led her by the arm still, and then we went through a dirty lane. She had a long white smock, very clean and fair, and it trailed in the dirt and her coat behind. I took her coat and did carry it up a good way, and then it hung too low before. I told her she should do me a favour to let me wait on her, and she said I should. Then, said I: 'I mean to wait *upon* you and not under you, that I might make this belly a little bigger to carry up this smock and coats out of the dirt.' And so we talked merrily and then she began to lean upon me, when we were past the dirt, and to be very familiar with me, and methought she began to love me. And when we were alone, out of sight, methought she would have kissed me.[30]

At this point – 3.00 a.m. – Forman woke up and, fortunately for us, recorded his dream.

If Elizabeth kept her sexual impulses under control, at the different level of her emotions she was not so restrained, at any rate in the earlier years of her reign. She cast her eye appraisingly over the handsome gentlemen at court, when there was still a universal assumption that she would marry, and quickly. At this stage she did not take the foreign suitors seriously (if she ever did). As the Habsburg alliance was still, up to a point, the foundation of English foreign policy, the Archduke Charles, son of the Emperor, was the leading suppliant. But he was unwilling to appear in person unless a match were virtually concluded, and Elizabeth always resolutely refused to go beyond the merest preliminaries until she had subjected the suitor to a physical inspection; no doubt she remembered the 'Flanders mare'. But the English eligibles were on the spot, visible daily. For a time Sir William Pickering was thought to be her choice; so much so that the Earl of Arundel, who also felt he had a chance, angrily declared that, if Pickering were elected, he himself would sell his estates and emigrate. Pickering was in his early forties at Elizabeth's accession, probably a confirmed bachelor (he died in 1575, still unmarried); he had done well in the last years of Henry VIII and in Edward's minority, serving as ambassador in Paris and elsewhere, and acquiring some choice Church estates, including the famous Cistercian abbey and sheep-farms of Vale Crucis, near Llangollen, which were to go to the Wottons via his illegitimate daughter Hester. He had an excellent house in St Andrews Underhill, with a copious library, which Elizabeth admired. He was tall, athletic and personable, in marked contrast to the Archduke who (Elizabeth was told), had an enormous head, bigger even than the Earl of Bedford's. But nothing came of the Pickering business, or of Arundel's supposed chances; or of anything else.

What the Queen did do, apparently because she needed it, was to form a close, often intimate, and (with some upsets) permanent friendship with Robert Dudley. It was one of the most – perhaps the most – important relationships in her entire life, and in some ways completely mysterious. Apart from Elizabeth, none of his contemporaries seems to have liked Dudley; and it is a curious fact that no first-class modern historian has ever had the fortitude to write his life. Printed extracts from his vast correspondence are scattered through numerous compilations, but only his letters during the Low Countries campaign, 1585-8, have been systematically edited.[31] As everyone agreed, and as Elizabeth, when angry, sometimes pointed out to him, Dudley had bad blood. His grandfather, Edmund Dudley, had been President of the Council under Henry VII, his chief debt collector and his most unpopular servant; Henry VIII had executed him, immediately after his accession, amid howls of delight, though Dudley's 'confession', now printed, shows he did little more than carry out his master's explicit orders.[32] Edmund's son John, Duke of Northumberland, did considerably more to justify the universal execration in which he was held. Thus both his father and grandfather had been executed as traitors (as Elizabeth remarked occasionally), and it is interesting to note that his only surviving son, Robert Dudley, turned traitor after Elizabeth's death, though he was never brought to book. During his lifetime Dudley was accused of virtually every vice by popular rumour – the most common charge being the practice of poison – and after his death, Ben Jonson asserted that he had died from one of his own potions, administered inadvertently by his wife (the story is baseless). If anyone chanced to die in his company, or under his roof, rumours about poison immediately circulated. Elizabeth was well aware of these tales; indeed, they often found their way into print; and in 1584 he was subjected to a full-scale and brilliant attack on his character, *Leycester's Commonwealth*, which circulated widely and gave much pleasure.[33] No one ever sprang to his defence, except close connections, like Sir Philip Sidney, or dependent scribes.[34] Yet the Queen liked him, perhaps even at times loved him. Why?

It is a commonplace that highly intelligent, prudent and virtuous women rarely attach themselves to men of similar cast. It may be too fanciful to suggest that Elizabeth saw in Dudley a younger, more malleable version of the bold, bad and fascinating Lord Thomas Seymour; a Lord Thomas, as it were, fashioned for her own control and consumption. She and Dudley were almost exact contemporaries; indeed it was widely believed – even so reliable an authority as Camden accepted it – that they had been born on the same day. Maybe the Queen believed this too, though in fact Dudley was born on 24 June 1533, which made him some two months older. A more important link was that they had been in the Tower together under Mary. Shared prison experiences (including the fear of imminent death) tend to breed adamantine friendship; the 'Marian Gaolbirds' formed a bizarre little club in the earlier years of the reign, with Elizabeth as their patron. Then, too, Dudley was a handsome fellow. His enemies called him the Gypsy – a reflection on his moral character as well as his looks. He had dark brown hair with a reddish tint (the tint was more pronounced in his beard and moustache), fine brown eyes, and a long prominent nose, with a bridge to it, rather like the Queen's own: she seemed to have liked such noses, for Essex's was similar.[35] But perhaps his chief attraction, at this time, was his horsemanship: he rode superbly, and was a wonderful judge of horseflesh. Elizabeth was always a keen rider, but as a young woman she was a passionate devotee. During her first years as Queen, the pressure of political work, and public appearances, was enormous, and she seems to have taken every possible opportunity to take vigorous exercise by hunting on horseback. Dudley's appointment as Master of the Horse had been among her first. It had little political significance except that it brought him into daily contact with the Queen. They spent a good deal of time together, training, exercising, breeding and buying horses. On 7 September 1560, for instance, Dudley reported he was hunting with her every day from morning till night: 'She doth mind out of hand to send into [Ireland] for some hobbys for her own saddle, especially for strong, good gallopers which are better than her geldings, which she spareth not to try as fast as they can go. And I fear them much, but yet she will prove them.'[36]

Already, in May 1559, she had made him a Knight of the Garter, and it was evident he was playing a prominent role in the arrangement of public cere- monial, for which he had a conspicuous talent. In after years, Elizabeth sometimes angrily complained (when examining her household accounts) that the display of her court during her first years had been far more magnificent than at any sub- sequent period, and achieved at less cost – thus paying an oblique compliment to Dudley's taste and management. Elizabeth never placed more emphasis on display than was seemly, but she recognized it was important, especially to a virgin Queen, and Dudley's efforts gave him an increasingly influential footing in the household. Dudley might have no capacity for attracting sincere friend- ship; but he was adept at clientage, the late-medieval device under which am- bitious men formed themselves into joint-stock companies, under an influential chairman. He soon had numerous followers at court, and got a grip of its in- ternal machinery which never really weakened: 'In the Privy Chamber next to her Majesty's person, the most part are his creatures (as he calleth them), that is, such as acknowledge their being in that place from him; and the rest he so overruleth that ... nothing can pass but by his admission.'[37]

Elizabeth, of course, was well aware of this. Sometimes she drew the line. She was never remiss in reminding Dudley, even after she made him Earl of Leicester, that, while she tolerated his clientage, he himself was entirely *her* 'creature'. Thus, Sir Robert Naunton records that when Bowyer, a gentleman of the Black Rod, tried to stop one of Leicester's men from entering the Privy Chamber – he had not taken the security oath – Leicester interfered, and told Bowyer he would lose his job. 'But Bowyer, who was a bold gentleman, and well-beloved, stepped before him, and fell at her Majesty's feet, related the story and humbly craved her Grace's pleasure: and whether my Lord of Leicester was king or her Majesty queen? Whereunto she replied, with her wonted oath:

"God's death, my Lord, I have wished you well; but my favour is not so locked up for you, that others shall not partake thereof; for I have many servants, to whom I have, and will at my pleasure, bequeath my favour, and likewise resume the same; and if you think to rule here, I will take a course to see you forthcoming. I will have here but one mistress and no master; and look that no ill happen to [Bowyer], lest it be required at your hands." Which words so quelled my Lord of Leicester, that his feigned humility was long after one of his best virtues.'[38] But in general she allowed Dudley a good deal of scope in the palaces, reasoning that the thuggery and rivalry that inevitably went on were better controlled by one senior operator than fought over by rival gangs.

Dudley first came into political prominence in the summer of 1560, when Cecil was absent in Scotland negotiating the Treaty of Edinburgh. Elizabeth was always adept at preserving the principle of balance in her government. The successful Scottish affair had brought considerable kudos to Cecil, as well as to the old aristocracy, led by young Norfolk, who had been prominent in the campaign. She thought it necessary to favour a 'swordsman' to balance the 'scribes', led by Cecil; and to emphasize that it was in her power to raise a new nobility, to curb any overweening pretensions on the part of the old. At any rate, when Cecil and Norfolk returned to court, they found Dudley in great favour. They themselves got precious little thanks for their efforts, and nothing beyond the nominal £4 a day expenses to which they were entitled.[39] Moreover, there was talk that Dudley's wife, Amy Robsart, was about to die, and that, when she did so, Elizabeth would marry Dudley. Meanwhile, the two supposed lovers were out all day, hunting.

Some historians believe, as indeed did many at the time, that during this summer of 1560 Elizabeth, for the first and last occasion in her life, almost surrendered to passion, and allowed her feelings to rule her head.[40] But this seems to me unlikely. Dudley's wife rarely came to court – she was almost certainly suffering from cancer – but her existence was an absolute obstacle to marriage, or thought of it. During August 1560, Amy Robsart's condition grew much worse. Rumours about Elizabeth and Dudley were spreading: on the 13th one Anne Dowe of Brentford was sent to gaol for asserting the Queen was with child by him (the first of many such convictions). Amy actually died on 8 September, supposedly of a fall, at Cumnor Place in Oxfordshire. As Dudley was supposed to benefit from her death, poison was immediately suspected. The scandal was intense, and Elizabeth found some difficulty in getting anyone to represent her at the funeral, eventually falling back on 'Old Crow', Lady Norris, one of her closest friends, who lived not far away. But there is no reason to suppose murder was committed. Elizabeth was kept well informed of Amy's condition; she told the Spanish ambassador, Bishop de Quadra, the day before death occurred, that Amy was dying. A recent medical analysis shows that the fall was entirely compatible with the progress of the disease.[41] While Dudley was often accused of being a poisoner, no one, then or since, has been able to produce any actual evidence that he used poison, or was skilled in its arts. Poison was the great popular obsession of the Renaissance Age, but from what we know of Amy's condition over many months, its administration in her case would have been beyond the skill of even the most devilish sixteenth-century practitioner.

In any case, once Dudley's wife had died in such circumstances, for the Queen to marry him was out of the question. She did not consider it. During September she was much more preoccupied with the reissue of the coinage, which she timed and supervised personally. Cecil, also, had taken a hand. From a letter he wrote to the Earl of Bedford in August, it appeared he was thinking of resigning.[42] On 6 September he broached his fears to Ambassador Quadra, complaining, so the latter reported

> that the Queen was going on so strangely that he was about to withdraw from her service . . . he perceived the most manifest ruin impending over the Queen through her intimacy with Lord Robert. The Lord Robert had made himself master of the business of the state and of the person of the Queen, to the extreme injury of the realm, with the intention of marrying her, and she herself was shutting herself up in the palace to the peril of her health and life.[43]

This last statement is certainly untrue, since we know Elizabeth was out hunting every day. The conversation was a calculated diplomatic indiscretion, with the object of bringing Spanish pressure to bear on the Queen not to make a fool of herself. Cecil's letter to Bedford probably had the same purpose, as did others he wrote to powerful friends at the time. He also wrote to English ambassadors, such as Throckmorton in Paris, telling them, in exaggerated terms, what was going on, and hinting that any reports they could forward showing that a Dudley marriage would be received with hostility on the Continent would be useful. They duly responded. Throckmorton, for instance, relayed the tale that Mary Queen of Scots had sneered: 'The Queen of England is about to marry her horsemaster.'[44] All this was brought to Elizabeth's attention, and how it must have rankled!

Cecil followed up such efforts by first exaggerating, then exploding, a complex manoeuvre to reconcile England to the Church of Rome. This was allegedly timed to coincide with the re-opening of the Council of Trent; the invitations, which included England, went out in November 1560; and efforts were being made to persuade Elizabeth to accept a papal representative, Abbot Martinengo. As an appendage, the rumour was spread that the Queen was to marry Dudley with the Pope's blessing, and reunion with Rome would follow. All this was speculation, resting chiefly on the conviction that Dudley, like his father, had no fixed religion but was willing to adopt any which seemed personally and politically convenient. But Cecil gave substance to the fears by 'discovering' a plot in the household of Sir Edward Waldegrave, a known papist. He later admitted this was a fake – 'I swear to God that I meant no evil to any of them, but only for the rebating of the Papist's humour which, by the Queen Majesty's lenity, grew too rank'[45] – but it served its purpose.

Elizabeth did not need this kind of pressure to convince her that her elevation of Dudley had gone too far; it, too, had served its purpose, and as early as mid-October 1560, she redressed the balance again. After much nagging by Dudley, a patent to make him an earl had been drawn up; she now cut it into tiny pieces with a knife. The story circulated in November and was much relished. On 15 December old Parry died, apparently from a fit of bad temper. This left the best plum of all, the Mastership of the Wards, at her disposal; she gave it not to Dudley, but to Cecil, and she followed it a few months later with substantial grants of lands.[46] Cecil wrote with some satisfaction to Throckmorton: 'Whatever reports or opinion be, I know surely that my Lord Robert hath more fear than hope, and so doth the Queen give him cause.'[47] Or, as Bedford put it: 'The great matters whereof the world was wont to talk are now asleep, having had some fits both hot and cold.'[48]

But if Elizabeth never had any intention of allowing the political balance to be upset, or to permit Dudley to emerge as the greatest single potentate at court, she was equally unwilling to dispense with the services of a clever and unscrupulous operator who (unlike Cecil, who had strong opinions and a conscience) was entirely at her bidding. Dudley, too, was learning the political game fast, and was building up connections not just with underlings but with leading political figures. He swung violently on to the Protestant tack, and from this point began to interfere systematically in ecclesiastical appointments, becoming in time the most important single patron of Protestant sectaries. These operations, which were troublesome and consumed a good deal of time, were well worth while: they brought him direct political influence, notably in the Commons, *ad hoc* allies in the shape of strongly Protestant peers like the Earls of Bedford and Huntingdon, and even cash rewards, for the recipients of benefices were expected to be grateful. They also made him an enthusiastic exponent of an activist foreign policy, and he was the leading spirit in the

English intervention in the French religious war during 1562-3. Dudley's advocacy, indeed, may well help to explain why Elizabeth embarked on the 'Newhaven Adventure' with such uncharacteristic lack of hesitation. She had brought forward Dudley's elder brother Ambrose, in December 1561, making him Earl of Warwick, and following this with massive grants of lands in the Midlands, drawn from the confiscated estates of his father, Northumberland. Warwick, of course, was given the Newhaven command, and though Dudley himself was not permitted to serve, he was handsomely favoured in other ways. During 1562 the Queen allowed him, for the first time, to plunge his hands deep into the royal till. This was not by any means entirely a matter of personal affection, let alone womanly improvidence. If the Queen wished to build up a powerful 'new' man, for reasons of political balance, she had to give him the wherewithal to maintain his position, and feed his party.[49] Early in 1562 Dudley, like his brother, got chunks from his father's old estates; in the summer he was awarded a licence to export 80,000 undressed white cloths. This was a valuable perk, for portions of it could be sold, as and when required, to City men for cash. In October he got an annual pension of £1,000, chargeable on the London customs.[50] The same month, immediately after Elizabeth recovered from the crisis of her attack of smallpox – while, indeed, she was still very ill – Dudley was brought on to the Council. She even discussed a plan to give him some form of plenary powers. But this was the product of delirium; when it came to the point she balanced his promotion by giving a councillorship to his enemy among the 'old' nobility, the Duke of Norfolk. All the same, Dudley was now at the centre of the political machine, and operating almost on a parity with Cecil himself. Both found it advisable to establish a courteous, if never a friendly, relationship with each other.[51]

But Dudley was, and remained, much more than a force for political balance. Though contemporaries could not see what the Queen admired and valued in him, I do not find it too difficult. He was a man of immense energy, and it found innumerable outlets. If his brain was shallow rather than deep, and his interests wide rather than dedicated, none the less his range of accomplishments was impressive. He was a master of all field-sports, something the Queen found far from negligible. At this period, his paunch had not yet appeared, nor the jowls of his cheeks, nor had his neck thickened; there were no angry red veins on his pink and white skin: he looked, and was, a superlative athlete. He possessed the manifold skills of the joust, and had a sound working knowledge of all aspects of chivalry, heraldry and knightly conduct. He understood the technology of warfare and how to handle weapons – was, indeed, an experienced soldier. But he was not just an extrovert, a bluff man-at-arms like Elizabeth's cousin, Hunsdon, or the barely literate Pembroke. He was, for instance, a great patron of architects and gardeners. Under his direct supervision, the old castle at Kenilworth was transformed into a Renaissance-Gothic palace, while still keeping all the majesty and operational resources of a major fortress. Enormous numbers of skilled craftsmen were at his beck and call. Almost overnight he could throw up a ceremonial garden, or the elaborate theatrical extravaganzas which delighted the Elizabethans (not least the Queen) and on which they spent fortunes. He patronized poets, playwrights, actors, musicians, singers, clowns, scholars, divines and artists – and he knew enough about the trade of each of them to pick the best and make full use of their skills. He was a fluent and attractive letter-writer, and a conversationalist with an infinite range of topics. Like the Queen, he had been taught to speak excellent Italian. He could dance and sing. By comparison, Norfolk seemed gauche, and Cecil pedestrian and sententious. For Elizabeth he represented the pleasure-principle as well as the duty-principle; he could switch from affairs of state to the latest entertainment, or book, and back again, without changing gear – and Elizabeth always liked to mingle business with pleasure. Ascham had taught her to look for the Complete Man. In Dudley she came nearest to finding him, for he could participate in the whole range of her interests. If he was greedy for money, he spent a good deal of what he got on keeping her spirits up; she not only knew, but insisted on this – it was part of their bargain, the way she operated with the men she created. And he was indeed her creation: from first to last he was *hers*, for he was nothing without her continual support. Moreover, he accepted this role – as, later, Essex tragically failed to do. Though he might grumble and agitate, he always, in the end, did as she wished, at any rate when he was near her; only when her piercing gaze was removed was he ever tempted to disobey orders. All in all, then, Elizabeth got value for her money and affection. She was a lady Pygmalion who had brought an idealized male statue to life; if the workmanship was imperfect, it was the best she was ever likely to get.

It is not surprising, then, that in the agony of smallpox, Elizabeth thought wildly of a major role for Dudley in settling her succession. But her illness focused the minds of everyone else, in the most vivid manner, on the problem. Not that the question of who was to succeed her, if she remained unmarried and died without an heir, had ever been far from the thoughts of public men. On the contrary: it tended to dominate politics, especially when parliament was sitting. Elizabeth's relations with parliament form a very important part of the political history of her reign; they also provide innumerable insights into her character and methods. Indeed, they reveal her in a characteristic posture:

struggling to preserve the essentials of an unwritten constitution, as she understood it, by making liberal gestures to the forces of change. We no longer think
of the Tudor age as a pause or hiatus in the development of parliament, sand-
wiched between the rapid constitutional development of the late fourteenth and
fifteenth centuries, and the breakdown of the divine-right monarchy in the
seventeenth. Parliamentary institutions, and their relationship to the crown,
evolved continuously throughout this period. The more we discover about the
actual workings of parliament, the more we perceive its importance in the state.
It is true that Henry VII disliked the institution, and sometimes threatened to
govern 'after the French fashion'. But he did not do so; he could not have done
so. Under his son, Thomas Cromwell used the machinery of parliament, and
especially the statute, to carry through the religious revolution, and align the
nation behind the King's cause. This process was irreversible; it was never
afterwards possible to effect structural changes in religion, or other central
aspects of the national life, by any alternative method. Nor were Henry VIII's
parliaments docile assemblies; during his time we first hear of divisions of the
Lower House, of government Bills 'dashed', or amended, or withdrawn under
parliamentary pressure. Parliament was an independent and operative factor in
the crises of Edward VI's minority. It was never wholly under the control of
Mary and her ministers, despite her efforts to pack the Commons. As we have
already seen, it decisively influenced Elizabeth's religious settlement. Moreover,
it was increasingly the Commons which took the initiative in legislation, or
offered resistance to the demands of the executive.

The Commons consisted of two knights for each shire, and two burgesses
from each enfranchised borough (London had four). The county electors were
those with a minimum 40s. a year freehold, a qualification which held until
1832; with the growth of population and wealth, they were becoming more
numerous. Thus, at the Yorkshire election of 1597 over 6,000 voters were
present, though this was exceptional.[52] Knights of the shire, especially the senior
of each pair, carried more weight and prestige than burgesses, and senior
political figures usually held county seats, but membership of the Commons in
any capacity was increasingly sought after. It was no longer the rule for MPs
to be paid their expenses – on the contrary, they were beginning to fork out to
get themselves elected. The country gentry had begun to invade the borough
representation in the fifteenth century, and under Elizabeth they supplied the
great majority of the 'burgesses'. During her reign only London, Bath, Bristol,
Ludlow and Worcester invariably returned local citizens.[53] Towns needed the
support and protection of powerful local magnates, and obliged them by
offering seats to their followers. Some boroughs – Gatton in Surrey, for

example – were already 'rotten', that is, in the permanent grip of a lord. The desire of magnates to find seats for their men, as a reward for services, and to enhance their own prestige, led them to put pressure on the crown to en-franchise new boroughs. Thus, in the sixteenth century, the Commons increased by 56 per cent – from 296 to 462. Most of these new seats were created by Elizabeth. It was one cheap way of rewarding the services of courtiers and officials, though she recognized its dangers. So she added eighty-seven new members, though after 1586, when she made one last concession to Leicester by enfranchising his borough of Andover, she flatly refused to create any more.[54] The fact is the genuine burgesses were, and had always been, far more sub-servient to the crown than gentry MPs, and the new boroughs were gentry preserves. The gentry, as a body, were prepared to stand up to the monarchy. As James Harrington later observed: 'By these degrees came the House of Commons to raise that head which since has been so high and formidable to their princes that they have looked pale upon those assemblies.'[55]

The crown retaliated by building up its own representation. It is significant that the conservative Pilgrims of Grace complained in 1536: 'The old custom was that none of the King's servants should be of the Common House; yet most of that House were [now] the King's servants.' Elizabeth did not, like her sister, generally interfere in elections by sending out letters of instructions to the sheriffs (who managed the poll). Sometimes she, or her Council, intervened in particular cases: thus she got James Morice returned for Colchester in 1586 – 'It was so ordered by her Majesty', noted the town's recorder. (Morice was a trouble-some fellow, but a man of weight; Elizabeth seems to have preferred ability and high standing to docility.) When she used her authority to try to correct more general trends, such as the growth in number of 'carpetbagger' MPs, she was ineffective. But the crown was not without resources. The Chancellor of the Duchy of Lancaster and the Warden of the Cinque Ports, both important government officials, controlled a number of seats. No Commoner member of the government, leading courtier or senior official ever had much difficulty in getting returned, usually to a senior county seat. The court element rose steadily: 54 in 1559, 75 in 1584, and about 100 in 1601 – nearly a quarter of the House.[56] Elizabeth's authority was such, and the spread of her government so wide, that she could always count on being strongly represented, even without resorting to electioneering.

What was more difficult to determine was the actual power of parliament, and especially the Commons. Theoretically, the great legislative engine was the Lords: there the Queen herself sat, at the beginning and end of each session, with her peers, bishops, judges and officers of state. The Lords were commodiously housed, with the full panoply of power; their clerk was the Clerk of the Parliaments, and they kept their own records. The Commons had originally sat in the Chapter House of Westminster; since Edward VI's days they had been crowded into the upper part of St Stephen's Chapel (where they remained until it was burned down in 1834). They had a small lobby, one committee-room, and no place at all for their records. Often their committees had to meet in private houses in Westminster or the City. In St Stephen's, they sat on raised benches, with the Speaker at the top end; the Privy Councillors sat on his right, other officers of state on his left; the younger members crowded towards the door – it was from there that the trouble usually came. They were supposed to meet from nine to eleven in the morning, breaking up when the courts sat; gradually, as their debates lengthened and business expanded, they met earlier, and continued to sit until dinner time at noon, or even beyond. Their business, as the crown saw it, was to vote supply, and petition for the redress of domestic grievances in their localities; nothing else. They were not expected to sit for more than two or three weeks, especially if necessity drove the crown to summon parliament for the late spring. No Tudor government wanted a 'long, hot summer' of politics, especially since it was generally believed that if London was crowded in the hot weather, plague would inevitably ensue. Elizabeth did not like prominent people hanging around the capital, unless there was specific state business to transact. It was the practice for the Council to summon MPs and other notables to the Star Chamber at the end of each session, and tell them to get back to their localities with all speed. All the same, by 1600 a London 'season' had developed, and enacted itself even if parliament were not sitting.[57]

Elizabeth was also anxious to prevent the Commons from legislating about, or even discussing, a wide range of state business: foreign policy, religion, the actual operations of government departments, such as the Exchequer, which she insisted were within the scope of the prerogative, and above all the question of her marriage and the succession. She expected the Commons to vote her taxes – fixed, as she always insisted, at the very minimum required to carry on government – and otherwise to allow themselves to be managed. She opened parliament in state, with a grand service at the Abbey, arriving on horseback for her first two parliaments, thereafter by barge or litter. The Commons were summoned to the Lords to hear a lengthy statement by the Lord Keeper or Chancellor, drafted by Elizabeth, outlining government business. Sometimes the Queen spoke too. Then the Commons elected a Speaker, and he and other prominent MPs attended her to request the privilege of freedom of speech during their debates. She granted this, usually with a qualification (e.g. in 1559) that they 'be neither unmindful nor uncareful of their duties, reverence and obedience to their Sovereign'.[58] In 1563 she used the formula, in granting the parliamentary freedoms, 'so that [provided] they be reverently used'. Once, in 1571, she added that she wished 'they would be more quiet than they were at the last time', and that 'they should do well to meddle with no matters of state but such as should be proposed unto them, and to occupy themselves in other matters concerning the Commonwealth'.[59] Sometimes the most emphatic warnings against what she considered to be abuse of the freedom of speech were given. She instructed Lord Keeper Puckering to tell the Commons in 1583:

For liberty of speech, her Majesty commandeth me to tell you that to say yea or nay to Bills, God forbid that any man should be restrained, or afraid to answer according to his best liking, with some short declaration of his reasons therein, and therein to have a free voice – which is the very true liberty of the House: not, as some suppose, to speak there of all causes as him listeth, and to frame a form of religion and a state of government, as to their idle brains shall seem meetest. She saith, no king fit for his state will suffer such absurdities. And though she hopeth no man here longeth so much for his ruin as that he mindeth to make such a peril to his own safety, yet, that you may better follow what she wisheth, she makes, of her goodness, you the partaker of her intent and meaning.[60]

This is the nearest Elizabeth came to defining her theory of parliament's freedom and function – and a very narrow definition it is, too. What is more it was further qualified by her prohibition against any form of political discussion which did not take place within the actual walls of St Stephen's, and during the prescribed hours. Strictly speaking, MPs were not allowed to talk about public matters over dinner in the taverns which surrounded Westminster, or in the Inns of Court, or even in private houses. She 'wept with rage', according to the Spanish ambassador, when she heard that prominent people had been meeting to debate the succession in Arundel's London house. Of course such discussions took place, but they were perilous. If she wanted to arrest an opposition MP, she usually made sure he had been witnessed holding forth outside the sanctuary of parliament.

Elizabeth was always in London for parliamentary sessions. There was one exception, in 1586, when the execution of Mary Queen of Scots was the salient topic. Then she remained at Richmond, to emphasize her detachment from the measures to be taken against her regal cousin. On all other occasions she lived in Whitehall, and followed the debates from hour to hour, using a series of messengers and informants. When she wished to respond or object to what was going on, she did so with great speed, summoning the Speaker late at night, or first thing in the morning, and flatly refusing, on one occasion, to accept his plea of sickness as an excuse. She always indicated whom she wanted chosen as Speaker, though she was careful to pick suitable and popular men. She was furious in 1566 when Richard Onslow, her Solicitor-General, was only elected after a division, and by a majority of a mere 82 to 70.[61] The Speakers were usually amenable, establishment men; their job was a step towards high office. But she was not above using her wiles to keep them sweet. Thus Speaker Yelverton (a very independent-minded man) records in 1597:

> After her Majesty had confirmed me for Speaker, and after that I had then ended my oration, her Majesty passing by me, pulled off her glove and gave me her hand to kiss, and [an archery metaphor] said: 'You, sir, are welcome to the butts, sir', and laid both her hands about my neck, and stayed a good space, and so most graciously departed; and in her Privy Chamber after, amongst her ladies, said she was sorry she knew me no sooner.[62]

These feminine tricks – there were no Women's Lib inhibitions about Elizabeth – were highly effective, and frequently used. Sometimes, especially at the break-up of parliaments, she gave her hands to scores of MPs to be kissed, remembering their names and localities. She had a habit, when they addressed her, of rising from her throne at a compliment, and making a low bow or curtsy, which she enacted slowly and with exquisite grace, and which was much appreciated. She also perfected a stately sweeping gesture of her arms, which passed into the repertoire of English monarchy, and was last effectively employed by Queen Mary, consort of George V. When, at the end of each session, the passing of the subsidy bill was announced, the Clerk of the Parliaments intoned: '*La Royne remercie ses loyaulx sujects, accepte leur benevolence, et aussie le veult*', and a curious ritual was enacted. She 'rose up and bended herself to the commonalty, opening her arms and hands, and then the commonalty kneeled, and then she sat down and they stood up again'.[63]

But, in the last resort, Elizabeth simply used her prerogative to curb the ambitions of parliament. She could, and did, veto Bills which had passed both Houses: six in 1563, seven in 1576, one in 1581, nine in 1585, one in 1593, and twelve in 1597. When, at the final ceremony in the Lords, the titles of the Bills were read out, and the embossed documents were held up, she either banged them with her sceptre – in which case the Clerk called out '*La Royne le veult*' – or she kept it stiffly to her side, and the Clerk replied '*La Royne S'avisera*'. She did this either because she disliked the Bill or, in some cases, because it had been passed in haste and she had not had time to study it. But there could be no question that she kept this aspect of her powers intact.[64]

This, however, was a fall-back position. In general, Elizabeth's handling of her parliaments started from the assumption, in which she genuinely believed, that she herself (properly advised) was the best judge of the nation's interests. Governments did not, on the whole, publish the salient facts on which political opinions could be formed; only the Queen and her closest councillors were privy to all of them. Just as parliament alone could vote and raise extraordinary revenue – here she did not interfere, except graciously to accept what they chose to give her – so she and her advisers were alone competent to settle affairs of state. As she constantly reiterated, members of parliament must trust her to do her best for them, and for the nation; that was why God had placed her on the throne, and endowed her with special blessings to discharge her duty. She struck this note – the appeal for trust – in her very first speech to parliament, in 1559, later recorded by the parliamentary diarist, Sir Simons D'Ewes. Her words might almost form the prologue to a play, and fittingly introduce the drama of Elizabeth and her parliaments: 'What credit my assurance may have with you I cannot tell, but what credit it shall deserve to have, the sequel shall declare.'[65]

She asked, therefore, for a permanent vote of confidence; but of course she rarely got it. And where parliament was least disposed to trust her was over the two issues closest to her person: her marriage and the succession. Nor can the parliamentarians be blamed. Her unwillingness to settle either matter was notorious, and their lives and properties were at stake if things went wrong, and England was landed with a fanatical Catholic sovereign or, more likely, rent by civil war. So, almost from the start of her first parliament, the marriage problem was raised, under the heading 'Request for her Highness for marriage'. Elizabeth's reply was good-tempered, written by herself, and 'read to the House by Mr Mason, to the great honour of the Queen, and the contentation of this House'. But it was no more than an assurance. She promised there would be no repetition of Mary's Spanish marriage. Her one concern was to do right by her people, country and God; no one need worry that 'the realm may, or shall have, just cause to be discontented. And therefore put that clean out of your heads.' But she also made no bones about her preference: 'And in the end, this shall be for me sufficient, that a marble stone shall declare that a Queen, having reigned such a time, lived and died a Virgin.'[66]

The nation did not yet grasp that she meant what she said about remaining a virgin, which seemed *contra naturam* in a male-oriented society. So, naturally, they could not for long put the issue clean out of their heads. And Elizabeth's attack of smallpox in October 1562 brought them, as they saw it, to the brink of the chasm. The strain which infected her was very virulent: it killed many, including the Countess of Bedford; and Sir Henry Sidney's wife, who attended the Queen and caught it from her, was disfigured for life. The disease struck Elizabeth at Hampton Court on the 10th; the rash failed to appear and she got steadily worse. For twenty-four hours she lost consciousness completely, and for a week there was a real possibility she would succumb. As she put it to a parliamentary committee afterwards: 'Death possessed almost every part of me.' Cecil was summoned from London at midnight, and the Council was in emergency session for days on end. If the Queen died, who was to succeed? Our only evidence for the discussion comes from the not very reliable Bishop de Quadra, the Spanish ambassador, and suggests complete division. The Protestant faction, which now included Dudley as well as Bedford, wanted the Earl of Huntingdon; others, probably including Cecil, preferred the leading Suffolk claimant, Lady Catherine Grey; Winchester favoured referring the decision to the judges, whom Quadra said were mostly Catholic (they were certainly ultra-conservative). Nobody wanted Mary Queen of Scots, though she had support outside the Council.[67] This lack of agreement suggested that the outcome might well have been civil war, and, when it was later reported by Cecil to the Queen, strengthened her determination to keep the issue firmly under her own personal control.

But this did not prove easy. The last thing Elizabeth wanted to do, when she recovered, was to summon parliament, which was certain to take up the matter. She was already having trouble keeping her leading magnates from marshalling opinion: Quadra reported that, following the conclave at Arundel's house, she and the Earl had a first-class row at which he insisted that he and his peers had a perfect right to interfere in a matter that affected them so deeply.[68] But parliament was needed to vote money: the Scottish, and now the French, wars had already cost £750,000, and the Queen's credit in Antwerp was under strain.[69] It met on 12 January 1563, and was both more radical and more Protestant than its predecessor. What is more, although the Protestants in the 1559 parliament had been numerous and powerful, they had been closely attached to the Cecilian faction at court, and therefore susceptible to government influence. In 1563, they formed a much more independent group. A manuscript, dating from the second session of this parliament in 1566, and entitled *A lewd pasquil set forth by certain of the parliament men*, describes forty-three of this group, and indicates the formidable quality of the men with whom Elizabeth had to deal.[70] There was Paul Wentworth (younger brother of Peter, who did not come into the House till 1571), known as 'Wentworth the Wrangler', a first-class debater and controversialist, William Strickland, 'the stinger', and James Dalton, 'the denier', also leading orators; Thomas Norton, 'the scold', perhaps the greatest of Elizabethan parliamentarians, William Fleetwood, later Recorder of London, 'the pleader', and Robert Bell and Christopher Yelverton, both to become in time Speakers of the House, and judges. These men could not be dismissed as bigoted sectarians. Norton was the translator of Calvin and Peter Martyr, and the joint author of the first fully-fledged Elizabethan play, *Gorboduc*; Yelverton was known as 'the poet'. All were scholars, jurists and men of affairs, though their average age was low. The lampoonist refers to them and their immediate followers as 'the choir', to which the solid majority of the House responded with a parrot-like chorus.

These men might have been expected, as did the 1559 parliament, to make religion their central concern. But a revived Convocation (the deliberative assembly of the two provinces of the English Church) diverted the attention of the Protestant clergy, and parliament did not attempt to push the formularies and doctrine of the new Anglican Church in a Puritan direction. It is true they were anxious to put legal pressure on the Catholics, and took steps to this end. Cecil noted: 'A law is passed for sharpening laws against papists, wherein some difficulty hath been, because they be made very penal; but such be the humours of the Commons House, as they think nothing sharp enough against the papists.'[71] This was bad enough, for it made death the penalty for refusing the Supremacy Oath the second time, and thus threatened – as Elizabeth feared – to bring the Catholics into open revolt. But at least it did not force her to take positive action. She was able to save the lives of former bishops like Bonner by declining to put the oath to them a second time. She was still determined, if humanly possible, to prevent the active persecution of Catholics, though characteristically she placed the onus for staying the government's hands on the quaking shoulders of Archbishop Parker, whom she forced to issue instructions in his own name, not hers.

But if parliament was comparatively inactive on the religious front, this was because MPs, then as now, find it difficult to become obsessive about more than one thing at a time. And in 1563 it was Elizabeth's marriage, and the succession, that riveted their attention. Their very first act was to appoint a committee to draw up a petition to the Queen, asking her to determine the succession. She was anxious, at all costs, to keep the subject off the floor of the House, because she rightly believed that if parliament passed legislation on the subject it would rule out Mary's claim – the one which (if any) she favoured. About this time she conceived the bizarre proposal to marry Mary off to Dudley, and settle the throne on their heir. This would not work because Mary did not want to marry 'the horsemaster' either. In any case, parliament's stomach heaved at the thought of a Scottish succession. Sir Ralph Sadler, the great pundit on Scotland, summed up the prevailing anti-Scottish mood: 'the stones in the streets would rebel against it.'

To forestall the prospect of legislation, Elizabeth resorted to cunning oratory. She received the petitioners and their scroll, in gracious fashion in the great gallery at Whitehall, a little after dinner on 26 January. Of course, she emphasized, she was just as much worried by the problem of the succession as anyone else – more so in fact. She won sympathy by describing her illness. Even while desperately sick she had been pondering the future: 'yet desired I not then life (as I have some witnesses here) so much for mine own safety as for yours.' The burden on her was inconceivable. They wanted her to determine the succession. But suppose she made the wrong choice? If she made a mistake, the worst that could happen to them would be to lose their bodies – but 'I hazard to lose both body and soul.' She, unlike them, was responsible to God. Strictly speaking, they had no right to petition her on this subject, which she must settle unaided. But (a characteristic note, this) she was prepared to distinguish between MPs who acted out of love and loyalty, and mere foolish troublemakers:

Lastly – because I will discharge some restless heads, in whose brains the needless hammers beat with vain judgment, that I should mislike this their petition – I say that of the matter and sum thereof I like and allow very well. As to the circumstances, if any be, I mean upon further advice further to answer. And so I assure you all that, though after my death you may have many stepdames, yet shall you never have a more natural mother than I mean to be unto you all.[72]

This was acceptable, so far as it went, but that was not very far. As Elizabeth doubtless knew, the 'needless hammers' would continue to beat on the point. There was some talk of a statute to limit the succession to four families, with the Queen to indicate her choice; this was a reversion to Henry VIII's plan, which had not worked very well. Cecil also produced a scheme – he was to bring it forward again from time to time – to set up a Regency Council, in the event of the Queen's death, until parliament met and pronounced on the succession. But to Elizabeth, of course, this was a Utopian formula, which would be rendered nugatory, like her father's Will, by the fierce passions of faction. Nothing came of these plans. But the Commons wanted an answer to their petition. For the first time they hit upon the device of linking their demands to the subsidy, and provided the money bill with a lengthy and tendentious preamble, which in effect reiterated the points made in their petition. But they had made the mistake, on which Elizabeth gratefully swooped, of passing the

Bill before confronting her a second time. Thus the session could be ended without the necessity for a definite answer to either document. For Easter Eve (10 April) when parliament broke up, she had prepared a careful speech, which she had Lord Keeper Bacon read out to Lords and Commons in her presence. In her first two drafts the anger showed: thus she wrote of 'the two huge scrolls' thrust at her. In the finished speech, this was toned down to 'the two petitions that you presented'. She again asked for time; there was still a strong chance that she would marry:

> if any here doubt that I am, as it were by vow or determination, bent never to trade that way of life [that is, the virgin state by marrying], put out that heresy, for your belief therein is awry. For though I can think it best for a private woman, yet do I strive with myself to think it not meet for a prince. And if I can bend my liking to your need, I will not resist such a mind.[73]

Having, in effect, left the Commons unanswered, Elizabeth did not want to increase the discontent by dissolving parliament, though its other business was concluded. So she merely prorogued it, the supposition being that it would meet again immediately some definite step was taken, either towards marriage or a settlement of the succession. In fact, nothing at all was determined, though desultory negotiations with the Archduke Charles continued. Parliament was kept in being by a series of prorogations. Elizabeth was blamed for her hesitations by her ministers and everyone else. But she deserves some sympathy, even if one discounts her undoubted right to choose to remain single. No one ever produced a Protestant candidate for marriage who could secure general support. The Archduke was a Catholic, and determined to remain one; no one ever devised a formula which reconciled his beliefs with the security which a predominantly Protestant country required. As for the succession, there was not only no unanimity, but no possibility of securing it. To postpone any decision, as Elizabeth did, was no solution, but at least it avoided an actual crisis. She had better grounds than Mr Micawber for supposing that something would eventually turn up, as in a sense it did.

But MPs could not be brought to see matters in this light. When they finally returned to Westminster on 30 September 1566, they felt they had good reasons to express a mood of impatience, indeed insistence. This was to be one of Elizabeth's most difficult parliamentary sessions. The Commons were virtually all experienced men, who had got their teeth, as it were, into the parliamentary game, and were not prepared to be bamboozled a second time. The succession issue was now more acute. Elizabeth was older; in December 1564 she had again been seriously ill (probably with gastroenteritis): 'For the time,' wrote

Cecil, 'she made us sore afraid.' In the meantime, Mary had married Lord Darnley, against the strenuous opposition of Elizabeth and the English government. In March 1566 she had been involved in the disgraceful murder of David Rizzio, and was thus building up an unenviable reputation which made her the last creature on earth most English people wanted to see on their throne. But in June she had produced a healthy male heir, the future James I, and much international opinion conceded him the eventual succession. The Scots minister in Paris, Patrick Adamson, saluted him in a poem as 'Prince of Scotland, England, France and Ireland'. The succession problem was thus invading the field of polemical literature. To Elizabeth's fury, an anonymous pamphlet was published setting out the case for Catherine Grey. She discovered that it was the work of John Hales, a senior Chancery official, and had been written with the approval of his chief, Lord Keeper Bacon. Bacon was excluded from the Council and the court, and Hales was put in the Tower for a spell.[74] But this did not halt the torrent of speculation and propaganda. More tracts appeared, supporting rival claimants. The clergy were agitating; so were the City merchants. In an age fascinated alike by genealogy and legal quiddities, the subject had a kind of polemical glamour, as well as intrinsic importance. The law students at Lincoln's Inn were discovered to have held a moot about it, and pronounced Mary's claim invalid. One Mr Thornton, a teacher at the Inn, was clapped in gaol. The finger of criticism was now pointing at the Queen herself, and her advisers. Thus, in his diary for 6 October 1566, Cecil noted: 'Certain lewd bills thrown abroad against the Queen's Majesty for not assenting to have the matter of succession proceeded in parliament', adding – shocked by the unfairness of it all – 'and bills also to charge Sir William Cecil, the Secretary, with the occasion thereof.' As Cecil well knew, Elizabeth was absolutely isolated on this issue, just as she was completely alone in upholding the principle of religious toleration.[75]

But she could not delay parliament any longer: once again, money was needed. Moreover, Elizabeth was in the embarrassing position of being obliged to ask for a further subsidy in time of ostensible peace. Once MPs reassembled, the ominous signs of revolt multiplied. There was the narrow division over electing Speaker Onslow (his predecessor had been installed by acclamation), not because of his views – the Spanish ambassador called him a 'furious heretic' – but because he was a government official, and MPs did not want to be managed. The Commons tried, ineffectively, to force all MPs to take the succession oath, which would have had the effect of excluding the small group of pro-Catholics, whom Elizabeth looked on almost as allies. There was an angry debate over the subsidy Bill, in which the integrity of Edward Baeshe, Surveyor of Victuals for the Navy was (no doubt with justice) attacked. This was, Elizabeth considered, a straightforward infringement of the royal prerogative. Worse, this time the Commons made no bones about linking the subsidy, before they had granted it, to the succession question. Elizabeth told Quadra that the Commons were offering her £250,000 in return for her agreement to resolve the issue, and that she would not have it.[76]

Moreover, it was not only the Commons who were getting out of hand. Having acted on 17 October – 'A motion, made by Mr Molyneux, for the reviving of the suit for the succession and to proceed with the subsidy, was very well allowed of the House' – they linked up with the Lords to produce concerted pressure. The Lords were only too willing to oblige them. Elizabeth's control of the Upper Chamber, hitherto reasonably secure, abruptly collapsed. Bacon, now restored to favour, was away, paralysed by gout. The leadership devolved on Winchester, but he was now nearly ninety, and suffering from 'decay of memory and hearing, griefs accompanying hoary hairs and old age'. On Friday, 25 October, the Lords joined the Commons, with Winchester's sole dissent. That week-end there was a terrific row, or series of rows, at court. The Queen castigated all the leading lords in turn. She told Norfolk, the only Duke, who might have been expected to set an example against the plebeian agitation, that he was little better than a traitor and a conspirator. The Earl of Pembroke, she said to his face, was talking like a 'swaggering soldier'. As for Leicester, she said bitterly that she had counted on him even if all the world abandoned her; his response that he would die at her feet gave little satisfaction – she did not want men dying at her feet, merely some intelligent political support. When her cousin by marriage the Marquess of Northampton put in his word, she drew scathing attention to the chaos in his marital affairs (he had had to appeal to parliament to extricate him from a charge of bigamy). Let him worry about his own mess instead of poking into her business! Cecil's diary reveals that Leicester and Pembroke were thereupon 'excluded from the presence chamber'; and Elizabeth told Quadra that Winchester was the only one on whom she could count – and he was useless.[77]

The Commons were now staging a go-slow. For nearly a month nothing had been done about the subsidy, or any other government business. MPs were meeting only for an hour or so each day, and then dispersing to talk about the succession in taverns. Cecil wrote two elaborate memos, exercises in the esteemed and old-fashioned art of syllogism, but not much to the purpose. The view was gaining ground that the best thing, in the circumstances, was to prorogue parliament for six months, and allow tempers to cool. But this would be a confession of failure – an 'Addled Parliament'. At a Council meeting early in

November, attended – a rare event – by Elizabeth herself, Sir Ralph Sadler warned her that, if parliament were dispersed, the political crisis would spread from Westminster to the nation. For the Queen to take a subsidy without settling the succession would lead constituents to ask MPs: 'What is done?' And the MPs would have to answer: 'We have done nothing but give away your money; the Queen hath that she looked for, but hath no care for us.'[78]

This striking speech seems to have had considerable effect. Sadler was a newcomer to Elizabeth's Council, but he was an elder statesman, a respected servant of her father, and a man with no particular axe to grind. He touched the Queen on her tenderest spot – the risk of forfeiting her popularity. At any rate she determined to act, and when Elizabeth made up her mind, she could move with great speed and decision. She had watched the parliamentary situation deteriorate, over the past four weeks, with growing dismay and anger. She seethed with resentment at the betrayal of the Lords. She was conscious she was alone, but in no way daunted. One woman could outface and cow a masculine multitude, provided she used her brains, her presence, her regality and her imperious will. She was, in fact, working herself up to make one of her greatest speeches. Her rough notes of the first draft – with many deletions and underlinings – survive. The tone is one of pent-up fury:

If the order of your cause had matched the weight of your matter, the one might well have craved reward and the other much the sooner satisfied. But when I call to mind how far from dutiful care – yea, rather, how nigh a traitorous trick – this tumbling cast did spring, I muse how men of wit can so hardly use that gift they hold. I marvel not much that bridless colts do not know their rider's hand, whom bit of kingly rein did never snaffle yet. Whether it was fit that so great a cause as this should have had his beginning in such a public place as this [parliament] let it be well weighed ... Was it well meant, think you, that those that knew not how fit this matter was to be granted by the Prince, would prejudicate their Prince in aggravating the matter, so that all their arguments tended to my careless care of this my dear realm?[79]

Here was the gist of Elizabeth's complaint – the impudent assumption that parliamentarians were more concerned for the future of the kingdom and its people than she herself, divinely anointed to discharge this very duty. She had a powerful, and overwhelming, sense of responsibility; she could not bear to hear it impugned. These bitter words she wrote out were not spoken, but the sense remained. On 3 November she summoned thirty members from each House to Whitehall Palace. She declined to have the Speaker, jesting angrily that she alone intended to do the talking on this occasion. A record of her speech survives.[80] Some sections, I surmise, she memorized, others were spoken from rough notes; some may have been quite spontaneous, as she got into her stride. As often, when we examine the verbatim records of the Elizabethan age, we realize that the language of Shakespeare and Marlowe did not spring, as it were, straight from the fountain of genius, but was merely a heightened version of the words and expressions and cadences which educated men and women used in the course of business. For Elizabeth, indeed, the world of politics was a stage: and here she confronted a sullen and hostile audience of sixty women-despising men, decked out in their best clothes, full of their importance in the state and their monopoly of prudence and wisdom.

The succession, she began, was a very delicate and complex matter. It was not something that could be broached in a hurry, and debated in public. It required careful and prudent thought, and private deliberation. The Commons had made the first mistake by bringing it on to the floor of the House. But the men who did this were rash and inexperienced. It was, therefore, the duty of the Lords to put a stop to their agitation, and impose order. Instead, they ran with the pack, and added their own weight to the folly of the Commons. The bishops behaved just as badly, 'with their long orations', as though they were not already fully aware of all the circumstances the Commons brought to their attention. No one had acted maliciously: no – they had been simple-minded, and allowed themselves to be seduced by hotheads and fools. But the result was deplorable, because it gave the nation the impression that the Queen was impervious to the dangers which threatened it. But everyone present knew this was not true!

> Was I not born in the realm? Were my parents born in any foreign country? Is there any cause I should alienate myself from being careful over this country? Is not my kingdom here? Whom have I oppressed? Whom have I enriched to other's harm? What turmoil have I made in this Commonwealth that I should be suspected to have no regard to the same? How have I governed since my reign? I will be tried by envy itself. I need not to use so many words, for my deeds do try me.

She, then, was as good a patriot as any of them. As to the substance of the matter, she had already told everyone she would marry if it were possible. 'I can say no more, except the party were present.' But her promise had not been believed, 'though spoken by their prince'.

> A strange order of petitioners, that will make a request and cannot be otherwise ascertained but by their Prince's word, and yet will not believe it when it

is spoken! But they (I think) that moveth the same will be as ready to mislike him with whom I shall marry, as they are now to move it.

This was a shrewd point and more was to follow. If people could not agree on her husband – while still pushing her into marriage – they could not agree on her successor either, while urging her to name the person. She was not going to re-create the horrible days of Mary Tudor, when she herself, as 'the second person', had been in peril of her life: 'So shall never be my successor.' In any case, who was that person to be? She had consulted a great many learned and legal gentlemen, and they could not give her a clear answer. The parliament men said they had no other interest but 'the surety of their country'. But they could not agree either: 'They would have twelve or fourteen limited in succession, and the more the better.' She did not claim to be a divine, but she had studied history, and knew what trouble 'had fallen out for the ambition of kingdoms . . . what cocking there hath been between the father and the son for the same.' Of course she *could* settle the succession. But with so many contenders, the result might be civil war, and *they* would suffer. On the other hand, if she allowed them to debate the matter openly, what would be the result?

> There be so many competitors – some kinsfolk, some servants, and some tenants; some would speak for their master, and some for their mistress, and every man for his friend – that it would be an occasion for a greater charge than a subsidy.

The debate would bitterly divide the nobility and all public men, who would spend their money building up parties – and in the end might well lose their lives, too. Well, she would not allow it.

> As for my own party, I care not for death; for all men are mortal. And though I be a woman, yet I have as good a courage, answerable to my place, as ever my father had. I am your anointed Queen. I will never be by violence constrained to do anything. I thank God I am endued with such qualities that if I were turned out of the realm in my petticoat, I were able to live in any place in Christendom.

The thought of their Queen deserting them, and looking for a job on the Continent, must have been enough to silence these sixty formidable gentlemen – had they not already been stunned by her vehement tirade. She ended by announcing that she might, indeed, determine the succession, at 'a convenient time' and provided it did not imperil their lives. But when and if that time came, there would be no need for a petition – she would present it to them 'as your Prince and Head, without request: for it is monstrous that the feet should direct the head'. The meeting then dispersed, without the parliamentarians being allowed to say a word. Cecil, on Elizabeth's instructions, relayed her speech to the Commons. No doubt he watered it down somewhat, but when he had finished, the Clerk added: 'Whereupon all the House was silent.' Well it might be!

The speech succeeded in its primary object, which was to bring the Lords to heel. This was essential: control of the Upper House was the fulcrum of Elizabeth's parliamentary authority, indeed of her whole political position. She was able to tell the Spanish ambassador, with some satisfaction, that the Lords had come to her individually, to ask pardon.[81] It was a different matter with 'the Protestant gentlemen', as she termed the Commons. They soon recovered their nerve. After all, most of them (unlike the Lords) had not actually been present to hear her thunders. It is true they now relaxed their pressure on the Queen to marry. While she might remain, as Walsingham put it, 'the best match in her parish' – that is, the civilized world – MPs were beginning to realize that she was not to be bullied into making her choice, and if any pressure were to be applied, it was best left to the Council; henceforth, the Commons were to push the marriage issue into the background. But the succession was becoming more, not less, urgent, and the Commons would not leave it alone. Thus a further row developed in which, for the first time, the succession merged with the wider issue of the powers and liberties of the Commons. A motion to limit the succession, moved by the antiquarian William Lambarde – the study of history and the growth of parliamentary authority were intimately connected – brought an immediate riposte from the Queen: an 'express commandment' to drop the subject. On 11 November, Paul Wentworth moved an answering motion: 'Whether the Queen's commandment were not against the liberties.' The seconder was James Dalton, and a long debate followed of which, alas, we have no account. This day was a landmark in parliamentary history, for what was at stake was the right (and duty) of parliament to discuss all or any affairs of public concern – something the Queen vehemently denied. The next day she summoned the Speaker and sent him back with a message which was also a threat: she vetoed all discussion of the succession, 'And if any person thought himself not satisfied, but had further reasons, let him come before the Privy Council, there to show them.'[82] Indeed, the Council was already involved, for Dalton had made a Commons attack on the Scots ambassador in Paris, for publishing a presumptuous poem; the Scots ambassador in London had complained about it, and the Council had hauled Dalton before it. It seemed that government and Commons were on a collision course.

At this point Cecil intervened. He was an MP of long standing, and shared the preoccupations of the House; he was also the Queen's closest adviser. On 16 November he completed the final draft of a further Commons petition, dealing with its liberties. It was couched in adulatory terms, but it reminded the Queen that, in attempting to 'diminish or abridge' the liberties of MPs she was acting against constitutional tradition. MPs, it added, were sure this was not her intention. The most significant thing about this petition was that it was never presented. Cecil showed it privately to Elizabeth, and persuaded her to back down, as it were of her own volition. On 25 November a message was sent via the Speaker that she was 'pleased to revoke and cancel those command-ments as needless to be sent'. Two days later she instructed Leicester that the Council was to drop the Dalton case and 'not proceed further to any question or trial' (she did not like the poem either). And, to crown all, she decided to remit one-third of the subsidy, as a good-will gesture. Her conciliatory moves went down very well, 'taken of all the House most joyfully, with most hearty prayers and thanks for the same'.[83] And MPs perversely, having won their point, decided not to discuss the succession after all.

Maybe Elizabeth had foreseen this would be their reaction. The Commons appeared to have won a victory on a fundamental matter of principle – their liberties had not been 'abridged' – whereas Elizabeth had merely got them to concede a point of detail – to drop the succession issue on this occasion. But that was not how she saw politics. She believed in living from hand to mouth, and that sufficient unto the day was the evil thereof. For her, a week was always a long time in politics. A conflict postponed might never, in the end, take place. Soon the MPs would disperse to their shires and towns; the next House of Commons might be more amenable – who could say? In any case, she was determined that her concession should not, as it were, be graven on the tablets. When the Commons, in presenting the subsidy bill – now passed – wrote in a long preamble, recording its victory over free speech and Elizabeth's promise to 'declare the succession in such convenient time', she put her foot down – or, rather, seized her pen.[84] At the bottom of the last sheet, using her 'running hand', she added a trenchant comment:

I know no reason why any my private answers to the realm should serve for prologue to a subsidies-book. Neither yet do I understand why such audacity should be used to make without my license an Act of my words. Are my words like lawyers' books, which nowadays go to the wire-drawers to make subtle doings more plain? . . . I say no more at this time; but if these fellows were well answered, and paid with lawful coin, there would be fewer counterfeits among them.

The preamble was scrapped, and does not appear in the embossed subsidy-roll. The episode served to remind MPs that the Queen had a perceptive eye for detail and did not easily fall a victim to sharp practice. If they were gaining in experience of parliamentary tactics, so was she.

The parliamentary session of 1566–7 was not a happy one. The Commons held up, or drastically amended, some important government Bills, and, among other things, expressed its discontent about the administration of the criminal law, and the Queen's proposals for improving it. Towards the end, Cecil wrote a lugubrious little memo to himself, noting the paucity of business done, and as a result what he termed: 'Dangers ensuing. General discontentations. The slender execution of the subsidy. Danger of sedition in summer by persons discontented.'[85] When the Houses met for the closing ceremony on 2 January 1567, Elizabeth added a few remarks of her own after the Lord Keeper's speech. The Commons should not make the mistake of thinking they could take refuge in numbers, or troublemakers believe they might mask themselves behind the appearance of unanimity: 'I would not you should think my simplicity such as I cannot make distinctions among you … Let this my discipline stand you instead of sorer strokes, never to tempt too far a Prince's patience' (she had originally intended to use the word 'power').[86] On the other hand, on two occasions a collision course had been avoided. Some hard words had been used on both sides, but no heads had been broken and the essential unity of the realm maintained. Elizabeth had shown she could bend with the winds of change while still holding her essential ground – something her Stuart successors never could combine. She did not part with her parliament in a particularly friendly spirit, but she retained the basic affection of MPs and, equally important, their respect. Anyone who sat in that parliament must have returned to his home with the strong impression that the realm was under the authority of a sovereign of conspicuous ability, resolute character, and great resourcefulness. It was just as well this feeling was abroad, for England was about to undergo a time of trial, when loyalties would be tested.

6

Monstrous Dragons and Roaring Lions

Elizabeth's vision of Europe was of a stable international community, in which princes honoured each other's titles, governed their subjects according to ancient custom and law, and were content to remain within their established historical frontiers. She hated change, and when she moved her object was essentially to restore the *status quo*. Thus, in the text of the Treaty of Berwick, she defended her intervention in Scotland by stating that her sole concern was 'the preservation of the Scots in their old freedoms and liberties'.[1] Her occupation of Le Havre, she argued, was motivated by a similar desire to uphold an agreed and legal settlement defining the political and religious rights of the Huguenots. Whatever arrangements, in politics or religion, which had been honoured by history and confirmed by time – these had her approval and support.

But of course she lived in an era of revolution and ideological conflict. When men began to organize themselves in religious parties, each of which believed itself in absolute possession of the truth, no frontier or constitution could be stable, and no custom was secure. Elizabeth's idealized vision was unattainable, and the forces that shattered it struck with violence and without warning. All the nations of Europe were close to the brink of civil conflicts which reflected the great international war of faith; the Continent was crusading against itself. In England, thanks to her father's quest for an heir, religious change had been imposed, or directed, from above, and legalized by statute; there, at least, civil war – so far – had been avoided. Elsewhere, Reform collided with established authority. Germany was to become a battlefield. Italy was already a theatre of violent persecution. In Spain, royal armies clashed bloodily with armed sectaries, Moors and Jews. In 1559 the religious revolution had struck Scotland with pent-up force. From 1560, and for the next thirty years, it convulsed France. In 1566, it came to the Low Countries.

This collection of semi-independent cities, and small oligarchical states, was an appendage of the Burgundian empire which had been absorbed, by marriage, into the Habsburg family trust. To the English these territories were of considerable economic, military and emotional importance. The trading and financial system radiating from Antwerp was closely meshed with the English economy, especially in wool and textiles. England, in her perpetual cross-Channel struggle with France, had formed military alliances with the towns and states bordering on the Rhine ever since the early twelfth century; it was the basis of the Anglo-Habsburg connection. Moreover, the English recognized in the inhabitants of these lands people with whom they had strong constitutional affinities. Their ancient charters, liberties and immunities formed a hotch-potch of history which appealed to the political cast of the English mind. With the Netherlanders, the English had emotional bonds which transcended mere self-interest.

The Emperor Charles v, a Burgundian internationalist, had respected the character of his Low Countries inheritance; it was a different matter with his son, Philip ii, a Spaniard by birth, education and temperament, and a papalist by conviction. Now that the German territories had been hived off from the Habsburg Spanish properties, he sought to impose on what remained a uniformity, especially in religion, that was alien to its nature. And he did this at a time when many of the towns and counties of the Low Countries were moving firmly into the Protestant camp. He took the view that the universal observance of the Catholic religion was essential to civil obedience, and that it was his interest and duty to enforce it. But of course this conflicted not merely with the religious views of many of his Netherlands subjects, but with their political liberties and historical traditions. He was in effect trying to turn a ramifying and diverse family estate into a unitary empire. From the early 1560s the signs of strain began to appear. His regents invaded liberties and ignored immunities, were in breach of specific charters and upset delicate constitutional machinery. The local nobility were excluded from the Council of State, and men were fined, imprisoned and burned for religious offences. These things were hateful to the English, and not least to Elizabeth. Indeed, they had to cope with the physical consequences. Flemish refugees poured into the country in large numbers; by 1563, for instance, there were nearly 20,000 of them in London, Sandwich and other centres, and a further 10,000 had crossed over by 1566.[2] Some of these were welcome, but they necessarily provoked social pressures, and it was a sign of Elizabeth's concern that she permitted the development of a pamphlet industry, written and printed in England for circulation in Flemisn cities, criticizing the Habsburg régime.

The inevitable explosion came in the summer of 1566. As in Scotland, it was detonated by mass preachings. Crowds of up to 20,000, from June onwards, assembled to hear fiery open-air sermons by Calvinist ministers. On 10 August, the first iconoclastic riots took place. On the 20th the mob destroyed the ornate interior of Antwerp Cathedral; during that night, thirty other churches were sacked, and in the following week 400 were plundered in a single Flanders province.[3] Philip II's response was to reinforce his garrisons and order a general repression of the revolt. By the spring of 1567, the heavy military hand of Spain had reasserted its grip. Valenciennes, the last centre of resistance, surrendered on 24 March, and fearful cruelties were inflicted on its inhabitants. On 15 April the Duke of Alva left Madrid to take charge, and the following month he published an edict which laid down an extraordinary number of offences to be punished by hanging.[4] Many more thousands of refugees crossed to England, bringing with them horrific tales of slaughter and persecution. This was not the only, or indeed the chief, aspect of the situation which worried the English government. Hitherto, the Habsburg garrison in the Low Countries had been limited to about 3,000 men, largely recruited locally. In August 1567 Alva brought the main Spanish army to Brussels, and settled it in permanent quarters. It was rapidly expanded by the enlistment of German, Walloon and Italian levies, rising to 25,000 and eventually to 50,000. These men were organized into huge divisions of 3,000 men each, heavily armed and, provided they were paid regularly, superbly disciplined. Europe had seen nothing like them since the days of the Roman legions. Such a phenomenon necessarily provoked a basic reconsideration of English foreign policy. Until now, for many centuries, France had constituted the chief danger to English security from across the narrow seas; the military resources of the Low Countries, such as they were, were considered actual or potential allies. Alva's army was now seen as a striking force, based, as Cecil put it, 'in the very counterscarp of England'.[5]

The diplomatic revolution which Philip's operations in the Low Countries brought about was slow in coming, and some English statesmen were quicker to grasp it than others. Elizabeth herself had been brought up in the tradition that the Habsburg alliance was the keystone of England's Continental policy. In this, as in all other respects, she was reluctant to consider change, especially one of so fundamental a nature; she continued to believe, up to and even beyond the dispatch of the Armada, that a settlement of all outstanding differences with Spain was not only possible, but right and natural. Cecil agreed with her. 'No prince of England', he wrote in a memo to the Queen in spring 1566, 'ever remained without good amity of the House of Burgundy, and no prince ever had less alliance than the Queen of England hath, nor any prince ever had more cause to have friendship and power to assist her estates.'[6] It is significant that he still saw the Spanish connection in the obsolete terms of the Burgundian alliance, that is, a defensive confederation of the states on France's northern and eastern borders. Younger men were quicker to perceive that change had brought a new set of realities. Where Cecil was still obsessed by the potential power of France, they were more concerned with the actual power of Spain: it was around these two propositions, both of which were valid, that the foreign policy debate revolved. Sir Francis Walsingham, who was emerging in the late 1560s as a formidable expert on Continental affairs, put the matter succinctly:

> The house of Burgundy, till of late days, was ever inferior to England and so depended thereon, but now being tied to the house of Austria, he is grown to the greatness as of inferior he is become superior, of a good quiet neighbour a most ambitious and dangerous neighbour, which we shall speedily find if we do not speedily provide for it.

He added an ideological note: since the Habsburgs had become 'the Pope's champion, and professed enemy of the Gospel', England should consider a French alliance, which would be 'an advancement of the Gospel there'.[7]

The last point, strongly as it was endorsed by Leicester and the Protestant faction at court, and by the majority of MPs, made little appeal to Cecil, and none at all to Elizabeth, who was notoriously lacking in the proselytizing or crusading spirit. Throughout the 1560s Cecil still angled for a Habsburg marriage, with Elizabeth's theoretical approval. But other factors were gradually pushing them in the direction Walsingham wished them to take. On 21 July 1567, Cecil noted that Alva's operations 'hath caused the Queen's Majesty to give some hearing to such as think her security cannot have continuence if the planets keep this course'.[8] In June 1568, her ambassador in Madrid, Dr John Man, was expelled, and never replaced; the following September, De Silva, the only Spanish ambassador with whom Elizabeth was on friendly terms, was recalled. The religious struggles in the Low Countries and France were beginning to impinge on the delicate area of coastal and oceanic trade, for French and Netherlander seamen (as in England) were predominantly Protestant and violently anti-Spanish. Since the voyages of the Cabots, under Henry VII, England had played very little part in maritime discovery. The chief challenge to the naval power, and overseas possessions, of Spain had come from France. But during the 1560s, the divisions in France led to a decline in state naval activity and commerce, leaving the field clear to Huguenot privateers, now joined by a growing number of Dutch adventurers. This posed a serious problem of piracy, for the Channel was the main line of communications between Spain and her possessions in the Low Countries, and England was traditionally the international custodian of its waters. The Privy Council papers for 1564–6 show that the English government made determined efforts to put down the traffic.[9] This was in response to a long list of complaints by the Spanish authorities in the Netherlands, and a six-month closure of their ports to English shipping.[10] But the activities of pirates, and Spanish remonstrances, continued; the latter blamed the remissness of English Admiralty judges. The English, too, were becoming directly involved, since during the Newhaven Adventure, English ships had been issued with letters of marque to prey on the French; West Country seamen had acquired the taste for plunder, and indulged it increasingly against Spanish traffic.

Thanks to the efforts of Cecil and Elizabeth, indeed, English naval and maritime power was growing, and seeking fresh outlets. The Low Countries were now the world centre of cartography and navigational expertise and instrument-making, and refugees brought these skills to England. In 1564 Mercator, for instance, published his *Map of England and Wales*, and the increasing interest in geography encouraged an outward-looking attitude to the world.[11] In theory, the new worlds of the western hemisphere were the exclusive property of Spain and Portugal, by Papal *diktat*. But the English, like the French, did not accept this arbitrary division; in 1561 Cecil, who was a stickler for international law, especially in the maritime sphere, firmly told the Spanish ambassador that the Pope had no authority for his award. There was, too, a curious tradition that, beyond a certain imaginary line in the Atlantic, the normal rules of peace and war were suspended, and free enterprise alone reigned. No one could agree where this line was, but it was generally accepted that the Caribbean lay beyond it.[12] If there was 'no peace beyond the line', why should not English adventurers take advantage of it? In 1562 John Hawkins of Plymouth carried out his first triangular trading voyage: off the coast of West Africa, he bought slaves from Portuguese traders, acquired more by raiding villages, and shipped them to Hispaniola, selling them for gold, silver, pearls, hides and sugar.[13] He brought back with him certificates of good behaviour from the Spanish authorities in the New World, though when he tried to sell part of his cargo in Seville it was confiscated – indicating that the government in Madrid took a different view of his activities. Even so, the voyage was commercially successful, and when he undertook a second voyage, in 1565, Elizabeth herself invested in it; she ventured her own ship, the *Jesus* (formerly of Lubeck), and Hawkins was able to claim, with some exaggeration, that he was 'in an armado of the Queen's Majesty of England'.[14] This voyage, too, was successful. When he prepared a third voyage, in September 1567, the Spanish ambassador, De Silva, protested to the Queen, and asked her to order him not to trade in prohibited places. When Cecil asked for a list of these places, De Silva said they comprised all the West Indies, islands and mainland.[15] Elizabeth repeatedly assured him Hawkins would not break Spanish law, and that she would execute him if he did; but in fact she knew perfectly well that his object, as he put it, was 'to laid negroes in Guinea and sell them in the West Indies'; moreover, she again had money in the project. No evidence survives that she actually gave her authorization to him to sail, but she was clearly a tacit accomplice.[16]

The voyage was a disaster. Hawkins set sail on 2 November 1567 with a small fleet which included the *Minion*, another of Elizabeth's ships, as well as the *Jesus*. He successfully took on his slave cargo in Africa, but the Spanish governors in the Indies had now received instructions to treat him as hostile. At Rio de la Hacha, he had to fight a pitched battle on land, and burned down the Treasurer's house; and when he put in to the Mexican port of St Juan de Ulloa, for repairs, on 20 September 1568, he was treacherously attacked by the Spanish fleet, under flag of truce. He escaped in the *Minion*, as did the young Francis Drake in the *Judith*, but the other ships, including the *Jesus*, were lost, and Hawkins reported 120 men missing. The story of this voyage caused an angry sensation in the English maritime counties, and laid the basis for the unrelenting hostility between English and Spanish seamen that now began to colour Elizabeth's foreign policy.[17]

It also made an immediate contribution to the first real breakdown of Anglo-Spanish relations, and to the growing political crisis in England. Elizabeth, as we have noted, was increasingly perturbed by the size of Alva's army in Flanders. But this army had to be paid in cash; the quickest, and hitherto the safest, means to transmit the huge quantities of sacks of silver required was to ship them via the Channel to Antwerp. Some time in November 1568, four small Spanish coasters sought shelter from storms and French pirates in Plymouth Harbour; later, a fifth turned up in Southampton.[18] Under Admiralty law, a claim for salvage was in order. But this was not immediately prosecuted. Indeed, De Spes, the new Spanish ambassador, arranged for the cargo to be put in bond ashore, for overland shipment through Dover. Then the Spanish squadron commander asked permission to open one of the chests to draw money to pay his expenses, and it was discovered that the ships contained £85,000 in specie for the payment of Alva's troops. Moreover, documents in the chests made it clear that the money actually belonged to Genoese bankers, and did not become Philip's property until it reached its destination.[19] Elizabeth ordered inquiries to be made at the Antwerp branch of the bankers as to the precise legal position of the money, and whether they had any proposals to make to her. The bankers regarded her as much better security than Philip, and in view of the fact that she had her hands on the money, and the possibility of a salvage claim, they replied that they were willing to advance the loan to her instead. Elizabeth was short of cash, especially as she had remitted one-third of the last parliamentary subsidy in 1566 (which, oddly enough, came to almost exactly £85,000). At this point, on 3 December 1568, Cecil received an indignant letter from William Hawkins, who had received advance notice of the disaster which had overtaken John at St Juan, and who knew all about the treasure ships. He urged Cecil to 'advertise the Queen's Majesty thereof, to the end that there might be some stay made of King Philip's treasure here in these parts till there be sufficient recompense made for the great wrongs offered, and also other wrongs done long before this.'[20]

The conjunction of events proved too great a temptation to Elizabeth, once she was satisfied about the legal position. But the crisis was heightened by De Spes's own angry behaviour. Although Elizabeth did not tell him until 28 December that she intended to borrow the money herself, he had gathered as much a week before, and had immediately written to Alva asking for all English ships and merchandise in the Low Countries and Spain to be seized. He further advised that Spain should throw her whole support behind the claims of Mary of Scotland. The first acts against English ships thus took place on 29 December, long before the official intimation of Elizabeth's intentions could have reached Alva. She got the news on 3 January 1569, was naturally extremely angry, and four days later ordered a similar seizure of Spanish ships and goods in English ports.[21] De Spes was placed under house arrest, ostensibly on the grounds that his predecessor, Bishop de Quadra, had left a lot of unpaid debts behind.

The war of economic attrition, as Cecil and Gresham had calculated, greatly favoured the English. Spanish property seized in England was many times more valuable than English property in Spain and the Low Countries. Gresham and the City merchants had for some time been agitating against the Antwerp monopoly, and the closing of the port to English ships clinched the matter; in spring 1569, the cloth fleet was sent to Hamburg under naval escort. Wind and weather were constantly driving Spanish vessels into English ports, and adding to the bag. By July, Alva was writing urgently to Philip warning him that the economy of the Low Countries was on the verge of collapse, and that a permanent break with Elizabeth must be avoided at all costs. But the situation could not be seen entirely in economic terms. In a memo written for Elizabeth in February 1569, Cecil dwelt gloomily on the grave consequences of a conjunction of Spanish hostility and internal subversion. Hitherto Spain had been preoccupied not only by the situation in the Low Countries but by the Turkish menace in the Mediterranean, but the latter had now receded, and Spain was in a position to divert resources to the English theatre. The unsolved problem of Mary Queen of Scots was an encouragement to 'secret and great numbers of discontented subjects of this realm, that gape and practise for a change by her means to be rewarded by her'. He was particularly worried by the situation north of the Trent:

It is also necessary to inquire and regard the state of the country northward, where her [Mary's] person is, and to keep suspected persons in some awe from hearkening to practices and the common people from riots and mutinies, which are the cloaks and preparatives of rebellion.[22]

In short, the breach with Spain constituted a serious risk that Philip might be tempted to intervene actively in English affairs, and provoke a challenge to Elizabeth's own authority of the kind which he himself faced in the Low Countries, and which she had so skilfully exploited in Scotland. Her régime was now over a decade old, and had never yet been tested. How strong was her hold over the English people; and, in particular, to what extent could she count on the loyalty of the nobles and gentry who formed the ruling class? To discover this, we must look more closely at her actual system of government.

Tudor government has been termed a 'despotism' by historians, but it is difficult to identify the physical machinery which made it possible to behave in a despotic manner. Elizabeth was always painfully conscious of the gap between her theoretical sovereignty and her ability to get things done as she wished. It was one reason why she was so opposed to activist policies of any kind. It is true the Tudors exacted some formal signs of reverence which their predecessors had lacked. They were no longer addressed as 'Your Grace', but as 'Your Majesty' – a verbal inflation not to much purpose. Elizabeth's greatest subjects spoke to her on their knees, though they were allowed to squat on their heels or stand if the interview was prolonged. In practical terms, the Tudors had to observe the law, and the supreme form of law was the parliamentary statute, which made them dependent on an unpredictable and sometimes uncontrollable assembly. Elizabeth often acted by proclamation, but her authority to do so was governed by the Statute of Proclamations, 1539, a proposed tyrannical device which had been considerably watered down by parliament.[23] Its second clause forbade proclamations to deal with inheritances, possessions, offices, liberties, privileges, franchises, goods or chattels, or to infringe the Common or statute law, or to exact the death penalty (except for heresy). Its preamble, indeed, which reflected the government's original intention, is flatly contradicted by its actual provisions drawn up in parliament; by this analysis the Tudors were would-be, but unsuccessful, tyrants.[24]

Outside the central administrative area of England, the crown exercised considerable powers through its prerogative courts. The Council of the Marches of Wales, which had been operating from Ludlow since the 1530s, controlled the twelve Welsh counties, plus Hereford, Monmouth, Worcester, Shropshire,

Gloucester and (until 1566) Cheshire. It was the only court authorized to use torture.[25] In York, the Council of the North exercised similar powers in the northern counties and the borders.[26] These bodies operated with considerable success, and remarkably little criticism, under Elizabeth. But this was due to a great extent to the qualities of the men she chose to run them, and their long continuance in office. Thus, the 3rd Earl of Huntingdon, for instance, held the Presidency of the North for twenty-three years; Sir Henry Sidney was President of Wales from 1559 until his death in 1586. One secret of Elizabeth's success was undoubtedly her ability to pick good men, and to give them her confidence for life. Huntingdon and Sidney operated more through their personalities, influence and diplomatic skill than by virtue of any extraordinary powers they possessed; indeed their courts had to observe Common Law procedures in all serious cases.

Outside these border areas, the law was administered by some 1,500 Justices of the Peace, for the most part local gentry; all were unpaid. Elizabeth took a close interest in their selection, scrutinizing the lists from time to time. They were drawn from the same class as the Commons, and were in many cases the same people. Contemporaries saw the JPs as the surest safeguard against baronial arrogance; thus Ralegh was to write:

> The Justices of Peace in England have opposed the injustices of war in England; the King's writ runs over all; and the Great Seal of England with that of the next constable's will serve the turn to affront the greatest lords in England that shall move against the King.[27]

But when examined individually, the JPs did not seem so reliable a buttress of the crown. Thus, when the bishops made a survey of religious loyalties in 1564, they discovered that, of 850 JPs surveyed, only about half supported the régime in religion; 264 were set down as neutral, and 157 as definitely hostile. No changes were thought possible, or desirable, in the light of this report.[28]

To back up the JPs, there was the Council itself, as the executive arm of government, and its regular court, which sat in Edward III's Star Chamber in Westminster Palace. These were two separate institutions. The Council, sitting as the government, could exercise very wide powers indeed; it could even authorize torture, though this was done rarely and with a good deal of fuss and opposition. It could summon the greatest man in the kingdom before it, and force him to kneel down while a lecture was delivered; moreover, under Elizabeth it was becoming increasingly a small professional body of politicians and administrators – Gilbert, Earl of Shrewsbury, was the last great territorial magnate she allowed to sit on it.[29] But it was overburdened by private cases – it could provide quicker and more equitable remedies than the ordinary courts – and although it sat more and more frequently, often every day including Sundays, it was not the all-seeing eye many supposed. The Star Chamber, since the 1540s, had its own separate clerical staff and records, and consisted of available Privy Councillors and the two Chief Justices. It met on Wednesdays and Fridays during term time, from 9.00 a.m. until dinner, when it consumed an elaborate and monstrously expensive meal, costing well over £1,000 a year, and paid for from the fines it exacted. Cases were prepared very carefully before they reached Star Chamber, and once in session, it operated with great speed and the minimum of legal fuss; it was therefore highly popular. Its function was primarily to keep the peace, by enforcing the crown's public authority, or by interposing between private parties engaged in violence, slander or libel. It punished contempt of court, false jury verdicts, perjury, conspiracy, 'subornation and maintenance', and breaches of proclamations. It could not inflict death or loss of property. But it could impose terms of imprisonment, whipping, pillorying, public confessions, loss of ears, and fines. These last were often enormous, but under Elizabeth they were usually 'taxed' (that is, reduced by nine-tenths) after the offender had been thoroughly frightened. Star Chamber did not deal with noblemen, but it could encourage lesser men whom a nobleman had abused to take a civil action before it, award them the verdict, and thus strike a blow at the great man's prestige. This, indeed, was its fixed policy. As Lord Buckhurst, on behalf of the government, told the Earl of Shrewsbury in 1592:

> Your lordship must remember that in the policy of this Commonwealth, we are not over-ready to add increase of power and countenance to such great personages as you are. And when in the country you dwell in you will needs enter in a war with the inferiors therein, we think it both justice, equity, and wisdom to take care that the weaker part be not put down by the mightier.[30]

Nothing could be clearer. But this was a statement of intentions. The **practice** might be different. The huge, ten-fold increase in civil litigation that occurred under Elizabeth indicates, among other things, that men were turning from violence, and towards the courts, to settle their disputes. But Elizabeth could not always enforce the peace she craved. Any kind of violence at court was strictly forbidden and could be savagely punished under martial law: her father had ordered the chopping off of the hand of a leading courtier, and had remitted the sentence only when the palace butcher was about to enforce it. But the

Earl of Sussex was driven to complain to Elizabeth in 1565 that his enemy, Leicester, was allowed to have armed retainers at court, while he had to go unprotected; he begged that Leicester's men be disarmed, or that the Queen provide him with an escort to his barge, 'where I may after shift for myself as I can'.[31] Sometimes rows broke out even in her Presence Chamber; after one, Charles Yelverton told Sir William Cornwallis: 'Sir Knight, had I you out of this place, I would pluck that periwig off your poxy pate.' They would not, then, come to blows in the palace precincts; but Elizabeth had to turn a blind eye when a *réglement des comptes* took place in the fields outside London. In the 1580s a violent feud raged between the Earl of Oxford and Thomas Knyvett, a senior gentleman of the Privy Chamber; incidents occurred all over London, four men were murdered and four wounded. But when Knyvett killed one of Oxford's men, Elizabeth's chief concern seems to have been to hush up the incident: she instructed Hatton to bring pressure to bear on Lord Chancellor Bromley to have the case tried privately during the legal vacation, and to accept a plea of self-defence – 'My good Lord, it is very necessary you take care to please the Queen in this case.'[32] Evidently Elizabeth sometimes felt it prudent to settle for the illusion, rather than the reality, of lawfulness. She and Cecil believed that wider education, and the development of polite manners, would prove more effective in raising standards of conduct than a blind enforcement of the law.

Indeed, outside the metropolitan area, it was sometimes beyond their power to impose peace. Local feuds between leading gentry – the Stanhopes and Markhams in Nottinghamshire, the Fiennes and the Dymokes in Lincolnshire, the Danvers and the Longs in Hampshire, the Muschamps and the Collingwoods in Northumberland – raged for years and sometimes generations, influenced the elections of MPs, the appointments of sheriffs and other officials, and occasionally had an important bearing on central politics. Powerful men did not necessarily feel they were subject to the law. When Lord Chandos was summoned before the Council of Wales for terrifying juries, threatening an under-sheriff with guns, and protecting highway robbers, he replied: 'I had thought that a nobleman might have found more favour in your court, than thus hardly to be dealt with (as I am) like a common subject.' John Fortescue protested to Lord Grey de Wilton about his habit of hunting over Fortescue's lands, and got the reply: 'Stuff a turd in your teeth, I will hunt it, and it shall be hunted in spite of all you can do.' Bess of Hardwicke and her last husband involved themselves in violent feuds which spread over five counties and two decades, and she sent her messengers, like heralds, to issue challenges and defiance to her enemies. Most of these offenders were eventually brought to book – it is why they appear in the records – but it was often a fine calculation for Elizabeth to make, whether it was preferable to allow riot to go unpunished or to risk antagonizing powerful men (or women).[33]

It is a mistake to think, moreover, that the Tudors had already stamped out private armies. It is true that to maintain men in livery required a licence; but these were granted in appropriate cases. The crown had no alternative, for its standing forces were minute, and well-affected lords provided the bulk of the armed forces in time of trouble. The militia itself was liable to prove useless; in 1573, Elizabeth ordered picked men to be drawn from the general levies, professionally trained and armed at public expense; but these 'trained bands' were usually recruited from the dregs or those who wished to escape the draft; at the time of the Armada, for instance, all the best troops – numbering 1,500 foot and 1,600 horse – were supplied by the nobility and gentry. Until the end of the reign, it was rare for the crown to maintain local depots of arms and ammunition. So great men were allowed to furnish their own armouries. The Cliffords, Earls of Cumberland, manufactured their own gunpowder. So did Leicester. At Kenilworth, it was reported that he had stored enough cannon, shot and small-arms to equip 700 men.[34] Elizabeth was particularly anxious that the armed servants of her lords should be humble professionals, rather than local gentry. She did not want pyramids of power growing up in the counties. Fulke Greville wrote that she 'did not suffer the nobility to be servants one to another, neither did her gentry wear their liveries as in the ages before.'[35] In 1561 she insisted that no JP might be a retainer, and in 1572 she issued a proclamation rigidly enforcing the law restricting livery to household servants. But many JPs, for instance, wore Leicester's livery; and the further from London, the more likely it was that substantial men would take service under leading lords, sometimes paying for the privilege (and spoils).

Elizabeth's nobility was thus only partly disarmed; its acquiescence in her authority, and still more its active support, had to be won and maintained by a continual process of conciliation – that is, by making the nobility, and other major landowners, participants in the process of government, and sharers in its rewards. Elizabeth's resources were limited. Her genius lay in distributing them to the widest possible number, in such a way as to cause the maximum gratification, and the least offence, while conserving the wealth, authority and prestige of the crown. She was exceptionally conservative in her awards of honours, thus preserving their value, and making them all the more welcome when (reluctantly and belatedly) they were given.[36] She made no dukes, created only one marquess (in fact a restoration), and very few earls. She kept the peers down to about sixty and brought very few 'new' men into the Lords· 'a concurrence of old blood with fidelity [was] a mixture which ever sorted with the Queen's nature.'[37] Cecil had to wait over fourteen years before he got his peerage, and it was denied to some of her greatest servants. Sir Nicholas Bacon was not even made Lord Chancellor, having to content himself with the lesser title of Lord Keeper. Lord Hunsdon, her own cousin, despite a lifetime of service, was offered an earldom only on his deathbed, when he refused it, complaining it had come too late. Sir Henry Sidney had to be content with a knighthood, despite his long service in Wales (during part of which he was also Deputy in Ireland). So did Hatton, Walsingham, Ralegh, Sir Robert Cecil and many others. At one point she told Burghley that the Lords were getting too few in number, and asked him to submit a list of possible creations (including promotion to an earldom himself). But he declined the earldom, as he did not wish to arouse needless jealousy, and she ignored his other suggestions.[38] Indeed, Elizabeth's reluctance to create peers (another characteristic she shared with Henry VII, under whom their numbers fell from fifty-seven to forty-four), increased with age; in the last thirty years of her life she created (or admitted) only two peers, and made one promotion to an earldom. She told the Earl of Essex, who wanted Sir Henry Sidney's son, Robert, made a peer: 'What shall I do with all these that pretend to titles? I could be willing to call [Sidney] and one or two more, but to call many I will not. And I am importuned by many of their friends to do it.'[39] Most modern prime ministers have used the same excuse; in Elizabeth's case, however, she was consciously adopting a deliberate, long-term policy to maintain the social hierarchy as a stable and beneficient political system, with the monarchy at its apex. She was the last sovereign to do this in a systematic manner and, not surprisingly therefore, the last to exercise a monarch's executive power with a consensus of approval.

She was equally conservative with knighthoods and claims to bear arms. The College of Heralds, under her close supervision, dealt with the latter, carried out on-the-spot visitations to inspect records, and frequently rejected claims – a tremendous humiliation for the families concerned. At the end of her reign, she had fewer (550) knights than at the beginning, despite the rapid growth in population; moreover, of these, 25 per cent had been created by Essex, on active service, against her express injunctions. She liked to make knights only for distinguished service, or (as Sir Thomas Smith put it), 'according to the yearly revenue of their lands'.[40] A knighthood had thus a very considerable value, denoting senior military rank or extensive possessions. Men grumbled at the time, but they saw the point later, when James I created 906 knights in his first four years, 'a scum of such as it would make a man sick to think of them'.[41] (He could not pronounce the name of one gentleman he dubbed, and told him:

'Prithee rise up and call thyself Sir-What-Thou-Wilt.') Though Elizabeth was persuaded by the Council not to revoke the Essex creations, she refused to recognize some of them in practice: thus, Sir Gelly Meyrick, sentenced to death for his part in the 1601 rebellion, was refused the knightly privilege of beheading, and was hanged, drawn and quartered.

Apart from titles, Elizabeth had a variety of devices to keep men sweet. Oddly enough, the most powerful, especially those of the ancient nobility, were the most easily dealt with in some ways. All had been accustomed, on succeeding, to receive particular honorific and quasi-hereditary offices; she refused to admit their hereditary character, and thus bestowed as a privilege what they had come to regard as a right. They seem to have accepted this. Thus, when deciding how to reward Shrewsbury for the onerous burden of keeping Mary of Scotland in his custody, Elizabeth was told by a councillor: 'I think this would content him: £200 in fee-farm, and that it would please her Majesty to bestow the reversion of such offices as he hath upon his children, as Queen Mary did after his father's death.'[42] Generally speaking, Elizabeth rewarded her senior peers with embassies, military commands, lord lieutenancies, and garters – thus, in this respect, adumbrating the modern honours system as devised by William Pitt the Younger.

For the rest – including her most active servants – Elizabeth was expected to provide something more tangible. It was a matter of self-respect, as well as hard cash. When Sir Henry Sidney was asked to resume the unpopular deputyship of Ireland in 1582, he asked for something (no matter what) 'that it may be known and made apparent to the world that her Majesty hath had gracious consideration of his service past and for his better encouragement thereafter'.[43] Elizabeth's difficulty was to make the available places in her gift go round among those who felt themselves entitled to one, to provide, as the borough-mongering Duke of Newcastle was later to put it, 'enough pasture for all the sheep'. Cecil calculated that there was an inner core of 100 notables; just over 800 tax-payers were listed as paying more than £20 a year; counting those holding Commissions of the Peace, plus younger sons and other aspirants, those who had some claim to preferment probably numbered 2,500.[44] As against this, Elizabeth had at her disposal about 1,200 places that could properly be occupied by gentlemen, and an equal number for those of lesser pretensions. At court, there were 175 elite jobs for men, 12 for women, plus 60 gentlemen-pensioners. The central administration, revolving round the Treasury and the Exchequer, had a staff of 65 at Westminster, plus 200 more in the country. The Court of Wards had just under 60, and the Secretariat about 50, including Queen's Messengers. Regional administration, including the Duchy of Lancaster and the Presidencies, supplied about 75 more. In the law courts, there were jobs for about 50 judges, sergeants, masters and court officers, but these nearly always had to go to professional lawyers. The Admiralty and the Ordnance had something like 200 posts; there were 36 garrisons, but, with the exception of Berwick, they rarely consisted of more than a dozen men. The crown lands employed about 600 men, stewards, bailiffs, keepers, foresters and so forth, who got small wages but valuable perks and privileges. Finally, there was the Church. In all, and allowing for pluralism, there were about 1,000 worthwhile jobs paid by the Queen.[45] Very few, if any, were absolute sinecures; and permission had to be secured from the top to serve by deputy. Elizabeth's servants, on the whole, earned their keep. And their keep was not generous: 400 got less than £20 a year, 200 less than £50; there were 71 between £50 and £100, 77 between £100 and £200, 20 over £200 and only nine over £300. Courtiers on the whole were worse paid than civil servants, but both types could add to their income by accepting gifts to expedite petitions or business. This traffic hovered uneasily between accepted usage and sheer bribery; the evidence seems to show that the latter increased towards the end of the reign, but this may simply be because more letters and papers have survived for the later period.[46] It has been argued that it was Elizabeth's meanness which led to the growth of corruption; but the fact is that corruption became far more wide-spread and flagrant once James I, who was profligate in all respects, came to the throne. On the whole, and by the standards of the time, Elizabeth's administration was hard-working and honest, not least because she was hard-working and honest herself.

In addition to offices, there were various cash rewards in the Queen's gift. She rarely made outright gifts of money. More often she made over assignments against an irregular (or unpopular) source of income. Thus a man might be given the right to collect fines from recusants, or the forfeiture of their goods or property; some, like Sir Philip Sidney, declined to operate in this sordid business; others, like Ralegh, were less squeamish. The crown employed, and paid according to results, every kind of debt and tax-collector, men who nosed out ancient and forgotten rights, ranging from concealed tenants-in-chief to legal bondsmen; when these were discovered, and compounded by fine, the informer got a cut. Men who earned their living this way were highly unpopular. Crown monopolies, and the right to farm the customs, were also unpopular, but in these cases the odium was worth it, for the rewards were huge, and such prizes only went to leading political figures in the régime – Leicester, Huntingdon, Walsingham, Hunsdon, Burghley, Sussex, Ralegh and so on. They were the principal means by which the Queen enabled her chief supporters and ministers to keep up their state. She also controlled a variety of time-honoured arrangements by which the favoured exploited parts of the crown lands. The most valuable were fee-farms – in effect, perpetual leases at nominal rents, that could be sold for cash. But they rarely exceeded £100 a year, and went only to senior figures. Sometimes, the favour took the form of a change of tenure, from fee-simple to socage, which meant the possessor escaped the Court of Wards and other feudal financial traps. Or the Queen would grant the right to dispark, or cut timber; and she had a vast number of ancient offices, which were paid nominally or not at all, on the royal estates – stewardships and bailiwicks and so forth. These carried local prestige and often valuable hunting rights. Last of all, she had a variable number of pensions and annuities to dispose of (there were about 350 in 1573). Leicester's £1,000 on the customs was unique; Hatton's £400 a year was next in size, and Lords Buckhurst and Howard of Effingham had £200 each; nearly all the rest were below £30 a year, and many of them went to Elizabeth's ladies. All these, of course, could be sold for lump sums, and often were.

For the powerful – but only for the powerful – there was a further privilege, exercised at the Queen's absolute discretion, and in a manner which was dangerously unpredictable. This was her willingness to allow leading courtiers, ministers and office-holders to accumulate debts to her. It was one way in which she enabled her principal servants to behave like Renaissance magnificos; but, after their death, she insisted their heirs repaid the money in annual instalments, and even during their lifetime the threat of enforced repayment hung like a sword over their heads, and was an inducement to compliance – rather like the huge recognizances which her grandfather, Henry VII, imposed on his magnates. Hatton's last years were clouded by the size of his indebtedness to the crown, and he died owing £42,139. 5s. as collector of First Fruits and Tenths from the clergy.[47] Huntingdon owed Elizabeth £20,000 at his death, and Leicester £70,000 (though the latter sum was rumour).[48] When Essex fell out of line, his crown debts were instantly raised (he owed at least £11,000, some of it accumulated by his father).[49] Modern writers have accused Elizabeth of being hard-hearted in dunning the heirs of her favourite servants; her contemporaries took quite the opposite view. Thus, in the 1571 parliament, John Popham MP bitterly attacked the crown for allowing officials to get into its debt and to use the money for private ventures – he was referring to a recent scandal involving £30,000.[50] But it was difficult for MPs to take a high line on this issue, since they themselves were the beneficiaries of another form of royal favour – gross under-assessment for income tax. There was nothing new in this. Early surviving tax-lists (e.g. from 1436) show that the practice went back 150 years or more.[51] Sir Walter Ralegh, always ready to blurt out in public matters about which others kept hypocritically silent, reminded the 1597–8 parliament that the tax-system was grossly unfair: 'When our estates that are £3 or £4 in the Queen's Book [the Exchequer assessments], it is not the hundredth part of our wealth.'[52] The higher the rank, the less relationship the assessment bore to reality. Thus, in 1559, the Earl of Derby was assessed for £2,000 (about a third of the true figure); in 1566 this had been halved, though his income had increased; while the Earl of Oxford, assessed for £1,600 in 1559 was not asked to pay anything seven years later. Winchester, one of the richest men in England (and also one of the assessors) was put down at a mere £800. In any case, the really big men did not pay up. In 1559, Norfolk got a tax-demand for £160, in respect of the first *tranche* of the subsidy; he discovered that Dudley had received a writ of discharge from Elizabeth and, furious, refused to pay his share. Indeed, it looks as though he never paid any income-tax. Cecil may have paid up; but then he was only asked to contribute £8 13s. 4d. (he was an assessor too). In 1589, said Burghley, Elizabeth was amazed, when scrutinizing the subsidy rolls, to see the flagrant discrepancies between the assessed and real wealth of people she knew.[53] But of course she was perfectly well aware of the practice; may be she thought it had got out of hand. But nothing was done; it would have been too unpopular.

By such means Elizabeth kept the 'political nation' content. Her methods were often devious, indeed dubious; the system was infinitely complex and thoroughly ramshackle; and, radiating as it did from a single person, imposed great strains on the Queen, even though she used Cecil as a controlling agent (he usually drew up the actual terms of the leases, and so forth, she granted). But it worked surprisingly well. The vast majority of her magnates stood solidly by her for nearly half a century, often in times of great stress. No conspiracy against her came within measurable distance of success. In forty-four years she found herself obliged to execute only three of her nobility, all of whom went to the scaffold with the full approval of their peers. She had to work hard to maintain the aristocratic consensus; but it never deserted her.

There was, however, one serious weakness in the system: the chink in the armour represented by Mary Queen of Scots. Rebellion needed a royal focus, and while Mary lived she provided it. Though the Treaty of Edinburgh marked the first great step towards the solution of the Scottish problem, Scottish affairs continued to plague Elizabeth and her ministers. Often they confessed themselves baffled by the volatility and complexity of Scots internal politics. 'Scotland is a quagmire,' wrote Cecil, 'no one seems to stand still.'[54] But he understood it better than most; when he was ill in 1564, Elizabeth wrote him a letter (in

Latin) asking his advice; she was, she said, 'in a labyrinth about Scottish matters'.[55] Once Mary was back in Scotland, the question of whom she would marry became of considerable importance to Elizabeth. Naturally, she herself wanted Mary to choose an English subject. Lord Darnley, son of the Earl of Lennox, technically qualified in this respect, but he was Scots by background and association, and in addition had a claim to the English throne. Why Elizabeth allowed Darnley to leave England for Scotland in February 1565 is difficult to explain; it was probably Leicester's influence, since he had no desire to support Elizabeth's impractical scheme to marry Mary himself. At all events, once Darnley arrived in Edinburgh Mary promptly decided to marry him, and ignored Elizabeth's protest, signed by all the members of the English Council, that such a match would be 'unmeet, unprofitable and perilous to the sincere amity between the Queen's and their realms'. On 28 July Mary proclaimed Darnley King, and married him the next day. Elizabeth's only response was to order a show of force in the north. When Mary broke with the pro-English faction in Scotland, led by her half-brother, the Earl of Moray, 'put him to the horn', and drove him and his followers into exile, all Elizabeth felt she could offer them was asylum: they reached England in October 1565. She was advised, on this as on many subsequent occasions, that the only way to keep Scotland quiet was to supply the pro-English faction with enough money and arms to allow them to neutralize Mary's hostility. The sums involved were not large: perhaps £10,000 a year would do the trick. She recognized the wisdom of this advice; but she was always worried by the possibility of French retaliation if she intervened openly in Scottish affairs – and that might prove really expensive, even dangerous. She received the exiled Moray in audience, in the presence of two French envoys, and told him (to their satisfaction):

> that whatsoever the world said or reported of her, she would by her actions
> let it appear she would not, to be a prince of the world, maintain any subject in
> any disobedience against the prince, for besides the offence of her conscience
> which would condemn her, she knew that Almighty God might justly
> recompense her with the like trouble in her own realm.[56]

This was her official, international position. Privately, she instructed her Scottish envoy, Thomas Randolph, that her intention was 'covertly, though not manifestly, to procure the restoration of Moray and others to their country'. She had a justifiably low opinion of Mary's political judgment, and no doubt calculated that she would come to grief sooner or later.

And this, of course, is what happened. The Scots nobility resented their exclusion from her councils, and the favour shown to her secretary, David Rizzio. By 13 February 1566 Randolph was reporting to Leicester:

> I know now for certain that this Queen repenteth her marriage, that she hateth the King and all his kin . . . David, with the consent of the King, shall have his throat cut within these ten days. Many things grievouser and worse than these are brought to my ears, yes, of things intended against her own person![57]

I doubt if Leicester showed this letter to Elizabeth. The murder of Rizzio she might condone in advance, but there could be no question that she would have warned Mary of any plot against her life. Elizabeth's ministers, however, were kept fully informed. Rizzio was slaughtered on 9 March, but the political aims of the plot misfired, and within a week Mary was back in control of Edinburgh at the head of 8,000 men; she sent Elizabeth a passionate and graphic description of her experiences, which must have convinced the latter that she had learned very little from them.[58] But she asked Elizabeth to let bygones be bygones; she restored Moray, and later Maitland, to office, balancing them by favour shown to the Catholic and Anglophobe Earl of Bothwell; and the birth of the future James I in June 1566 was well received at the English court.

Mary, however, was incapable of playing the role of a responsible sovereign. It was the principal charge Elizabeth held against her. Like Mary, she had a high regard for her position and prerogatives, and exploited them to the hilt; but, unlike Mary, she always recognized that they had to be earned by placing the interests of her nation and her people before her personal inclinations. Monarchy involved obligations and duties, as well as rights; this was something Mary could never understand. And, of course, Elizabeth was a professional, Mary a self-willed amateur. By the winter of 1566, Mary was anxious to rid herself of her husband. It was, wrote her secretary, Maitland, to the Scots ambassador in Paris, 'heartbreak to her to think he should be her husband, and how to be free of him she sees no outgate'.[59] Bothwell supplied her with the 'outgate'. On 10 February 1567 Darnley was murdered at Kirk O' Fields, outside Edinburgh. An official Scottish version, designed to exonerate Mary and Bothwell and prepare the way for a fake trial at which he would be acquitted, was sent off post-haste to Elizabeth. But the latter's own agents, bringing a much more sinister story, reached her first. Her response was to write Mary a letter, beginning 'Madame' (not the customary '*Ma chère Soeur*'), indicating that she thought Mary guilty: 'I should not do you the office of a faithful cousin and friend if I did not urge you to preserve your honour rather than look through your fingers at revenge who had done you "*tel plaisir*", as most people say.'[60]

The irony and contempt were unmistakable. Indeed, it was doubtless at this point that Elizabeth finally decided that Mary must be ruled out of the succession completely, as unfit for any throne, let alone the throne of England; the problem now was to get possession of the young James, or at least ensure he was decently brought up. Cecil was able to show Elizabeth a well-informed dispatch: ' . . . she cares not to lose France, England and her own country for [Bothwell] and shall go with him to the world's end in a white petticoat ere she leave him.' Though the English Council agreed, with Elizabeth's approval, to try to prevent the new marriage at all costs, in fact Bothwell had carried Mary off before this decision was reached, and they were married on 15 May. Elizabeth did nothing beyond paying out more rope with which Mary could hang herself. Bothwell's forces were defeated at Carbury Hill on 15 June, and Mary was brought prisoner to Edinburgh; the crowds shouted 'Burn the whore!' and she spat back that she would hang and crucify the lot of them.[61]

The collapse of Mary's régime placed Elizabeth in an ideological dilemma. On the one hand, she wished to secure the person of James – and, still more, prevent the French from getting him; but this was unacceptable to the Scots lords, except on condition that she would acknowledge him as heir-presumptive to the English crown, something she was not prepared to do on principle. On the other hand, she was strongly opposed to Mary's enforced abdication – the royal trade unionist in her coming out again and wished her to be restored, in some nominal sense, to her throne. She seems to have dithered and vacillated surprisingly during these months. On 29 July she told Sir Nicholas Throckmorton, who had been sent north as ambassador, that if the Scots deprived 'their sovereign lady' of her rights, she would revenge her as an example to all posterity, quoting St Paul to boot. In August, in what Cecil termed 'a great offensive speech', she accused him of making no preparations 'to revenge the Queen of Scots' imprisonment and deliver her'. She 'began to devise revenge by war'.[62] She seems to have been more inclined to bad-temper than usual, as she was suffering from a painful 'crick in the neck'. But of course her words were pure hyperbole. She had no intention of invading Scotland to restore Mary; this, indeed, would have shattered the English consensus. Probably she was worried by French reactions if she failed to make the appropriate noises. But in October 1567 religious war broke out again in France, removing any threat from that quarter, and thereafter Elizabeth accepted the situation in Scotland, where Moray, as regent to the young King, was acquitting himself, as Cecil put it, 'very honourably to the advancement of religion and justice without respect of persons'. Indeed, in April 1568 Elizabeth agreed with Moray to buy part of Mary's jewels – in particular, an enormous six-row string of pearls, much coveted by Catherine de Medici, in the form of a rosary; some of the pearls were as large as black grapes. They reached her on 1 May, when she displayed them to Leicester and Pembroke. Just over a fortnight later, on 16 May, the Scots Queen, who had escaped from her island prison on Lochleven, roused her forces. But she was decisively defeated at Langside, and crossed the English border as a refugee. She had shaved her head to escape detection, and was virtually friendless and penniless.

All the same, Mary was the cynosure of many eyes on both sides of the border, and a political factor of great potentiality. What was to be done with her? When news of her arrival reached court, Elizabeth summoned, and attended, two long meetings of the Council. She let the Spanish ambassador know that she had spoken up strongly for Mary, and intended to treat her as still a sovereign. But this was for Philip II's consumption.[63] In reality, the plan of the English government, as outlined in a Cecil memo, was to bring her to trial for her alleged complicity in the murder of her husband. This was to be done by virtue of the English claim to sovereignty in Scotland, 'for that of ancient right it appertaineth to the crown of England, as by multitude of records, examples and precedents may be proved'. If Mary was found innocent, she might be restored; but of course she would be found guilty – she *was* guilty! – and in that case it was for the Queen to decide. In any event, she was to be held incommunicado, in a safe place, while the investigations were made.[64] Privately, at least, Elizabeth accepted these recommendations, and was stiffened in her determination by news that Mary's first act, on reaching England, had been to resume her correspondence with Bothwell, and closet herself with two of his associates. Sir Francis Knollys, who had been sent north to supervise her custody, reported that she had threatened to summon help even from Turkey rather than submit to Moray, and that she refused to admit that her conduct was open to criticism in any respect whatever.

Obviously, Elizabeth was anxious to break the potential threat of Mary to her throne by destroying her reputation in a public judgment. But she did not want a trial as such – queens, even delinquent ones, were not to be tried – but an inquiry, and one, moreover, whose terms of reference Mary could be persuaded to accept. She had Mary moved to Bolton Castle, and sent her a message:

that if she would commit her cause to be heard by her Highness's order, but not to make her Highness judge over her, but rather as to her dear cousin and friend to commit herself to her advice and counsel, that if she would do thus, her Highness would surely set her again in her seat of regiment, and dignity regal . . .

The procedure to be followed was that the rebellious Scots lords would be asked to present their case against Mary; if their grounds proved sufficient, Mary would be restored to her throne conditionally, the lords being allowed to 'continue in their honours, estates and dignities'; if their grounds were inadequate, Mary would be restored unconditionally, 'and that by force of hostility, if [the lords] should resist'. Elizabeth imposed further safeguards: that Mary should renounce her claim to the English throne, during the life of Elizabeth or her issue, should forsake her league with France, and accept the Book of Common Prayer 'after the form of England'.[65] After some hesitation, Mary accepted these terms. But of course they were offered to her on the firm assumption she was guilty, and Elizabeth never had the slightest intention of carrying out the conditional restoration. As Cecil assured Moray on 25 September 1568: 'It is not meant, if the Queen of Scots shall be proved guilty of murder, to restore her to Scotland, howsoever her friends may brag to the contrary, nor yet shall there be any haste made of her delivery.' Elizabeth, in fact, was lying; but then she knew she was dealing with a consummate liar, who held herself to be regally and morally absolved from telling the truth, and who had no intention of abiding by the conditions she had accepted.

All three sides, Scots, English and Mary, appointed their commissioners for the inquiry, which opened at York on 4 October. Moray headed the Scots team, Elizabeth was represented by Norfolk, Sussex and Sadler, and Mary's chief spokesman was John Leslie, Bishop of Ross. A digest of the evidence against Mary had already been forwarded to Elizabeth in the summer; but Moray was evidently unwilling to produce the original papers unless he was reasonably satisfied a guilty verdict would be found. Elizabeth reassured him, and on 25 November she decided to bring the inquiry under her personal supervision by transferring it to Westminster; her commissioners were augmented by adding Cecil, Leicester and other grandees. Four days later, Moray brought forward his famous 'eik', or additional proofs, in the form of the Casket Letters, and now openly accused Mary of murder.

What was this proof? The casket itself was described in the Journal of the Commission as 'a small gilded coffer not fully one foot long, being garnished in many places with the Roman letter "F" set under a royal crown'. It contained eight letters, two marriage certificates, and twelve sonnets – twenty-two documents in all; and, if authentic, they collectively proved Mary's complicity in the murder beyond any shadow of doubt. The casket (which does not correspond exactly to the description in the Journal) survives, and is now in the Lennoxlove Museum in Scotland. All the original documents have since disappeared. One, it seems, was never returned to Scotland after the inquiry;

the remaining twenty-one vanished in 1584. Copies of four letters made at Westminster survive in the London Public Records Office; four more are in the Cecil papers at Hatfield; and a copy of one of the marriage contracts is in the British Museum. No contemporary copies of the other documents survive, though Elizabeth had extracts published unofficially in 1571.[66] At the time, Mary flatly and vociferously asserted that the letters were forgeries, and many historians since – working of course from the copies – have doubted their authenticity.[67] The problem is now insoluble, unless of course the originals reappear. But the important thing to bear in mind is that all the English commissioners, including men like Norfolk, Arundel, Northumberland and Westmorland, who later showed considerable sympathy for Mary, and who saw the documents, accepted them as genuine. This was the harsh political fact, as opposed to later speculation. Moreover, Mary produced no answer to the charges, beyond a blanket denial, and the claim that the letters were forged. Despite repeated requests by Elizabeth, she declined to make a formal reply, unless she had guarantees about her future. As Knollys reported: 'it is vain to look for her answer as standing to her justification formally ... without her assurance beforehand that howsoever the matter fall out that yet the good judgment will fall on her side.' In short she wanted Elizabeth to promise a not-guilty verdict in advance.[68] There was no question of this; but, equally, Elizabeth did not think it prudent to pronounce a guilty verdict. On 14 December 1568, at Hampton Court, she had the commission's proceedings read out before a large assembly of magnates, who afterwards thanked her for displaying the case to them 'wherein they had seen such foul matters as they thought truly in their conscience that her Majesty's position was justified'. But, having many other matters on her plate, she brought the inquiry to an end on 11 January 1569, with the conclusion that the Scots nobility had not been guilty of rebellion, but that Mary's guilt had not been fully established either. Mary, now in effect a prisoner (though a highly privileged one), was handed over to the custody of the Earl of Shrewsbury, and housed in his castle at Tutbury in Staffordshire. Elizabeth had avoided the risk of judging her captive a murderess, which would have closed her options, while ensuring that the accusations would be rapidly spread and widely believed. Perhaps to her chagrin, however, the courts of Europe were not inclined to admit that Mary's behaviour, however wicked, destroyed her potential value to them. Politics came before morals.

One reason why Elizabeth was anxious to terminate the commission without the international complications that a guilty verdict would bring was that she was becoming increasingly perturbed by the behaviour of the Duke of Norfolk.

He was a unique piece on the political chessboard of England. Not only was he the only duke, standing in honour and title next to Elizabeth herself; in a sense he was, despite his youth (he was still only thirty in 1568), a relic from an earlier age, lumbering about Renaissance England like the survivor of a prehistoric species. His father, the doomed Earl of Surrey – 'the most foolish proud boy that is in England' – had boasted of his Plantagenet blood, and had quartered the royal arms; his mother was daughter of John de Vere, 16th Earl of Oxford. He had married three times, and buried three wives: a Fitzalen of Arundel, an Audley of Audley and a Dacre of Westmorland, all of whom had added to his already great possessions and connections. At his vast house of Kenninghall, twenty miles from Norwich, surrounded by its 700-acre park, he controlled the last of the great medieval liberties, 600 square miles of territory exempt from the normal procedures of royal justice.[69] When Elizabeth made him Scottish commander in 1559, he took with him 1,650 armed men from Norfolk, most of them his own tenants. This had been his first visit to what he termed 'the inly-working north', and led him to form fatal connections: his own with the Dacres, and the marriage of his two sisters to the Earl of Westmorland and Lord Scrope. Elizabeth showed him the favour appropriate to his rank. He was licensed to keep 100 men in livery and, in addition to income-tax concessions, to import Turkey carpets duty-free. He moved from London to Norwich, and about his business, accompanied by 500 retainers on horseback. In the City, he transformed the Charterhouse into the finest of town palaces; and his house in Norwich was the greatest town house of the provinces: it had a bowling alley, the first of its kind in England, a tennis court and a play-house. Norfolk's accounts show he was often short of ready cash: the reason was that he was buying land faster than any man in the kingdom. He had the acquisitiveness and ambitions of a would-be prince.[70]

As the paladin of the ancient nobility, Norfolk hated Leicester. The two fought many local battles over patronage; once they had almost come to blows in the Whitehall tennis court. Leicester spread rumours that Norfolk protected recusants in Norfolk, and was not a loyal Anglican. It is true that the Marian bishop White of Winchester had been among his tutors, but so had Foxe himself. Norfolk's second marriage had been contracted in defiance of the old Church, and he was never a papist. He died a sworn Anglican, with Foxe beside him on the scaffold, and there is nothing to show that his treason was motivated by religious faith. Elizabeth began by trusting him, made him a councillor to balance Leicester, and permitted him a freedom of speech which she accorded to no other aristocrat. He seemed to her, and to others, aloof from the faction-fight and the scramble for offices and favours, raised by his very magnificence from the self-seeking world of court politics, and grandly disinterested. He was, therefore, a natural choice to be her chief representative on the commission investigating the guilt of Mary Queen of Scots. She had no reason to distrust him. In 1559, as Earl Marshal of England, and head of the heraldic profession, he had pronounced decisively against Mary's quartering of the royal arms, judging it maliciously prejudicial to Elizabeth, and also 'falsely marshalled, contrary to all law and order of arms'. At York, he had been convinced and appalled by the evidence against her. As he wrote to Elizabeth, he was shocked

> to discover such inordinate love between her and Bothwell, her loathsomeness and abhorring of her husband that was murdered, in such sort as every good and godly man cannot but detest and abhor the same ... the matter contained [in the letters] being such as could hardly be invented or devised by any other than herself.

Yet, only five days after this letter was written, on 16 October 1568, Norfolk went hawking with Secretary Maitland, and the latter suggested Norfolk should marry the Scots Queen. The Duke fell for the bait at once, despite the fact that he carried in his instructions an explicit command from Elizabeth that anyone with whom Mary contracted a marriage, or anyone advising one, 'shall be *ipso facto* adjudged as traitorous and shall suffer death'. The truth is, Norfolk, like his father, was a foolish man, consumed by dynastic pride: the prospect of a kingdom dangled before his eyes was irresistible. Moreover, he was the last man in the world to carry through such a dangerous project with success, lacking both the ability to keep his mouth shut, and the courage to pursue his aim with constancy and fortitude. Within a week or two Elizabeth got wind of the scheme: it was one reason she brought the commission back to London. She might not have been so suspicious had it been a question of love. But it was nothing of the sort; Norfolk had never met Mary, and was never to set eyes on her. His calculation was coldly political and materialistic, like his previous marriages. And, from Elizabeth's point of view, the conjunction of Mary's claim, and Norfolk's power and wealth, was the most perilous that could be devised.

When Norfolk returned to court late in November, his relations with the Queen underwent a radical transformation. Hitherto, they had been conducted on a level of sincerity, even frankness. Now, she asked him point-blank about the truth of the rumours, and he responded with a deliberate lie. No reason, he said 'could move him to the like of her that hath been a competitor to the crown; and if her Majesty would move him thereto he will rather be committed to the Tower, for he never meant to marry with such a person, where he could not be sure of his pillow.'[71] This exchange ended a very special relationship.

From now on, Elizabeth knew him to be a liar. He, conscious of his lie – and half aware of the Queen's knowledge – became increasingly uneasy, and hence more devious, in her presence. He had ceased to be a superlord, above the political battle. At York he had descended to the level of a Leicester, and become an operator. A combination of guilt, cowardice and folly was to turn him into a conspirator.

There can be no doubt that it was through Cecil's intelligence service that Elizabeth had heard of Norfolk's marriage plan; and it was against Cecil that Norfolk first turned. This was a *renversement d'alliance* with a vengeance. Throughout his career, Cecil was always careful to keep on good terms with the old nobility, indeed with all the great men of the kingdom; letters to and from them form a large part of his vast correspondence (which ran, in terms of letters received, at the rate of 60–100 a day). Though he might tell his son that nobility 'was but ancient riches', he, like the Queen, believed in birth and hierarchy as the basis of the stable society they both sought to preserve. Cecil had a particular veneration for Norfolk as the head, as it were, of the English aristocratic profession; they shared a passion for genealogy; they had co-operated closely in the Scottish business; and Cecil, as Master of the Wards, was directly involved in a complex suit over the Dacre wardships – the lands at stake were very valuable – in which Norfolk, through his third marriage, was a principal party. Since the decision in this last suit was Cecil's, Norfolk had every reason to remain his friend. The fact that he now turned on Cecil says a good deal about the collapse of his judgment; and the further fact that he did so in conjunction with his despised enemy, Leicester, indicates that he had lost his self-respect. From being a man who had stood aloof, and above faction, Norfolk was sinking low indeed.

The conspiracy against Cecil, which got under way in January 1569, involved a large section of the Council. But it was a ramshackle coalition of men of diverse attitudes, and diverse motives; there was no leader, and no real unifying force. Leicester envied Cecil's grasp of the government machine, and saw him as the chief obstacle to his own paramountcy (in fact, Elizabeth was an even more formidable one). Norfolk knew that Cecil must be got out of the way if his marriage to Mary was to stand a chance. Some of the older councillors such as Winchester, Arundel and Pembroke, regarded Cecil as the chief agent of the breach with Spain; they thought the seizure of the treasure-ships a reckless blunder which had undermined the basis of English foreign policy, disrupted trade, and might lead to national bankruptcy. It was still unclear, in January–February 1569, whether England would get the better of the mutual embargoes, and Cecil's judgment had not yet been vindicated. Moreover, Cecil was passing through a phase of great unpopularity. Though Gresham and many big merchants were behind him in the trade war, he had quarrelled with the Lord Mayor of London and others who had had their ships and property seized by Spain, and 'many did also rise against his fortune, who were more hot in envying him than able to follow him, detracting his praises, disgracing his services, and plotting his danger'.[72] Moreover, Cecil had been responsible for the organization of a state lottery, designed to raise money to repair harbours and carry through other public works. Tickets were 10s., and prizes totalling £100,000 (with a first prize of £5,000) were advertised. But the lottery was under-subscribed; the prize money had to be reduced to £6,000, and when the first lots were drawn, at the West Door of St Paul's, from January onwards, there was angry grumbling at Cecil, and rumours of a fiddle. This gave the plot, as it were, the flavour of a popular base.[73]

It also had a foreign connection. Norfolk, in his efforts to raise loans to buy land, had been using the services of an Italian banker, Ridolfi; he and others, at this stage, thought Ridolfi was an ordinary man of business, though his capital had, in fact, been supplied from papal and other sources to serve as a financial 'float' to organize subversion in England. Ridolfi had links with the Spanish embassy, and through him Norfolk and Arundel let De Spes know that they were

> gathering friends, and were letting the public know what was going on, in the hope and belief that they will be able to turn out the present accursed government and raise another ... Although Cecil thinks he has them all under his heel, he will find few or none of them stand by him.

In fact the one person who mattered stood by him in no uncertain fashion, and she was well informed in advance of what was going on: the need to collect a heterogeneous coalition to crush Cecil made leaks certain. The only contemporary account of the crisis is given by Fénelon, the French ambassador; Cecil's own version is provided by Camden (whom he briefed many years later), and his factotum, John Clapham, who wrote his life.[74] According to Fénelon, the drama was resolved on 22 February, Ash Wednesday, after Elizabeth had summoned a Council, to outface Cecil's enemies, and was furious when some did not turn up. She gathered Leicester, Norfolk and Northampton in her privy chamber, just before supper, with Cecil present. She turned angrily on Leicester, then berated Norfolk when he spoke up for him. Camden put the matter more tersely: a gathering of the plotting lords was surprised by the Queen, 'who, coming upon them in the very instant of time, restrained them by a beck'. Another version, which has a sinister ring of truth, emerged at

Norfolk's trial. In Henry VIII's days, when members of the Council decided, like a wolf pack, to destroy one of their number, they forced him to take off his cap and go down on his knees before the board: this was what happened to Thomas Cromwell (the Soviet politburo, it is said, uses similar rituals). According to this account, the councillors already had Cecil on his knees when Elizabeth burst in and told him: 'I pardon thee that and more. Stand up and go sit down in thy place.'[75] Leicester, immediately the Queen made her views clear (and a 'beck' would suffice), deserted his allies; Norfolk was irresolute, as well as pusillanimous; the rest ran for cover. The episode was a transparent display of the Queen's personal and absolute authority; thereafter, Cecil never had any real trouble (except, once, from Elizabeth herself). But it is characteristic of his prudence and political *nous* that he refrained from following up his political advantage. Indeed, he completely hushed up the episode until, many years later, he described it to Camden and Clapham. Not only was he extra careful, throughout this period, to secure explicit Council approval for all his acts as secretary, but he did nothing to revenge himself on the men who had tried to destroy him. In Norfolk's case, indeed, he held out the hand of friendship again. This accorded with his usual methods, and also with the urgent advice of Thomas Radcliffe, Earl of Sussex, one of the wisest of Elizabethan statesmen. As an 'old' aristocrat, a friend and admirer of both Cecil and Norfolk, and a bitter enemy of Leicester, he had been appalled by Norfolk's folly, and desperately upset to hear of his estrangement from Cecil. He begged Cecil to 'rip up this matter from the bottom with the Duke himself', and offered to ride to London, 'yea, to Jerusalem', to mediate. When, two weeks later, Sussex heard the two were reconciled, he was delighted, for he had high hopes of Norfolk as a statesman, 'whom the world hath always judged to be void of private inclines' (alas, this was no longer true).[76] Cecil, indeed, tried hard to save the Duke from his own ambitions; he wanted to scotch the scheme to marry Mary by getting Norfolk to take, instead, the recently widowed Mistress Cooke, youngest of his sisters-in-law; but, says De Spes, 'the Duke would not listen to it, for he had his thoughts high, having fixed his eyes upon the Queen of Scotland'. But at least Cecil was able to ensure that Norfolk won his case over the Dacre inheritance; three years afterwards, in the Tower, Norfolk belatedly recognized Cecil's disinterested friendship by entrusting him with his children's welfare.

At the time, however, though by now back on friendly terms with Cecil, Norfolk persistently ignored his advice. About 1 June 1569, he told Cecil of his plans to marry Mary; Cecil advised strongly against it, but said that in any event he must come clean and tell Elizabeth (he certainly told her himself). Norfolk might have taken more notice of Sussex, his best friend, but Sussex was in York, as President of the North. In June, he had his first exchange of letters with Mary, who saw him as the best means to get her freedom. She told him she 'remitted all my causes' to him, 'to do as for yourself', and signed the letter 'your assured Mary'. She sent him a cushion she had embroidered with a knife cutting down a green vine (Elizabeth). Norfolk was less gushing. His letters have a chilly and timorous tone. Both were acting out of pure calculation; as I have said, this was not a romance, but, as Walsingham put it, an affair of letters, 'for other eyeliking hath not passed between them'.[77] But while carrying on nervously with Mary, Norfolk was still more nervous about confronting Elizabeth with the truth. She, and everyone at court, knew about the intrigue by July, and he had several opportunities to broach the matter with her. Indeed, she invited him to do so. On 1 August, at Oatlands, she asked Norfolk, who had just returned from London, for the news. He said there was none. 'No? You come from London and can tell no news of a marriage?' Just then, Lady Clinton arrived with some flowers, and Norfolk slunk off. He went straight to Leicester's rooms, waited till he had returned from hunting, and asked his advice; Leicester – not a man to consult in the quest for disinterested counsel – said to leave it to him: he would soften up Elizabeth. In fact Leicester does appear to have hinted at the matter, twelve days later, at Sir William More's house at Loseley near Guildford, where Elizabeth was staying on summer progress; it was morning, and one of Sir William's children was 'playing on a lute and singing, her Majesty sitting upon the threshold of the door, my Lord of Leicester kneeling by her Highness' – a delightful picture of royal domesticity, and a well-chosen moment to speak. Elizabeth, after hearing Leicester, said she would herself tackle Norfolk later in the progress. On 15 August, at Farnham, she paid the Duke the rare compliment of asking him to dine alone with her; he said nothing, and at the end of the meal she 'gave me a nip' (according to Norfolk's account) and said 'she would wish me to take good heed to my pillow ... I was abashed at her Majesty's speech, but I thought it not fit time nor place there to trouble her.' If a tête-à-tête dinner was not a good opportunity, what was? Norfolk was a coward. But if he was abashed in her presence, he switched to bravado in her absence, telling Richard Cavendish 'before he lost that marriage he would lose his life'. He had further chances to speak to Elizabeth, but passed them. Finally, on 6 September, Elizabeth paid a sick call on Leicester, who was bedridden, and he told her everything. The same afternoon, in the great gallery at Titchfield, she swore at Norfolk and charged him on his allegiance 'to deal no further with the Scottish cause'. He babbled that he had but 'a very slight regard' for Mary; his own 'revenues in England were not much less than those of the Kingdom of Scotland, and that when he was in his tennis court at

Norwich he thought himself in a manner equal with some kings'.[78] It was characteristic of Norfolk to put the match in these mercenary terms, and his analogy with kings was not calculated to appease Elizabeth. From this point, the courtiers began to give Norfolk a wide berth, and he went back to London. It should be added that, throughout this time, he was actively intriguing to promote the marriage.[79]

The breach with Spain had led Elizabeth to instruct lord lieutenants and other provincial authorities to hold musters of all able-bodied men, and report back to the Council on their available strengths. The musters took place from June onwards, and the reports received by Cecil were deeply discouraging. On 28 June, at Durham, most of the able men were listed as 'naked', that is, foot-soldiers without arms or armour. The next day, at York, it was the same story, and in addition the men were described as mutinous. Reports from many southern and eastern counties (e.g. Suffolk) were little better. Against this gloomy background, the impending defection of Norfolk seemed more serious than it actually was. Elizabeth, indeed, told Leicester early in September that if she allowed Norfolk's marriage to take place, she would be in the Tower within four months.[80] Within a week, she had closed the ports, alerted the militia, and sent the Earls of Huntingdon and Hereford with a force of cavalry to cover Tutbury Castle, where Mary was installed; the custodian, Shrewsbury, was ordered to double the guard on her. On 23 September, Elizabeth ended her progress at Windsor and decided to wait there (it was a strongly fortified place) until the situation was clearer. The day she arrived, she heard that Norfolk had left London for Kenninghall, and she naturally assumed he had decided to raise a rebellion; Elizabeth had already sent him polite letters requesting his return to court. Now, on 25 September, she sent him an absolute command to come forthwith to Windsor.

Had Elizabeth been able to peer inside Norfolk's head, she would not have been so worried. His unwillingness to appear at court arose not from a rebellious spirit, but from his sheer terror at facing her. In the far north, it is true, treason was afoot. His brother-in-law, the Earl of Westmorland (head of the Neville clan), and the Earl of Northumberland (head of the Percys) were organizing great gatherings of gentry and yeomen, ostensibly for country sports. The plan was to have the Queen's officers in the North murdered, and for a rescue party to ride to Tutbury and release Mary; Charles IX of France, with whom they had been in contact, had promised to land about 5,000 men at Dumbarton. And Ridolfi had already handed over 12,000 crowns to the two Earls, for their military expenses. But Norfolk simply remained at Kenninghall, quaking. In reply to Elizabeth's first summons, he pleaded to be excused: 'My enemies found such comfort in your Highness's heavy displeasure that they began to make of me a common table-talk; my friends were afraid of my company'; he knew he was a 'suspected person' and feared the Tower, 'too great a terror for a true man'. Elizabeth answered that she had no intention 'to minister anything to you but as you should in truth deserve'; she sent him two more summonses, the second ordering him to travel by litter if (as he claimed) he was ill. His old tutor Foxe, Cecil, and others all begged him to obey. The Norfolk gentry showed no sign of stirring on his behalf, according to reports from Lord Wentworth, the lord lieutenant. At last Norfolk decided to submit, and sent an urgent message to his brother-in-law's headquarters at Topcliffe Castle, begging him to call the rising off, 'if not it should cost him his head, for that he was going to court'.[81] He asked Westmorland to stay at home even if the Percys rose. On 1 October Norfolk was placed in royal custody; by the 11th he was safely in the Tower – occupying the same room in the Constable's lodgings his grandfather had had for six years. Twenty of his men were rounded up, and Pembroke, Arundel and others placed under house arrest.

Elizabeth and Cecil had all along realized that the chief military danger came from the 'inly-working North', and that it would become acute only if the North rose in conjunction with Norfolk and other members of the southern aristocracy. As Camden later put it, 'all the whole court hung in suspense and fear lest [Norfolk] should break forth into rebellion; and it was determined [so the report went] if he did so, forthwith to put the Queen of Scots to death'. Once Norfolk was under arrest, it was important to reassure other powerful men in the South that this was not the beginning of a purge. Elizabeth sent letters to all lord lieutenants that Norfolk would not be treated harshly, the Queen 'being loath to have such a noble man abused with untrue reports'. Some 200,000 men had now reported for musters; and in the autumn all JPs were individually called to declare their obedience to the Act of Uniformity. Cecil was also working on an idea for all substantial Protestant gentlemen to form an Association, swearing a special oath to give their lives in Elizabeth's defence. On 16 October he summarized for her eyes, using his characteristic academic method, the situation as he saw it:

The Queen of Scots is and shall always be a dangerous person to your estate. Yet there are degrees of danger. If you would marry, it should be less; whilst you do not, it will increase. If her person be restrained, here or in Scotland, it will be less, if at liberty, greater. If by law she cannot marry while Bothwell lives, the peril is less, if free to marry the greater. If found guilty of her husband's murder, she shall be less a person perilous, if passed over in silence the scar of the murder will wear out and the danger greater. Now for the Duke, whilst unmarried his hope to match with her will continue; if he marry elsewhere (most necessary) all pernicious intents depending on him shall cease. If charged but not convicted of treason, his credit shall increase. I cannot see how his acts are within the compass of treason. Whereupon I am bold to wish your Majesty would show your intent only to inquire into the fact, and not to speak of it as treason.[82]

Elizabeth's problem, in short, was that the evidence against Norfolk was not strong enough to persuade a jury of his peers to convict him. But her freedom of action would obviously be greater if the Northern menace were dealt with. The question was: would it be more prudent to seek to avoid a confrontation with the Northern peers, or to bring the potential rebellion to a head and crush it once and for all? The two Northern Earls were not much keener on a fight than Norfolk; indeed it was his sister, Lady Westmorland, who played Lady Macbeth; when the Duke's message to stay the rising was received, she exclaimed to her husband: 'What a simple man the Duke is, to begin a matter and not go through with it!' Protestants held all the key government posts in the North, but the chief of them, Sussex, as a friend of Norfolk's, was not entirely trusted by Elizabeth, though, as he complained to Cecil, he had 'always hitched his staff to her door'. He admitted he had 'always loved [Norfolk] above all others'; but 'if he should ever forget his duty, which God forbid, I will never slack my service, and thereof her Majesty may be most assured'.[83] He was more closely in touch than the court with the actual feeling in the North; he was aware both of the timidity of the Earls and of their inability to agree on a common, and convincing, political programme. His advice was to avoid anything which might provoke them, or at least to wait until the fine autumn weather was over; the local members of his Council shared this view. As one of them, Sir Thomas Gargrave, put it to Cecil, on 2 November, it was preferable 'to nourish quiet until the winter, when the nights are longer, the ways worse, and the waters begin to slip their passage'.[84]

But Elizabeth, rightly in my view, chose to resolve the issue, and instructed Sussex to command the Earls, on their allegiance, to come to court. She was assembling massive military forces in the South and Midlands, was worried about their cost and their loyalty, and was painfully aware that to keep them inactive was to invite trouble; moreover, delay would increase the risk of foreign intervention. For the first fortnight in November, after Sussex had carried out her instructions, it was uncertain whether the Earls would obey or rise. They, too, had their men collected together. On 12 November, Lady

Westmorland appears to have clinched the debate by swearing that, if all dispersed to their homes, 'We and our country were shamed for ever, that now in the end we should seek holes to creep into.' On the 14th they rode to Durham and took it, and solemn High Mass was once more celebrated in the cathedral. This marked the transformation of the rising from a political to a purely religious basis. As such, it ensured a higher degree of popular support in the far north, but robbed the cause of a national appeal and devalued the role of the Queen of Scots. The ultimate success of the movement hinged on the ability of the Earls to place her on the throne. But her claims did not figure in their official proclamation, issued at Ripon on 16 November, which was addressed to members of 'the old Catholic religion'. There were few such south of the Trent.

Cecil's reports numbered the rebels at no more than 1,000 horse and 400 foot. He agreed with Sussex that 'the suppression of this rebellion lieth in celerity', and that the best course was to deploy a compact, well-armed force of local recruits from Yorkshire. Sussex thought he could make do with 1,000 horse, 500 pikemen and 500 arquebusiers – indeed, he would settle for 500 horse if they came quickly. But the northern musters reflected the unwillingness of the locals to fight on either side, or rather their inclination to insure with both. Sadler, from York, reported:

> There be not in all this country ten gentlemen that do favour and allow of her Majesty's proceedings in the cause of religion, and the common people be ignorant, full of superstition and altogether blinded with the old popish doctrine ... if the father be on this side, the son is on the other, and one brother with us, the other with the rebels.[85]

As a result, four large forces were organized south of the Trent to render assistance. Some 15,000 troops were assigned to defend Elizabeth in the Windsor area. Warwick was to command the Midlands forces, and Clinton those of Lincolnshire and East Anglia; Hunsdon was sent north immediately with a striking force, to be joined later by Clinton and Warwick. The co-ordinator seems to have been Leicester, who had no patience with Sussex's view that the Earls could be disposed of by a small professional force, and who was determined on a glorious and massive campaign north of the Trent. By the time, however, that these national forces were en route, the rebellion was virtually over. The Earls had not dared to attack York, but by-passed it, reaching Selby on 24 November. This was within striking distance of Tutbury, where they understood Mary to be held. But on the next day she was removed further south to Coventry, and meanwhile Hunsdon's force had come within range. The Earls then decided to return north, and their army promptly melted away. By 11 December Sussex was able to take the offensive, and four days later the Earls, who had given a unique demonstration of combined political and military ineptitude, decided the game was up and rode for the Scottish border.[86]

The only real fighting, indeed, took place almost as an afterthought. Leonard Dacre, the discomfited suitor in the case of the Dacre inheritance, had been at court when the rising began; he had ridden north to help to suppress it, and had in fact been commended by Sussex for doing so. After the Earls had fled, and any semblance of a cause was already lost, he suddenly seized Greystoke Castle, and other houses of the Dacre lordship, fortified his castle at Naworth, and summoned 3,000 border ruffians to his aid. He rejected an order from Lord Scrope to come to Carlisle and discuss what on earth he was trying to do. In mid-February, Hunsdon received instructions to take him by force, and a week later Dacre's men were dispersed in a cavalry action fought on the River Cleth – as Hunsdon put it, 'the proudest charge, upon my shot, that ever I saw'. It was the only battle fought on English soil during the whole of Elizabeth's reign, and it brought from Elizabeth a characteristic tribute. Cecil had drafted her a formal letter of congratulation to Hunsdon. At the foot, she added in her own hand:

I doubt much, my Harry, whether that the victory were given me more joyed me, or that you were by God appointed the instrument of my glory; and I assure you for my country's good, the first might suffice, but for my heart's contentation, the second more pleased me ... I intend to make this journey somewhat to increase your livelihood, that you may not say to yourself, *perditur quod factum est ingrato.*

Your loving kinswoman, Elizabeth R.[87]

This was the personal touch, the grand and rare unbending into familiarity, which even her most hardened servants found irresistible.

After the Earls had fled, the methods used to pacify the North have brought upon Elizabeth's head much censure from modern historians. Thus, one writes: 'Compared with the savage reactions of Elizabeth and Burghley, James II and Judge Jeffreys acted with compassion and restraint in their handling of the Monmouth Rebellion.'[88] This is an exaggeration. Elizabeth herself seems to have given no explicit instructions about the treatment of the rebels. Cecil drafted two memos on the subject, urging a degree of severity. Suspects should be 'pinched with lack of food or pain of imprisonment' into betraying their friends. All clergymen and secular office-holders who participated in the rising were to be harshly treated. Rebels without property should be hanged in the nearest market place to their birth, and serving-men of the Earls and other gentry near their masters' houses. But Cecil seems to have been chiefly concerned with exacting the maximum fines, to pay for the cost of suppression. He was thus opposed to martial law, unless essential, since this might mean escheated property would escape the crown.[89] How far these recommendations were approved by the Queen, and became official policy, is not clear. The punishments were carried out by the men on the spot, operating 400 miles from court, and in great haste and confusion. It seems that about 750 men were hanged, after courts-martial – so Cecil's advice was not followed in this respect.[90] Others were tried at special sessions in York, Durham and Carlisle, and in Church courts. Many clergy were deprived; 2,000 lesser fry were pardoned and fined, but many were found to be too poor to pay, and so got off. Northumberland was eventually handed over by the Scots, and executed. Westmorland got abroad and spent the rest of his life in exile. His wife, curiously enough, went unpunished, and eventually got a state pension. Many estates were confiscated, and carved up among leading figures in the royal armies. This, indeed, occasioned a good deal of bickering among the victors. Sussex and Hunsdon, reflecting Elizabeth's views, were in favour of leniency. It was Clinton and Warwick, and their bloodthirsty and grasping captains, who behaved with savagery. They had done no fighting, and had been late arrivals, but they made up for it by plundering and hanging. Sussex complained bitterly to Cecil that they 'have driven all the cattle of the country and ransomed the people in such miserable sort and made such open and common spoil as the like I think was never heard of, putting no difference between the good and the bad'. Hunsdon thought it was monstrous that Clinton and Warwick should carry off the prizes while Sussex, the real hero, should go unthanked:

> If the Earl of Sussex had not been where he was neither York nor Yorkshire had been at [Elizabeth's] discretion, and then the lusty southern army would not have returned laden with such spoils, nor put their noses over Doncaster Bridge. But others beat the bush, and they have the birds.[91]

Elizabeth's first concern was to ensure that the power of the independent-minded northern gentry was broken, and this, certainly, was achieved. Some went into exile; others became safe, absentee landlords in the South. The process took some time, but by the end of her reign there were no great men left in the North. Some lesser peers survived; the rest of the land fell into the hands of carpetbaggers, bureaucrats, lawyers and loyal local landowners of medium rank – all ultimately dependent on the crown.[92] As for the common people, Elizabeth showed her anxiety for a policy of reconciliation, especially over religion. The draft of a proclamation, to be read out in churches, put her point of view admirably. Parliament, she said, had given her the task of providing for the government of the Church, through archbishops, bishops and other ministers, 'according to the ecclesiastical ancient policy of the realm'. But she indignantly denied there was 'some general severity intended by us and our ministers against them only in respect of opinion in religion, when no such thing did appear or was any wise by us meant or thought of'. On the contrary:

> We affirm that we never had any meaning or intent that our subjects should be troubled or molested by examination or inquisition in any matter, either of their faith ... or for matters of ceremonies, as long as they shall in their outward conversation show themselves quiet and not manifestly repugnant to the laws of the realm ...[93]

At all events, this aspect of her policy was successful too. Elizabeth had noted that the rebellion showed the active and irreconcilable Catholic nobility in a bad light. They had stirred up the people without cause, deserted them without a fight, and left them to face retribution. Evidently the Earls had been bitterly disappointed by the response of the northern Catholics, most of whom had shown sympathy but remained inert.[94] Elizabeth saw – and this became an important element in her religious policy – that when it came to the point those of the 'ancient faith' were better Englishmen than Catholics.

The suppression of the Northern rising immeasurably strengthened Elizabeth's position. It confirmed her judgment that it was preferable to face the risk of a religious-inspired revolt, and crush it, than to allow the threat to remain under the surface. Henceforth, she never had to fear the emergence of a regional power-base, co-operating with her foreign enemies. England was now solid; and the Counter-Reformation would have to turn to Ireland to raise men against her. Yet the Northerners' defeat left a number of problems un-resolved, notably what to do with Mary Queen of Scots. In the aftermath of the Northern rebellion, Scotland had again dissolved into chaos with the assassination of the Regent Moray on 23 January 1570. While the bulk of the Scots nobility supported the infant King James, a Marian party formed under her former Secretary, Maitland, and the Scots despatched raiding parties across the border. In April 1570, Sussex was ordered to carry out retaliatory action, and he reported at the end of the month that he had destroyed all fortified residences over a large area of southern Scotland. But was Elizabeth to continue to recognize Mary, or accept James as King? On 29 April she attended a full

meeting of the Council, and told them 'that she herself was free from any determined resolution and that she would first hear their advice and thereupon make
choice of what she should think meetest for her honour'.[95] The Council was
divided, with the old aristocrats, plus Leicester, favouring a pro-Marian policy,
while the 'scribes', such as Cecil, Bacon and Mildmay (reinforced by the advice
of Sussex), wanted to support the King's party, now led by the Earl of Morton.
Elizabeth was divided, too, in her own mind – so much so that, at one stage,
Bacon threatened to boycott the Council, on the ground that she did not recognize good advice when she got it.[96] She drew up, as the price of her support for
Mary, a severe set of terms which Mary was to accept; Cecil was dispatched to
Chatsworth, where the Scots Queen was currently held, to secure her com-
pliance. This, for what it was worth, was eventually forthcoming in October.
But in the meantime Elizabeth sent material assistance to the King's party, and
kept it in play.

So far she had successfully postponed any real decision on what to do with
Mary, and despite much pressure from various quarters, had kept the matter
entirely in her own hands. But her options were beginning to narrow. On
25 May 1570, the feast of Corpus Christi, the Papal Bull, *Regnans in Excelsis*,
was found nailed to the door of the Bishop of London's house in St Paul's
Churchyard. It excommunicated Elizabeth, and absolved her subjects from their
allegiance. John Fenton, who put it there, was arrested, confessed on the rack,
and was duly tried and executed on the scene of his act – as the Spanish ambassador put it, '*Le hicieron quartos vivo con grandissima crueldad.*' The episode of the
Bull was curious in a number of respects. It was the last time the papacy used
the old medieval methods to bring a heterodox monarch to book. Pius v was
inspired to issue it by reports, which were already hopelessly out of date, that
the English Catholics were rising; it was in fact published by the Papal
Chancery on 25 February, the very day Hunsdon finally crushed Dacre's forces.
No news of the Bull reached England, and Fenton's gesture was the first the
government knew of its existence. Elizabeth wrongly assumed that it had been
issued with the full approval of the Kings of France and Spain, as the prelude to
joint intervention. In fact they knew nothing about it either, and both were
furious to discover that the Pope had taken such a decisive step without consulting them. The Bull was confused and mendacious (for instance, it implied that
the papacy had never recognized Elizabeth's title, whereas in fact both Paul iv
and Pius iv had done so without qualification), and as a piece of international
diplomacy it was woefully inept.[97] Yet it was a watershed all the same, for it
brought to an end Elizabeth's efforts to reach a *modus vivendi* with the papacy,
and supplied – for the future if not for the present – specific ideological grounds

both for domestic subversion and foreign invasion. Despite Elizabeth's wishes, England was being slowly pushed into the arena of international religious conflict.

The Bull, too, altered the parliamentary balance at Westminster, for it encouraged the Protestants to adopt a posture of aggressive defence, and demand harsher treatment of the Catholics – not least Mary of Scotland. The Puritan faction, with its strong flavour of Calvinist theory in both Church and state, was now beginning to organize itself, among ministers of religion as well as MPs. The 1569 rebellion had been suppressed by raising forced loans, and as early as February 1570 Cecil had urged Elizabeth to call parliament to provide a subsidy. She delayed for a year, but by the spring of 1571 the demands of the Treasury were imperative, and parliament met on 2 April. Its mood was strongly loyalist: in deference to the Queen it declined to discuss her marriage at all, and pushed the succession question into the background.[98] But in the light of the Bull, the Northern rising, and the activities of Norfolk and the Queen of Scots, it wanted the strongest possible measures against active Catholics and all forms of treason. In preparation for the parliament, Cecil had been created a peer, as Baron Burghley, on 25 February; this was to ensure the successful management of the Lords. Burghley evidently played his part well, as the Queen congratulated the Lords at the end of the session for their 'diligence, discretion and orderly proceedings'. Some of the Commons, by contrast, 'showed themselves audacious, arrogant and presumptuous'.[99] In particular, they were not satisfied by a new Treasons Bill, which the government had persuaded a very reluctant Elizabeth to present. This strengthened the hand of the executive against actual and potential traitors; the Commons tacked on to it an additional Bill which would, in effect, have made Mary retrospectively guilty of any treason against the Queen, and barred both her and her son from the succession. The linked Bills were passed by a Commons majority of 170–138. Elizabeth disliked this legislation not only because it interfered with the succession, but because she always felt that the ordinary Common and statute law gave her ample powers to deal with treason, and that any additional, and mandatory, punishments and definitions merely narrowed her freedom of action. As she said, 'we misliked it very much, being not of the mind to offer extremity or injury to any person'. She insisted on getting the Bill re-drafted to exclude the treason charges against heirs of those who, unwittingly or no, benefited from treason. The Commons, having gained half a point, accepted the compromise, and the parliament broke up in a mood of amity.

It would certainly have taken a different line if facts already in the possession of Elizabeth and Burghley had been disclosed publicly. While it was still sitting, the two, and their closest confidants, had been unravelling the first details of the Ridolfi Plot. Ridolfi had come under suspicion in the autumn of 1569, because of his known connections with the Bishop of Ross, Mary's factotum, and because of his handling of large sums of money. He had been confined to Walsingham's house, under surveillance, on 7 October. But he was evidently a plausible rogue, and had persuaded Walsingham that he would make a valuable double agent. On 11 November 1569 he had been released on a bond of £1,000; the bond was returned to him in January 1570, and in the following October Walsingham recommended him to Cecil for confidential work in Flanders.[100] Before Ridolfi finally left England on 25 March 1571, to arrange the Continental end of his conspiracy, he had an interview with Elizabeth at Greenwich and got from her what was termed a 'very favourable' passport. Essentially Ridolfi was a freelance contact-man, working for money, whose object was to co-ordinate the activities of those anxious to overthrow Elizabeth and replace her with Mary. He thus had dealings with Mary herself, Norfolk, the Pope, Alva (in the Low Countries) and Philip II. He had outlined his general scheme to the Pope as early as 1 September 1570. A month before, Elizabeth had allowed Norfolk to be transferred from the Tower to house-arrest in his town palace, the Charterhouse. There, on two occasions, Ridolfi had been smuggled in, and had talked with Norfolk in the Long Gallery. Despite his imprisonment, Norfolk had remained in contact with Mary, corresponding in cyphers placed in leather bottles. He listened to what Ridolfi had to say, but, characteristically, refused to write or sign anything. Instead, he committed the business to his secretary, William Barker, who was authorized to deal with the Bishop of Ross and Ridolfi. Evidently Norfolk felt that, so long as he himself committed nothing to writing, he could not be accused of treason. But Ross stated later that 'he heard the Duke so precisely affirm his contentation and agreement' to the proposals that he had, in effect, committed himself absolutely. Letters, in his name, and on behalf of the English Catholic nobility, were drafted for Ridolfi to carry to the Pope and Philip II. Philip was to supply, from Alva's army, 6,000 arquebusiers and 25 field-pieces; they would be landed at Harwich, where Norfolk would meet them, having raised 20,000 foot and 3,000 horse. The Duke declined to see the text of these letters, but agreed with their general sense. Ridolfi carried the letters to Alva, the Pope and Philip II in the summer of 1571. Only the Pope took him seriously. Alva dismissed him as a '*gran' parlaquina*', a 'babbler' – as he undoubtedly was – and Philip thought the scheme a fantasy. He received Ridolfi only because he had the Pope's backing.[101]

Yet Elizabeth and her government were bound to take the plot seriously when it came to light. Early in April 1571, while Ridolfi was still doing his rounds in Europe, a Catholic agent, Charles Bailly, was arrested at Dover when his luggage was found to contain prohibited books, and letters for Ross. Burghley had Bailly gaoled, and set a double-agent on to him in the cells. By this means, his communications with Ross, in cypher, were intercepted, and on the rack he betrayed the cypher. Ross was interrogated, then committed to the Bishop of Ely's custody in Holborn. By May Bailly was beginning to confess. More evidence was received early in the summer; after Ridolfi had called on the Grand Duke of Tuscany, and told him of his plans, the Grand Duke immediately informed Elizabeth. Burghley advised Elizabeth not to go on summer progress, but she insisted, and indeed even stayed (on 24 August) at Norfolk's house in Walden, Essex, where representations were made to her, by his staff, that he be given full liberty. Two days later, a bag of money, containing 300 French gold crowns, and 300 English angels, plus cypher letters, was dispatched from Norfolk's London house for Mary's supporters in Scotland; an unwitting intermediary, one Thomas Browne, a Shrewsbury draper, was asked to carry the bag, and was told it contained £50. He thought it too heavy, broke the seal, and reported the matter to the authorities. This was the decisive link in the chain of evidence needed to implicate Norfolk. Elizabeth, furious to discover that Norfolk had been working against her even while she was a guest in his house, ordered that his secretaries, Barker and Higford, be arrested and racked. Higford admitted that the key to the cypher would be found in the Charterhouse, 'under a mat, hard by the window's side where the map of England doth hang'.[102] No cypher was found there but – far worse – a cyphered letter from Mary herself. On 7 September, Burghley had Sadler and Dr Thomas Wilson dragged out of bed in the middle of the night, and ordered them to escort Norfolk to the Tower:

> So, having prepared a foot-cloth nag for him, I, Sir Ralph Sadler, on the one side, and I, Dr Wilson, coming immediately after, with only our servants and friends accompanying us, he was betwixt four and five of the clock quietly brought into the Tower without any trouble, save a number of idle, rascal people, women, men, boys and girls, running about him, as the manner is, gazing at him.[103]

The same day Burghley discovered the cypher-key behind some tiles in the Charterhouse, and a letter from Mary to Ross, revealing Norfolk's close connection with the plot, was immediately decoded. Various of the Duke's books were found to contain letters and cyphers; another turned up under a tile on the roof. Barker and Higford told all they knew. Mary, confronted with the evidence, promptly washed her hands of Norfolk. She said she had only tried to get back her Scottish throne, and those who confessed she had attempted more 'were false villains and lied in their throats'. As for Norfolk, he was Elizabeth's subject, 'and for him she had nothing to say'. Ross claimed diplomatic immunity, but after the civil lawyers reported to Burghley that he had no case under international convention, he was threatened with torture and promptly blurted out all – and more than all. He told Dr Wilson that Mary was not fit for any husband, had poisoned her first, had been a party to the murder of her second, and would not have kept faith with Norfolk even if she had married him. Wilson reported this to Burghley, adding: 'Lord! what people are these! What a Queen! What an ambassador!'[104]

By 13 October, enough evidence had been collected for the Council to summon the Lord Mayor of London, and other dignitaries, to Star Chamber, inform them of the plot, and demonstrate that Norfolk was guilty. He himself wrote out a confession on 10 November, though he contrived to leave Ridolfi out of it. There was no great anxiety to bring Norfolk to trial, but as Hunsdon said, 'Her Majesty and he cannot continue in one realm.' A few days later Burghley drew up charges against him under thirteen heads. The most serious was Number Eleven, that he was 'principal counsellor and director to Ridolfi' to persuade Alva, Philip II and the Pope to invade the realm, 'and to have maintained the Scots Queen in this realm by force'. Of course he was not Ridolfi's 'principal counsellor and director', but he was certainly privy to his schemes and gave them his approval. Elizabeth felt most strongly about Charge One – 'The disclosing of the Queen Majesty's counsel when he was in commission at York, in favour of the Queen of Scots both to cover her faults and to further of her marriage'; this was his original betrayal of her trust, from which all else sprang. She also felt bitter about Charge Eight, his breaking of his word never again to have dealings with Mary. All the charges were true, though Five and Thirteen only technically so. Norfolk's partial confession further damaged him, not least among his fellow peers, since it contained flat lies which were exposed by other evidence.[105]

The first sign that Norfolk was doomed came in September when commissioners were empowered to inventory his goods and lands. His household was broken up and Kenninghall closed down. The usual Tudor vultures gathered to fatten on a traitor's possessions. Hunsdon consulted Burghley about being made keeper of the Charterhouse; he thought it too grand for him to 'ask it as a gift'. On 22 November, a preliminary hearing of the charges against Norfolk took place before Middlesex sessions, and a true bill was found. De Spes, the Spanish ambassador, was expelled on 13 December, and in the wake of his departure, it was discovered that one of his servants had been conspiring with two Englishmen, Mather and Berney, to murder Burghley. They, and others, were roped in, and the Tower was now fuller than at any time since the aftermath of the Wyatt rebellion. On 16 January 1572, Norfolk was tried in Westminster Hall, before Shrewsbury, as Lord High Steward, twenty-six peers, senior judges and members of the government. It lasted from 7.00 a.m. to 6.45 p.m., without a break; then, after an interval to consider the verdict, the peers reassembled at 8.00 p.m. to pronounce Norfolk's sentence; all gave verdicts against him. The atmosphere was painful: the peers plainly resented the manner in which Norfolk, the senior member of their order, had betrayed all his loyalties. He replied that, seeing the Lords had pronounced him unfit for their company, 'I trust shortly to be in a better.' Shrewsbury, with tears in his eyes, gave sentence:

> Thou shall be had from hence to the Tower of London, from thence thou shalt be drawn through the midst of the streets of London to Tyburn, the place of execution. There thou shalt be hanged, and, being alive, thou shalt be cut down quick; thy bowels shall be taken forth of thy body and burnt before thy face; thy head shall be smitten off; thy body shalt be divided into four parts or quarters; the head and the quarters to be set up where it shall please the Queen's Majesty to appoint; and the Lord have mercy upon thee.

There was, of course, no question of this sentence being carried out in all its savagery; even common criminals were rarely cut down quick, and the Duke's rank entitled him to the axe. The question was: would Elizabeth execute him at all? She alone was in favour of mercy; on four occasions she was brought warrants to sign for the sentence to be carried out, and then cancelled them. Two letters from Burghley to Walsingham show her state of mind in the early months of 1572. Thus, on 23 January:

> The Queen's Majesty hath been always a merciful lady and by mercy she hath taken more herein than by justice, and yet she thinks that she is more beloved in doing herself harm.

Again, on 11 February:

> I cannot write you what is the inward cause of the stay of the Duke of Norfolk's death, only I find her Majesty diversely disposed. Some time when she speaketh of her danger, she concludeth that justice should be done, another time she speaketh of his nearness of blood, of his superiority of honour, etc, she stayeth. As upon Saturday she signed a warrant ... for his execution on Monday, and so all preparations were made ... and concourse

of many thousands yesterday in the morning, but their coming was answered by another, ordinary execution ... And the cause of the disappointment was this. Suddenly, on Sunday, late in the night, the Queen's Majesty sent for me and entered into a great misliking that the Duke should die the next day ... and said she would have a new warrant made that night to the sheriffs, to forebear until they should hear further. And so they did.[106]

The 'ordinary execution' thus substituted for Norfolk's was that of Berney and Mather, thrown to the hangmen, as it were, to appease the London Protestant mob. But on 20 March Elizabeth fell seriously ill – gastroenteritis again, after eating bad fish. Burghley and Leicester together spent three days and nights at her bedside, and the upshot was that parliament was hastily summoned, the writs going out a week later, for a session on 8 May.[107] Once parliament met, Norfolk was finished, for he, in turn, had to be thrown to the wolves, to save a yet greater person, Mary of Scotland, from trial and execution.

Indeed, the Commons made its feelings plain from the first day. Bell, elected Speaker, announced in his opening address: 'This error was crept into the heads of a number: that there was a person in this land whom no law could touch.' The business of Mary was 'the great cause', 'the great matter'. On 15 May the central debate began with a rousing speech by Thomas Norton, calling for the execution of both Norfolk and Mary; when he sat down there were strident cries of 'Yea, Yea!' Only one member, Arthur Hall, spoke against the proposal, and 'The house misliked so much of his talk that with shuffling of feet and hawking they had well nigh barred him to be heard.' The next day the question was moved whether he was fit to be a Member – the Protestant majority supporting freedom of speech principally for themselves. A motion was pressed for a Bill of Attainder against Mary, 'by the whole voice of the House'; she should be proceeded against 'with all possible speed ... in the highest degree of treason, and therein to touch her as well in life as in title and dignity'.[108]

MPs were not just thirsting for blood. They genuinely felt that the Queen's lenity might imperil their lives. George Ireland said, 'for his part he would as lief be hanged in resisting the Queen of Scots as hanged thereafter'. They were thinking of a situation in which Elizabeth might die, or be assassinated, and Mary and Norfolk would sweep to power. Norton, too, spoke of the risk they would be 'hanged thereafter', if traitors were not deterred by severity. He thought the best course was to press for the immediate execution of Norfolk, which would fatally weaken Mary's party: 'Those that labour to save the Duke do it surely with intent to be themselves saved by the Duke.' Robin Snagge spoke of 'a most dangerous state, when traitors live more surely than true men'.

It says a lot for Elizabeth's courage and determination that she tried, at first, to resist this virtually unanimous clamour on all points. But slowly she was brought to recognize that the Duke would have to be sacrificed if Mary were to be saved. A huge dossier survives in which everyone of importance in the régime – bishops, peers, judges, MPs – set down their reasons, for presentation to the Queen, why Norfolk should die. No senior figure argued to the contrary: Elizabeth was faced with the entire Protestant consensus of the nation. On Wednesday, 28 May, at 8.00 a.m., she saw a joint committee of the Houses, which had come to press their case. She sent them away unsatisfied, but hints were dropped that she would give way over Norfolk if the agitation for the immediate execution of Mary were dropped. The House of Commons responded. Mary might be, as Peter Wentworth put it, 'the most notorious whore in all the world' or, as St Leger called her, 'the monstrous and huge dragon and mass of the earth, the Queen of Scots'. But since Elizabeth would not yet move against her, let the House, to quote St Leger again, proceed 'with the execution of the roaring lion: I mean the Duke of Norfolk'.[109] On Saturday, 31 May, the debate concluded; the House refrained from a formal vote, out of deference to the Queen, but its message was clear, and she accepted it. That afternoon she gave final orders for his execution, and the erection of a scaffold. On the Sunday evening, the next day, she herself paid a visit to the Tower, to see that seemly and dignified preparations had been made: the Lieutenant of the Tower, Skipwith, noted in a report to Burghley, 'When I had written this much, the Queen came.'[110] She did not see Norfolk. He had long since made his final dispositions, asking the Queen for his children to be committed to Burghley's care, and later thanking her for granting this request. On Monday morning, 2 June, 'straight after 7 o'clock', England's only duke was executed; 'his head was at one chop cut off and showed to all the people'.[111] His final words had been conciliatory: 'For men to suffer death in this place is no new thing, though since the beginning of our most gracious Queen's reign I am the first, and God grant I may be the last.'

To this Elizabeth would certainly have said 'Amen'. Indeed, Norfolk's execution, though she recognized it was inevitable, strengthened her determination to keep the fate of Mary entirely in her own hands. Parliament passed a Bill (26 June) barring Mary from the succession, as an alternative to executing her; Elizabeth vetoed it. There is no doubt that she so acted against the will of all her councillors. As Burghley put it to Walsingham:

All persons shall behold our follies, as they may think, imputing these lacks and errors to some of us that are accounted inward counsellors, where indeed the fault is not. And yet they must be so suffered and so imputed for saving the honour of the highest.

When parliament broke up, he noted dolefully:

All that we had laboured for and had with full consent brought to fashion, I mean a law to make the Scottish Queen unable and unworthy to wear the crown, was by her Majesty neither assented to nor rejected, but deferred until the Feast of All Saints.[112]

Elizabeth herself was inclined to take a more optimistic view. The events of 1569–72 had greatly strengthened her internal position. The execution of Norfolk, disagreeable though it had been for her, had shown that no one was above the law. Mary was in a different category because her death was certain to evoke an international response, and Elizabeth was by no means yet convinced it was worth it. She had, of course, no personal sympathy for Mary, whom she believed far more culpable, and indeed wicked, than the foolish Duke of Norfolk. But she still hoped to keep England at peace; and she trusted in the English people to render the worst schemes of Mary and her allies impotent. Indeed, it was almost certainly at the end of this parliament, in the early summer of 1572, that she set her convictions down in sonnet form, later published in her own lifetime in Puttenham's *Arte of English Poesie*:

> For falsehood now doth flow, and subjects' faith doth ebb;
> Which would not be if Reason ruled, or Wisdom weaved the web . . .
> The Daughter of Debate, that eke discord doth sow,
> Shall reap no gain where former rule hath taught still peace to grow.
> No foreign banish'd wight shall anchor in this port;
> Our realm it brooks no stranger's force, let them elsewhere resort.
> Our rusty sword with rest shall first his edge employ,
> To poll their tops that seek such change, and gape for joy.[113]

The verse is little more than doggerel, but it has memorable phrases, and it expresses her policy and attitudes admirably. England would pursue peace, but need not fear war. At heart Elizabeth was always a simple patriot, though not a simple-minded one. She often took a far more sophisticated view of where true patriotism lay than her more alarmist, and aggressive-minded, ministers.

Indeed, in this instance, it can be argued powerfully that Elizabeth's determination to keep Mary alive not only avoided the near-certainty of war, but led to a progressive clearing of the international horizon. Now that the domestic front was secure, Elizabeth was still faced with three theatres of danger, each interrelated to the others: Scotland, France and Spain. The key really lay in

France, for if the House of Valois adopted a posture of benevolent neutrality, and still more active friendship, towards England, there could be no question of Scotland constituting a serious menace, and little chance that Spain alone would lead the Counter-Reformation crusade against Elizabeth. Since the breach with Spain over the treasure-ships, England had moved closer to France, and from 1570 negotiations were undertaken to explore the possibility of a marriage between Elizabeth and Charles IX's brother, the Duke of Anjou, or an Anglo-French diplomatic league, or both.

It was at this point that Francis Walsingham first began to play a leading role in Elizabethan government. He seems to have been born in 1532, the only son of a Kentish gentleman from the junior branch of an old Norfolk family. Like Cecil, he had studied under Cheke at Cambridge, and he had made many connections with the Elizabethan Protestant establishment. His stepfather was a Carey, related to Elizabeth herself, and his brother-in-law was Sir Walter Mildmay, Chancellor of the Exchequer. In some ways Walsingham was the best-educated and most sophisticated of the Queen's servants. He spent the years 1550–2 travelling in Europe, learning modern languages, and after a spell at Gray's Inn, he moved to Padua, the most liberal of the Continental universities, where he served as Consularius to the English students in the Faculty of Civil Law. He spoke wonderful French and Italian, and had a good grasp of German and Spanish; and his knowledge of international procedures in diplomacy and law made him one of the most accomplished envoys of his day. He may have sat in parliament as early as 1559; he was certainly there in 1563, occupying Throckmorton's old seat at Lyme Regis. Thereafter, until his death, he was regularly a member of the House (except when abroad), though he was by temperament more a government servant than a Commons man. He married twice, the second time (in 1568) to an Isle of Wight heiress, who brought him Carisbrooke Priory; and the same year, aged thirty-six, he emerged as Cecil's confidential lieutenant, in charge of secret service work and the production of government pamphlets. In the summer of 1570 Elizabeth sent him on a special mission to the French court, and at the end of the year he was confirmed as English ambassador in Paris.[114]

Although Walsingham had been brought to the fore by Cecil, he was in his opinions much closer to the Protestant activism which Leicester had adopted. Where the Queen and Cecil were essentially empiricists, making minor adjustments to policy as needs dictated, Walsingham tended to think in the long term, and evolve ambitious, even grandiose, projects. He was convinced that the old Burgundian alliance was dead, and Spanish hostility certain; the problem as he saw it was how to meet this hostility without adding to the power of France.

'Let her Majesty well assure herself', he wrote to Burghley in June 1571, 'that Spain will never forget the injuries they have received, as shall well appear when opportunities for revenge shall be offered. I wish, therefore, they were reduced to that state they had more will than ability to execute their malice.' Spain would attack sooner or later, he confided to Leicester the next month. England must act with France in the Low Countries, but she should ensure that the Protestant provinces remained independent and allied with the German Protestant states, to balance any increment in French power.[115] The Prince of Orange was the man to back, and in the summer of 1571 he supported the plan, called 'the enterprise of Flanders', which Orange's brother, Louis Count of Nassau, put to Charles IX – a Franco-English-German assault on Spain, to partition the Netherlands three ways. 'I do not doubt', he wrote to Leicester

> but that your Lordship will do what you may so to deal with her Majesty as that some of the Count's requests may take place, whereby the fire that is now akindling may grow a flame and we take comfort from the heat thereof . . . The proud Spaniard (whom God hath long used for the rod of his wrath), I see great hope that they will now cast him into the fire, that he may know what it is to serve against God.[116]

From this it can be seen that Walsingham was, to some extent, an ideologist in politics; as he once put it, 'I wish God's glory and next the Queen's safety.' But he was also a disciplined functionary, with a high sense of personal honesty, and he always faithfully carried out Elizabeth's mandates, even when he dis-agreed with them vehemently: as he said when he departed for Paris, 'I left my private passions behind me.'

During 1571 it became apparent that Elizabeth was not serious about the Anjou marriage. In the first place she insisted that the Duke, known to be a zealous Catholic, would not be allowed to hear Mass, as her husband, even in secret. She said this was a matter of her personal conscience (an evident lie) and when Burghley argued with her on the point, she shifted her grounds, and said the Mass would offend her 'faithful subjects'. The moment any progress was made on the religious issue, she raised fresh difficulties. Burghley gives a vignette of her in a letter to Walsingham dated 5 June 1571:

> And so with some long laborious persuasions her Majesty was induced to agree that the articles [of marriage] be made ready and showed . . . But ere I could finish them I was commanded to conclude them with a request to have Calais restored, a matter so inconvenient to bring forth a marriage as indeed I thought it meant to procure a breach.[117]

As, of course, it was. Elizabeth always used what Burghley called 'the toy of Calais' to frustrate plans to marry her to a Frenchman. She was relieved to hear, early in 1572, that Catherine de Medici insisted that her son be allowed to hear Mass openly, as reported by Sir Thomas Smith, who had been sent to join Walsingham in Paris. 'Why Madame,' retorted Smith angrily to Catherine, 'then he may require also the four orders of friars, monks, canons, pilgrimages, pardons, oil and cream, reliques, and all such trumperies!' This was the end of the Anjou project, and when it was suggested that his younger brother, Alençon, who was less of a zealot, might do as well, Elizabeth immediately raised personal objections: he was too young, and too small. Burghley said he was the same height as himself. Elizabeth snorted: 'Say rather the height of your grandson.'[118]

Nevertheless, Walsingham and Smith pressed ahead with the plan for a league. Here Elizabeth proved much more flexible. The English wanted the treaty to include a clause (known as the *etiamsi religionis causa* clause) under which both countries contracted to come to each other's assistance, even if attacked on religious grounds. The French were reluctant to agree to this publicly, and Elizabeth was eventually persuaded to accept a 'letter close' from King Charles, which embodied the promise, and to omit it from the text; she also compromised on the Scottish clauses, under which the English and the French agreed to work jointly towards a solution of the Scots problem. The final treaty, signed at Blois on 19 April 1572, made no mention of Mary Queen of Scots, and no provision for her welfare: an Anglo-French commission was to reconcile the warring factions in Scotland, and the English were to be allowed to invade if Elizabeth's enemies sought refuge in Scottish territory.

These provisions prepared the way for a favourable settlement in Scotland. The King James faction, led by Morton, and the Marian faction, led by Maitland, were still fighting when the Treaty of Blois was signed. The Anglo-French commissioners duly arranged an armistice in the autumn of 1572, by which time the Marians were virtually confined to Edinburgh Castle. After it expired, early in 1573, most of Mary's remaining supporters outside Edinburgh deserted her, and in April Elizabeth was persuaded to authorize Sir William Drury, Marshal of Berwick, to move north with a siege-train. On 17 May he began the bombardment of the castle, and it surrendered at the end of the month. Maitland was found dead in his room; Kirkaldy, the commander of the garrison, was hanged, and the Marian party was dispersed. Strictly speaking, the English intervention broke the Treaty of Blois, but the spirit in which it was negotiated made it certain that the French would not intervene: they had abandoned Mary as virtually a lost cause. Henceforth, Elizabeth's problem in Scotland was how to control the government of the young King, something which could be accomplished by the prudent distribution of quite small sums of money.

The other positive provisions of the Treaty of Blois remained dead letters. There was, indeed, a real risk that the Anglo-French understanding might be shattered by the massacre of the Huguenots which took place in Paris on St Bartholomew's Day, 24 August 1572. Walsingham himself was threatened and he reported angrily to the Council: 'considering how things presently stand, I think it less peril to live with [the French] as enemies than as friends.'[119] The slaughter horrified English opinion, especially in the south-east. Huge indignation meetings were held in London. Indeed, the Bishop of London asked Burghley to advise the Queen to have Mary's head cut off instantly, to appease public wrath. But Elizabeth kept her temper and her judgment. The crime revolted all her insular instincts; it was the kind of senseless state violence, compounded by treachery, that she found most abhorrent. But she was not prepared to give way to sentiment, lose a valuable ally, and so again expose her flank to Spanish enmity. She refused Walsingham's request for his immediate recall: 'it cannot, without some note of the breach of amity, be done'. She declined, at first, to receive the French embassy which came with an explanation of the episode; but, three days later, on 8 September, she saw them at Woodstock. The accounts of their reception, by Fénelon and Burghley, differ on some details, but it is clear that her mood was chilly, rather than angry; and there is no truth in the traditional version that she and the court were dressed in deep mourning. She received Fénelon in silence, advanced to meet him, and then drew him into a window seat. According to the French account, she expressed the hope that their King would clear himself in the eyes of the world. Burghley attributes to her much stronger words: 'she could not allow the manner of cruelty used in any kingdom or government . . . If the King shall not use his power to make such amends for so much blood so horribly shed, God who seeth the hearts of all, princes as others, will show His justice in time and place.'[120] Elizabeth, in fact, took the sensible line that, while making her feelings plain, she was bound, as a matter of form, to accept the official explanation provided by a friendly government, and exert her influence to protect Huguenot interests. This could be accomplished more effectively by diplomatic pressure than by displays of public indignation. Fénelon got the point. 'I can assure you, Madame,' he reported to Catherine de Medici, 'that the late accident hath wounded the Queen and her subjects so deeply that only a very skilful surgeon and a very sovereign balm can effect a remedy.' France responded, indeed, by acquiescing in Elizabeth's handling of Scottish affairs; and Elizabeth made a reciprocal gesture by sending the Earl of Worcester to represent her at the christening of Charles ix's daughter.

She had good reason to maintain the understanding with France despite the emotion aroused by the massacre. One of the objects of the Treaty of Blois, from her point of view, was to exert pressure on Spain to end the breach with England. St Bartholomew's came at a time when Philip ii was beginning to nibble at the bait, and by keeping cool and preserving an outward front of amity with France, Elizabeth persuaded him to swallow it. In October 1572 Antonio de Guaras, who had been acting as unofficial Spanish agent in London, came to her with proposals for an Anglo-Spanish rapprochement, and a personal letter from Alva. This was what she had been waiting for. In November she authorized Burghley to draft heads of agreement, and in January 1573 Alva, on Philip's behalf, accepted them. A provisional agreement was initialled by both parties on 5 April 1573, and commercial trade and contacts resumed.[121] In July 1574, Mendoza arrived with powers to negotiate a wide-ranging treaty, and on 28 August, during Elizabeth's summer progress, it was signed with some solemnity at Bristol. The Spanish claim was set at £89,076, the English at £68,076, leaving England with £21,000 to pay – a very advantageous settlement from Elizabeth's viewpoint. During the following months, further agreements were reached on the position of English Catholic refugees in Flanders, on English merchants trading with Spanish territories, and other vexed matters. As an ocular demonstration of the new understanding, the Spanish fleet paid a friendly visit to Portsmouth and the Isle of Wight in October 1575.[122]

Thus, from the desperate days of 1569, the Elizabethan state had sailed into comparatively sunny waters. How much of the credit should go to Burghley, and how much to Elizabeth herself, is a matter of opinion. Certainly he supplied the detailed expertise, and the constant energetic hard work, needed to promote these diplomatic ventures. Often he had to bring relentless pressure on Elizabeth to act, even on policies to which she had already agreed in principle. But often, again, her hesitations and her dislike of precipitancy played a positive role. And there can be no doubt that the main lines of policy reflected her deepest convictions. She had not been afraid to act, when to do so was prudent and necessary. But she had refused to be stampeded into an ideological war and had placed above any other consideration – save that of absolute national security – the need for reconciliation with her opponents at home and abroad. At the heart of her evasiveness and vacillation, there was a purposeful inner consistency: the search for domestic and international stability. By pursuing it steadily, she had restored a high degree of national unity, removed the threat from

Scotland, and reached an amicable *modus vivendi* with her two powerful neighbours on the Continent.

These were solid gains; nor were they unappreciated by the mass of Elizabeth's people. She was now beginning to be recognized, and not only in England, as a ruler of exceptional sagacity and prudence. From the early 1570s, as Camden relates, the people began to celebrate the anniversary of her accession, 17 November, as a public holiday:

> their Golden Day, as they termed it, [when] all good men throughout England joyfully triumphed, and with thanksgivings, sermons in churches, multiplied prayers, joyful ringing of bells, running at tilt, and festival mirth, began to celebrate the seventeenth day of November ... which, in testimony of their affectionate love towards her, they never ceased to observe as long as she lived.[123]

A special service was drawn up by Elizabeth herself for the annual celebration, which from 1576 was added to the rota of Holy Days. Being a realist, she chose for the Second Lesson a passage from the 13th chapter of St Paul's Epistle to the Romans. It was one she knew by heart; it expressed a good deal of her political philosophy; and she picked it to remind her people that the felicity they enjoyed was not fortuitous. It rested, and must continue to rest, on the principles of hierarchy and obedience, the true foundation of civilized tranquillity:

> Let every soul be subject unto the higher powers: for there is no power but of God; and the powers that be, are ordained by God. Whosoever resisteth the power, resisteth the ordinance of God: and they that resist, shall receive to themselves condemnation. For magistrates are not to be feared for good works, but for evil ... For he is the minister of God for thy wealth, for if thou do evil, fear: for he beareth not the sword for naught: for he is the minister of God to take vengeance on him that doeth evil. Wherefore ye must be subject, not because of wrath only, but also for conscience sake.[124]

From obedience sprang peace, and from peace prosperity: that was Elizabeth's simple little moral. But she was not content merely to prepare the ground from which the Renaissance of her age flowered; she wished to be at the centre of it herself, an actress and a participant in all its manifestations. We must now look more closely at her way of life and the manner in which she epitomized her society.

7

God's Virgin

Elizabeth is the first English monarch whom the evidence permits us to know with a fair degree of intimacy. There are some baffling *lacunae*, and some evident contradictions, but in general we can build up a convincing picture of her as a human being. We know something about her daily routine. She once described herself as 'not a morning woman', and this was true in the sense that she did not like to be seen, except by her women, early in the day before her toilette was complete.[1] Often she rose late because she had been working at night. Thus, in the middle of the night of 24 November 1586, she drafted fresh instructions to postpone the prorogation of parliament, and had them sent to Burghley before seven o'clock the next morning.[2] During the same parliament, on 27 February 1587, she summoned the Speaker late at night to question him about legislation, tabled that day, which she found offensive.[3] On 8 October 1597, at 11.00 p.m., she invested Sir Robert Cecil with the seals of the Chancellorship of the Duchy of Lancaster, to enable him to get off letters quickly during the night to influence the forthcoming elections.[4] Harington says she often kept Burghley, and sometimes other councillors, up till a very late hour talking politics; and her insomnia meant that she was inclined to take (or, more likely, reverse) decisions in the small hours, while restless in bed. In the summer of 1597 Sir John Stanhope reported to Robert Cecil: 'I found her Majesty and the Lords closed up in the Privy Chamber until it was candlelight.' Evidently Elizabeth liked to sleep after dinner (she took short naps at other times), and then resume work. Stanhope says: 'I left the Queen at six very quiet and, as I guess, will not stir till very late; but I will attend the time and present it [more business], if she do but breathe a little while afore her going to bed.'[5]

With late hours, Elizabeth took her time dressing the next morning. Sometimes she would slip out, not fully dressed, to go for a brisk exercise-walk in seclusion. This was why she built the terrace at Windsor, and in 1577 the wall was heightened, 'to prevent persons in the dean's orchard seeing into the Queen's walk'.[6] She also had a habit of hanging about her bedroom window-seat in the morning, and peering out to overhear gossip. Thus, at Windsor once, she overheard a carter complaining that 'he knew the Queen was a woman' since she had three times countermanded orders to move her stuff; she sent him an angel [10s.], 'to shut his mouth'. In May 1578, early one morning, Gilbert Talbot, son of the Earl of Shrewsbury, caught her looking out of the window:

> My eye was full towards her; she showed to be greatly ashamed thereof, for that she was unready and in her nightstuff. So, when she saw me after dinner as she went to walk, she gave me a great filip on the forehead, and told the Lord Chamberlain . . . how I had seen her that morning, and how much ashamed thereof she was.[7]

Sometimes, if a little more suitably attired, she was prepared for a chat during these morning gazings. Francis Bacon reports that, looking through her window one morning, she spotted Sir Edward Dyer, who had been importuning her for a job, walking moodily about her garden. She asked him, in Italian, what he thought about when he thought of nothing. He said, of a woman's promise. Elizabeth replied: 'Anger makes dull men witty, but it keeps them poor'; then, 'the Queen shrunk in her head', before he had a chance to reply.[8]

She took her breakfast in her bedroom, or an adjoining chamber, alone, as she did (as a rule) with all her meals; she was served with some formality, but was not to be seen, except by her ladies, at mealtimes. Her breakfast cost 8s. 6½d. (as we learn from the daily account, signed by her own hand, for 19 November 1576), her dinner 45s. 0½d., her supper 32s. 9d.[9] Unlike most of her subjects, and courtiers, she observed fast-days and days of abstinence, but on Wednesdays and Fridays (both fish-days), she had a choice of lings, pike, salmon, haddock, whiting, gurnards, tench, birts, sturgeon, conger eel, carp, eels and lampreys, chine of salmon and perch. She was fastidious in some ways: her manchet, or fine white bread, came from wheat grown at Heston, as it was accounted the purest.[10] She preferred lighter dishes – chicken and game-birds – to red meat. Often, particularly towards the end of her life, when her teeth decayed, she made do with pottages, gruels and other soft foods. But, along with many other English people, she retained a passion for rich cakes (it was one reason why her teeth were so poor), made from Corinth currants, of which England imported the whole crop, 'so that the very Greeks that sell them wonder what we do with such great quantities thereof, and know not how we shall spend them except we use them for dyeing, or to feed hogs'.[11] Her godson, Sir John Harington, sometimes cheered her up by devising recipes for special sweetmeats. But in general she was very abstemious. She particularly disliked old, strong ale or beer, of the type known as 'March ale' (it was brewed in March), what one contemporary called 'old beer that will make a cat speak and a wise man dumb'.[12] At her houses, and on progress, she insisted that her beer be light and newly-brewed. John Clapham records:

> She was in her diet very temperate, as eating but few kinds of meat and those not compounded. The wine she drank was mingled with water, containing three parts more in quantity than the wine itself. Precise hours of refection she observed not, as never eating but when her appetite required it.[13]

Washing, dressing and adorning herself probably took two hours or more. She washed her hair with lye, a compound of wood-ash and water, which she kept in pots with attached comb-cases and looking glass; she cleaned her teeth with a tooth-cloth and gold-and-enamel picks, and washed her mouth with marjoram. She dyed her hair, and used a range of reddish or blonde wigs, and a good many cosmetics – though some of the stories about her painting are exaggerations, or even malicious fictions. Her face-paint was a mixture of white-of-egg, powdered egg-shell, alum, borax and poppy-seeds, moistened with mill-water. For her dresses she generally stuck to black and white – often white alone – with silver diaphanous veils, and looped over them great sets and strings of large pearls. The white or black base of her dresses was picked out with silver and gold thread, and often embroidered with symbols in russet, tawny, orange, peach and pink: she rarely wore blue, green or yellow.[14] Unfortunately, very few of her dresses, as described in the inventories, correspond with those we see in her portraits. By her death she had acquired many hundreds, some of which she never wore, and most of which had been presented to her as New Year gifts. The portraits, of course, show her in her great set-pieces, which took hours to put on and arrange, and which she wore only for public appearances and for receiving ambassadors before the full court in the Presence Chamber. Usually she dressed much more simply, for dress with her was not a passion, but an act of state. Sometimes, towards the end of her reign, she wore the same simple dress five days running. Her personal tailor was Walter Fish; she had a furrier, or 'skinner', called Adam Bland. Henry Hérne was her hosier; but after 1559, when one of her ladies knitted her a pair of silk stockings (an Italian fashion which was quite new in England), she normally employed her maids to make them. Her shoemaker, Garrett Johnston, apparently provided her with a new pair each week (the old were distributed among her ladies).[15]

Her collection of jewellery was vast – the envy, even, of the popes. Some of it was inherited: Henry VIII's giant sapphire surrounded by rose rubies, for instance, was re-set by her German jeweller, Master Spilman. Some were presents from foreign courts, especially France.[16] Christopher Hatton gave her some of her finest sets, with up to seven matched pieces.[17] She had at least eleven jewelled watches in 1587, in the shapes of crosses, flowers, pendants and reliquaries.[18] She loved ostrich-feather fans with jewelled handles, or jewels which told a story, made a pun, or were acrostics of 'Elizabeth'; she was especially fond of jewels in the shapes of ships and animals.[19] She often gave away jewels – cameos of herself, for instance, were distributed to her god-children, and sometimes more elaborate affairs presented to ministers for special services. Thus, Sir Thomas Heneage, Treasurer at War during the Armada, received a splendid jewel (now in the Victoria and Albert Museum), with a bust of Elizabeth on the front, a storm-tossed Ark on the back, and inside a miniature of her by Hilliard (who probably designed the whole thing).[20]

When she was dressed to be seen, Elizabeth launched herself into a varied routine, which mingled exercise, study and business. Edmund Bohun describes her life at Richmond:

> Six or seven galliards of a morning, besides musics and singing, were her ordinary exercise. . . . First in the morning she spent some time at her devotions, then she betook herself to the dispatch of her civil affairs, reading letters, ordering answers, considering what should be brought before the council, and consulting with her ministers. . . . When she had thus wearied herself she would walk in a shady garden or pleasant gallery, without any other attendants than a few learned men; then she took coach and passed, in the sight of her people, to the neighbouring groves and fields, and sometimes would hunt and hawk; there was scarce a day but she employed some part of it in reading and study.

Harington said that 'Her Highness was wont to sooth her ruffled temper with reading every morning . . . She did much admire Seneca's wholesome advisings, when the soul's quiet was flown away.'[21] There is abundant testimony that Elizabeth did some scholarly work virtually every day. Ascham, for instance, stated: 'I believe that, besides her perfect readiness in Latin, Italian, French and Spanish, she readeth here now at Windsor more Greek every day, than some prebendary of this church doth read Latin in a whole week.'[22] She was particularly fond of translating, and quite a number of her efforts are listed. Thus, in 1593, when angered by Henri IV's decision to turn Catholic, she calmed herself by turning Boethius's *Consolations of Philosophy* into English, taking a total of twenty-six hours to do it.

Elizabeth was busiest when parliament was sitting. But this was comparatively rare. In 44 years she held only 10 parliaments (with a total of 13 sessions) of an average of 10 weeks – the longest was her first, in 1559, which took 14 weeks and six days. Thus parliament sat for a total of less than three years during her reign.[23] But Council meetings were held virtually every day, and though Elizabeth rarely attended them, she always required a report, and in addition held private consultations daily with one or more of her ministers, especially the Principal Secretary. He needed to handle her carefully. Robert Beale, Walsingham's right-hand man and Clerk of the Council, noted in his 'Treatise on the office of a counsellor and secretary to her Majesty':

> Have, in a little paper, note of such things as you are to propound to her Majesty and divided it into titles of public and private suits . . . Learn before your access her Majesty's disposition by some of the Privy Chamber, with whom you must keep credit, for that will stand you in much stead . . . When her Highness is angry or not well disposed, trouble her not with any matter which you desire to have done, unless extreme necessity urge it. When her Highness signeth [papers] it shall be good to entertain her with some relation or speech whereat she may take some pleasure. . . . Be not dismayed with the controlments and amendments of such things which you shall have done, for you shall have to do with a princess of great wisdom, learning and experience. . . . avoid opinion of being new-fangled and a bringer-in of new customs.[24]

Her favourite method of taking counsel was to hold individual interviews with her chief ministers, assemble them together the next day, and hear them again collectively; and then, according to Harington

> if any had dissembled with her, or stood not well to her advisings before, she did not let it go unheeded, and sometimes unpunished. Sir Christopher Hatton was wont to say that the Queen did fish for men's souls, and had so sweet a bait, that no one could escape her network.

Sometimes, Harington adds, she wrote down ministers' opinions, 'having drawn them out', and showed the results to them a month later. Her moods, in political discussion, were volatile:

> When she smiles, it was a pure sunshine, that everyone did choose to bask in, if they could; but anon came a storm from a sudden gathering of clouds, and the thunder fell in wondrous manner on all alike. . . . I never did find greater show of understanding and learning, than she was blest with.[25]

No one, indeed, doubted her intelligence; the universal complaint was of her vacillation. Like many before and since, who have to carry the solitary weight of grave responsibilities, Elizabeth sometimes revolted against the business of taking, hour by hour, and day after day, an endless series of decisions. Sir Thomas Smith wrote a despairing letter of complaint to Burghley in 1574:

It maketh me weary of my life ... the time passing almost irrecuperable, the advantage lost, the charges continuing, nothing resolved. ... I neither can get the other letters signed, nor the letter already signed, which your lordship knoweth, permitted to be sent away, but day by day, and hour by hour, deferred until anon, none, and tomorrow ...[26]

A letter survives, endorsed by a clerk:

A letter which her Majesty willed me to write to her Secretary, and to send it by post, but before I had fully ended the letter she sent me to bring it to her before it was closed, which I did upon the point of six o'clock, and then her Majesty having read it and scanned it three or four times and sometimes willing me to send it away, and sometimes altering that purpose, commanded me at last to stay both the letter and the post.[27]

No wonder Burghley once complained: 'The lack of a resolute answer from her Majesty driveth [me] to the wall.'[28]

Of course it must be remembered that, in addition to public business, the Queen was constantly solicited for decisions and favours on a multitude of private matters. The moment she stepped beyond her Privy Chamber or (in the larger palaces) the series of withdrawing chambers which surrounded her bedroom, to go to the gallery, or the gardens, or other parts of her houses, she was liable to be importuned. Often her ladies, or other servants, were bribed to show her letters asking for jobs. Sir Robert Sidney, who had asked for the Cinque Ports by this means, was informed by his agent:

Lady Scudamore got the Queen to read your letter. ... 'Do you not know the contents of it?' said the Queen. 'No madam,' said she; when her Majesty said: 'Here is much ado about the Cinque Ports.' I demanded of my Lady Scudamore what she observed in her Majesty while she was a-reading of it; who said that she read it all over with two or three 'Poohs!'[29]

The outer rooms of the palaces swarmed with suppliants, trying to get in and often succeeding. The Privy Chamber, and the inner rooms beyond it, were very closely guarded; the Presence Chamber, which was much bigger and more frequented, was more difficult to control. When Elizabeth was sixty-seven, a mad sailor, who had written her a passionate love-letter, managed to penetrate it, and drew his dagger there; he proved so strong he broke all the manacles they forged on him in Bedlam.[30] Porters, who were responsible for access, were important, indeed self-important, people (but they could be bribed, too). The Council Porter, Robert Laneham – who, needless to say, was a Leicester man – has left us a boastful vignette of himself at work:

Now, sir, if the Council sit, I am at hand, wait at an inch, I warrant you. If any make babbling, 'Peace!' say I, 'wot where you are?' If I take a listener, or a prier-in at the chinks or at the lockhole, I am by and by in the bones of him. But now they keep good order; they know me well enough. If there be a friend, or such one as I like, I make him sit down by me on a form or a chest; let the rest walk, a' God's name![31]

Elizabeth was protected by three sets of guards, in theory at least. The oldest, the Sergeants-at-Arms, twenty in number, were grand people, invested with the SS collar, and had become honorific by her day. The Yeoman of the Guard (the 'new' guard) had been founded by Henry VII in 1485, and were the working guards of the palace. In addition there were the Gentlemen Pensioners (or 'spears'), a horse guard established by Henry VIII in 1509. These were gentlemen, who consorted closely with the Queen, supplied her best performers for tilts, and escorted her to chapel and in public processions on foot, carrying gilded battle-axes. They were tall, handsome and gave themselves airs: Mistress Quickly, in the *Merry Wives*, naively ranked them even higher than earls. The captaincy of this guard, held successively, for instance, by Hatton and Ralegh, was one of the most valued of the higher non-political posts; Ralegh claimed it gave him better access to the Queen than many councillors enjoyed.[32] In fact, despite the obsession of both Burghley and parliament with her protection, the security which surrounded the Queen was far from perfect, probably because she found precautions intolerable. One would-be assassin, Dr Parry, was able to approach her in the Privy Garden, and failed to make his attempt because he was overawed by her likeness to her grandfather, Henry VII. Recorder Fleetwood of London reported to Burghley in January 1581 that the Queen, in Islington, 'for taking of the air', had been suddenly 'environed with a number of rogues'.[33] On one occasion, at Greenwich, while in her barge, she was nearly killed when a fowler accidentally discharged his piece, hitting one of her oarsmen; he was charged, convicted, taken to the site of the accident to be hanged, and then pardoned at the last minute.[34] Burghley prepared a memo on 'certain cautions for the Queen's apparel and diet' (poisoned gifts of perfumes, gloves and so forth, as well as food, were suspect), and in theory everything the Queen ate and drank was tasted beforehand. But Elizabeth often ignored these rules, especially on progress; on at least one occasion she entered a private house, without warning, ate some untasted food there, and was so pleased with it that she had the rest of the dish carried back to her lodgings. She was not an easy woman to guard.

Her immediate personal staff was small for a monarch. She had only two (sometimes three) Gentlemen of the Privy Chamber, and five to ten grooms, far fewer than her predecessors. But she may have had more women: two senior ladies and five junior ones (all married), and four socially-inferior ones, or 'chamberers', known as 'the Queen's women', plus six maids-in-waiting always in attendance, who lived in the Coffer Chamber under the Mother of the Maids, and were frequently rebuked by the Vice-Chamberlain for making a din at night. Among other menial duties, the maids waited on her at table and fetched things, not always to Elizabeth's satisfaction. Harington was told (23 May 1597) that Lady Mary Howard was in trouble

> foreasmuch as she has refused to bear [the Queen's] mantle at the hour her Highness is wonted to air in the garden, and on small rebuke did vent such unseemly answer as did breed much choler in her mistress. Again, on another occasion, she was not ready to carry the cup of grace during the dinner in the privy chamber ... [The Queen] swore out with all such ungracious, flouting wenches.[35]

There were also older ladies, with lodgings at court, who attended in the Presence Chamber, and Esquires of the Body, who slept in this room, and took charge after the 9.00 p.m. ceremony of 'Good Night', after which all were supposed to be asleep. Elizabeth scorned the curious collection of amusing freaks kept at most European courts, and she was not as much attached to fools as her father, whose jester, Will Somers, was very close to him. But she employed a family of hereditary fools, the Grenes, and later an Italian jester, called Monarcho, who was well known and is mentioned in *Love's Labour's Lost*. Other favoured servants were the Italian footman in the Privy Chamber, Ferdinando – evidently privileged for he was referred to as 'Mister' – a woman-dwarf, Ippolita the Tartarian ('our dearly beloved woman'), another Italian dwarf-woman called Thomasina, and a little blackamoor, who wore baggy trousers and a jacket of black taffeta and gold tinsel.[36]

Elizabeth ran her court in a highly decorous and disciplined fashion. She set high standards herself. It is true she sometimes slapped her maids, but this was in an age when parents flogged their children of both sexes until they were married and when children (even after marriage) normally stood or knelt in their presence. It is also true that the Queen swore, heavily and often, thus inaugurating an English upper-class tradition of ladies swearing which persisted well into the eighteenth century. Her habit was well known, and much deplored by Puritan divines. One of them, Mr Fuller, asked permission to send her a book he had written, and this was granted. It turned out to contain, her lady-in-waiting was horrified to discover, an essay demonstrating God's command against swearing

> and yet notwithstanding, your gracious Majesty, in your anger, hath used to swear sometimes by that abominable idol, the Mass, and often and grievously by God, and by Christ, and by many parts of his glorified body, and by saints, faith, troth and other forbidden things; and by your Majesty's evil example and suffrance, the most part of your subjects and people of every degree, do commonly swear and blaspheme, to God's unspeakable dishonour, without any punishment.[37]

The lady told Burghley of the book being presented and

> it lying on a chair, as he went out he took it with him, and then her Majesty coming to the chair, asked the lady for the book; and she answering that my Lord took it, her Majesty willed her to call for the book and said 'I will have it again', but the lady durst never ask it.[38]

Nevertheless, there was remarkably little scandal at court, as a multitude of foreigners testified. They also commented on the orderliness with which court ceremonials were carried out. 'One thing above all surprised me,' wrote the Venetian Secretary, Gaspar Spinelli, 'never having witnessed the like anywhere, it being impossible to represent and credit with how much order, regularity and silence such public entertainments are conducted in England.'[39] Elizabeth kept a very sharp eye on such things, and never hesitated to rebuke offenders. Thus, at a City ceremony, Recorder Fleetwood reported to Burghley:

> Her Majesty was wonderfully well pleased in all things, saving that some young gentlemen, being more bold than well-mannered, did stand upon the carpet of the cloth of state, and did almost lean upon the cushions. Her Highness found fault with the Lord Chamberlain and Mr Vice-Chamberlain, and with the gentlemen ushers, for suffering such disorders.[40]

Sunday was the great day for court ceremony; visitors could watch her coming to, and going from, chapel in state, and afterwards saw her dinner being served (though she actually ate it in private). Lupold von Wedel, a German nobleman and experienced traveller, described the scene on 18 October 1584:

> Before the Queen marched her lifeguard, all chosen men, strong and tall, two hundred in number, we were told, though not all of them were present. They bore gilt halberds, red coats faced with black velvet in front and on the back they wore the Queen's arms, silver gilt. Then came gentlemen of

rank and of the Council, two of them bearing a royal sceptre each, a third with the royal sword in a red velvet scabbard, embroidered with gold and set with precious stones and large pearls ... The people standing on both sides fell on their knees, but she showed herself very gracious, and accepted with a humble mien letters of supplication from rich and poor. Her train was carried behind her by a countess, then followed twelve young ladies of noble birth ... Then the Queen returned as she had come and went to her room, and when on her passing the people fell on their knees, she said in English: 'Thank you with all my heart.' Then eight trumpeters clad in red gave the signal for dinner, and did it very well.[41]

Foreigners were particularly impressed by the excellence of the music and singing in the chapel royal. Henry Remelius, ambassador from Denmark in 1584, heard the Office at Greenwich 'so melodiously sung and said ... as a man half-dead might thereby have been quickened'.[42] A French ambassador, Champagny, said of the service at Eltham, 'in all my travels in France, Italy and Spain, I never heard the like ... a concert of music so excellent and sweet as cannot be expressed'.[43]

The standards of the chapel royal, and indeed of English music in general, were not maintained without great difficulty, and against strenuous opposition. Indeed, Elizabeth may be said to have saved English music, which had been internationally famous since the early fifteenth century, from Puritan destruction. The Reformers objected to elaborate polyphonic music, in which the words were drowned in a multitude of notes; as Cranmer said to Henry VIII, there ought to be, 'for every syllable a note, so that it may be sung distinctly and devoutly'. They preferred instead the simple settings for the metrical psalms, which could be sung by massed congregations: Bishop Jewell told Peter Martyr in 1560 that 'sometimes at St Paul's Cross there will be 6,000 people singing together' – rather like Welsh rugby crowds today. It was all part of the Puritan demand for participation, as opposed to a hieratic performance, in religious ceremonies. Elizabeth did not dislike the psalm-singing, indeed she translated some of the psalms herself. But she was determined to keep up the polyphony. Under the 1559 Act of Uniformity she issued injunctions that no changes should be made in churches with endowed choirs, 'by means whereof the laudable science of music has been had in estimation, and preserved in knowledge'. She insisted that 'for the comfort of such that delight in music ... either at morning or evening there may be sung an hymn, or suchlike song to the praise of Almighty God in the best sort of melody and music that may be conveniently devised ...' To this we owe the Anthem, so notable a feature of

Anglican church music.[44] Indeed, in some respects – thanks to Elizabeth's firmness – reform proved an asset, for the music of all texts had to be reset to English words.

Elizabeth was a notable performer; next to philosophy, music was her greatest pleasure and passion. She 'composed ballets and music, and played and danced them'. Tallis and Byrd, dedicating their *Cantiones Sacrae* to her in 1575, praised not only her playing (on the lute, lyre and virginals), but also her elegant voice. The great schoolmaster, Richard Mulcaster, wrote in Latin elegiacs (I quote from an eighteenth-century translation):

> *The Queen, the glory of our age and isle*
> *With royal favour bids this science smile;*
> *Nor hears she only other's labour'd lays,*
> *But, artist-like, herself both sings and plays.*[45]

She probably regarded the music composed for her chapel royal as a greater glory of her realm than the poetry and plays of her age. In addition to Tallis and Byrd, she employed John Bull, Thomas Morley and the great organist Christopher Tye (Anthony Wood recorded: 'The Queen would send the verger to tell Dr Tye that he played out of tune; whereupon he sent word that her ears were out of tune'). At her accession, she inherited 32 adult chapel singers, 12 boys, and 41 instrumentalists, about half of them from famous North Italian musical families. These families, such as the Bassanos and Laniers, continued in her employ throughout her reign (there were six Bassanos and six Laniers still at court in 1603), but she also sent her agents to all provincial cathedrals and collegiate churches, to recruit singers, especially boys. Elizabeth's love of music undoubtedly influenced her religious policy, for all the foreign musicians and composers, and a great many of the native ones, were Catholics. One reason why she liked the Earl of Worcester, whom she eventually made Master of the Horse, despite the fact that he was (as she put it) a 'stiff papist', was that he was devoted to music, and Byrd's best patron. She drew the line at Dowland, because of his publicly-known Catholicism, and refused to employ him; but she protected most Catholic musicians, and even allowed Byrd to compose in Latin as well as English.

The appearance, no less than the voices, of Elizabeth's chapel boys incensed Puritans; they were part of 'the enormities of the Queen's closet'. The Puritans drew the connection between the chapel royal and the theatre. Thus, in 1569, an angry pamphlet called *The Children of the Chapel Stripped and Whipped* – the Puritans were always anxious to whip someone – noted: 'Plays will never be suppressed while her Majesty's unfledged minions flaunt it in silks and satins . . .

they had as well be at their popish services in the Devil's garments.'[46] But on this point Elizabeth never gave way. In 1601 two Catholic visitors from Italy attended the Epiphany service in her chapel. They were delighted with the splendid music and singing, and observed that, though a table had replaced the altar, it was covered in damask cloth; there were two candles (admittedly unlit), holy books covered in gold, and priests wearing golden copes. Elizabeth herself presented offerings of gold, frankincense and myrrh, and though the two visitors scandalized their co-religionists by thus attending a heretic service, their description makes it clear that it was much more splendid than they had been used to at home.[47]

So Elizabeth maintained the fine musical traditions upheld by her gifted father. There were probably more musicians at court at her death than at her accession. In 1601 Morley edited *The Triumphs of Oriana*, a collection of madrigals written in her honour by no less than twenty-three grateful English composers.[48] She arranged for free concerts of music to be held at the Royal Exchange, every Sunday and holiday from Lady Day to Michaelmas – an early adumbration of the 'Proms' – and saw to it that even the poor could enjoy the art: indeed, the most popular of all English rounds, *Three Blind Mice*, dates from her day (it was not published till 1609). Most of her leading servants loved music – Hatton particularly. Drake dined to music even on his lonely world voyage, and when he went on the Portugal expedition of 1589 he took with him five boy singers loaned by Norwich (another leading musical centre where free concerts were held). Indeed, by a historical paradox, it was Elizabeth's vigorous patronage of music on traditional lines which probably delayed, in England, the introduction of the Italian opera.[49]

Behind the outward decorum, and the real splendour, of Elizabeth's court, there was a less satisfactory tale of waste, sloth and mismanagement. Tudor courts were enormous – the dining hall at Whitehall could seat 1,500 at one sitting. Successive sovereigns took steps – often backed up by ferocious threats and punishments – to pare down the numbers, and reduce the ever-swelling cost. But reforms were short-lived, and invariably futile in the long run. It was not possible to conduct an institution designed to radiate magnificence on strict business principles. Under Henry VII, the expenses of the Household went up to £15,000 a year; he reduced them by £2,000 towards the end of his reign (this was one reason Edmund Dudley was so hated by the court), but on his son's accession they jumped to £16,000, and were £40,000 at his death. Elizabeth performed prodigies to keep the cost, by her death, down to £55,000. But the problem was insuperable. Official regulations were ignored, or eroded by time, the bribery of senior servants and controllers, favouritism and 'exceptions', which rapidly became the rule and soon hereditary. Petty theft became legitimized by usage and was built into the system, and eventually became a time-honoured right, as the basis for another archaeological layer of theft. The death of a monarch was, in theory, the occasion for a purge, and a fresh start. In fact it became the opposite: the new monarch moved in with his or her personal household, and the old clung on, doubling up to perform the same duties. Thus, Edward VI ended up with more Yeomen of the Guard than his father, extra kitchen boys, another twenty-four musicians, more buttery officers, the swollen totals now becoming the authorized, official number.[50]

One major source of abuse was that the high-born at court, instead of eating in the great hall, had their meals served separately in their rooms, leaving the hall to clerks and minions. The catering department found this costly and inefficient – it led, among other things, to a proliferation of kitchens, and a steady increase in serving men and wenches – and it infuriated the monarch, but then the monarch had begun it all by dining separately himself.[51] The Board of the Green Cloth controlled everything, in enormous detail, but its minute and painstaking accounts concealed an abyss of financial confusion, bureaucratic incompetence, and sheer human inertia. Once a cooked dish, however large, left one of the senior tables, it was gone for good – taken home, given to hangers-on, devoured by dogs. Elizabeth's establishment consumed annually 600,000 gallons of beer, 300 tons of wine, 1,240 oxen, 8,200 sheep, 13,260 lambs, 2,752 dozen chickens, poultry and capons, 60,000 lbs of butter, and 4,200,000 eggs.[52] There was a huge and growing difference between the authorized amount spent on food and what it actually cost – in 1576 Elizabeth signed for £15,441 19s. 10¼d. but £21,096 10s. 4¼d. was paid out. Estimates of 'waste', being 'neither comprised within her book of ordinance, nor spoken of within any of the incidents before recited', came to £1,858 8s. 5d. 'Leakage' of ale and beer cost £292 10s., 'wastage and spilt in drawing' £187 9s., 'ullage and leakage of wines' £253. £30-worth of 'muttons' was actually written off as stolen, for once euphemism being abandoned. Extra 'bouches of the court', as they were termed – snacks of high-quality bread and ale – were supplied to powerful individuals, morning, noon and night: for ten people alone these came to over £53 a year.[53]

Senior courtiers brought their own teams of servants to court, and these expected to be fed free, and indeed waited upon. High-born domestics relegated their duties to servants, and the servants, the older and more senior they became, recruited others to do the actual work. Everyone was good at giving orders to the man below him; all hated doing manual work, cleaning up messes, scrubbing, washing and polishing. Hence, despite the enormous numbers, only a few were really scullions and menials. If the monarch wanted a midnight snack, relays of officials and servants ceremonially passed on the order into the stygian depths of the hierarchy; it might take an hour or more to arrive. When Elizabeth complained that the food served to her at Windsor was cold, an elaborate investigation eventually revealed that, despite the existence of innumerable kitchens in the Castle, her meals were actually being cooked in the public oven in Peascod Street, and carried half a mile to her table. Things were no better at Richmond.[54]

Elizabeth was particularly incensed at the wastage in the court, because its supplies were bought up at fixed or cheap prices in the localities, and this system of purveyance was rightly a subject of constant criticism; she felt that the extravagance of the court was not merely impoverishing herself but undermining her popularity. A record survives of conversations she held, towards the end of her reign, with Richard Brown, an officer of the Green Cloth.[55] Elizabeth complained that, at her accession, the bills came to only £40,000. 'Brown answered, that then all the provisions were cheaper. The Queen said, that may be so, and I saved by the late composition (so I am informed) £10,000 a year, and therefore I charge you examine the difference of some year at the beginning of my reign with one year's expenses now, and let me understand it.' Brown found there had been a rise of £12,000 a year just on bread, beer, heating, lighting and some wages, 'and no sufficient warrant for the increase':

> The Queen's Majesty being informed of the difference, and being therewith moved greatly, said, And shall I suffer this, did I not tell you, Brown, what you should find? I was never in all my government so royally, with numbers of noblemen and ladies attended upon, as in the beginnings of my reign, all officers of my court being supplied, which now are not ... And shall not these now that attend, and have the like allowances, not rest contented? I will not suffer this dishonourable spoil, and increase that no prince ever before me did, to the offence of God, and great grievance to my loving subjects, who, I understand, daily complain, and not without cause, that there is an increase daily of carriages and of provision taken from them, at low prices, and wastefully spent within my court to some of their undoings, and now myself understanding of it, they may justly accuse me, to suffer it; with many other discontented speeches, delivered with great vehemence.[56]

Death intervened before her orders for reform could be carried out; in fact, she did well to confine the increase to within such comparatively modest limits, during a period of steady inflation. She thus acquired a reputation for parsimony which was not wholly deserved (people soon grumbled far more when James I went to the opposite extreme). Sir Thomas Wilson, in his *The State of England, Anno Domini 1600*, writes that she was considered 'liberal' in her young days, 'but her years hath now brought with it (the inseparable quality thereof) nearness'. Once, as a young Queen, she was rebuked by Winchester for being 'too liberal in gifts before her Majesty knoweth what it is she giveth'. Later, under his and Burghley's guidance, she saved money, so that she had a 'war chest', as the latter called it, of £300,000 at the start of the Armada campaign; Burghley boasted of 'the parsimony of her Majesty [that] hath been a great cause of her Majesty's riches, able to perform these actions whereof heads are inquisitive'.[57] Of course, it depended from what point of view one was judging the Queen's actions – as a potential recipient, or as a harassed minister looking for essential cash to pay fleets and armies. One general complained:

> Amongst her manifold and rare virtues of nature and art, this was the only detraction, that she had not power to give where it was merited … If she had disposed of twenty or thirty thousand pounds to the comfort of her long-worn, threadbare, poor old servants, and paid her debts, she had died, as she lived, the mirror of her sex.[58]

Against this, the accounts show that she often gave money and other rewards to her servants, of which no other record survives.[59] And sometimes her charities were very substantial. When Nantwich, in Cheshire, was almost destroyed by fire in 1585, she organized a nationwide fund, and contributed £1,000 herself, out of a total raised of £3,142.[60] At any rate, when her ministers were asking parliament for taxation, they were always able to point to her own modest expenditure. Thus in 1593 the Chancellor of the Exchequer told the Commons: 'As for her own private expenses, they have been little in building; she hath consumed little or nothing in her pleasures. As for her apparel, it is royal and princely, beseeming her calling, but not sumptuous nor excessive.'[61] This seems to suggest that parliament as a whole found no fault in a 'near' monarch.

The system of exchanging gifts at the New Year provides no real guide to Elizabeth's generosity, or indeed rapacity. It had become formalized long before her time. Five rolls of New Year's gifts have been preserved, the earliest from 1562, the last from 1600.[62] Members of the nobility and senior officials presented her with purses of gold, according to their wealth and station; in return they got carefully graded quantities of silver-gilt plate. The Archbishop of Canterbury usually paid the most, £40; earls, £20; and so on down to court ladies, who gave £4, £3 or less. The sums collected came to between £700 and £1,200. Some professional courtiers were excused the present but still received plate, as what was termed 'a free gift'. The Queen handed out plate weighing between 4,000 and 5,500 ounces. Shortly after she died, the Earl of Huntingdon described how the system worked. He bought a purse for 5s., and put in it twenty pieces of new-minted gold at £1 each. At 8.00 a.m. on New Year's day he took it to the Presence Chamber and handed it to the Lord Chamberlain. Then he collected a ticket at the Jewel House (paying 6d. into the ticket box), stating how much plate he was to receive. He went into the Jewel House, chose his plate and marked it. In the afternoon, he went back to collect it, paying the gentleman on duty a tip of 40s. in gold, another 2s. to the ticket-box, and 6d. to the porter. Of course many people gave the Queen presents in addition – jewels, clothes, gloves, and a multitude of knick-knacks. Hatton's presents were enormously costly and much relished for their ingenuity. But then he got more plate than anyone else – 400 ounces as a rule. There was something mechanical and mercenary about these exchanges, which Elizabeth was too conservative to modify. Personally, she liked being given presents very much indeed, particularly if they were unexpected, but she enjoyed them more for their taste, wit and appropriateness than for their intrinsic value. When Michael Hicks, Burghley's secretary, was asked to vacate his house for a day so that Elizabeth could be put up, he was told his wife should leave a gift for Elizabeth – a shawl or ruff, or something of the kind; it was not to cost much, but should be well chosen. Sometimes, when Elizabeth stayed in a private house, she took on leaving, as a compliment to the host, a silver spoon. She accumulated vast quantities of valuables; but they were constantly being inventoried, sold, melted down, re-set, given away, or otherwise put to use.

The court was a mercenary place because it expressed the realities of society. It was where power resided, and where wealth was to be made. In their more idealistic moods, Elizabeth's contemporaries denounced the atmosphere in which anxious men spent their money in the constant, often desperate, search for place and favour at court. As Spenser put it:

> *Full little knowest thou that hast not tried,*
> *What hell it is, in sueing long to bide:*
> *To lose good days, that might be better spent;*
> *To waste long nights in pensive discontent;*
> *To speed today, to be put back tomorrow;*
> *To feed on hope, to pine with fear and sorrow . . .*
> *To fawn, to crouch, to wait, to ride, to run,*
> *To spend, to give, to want, to be undone,*
> *Unhappy wight, born to disastrous end,*
> *That doth his life in so long tendance spend.*[63]

Yet no ambitious man could afford to ignore the court. Wealth and station could be acquired more quickly there than anywhere else in the kingdom. And Elizabethans had a horror of poverty which is almost palpable in their writings, a constant fear of falling in the social scale. Ralegh put the matter admirably in his advice to his son, Carew:

> Public affairs are rocks, private conversations are whirlpools and quicksands. The adventure lies in this troublesome bark; strive, if thou canst, to make good thy station on the upper deck; those that live under hatches are ordained to be drudges and slaves ... Poverty is a shame amongst men, an imprisonment of the mind, a vexation of every worthy spirit.[64]

As captain of the troublesome bark, Elizabeth was anxious that the upper deck should be staffed largely by the ancient nobility. She wanted her first parliament to enact an ordinance

> to bind the nobility to bring up their children in learning at some University in England or beyond the sea from the age of 12 to 18 at least ... The wanton bringing up and ignorance of the nobility forces the Prince to advance new men that can serve ...[65]

In accordance with the same policy, she did her best, throughout her life, to ensure that old families kept their estates together. After the old Marquess of Winchester died, she brought pressure on his heirs not to divide his patrimony. Burghley, as her chief factotum, and especially in his function as Master of the Wards, constantly intervened to prevent lands being sold to pay current debts; he always argued, with great justice, that debts could usually be paid in the end provided the family kept its estates. He tried to bring up his Wards, such as Essex and Oxford, in accordance with this principle, not always successfully: Oxford eventually lost nearly all his lands, and died on a royal pension. The protective legal machinery of the entail and the strict settlement – devices invented by Chancery lawyers in the mid-seventeenth century – did not exist in Elizabeth's day. If mortgages were allowed to fall due (and the rates of interest were ferocious) time-honoured estates would vanish into the hands of moneylenders. Burghley, 'by occasion of his office, hath preserved many great houses from overthrow by relieving sundry extremities'.[66] He has been well called 'the family solicitor to the kingdom', acting on conservative lines laid down by the Queen.[67] Sons inheriting their father's lands often found themselves faced by an abyss of debts and menacing claims, gross malpractices by trusted servants, and the depredations of relatives, especially females. The 9th Earl of Northumberland complained bitterly that he was

> so well left for movables as I was not worth a fire-shovel or a pair of tongs;

what was left me was wainscoting or things riveted with nails; for wives commonly are great scratchers after their husband's deaths, if things be loose.[68]

Generally speaking, with good estate management, the old families found no real difficulty in surviving and playing their part at court; and Elizabeth would give a helping hand if occasion required. Her activities in trying to prop up the social pyramid intensified the violent snobbery of the age, which found its battlefield in her palaces. But pride sprang as much from claims to ancient free status, or gentility, as from title to nobility. Richard Bertie, who married the widowed Duchess of Suffolk (he had been her horsemaster), complained bitterly to Elizabeth when Arundel, the worst snob of all, told her Bertie was not a gentleman. Had not the Fitzalans once been mere bailiffs of London?

As I have no cause, so I am no whit ashamed of my parents, being free English, neither villeins nor traitors. And if I would after the manner of the world bring forth old abbey scrolls for matter of record I am sure I can reach as far backwards as Fitzallan.[69]

When Burghley, rebuking Sir John Holles in a Star Chamber suit for abusing his tenantry, added that his forebears were usurious merchants, he got a tremendous blast in reply:

Touching my ancestors, I am not so unnatural as not to acknowledge them, nor so foolish proud as not to confess them as they were. I will hold myself to their name and, if I cannot prove them gentle, I will not take myself to another man's pedigree nor usurp others' arms.[70]

After all, as he hinted, who was Burghley? Or, for that matter, who was Elizabeth? She did not, indeed, press the matter of ancient nobility too far; she was not in a position to do so. She merely insisted that those around her should look, and behave, and dress like gentlemen. She often commented on their clothes and appearance, and many who flocked to her court carried most of their fortune on their backs. So a man's outward apparel and deportment was the real key at court. As Sir Thomas Smith put it:

As for gentlemen, they be made good cheap in England. For whosoever studieth the laws of the realm, who studieth in the universities, who professeth liberal sciences and, to be short, who can live idly and without manual labour and will bear the port, charge and countenance of a gentleman, he . . . shall be taken for a gentleman.[71]

Even accents did not matter much. The courtiers carried their country about with them on their tongues. Hatton wrote 'axe' for 'ask'; Leicester's letters show he often added superfluous 'h's (as 'hit' for 'it'), and dropped them too.[72] At court, Lancashire and Yorkshire dialects and pronunciations jostled with Somerset (regarded as the worst) and Lincolnshire. Elizabeth came from an academic background where scholars were increasingly interested in spelling reform and unity of pronunciation (the two were intimately connected): thus Sir John Cheke and his pupils strove to create uniform rules, though he himself spoke Lincolnshire. Elizabeth almost certainly spoke with an upper-class London accent – she drawled her vowel sounds – and efforts were being made, during her reign, to make this the norm in polite society. The *Orthographie* by John Hart, an official in the Court of Wards, which was published in 1569, took a strong line that the court accent, which he equated with correct London speech, was the only 'proper' way to talk English. The most persistent spelling reformer, William Bullokar, seems to have deliberately changed his native East Anglian accent into a court/London one; and when the great headmaster of Merchant Taylors', Richard Mulcaster (who came from Carlisle), was visited by the school governors, they had only one complaint: the ushers, 'being Northern men born, had not taught the children to speak distinctly, or to pronounce their words as well as they ought.'[73] But it was useless to attempt to get men like the Earls of Derby and Shrewsbury to speak except in the accents of their localities, and even among 'new' men a provincial accent seems to have done no harm. John Aubrey records that Sir Walter Ralegh 'spake broad Devonshire to his dying day'.[74]

However she may have wished to confine power to ancient families, Elizabeth in fact was forced to turn to these new men, in her constant search for ability and brilliance at court. But we must make a distinction. She did not, like her father, draw men from the lower rungs of society: there is no equivalent, in her government, to the rise of a Wolsey or a Cromwell, partly, no doubt, because the Church, traditionally the quickest way to favour for a really humbly-born man, scarcely touched the court at any point. Aspirants at her court would not be noticed at all unless they already had the appearance of gentlemen; and they had to be able to show that their families had some claim to landed status (though the proofs were not always rigorously examined).

Nor, in any case, did they rise to sudden favour overnight. The image of Elizabeth as a woman who picked men out from the ranks for their looks is wholly false. She wanted good looks, but she wanted strong evidence of real capacity too, and this invariably took years to display before promotion came. The rise of Sir Christopher Hatton is an excellent case in point. His relations with Elizabeth have been distorted by the fact that his first biographer, Sir Robert Naunton, had a family hostility towards Hatton. Naunton married the granddaughter of Sir John Perrot, Hatton's one known enemy (Perrot had seduced Hatton's illegitimate daughter), and the Perrot family believed Hatton mainly responsible for the fact that Sir John died in the Tower. Thus Naunton represents Hatton as a courtier picked for his looks and talent for dancing, 'a mere vegetable of the court that sprang up at night and sank again at his noon'.[75]

This version has been reproduced through the centuries; but the truth is more interesting. Hatton came from a family of small Northamptonshire squires, and received a conventional education at St Mary's Hall, Oxford, and the Inner Temple. It was part of Elizabeth's policy to revive the ancient entertainments of London and the court, which had been falling into disuse for lack of money: Dudley was her prime instrument in this process. In 1561 Dudley was elected Governor of the Christmas celebrations in the Inner Temple, and Hatton, then about twenty-one, was the Master of the Game. He may have met Elizabeth on this occasion, in his capacity as a student official, when *Gorboduc*, presented by the Inner Temple on 6 January 1562, was performed before Elizabeth, at her express command, a fortnight later.[76] Court masques consisted of 'interludes' or actual scripted performances, and dancings, in which performers mingled with spectators, and Elizabeth probably danced with Hatton on this occasion. Naunton was thus doubtless correct in saying that 'Sir Christopher Hatton came into Court . . . as Perrot was used to say, "by the galliard", for he came thither as a private gentleman of the Inns of Court in a masque.' Elizabeth showed a lifelong interest in formal dancing which, to be done to her satisfaction, required some of the training and practice of a modern ballet-dancer. The galliard in particular was extremely difficult to master. In its simplest form it was five steps, with a leap in the air and beating of the feet together after the fifth; it was thus called the *cinquepace*, and the leap the *cabriole* or caper. But refinements soon put it beyond the reach of most. As the old soldier Barnaby Rich complained:

> Our galliards are now so curious that they are not for my dancing, for they are so full of tricks and turns that he which hath no more than the plain *cinquepace* is no better accounted of than a very bungler; and for my part they might as soon teach me to make a capricornus as a caper in the right kind that it should be.[77]

Elizabeth insisted on all the refinements. She herself, according to Sir James Melville, danced the galliard more 'high and disposedly' even than Mary Queen of Scots or, as another eye-witness put it, 'after the Florentine style, with a high magnificence that astonished beholders'. And she liked to watch others dance it as well: this was how her eye fell on Hatton. But she was not impressed by dancing alone. The Earl of Oxford was the finest dancer in the kingdom, but that did not save him from disgrace when he proved himself a fool and a scoundrel. And when it was pointed out to Elizabeth that an Italian dancing master performed even better than Hatton she snorted: 'Yes, but it is his trade.' Hatton looked and behaved like a gentleman, which was what mattered to her in the first place.

Even so, his rise was gradual. It was not until two-and-a-half years later that he was appointed a gentleman-pensioner, and several months more elapsed before he received his first official task at court – as a member of a delegation to greet the new Scottish ambassador. He was, in a way, a Leicester writ small, the master of many approved accomplishments. In November 1565, he was one of the stars at tilts held before the Queen, performing the tilt proper (with lances on horseback), the tourney (also on horseback but with swords), and the 'barriers' (on foot with pike and sword). The next year he wrote part of a Shrovetide play for the Queen, and performed other minor functions. At the end of that year he got his first diplomatic appointment away from court, accompanying the Earl of Bedford to Scotland for the christening of Prince James. But he had to wait two more years before he got his first parcel of crown lands (April 1568), and another year before being made a Gentleman of the Privy Chamber. Not until 1571 did he sit in parliament, and not until 1572 did Elizabeth give him his first important post, as Captain of the Bodyguard. Thus, between being noticed by the Queen, and achieving real recognition as a leading courtier, Hatton had to put in a decade or more of hard work, during which his behaviour, honesty, loyalty and gifts were closely scrutinized. Then, admittedly, the honours and the wealth flowed in steady procession; but it had been a taxing apprenticeship.[78]

Elizabeth seems to have valued Hatton for a number of hard-headed reasons. The fact that he was presentable and efficient at court was taken for granted, though later, his experience, mastery of all court functions, and capacity for detailed planning, made him an excellent Vice-Chamberlain, in charge of progresses and major ceremonies. More important was that his views on religion came very close to Elizabeth's own; as Camden put it, he 'was of opinion that in matters of religion neither fire nor sword was to be used'. He helped to protect Catholics, with Elizabeth's support, from the worst excesses of Puritan zealots, and this led many to suppose he was a secret Catholic himself. But the evidence shows he was a straightforward Elizabethan Anglican. Whitgift, Elizabeth's favourite prelate, was his friend and ally; and Whitgift's ablest lieutenant, the future Bishop Bancroft, started his career as Hatton's chaplain.

Indeed, it was very likely at Whitgift's suggestion (he did not want the job himself) that Elizabeth eventually made Hatton Lord Chancellor in 1587. But before that he had had to demonstrate outstanding capacities as a parliamentarian, and a manager of government business in the Commons. His first surviving letter to Elizabeth (October 1572) shows that he had played a formidable role in the spring parliament of 1572. The records of his speeches show him to have been a first-rate orator, concerned to combine the rapid dispatch of government business with a conciliatory attitude very much to Elizabeth's taste. Indeed, in many ways Hatton stepped into Burghley's place on the government bench, when the latter went upstairs to manage the Lords (it was one reason why Elizabeth kept Hatton in the Lower House until he automatically went to the Lords on becoming Chancellor). In the Commons, Elizabeth could rely on Hatton not only to interpret her wishes faithfully, but to pursue her conservative-liberal methods.[79] He was admirably cast to be used on Elizabeth's confidential business, especially in religious affairs. She came to admire his tact and his (almost invariable) good temper. If, to some extent, she consciously trained him as a political instrument of her own, his merits came to be recognized by all her other great servants. Burghley had nothing to do with his early rise, and might have been expected to resent the emergence of a major power in Northamptonshire, his part of the country; in fact they became very good friends, and Burghley once paid a remarkable tribute to Hatton: of all the court and government, he said, Hatton was the least apt to bear resentment, raise difficulties, or pursue a quarrel.[80]

Naturally, Elizabeth's appointment of Hatton as Lord Chancellor aroused resentment among the legal profession; as Camden said, 'The great lawyers of England took it very offensively ...' Hatton had received no more legal training than any other gentleman who attended an Inn, but by then he had acquired considerable equity experience in Star Chamber, and he proceeded to behave with the circumspection and tact Elizabeth had foreseen. He took on a high-powered legal adviser, and in Westminster Hall he had four Masters of Chancery to sit on the bench with him (two of them attended him, after the court had risen, to prepare cases in the afternoons). Camden, echoing Burghley's approval of his conduct, described him as 'one who in the execution of that high and weighty office of Lord Chancellor of England could satisfy his conscience in the constant integrity of his endeavours to do all with right and equity'. It was such talents, rather than his looks, which commended Hatton to the Queen.

Nevertheless, it should be added that there was a darker side to Hatton's relationship with Elizabeth, illustrating the way in which the scramble for money and places shaded off into the legal underworld, and made the court, as Ralegh put it, 'glow and shine like rotten wood'. Through one of his dependants, William Tipper, a London grocer, Hatton became involved in an abusive tax, called 'hosting', an *ad valorem* charge levied on foreign merchants in London, which Sir Thomas Smith, the Secretary, held to be illegal, contrary to all commercial treaties and, indeed, against Magna Carta. Hatton was a monopolist, especially in the wine trade, and, again through Tipper, concerned himself in the highly unpopular, though not strictly illegal, business of 'discovering concealed lands'. To some extent Elizabeth felt herself obliged to cast the cloak of her approval over these activities. Moreover, she allowed Hatton more latitude than anyone else in nibbling at episcopal and other Church estates. Like many before him, Hatton cast envious eyes on the splendid London estate of the bishops of Ely in what is now called Hatton Garden. It consisted of a large kitchen-garden, a seven-acre vineyard, five acres of arable, plus a hall, chapel and other buildings. Hatton began to agitate for it as early as spring 1575, with Elizabeth's active assistance: she wanted him to have a splendid London house for entertaining purposes. She hated Cox, the Bishop, and the lands of his see were reputed to be the richest in England; moreover, Cox was supposed to be building up his own private fortune by exploiting them. Elizabeth's alleged letter to Cox, beginning 'Proud Prelate' and ending with the threat that, unless he acceded to her desires, 'I will unfrock you, by God!', is a forgery, inserted as a joke in the *London Register* of 1761, though it still occasionally makes its appearance as genuine.[81] The truth is scarcely less discreditable, for Elizabeth used one of her creatures, Lord North (who had his eye on another estate of the bishop's), to write a threatening letter on her behalf: 'This last denial being added to her former demands, hath moved her Highness to so great disliking as she purposeth presently to send for you, and to hear what account you can render for this strange dealing towards your gracious sovereign.' It went on to warn Cox that his depredations of the episcopal estates would be exposed before the Queen and Council, and there is an implicit suggestion in the letter, which is couched in the most violent terms, that Cox might be deprived of his see.[82] Cox had to accept a complex legal arrangement, under which he conveyed a mortgage of Ely House to Elizabeth, who passed it on to Hatton. The latter did not get formal grant of the property until 1578, and Cox evidently fought a bitter rearguard action, for the conveyance was still not complete when he died in 1581. Elizabeth retaliated by keeping the see vacant for nineteen years. Nor was this the only instance of Hatton filching Church lands: in 1575, the Dean and Chapter of Peterborough were threatened by the Council for delay in assigning favourable leases to Hatton.[83] There seems to me a strong likelihood that his involvement in Church appointments was accompanied by simony.

Elizabeth's favourites, indeed, were not scrupulous men. She knew it, she connived in their methods, and sometimes helped them openly. Leicester, Hatton and Essex all at times crossed the borderland which separated accepted practice from ruffianism. Burghley was much more high-minded, but then the Wards, and the Treasury (which he acquired in 1572), gave him an ample, assured and legal income. Even Walsingham, equally high-minded and basically un-interested in money, did not hesitate to use his power to bully on behalf of others. Thus, in 1581, we find him forcing the joint holder of the signet in the Welsh Marches (an active official) to hand over a half-share of the fees, in the form of a sinecure, to Walsingham's relative Fulke Greville; and he was assisted in this manoeuvre by the supposedly saintly Sir Philip Sidney.[84] Another favourite of Elizabeth's, Sir Walter Ralegh, was a life-long operator in every form of Tudor skulduggery and rapidly made himself, and remained, one of the most unpopular men in the kingdom.

Ralegh's dealing with Elizabeth illustrated her methods and attitudes – and reservations – almost to perfection. Like Hatton, he had the essential qualifica-tion of gentlemanly status; indeed, he could truthfully claim that the Raleghs were an ancient Devon family which had been more prominent in the thirteenth than it was in the sixteenth century. In his own day the Raleghs were poor but had extensive connections – with the Gilberts, Drakes, Champernownes, Carews and Thynnes, all important or growing West Country families, and most of them with seafaring and trading interests.[85] Ralegh's enemies, like Essex and Oxford, might term him 'Jack the upstart' and 'the knave', but there was no doubt about his status; indeed, as Naunton observed, 'the Queen in her choice never took into her favour a mere new man, or a mechanic.'[86] The emphasis here should be on the 'mere'; Elizabeth was always pleased to see a penniless man of ancient stock raise himself by his intelligence and courage – and help the process.

Nevertheless, Ralegh, like Hatton, had to work extremely hard at it. Long before he met the Queen (he was probably born in 1554, and twenty years her junior), he had acquired a variety of experiences – as a soldier fighting for the Huguenots, aged fifteen or sixteen, as a student at Oriel, Lyons Inn and the Middle Temple, as a poet, as a suppliant on the invisible outer fringes of the court, as a sea-captain under Gilbert, when he saw his first naval action, as the commander of 100 City footmen in the suppression of the Munster Revolt in 1580. He had twice been in gaol for affrays, and, in his turn, he had hanged scores of Irish rebels. Ralegh had been in correspondence with Burghley and

Walsingham over Irish affairs – writing over the heads of his superiors, to their
fury – before he made any mark at court, and it was as a result of his Irish
experiences and strongly-held opinions that he first caught Elizabeth's
attention. What seems chiefly to have impressed her was not so much his striking
looks (though these helped) as his formidable intelligence, and his capacity to
state his views in the most forthright and eloquent fashion. As Naunton put it:

> true it is, he had gotten the Queen's ear at a trice, and she began to be taken
> with his elocution, and loved to hear his reasons to her demands. And the
> truth is, she took him for a kind of oracle, which nettled them all.[87]

The story of his cloak is apocryphal, though it has a certain poetic truth:
Elizabeth would have relished the idea of a poor would-be courtier sacrificing
a new garment (probably not yet paid for) for her comfort at a time when his
outfit was his only capital. But we first hear of it from Fuller's *Worthies* (under
'Devonshire'), and it is significant that Naunton, a younger contemporary of
Ralegh's, does not relate so striking an anecdote in his potted biographies.[88]
Nor does it seem likely that he and Elizabeth exchanged messages by writing
with diamond rings on the palace window-panes, as tradition relates.

Indeed, all the known facts about Ralegh's rise fit in exactly with Elizabeth's
character. She never surrendered herself to men, but she was fascinated by a
combination of appearance, bravado, intelligence and energy, all of which
Ralegh had in abundance. He was 'a tall, handsome and bold man', said Aubrey,
'damnably proud'. When he caught her eye, aged twenty-six, he had already
acquired an extraordinary store of miscellaneous information, and had thought
deeply about the problems of man and nature, in the empirical manner Elizabeth
found most satisfying. Typical of his appeal to her was his striking demonstration, before a sceptical court, of how to determine the weight of tobacco smoke;
and, once he had made his mark, he took into his service the Oriel mathematician
and scientist Thomas Hariot, to feed him new ideas and experiments with
which to keep up Elizabeth's interest. He recognized in her a fellow intellectual,
someone who shared his insatiable curiosity; and also a woman, barred by her
sex from activity and adventure in a wider world, who loved to experience
vicariously the life of a thinker who was also a man of action. It was in this
capacity that she employed him: as a pioneering plantation landlord in Ireland,
where he was given 12,000 acres in Cork and Waterford; as Warden of
the Stannaries, where he helped to regulate the Cornish tin-mines; as lord
lieutenant and vice-admiral of Cornwall, where he played a leading part in
organizing the offensive and defensive power of the Western counties; as
Captain of the Guard, in succession to Hatton; as an explorer and commercial

adventurer, a man of vision who thought of colonizing America as easily as Ireland.[89]

But she also perceived in him a degree of recklessness which made him unsuitable material for the highest office. Here he differed strikingly from Hatton. His aggressive pride was sometimes intolerable. Thus we find him writing, characteristically, in 1589:

> If in Ireland they think I am not worth the respecting, they shall much deceive themselves. I am in place to be believed not inferior to any man to pleasure or displeasure the greatest; and my opinion is so received and believed as I can anger the best of them ... by the honourable offices I hold, as also by that nearness to her Majesty which I still enjoy, and never more.[90]

Damnably proud indeed! – and the man at court least inclined to conceal it. No wonder he was reported to be 'the best-hated man of the world, in court, city and country'.[91] In fact he was popular in the West Country, whose interests he was seen to uphold; elsewhere he was hated for his arrogance and greed, as a monopolist of great notoriety, and a dealer in the confiscated lands of Catholics. The trouble with Ralegh was that he took such hatred for granted, even relished it, as a sign of success. As he put it in his first published verse:

> *For whoso reaps renown above the rest*
> *With heaps of hate shall surely be oppressed.*

The Queen did not like this attitude. She put up with Leicester's unpopularity – though she deplored it – because she knew it was, to some extent, undeserved, and that he did his best to alleviate it by smooth talk and honeyed letters. But the way in which Ralegh gloried in odium seemed to her stupid and dangerous, and not to her credit. He was also, in strict contrast to Hatton, notoriously tactless, blurting out in the Commons home truths which others took pains to conceal. Thus, he told the House that he often 'plucked at a man's sleeve' to prevent him voting in a division, which he took to be a common practice and of no great importance (cries of 'Oh! Oh!'). He conspicuously lacked the English hypocrisy which Elizabeth, too, despised but which she knew to be necessary to oil the machinery of state. Of course this realism, even cynicism, was the reverse side of the medal to his intellectual adventurousness, which she so much appreciated: the man was a unity, with the indivisibility of genius, as she recognized. He continued to fascinate her mind until the end. But he lost her personal regard in 1590 when he foolishly and secretly married her maid-in-waiting, Elizabeth Throckmorton, a woman of undisciplined habits and small fortune whom the Queen would not have chosen for him, and he was never completely restored to favour, though he rendered her tremendous services in her last decade. Even before his marriage, she had pointedly declined to give him a major office of state, and to admit him to the inner circle of her advisers. She never made him a Privy Councillor. In the 1590s he campaigned in vain for various offices, getting in the end no more than the Governorship of Jersey, which proved a great disappointment. In financial terms he did very well, obtaining (among many other things), Sherborne Abbey in Dorset, and a splendid apartment in Durham House: here was his famous turret-study overlooking the Thames, 'the prospect from which', wrote Aubrey, 'is as pleasant perhaps as any in the world'. But she would not allow him real responsibilities in matters of state: he was not, in the true sense, responsible enough. So Ralegh remained a maverick at court, part of an intellectual circle which Elizabeth enjoyed and patronized, but which she did not allow to overlap the centre of power.

This intellectual circle, which originally radiated from Leicester, expanded, contracted and mutated itself throughout her reign. It had many ramifications, extending, on the one hand, to Sir Philip Sidney, and the group of friends, poets and scientists who surrounded his beautiful sister, the Countess of Pembroke, in Wiltshire; and, on the other, to the growing numbers of historians, cartographers, theorists and adventurers who were working towards the English domination of the high seas and oceans in the latter part of her reign. Intellectual England of the later sixteenth century was still a very small world; its members impinged on Elizabeth's life at a number of points. She did not identify herself with any particular faction – she was much too prudent for that – and her other responsibilities did not permit her the time to become deeply involved in the higher speculations of the age. But she constantly saw and patronized those who were pushing forward the frontiers of knowledge. At Richmond, her favourite palace, she was within easy reach of Walsingham's house at Barnes, where members of the Sidney circle, and other intellectuals, were his frequent guests and visitors; of Syon House, where the 'Wizard Earl' of Northumberland received Ralegh, Hariot, Marlowe, Donne and other men of learning; and of Mortlake, where the great mathematician, Dr John Dee, had created a laboratory and a library of over 4,000 volumes – bigger than anything in England, and the second largest in Western Europe, containing what has been termed 'the whole Renaissance'.[92]

Dee had taught science to the young Dudley, and it was through this connection that he became the Queen's friend.[93] Dee's relationship with Elizabeth has damaged her reputation as an intellectual, for he has traditionally been represented as a magician and astrologist – 'Doctor Dee the great conjuror', as his enemy John Foxe called him in the *Acts and Monuments*. In fact he was an experimental and theoretical scientist of outstanding originality, worthy to rank with Copernicus. Indeed, it was the interest he shared with Copernicus in the early Christian Hermetic texts which led to his obsession with astrology, cabalistic art and other supposed keys to knowledge. Such explorations were coming under criticism in his own day, and were later to be seen as wholly unprofitable, though even in the late seventeenth century Newton himself did not despise them. Dee's use of them sprang from his impatience with the methods and instrumentation of empirical research at his disposal. But he was a true scientist all the same.[94] He was six years older than Elizabeth, and had made a prodigious sensation at Rheims College in Paris in 1550 when, aged only twenty-three, he had given the first lectures on Euclid at a Christian university. His range of interests was wide even for the Renaissance age, and he turned his back upon an Oxbridge career precisely because he thought its curricula and preoccupations too narrow – no doubt one chief reason why his posthumous reputation has suffered. In essence, he sought to prevent the separation of the two cultures, believing (along with Sir Philip Sidney and his friends), that poetry, geography, mathematics, classical studies, philosophy and physics were all legitimate methods to determine an ultimate truth which was at once Christian and rational. As Sidney himself put it:

> all lead and draw us to as high a perfection as our degenerate souls, made worse by their clayey longings, can be capable of. For some, thinking this felicity was principally to be gotten by knowledge, and no knowledge to be so high and heavenly as acquaintance with the stars, gave themselves to astronomy; others ... became natural and supernatural philosophers; some with an admirable delight drew to music; and some the certainty of demonstration to mathematics. But all, one and other, having this scope – to know, and by knowledge to lift up the mind from the dungeon of the body to the enjoying of his own divine essence.[95]

In understanding Elizabeth, it is important to realize that, behind the woman of state, obsessed by finance, relations with Spain, the problem of Mary Queen of Scots, the internal political balance, marriage plans and the importunings of court suitors, behind, too, the woman of pleasure who loved dancing and adulatory verse, there was a powerful intelligence, working on similar lines to Sidney's, and concerned (if less fundamentally than he) with the search for eternal verities, and the escape from 'the dungeon of this body'. It was her own form of Christianity. She lived vicariously the intellectual life through Dee, as she touched heroic adventure through Ralegh. Highly original speculation was always a risky business in her day. Dee noted in his autobiographical fragment that the Queen gave him her full protection, and 'promised unto me great security against any in her kingdom, that would by reason of any my rare studies and philosophical exercises, unduly seek my overthrow'.[96] At Greenwich, in June 1564, he presented her with his *Monas Hieroglyphica*, 'whereupon her Majesty had a little perusal of the same with me, and then in most heroical and princely wise did comfort me and encourage me in my studies philosophical and mathematical'. She visited him on many occasions, received him at court, and begged him to stay there (he declined because it interrupted his studies), and in March 1575 paid him a state visit of approval: 'The Queen's Majesty, with her most honourable Privy Council, and other her lords and nobility, came purposely to have visited my library.'[97] Dee had long ago pressed on Queen Mary the idea of a Public Record Office to preserve state and other manuscripts; turned down, he tried to create his own, and his collection was used by Camden, Hakluyt, Stow, Holinshed and the royal heralds, among others. He served Elizabeth in a practical manner by thus combining antiquarianism with the physical sciences. Thus he worked with Christopher Chancellor and Frobisher on preparing the cartography and instrumentation for their voyages; Walsingham, Leicester, Hatton and Dyer – all backers of Drake's world voyage – came to seek his advice and documentation before Drake set off in 1577. His advocacy was one reason why Elizabeth gave the expedition her approval. But at the same time he was preparing the historical basis for claims Elizabeth might advance in the wake of her explorers and mariners. The same year he predicted the formation of what he called an 'Incomparable British Empire', both political and religious, underwritten by a huge navy and based on historical claims dating from King Edgar, whom he termed 'the Saxonical Alexander'. He explained to Elizabeth, on 3 October 1580, that she was legally entitled to enormous areas in the northern hemisphere, adding that 'the Lord Treasurer has greatly commended my doings for her title'; such an empire would resolve, by peaceful means, the divisions of Christianity on a basis of tolerance.[98] The oceanic adventures of Elizabeth's reign are too often portrayed exclusively in terms of near-piracy and the ruthless quest for spoils and gold, with Elizabeth as a covert and mendacious abettor; they were also, as we see from the Dee connection, part of the Renaissance search for truth, with profoundly moral and pacific objectives, which appealed strongly to Elizabeth's intellect and character.

Indeed, it is probable that what we would today term the superstitious side of Dee's work made the least appeal to her. She could not, of course, ignore this world, which dominated the thinking of so many of her subjects; superstition was closer to their daily lives than reason, or indeed religion. Most of her contemporaries believed in astrology, and so did she in the sense that she was not prepared to rule it out as a possibility. It had the approval of many clergymen, who were regular clients of such professionals as Simon Forman. Bishop Aylmer of London assured her she had nothing to fear so long as Virgo was in the ascendant.[99] As the epitome of Virgo – 'God's virgin', to quote Rossetti[100] – she used this as a collateral reason not to get married. Politics and prophecy were closely related. Norfolk's actions may have been influenced by a prophesy against her.[101] Politicians took such things seriously. In 1581 parliament made it a statutory felony to erect figures, cast nativities or calculate by prophecy how long Elizabeth would live, or who would succeed her.[102] Babington plotted against her on the basis of a prophecy attributed to Merlin, and she received constant warnings of a similar kind. Hatton gave her a protective ring, and she in turn gave Essex an Edward III noble, reputed to have such properties, when he went on the Islands Voyage in 1597.[103] Many hostile dolls were made of her, and assaults committed on her images and portraits.[104] This was the atmosphere she lived in, and Elizabeth accepted it with her customary tact, realism and unwillingness to offend contemporary standards. She consulted Dee about the famous comet of 1577, but she ignored superstition, and the pleas of her courtiers, by insisting on going to look at it through a window, saying *Iacta est alea*, the dice is thrown.[105] Like the best of us, Elizabeth hovered towards credulity in moments of extreme danger; but as a rule she was a supreme Renaissance woman, ready to look the unknown world in the face and penetrate its mysteries. Dee, Ralegh and many other explorers carved windows for her into this world, and that was why she liked their company.

Elizabeth was an adventurer and traveller in the mind; for this, Richmond was her chosen place, her reading, her gift of languages, the brilliant men she patronized and who came to visit her, the instruments and agents in these transferred experiences. Did she ever wish to travel in fact? There is no evidence. Her father and grandfather had been cosmopolitans, to some extent. Virtually all the great men at her court had crossed the Channel. Most of those she esteemed were familiar with European courts and universities. It was already accepted that the education of an ambitious young gentleman was incomplete unless he had travelled in France, Germany and Italy. The times were enviable: when Sir Philip Sidney was in Venice and decided to have his portrait painted, he could choose between Titian, Veronese and Tintoretto (Veronese was elected).[106] Yet Elizabeth not only never went abroad: there is nothing on record that shows she had the slightest desire to do so; such voyages were not for women, and she was very angry when court ladies followed Leicester to the

Low Countries. She may, perhaps, have taken the view of her Treasurer: 'The old Lord Burghley, if anyone came to the lords of the Council for a license to travel, would first examine him of England. And if he found him ignorant, would bid him stay at home and know his own country first.'[107] Yet in England, too, Elizabeth showed no practical willingness to travel beyond the south, and east and Midlands, from which she drew her strength. She went as far as the Severn and Trent, but never crossed them. Projects to visit, for instance, Shrewsbury and York, were discussed, planned, but never carried out.

Nevertheless, within the geographical limits she apparently set herself, Elizabeth moved about a good deal. Her court was itinerant. It had to be so, for a variety of reasons – economic, hygienic, political. Its vast, voracious and filthy presence emptied the surrounding land of food and filled the streams with sewage. If it stayed too long in any one place, epidemics, it was thought, were bound to break out. Yet if it did not come in solemn cycle, its absence was vociferously deplored by tradesmen and local operators. Then, there were certain ceremonies which had, as a rule, to be performed in specific places. The court year began in November, when Elizabeth was back in Whitehall for her Accession Day tilts, the legal term and (when sitting) the parliamentary session. Whitehall was the normal place for Christmas, too, though (especially during the years of danger, or plague), she sometimes spent it at Greenwich, Richmond, Hampton Court, or even Windsor. These palaces were fully equipped for the Christmas festivities, including the play-season, which lasted from 26 December to 2 February, with extra plays at Shrovetide. She spent part of the late winter away, if parliament was not sitting, at the outer Thames palaces, at Oatlands and Nonsuch. She was back in Whitehall for the spring, performing the Maundy washing of feet, like the Pope: 'You see,' she said to the Spanish ambassador, 'in essentials we monarchs think alike.' She spent the rest of the spring and early summer in little, or 'by-progresses', but usually with a visit to Windsor for the Garter ceremony; it was performed by deputy, but she saw the plays which accompanied it. Then there were spells at the river-palaces. July, August and September were set aside for major progresses, if the times permitted, the court ending up in early autumn at Oatlands, Windsor, Reading or Nonsuch, before returning to London to start the cycle again.[108]

The progresses enabled Elizabeth to cover a good deal of ground. In 1561 she made a prolonged tour of Hertfordshire, Essex and Suffolk. In 1564 she went to Cambridge and East Anglia, in 1566 to Oxford and the Midlands. In 1568 she was in Northamptonshire, the following year in Surrey and Hampshire. In 1572 she ranged widely in Hertfordshire, Bedfordshire, Warwickshire, Leicestershire and Berkshire. In 1574, she went westwards to Bristol, for the signature of the treaty with Spain, covering much of Gloucestershire and Wiltshire. The next year came the grandest progress of all, through the Midlands, culminating in the fortnight's entertainment Leicester arranged for her at Kenilworth Castle. In 1578 there was another memorable voyage through East Anglia. The 1570s were the vintage years of the Elizabethan progress; during the crisis years of the 1580s her movements were restricted, but she stepped them up in the 1590s, partly at least to prove she was not growing too old to travel. Always, whatever the situation, she spent some weeks travelling around the Home Counties, where the source of her popularity and strength lay. Many of her movements are minutely chronicled, from the surviving documents, in Nichols' *Progresses*: he lists 241 places she visited for a night or more, and 148 different households with whom she stayed, and his catalogue is necessarily incomplete.[109] Over a large part of south-east and central England Elizabeth was a known, if not quite a familiar, figure: there can have been few people in these areas who did not get a chance to see her.

The itineraries, or 'gestes', for progresses were first drawn up by the Vice-Chamberlain in consultation with Elizabeth, and arranged by letter with town corporations and owners of private houses. There followed a visit by the royal Harbinger and two ushers of the Bedchamber, who inspected arrangements and accommodation. Road masters, security officials and equerries surveyed the route. Getting the progress on the road entailed prodigies of organization. One contemporary says it required 400 carts and 2,400 pack-horses to move a full progress – at the rate of 10–12 miles a day – and the cost had to be worked out to the nearest penny.[110] These huge convoys smashed up the primitive roads, though they were also an incentive to road-improvement. Sometimes the going was rough. Writing from Benenden, in Kent, in 1573, Burghley complained: 'The Queen had a hard beginning of her progress in the Weald of Kent and namely in some parts of Sussex, where surely were more dangerous rocks and valleys, and much worse ground, than was in the Peak [District].' Elizabeth herself travelled mainly on horseback, occasionally by litter, but two empty coaches, built by her Dutch carriage-master, William Boonen, followed in attendance if she and her ladies wanted a change. At the boundary of each shire she was met by the sheriff and the chief gentlemen of the county, who often accompanied her throughout her stay; and at town boundaries the mayor and corporation, in regalia, received her to hand over the keys. There were invariably speeches of welcome, often lengthy, but sweetened by purses of gold. When it rained, Elizabeth usually insisted on carrying on, and then ruffs – which came in towards the middle of her reign – collapsed in ruin and festooned the bedraggled shoulders of men and women alike.

Elizabeth always had the magic touch for these ceremonies. At Warwick, in 1572, Mr Aglionby, the recorder, made a long speech, and when he had finished, the Queen said: 'Come hither, little Recorder. It was told me you would be afraid to look upon me, or to speak boldly; but you were not so afraid of me as I was of you; and I now thank you for putting me in mind of my duty, and that should be in me.'[111] Here, she had the neighbouring village youths and maidens dance in the courtyard of the castle, 'which thing, as it pleased well the country people, so it seemed her Majesty was much delighted, and made very merry'. When a firework display accidentally burned down a house near the castle, Elizabeth had the poor owners, Henry Cooper and his wife, brought to her, and raised a collection of £25 12s. 8d. for a new roof. She often stopped the progress to talk to the crowds, sometimes went into private houses without warning and had a snack or a drink. The Spanish ambassador, following her 1568 progress, reported that she 'ordered her carriage . . . to be taken where the crowd seemed thickest, and stood up and thanked the people'. She inspected local manufactures: thus, at Norwich in 1578, she visited children employed on worsted knitting. The contemporary account of this visit notes: 'She took the mayor by the hand and used secret conference, but what I know not.' Afterwards, she knighted him, saying 'I have laid up in my breast such good will as I shall never forget Norwich.' And when she left its boundary, she 'did shake her riding rod and said, "Farewell, Norwich", with the water standing in her eyes'.[112] The poet Thomas Churchyard had been in the city for three weeks, rehearsing the local children in pageants; at the last minute it looked as though his efforts would be crowded out of the programme, but the Queen insisted on seeing them. She had an extraordinarily high tolerance for tedious entertainments; but then she was always anxious to please, if it could be done with dignity. In the case of Norwich she was particularly delighted to get such a warm reception, for this city had been a centre of Kett's rebellion, and it had, of course, been the home town of the Duke of Norfolk whom she had executed. She usually had a local compliment to pay: thus, in Bristol, she called St Mary Redcliffe's 'the finest and goodliest parish church in England' – which, indeed, it still is – and a wooden statue of her, carved and painted to mark her visit, is preserved in the church. For such gestures she was well briefed by Burghley: we find him studying Lambarde's *Itinerary of Kent* so that he could instruct her on the local marvels there.[113]

Elizabeth's progresses have often been represented as a monstrous burden on town and countryside, and in particular on the individuals who entertained her. But the evidence shows that she was welcome everywhere, and that the towns – the Tudors were always popular in the towns – fought hard to get a place on the itinerary. Who paid for what is hard to determine. Puttenham, in his *Arte of Poesie*, says that Henry VII always paid himself if he took more than one meal, or spent the night, and was angry if more were proffered. He adds: 'Her Majesty hath been known oftentimes to mislike the superfluous expense of her subjects bestowed upon her in times of her progresses.'[114] When she took a meal *en route* she always provided for herself, and she brought her own wine, and often her own beer as well (to make sure it was not too strong). Most of those who went with her lived in tents, and were fed at court expense. The food was bought on the spot, at low rates fixed by the court; but local juries were empanelled to assist her Clerk of the Market with tariffs, and to supervise weights and measures. Everyone, including the Queen and Burghley, disliked the purveyance system, but no one could think of a better, and the fact that the progresses were popular suggests that Elizabeth took care not to exploit it. Cities and towns had to pay for gifts to officials, and a present for Elizabeth; but part of the cost of entertainment was borne by the Revels Office, which loaned tents, costumes and properties, and paid for light, rushes and fuel.[115]

As for individuals, I have found no case where a host resented Elizabeth's coming, or complained openly at the expense. As sovereign, she had an absolute right to occupy the house of any subject who was a tenant-in-chief, since all manors were held ultimately of the crown, but it is significant that the legal position did not have to be spelled out until James I came to the throne and abused it.[116] Owners were chiefly concerned to receive enough warning, so that sufficient preparation could be made. Buckhurst, whose splendid house at Knole was being rebuilt, wrote anxiously to the Chamberlain, Sussex, in 1577, for 'some certainty of the progress, if it may possibly be'. Other peers, he explained, had bought up all the surplus provisions in Kent, Surrey and Sussex, but he could send to Flanders if need be. However, unless Elizabeth could be 'presently determined' on when she was coming, he could not perform 'which is due and convenient': 'May it please God that the house do not mislike her; that is my chief care . . . But if her Highness had tarried one year longer, we had been too, too happy; but God's will and hers be done.'[117] Sir William Cornwallis, writing to Walsingham in 1583, on behalf of the Earl of Northumberland, whose house at Petworth the Queen planned to visit, also begged for a definite date, but added hastily: 'Notwithstanding, Sir, this is very true, yet it may not be advertised, lest it might be thought to give impediment to her Majesty's coming, whereof I perceive my lord very glad and desirous.'[118] The Thynnes of Longleat successfully deferred a royal visit; but this was because they wanted Elizabeth to see their elaborate house when it was finished. Generally, owners were anxious to accommodate the Queen, and disappointed if she passed nearby without staying; Lady Norris bitterly upbraided Hatton and Leicester in 1582 for advising the Queen not to call at Rycote because of the 'foul and ragged way'. The only recorded case of stinginess is that of Sir William Clarke in 1602, who 'neither gives meal nor money to any of the progressors. The house her Majesty has at commandment, and his grass the guard's horses eat, and that is all.'[119]

As a rule, the hosts rivalled each other to put on splendid entertainments. In East Anglia in 1578, Sir William Cordell of Long Melford 'did light such a candle to the rest of the shire'. At Hawstead, Sir William Drury had a new stone fountain erected, surmounted by a giant statue of Hercules, who peed into the water. At Elvetham, Lord Montague built an artificial crescent-shaped lake for a water-pageant; at Mount Surrey an artificial cave was excavated to contain a hidden orchestra; and Sir Francis Carew retarded a cherry-tree by covering it with a tent, so that the Queen could have out-of-season fruit. These displays were not conspicuous consumption for its own sake: they were deliberately put on to epitomize the ancient tradition of country hospitality, and to delight the neighbourhood, for whom a royal visit might well be the most remarkable event in their lives. The actual cost has been distorted by a statement in Burghley's anonymous biography that he forked out some £2–3,000 whenever the Queen came to Theobalds (she was there at least twelve times). This assertion is frequently repeated even today, but Burghley's own accounts show it is a gross exaggeration. Elizabeth's fourteen-day visit to Burghley in 1575 cost him £340 17s. 4d.; a shorter visit in 1578, £337 7s. 5d.; a ten-day visit in 1591 came to £998 13s. 4d., to which Burghley added £100 'for a gown for the Queen'.[120] Such accounts as survive indicate that the cost varied greatly, depending on what items were included to cover the royal visit. Often, major work on the house and gardens was included under this head, though the money would have been spent anyway. Lord North spent £762 5s. 2d. entertaining Elizabeth for two nights and three days at Kirtling: of this, £120 went on a jewel for her, £88 on meat, and £5 for a cartload and two horse-loads of oysters; 2,522 eggs were eaten. Sir Nicholas Bacon, who had Elizabeth at Gorhambury for four nights in 1577, spent a total of £577 6s. 7½d., including £12 for hiring cooks from London. The discrepancy between this, and larger amounts spent by others for shorter stays, indicates that ruining yourself for Elizabeth was entirely optional. Wealthy neighbours were roped in to help. When Lord Keeper Egerton entertained the Queen on a grand scale at Harefield in 1602, he himself spent £1,225 12s. for provisions, out of a total (including the bills for gifts and temporary buildings) of over £2,000 – the highest figure for a visit I have been able to find. But local gentry provided 86 stags and bucks, 11 oxen, 65 sheep, 41 sugar loaves, and game, fish, oysters, sweets, wine, wheat and salt.[121] One reason why people enjoyed entertaining Elizabeth was that she was very appreciative, and made remarkably little fuss (except over strong beer); another was that she enforced high standards of behaviour among her court and servants. Henry VIII had had to issue an angry ordinance in 1526, because of what he termed 'the spoliation of houses' on progress: locks had been smashed, tables, benches and even cupboards stolen, and produce of all kinds eaten without permission, or destroyed. Nothing like this is reported under Elizabeth; the only occasion when the progress got out of hand was in 1574 when it put up without warning at Berkeley Castle, in Lord Berkeley's absence, and twenty-seven deer were killed in a single day. This was Leicester's doing, and Berkeley (they were enemies) was rightly furious. But in most cases Elizabeth left a happy memory behind.[122]

The chief onus of entertaining her fell, as was natural, on her greatest servants (Egerton was a case in point). This was one chief reason why she rewarded them so handsomely, or rather enabled them to reward themselves at public expense. Leicester's entertainment of her at Kenilworth in 1575 – the most spectacular of the entire reign – lasted seventeen days, and the cost (alas, unknown to us) must have been enormous. One of the Earl's men, the Porter Robert Laneham, wrote a detailed description of the ceremonies, which included masques by Gascoigne and elaborate *son-et-lumière* set-pieces, all conducted in fine, hot weather.[123] According to the French ambassador, Leicester bore the whole cost himself; but then most of his vast income came through Elizabeth's favour.[124] Elizabeth deliberately encouraged two or three of her leading ministers to build spacious houses so that the court could be properly accommodated, and the business of government carried on from there, if necessary for long periods. Burghley greatly enlarged the house he had inherited (now Burghley House) near Stamford. But for entertaining the Queen he built another, Theobalds (she called it Tibbuls), near Waltham Cross, which was conveniently near London, and within riding distance of the country seats of other ministers. He seems to have designed it himself, and it became the quintessence of the grand Elizabethan provincial palace, and the archetype for many more.[125] As his biographer says, 'at the first he meant [it] for a little pile, as I have heard him say, but, after he came to entertain the Queen so often there, he was enforced to enlarge it rather for the Queen and her great train ... than for pomp and glory'. Burghley himself confirmed this statement in a letter dated 14 August 1585: 'begun by me with a mean measure, but increased by occasion of her Majesty's often coming.'[126] She herself played a part in the design and decoration of the house, since it was apparently on her instructions that her bedchamber was enlarged and lined with artificial trees, so lifelike, said a visitor in 1592, that the birds flew in through the windows, perched on the branches, and sang; the whole ceiling was laid out as an astronomical clock, with the sun and stars performing their courses mechanically. There were five different galleries, where the Queen could walk in wet weather, one of them lined with maps of all the counties of England, with family trees of the principal gentry in each; on fine days she could walk on the roof, made specially flat for this purpose, or in the gardens, of which there were four. The house cost Burghley £25,000.

Hatton used Theobalds as the model for his palace of Holdenby – 'done', as he wrote to Burghley, 'in direct observation of your house and plot at Tyball's'. It was the biggest house in England, next to Hampton Court, formally dedicated to Elizabeth, and undoubtedly constructed at her behest and direction. Indeed, accordingly to Barnaby Rich, Hatton hardly ever visited it, except in the company of the Queen. But, even when Hatton was away, any properly-dressed gentleman could drop in, be fed, and even lodged. The house, indeed, was an exercise in state public relations, conducted through a private individual. When Burghley inspected it, he wrote admiringly to Hatton that it was even finer than Theobalds, 'no otherwise worthy in any comparison than a foil'. And he added: 'God send us long to enjoy Her, for whom we both meant to exceed our purses in these.'[127] This last remark was something of a private joke: both houses were, in effect, paid for out of public funds. Indeed, Hatton was already £10,000 in debt when he began Holdenby in 1578, and it was financed by an extraordinarily complex series of deals with Elizabeth, involving the swopping around of manors, leases, counter-leases, loans and mortgages. Visitors to Holdenby were under no illusion how the house had come into existence. Thus, Ben Jonson, who was there in 1603, wrote, echoing Perrot's dancing crack at Hatton:

> They come to see and to be seen,
> And though they dance before the Queen,
> There's none of these doth hope to come by
> Wealth to build another Holmby.

In a sense, Theobalds and Holdenby can be described as surrogate royal houses, and since Elizabeth had so large a hand in their conception, she can rightly be described as one of the most important figures in the architecture of her age. Unhappily, virtually nothing now survives of either. Elizabeth built these houses by deputy; James I took them over in fact (he exchanged Theobalds, which Burghley had bequeathed to his younger son, Sir Robert Cecil, for Hatfield, and took over Holdenby as part-cancellation of Hatton's still unpaid debts).

As a result, both houses fell into ruin during the Civil War, and were later demolished. The story of their rise and fall is one more illustration of the fact that Elizabeth was the last English sovereign who knew how to operate the system of personal monarchy successfully.

However, though Holdenby and Theobalds are lost, so many country houses where she did stay still survive, at least in part, that we tend to think of Elizabeth as chiefly preoccupied with her popularity in the counties. Not so. There were several more important considerations in planning her routine. She had to maintain her esteem in leading cities and towns: hence the elaboration of her visits to such places as Norwich, Bristol, Southampton, Worcester, Warwick, Canterbury and so forth. She also had to pay particular attention to the seats of learning. Education was a prime concern of Elizabethan government and of the Queen personally. She took a direct interest in the management of such schools as Eton and Westminster, which were of royal foundation or had developed from royal abbeys. Many schools were directly linked to government: thus Shrewsbury, one of the largest and best of her day (Philip Sidney and Fulke Greville were contemporaries there), owed its significance to its connection with the court of the Welsh Marches at Ludlow. Both government and parliament pushed the development of the grammar school system, which perhaps played a more positive role in English education under Elizabeth than at any time before or since. Elizabeth and her ministers believed that an educated ruling class, in both town and county, was essential to the maintenance of civil stability. What happened at Oxford and Cambridge was, to her, of direct concern to government, since it influenced patterns of thought and behaviour in public affairs, especially in religion. Thus, though Elizabeth was only involved in the foundation of one college, Jesus at Oxford, she saw to it that her leading ministers took a personal interest in many of the houses, and the Chancellors of the universities – Leicester and Hatton at Oxford, for instance, and Burghley at Cambridge – were always men she could trust. Their positions were not sinecures, and they, and she, directly intervened in Oxbridge affairs on many occasions.

The government took extraordinary care in arranging her visits to the universities. It was considered vital that the régime should be popular, and the sovereign venerated, in the seats of learning. Burghley, for instance, meticulously planned her visit to Cambridge in 1564, corresponding at length with the Vice-Chancellor, briefing heads of houses, drawing up the programme of events in great detail with them, and even issuing instructions about gifts to be offered to her. He wrote: 'I am in great anxiety for the well-doing of things here,' and he instructed officials 'that order should be diligently kept of all sorts;

and that uniformity should be shown in apparel and religion, and especially in setting at the communion table.' Rushes and sand were put in the street, lanes were boarded up to control the crowd, and the scholars were instructed to shout *Vivat Regina!* while 'lowly kneeling'. Elizabeth's behaviour was thoroughly characteristic. She wore a black velvet gown, slit with pink, and a gold-spangled hat with bushy feathers. On her arrival, she accepted the staves of office of the university authorities, and handed them back with a joke: 'willing [the vice-chancellor] and other magistrates of the university, to minister justice uprightly, as she trusted they did, or she would take them into her own hands and see to it.' She was delighted with King's Chapel, which she said was the best in her realm. There was a Latin sermon delivered by Dr Andrew Perme, and she told him, half-way through, to put on his hat; afterwards, she said it was the first sermon she had ever heard in Latin, 'and, she thought, she should never hear a better'. Then she sang a song, 'in prick-song', and in the evening saw a play by Plautus. The next day, a Monday, lectures were specially held for her to attend (it was vacation), and she heard a formal disputation in Great St Mary's, where she noticed, and publicly criticized, some of the masters' gowns. That evening she saw *Dido*, and the following day, having cancelled a disputation in order to hold a Council meeting, she heard *Ezechias* performed in English. As a compliment, she postponed her departure a day, and said she would have stayed longer, 'if provision of beer and ale could have been made'. She toured the colleges, heard a divinity debate, and made a speech in Latin, in which she promised to build a college. At the end of it, the crowd shouted *Vivat Regina!* to which she replied *Taceat Regina!* and said she wished that 'all they that had heard her oration had drunk of the flood of Lethe' – 'and so her Majesty cheerfully departed for her lodging'. On her last evening the students wanted to give her a Sophocles tragedy in Latin; but she said she was too tired, and had to get up early the next morning.[128] It was all a typical Elizabeth performance, a blend of formality and fun, wit, erudition, humanity and sharp criticism (Elizabeth knew many of the dons by name, and often rebuked or commended them for their writings and sermons), carried through in relaxed style.

In a sense, indeed, Elizabeth was an actual performer. Reconstructions of the physical arrangements made for plays given before the Queen make this clear. Thus, for the performance of the Plautus play, the *Aulularia*, in King's College Chapel, the seating was arranged so that only Elizabeth herself had a perfect view of the stage: this was intentional, for the spectators were just as interested in watching her, as in seeing the performance.[129] The action on stage was a play within a play, with the Queen as heroine – just as Claudius, in *Hamlet*, is the cynosure while the players are acting. The point was made even more strongly at Oxford, in 1566, when Elizabeth stayed at Christ Church, and saw Richard Edward's *Palamon and Arcyte*. A special door was cut in the wall to ensure that Elizabeth was able to move in complete privacy between her lodgings in the college and her seat directly facing the stage: thus she was able to make a dramatic entrance, and the first the audience saw of her was when she took her seat. Others played subsidiary roles: at Cambridge in 1564, Leicester and Burghley sat on the stage holding the prompt-books: they, too, were to be seen – though there was no question of their upstaging the Star! For these university performances, the government paid for the erection of the stage, expensive properties, and much else. At Christ Church, the hall had been specially panelled in gilt, and the beams painted, so that, said an eye witness, it looked like 'an ancient Roman palace' – this, too, was at the Queen's expense.[130] The régime thus underwrote the cost of theatrical performances, since, when the Queen was present, it had a political interest in their success, not only in the universities but at the court in London. Under Elizabeth, a court play including the accompanying masque, cost about £400.[131] The Queen was, in a practical sense, a backer, or 'angel', of the Elizabethan theatre, and the public, who later saw plays, first presented at court, in the commercial houses, was the beneficiary of a substantial crown investment in the original productions.

Indeed, in all the activities of Elizabeth's court – ostensibly mounted for the exclusive enjoyment of the favoured few – the great mass of the public was always kept in mind. Hers was a popular monarchy. The performance was aimed at them. It was one of the greatest grievances against James I that he so rarely showed his face to his subjects (threatening, when criticized, to 'take down my breeks and show my arse'). Much as Elizabeth sought the applause of the provincial towns and the universities, it was to the theatre of metropolitan London that she directed her chief efforts. She spent far more time there than anywhere else; she moved constantly about Westminster and the City, for dinners, weddings, supper-parties, plays and musical entertainments, bull- and bear-baiting, river-fêtes, military exercises and tilts – which were held in Cheapside and elsewhere as well as in the Whitehall tiltyard – in addition to special occasions, like the opening of the new London Exchange, when she dined in state at Sir Thomas Gresham's palace. She must have known London intimately, and its citizens found her a familiar presence, arriving to dine at a great City house to the sound of eight trumpeters, with drums and fifes and flickering torches, often with the peal of artillery. All her leading men kept up great state in Westminster and the City when she was in residence. Only the Charterhouse, occupied in succession by Lord North, the Duke of Norfolk and Lord Thomas Howard, survives to show us what an Elizabethan town palace was like. But in her day there were over a score of them – Lord Burghley in Cecil House north of the Strand; the Lord Chancellor in York House, east of Charing Cross; Ralegh in Durham House nearby; Sir John Thynne, Sir Edward Hoby, the Earls of Derby, Hertford and Lincoln east of King Street, Westminster; Lord Grey, the Earl of Sussex, Lord Dacre in and around Tothill Street; Howard of Effingham in Chelsea, Lord Burgh and the Archbishop of Canterbury in Lambeth; Lord Hunsdon in Somerset House; the Earl of Bedford in Russell House off Ivy Lane; Dudley in Leicester House (later the Earl of Essex's town palace) near St Clement Danes; the Earl of Southampton in Chancery Lane; Pembroke in Baynard's Castle near the Fleet Ditch; Gresham off Bishopsgate Street; Walsingham in Houndsditch; Sir Thomas Heneage near St Mary Axe; Lord Lumley north of the Tower. In these great mansions the Queen dined, supped, danced and saw entertainments, passing to and from them, by the river or through the streets, in the sight of multitudes. 'God's Virgin' was also, perhaps more so, the people's virgin.

Indeed, the phrase she used more often than any other – it occurs, throughout her reign, in innumerable eye-witness accounts – was 'Thank you, my good people', her customary refrain (with variations) when acknowledging the cheers of the crowd. Nor was this simply a matter of public relations. Elizabeth received, almost every day of her reign, individual and collective petitions from the obscure. She saw herself as embodying the popular sovereignty of the Plantagenets, which itself derived from the far more ancient traditions of the royal house of Wessex; she had, and she was proud of it, a direct nexus with ordinary men and women. Her insistence on this point sometimes disconcerted her ministers, even those who knew her best. Complaints about the behaviour of the powerful, including those she trusted most, sometimes took a long time to get through to her – sometimes, perhaps, they never got through at all – but when a grievance was brought to her notice, she could act against the whole weight of her government. Thus, in 1590, Richard Carmarthen, a comparatively humble tide-waiter, or customs official, in the port of London, finally succeeded in drawing her attention to the scandalous farming of the London customs by 'Customer' Smythe. Carmarthen had been campaigning for reforms for twenty years, but Smythe's profits – which were made at the expense both of the Queen and of ordinary people – were to some extent shared by members of the government, notably Leicester, Walsingham and Hatton. Burghley approved of the system partly on purely conservative grounds, and partly because an efficient customs administration would be unpopular with a large section of the monied merchant community. Together, these powerful men kept Carmarthen from seeing the Queen for five years. When Elizabeth got to hear of the matter,

Carmarthen had, in fact, been put in prison as a nuisance; she ordered his immediate release, and directed that he not 'be imprisoned for discovering that which might be profitable to her'.[132] Camden's account of this obscure episode, once discredited, has now been fully substantiated by research in the state papers, and it is worth quoting. Walsingham and Burghley, it seems, protested that she should 'hearken to the accusation of so inconsiderable an informer'. Elizabeth replied:

> That it was the duty of a prince to hold an equal hand over the highest and the lowest. That such as accuse magistrates and counsellors rashly . . . are to be punished: those which accuse them justly are to be heard. That she was Queen of the meanest subjects as well as of the greatest; neither would she stop her ears against them, nor endure that the farmers of the customs should, like horseleeches, make themselves fat upon the goods of the commonwealth whilst the poor Treasury waxed lean and was exhausted; nor that the Treasury should be crammed with the spoils and pollings of the poorer sort.[133]

Here, I think, we can detect an echo of Elizabeth's actual words, spoken in some anger: she seems to have used similar phrases on other occasions. She always distrusted public servants who sought 'popularity': that was for the monarch alone. Sir Walter Ralegh recorded that 'she much desired to spare the common people', and says that when he defended popular interests in the House of Commons, 'I did it by her commandment.' After her death, he had the temerity to point out to King James that 'Queen Elizabeth would set the reason of a mean man before the authority of the greatest counsellor she had . . . she was the Queen of the small as well as the great, and would hear their complaints.'[134] These were not just empty phrases; they evidently had a real meaning for her contemporaries. If Elizabeth was the centre of an elitist society, distinguished by brains as well as birth and wealth, if she was the apex of a hierarchical pyramid whose gradations she sought strenuously to maintain, she was well aware that its solidity rested on the loyalty of the base. This was something she bore constantly in mind as, during the 1580s, her régime and her country were impelled, by forces which proved irresistible, towards a great **Continental war.**

8

Daughters of Debate

As the 1570s progressed, it seemed possible, at least to Elizabeth, that she might contrive to keep her country out of war. There were, of course, all kinds of theoretical, and some practical, reasons why the religious disputes now convulsing Europe must and would engulf England. But she hoped that, by exercising tact, and patience, and by rejecting the monstrous logic of inevitable war, she could, as Burghley put it, 'win time, wherein many accidents may ensue'.[1] Meanwhile, England was enjoying peace and a growing measure of prosperity. Population and incomes, the volume of trade and of manufactures, were all rising. Sir Walter Mildmay, addressing the Commons, was able to point to the striking contrast between England and her Continental neighbours. Abroad, there was nothing but 'depopulations and devastations of whole provinces and countries, overthrowing, spoiling and sacking of cities and towns, imprisoning, ransoming and murdering of all kinds of people'. But in England, 'the peaceable government of her Majesty doth make us to enjoy all that is ours in more freedom than any nation under the sun at this day'.[2] England, added Burghley, was 'a centre of happiness, where the circumference is in open calamity'.[3] Holding herself aloof, above the European struggle, Elizabeth appeared at this time, as Camden records, as a mediatrix and arbitrator of the nations:

> Thus sat she as an heroical princess and umpire between the Spaniards, the French and the States; so as she might well have used that saying of her father, *cui adhereo, praeest*, that is, the party to which I adhere getteth the upper hand. And true it was which one hath written, that France and Spain are, as it were, the scales in the balance of Europe, and England the tongue or the holder of the balance.[4]

The parliament of 1576, against this background, passed virtually without incident. It was the most amenable and good-tempered of all Elizabeth's assemblies, and she closed it with an elegant speech, of which she was evidently proud. Good-naturedly, she sent a copy of it to her young godson, the future Sir John Harington, with a note in her own hand:

Boy Jack, I have made a clerk write fair my poor words for thine use, as it cannot be such striplings have entrance into parliament assembly as yet. Ponder them in thy hours of leisure, and play with them till they enter thine understanding; so shalt thou hereafter, perchance, find some good fruits hereof, when thy Godmother is out of remembrance.[5]

Yet the security was really an illusion. The peace-treaty which Spain, France and England had signed at Cateau-Cambrésis in 1559 had been the last, unsuccessful, attempt to rebuild the concert of Europe. The old medieval certitudes of a unified Christian world – such as they were – had vanished, and nothing had yet been devised to replace them. Until about 1550, there had been certain common assumptions about the inter-relationships of states; the united Church had been there to point them out, and to descant upon them from its great corpus of canon and civil law. But once the breakdown of the papacy's international authority was consummated, there was no agreed theory, let alone practice, of the law of nations. Elizabeth was dead before thinkers like Bacon, Suarez and Grotius began to construct a new code on a secular basis. Her reign thus coincided with a dangerous vacuum between two systems.[6] The papacy was no longer an intermediary but an embattled and bellicose partisan. There was no agreement on what ambassadors were supposed to do, on their rights, immunities and modes of procedure. Moreover, as yet, no state, save the papacy, maintained central diplomatic archives in such a way as to enable them to be consulted for day-to-day diplomacy. Often treaties and agreements were mislaid, and variously interpreted by the contracting parties. Official embassy files were virtually non-existent; departing ambassadors simply regarded them as private papers, and took them away, where they ended up in family archives, or were lost. Ministers treated state papers in the same way: when Walsingham died, the government felt it had no alternative but to take charge of all his papers, in the hope of finding whatever was needed. Elizabeth had no files of her own, no private office; she kept letters, memos and other up-to-date scraps of paper in her 'great pouch', which hung at her waist, or in her bedroom, then threw them away when they no longer seemed relevant. With the decline of spoken Latin, and the growing nationalism in the use of modern languages, linguistic barriers rose higher. Bad communications made diplomatic reflexes slow; often angry decisions had been taken, and men and ships moved, before a reply to admonitory letters could be received. London was over a week from Paris, four from Rome and Madrid.[7] Ambassadors and their governments were sometimes working at cross-purposes, and according to different time-scales.

In any case, formal diplomacy was ceasing to function. In an age of religious warfare, ambassadors were increasingly picked for their sectarian zeal; they declined to see themselves as channels of communication, and assumed the role of missionaries, and so conspirators. Sometimes they were prominent members of the governments they served, and picked for that reason. Since maintaining a regular ambassador was a symbol of alliance, envoys did not know what to do when cold war supervened. They drifted into contacts with elements trying to subvert the régime to which they were accredited. Sir Thomas Challenor was Elizabeth's last non-ideological ambassador to Philip II. His successor, Dr Man, was a bigoted Protestant Dean of Gloucester, and when he was expelled no one replaced him: a heretic could not operate at an ultra-Catholic court. The best appointment would have been Jane Dormer, a highly-intelligent lady of gentle birth, well known to Elizabeth from her youth, who had married Ambassador Feria and gone to live in Spain. She did her best to help captured English seamen and protect English interests at a personal level, but of course she was barred from any official role by her religion, sex and connections.[8] Philip's ambassadors to Elizabeth did more to promote enmity than to salvage the old Anglo-Habsburg relationship. Bishop Quadra, who replaced Feria, was deep in conspiracy with English, Scottish and Irish malcontents before he had been in London three months; Guzman de Silva tried hard at a personal level; Elizabeth herself liked him, and he was the only Spaniard to appreciate Burghley's pacific intentions, but even he felt that, in the long run, there could be no settlement with heretics. His successor, Guerau De Spes, regarded himself as placed in an enemy country, took a leading part in the Ridolfi Plot, may have been involved in an attempt to poison Burghley, and was sent back in disgrace. The merchant Antonio de Guaras, who then acted as chargé d'affaires, landed in the Tower. Philip's last ambassador, Bernadino de Mendoza, was a fire-eating cavalry commander and an open enemy of the Elizabethan régime. He was at the centre of the Throckmorton Plot, and was expelled, his parting words being that, the next time he came to England he would be at the head of an army. He was next sent to France, where he ended up discharging the more congenial duty of defending its capital against its King.[9] After 1589, Elizabeth had regular diplomatic contacts only with the Protestant King of France, the Protestant Dutch, and the Turks, where Sir William Harborne had been sent in 1583. This last contact, indeed, was a symbol – and more than a symbol – of the break-up of the old Christian world, for as recently as 1565, when the Turkish siege of Malta was lifted, Elizabeth had ordered services of thanksgiving, to be held thrice weekly for six weeks, in which Malta was referred to as the 'Bulwark of the Faith'; fifteen years later Walsingham was inciting the Turks to attack Christian Italy and Sicily.[10]

The diplomatic breakdown, and the atmosphere engendered by violent religious persecution, led to a collapse in the already precarious ethical standards of conduct between states, and particularly between princes. It was taken increasingly for granted that rulers, however divinely ordained, would lie and break their word, if it seemed convenient. Sir Robert Cecil wrote to a Scots correspondent:

> Trust no more than you think is wisdom for a prince to observe, for what formalities soever princes observe in these days of giving such words, I see most of them think they are bound to nothing that is evil for themselves; wherein they say they break not as out of lack of honesty, but because as kings they are tied to do that which concurs with their commonwealth's utility, for whom they were born, and not for themselves.[11]

Cecil's father, brought up in a sterner moral tradition, nevertheless allowed that lying was permissible in the right circumstances:

> All princes and especially such as profess the sincerity of true religion [that is, were Protestants] ought so to regard their leagues and promises as, although through necessity they are urged in certain manner to violate the same, yet not in so open and so violent a sort as it shall manifestly appear to the whole world.

Moreover, under threat, he considered that a state was divinely authorized to use any means:

> All forces and resistance begun upon urgent and necessary occasions for the safety of any state whose ruin is greedily sought after, is allowed of God, conformable with nature and disposition of men and by daily experience continued through the whole world.[12]

Machiavelli was officially banned in England, but his works circulated and were frequently quoted by clerics and secular writers alike; and his sentiments permeated political society. 'I must distinguish', wrote Burghley, 'between discontent and despair, for it is sufficient to weaken the discontented, but there is no way but to kill desperates.'[13] No wonder poor old Bishop Mandell Creighton, writing his *Life of Queen Elizabeth* in the 1890s, once piously suggested that Tudor history should be banned, since no one could study it without imperilling his soul!

Yet the Spaniards, indeed Catholics generally, were thought to be far worse. Challenor was shocked when the Duke of Alva told him that, if you found your enemy in the water up to his waist, you should help him out; but if he were up to his neck, you should push him under.[14] The paladins of the Catholic cause were regarded as monsters, in their private as well as their public life. What about the Monstrous Dragon herself? Philip II was portrayed in Protestant propaganda as a domestic ogre. In 1562 his son and heir, Don Carlos, had a fall and was supposedly 'cured' by having the bones of a pious Franciscan, who had died a century before, placed in his bed. Maybe he suffered brain-damage, but in any event he turned violent. Philip, wearing full armour, arrested him at dead of night, put him on trial, walled him up in his quarters, and later announced he had died. The Prince of Orange, William the Silent, openly accused Philip of murdering his heir, adding for good measure that he had also killed his wife, Isabella of France, who in fact had died in childbirth the same year, 1568. Philip himself deliberately and openly plotted the murder of Orange, placed a price on his head, and in 1584 saw his plans carried out. He had already had two of the greatest members of the Flemish nobility, Counts Hoorne and Egmont, condemned to death in defiance of all tradition and statute, and decapitated by the sword; two years later, in 1570, Egmont's younger brother, the Baron de Montigny, who had gone to Madrid under safe conduct, was secretly tried and garotted under Philip's personal supervision (it was officially announced he had died of natural causes). Philip accepted a plan for the murder of Elizabeth, Walsingham, Hunsdon, Sir Francis Knollys, and Robert Beale, adding: 'It does not matter so much about Cecil, though he is a great heretic, but he is very old ... it would be advisable to do as [the would-be assassin] says with the others.'[15] The French Catholics, of course, were committed to assassination, wholesale and in detail: the Duke of Guise made no secret of the fact that he was prepared to pay the murderer of Elizabeth. The Pope set the pattern and example for all. In 1580 the Papal Secretary of State was instructed to write to the nuncio in Madrid, who had asked whether English Catholic exiles and Jesuits would incur sin if they assassinated Elizabeth. His letter ruled:

> Since that guilty woman of England rules over two such noble kingdoms of Christendom and is the cause of so much injury to the Catholic faith and loss of so many million souls, there is no doubt that whosoever sends her out of the world with the pious intention of doing God service, not only does not sin but gains merit, especially having regard to the sentence pronounced against her by Pius V of holy memory. And so, if those English gentlemen decide actually to undertake so glorious a work, your Lordship can assure them that they do not commit any sin. We trust in God also that they will escape danger.[16]

The threat to Elizabeth was thus a real one, and universally known to be so. Moreover, there were few members of her government, and fewer still in parliament, who were under any illusion that her, and their, régime was likely to survive her murder. No imaginable successor would be able to command the confidence of the country; the result would be civil war, the intervention of one or more Catholic powers, a compromise at best, leading inevitably to the triumph of Rome. Then they would be hanged or burned alive. Nor was it just a question of their own lives. They had no doubt that the fall of England would mean the end of reformed religion. As Burghley, less of an alarmist than many other members of the government, put it, if England were forced back into the Catholic camp, 'all other parts of Christendom that are opposite to Rome will fall themselves without any great force or long war'.[17]

There was thus a powerful impulse among the English ruling class to seek the arbitration of the sword, which many believed must come sooner or later. All the evidence suggested that the power of Spain was growing. The number of professional troops under Spanish command in the Low Countries was steadily increased; there was no doubt whatever that, without foreign help, they would slowly but surely extinguish the independence of the Dutch and Flemish communities, and would then become available for a religious crusade against England. This was bad enough, but equally ominous was the growth of Spanish naval power. Philip's treasure fleets brought ever-larger cargoes of silver and gold from central and southern America to Seville, and the actions of French and English ships in the Caribbean had, paradoxically, led to a strengthening of Spanish power in the area, as the Spanish government ordered the construction of more warships, large, defensible merchant vessels, forts, dockyards and harbours. In 1571 the overwhelming Spanish naval victory over the Turks at Lepanto, where Philip's armada was commanded by his illegitimate half-brother, Don Juan of Austria, made possible the steady redeployment of the Habsburg naval resources – which included warships from many large Italian towns, such as Genoa – from the Mediterranean to the Atlantic theatres, and if necessary to the Channel. Moreover, it led to a redeployment in Philip's own mind: henceforth he saw his divinely-appointed task to be not so much the destruction of the infidels of the south and east, as the restoration to true faith among the heretics of the north.[18] Events seemed to encourage this design. In 1580 the childless King of Portugal died, leaving Philip himself, if not his legal heir, at least in a position to establish his claim *de facto*, which he proceeded to do without difficulty. Efforts to assert the rights of the anti-Spanish claimant, Don Antonio, sponsored by France and to some extent by England, proved futile; his base in the Azores fell to Spain in 1582, and in the process the French fleet was virtually annihilated, thus removing France, as a major factor in the naval balance, for more than a generation. By absorbing Portugal, Spain became a first-class Atlantic power; Philip acquired twelve enormous galleons, and promptly laid down nine more in Portuguese yards; Lisbon gave him an assembly port for fleets, and the Azores a valuable link in his Atlantic communications. Between this accumulation of naval forces, and Spanish control of the Channel and the Narrow Seas, there now stood only the English navy.

Confronted by the growing power of Spain, and by the distressing evidence of Philip's intentions towards her, what was Elizabeth to do? She wanted to avoid outright war at almost any cost; she was always careful to ensure that Spain had the least possible legal justification for any hostile action. On the other hand, it was a paramount English interest to take any measures, short of war, to delay or reverse the build-up of Spanish naval and military power. Now there was one sphere in which England was strong, and Spain notoriously and chronically weak: state finance. Philip lived, and ruled his great empire, by borrowing. His capacity to borrow from the Italian bankers depended on his credit and this, in turn, was maintained by the safe and regular arrival of bullion from America. If his credit collapsed, he could not pay his legions in the Low Countries, which absorbed enormous quantities of cash; and the legions, though superbly disciplined, had perfected the organized indiscipline of the mutiny when their wages were unpaid. Spain was a vulnerable giant, as had indeed already been proved by Elizabeth's appropriation of Philip's borrowed treasure in 1569 – a calculated escapade from which she had emerged in a highly successful manner.

Two factors, therefore, now shaped Elizabeth's strategy, which seems to me to have been far more conscious and deliberate (and personal) than many historians have supposed. The first was the need to weaken Philip's credit, and so impede his conquest of the Low Countries. The second was to carry out this operation in such a way as to leave the legal issues doubtful. Bearing these two factors in mind, the answer seemed to be action against the treasure fleets and the bullion-assembly ports, not in European waters, where war would be the inevitable outcome, but over the imaginary mid-Atlantic line beyond which all men and nations were assumed to be in potential or actual conflict. Elizabeth had been moving towards this strategy from the early 1570s. The Spanish treachery at San Juan de Ulloa was regarded by English seamen as a legitimate excuse for revenge and depredations in the Caribbean. In Elizabeth's view this attitude was reasonable; though she might not avow it herself, she was not willing to inhibit or punish those who gave it physical expression. In 1572–3, Francis Drake had carried out a surprise raid on the Panama isthmus, seizing a bullion convoy near Nombre de Dios, and returning with it safely.[19] As a consequence, Spanish defences in the area were reorganized and strengthened, and further English attempts, by John Oxenham in 1575, and Andrew Barker in 1576, were wholly or partially unsuccessful. By early 1577 it was clear from English intelligence that the next step should be an assault on Spain's virtually undefended possessions on the Pacific coast, where most of the silver was actually mined before being transported overland through Panama to the Caribbean.

A good deal of mystery still surrounds the origins and planning of Drake's great voyage of circumnavigation, 1577–80.[20] Drake was evidently a moving spirit from the outset. He was already one of England's most experienced seamen, with a proved capacity for daring and generalship, at any rate in the command of small forces, and – what was more rare – an aptitude for careful preparation. Moreover, he was an ideologue, with a profound and burning faith in the justice of the Protestant cause. His father, Edmund, had been driven out of Devon by the Catholic rising against the First Prayer Book in 1549; he went to live in a hulk on the Medway, where he became a preacher and Bible reader to the seamen and shipwrights. After Elizabeth's accession he got a benefice nearby, at Upchurch. Drake was the eldest of twelve children; his nephew was later to write, 'as it pleased God to give most of them a being on the water, so the greatest part of them died at sea'.[21] He was brought up as a fundamentalist Protestant, and as a young man he fell avidly on Foxe's great book, which to him was both the true history of his country's past, and a guide to its future. He took it with him on his voyages, coloured the illustrations with his own hand (he was a gifted water-colourist, who made accurate panoramic studies of harbours and anchorages), and read extracts from it to his prisoners. He believed, along with many other seamen, that God had specially appointed the English to restore His Church, and that naval power was a salient factor in this divine dispensation.[22] His views and experience thus fitted neatly into the more grandiose, elaborate and intellectualized schemes of Dr Dee and the Mortlake–Richmond–Barnes circle.

How far Elizabeth was involved in the detailed preparations for the voyage is not clear. The project was discussed at length by her intimates in the spring and summer of 1577. Earlier that year Dee had published his *Perfect Art of Navigation*, which convinced Drake that the voyage was a possibility. It is significant that the book was dedicated to Hatton, by now very close to Elizabeth, who took a leading part in financing the voyage and smoothing political difficulties. Drake's own ship, the *Pelican*, was renamed the *Golden Hind*, in honour of Hatton's heraldic beast, and Hatton invested heavily in the scheme, both on his own behalf and on that of the Queen (probably £1,000 in each case). William Winter and his brother George put in £750 and £500 respectively, Hawkins £500 and Drake himself £1,000. Other shareholders were the High Admiral, Lincoln, Leicester and Walsingham. The Queen was perfectly well aware of the objects of the expedition, and gave it her explicit, though confidential, blessing. In 1929, a draft plan for the enterprise (unhappily damaged) and a report by John Winter were discovered in the British Museum.[23] This plan, which was top-secret, and addressed to Leicester, Hatton and Walsingham, states unequivocally: 'The Queen's Majesty may be made privy to the truth of the voyage, and yet the colour to be given out for Alexandria, which in effect is already done by a license procured from the Turks.' Drake went on record, under oath, that Elizabeth had 'adventured . . . towards his charges' and he added that he 'was sent for unto her Majesty by Secretary Walsingham'; she told him that she 'would gladly be revenged on the King of Spain, for divers injuries', and that Drake 'was the only man who might do this exploit'. What is not clear is whether the voyage was designed solely to rob Spain and damage Philip's credit – which, of course, would have the welcome effect of improving Elizabeth's own with the international bankers, who had to lend their money to somebody – or whether it had the wider aim, in accordance with the ideas Dee had discussed with Elizabeth, of preparing the way for an English empire on the Pacific coast of North America.

It is, however, quite clear that Elizabeth tried to keep Burghley in ignorance both of the object of the voyage, and of her own involvement. Burghley believed in the international system of maritime law, such as it was. He never countenanced the theory of 'no peace beyond the line', even though he would not admit the validity of the Papal award of the Americas to Spain and Portugal. As he said: 'I hate all pirates mortally.'[24] Elizabeth, said Drake, gave him 'special commandment that of all men my Lord Treasurer Burghley should not know about it'.[25] As it happened, Burghley did know about the voyage, at least in outline. One of the gentlemen-adventurers on the fleet, Thomas Doughty, was a private secretary to Hatton, and privy to the plan. He had probably had previous connections with Burghley, and may have been placed in the expedition to act as Burghley's informant, though there is no evidence of this. At all events, he communicated the plan to Burghley, and when the expedition was at sea he was foolish enough to boast to Drake himself of what he had done. Drake had already had trouble from Doughty, and the revelation about the Burghley connection sealed his fate; he was tried and beheaded. No doubt Drake felt that, if the expedition was a failure, Elizabeth might disavow him, and that in any subsequent prosecution Doughty would prove a hostile, possible fatal, witness.

He killed Doughty to safeguard the enterprise, as well as his own interests. His action was high-handed but understandable.

The expedition, however, was an enormous success. Drake crossed the equator, the first time he or any of his men had done so, and pushed through the Straits of Magellan in the record time of sixteen days (Magellan had taken thirty-seven, and others much longer). Once in the virtually undefended Pacific he was 'as a pelican alone in the wilderness'. Off Panama he took the treasure-ship *Cacafuego*: 'we found in her great riches, as jewels and precious stones, thirteen chests full of *reals* of plate, four-score pound weight of gold, and six and twenty ton of silver'. There were other captures, taken without difficulty; and from Panama Drake went north to California, which he prospected for future colonizing, and then west into the waters of the real Indies, picking up booty and prisoners on the way, and returning via Africa. The *Golden Hind* was small – only about 135 tons – but it was heavily armed, and Drake kept his cabin in great splendour. His captives were treated with civility and even generosity: Drake had a habit of handing out purses of *reals* to the humbler Spanish sailors and passengers, though they took less kindly to his practice of reading them elevating extracts about Protestant martyrs from Foxe's *Acts and Monuments*. One prisoner, Francisco de Zarate, left an intimate portrait of Drake on board his ship:

> When our ship was sacked, none of the English dared take anything without Drake's orders: he shows them great favour, but punishes the least fault . . . Each one takes particular pains to keep his arquebus clean. He also carried painters, who paint for him pictures of the coast in exact colours. He carried trained carpenters and artisans, so as to be able to careen the ship at any time . . . He is served on silver dishes with gold borders and gilded garlands, in which are his arms. He carried all possible dainties and perfumed waters. He said that many of these had been given to him by the Queen. He dines and sups to the music of viols.

The result of the three-year voyage was to inflict incalculable damage on Spanish naval and military prestige and, as foreseen, to make it appreciably more difficult for Philip to borrow money, especially in Italy. The spoils were vast: the value of the cargo when the *Golden Hind* reached Plymouth constituted a 4,700 per cent return on the original investment. Drake became a rich man. Leicester and Walsingham, by royal warrant, received £4,000 each, and Hatton £2,300. The Queen's share of the loot was not disclosed, since for obvious reasons the expedition's finances could not go through the regular Exchequer procedure; at no point was it publicly admitted that Elizabeth was an investor.

She made, however, no attempt to conceal the fact that she gave *ex post facto* approval to the enterprise. The proceeds were locked up in the Tower, and the indignant protest by Ambassador Mendoza that they were the property of Philip was rejected. In all, Elizabeth received about £160,000, equivalent to a normal parliamentary subsidy. She did not, as is often supposed, knight Drake herself. But she had dinner on board the *Golden Hind* for the ceremony, and then handed the sword to the Seigneur de Marchaumont, the French envoy of the Duke of Alençon, who carried out the dubbing for him; thus she contrived to spread the umbrella of French approval over the venture.[26] Later, she accepted a present of Drake's illustrated log: 'Drake', said Mendoza angrily, 'has given the Queen a diary of everything that happened to him during the three years he was away.' The log, alas, has disappeared.[27] So, too, has the *Golden Hind*, which Elizabeth ordered to be kept as a national memorial in the Thames; it was already rotting to bits by 1599, though it may survive in the shape of the earliest English ship-model, in the Ashmolean Museum, Oxford.[28]

All the same, Elizabeth was evidently very concerned that her secret involvement in the scheme *ab initio* should not emerge. She set a high practical value on her international reputation as a law-abiding monarch; it was one thing to be seen to be the beneficiary of a great naval exploit, quite another to be exposed as a calculated investor in an enterprise hovering on the verge of legality. Above all, it was essential that Spanish propagandists should not discover that she had deliberately concealed her prior knowledge of the scheme from her chief councillor: this was tantamount to a confession that she knew she was doing wrong. Hence she was anxious, not only at the time but for long afterwards, that the truth about the Doughty affair should not emerge. When Drake returned, Doughty's brother, John, tried to prosecute him in the Earl Marshal's Court on a charge of murder. Drake went to the Queen's Bench, with a plea that the Marshal's Court had no jurisdiction, but the Lord Chief Justice ruled that the case could proceed. At this point the process was mysteriously dropped, no doubt at the intervention of the Queen, using – as she often did in such matters – Hatton as her instrument. John Doughty, getting no justice, talked wildly in taverns, was indicted for conspiring with a Spanish spy to have Drake assassinated, and was imprisoned without trial. After sixteen months he petitioned to be tried or released (there was, of course, no *habeas corpus* in sixteenth-century England), but the petition was rejected and no more was heard of him; perhaps he died in prison.

Six years after Drake's return, one Peter Carder, who had been shipwrecked early in the voyage (but after Doughty's execution) finally made his way back to England. He recorded:

My strange adventures ... being known to the right honourable the Lord Charles Howard, Lord High Admiral of England, he certified the Queen's Majesty thereof with speed, and brought me to her presence at Whitehall, where it pleased her to talk with me a long hour's space of my travels ... and among other things of the manner of Mr Doughty's execution; and afterwards bestowed 22 angels on me, willing my lord to have consideration of me; with many gracious words I was dismissed.[29]

Evidently Elizabeth was still worried by the Doughty episode as late as 1586 – the crisis with Spain was then, of course, moving towards a climax. It would have been extremely inconvenient for her to have the whole truth come out. As Drake himself put it, 'her Majesty did swear by her crown that if any within her realm did give the King of Spain hereof to understand they should lose their heads therefore'. This assertion of Drake's, itself incriminating Elizabeth, was recorded in a *Narrative of the Voyage* written by one of his men, John Cooke.[30] John Stow was allowed to consult it for his short, harmless account of the circumnavigation; but it was not printed until 1855. Thus Elizabeth's secret was preserved, and the Spanish government was never able to nail her over the Drake voyage, any more than over the treasure ships of 1569. Burghley, who might have told a great deal, did not choose to mention the matter in any of his surviving letters or memos; he may well have thought that, since Elizabeth had got away with it, she was entitled to silence.

Attacks on the treasure-lanes were a relatively cheap and easy method of holding Spanish power in check. But they could have no decisive influence on what was, for England, the key to the struggle – Spain's attempt to assert absolute dominion over the Low Countries – so long as Philip II retained the will to carry on his policy by force. However great his financial difficulties might be, he could somehow keep his army in being provided he gave the Low Countries priority over any other Spanish interest. And this is precisely what he proceeded to do – against logic, and common sense, and all the evidence. Elizabeth continued to believe that, sooner or later, Philip would recognize that a compromise was desirable, and accept a constitutional settlement which restored the ancient liberties of the States, preserved his nominal suzerainty, permitted the withdrawal of the standing army, and so removed the threat to England. But she, like many other people, underrated his obstinacy and the ideological forces which sustained it. To him, an empire based on tolerance and diversity was a contradiction in terms. Uniformity of religious belief was essential to civil obedience; the Habsburg dominion was Catholic or it was nothing. It was not a matter on which he had any freedom of choice; the mandate of duty was overwhelming. The deeper he committed himself to the struggle, the greater his losses, the more painful his reverses, the more positive his conviction became. Many years later, in his Preface to his *History of the World*, Ralegh was to write eloquently on the futility of Philip's efforts to solve by military means what was essentially a political problem:

> He hath paid above an hundred millions, and the lives of above 400,000 Christians, for the loss of all those countries, which for beauty gave place to none, and for revenue did equal his West Indies; for the loss of a nation which most willingly obeyed him, and who at this day, after 40 years war, are in despite of all his forces become a free estate and far more rich and powerful than they were when he first began to impoverish and oppress them.[31]

To which Philip might have replied: what does it profit a man to gain the whole world and suffer the loss of his soul? Elizabeth, in short, was dealing with an obsessive.

The measure of Philip's obsession is the extent to which Elizabeth, against all her will and instincts, was slowly dragged into the business of frustrating him. In a way her own pacifism was almost as fanatical as his quest for absolutism. Moreover, it was reinforced by two common-sense arguments of great cogency which sprang from the very centre of her convictions. The first was that financial stability was essential to underwrite peace at home and her capacity to influence events abroad. She and her ministers had worked hard and successfully to secure it. It would be rapidly undermined by involvement in war – the road to ruin, in her opinion, for all monarchies – or even if England accepted the role of paymaster for other belligerents. To this the activists in her government answered: what purpose did a full Treasury serve, if by parsimony the security of the state were destroyed? War was coming anyway: a thousand spent today might save ten thousand tomorrow, and a million in ten years' time. Her second argument she advanced equally tenaciously, and it provoked corresponding resistance. Leaving aside the religious issue, what was the real object of English policy towards the Low Countries? It was, surely, to restore the *status quo* before Philip began his foolish policy of insisting on conformity. England's security demanded that these strategic territories, so close to her vital interests, should be administered by a second-rate power (like Burgundy) or, if part of a major empire like Spain, should retain a wide measure of self-government: they should enjoy Spanish protection against France, but at the same time dispose of sufficient constitutional safeguards to allow their commercial interests – which lay in friendship with England – to override purely Spanish objectives. If Spanish power in the Low Countries were destroyed, with English assistance, what would be the outcome? Either a small and vulnerable independent state, forced into the position of a puppet of France or, more likely, an open French move into the vacuum left by the retreat of Spanish power. England's peril would then be far more acute. One of the virtues, from England's point of view, of the traditional Habsburg status in the Low Countries was that it enclosed France, as it were, in a restrictive vice from north and south. If the vice were dismantled, the real power of France would become immediately apparent; and indeed it can be argued that Elizabeth's fears were abundantly justified in the late seventeenth century, when England had to struggle desperately to maintain Dutch independence against a reinvigorated and united France. However, at the time, the reply to her was obvious, and difficult to meet: was it not foolish to guard against hypothetical and future dangers, at the expense of neglecting a real and present peril? France was weak; Spain strong. France was willing to compromise on any number of issues; Spain on none whatsoever. France was passive, if not actually pacific; Spain was active and aggressive, the prime mover in the convulsion which was disturbing the balance of power.

However, it says a good deal for the force of Elizabeth's arguments, and the capacity with which she deployed them, that even men like Walsingham and Leicester, committed as they were to an anti-Spanish policy, accepted the potential danger from France as an ever-present factor to be met in the overall scheme for English policy. It is these reservations on their part, no less than Elizabeth's own, which add to the complexities and confusion of English diplomacy in the 1570s and 1580s, the long hesitations, and the lack of real conviction behind decisions once taken. There were solid reasons for Elizabeth to fear France more than Spain. She was bigger, more populous, richer and, above all, nearer. In 1492 she had absorbed Brittany, England's ally: since the fall of Calais, in 1558, she had controlled the whole southern coast of the Channel, for the first time in history. The French fleet – still a factor until 1583 – would have the wind behind them up the Channel. The main English fleet might be bottled up by weather in the Thames and Medway, and thus unable to join with the advance guards from Plymouth and Portsmouth. This had happened in 1545. Or, if the English fleet were concentrated in the West, the weather might force it to eat the West Country bare, while delaying the arrival of supply ships sent from the Thames – this, indeed, did happen in 1588. In every respect, military as well as naval, the threat of an invasion of England was far more serious when mounted from France than from Spain, whose ships would have to concentrate as far away as Corunna, Lisbon or Cadiz, and were highly vulnerable at their assembly points.[32] If France replaced Spain in the Low Countries, the danger of a cross-Channel invasion would become far more acute, and a large proportion of the shire-levies in the southern and eastern counties would have to be maintained virtually on permanent stand-by, inflicting huge cost on the Treasury and damage to the economy.

Indeed, it was fear of France, rather than Spain, which first led to a physical English involvement in the Low Countries struggle. Early in 1572, seeking a reconciliation with Spain, Elizabeth had expelled the Protestant Dutch free-booters, who had been operating against Spanish traffic in the narrow seas, from English ports and harbours. Paradoxically, this pro-Spanish gesture inflicted permanent damage on Spanish interests, for the freebooters, deprived of their bases, seized Brill on 1 April, and began a new, and much more militant, phase in the revolt against Philip's dominion. The French, taking advantage of Philip's difficulties, began to push forward into Flanders, with the object of seizing ports. It was to prevent the French getting a toehold in Flushing that Elizabeth and Burghley first authorized the departure of a force of English volunteers, under Sir Humphrey Gilbert, to take an active part in the fighting. A document in Burghley's hand, entitled 'A Memorial for Matters of Flanders', makes it clear that the expedition was aimed at a potential French threat, rather than an actual Spanish one.[33] Alva, then still in command, protested strongly that the volunteers were dispatched with Elizabeth's knowledge and on her orders, which was true. But the memo makes it clear that, if the French threat materialized, Elizabeth would secretly assist Alva 'by all honourable means' – whatever that may imply – 'in the defence of [Philip's] inheritance', provided the ancient liberties of the state were restored.

But of course these conditions were not met, and the English force became in fact, if not wholly in intention, committed to the Dutch cause against Spain. It was a significant point of departure, from which Elizabeth was never, despite her efforts, able to retreat: an option had closed. It was also the real birth of the modern British army, an episode from which we can trace, sometimes tenuously, a continuous process of evolution in structure, hierarchy and tactics – even in the words of command. Gilbert's troops still included a few bowmen; but they responded to the order 'As you were' just as British soldiers do today.[34] Hitherto, in Elizabeth's reign, Englishmen with a taste for soldiering had been hard put to find employment. In 1566 some, like Richard Grenville, had been forced to go as far as Hungary to fight the Turks; others, like Ralegh himself, had found activity with the Huguenots. Now England, as a state, was com-mitting herself to Continental warfare, in the shape of a small contingent which was later to swell into a formidable army. It was thus appropriate that Elizabeth herself was present when the troops marshalled for embarkation, as one of their captains, Roger Williams, records:

At this time there was a fair muster of Londoners before the Queen's Majesty at Greenwich. Amongst the Londoners were divers captains who had served, some in Scotland, some in Ireland, others in France. And having nothing to do, and with the countenance of some great men who favoured the cause, and the small helps of the deputies of Flushing, Captain Thomas Morgan levied a fair company of 300 strong; amongst whom were divers officers who had commanded before, with many gentlemen, at the least above one hundred, of whom myself was one.[35]

If Elizabeth gave her sanction to this expedition, she flatly refused to see it as evidence of a continuing, let alone a growing, commitment to help the Dutch. Indeed in some ways she hated the Dutch, as rebels and nuisances. Under Governor Luis de Requescens, who succeeded Alva, Spanish policy appeared to be changing in favour of moderation, and Elizabeth hoped once more to be able to play the role of benevolent mediatrix. She turned on the Dutch, who had been seizing English shipping in harbour, and boarding it at sea: in spring 1576, the young Earl of Oxford, for instance, had been robbed and stripped to his shirt only six miles from Dover. There were many good reasons why this arrogant and worthless peer should be ill-treated, but they were not among the excuses advanced by the Dutch freebooters, for whom he was simply a rich Englishman. Elizabeth sent Winter and the fleet to patrol the coastal waters, and for a time a virtual state of war existed between England and the States. But Requescens died early in March 1576; his troops, without pay, mutinied, and rampaged throughout the summer, sacking Maastrich and Antwerp. The effect was to unify both Catholics and Protestants in the Low Countries: on 5 November the Prince of Orange was able to persuade them all to sign the Pacification of Ghent, under which they undertook to unite to drive out the Spanish. Don Juan of Austria, the victor of Lepanto, arrived the same month to take up the governorship. Unable to pay his men, and so to use them, he negotiated with the States and signed an agreement (the 'Perpetual Edict') in February 1577. This, in theory, gave Elizabeth everything she wanted in the Low Countries: peace with the traditional *status quo*. But Philip, and for that matter his half-brother, signed the peace only because for the moment they had no alternative. As soon as the fragile unity of the States dissolved, Don Juan renounced the pacification; Philip contrived to meet the arrears of pay; the Spanish went back to the offensive; and at Gembloux, in 1578, the Netherlanders were badly beaten. From this point, it was only a matter of time before the Spanish forces, under Don Juan and his successor the Prince of Parma, reduced the forces of resistance to submission – unless, of course,

Elizabeth intervened, not by mediation, but by substantial financial and physical support.

There were a number of ways, alone or in combination, by which Elizabeth could render assistance. The worst possible alternative, in her eyes, was direct English military intervention, though in a sense she was already committed to it. Then there was the possibility that she could subsidize German mercenaries, supplied by the Palatinate prince, Frederick the Pious – so-called by the Protestants; Catholics had a different name for him – and by his son, the greedy and bellicose John Casimir the Good. A third alternative was to supply money, and arms (by this time England was in a position to export arms in growing quantities) to the Prince of Orange and other Dutch Protestants. A fourth was to use the Duke of Alençon (who, since his brother, Anjou, had become King of France as Henri III, had succeeded to the title of Duke of Anjou) as a comparatively independent French potentate, to be subsidized as an ally of the Dutch without necessarily thereby increasing the risk of French penetration of the Low Countries. The existence of these various possibilities, the fact that each had drawbacks and possibilities, enabled Elizabeth to baffle friends and enemies alike as to her real purposes, and to delay committing herself.

We get a characteristic glimpse of her in action when the Spanish envoy, the Sieur de Champigny, Governor of Antwerp, visited London in 1576 to ask her point blank if she intended to assist the Dutch rebels with money and men. If the answer was 'yes', he was told to say, the only outcome would be war. But there was no question of his getting a straight answer, yes or otherwise. First, after a delay of a fortnight before seeing him at all, she said she was bitterly hurt by Philip II's failure to write to her. It was remiss. Then she complained that for Spain to try to establish absolute dominion in the Low Countries was intolerable for England. Such a thing her beloved father would never have tolerated, and she, though a woman, 'would know how to look to it'. Champigny's master must not presume that the English were a nation of women. On the other hand, the behaviour of the Dutch was intolerable – they were pirates, malefactors and breeders of sedition. She herself, she said, had a tremendous personal liking for Philip II – and she smiled.[36] This was a semi-public audience, and left Champigny bewildered. A month later, on 2 March, she saw him again in her Privy Chamber, and made him sit by her, alone, for a tête-à-tête. No one at all would know of their conversation, she said, 'not even my petticoat'. She proposed mediation (as though there was anything new in this), and promised to make a formal proposal to this effect in a Latin letter. She would emphatically be unwilling to help the Dutch if Philip made them a fair offer to maintain their ancient privileges; otherwise she would have no alternative but to consult the 'interests of my people'. While this interview was going on, she deliberately stormed at Walsingham, and boxed the ears of a maid-in-waiting. Champigny – no fool – left impressed.[37]

But if Philip's envoys saw her as a mistress of infinite subtlety, her own servants, often growing weary of such performances – virtuosity for its own inconclusive sake – saw only her capacity for vacillation and delay. Thus Sir Thomas Smith wrote to Burghley:

> For matters of state I will write as soon as I can have any access to her Majesty, the which, as it was when your Lordship was here, sometimes so, sometimes no, and at all times uncertain and ready to stays and revocations . . . This irresolution doth weary and kill her ministers, destroy her actions, and overcome all good designs and councils . . . I wait whilst I have neither eyes to see nor legs to stand upon. And yet these delays grieve me more and will not let me sleep in the night . . . Yea or nay can I get, and, as I hear, her Majesty hath forbidden Mr Hatton and my Lord of Leicester to move suits.[38]

It is hardly surprising that Walsingham, in his exasperation, actually advised the Dutch on the best way of dealing with his sovereign, suggesting that their chances of getting help from England would increase *pari passu* with the energy they sought it from France.[39] This advice was taken and to some extent it worked. The Dutch got their first handout of Elizabeth's cash at the end of 1576 – £20,000, not in the form of paper or bonds but in chests of sterling silver, something which caused a sensation at the time. But this was in response to the sacking of Antwerp and the imminent prospect of French intervention. Elizabeth, as always, tended to operate on a week-to-week basis, reacting to any abrupt deterioration in the military balance, but drawing her horns in the moment the skies cleared and mediation seemed conceivable again. At all times she preferred diplomacy to action, sending envoys constantly to Flanders to talk with the various interested parties – usually to no purpose – and holding long discussions with Dutch and Spanish representatives at court, as an excuse for postponing decisions. She again appeared ready to act after Don Juan's victory at Gembloux, promising to give her bond for the payment of 11,000 mercenary troops under German commanders, on condition the Dutch guaranteed to pay the bill eventually. But it then emerged she demanded an English occupation of certain Dutch cautionary towns as security for repayment, or alternatively plate and jewels to an equivalent amount, and the proposal was rejected. Instead, the Estates signed an agreement with Anjou, under which he undertook to supply specified numbers of troops for a fixed period in return for three towns, any land he could conquer beyond the Meuse, and the title of Defender of Belgian Liberty against Spanish Tyranny.

This compact at once set Elizabeth off on a fresh tack: a renewed proposal for a marriage with Anjou, or a reinvigorated league with France, or both. For a woman with Elizabeth's reputation, the Anjou marriage scheme did not have a very convincing ring about it. He was, in addition to being the last, the youngest, smallest and ugliest of her suitors. His portrait in the Bibliothèque Nationale, Paris, does him considerably more than justice, though it has the merit of evoking the shifty and often purposeless cunning of this Valois-Medici offspring. In fact, he was badly scarred by smallpox, and at one time Burghley thought of recruiting two specialists alleged to be experts in removing the stigmas of the disease, in the hope of tidying the Duke up. There was no doubt that Anjou himself was keen on the match, but he could have been under no illusions about the likelihood of its coming off. As Walsingham put it to Leicester:

> To think that Monsieur could not be content to marry with our mistress were a vain opinion, being as she is the best marriage in her parish, but to say that he doth hope after it, considering his former trial in the attempt thereof, is very doubtful.[40]

On the other hand, her ministers considered that at least it held out a possibility that Elizabeth would take some useful action, since for the moment she seemed to rule out direct help to the Dutch completely. Burghley wrote in great depression to Walsingham (July 1578):

> Mr Soames [the bearer] can tell you how sharp her Majesty hath been with some of us here as counsellors, whereof you, Mr Secretary, are not free from some portion of her words ... And yet we must all dutifully bear with her Majesty's offence for the time, not despairing but, howsoever she misliketh matters at one time, yet at another time she will alter her sharpness, especially when she is persuaded that we all mean truly for her and her surety, though she sometimes will not so understand.

The letter is dated from Havering, in Essex, 'where I am kept only to receive some chidings upon daily debate of these matters'.[41]

Early in January 1579, Anjou's agent, Jean de Simier, arrived with full powers to negotiate the marriage treaty, 'a most choice courtier', says Camden, 'exquisitely skilled in love-toys, pleasant conceits and court dalliance'. This was all very much to Elizabeth's taste, and the negotiations, ostensibly, went well. A draft marriage treaty was drawn up, a passport issued to Anjou, and in

August he arrived for a twelve-day visit. Elizabeth liked him, or pretended to; he became 'our frog'. But the public, especially the London public, was hostile to any idea of marriage with a French Catholic. Many of the Protestants at court were equally upset. Sir Philip Sidney wrote the Queen a long letter of protest, dwelling on the treachery of French Catholics (he had been, like Walsingham, in Paris during the St Bartholomew Massacre), and the offensiveness of the marriage to English Protestants, 'your chief, if not your sole, strength'.[42] The letter was, thought Elizabeth, an impertinence, but it was courteously worded, and brought Sidney no more than a scolding. It was a different matter when, while Anjou was still Elizabeth's guest at Greenwich, John Stubbs, brother-in-law of the leading young Puritan preacher, John Cartwright, wrote and actually published a sensational pamphlet, *The Discovery of a Gaping Gulf whereunto England is like to be swallowed by another French marriage if the Lord forbid not the bans by letting her Majesty see the sin and punishment thereof.*[43] One of the characteristics of the Puritans was the extraordinary violence of their language. They made, indeed, a positive virtue of crude phraseology, especially in their castigation of women, whom they regarded (on the supposed authority of the Bible) as natural vessels of iniquity and, in matters of state, vain and foolish. Stubbs's pamphlet was in the tactless tradition of Knox. The Queen, he argued, was much too old even to think of marriage: at forty-six, she was most unlikely to produce a living child, the whole object of the operation, in so far as it had one. As for the Duke, the very marrow of his bones had been eaten by debauchery: he was 'the old serpent himself in the form of a man come a second time to seduce the English Eve and to ruin the English paradise'. And more to the same effect.

For once Elizabeth lost her temper completely. As she had no intention of marrying Anjou, and was merely going through the motions as an act of state policy to protect English interests and, not least, save her subjects' money, the insinuation that she was behaving like a love-sick maiden and sacrificing national objects for the sake of her selfish personal inclinations was particularly hard to bear. It was the same charge that produced her explosion in the 1566 parliament. Moreover, she feared that Stubbs had been put up to his foolish exploit by far more significant figures. Without consulting anyone but the judges, who could normally be relied upon to give reactionary advice, she had Stubbs, his printer, and his publisher, William Page, sent to the Tower, and announced that all three would be hanged. In fact this proved legally impossible. A proclamation issued on 27 September, which defended the Queen's intentions and attachment to the lawful religion, castigated the pamphlet as a lewd and seditious book, and ordered all copies to be seized and burnt. But the only charge on which she could get the accused was under a statute of Mary's designed to protect her husband, Philip II no less, and even this had to be interpreted in such a loose way as to suggest that Anjou was already Elizabeth's husband.[44] 'Lawyers', wrote Camden, 'murmured that the proceedings were erroneous', and Thomas Mounson, a judge of the Common Pleas, resigned rather than be a party to the verdict. All three men were sentenced to lose their right hands. Singleton, the printer, was pardoned, but Stubbs and Page were brought from the Tower, on 3 November, to a scaffold before the palace at Westminster. Camden was present in the vast crowd, and recorded that 'their right hands were struck off with a cleaver driven through the wrist with a beetle'. Page, as the stump was seared with a hot iron, shouted: 'I have left there a true Englishman's hand.' Stubbs waved his hat with his left hand, called out 'God save Queen Elizabeth', and then fainted. The people watched these barbarous proceedings in chilly and disgusted silence.[45]

Elizabeth's savagery on this occasion, for which she must take sole responsibility, was uncharacteristic and wholly indefensible. But, as always, she was quick to see she had made a mistake, and grossly misjudged public opinion. (Stubbs was later received at court, and in 1581 became a member of parliament.) The hostile public reaction to the punishment was used by her as an excuse for playing down the marriage scheme, owing to 'the mislike of our faithful subjects', as she put it. She threw the onus for any change of policy on the Council, which sat from 8.00 in the morning until 7.00 at night, 'without stirring from the room, having sent the clerks away'.[46] The Council, reporting back to her, said it reserved judgment on the marriage until they knew which course she proposed to follow. As she had hitherto said, on many occasions, that she would decide the marriage issue herself, this reply was not unreasonable; but she was furious not to receive a positive recommendation one way or the other, and made her feelings plain. The following day, accordingly, the Council sat again, and reported to her that they would approve the marriage 'if so it shall please her'. But she did not like this either, and replied that she 'thought not meet to declare to us whether she would marry with Monsieur or no'.[47]

Obviously Elizabeth, while determined not to marry at all, let alone Anjou, was anxious to prolong the uncertainty as long as possible, since it was a substitute for action and, moreover, cost her nothing. So Anjou departed without anything definite being settled, and was kept dangling on a string throughout 1580, and the spring of 1581. Walsingham, under a cloud during the Stubbs affair, since Elizabeth believed he had known the pamphlet was to be published and had done nothing to stop it, was known to oppose the marriage; so she accordingly sent him on embassy to France to promote it – a characteristic ploy.

He found Henri III very angry, and England's reputation suffering from Elizabeth's indecision and deviousness. He wrote scathingly to Burghley (21 August 1581):

> I should repute it a greater favour to be committed into the Tower, unless her Majesty may grow more certain her resolutions there. Instead of amity, I fear her Highness shall receive enmity, and we her ministers here be greatly discomfited . . .

Again, four days later:

> I would to God her Highness would resolve one way or the other touching the matter of her marriage . . . when her Majesty is pressed to marry, then she seemeth to affect a league, and when a league is yielded to, then she liketh better of a marriage. And when therefore she is moved to assent to marriage, then she hath recourse to the league; when the motion for the league or any request is made for money, then her Majesty returneth to marriage. As these things are delivered about her in discourse among the [French] secretaries, so they are all conveyed and distributed into other courts throughout Europe, where her enemies will make their profit to throw her into the hatred of all the world.[48]

Walsingham was not content to pour out his wrath into the sympathetic ears of colleagues. He was the bravest of her councillors and virtually alone in telling her his true opinions and feelings. She sometimes resented this, but on the whole she recognized the value of his plain-speaking and accorded him a respect (akin, occasionally to awe) which she reserved for no other member of her government, even Burghley. He left her in no doubt that she was behaving stupidly if she had no intention of marrying. As he wrote in a letter to her dated 12 September 1581:

> If you mean it not, then assure yourself it is one of the worst remedies you can use (howsoever your Majesty conceiveth it, that it may serve your turn) . . . Sometimes when your Majesty doth behold in what doubtful terms you stand with foreign princes, then you wish with great affection that opportunities offered had not been overslipped. But when they are offered to you (if they be accompanied with charges) they are altogether neglected . . . I see it, and they stick not to say it, that the only cause that moveth them here not to weigh your Majesty's friendship, is that they see your Majesty doth fly charges otherwise than by doing somewhat underhand . . . Heretofore your Majesty's predecessors, in matter of peril, did never look into the charges, when their Treasure was neither so great as your Majesty's is, nor

subjects so wealthy nor so willing to contribute ... If this sparing and improvident course be held still ... there is no one that serveth in place of a counsellor, that either weigheth his own credit, or carryeth that sound affection to your Majesty as he ought to do, that would not wish himself in the farthest part of Ethiopia rather than enjoy the fairest palace in England.[49]

If this letter provoked 'two or three poohs', we do not hear of them; it was evidently not resented. Elizabeth might be haughty in many ways, but no other Tudor, or for that matter Stuart, sovereign would have accepted this kind of lecture in the spirit in which it was given. It was one of her greatest qualities that she was not afraid to employ strong-minded men, and subject herself to the full force of their intellects.

In this instance, as she did not fail to point out, Walsingham was no more consistent than she, rather less so in fact, since he had once hotly opposed the Anjou marriage, and now saw it as part of a deal with France: 'Well, you knave,' she told him when he got back to England, 'why have you so often spoken ill of him? You veer round like a weathercock.'[50] Nevertheless, she saw his point, and if the final phase of the marriage negotiations was the most dramatic (and farcical) of all her courtships, the reason was undoubtedly Elizabeth's somewhat desperate efforts to put on a show to convince French, and Spanish, official opinion that she was still serious. To prepare the way for a second visit by Anjou, a high-ranking French delegation, including princes of the blood and Pinart, the Secretary of State, accompanied by 500 gentlemen, arrived by river at Whitehall late in April 1581. This was the occasion when the famous 'temporary' banqueting hall in Whitehall was erected, at a cost, according to Stow (who got his information from the designer), of £1,744 19s. The guests were put up in sumptuous lodgings scattered all over the Strand/Fleet Street area, held solemn meetings with the Council, and were entertained to a series of dinner-parties, given by the Queen herself, Leicester and Burghley. At Burghley's dinner, on 30 April, the English guests alone numbered thirty-seven and included all the Privy Council and six leading magnates. Burghley's elder son Thomas, and his young and clever nephew, Francis Bacon, were among the interpreters. The kitchen bill came to £204 7s., and the event cost Burghley over £350 – 20 per cent of his annual household costs. Flowers and rushes, Turkey carpets, furniture, pewter and Elizabeth's picture were brought up from Burghley House for the occasion.[51] There was bear-baiting on May Day and a fortnight later a 'triumph' in the Tiltyard: four knights – the Earl of Arundel, Lord Windsor, Philip Sidney and his friend Fulke Greville – representing

'Desire', attacked the 'Castle of Perfect Beauty', presumably a symbol of Elizabeth's virginity. It was a splendid spectacle to illuminate Anglo-French amity – but 'Desire' lost the battle. A marriage agreement was drawn up on 11 June, but it contained a proviso that its operation would depend on a personal agreement signed by Anjou himself, and this would mean a second visit. With this the French went home, none too happy; but Elizabeth, on learning in August that Anjou was at the end of his financial resources, and would soon have to give up his Low Countries venture, kept the marriage in play by authorizing Burghley to dispatch £30,000 in cash: it was sent by four envoys, each carrying his portion of the silver on a pillion.

The money at least allowed Anjou to return to England, where he disembarked at Rye on 31 October.[52] All the secret papers of his delegation fell into the hands of Burghley as a result of thefts by whores, introduced into the lodgings where the French were staying. This was doubtless deliberate, though if so Burghley took pains to conceal his part in it.[53] Mendoza, the Spanish ambassador, was scathing about the prospects of the marriage, and offered bets of 100 to 1 against it; no takers were reported. To raise the flagging credibility of her intentions – and thus gain a little more time, though for what she scarcely knew herself – Elizabeth put on scenes in front of the court which bordered on the vulgar. On 22 November at Whitehall

at eleven in the morning, the Queen and Alençon [Anjou] were walking together in a gallery, Leicester and Walsingham being present, when the French ambassador entered and said that he wished to write to his master, from whom he had received orders to hear from the Queen's own lips her intention with regard to marrying his brother. She replied: 'You may write this to the King: that the Duke of Alençon shall be my husband', and at the same moment she turned to Alençon and kissed him on the mouth, drawing a ring from her hand and giving it to him as a pledge. Alençon gave her a ring of his in return, and shortly afterwards the Queen summoned the ladies and gentlemen from the Presence Chamber into the gallery, repeating to them in a loud voice in Alençon's presence what she had just said.[54]

This was Mendoza's account, and the scene was played not only for his, and Anjou's, benefit, but for the courts of Europe. Evidently it took in the Prince of Orange who, when he heard the news, had the bells of Antwerp rung.[55]

By mid-December, however, Elizabeth decided that the farce had gone on long enough, and that it was time to get rid of Anjou, who was still hanging around her court. Without too much ceremony, she negotiated with him the sum he would accept (nominally in the form of a loan) to go away and fight the Spanish. This was very much to Walsingham's satisfaction, since all along he had preferred the idea of a subsidy to a marriage, though he woefully overrated the Duke's ability, or indeed willingness, to do anything effective with the money. Anjou agreed to take £60,000, half within fifteen days of leaving, half fifty days afterwards.[56] As he still delayed his departure – he may have lacked the actual money to hasten it – she gave him £10,000 in cash on 31 December. He finally left London on 1 February 1582, Elizabeth paying him the ostentatious, but not very convincing, compliment of accompanying him as far as Canterbury. She put on a great display of grief, and said she would never be happy until he returned. No one believed her. Leicester, always willing to oblige his mistress, was given the disagreeable duty of sailing with the rebuffed Duke from Sandwich, and depositing him in Antwerp. He reported sardonically that he left him 'like an old hulk run ashore, high and dry ... stuck upon a sandbank'. When this description was reported to Elizabeth she put on a fit of temper. She knew that everyone by now saw through her histrionics, but she resented Leicester's open mockery of her intended. The Earl, she said, was a traitor, like all his horrible family.[57] Privately, she was well satisfied. In all, Anjou got from her, over fifteen months, £90,000 in cash and bonds, a reasonable price (even assuming he did not use it to mount a military expedition) for a negotiation which had won nearly three years of time, 'wherein many accidents may ensue'. Her ladies reported that, when she heard the news that the Duke had actually left the country, she danced for joy in her bedchamber.[58] This was the last of her final suitor, and although his departure brought to her the knowledge that she could never again enjoy the pleasures (or exploit the political advantages) of a courtship, there was also the heartfelt sense of relief that the long farce was over. It was a relief shared by her statesmen, and endorsed by the historian who has to record the complex and repetitive saga of her pretend *fiancailles*.

But if the end of any prospect of Elizabeth marrying brought emotional respite for all concerned, in political terms it merely removed another of Elizabeth's options, and left wholly unresolved the question of what she was to do to keep the Protestant cause in the Low Countries alive. There had been, there were, and there continued to be, plans to 'annoy' the King of Spain – this was the term universally used by English ministers – in other theatres. Both England and France made desultory efforts to plant the Portuguese pretender, Don Antonio, in Lisbon, or the Azores, and so open up another costly internal war in the Spanish dominions. All came to nothing. Philip may not have been popular in Portugal, but neither was Antonio, and Philip's military grip on the

Portuguese territory and possessions was never really challenged. Moreover, after July 1582, the French had virtually no fleet. The Low Countries, therefore, remained the only part of the Continent where Spanish weakness could be exploited or, to put it another way, the growth of Spanish power could be checked. Following the defeat of the French fleet, Elizabeth sent Anjou a further £15,000, to prevent, as Burghley put it, 'that Spain should crow over us in the Low Countries'. But Anjou was a supine and incompetent commander, and in January 1583 disgraced himself by trying to seize Dutch towns, and being forced to flee back into France. On 7 June the following year news reached Elizabeth that he was dead. She was, or pretended to be, very sad, and put the court in mourning, exploiting the occasion by using it as an excuse for postponing decisions: 'Now melancholy doth so possess us', wrote Walsingham from court, 'as both public and private causes are at a stay for a season.'[59] Then, a month later on 6 July, came the appalling news that Philip's efforts to assassinate the Prince of Orange had at last succeeded.

For a generation, Orange had sustained the Protestant cause against Spain. He had been courageous, single-minded, straightforward and, within the limitations of his political and military resources, successful. His removal placed the responsibility for carrying on the defence of Dutch freedom squarely on Elizabeth's shoulders. If she failed to play her part, with money, or soldiers, or both, Protestant resistance would collapse. For the first time she began to recognize that a direct and official English military commitment might be inescapable. She had no love for the Dutch. While she sympathized with their conservative – as she saw it – struggle to preserve ancient liberties, she also, and perversely, saw them in the role of rebels against their legitimate sovereign. Moreover, she suspected from the start that they would be evasive and disingenuous in any financial dealings she had with them, and events fully justified her forebodings. Even by July 1583, the Dutch owed her, on the mere security of their bonds, £98,374 4s. 4d., and they tended to default even on their 10 per cent interest payments. They were always asking for more loans, and always anxious to proffer more bonds, but as Burghley sourly remarked, the Treasury was already full of Dutch paper, 'of which we have great store'. It was not as though the Dutch were poor. On the contrary, they were growing rich through the war, since the blockade of Antwerp and Ghent was diverting trade to Amsterdam and other more northerly ports. They lacked cash simply because their political organization made the raising of taxes difficult. Elizabeth thought the situation intolerable, as it was. Burghley wrote of 'her old rooted opinion that she hath, that all this war will be turned upon her charge, by the backwardness in payment by the States'.[60] How right she proved!

But if the situation was intolerable, it nevertheless had to be borne. After Orange's murder, Elizabeth instructed Walsingham to draw up a comprehensive paper on the situation in the Low Countries, with the various alternatives open to her, and in the discussions which followed she began to move slowly in the direction of intervention.[61] The Secretary wrote to Sir Edward Stafford, ambassador in Paris: 'it hath grown to half a resolution that the peril would be so great in case Spain should possess the said countries, as whether France should concur in the action or not, yet it doth behove her Majesty to enter into some course for their defence.'[62] Nevertheless, a great deal more pressure on Elizabeth was required before the 'half resolution' became a full one. If she intervened at all, she wished to do so in conjunction with France. But France's capacity as an effective ally was declining. Henri III was, indeed, offered the sovereignty of the Netherlands in return for military help, but he eventually refused it. His own kingdom was falling apart. The death of his brother Anjou meant that the crown, in the event of his own death, would go to the Huguenot Bourbons of Navarre, and the Catholic party in France was beginning to organize itself against this contingency, and was putting out feelers to Spain for the formation of a Catholic alliance. If any French aid materialized, it could be nothing more than a bonus. When Elizabeth summoned the English Council for a thorough debate on the problem, on 10 October 1584, it had before it a long working-paper by Burghley which outlined the arguments for and against intervention. It was a gloomy document because, although it concluded that the perils of an outright Spanish conquest on the Netherlands made intervention necessary, it pointed out that this would mean war with Spain, assisted by the papacy and Empire, fought in conjunction with the Dutch, who were disunited, leaderless and, by past experience, unreliable. The expense would be enormous, and English trade was bound to suffer.[63]

The debate which followed, summarized by Camden, showed that Elizabeth was not alone in her reluctance to commit the nation. Walsingham, who had no confidence in English military capacity to resist invasion once the barrier of the navy was breached, believed passionately that any fighting must be conducted on foreign soil. He was supported by Leicester and those whom Camden terms 'martial men'. But others

> held it the best course if the Queen would meddle no more in matters of the Netherlands, but most strongly fortify her own kingdom, bind the good unto her daily more straitly by her innate bounty, restrain the bad, gather money, furnish her navy with all provisions, strengthen the borders towards Scotland with garrisons and maintain the ancient military discipline of

England ... So would England become impregnable and she on every side most secure and dreadful to her neighbours.[64]

The result was a compromise, under which Elizabeth agreed to explore the terms – in money and cautionary towns; that is, towns held as security against payment of debts – under which the Dutch would pay for her assistance. Many months were spent in diplomatic missions and negotiations. Once again it was events which pushed the Queen into the hands of the activists. In April 1585 she got the news from intelligence sources that, four months before, Philip II and the Duke of Guise had signed an agreement, in which both would unite to exclude Navarre from the throne when Henri III died, and co-operate in other respects to promote the cause of the Catholic religion all over Europe. Thus, once again, the horrific spectre of a Franco-Spanish Catholic alliance was raised. Some councillors still opposed intervention. Walsingham recorded: 'I find those whose judgment her Majesty most trusts so coldly affected to the cause that I have no great hope of the matter.'[65] According to Clapham, Burghley's confidant, it was Leicester's persuasion which finally brought Elizabeth to take action: 'in the end he swayed the balance on the left side.' She put out feelers in Scotland and Germany for the creation of a counter-league of Protestant states, brought Sir John Norris back from Ireland to prepare an expeditionary force, ordered Ralegh to organize attacks on Spanish fishing-fleets in the Newfoundland Banks, and Drake to assemble ships for a West Indies expedition. Philip II played his part in making up her mind by seizing English ships in Spanish harbours, thus incidentally alienating the one economic interest in England which had hitherto flatly opposed war. Appalling tales reached London of Spanish ill-treatment of the imprisoned sailors.

One of Burghley's covert reasons for doubting the wisdom of direct intervention by England was, and remained, his fear that Elizabeth would never commit herself emotionally to the enterprise. He knew her to be a pacifist at heart. She would send too little, too late, and at the first hint of difficulties she would pull back. He was aware that she had her own private channels of communication with the Spanish, both in Madrid and Brussels, and that while these contacts continued she would always entertain the hope that Philip would do a deal. But the machinery of war was now in motion. The Duke of Parma's men made slow but steady progress; by the early summer of 1585, they threatened Antwerp. On 29 June Elizabeth met the Dutch delegation which had arrived in London to negotiate a military pact. She declined their offer of the sovereignty of the Netherlands. She did not want sovereignty, she wanted mortgages as security for her money. As Burghley put it to the Dutch delegates:

> We have told you over and over again that her Majesty will never think of accepting the sovereignty. She will assist you in money and men, and must be paid to the last farthing when the war is over; and until that period she must have solid pledges in the shape of a town in each province.[66]

The question of Antwerp was becoming urgent, but although Elizabeth had already signed the letters to levy men in the counties, she was reluctant to send a relieving expedition immediately, 'so loath is she', reported Walsingham, 'to enter into a war.' Indeed, she still seems to have thought it possible to dispatch aid without a public commitment:

> She refuseth to enter into the action otherwise than underhand, wherein the whole Council, howsoever they stand inwardly affected, so nevertheless outwardly concur in opinion that it is a dangerous course for her and that it is impossible that she should long stand unless she enter openly and soundly into the action.[67]

Nevertheless, on 12 August she was finally brought to sign an agreement: she would provide, at fixed rates of pay, 400 horse, 4,000 foot and 700 garrison troops, on the security of Brill, Flushing and the Ramekins Fort. Two days later news was received of the fall of Antwerp; she was 'greatly troubled', though since the city was expected to withstand siege for many weeks, her hesitation can hardly be blamed for its loss. Her response was to add another 600 cavalry and 1,000 footmen to her commitment. After a good deal of manoeuvring, she agreed on 17 September to assign the command to Leicester, and in October Sir Philip Sidney was appointed governor of Flushing, and Thomas Cecil of Brill. Most of the promised English troops had already crossed over and taken up their stations; Leicester himself did not join them until December.

Thus with infinite reluctance, and with every conceivable kind of reservation, Elizabeth went to war. Or, rather, she committed herself to conflict: there was no formal declaration of hostilities. War had in fact come in April 1585, when Philip seized English shipping. The nearest Elizabeth came to a formal admission that England and Spain were no longer at peace was in October, when she issued a 'Declaration' justifying her motives in sending troops to the Netherlands. It was an appeal to international public opinion, something in which Elizabeth – like so many English statesmen since – had a touching, and not always justified faith. Translations were made into Dutch, Italian and French, and distributed widely across the Continent. The actual drafting was done by Walsingham, assisted in places by Burghley, but the sentiments and the language were characteristically her own. The tone of the document is essentially moderate, its arguments notably conservative. Indeed, it still refers to Spain as England's 'ally'! The war Elizabeth was fighting, she said, was by nature defensive, a reaction to a Spanish occupation of states which were Philip's by rightful inheritance, but in other respects self-governing by law and tradition. The Spanish were strangers in these territories, 'men more exercised in wars than in peaceable government and some of them notably delighted in blood, as hath appeared by their actions'. They had 'broken the ancient laws and liberties of all the countries, and in a tyrannous sort have banished, killed and destroyed without order of law within the space of a few months, many of the most ancient and principal persons of the natural nobility that were most worthy of government'. Hence, 'we did manifestly see in what danger ourselves, our countries and people might shortly be, if in convenient time we did not speedily otherwise regard to prevent or stay the same'. The document hotly denied the charge that she had tried to have Parma murdered. On the contrary, she acknowledged 'those singular rare parts we have always noted in him, which hath won unto him as great reputation as any man this day living carrieth of his degree and quality'. Nevertheless, because of his and his master's actions, she had no alternative but to look to her defences.[68] Elizabeth was taking a revolutionary step, committing her country to the support of those rising against their lawful sovereign, and to an international action on behalf of the Protestant religion. But she cloaked it in traditionalist phraseology, which portrayed Philip as the innovator, and herself as the custodian of the 'ancient' and 'natural' order.

One collateral reason why Elizabeth entered the Netherlands commitment with such heart-searchings was that she was unsure how, and by whom, it was to be conducted. Should it be purely a businesslike military expedition? If so, Sir John Norris, her most experienced soldier, was the natural choice to lead it. On the other hand, she had taken the Low Countries under her 'protection'. This implied a political link, well short of sovereignty indeed, but an affair to be handled by someone much higher in the state, and deeper in her confidence. The choice, therefore, pointed to Leicester, and with many misgivings she made it. Leicester, at least, could always be relied upon to do what she wanted, and this was a tricky assignment, over which she intended to exercise close control. One of her greatest objections to war was that, with a woman sovereign, events were liable to slip beyond the grasp of the crown. But could Leicester, in practice, be relied upon? His trouble was that his fear of the Queen, and his corresponding willingness to obey her, declined in direct proportion to his distance from her forbidding presence. He was not, as she now discovered, a man to be sent on distant assignments. It does not seem likely that he deliberately planned to exceed his mandate. Though he had a taste and an aptitude for devious courses, he was not a long-term plotter. Rather, like the Queen, he tended to live from week to week, and respond to events as they arose. It was the Dutch who wished to change his role. Frustrated in their desire to have Elizabeth (or Henri III) as their sovereign, to accept the full legal, financial and military responsibilities for their actions, fobbed off with a vaguely-defined 'protection', they were anxious to elevate Elizabeth's deputy into a surrogate Burgundian prince. Leicester was tempted, and succumbed.

Some inkling of the transformation of the expedition reached the Queen even before Leicester departed. She was furious to learn that his wife (whom she hated anyway), as well as other ladies, were to accompany him. Not only that: they were taking with them enormous quantities of household stuffs, dresses and servants – even carriages. The carriages, in particular, rankled. Unfortunately, Elizabeth's emotional distaste for the whole enterprise was so strong that she declined, at least to begin with, to take any interest in the detailed preparations. She just did not want to know about them, and by the time she decided she did want to know – and object – the affair had got out of control, and Leicester was committed not so much to leading an armed force as to conducting a royal progress – in which, naturally, he was revelling.

Even by the somewhat bizarre standards of sixteenth-century warfare, Leicester's personal entourage gave his army a top-heavy appearance. We possess a list of over 1,100 persons forming what was called his 'train'. These included nearly 700 cavalry, under his immediate command, and their names read like a litany of Tudor history: Alleyn, Arundel, Ashton, Babington, Bertie, Bingham, Blount, Boleyn, Bowes, Catesby, Cave, Clifton, Davison, Devereux, Dyer, Fairfax, Fisher, Fox, Gardiner, Gorges, Harington, Heneage, Hoby, Killigrew, Knollys, Norris, Nowell, Paulet, Randolph, Roper, Russell, Sadler, Shirley, Stafford and Topcliffe. Hardly a family which had grown great or notorious in those times was without a representative. Not since the exhilarating days of Henry v had the English ruling class gone to war in so comprehensive a fashion. There was even, indeed, a Tudor, and many more fighting Welsh: two Morrises, two Prices, three Evanses, three Floyds, three Lloyds, five Morgans and no less than eleven Joneses.[69] Moreover, Leicester himself was surrounded by a household a monarch might have envied: his personal suite comprised 99 gentlemen-officers, yeomen and their servants, and over 70 lords, knights and gentlemen; he had a steward, 4 secretaries, 2 engineers, pages, grooms, trumpeters, footmen, chaplains, physicians and a whole company of actors. The vast quantities of baggage included no less than 44 beds for his kitchen staff alone.

When the Earl finally arrived in the Netherlands, he found that the Dutch had organized, on his behalf, a triumphal progress through the country, with state receptions and festivities of every kind. Leicester was only too ready to fall in with these arrangements – it was a heady experience recalling the great days of his father's protectorate, and his own old ambitions of marrying royalty – but even he must have been appalled at the expense, and the whole air of unreality, so remote from the grim struggle he was supposed to be waging. At The Hague he was treated like a prince, and held court under a panoply of state. At Haarlem over £1,000 was spent on triumphal arches and fireworks, £639 on food for a grand dinner, £169 on marchpane, sugar and confectionery; the English officers got hopelessly drunk and pelted the solid Dutch citizens with sweets and cakes. At Amsterdam, £1,100 went simply on buying a presentation jewel for Leicester, and he in turn was forced to give elaborate feasts, and dispense hospitality from a household of gigantic size. By the time he finally joined his troops, more than four months after his arrival, he confessed to Walsingham: 'I am weary, indeed I am weary, Mr Secretary.'[70]

At home, the court made desperate attempts to keep the news of these goings-on from Elizabeth. This was a mistake, for she was bound to find out sooner or later, and she always, above all, hated efforts to conceal things from her. By 27 January she heard that Leicester was being addressed by the Dutch as 'Your Excellency', a clear breach of her commandment that he was to accept no honours without her express permission. On 5 February, she learned that he had been offered, and accepted, the title of Governor-General, only one step away from a throne itself, and in flat defiance of her whole political policy. By 17 February she had got the whole truth, and the result was an explosion. She sent Sir Thomas Heneage to Leicester with precise instructions and a savage letter of rebuke:

We could never have imagined, had we not seen it fall out in experience, that a man raised up by ourself, and extraordinarily favoured by us, above any other subject of this land, would have, in so contemptible a sort, broken our commandment, in a cause that so greatly touches our honour ... Our express pleasure and commandment is that, all delays and excuses laid apart, you do presently, upon the duty of your allegiance, obey and fulfil whatsoever the bearer hereof shall direct you to do in our name: whereof fail you not, as you will answer the contrary at your uttermost peril.[71]

Leicester, on receiving this, panicked, and tried to blame his actions on others:

he had merely followed Burghley's advice, or William Davisons's (the latter, denying this, noted angrily in the margin of Leicester's letter: 'Let Sir Philip Sidney and others witness'). But Elizabeth was not deceived, since she now knew that Leicester had written to everyone else at court telling them what he was doing, and had deliberately kept her in the dark. What particularly angered her was that she felt she could trust nobody to carry out her wishes to the letter. The moment they crossed the Narrow Seas, the normal discipline and respect for her seemed to fly out of their heads. Heneage, who was afraid of Leicester, and perhaps more aware than Elizabeth of the complexities of Dutch politics, delayed getting Leicester to renounce the Governor-Generalship promptly, and earned a stinging rebuke in Elizabeth's own hand (27 April 1586):

> Jesus, what availeth wit when it fails the owner at greatest need? Do that you are bidden, and leave your considerations for your own affairs; for in some things you had clear commandment, which you did not; and in other things none, and did; yea, to the use of those speeches from me that might oblige me to more than I was bound, or mind, ever to yield. We princes be wary of our bargains. Think you I will be bound by your speech to make no peace of mine own matters without their [the Dutch] consent? It is enough that I injure not their country nor themselves, in making peace for them, without their consent. I am assured of your dutiful thought, but I am utterly at squares with this childish dealing.[72]

Eventually a compromise was reached, as it had to be, for a flat repudiation of Leicester's arrangements with the Dutch must have jeopardized the alliance at the moment when the fighting season was about to begin. But the affair of his title confirmed all Elizabeth's worst suspicions about the wisdom of the whole enterprise, and the double-dealing of the Dutch. Moreover, she now had another, and mounting, grievance: the rising cost of the expedition, and the apparent inability or willingness of anyone to furnish her with meaningful accounts. Elizabeth has often been accused of neglecting the interests of her soldiers, of willing the ends of warfare while refusing to provide the financial means. Thus, the historian of the British Army, Sir John Fortescue, wrote: 'There have been many sovereigns and many ministers in England who have neglected and betrayed their soldiers, but none more wantonly, wilfully and scandalously than Elizabeth.'[73] The records tell a wholly different story. Elizabeth had the greatest possible sympathy with her troops, and was anxious at all times that they should be paid in full. When, in 1588, English troops mutinied at Ostend, because of delays in paying them and atrocious victualling, she sympathized with their demands, ordered an inquiry and instructed her commanders to use moderate dealing with the men. [74] When mutineers striking for pay were hanged, it was usually done without consulting her. Her animus was directed not at the troops but, on the contrary, at the captains who exploited and cheated them – and her.

The captains were the key agents in sixteenth-century armies because they not only raised troops, or 'bands', but were the means of distribution by which they were paid. The system had been introduced by the Italians in the fourteenth century, and had gradually spread to all European armies. It meant that the captain was the essential intermediary between the troops and the government, and his aim, often enough, was to cheat both. Everyone, except the captains, hated the system, but they successfully resisted all attempts at reform. Elizabeth was well aware of its defects, since she had suffered from them during the Siege of Leith. At the beginning of the Netherlands campaign she tried to insist that the captains should only be paid in respect of men they actually commanded. The men were to be mustered regularly for pay, and the Treasurer at-War was to hand over the money only when the muster-master had ocular evidence that the number of men on the rolls corresponded exactly with the number actually on parade. This was called paying by poll. But in practice the Treasurer simply handed over the money to the captains, on the basis of a nominal roll which was, of course, inflated. Moreover the Treasurers themselves turned out to be crooked, or incompetent, or a bit of both. Her first, Richard Huddilston, was paid £2,000 a year – more than the highest-paid officers in the home government. But he was soon accused of fraud, and though Elizabeth refused to condemn him without more proof, Sir Thomas Shirley was sent out as joint-treasurer, and the pay held in a double-lock chest, to which each had a complementary key. Shirley, however, was even more dishonest, or more incompetent, than Huddilston, though it was some years before this was discovered. He was accused of making £16,000 a year on top of his salary, but nevertheless contrived to get himself hopelessly in debt. [75] With such men in charge of finance how could the captains be kept in check? Moreover, 'pay' meant full settlement. In practice, the money arrived, and was distributed, at irregular intervals, and went to the captains in part-settlement – called 'imprests' or 'lendings'. The system was encrusted with all the complexities of ancient usage and fiddling. In theory, the Treasurer attended a muster with the muster-master. The latter examined the rolls, checked the numbers, and made deductions from the total for soldiers 'dead, discharged or departed'. He also deducted for armour, clothing or victuals already supplied by the Queen, or money advanced from the Treasurer. The deductions complete, the residue was then paid by the Treasurer to the captain. It was vital, therefore, that musters be held frequently, for the muster-master was the one official who could be relied upon to uphold the Queen's interests – which were identical with the men's. But on active operations it was always difficult to hold musters, and it was in the captains' interests to delay them and survive by imprests. And when a muster was held, the men expected to be paid in full: otherwise they mutinied immediately. This fact gave the Treasurer, too, an interest in delaying settlement. As Leicester himself put it (15 March 1586): 'Without pay, there can be no muster, and till pay the old rolls come on, be the bands never so weak. And it is the thing the captain desireth, never to have fully pay, but to run on with imprests, for so shall his bands never be looked into.'[76] However, in dealing with his own regiment, Leicester behaved like any other captain, and he never seems to have been willing to risk his popularity with the captains by enforcing the Queen's commands.

Moreover, right from the start, he eliminated any prospect of accurate and systematic accounting by adjusting the rates of pay upwards. He raised his own from £6 to £10 13s. 4d. a day, and others accordingly. This massive increase may have been justified in an age of inflation – the Council having calculated the rates on the basis of out-of-date practice – and he could also argue that he himself had put in a great deal of his own money to furnishing the expedition. But the rise was unauthorized, and of course it completely nullified the financial calculations on which the cost of the expedition, and Elizabeth's commitment, had been based. From August 1585 to December 1587, she had contracted to pay a total of £296,000. She actually disbursed £298,760. So Elizabeth not only paid in full, she overpaid. But the sums the troops should have received came to £313,000 – so they went £15,000 short. As Elizabeth's liability was limited by the treaty, the Dutch should have paid the difference, as she insisted. Not only did they not pay it, but they used some of the money which should have gone to the English troops in Leicester's service to pay English volunteers who were serving under Dutch command. When the Dutch were asked for money they had specifically contracted to pay, they replied that it had already been advanced in loans to English captains. This may have been true, but in that case it should have been debited to the captains in the Treasurer-at-War's account. It was not: no such accounts were ever produced. From early in 1586, therefore, any possibility of realistic accounts vanished.

It says a great deal for Elizabeth's fortitude that, without much assistance from Burghley or anyone else, she did her best to get to the bottom of this mountain of ineptitude, confusion and fraud, poring over such accounts as filtered through to her, and writing angry letters. The trouble was that, once the money left her

Treasury, she completely lost control over what was done with it. Much of it was diverted to pay English troops in Dutch service, and no accounts of these payments were ever supplied, 'God knows by whose default', as she put it. She handed over the money scrupulously, as her own accounts show, but then reports came back that the troops were unpaid in many cases and almost starving. All the officials blamed each other, and only the common soldiers shared with her the role of victim. 'It is a sieve', she wrote in exasperation, 'which spends as it receives to little purpose.' As the campaign progressed, and the number of troops in actual service declined, the cost should have fallen too. But checks were unpopular, and were not made, and the cost therefore rose. The muster-master reported to her that he had detected many frauds, which he refused to countenance, but the captains then complained to Leicester, and he, 'finding indeed that it was not possible for them to maintain their bands without certain allowances, did mitigate or pardon the checks.'[77] Asked for more money, Elizabeth demanded to see the accounts on which the demand was based, but they were in arrears and so useless, or not forthcoming at all. 'Though it be continually alleged', she stormed, 'that great sums are due, yet why such sums are due, or to whom they are due, and who are paid and who not paid . . . is never certified.'[78] Each time she sent over a further large sum, she tried to impose a foolproof system, but each time her efforts were frustrated by Leicester. Her only recourse, therefore, was to decline to send more money, and order some of the troops to be disbanded. But when, in the autumn of 1587, this action was taken, it was discovered that the released troops, far from being paid in full, as she had ordered, had in fact been sent home penniless: 'Great numbers come [home] in lamentable case, alleging for their defence, when they are charged as vagabonds . . . that their captains have paid them neither wages nor lendings, but have also disarmed them, and sent them away without any food, money or passport.'

Thirty of them turned up at the court gate, starving. Elizabeth ordered an inquiry, and eventually directed that any ex-soldiers who could convince the local authorities that they were owed wages should turn up at the court, where they would be 'fully satisfied'.[79] It was the best she could do. Her efforts to get fraudulent captains brought to justice were futile. What is worse, many of them were knighted by Leicester – fourteen in one day – against her express injunction that he was not to use his vicarious powers of knighting except for conspicuous gallantry in the face of the enemy. From this experience she acquired a detestation of the captains which lasted for the rest of her life: it was one reason why she so much enjoyed Shakespeare's ridicule of Sir John Falstaff in *Henry IV* Parts One and Two. His combination of cowardice, greed, fraud and sloth seemed, to her, to present an accurate picture of what most, or at any rate many, captains were actually like.

As for the expedition itself, it accomplished little or nothing. It can be argued that it actually damaged the Dutch cause, though, on the other hand, it may have achieved a strategic purpose by diverting additional Spanish military resources to the Netherlands theatre. At all events, it brought little glory to English arms. When Sir Philip Sidney was killed in a skirmish outside Zutphen, the political nation went into mourning, and tales of his gallantry and self-sacrifice became instant legend. Elizabeth, being a realist, was not impressed by this pointless incident. A state funeral was held, but she did not attend, and it was left to Walsingham – Leicester, Sidney's godfather, having defaulted – to pay the hero's £6,000 debts. By the end of 1587, Elizabeth would have given a great deal to have got out of the Low Countries commitment altogether. It was threatening to destroy the financial foundation on which the whole of England's security rested. But this was impossible. She was now firmly chained to the chariot of war, which was beginning to gather speed and threaten her heartlands.

Elizabeth had been able to take offensive action against Philip's communications and his possessions in the New World, and to play on his weakness in the Low Countries, knowing that her own home base was reasonably secure. Since the suppression of the Northern Risings in 1569–70, there had been no overt challenge to her rule in England, and the North had since been steadily brought under the control of the régime. Philip himself did not take the Ridolfi Plot seriously, and he seems to have made little attempt in the decade of the 1570s to encourage disaffection in England. It is true that other forces were at work. Until 1575, all the Catholic priests left in England were Marian survivals, increasingly old men. But in the Catholic areas of the Low Countries, especially at Douai, and in Rome and Madrid, the English arm of the Counter-Reformation was being organized to bring a new generation of missionary priests into action. The first three left for England at the end of 1574, and by the end of 1580 about 110 of them, including many Jesuits, had been smuggled into the country. The clerical menace to Elizabeth was never very substantial, and we shall see how she dealt with it in a later chapter. Its effect was more to transform the nature of surviving English Catholicism than to create centres of active resistance, and the government dealt swiftly and effectively with any priests who engaged in open proselytizing and agitation. By the end of 1581, Campion and fourteen of his companions had been seized, tried and executed, and the first wave broken.

A more serious point of weakness was Ireland, where Elizabeth's un-willingness to adopt a radical solution, or to supply sufficient men and money to make even her temporary expedients work, left the country to fester in periodic cycles of rebellion and repression. In this case, the Counter-Reformation was able to make some impression. A Jesuit mission, under Nicholas Sanders, established itself in July 1579, and it organized military resistance which was not fully suppressed until the end of 1580. The English position in Ireland was slowly deteriorating but for the moment it did not constitute any real threat to Elizabeth's régime. The effect both of Jesuit activity in England and of unrest across the Irish Channel was, rather, to alarm Protestant opinion, and to increase the psychosis of encirclement and the fear of conspiracy which began to grip the English government as the cold war with Spain grew more intense.

There was a third area of weakness which Elizabeth, or at least her ministers, took much more seriously: Scotland. Early in 1578, James, who was now twelve, assumed the kingship and began to take an increasing interest in the faction struggles between groups of nobles who fought for possession of his mind. In September 1579, a Guise agent of Scots descent, Esmé Stuart, Seigneur D'Aubigny, landed in Scotland and soon established himself in the young King's favour. At the end of 1580, the Regent Morton, who had governed Scotland in the Protestant and pro-English interest since 1572, was dismissed and imprisoned, and six months later he was executed. Esmé Stuart was made Earl of Lennox and began to build up a Catholic party on the ruins of the old Marian faction. Elizabeth always showed extreme reluctance to mix herself in Scots internal affairs, or to supply the money which would make such interference needless. In 1582, Walsingham, in conjunction with the Protestant nobles, organized the so-called 'Ruthven coup', which led to Lennox's expulsion (he died in May 1583, from a combination of dysentery and gonorrhoea), but Elizabeth was unwilling to take Walsingham's advice that 'Money will do anything with that nation', or to accept the recommendation of her Council that £10,000 a year should be allotted to bribing the King, and the nobility.

Instead, in August 1583, she sent Walsingham north on a threatening mission. Loyally following his instructions, he behaved in a masterful and pro-consular manner. He told the Scots that his mistress had been too liberal with them; she had no need to offer bribes, or to seek their friendship; he himself would advise her not to give them 'a single testern'; she wanted to live at peace with them, 'and yet hath she not her sword glued in the scabbard'. It was a colonial governor rebuking a rebellious tribe. Using recent border incidents as an excuse, he read the young King a sharp lecture about suppressing his border bandits, but he also reminded him that monarchs were obliged to rule with the consent of their people, and in accordance with the law. The state of Scottish public life at this period was lamentable: James's officers asked Elizabeth for an immediate loan of £300 just to keep the king's personal guard in being, and his favourite, the Earl of Arran – whom Walsingham contemptuously refused to meet – took his revenge by hiring a harridan, called Kate the Witch (he paid her £6 plus a plaid), to sit outside the palace door and insult the envoy whenever he came in and out. Walsingham satisfied himself that the old Marian party was now a negligible factor: James himself was no longer interested in securing his mother's release – on the contrary, he wanted her kept in detention. But he warned Elizabeth that James was no friend of hers, or of the English:

> For as your Majesty has always doubted, so I think you shall find him most ingrate, and such a one as if his power may agree to his will, will be found ready to make as unthankful a requital as ever any other did that was so beholden unto a prince, as he hath been unto your Majesty.[80]

Walsingham considered that James had been brought up in 'pride and contempt' for Elizabeth on the instructions of his infamous mother, and what really worried him was that, now it was clear Elizabeth would never marry, men were beginning to turn to James as her natural successor. Here was the real danger from Scotland: 'I find that men begin to look to the sun rising and therefore it will behove her Majesty to make much of faithful servants.' No one then guessed that Elizabeth would live another twenty years, and would decline to acknowledge James (or anyone else) as her successor until her death. Scotland was seen, for the moment, as a post-feudal chaos, but for the future as a real threat to the régime in England, if ever Elizabeth should get into serious difficulties at home or abroad. It was the force of this argument which finally enabled Walsingham to persuade Elizabeth to authorize a financial agreement with James at Berwick in July 1586. He was to receive a pension of £4,000 a year, plus the Queen's assurance that she would not explicitly bar his succession when she died. In return, he promised to give no hospitality or aid to her enemies, and to come to her assistance if she were attacked.

But of course James's mother was a silent and non-contracting factor in this league. James might not want her release; but he could scarcely be expected to acquiesce in her execution, or to decline to express his resentment if it took place. France – now England's uneasy ally, in a sense – was in an analogous position. France could, and would, do nothing to liberate Mary, but she was bound in honour to do her best to protect the life of a woman who had been her queen. Elizabeth's dilemma was very awkward: she was engaged in a deepening struggle with Spain, once her chief protector against the pincers of the 'Auld Alliance'; now, both wings of that alliance were formally her friends, but each inhibited her from dealing resolutely with the chief internal threat to English Protestantism.

Moreover, Mary Queen of Scots was now a factor that Philip II was beginning seriously to exploit. From being an amused and sceptical spectator of the earlier French efforts to release her, he became an active agent in her cause. Hence Elizabeth was very much thrown under Walsingham's protection. As she felt unable to remove Mary by execution, she became increasingly dependent on the security and counter-intelligence screen which her Secretary wove about the throne. During the 1580s, Walsingham became the most important of her ministers, and they developed a close (though never exactly friendly) relationship. They differed profoundly on many political matters. Elizabeth was a traditionalist and a conservative, though enough of a realist to accept change when it became inevitable. Walsingham was an activist, an ideologue and a man attuned to the movements of his age. A generation or so later, he would have been a parliamentary leader, engaged in bringing about political revolution by statutory process. Though he rejected, on tactical grounds, the extravagances of the Puritan divines, there could be no doubt about his deep commitment to the Protestant religion, which was in his view – as it was later in Cromwell's – the true dynamic of English power in the world. The frills of tradition – except it be the English tradition of constitutionalism and law – meant nothing to him. In a remarkable essay, 'On Fortitude', written shortly before his death, he showed himself almost alone in his period to reject the externals of hierarchy:

As for titles, which at first were the marks of power and the rewards of virtue, they are now according to their name but like the titles of books, which for the most part the more glorious things they promise, let a man narrowly peruse them over, the less substance he shall find in them.[81]

He was austere, sardonic, incorruptible, absolutely fearless, and an indefatigable man of business. Moreover, he was at heart, like Elizabeth, a simple English patriot, and his patriotism expressed itself in (among other things) a resolute determination to keep her alive. His small, slight figure, invariably dressed in black, was a visible reassurance of her security, far more formidable and effective – as she was well aware – than the military peacocks who also thronged her court. It explains her willingness to permit Walsingham intellectual liberties in argument which she accorded no one else. And of course they had a special relationship over the money needed to finance his security networks and his intelligence system. What this cost altogether cannot be discovered, for the money came out of the Treasury on Privy Seal warrants 'for such purposes as the Queen shall appoint', and this covered other expenditures. Warrants dated

24 July 1582, on the Exchequer of Receipts, show that from then on he was paid, quarterly, £750 a year, 'as for very special considerations we have agreed', and the sums were 'to be accounted as given by our mere liberality' and in no other fashion. This annual establishment was later raised to £2,000 a year; and many of the very substantial gifts, leases and financial privileges Elizabeth made over to Walsingham were also clearly intended to finance his operations. In addition he used his own fortune and died a comparatively poor man, though – unlike most of her leading servants – his debts to her were greatly exceeded by her debts to him. His combined security and intelligence services probably cost £3–4,000 a year, and though they were run in a far from lavish manner, they gradually evolved into the most powerful instrument of its kind in Europe. By 1580 he had four agents in Spain – in Corunna, Lisbon, Madrid and San Lucar (covering Cadiz and Seville) – to give him advance warning of Spanish naval and military movements; twelve agents covered France; nine Germany; four Italy; three in the Low Countries; and three more in Algiers, Tripoli and Constantinople.[82] The purpose of this network was not merely to forewarn, but to save the English government money by enabling it to stand-to troops and furnish ships at the last possible moment compatible with safety, and to stand them down immediately the threat receded.

At home, Walsingham's security service was built up progressively in the 1570s. It operated in the ports, in the London taverns, in the French and Spanish embassies and, from 1575, in the household of Mary Queen of Scots. He never had any doubt whatever that the most sensible course for Elizabeth was to bring Mary to trial and execute her. He did not believe (and he was proved right in the end) that there would be any significant Scottish or French reaction. As early as January 1572, he wrote to Leicester: 'So long as that devilish woman lives neither her Majesty must make account to continue in quiet possession of her crown, nor her faithful servants assure themselves of safety of their lives.'[83] Mary knew this herself: as Sir Walter Mildmay reported to Walsingham, 'She told me that she found in you a plain and round nature, for when you said you would be against her, you were so indeed.'[84] For more than ten years, Walsingham worked hard to secure absolute proofs of Mary's determination to obtain her release by combining with England's enemies and plotting to murder Elizabeth. In February 1575 he had his first success when Henry Cockyn, a London stationer, revealed under threat of torture the details of Mary's secret methods of communication. All this was reported to Elizabeth, who did nothing.[85] In January–March, 1577, he unravelled the 'Don John' plot, in which the Spanish regent, plus the Duke of Guise, planned to land troops to release Mary.[86] Again, Elizabeth took no action against Mary, though 10,000 troops were mustered and stood-to for a month. Walsingham was able to give the government advance warning of the Catholic landings in Ireland in 1579 and 1580, and to demonstrate their connection with Mary's cause. Again, Elizabeth took no action against her cousin.

In May 1582 an international conspiracy was mounted in Paris: the Pope, the Dukes of Guise, Philip II, Esmé Stuart, the Archbishop of Glasgow, Father (later Cardinal) Allen, head of the English Catholic missions, and Father Parsons, co-ordinator of the English Jesuits, were all involved. Walsingham contrived to get hold of dispatches from Mendoza to Stuart, and (in October), a cypher letter from Mary to the Archbishop. From there he traced communications between Mary and Mauvissière, the French ambassador in London, and planted two double-agents in the French embassy. By April 1583, using these agents, Walsingham was able to suborn Mauvissière's secretary, and by this means he learned that two Catholic gentlemen, Lord Henry Howard and Francis Throckmorton, had been visiting the embassy secretly. Throckmorton was tailed for six months, then arrested (along with Howard) in November 1583. A list of Catholic noblemen, plans of harbours, and 'infamous pamphlets' were found in his papers. Throckmorton proved obdurate, even under torture, and Walsingham ordered the treatment – personally conducted by Thomas Norton, the great parliamentary orator – to be stepped up: 'I have seen as resolute men as Throckmorton stoop, notwithstanding the great show he hath made of Roman resolution. I suppose the grief of his last torture will suffice without any extremity of racking to make him more conformable than he hath hitherto shown himself.'[87] Walsingham was right: the next day the prisoner confessed as soon as he was put on the rack. Four separate attacks had been planned, in Scotland, Ireland, Arundel in Sussex and in Norfolk – the last by 5,000 Bavarian mercenaries. Moreover, these were serious proposals, not the fantasies of Ridolfi. Walsingham was deeply disturbed, especially as he realized that the information would not have been forthcoming without the use of torture. There could be no doubt, moreover, about Mary's complicity, since Walsingham's bag also included a man who had carried numerous secret letters to and from Sheffield Castle, where she was housed, and a letter she had written to Mauvissière on 26 February 1583 read: 'If you can, get access directly or indirectly to Throckmorton or Howard, for the third [Northumberland] I have never had to do with him; assure them in my name that I shall never forget their affection for me and their great suffering in my cause.'[88] Any jury would have convicted her on this evidence alone.

Confronted with Walsingham's findings, Elizabeth still flatly refused to put Mary on trial. But she agreed to expel Mendoza, and gave Walsingham the pleasure of carrying this out personally, at York House on 19 January 1584. One of the conspirators, Lord Paget, fled abroad; Throckmorton was executed; the Earl of Northumberland committed suicide in the Tower. Walsingham, disturbed at Mary's apparent ability to send and receive letters without his knowledge, despite his elaborate attempts to control her correspondence, finally persuaded Elizabeth to place her in closer custody. Sir Ralph Sadler succeeded the unwilling and incompetent Earl of Shrewsbury as her custodian in August 1584, and the following month Walsingham was able to show the Queen a captured document, setting out in detail the 'design' to replace her on the throne by Mary. This, too, had a marginal effect: Elizabeth ordered Mary to be removed from Sheffield to Wingfield, in Staffordshire, and later to the fortress of Tutbury, where, in April 1585, Sir Amyas Paulet, a severe and methodical Puritan gentleman, was put in charge of her.

Mary complained bitterly of these changes, which curtailed her hunting, and made it more difficult for her to keep up the appearance of a court. Nevertheless by any standards her custody was comfortable. She had, even at Tutbury, a personal staff of forty-eight, consuming enormous amount of food. The accounts show that vast quantities of sea-coal, charcoal and wood were used to heat the castle; the cold and damp about which she made such a tale were the common lot of all, high and low, and she might well have been less cared for as Queen-Regnant in Scotland.[89] Nevertheless, the shadows were closing in for her. At various times there had been suggestions that, in the event of an actual rising on her behalf taking place, she should be put to death. Now, on a confidential basis at least, the point was made explicitly, as Paulet made clear to Walsingham:

> I will never ask pardon if she depart out of my hands by any treacherous slight or cunning device, because I must confess that the same cannot come to pass without some gross negligence or rather traitorous carelessness; and if it shall be assault with force at home or abroad, as I will not be beholden to traitors for my life ... so I will be assured that by the grace of God she shall die before me.[90]

But ministers wished to go further than this. Since Elizabeth would not bring Mary to trial and execute her by due process of law, was it not possible to devise some public plan to eliminate her in the event of a rising – and the death of Elizabeth – so that she, and those who planned to assist her, would be denied any benefit of their scheme? This was Burghley's view: he thought the best deterrent to conspiracy was to show, in advance, that Mary, at least, would not survive such a crisis. It was at this point that parliament – indeed the 'political nation' as a whole – began to take a direct interest in Mary's survival. Once again, on this issue also, Elizabeth's options were beginning to narrow. The parliament of 1581 had been, like its predecessor, reasonably co-operative. But a new one was due, for financial reasons, in the autumn of 1584, and in the meantime the assassination of the Prince of Orange had brought home to everyone the peril in which Elizabeth stood, and the way in which national security and religious toleration could be damaged – perhaps fatally – by a single murder carried out on Catholic orders. Even before parliament met, the Council had drafted the terms of an oath under which all loyal English gentlemen swore individually to protect their Queen, and avenge her murder, or attempted murder, by pursuing those who committed or planned it, or who stood to benefit from it. They were to 'prosecute such person or persons to the death . . . and to take the uttermost revenge on them . . . by any possible means . . . for their utter overthrow and extirpation'.[91] In October, while the elections were in progress, copies of the Bond of Association, as it was termed, circulated all over the country, and thousands of signatures and seals were attached.

As Elizabeth had refused to carry out the law against Mary, her government and supporters had resorted to a form of lynch law. But of course their object was to force the Queen into regularizing the oath by permitting a statute on similar lines to go through parliament. In 1586 Elizabeth claimed she knew nothing about the Bond until shown the lists of signatures, but this is not true since she almost certainly took part in the drafting. As a matter of fact, if the worst came to the worse, she preferred her loyalists to deal with Mary under the Bond, since this meant she herself had to bear no legal responsibility for her death. But her supporters thought otherwise. For them the Bond was a *pis aller*, an emergency measure to be superseded by law as soon as parliament could act. They had the Englishman's deep respect for, and confidence in, a court operating under statutory authority: their children and grandchildren were later to insist on a similar trial to secure the death of Charles I, openly, as Milton put it, in the face of the world. The parliament which met on 32 November 1584 revealed what we should now term a marked shift to the left. The Puritan faction was there in strength and overlapped substantially with the government (since the death of the Earl of Arundel in 1580, the entire Privy Council consisted of active Protestants). And there were some brilliant new figures among a host of young enthusiasts for the régime: Francis Bacon, Walter Ralegh, Francis Drake, Robert Cecil, Thomas Bodley and Fulke Greville – what a galaxy of talent! There could be no question that Elizabeth would have to take this assembly seriously, and this was reflected at the outset when government spokesmen (Mildmay on domestic affairs and Hatton on foreign policy) took the

Commons into the régime's confidence over the whole range of state affairs. 'I never heard in parliament the like uttered,' wrote Recorder Fleetwood to Burghley, 'they were *magnalia regni*'.[92] The Queen told parliament that she did not want Mary's name mentioned, but she knew very well that the substance of Mary's case was bound to be dealt with. Her object, by now, was to ensure that any security statute underwriting the Bond of Association was moderately worded, and in particular did not involve James. As a matter of fact, when the Commons got down to discussing a Safety Bill drafted by the crown law officers, they realized how repugnant it was in practice to give legal authority to the lynch-law of the oath. It got a second reading, but they sympathized with Elizabeth's comment:

> she would not consent that anyone [i.e. James] should be punished for the fault of another . . . nor that anything should pass in that Act that should be repugnant to the Law of God, or the Law of Nature, or grievous to the conscience of any of her good subjects, or that should not abide the view of the world, as well enemies as friends . . . in foreign nations as at home.[93]

This was sound sense, and ordinary decency, as well as good diplomacy and international public relations, and the Bill was taken back for redrafting.

During the Christmas recess, and as an adjunct to any Safety Bill, Burghley produced – in its mature form – his long-considered and grandiose scheme for a constitutional body to take over the country in the event of the Queen's sudden death. It adumbrated the Commonwealth, and indicates how firmly the achievements of the parliamentarians in the period 1640–60 were rooted in the notions of Elizabethan statesmen. If the Queen were killed, Burghley's draft states, all officials would be empowered to continue in their places, and the Council would be expanded into a Grand Council invested with the executive functions of the crown. Parliament would be summoned, and the three estates would become sovereign until such time as all claims to the throne had been heard, and the estates had decided which person 'to have best right . . . in blood by the royal laws of the realm'. The decision would then be embodied in an Act, all other claims would cease under pain of treason, and the interregnum would end. In short, the scheme put the crown into commission. The mathematician and scholar Thomas Digges, who had a hand in it, enthused to Elizabeth that the plan was 'a cause to immortalize your Majesty's fame and renown with all posterity, being the first estate royal that ever in England established so rare a provision'. But, as Elizabeth made very clear, this was not the kind of immortality she sought. The proposal would make parliament a sovereign body, with the crown a mere convenience (as has, indeed, since happened). By accepting it, she would effectively surrender her inheritance. Anyway, remembering the experiences of Somerset and Northumberland under her brother, she did not think it would work; it was a formula for faction. Though Burghley argued it would diminish the chances of her being assassinated, she preferred to take the risk. Nor was she unduly alarmed when, at the end of January 1585, Dr William Parry, a member of the Commons, was discovered to be involved in a plot to assassinate her. He had worked for Burghley on the Continent, and may have been a double-agent, or mad, or both. At all events he was arrested and convicted amid loud cries of outrage. Two senior MPs moved that the Queen's permission be sought to pass a law for Parry's execution in a manner 'fitting his so extraordinary and most horrible kind of treason'. Elizabeth thanked them for their concern but 'would not agree to any other form of dealing' than 'the ordinary course of the law'.[94]

The effect of these developments, however, was to increase the pressure for a Safety Bill, and in the end Elizabeth – who had a strong lawyer's mind – played a notable part in its drafting. The lynch-law element was removed by providing for commissioners to investigate any rebellions or plots against the monarch on behalf of claimants, and pronounce judgment. After this due process of law, all subjects 'shall and may lawfully, by virtue of this Act and Her Majesty's direction' pursue to the death anyone the commission said was concerned in, or privy to, the offence. If the Queen were killed, the claimant would be excluded, but not his or her heirs, unless it was shown they were privy to the offence – thus James was protected. Burghley's grandiose scheme was boiled down to a clause setting up the statutory commission, whose sole job was to destroy the guilty. On Elizabeth's suggestion, the Bill neatly solved the difficulty over the Oath of Association by stating simply that those who had sworn it were to discharge their obligations according to the true intent of the Act. The statute, as passed, thus reflected Elizabeth's qualifications and her moderate approach. It enabled the subsequent trial of Mary to be conducted by a respectable judicial process, and allowed her son to succeed peacefully. Indeed, it remained the law of the land until the reign of Queen Victoria.[95]

The question now was, would Mary be deterred by the new statute from taking part in further conspiracies and, if not, how resolute would Elizabeth show herself in enforcing it? There was not much doubt on the first point. Mary never seems to have been deterred by anything, or to have been influenced by the slightest consideration of personal safety, in pursuing her efforts to obtain her liberty and the crowns she thought were hers. Maybe she believed in the divine protection she constantly invoked, or perhaps her long confinement – she had now been in custody nearly two decades – had destroyed whatever slender grasp on reality she had once possessed. She continued to plot, and Walsingham to survey her. He did not act as an *agent-provocateur*; what he did was to allow her controlled access to the outside world, and by this means to secure valid evidence of her intent to kill, or assist or connive in the killing, of his Queen. His methods seem to me to have been perfectly legitimate, and he was able to claim at Mary's trial: 'I call God to witness that as a private person I have done nothing unbeseeming an honest man, nor, as I bear the place of a public man, have I done anything unworthy of my place.'

At what point Walsingham got wind of the Babington Plot is not clear. It was, in fact, merely a new phase of what had become a permanent conspiracy, hingeing on the murder of Elizabeth, the release of Mary and her imposition on the English nation by force of Spanish arms. Presumably Philip believed that once Elizabeth was dead, resistance would collapse. This was a very implausible supposition, but then Philip, who was no longer represented in London, can have had little knowledge of the temper of parliament, and he was always fed with wildly optimistic estimates not merely of the numbers of English Catholics, but of their willingness to betray their country. The French, who of course had an embassy in London, were much better informed, and correspondingly less sanguine; but by this stage, one feels, they were merely going through the motions of assisting Mary. In any case, they were allowed legitimate contacts with her until September 1585, when Walsingham directed that her official letters were to go through him and Paulet rather than, as hitherto, through Chateauneuf, the French ambassador. Walsingham thus took personal charge of her one legitimate channel of communication. It was clear, however, from past experience, that she and her confederates would set up a secret one, and Walsingham was determined this time that he should control it also.

In December 1585 a conjunction of events made such a scheme possible. In response to Mary's complaints, Elizabeth ordered Mary's removal from Tutbury to the Earl of Essex's house at Chartley, 'doubting that the coldness of Tutbury Castle may increase her sickness'. At the same time, a Catholic spy, Gilbert Clifford, was arrested at Rye and brought to the Secretary; he agreed to act as a double-agent, betray Mary, and in particular to ensure that her letters were intercepted. One of Walsingham's agents, Thomas Philips (or Phelippes), was sent to Chartley to make arrangements at that end, while Clifford was released to ingratiate himself with the French embassy, and obtain advance information of when outgoing letters were to be sent. At Chartley, Philips discovered that no beer was brewed in the house but instead was sent once a week, in keg, from Burton. Letters to and from Mary could be conveyed in a waterproof package inside the stopper. This arrangement was explained to Clifford, who went to the French embassy, told Chateauneuf he had found a method of getting letters to Mary, and offered to act as courier. Chateauneuf gave him a harmless trial letter on 12 January 1586, which was conveyed to Mary four days later. Early in February she sent a batch in reply, which after going through the Walsingham machine, were delivered to the French embassy on 19 February. Convinced by this, Chateauneuf handed over a two-year accumulation of letters which were delivered to Mary in batches.[96] Thus the controlled secret channel of communication was established.

On 20 May 1586, Mary fell into the trap by sending two letters, one to Charles Paget (a supporter of hers in Paris), and one to Mendoza, now ambassador to the French court. She said she favoured the invasion plan, and would try to induce her son to co-operate.[97] This in itself was enough to convict her, but Walsingham was anxious to learn more about the invasion schemes, and allowed the letters to continue. On 22 May, a Father Ballard, who had been in contact with Mendoza, arrived in England, secretly tailed by one of Walsingham's men. He almost immediately saw Anthony Babington, a young Catholic gentleman who had for two years been one of Mary's staunchest supporters: the previous autumn he had drawn up a plan to murder the entire Privy Council in Star Chamber.[98] Babington was now tailed also, and it soon emerged that he had got, from Ballard, the details of the invasion plan, which included the murder of Elizabeth, and he was overheard discussing the lawfulness of killing the Queen. Walsingham's next move was to put Mary in touch with Babington, which he did by forwarding to her a letter from another of her agents, Thomas Morgan, commending Babington's loyalty and trustworthiness. In reply, she wrote to Babington on 25 June; her letter was seen by Walsingham four days later, then forwarded on to Babington. Babington's reply was his fatal letter outlining the plot, which was taken to Chartley by Philips himself on 9 July. In it he told Mary that he and six friends were preparing to murder Elizabeth. On 19 July Philips was able to write to Walsingham in triumph: 'You have now this Queen's answer to Babington, which I received yester-night.' The letter was in cypher, drawn up by Mary's two secretaries, Gilbert Curle and Claude Nau, from a minute of instructions written in her own hand. She burnt the minute immediately afterwards, and the original cypher does not survive either, for after Walsingham had it copied, it was forwarded to Babington, who must have destroyed it. Philips, indeed, hoped to get it back for use in evidence. As he wrote to Walsingham:

If your honour means to take [Babington], ample commission and charge would be given to choice persons for search of his house. It is like enough, for all her commandment, her letter will not so soon be defaced. I wish it for evidence against her, if it please God to inspire her Majesty with that heroical courage that were meet for avenge of God's cause, and the security of herself and this state. At least I hope she will hang Nau and Curle.[99]

The cypher letter itself was not tampered with, but Walsingham could not resist adding a postscript, in an attempt to induce Babington to disclose the names of his six associates. This ploy did not come off, for on 4 August Walsingham decided to arrest Father Ballard, and immediately Babington heard this he burnt his more incriminating papers and fled. On 14 August he was picked up in St John's Wood (then a real wood). Meanwhile, five days before, Paulet, acting on Walsingham's instructions, sent Mary out hunting under escort, seized her papers while she was away, and arrested her on her return.

There was no difficulty in getting sufficient evidence to convict Mary, even though her minute, and the original cypher letter, had been destroyed. On 18 August Babington was examined by Lord Chancellor Bromley, Hatton and Burghley, and immediately made a confession – the first of seven statements. It was not necessary to torture him: he seems to have believed he would win pardon by frankness. He admitted that he planned to murder not only the Queen but all her principle ministers. As Burghley wrote jokingly to Leicester: 'Your lordship and I were very great motes in the traitors' eyes, for your lordship there [in the Low Countries] and I here should first, about one time, have been killed. Of your lordship they thought rather of poisoning than of slaying.'[100] Babington made no effort to protect Mary, or anyone else. Indeed he provided a full summary of her letter to him. Nau and Curle also made full confessions. Both attested that the copy of Mary's letter was identical with the original. Nau admitted to writing it in French from Mary's minute, and Curle to translating it into English and putting it into cypher.[101] Another arrested conspirator, Dunne, also attested that the copy in evidence was accurate, though he awkwardly drew attention to the forged postscript.[102] Indeed, Mary's modern apologists no longer attempt to prove that she was the victim of forgery, and concentrate their case for her relative innocence on the political background to the letter. The crucial passage in Mary's letter reads:

The affair being thus prepared and forces in readiness both within and without the realm, then shall it be time to set the six gentlemen to work, taking order, upon the accomplishment of their design, I may be suddenly transported out of this place.[103]

This plainly signified Mary's acquiescence in Elizabeth's murder, and the letter goes on to express great concern about her own safety once Elizabeth had been dispatched. Mary's own words thus brought her within the meaning of the statute of 27 Elizabeth I, c. 1. She had done, in fact, precisely what the Act provided against.

Apart from Leicester, Elizabeth was the only person who knew about Walsingham's efforts to trap Mary. They evidently had her full approval. Walsingham's doubts centred on the risk that the Queen would tell others. On 9 July he had written to Leicester: 'I dare make none of my colleagues here privy thereunto. My only fear is that her Majesty will not use the matter with that secrecy that appertaineth.' He need not have worried; no one was better at keeping a secret than Elizabeth. But after Babington fled, she thought it necessary to tell Burghley, so that he could issue a proclamation against the conspirators.[104] As Walsingham had kept her fully informed for more than a decade on Mary's activities, this latest episode can have come as no surprise to the Queen, though she was naturally pleased that the evidence was so conclusive, and that her servants had handled the affair in such a discreet and efficient manner. She wrote a warm letter of congratulation to Paulet: 'Amyas, my most faithful and careful servant, God reward thee treblefold in the double for thy most troublesome charge so well discharged', and she did not scruple to refer in it to Mary as 'your wicked murderess'.[105]

As Elizabeth had been following day by day the evolution of the plot since December 1585, it is mistaken to maintain that its discovery plunged her 'into a panic of acute physical fear', as one recent account has it.[106] On the contrary, she was still anxious, if possible, to spare Mary's life. Just as in 1572 she had sacrificed Norfolk to appease the public, so now she hoped that the trial and execution of Babington and his associates would prove sufficient. Remembering the parliamentary proposal to execute Dr Parry in a new and spectacular fashion – an idea she had rejected at the time with some abruptness – she resurrected it in an effort to satisfy the blood-lust of the London mob. On 12 September, the day before the Babington conspirators were to be tried before the special commission provided for by the Safety Act, Burghley wrote to Hatton:

she commandeth me to write that when the judge shall give the judgment for the manner of the death, which she saith must be done according to the usual form, yet in the end of the sentence he may say that such is the form usual, but considering the manner of horrible treason against her Majesty's own person hath not been heard of in this kingdom, it is reason that the manner of their death, for more terror, be referred to her Majesty and her

Council. I told her Majesty that if the execution shall be duly and orderly executed, by protracting the same both to the extremity of the pains in the action, and to the sight of the people to behold it, the manner of the death would be as terrible as any new device could be. But herewith her Majesty was not satisfied but commanded me thus to write to you to declare it to the judge and others of the Council there.[107]

In fact Burghley was quite right; the process of hanging, drawing and quartering, if carried out according to the strict terms of the sentence, was of ample horror, for the felon was cut down while he was still alive, eviscerated and emasculated, and the members and entrails, still smoking, were burnt in front of his nose. In practice this was virtually never done, the executioner ensuring that the man was dead before beginning his butchery. All that was necessary to ensure that the punishment was carried out in full was for a councillor to instruct the hangman to stick to the book. This was done: we hear no more of Elizabeth's special 'manner'. In fact she had wildly miscalculated the attitude of the mob. Their animus was wholly reserved for Mary: they saw Babington and his fellows as mere catspaws in her wickedness. When the first batch of convicts – Babington and six others – were dispatched on 18 September with the full ritual of barbarity, the crowd which watched was revolted, and expressed its feelings in no uncertain way. Much relieved, Elizabeth promptly issued instructions that the remaining conspirators, due to be executed the next day, should be hanged until they were dead.[108]

For a time there was some doubt whether Elizabeth would allow Mary herself to be tried. At first she had issued strict instructions that Mary's name was not to be mentioned at the trial of Babington and the others; but the commissioners for the trial unanimously signed a written protest saying that this omission would make nonsense of justice; and the Queen then agreed that Mary should be referred to in the indictment of Babington, and in the use of his confession to convict two of his associates, 'without exacerbation or enlargement of the Queen of Scot's crime more than shall be requisite for the maintenance of the indictment'.[109] Once this was done, there could really be no question of Elizabeth refusing the nation the trial on which it insisted. She gave way on 9 September, when the writs setting up a high-powered legal commission, under the Act, were sent out. She also agreed, after much argument, to summon parliament. Burghley reported to Walsingham: 'We stick upon parliament, which her Majesty mislikes to have, but we all persist, to make the burden better borne and the world abroad better satisfied.'[110] Obviously, it was politically and diplomatically desirable that the trial of a woman, whom most of the world still regarded as a queen, should be seen to have the unanimous endorsement of the representative nation sitting at Westminster. At the same time, Elizabeth knew very well that parliament, once in session, would insist that the sentence be carried out. Mary's death became virtually inevitable once Elizabeth had conceded that parliament should be brought into play.

For the trial, Elizabeth had Mary moved to Fotheringay, where the Commissioners assembled on 11 October. The Queen had insisted on revising the terms of the Commission, drawing a snarl from Walsingham: 'I wish to God her Majesty would be content to refer these things to them that can best judge of them, as other princes do.'[111] But it was impossible to prevent her supervising all the details, and she was kept daily informed of proceedings by express post. Burghley, Walsingham and Hatton, all members of the commission, were appointed by her as the stage-managers (a sketch by Burghley of the seating arrangements for the trial survives); but the commission was wide-ranging: it included all the senior earls, a number of prominent barons, the judges, and the members of the Privy Council, including William Davison, who had been appointed additional secretary to Walsingham on 1 October. Two of the commissioners, Lords Lumley and Montague, were notorious Catholic sympathizers, and were appointed for this reason. Mary began by refusing to recognize the trial at all, but was persuaded to plead by Hatton. Two sessions were held on 14-15 October. Then the commissioners, leaving Mary behind in custody, returned to London for a final session, to review the evidence, in Star Chamber on 25 October. Evidently Mary did not impress such men as Lumley and Montague. Walsingham wrote with satisfaction to Leicester: 'In the opinion of her best friends, that were appointed commissioners, she is held guilty.' At the final session in Star Chamber, Curle and Nau were brought in person to confirm their written testimony, and it was their evidence, apparently, which secured a unanimous verdict of guilty. Walsingham summed up:

> [the evidence of the secretaries] brought a great satisfaction to all the Commissioners, insomuch that albeit some of them, as you know, stood well affected to her, yet, considering the plainness and evidence of the proofs, every one of them after this gave his sentence against her, finding her not only accessory and privy to the conspiracy but also an imaginer and compasser of her Majesty's destruction.[112]

In accordance with Elizabeth's desire, the judges present confirmed that the commission's verdict in no way prejudiced the claims of James to the English throne.

Elizabeth now had to steel herself to carry through the execution, or risk an open breach with the political nation. The next few months were among the most tense and anguished in her whole reign, and the evidence suggests to me that she came close to a breakdown and, at times, to a total loss of judgment. She was already under great strain. She was emotionally upset by Leicester's long absence in the Low Countries, and angered and bewildered by the accumulating evidence of his financial folly (or worse), and military incompetence in the conduct of the campaign. The country was drifting into the open war she had struggled so long to prevent. The Treasury was already under pressure, despite all her hard saving. No one in the Council appeared to share her apprehensions or her almost ungovernable distaste for executing a woman who was also her relative and a Queen. It must have seemed to her, at this time, that her policies were ending in failure, and she lacked anyone to offer her the sympathy she craved. She may also have been undergoing her climacteric, and it is even possible that, in her nervous state, she paid uncharacteristic attention to the prophecies of a Leicester embroiderer, Edward Sawford, who predicted that dire consequences would follow Mary's death.[113]

Yet the machinery of execution was already in motion. Parliament met on 29 October, and for no other purpose than to see the verdict of the commission carried out. To mark her detachment, and to escape the funereal atmosphere of Westminster, Elizabeth remained throughout its sitting in Richmond: as she said, 'being loath to hear so many foul and grievous matters revealed and ripped up, she had small pleasure to be there present'. Three councillors, including Burghley and Whitgift, deputized for her. Bromley, in his opening speech as Chancellor, was instructed by her to say that the object of the parliament was to give her advice on what to do with Mary, a problem 'of great weight, great peril and dangerous consequence'. A two-day debate followed in the Commons, and according to the clerk, all the speakers favoured execution. A joint committee of both Houses unanimously petitioned her to proceed to carry out the law, and sign the warrant for Mary's death. On Saturday, 12 November, twenty peers and forty MPs waited on Elizabeth in her Withdrawing Chamber at Richmond, and handed over their petition. It made no reference to the Oath of Association. Indeed, since parliament now had secured a legal verdict, under statute, why should it be necessary for Protestant gentlemen to take matters into their own hands? Let the state do its work.[114] Yet Elizabeth evidently still hoped that this was what might happen, and spare her the agony of signing Mary's warrant. She got the Speaker to insert a reference to the Oath in his remarks to her:

Either we must take her life from her without your direction, which will be to our extreme danger by the offence of your law; or else we must suffer her to live against our express oath, which will be to the uttermost peril of our own soul, wherewith no Act of Parliament or power of man whatsoever can in any wise dispense.[115]

After this, Elizabeth ordered the parliamentarians to draw near to her, and made an extempore speech. Considering her state of mind, it was a masterly little performance, tactful, very personal, blending reflections on kingship with inside information:

I had so little purpose to pursue [Mary] with any colour of malice, that it is not unknown to some of my lords here – for now I will play the blab – I secretly wrote her a letter upon the discovery of sundry treasons, that if she would confess them, and privately acknowledge them by her letters unto myself, she never should need be called for them into so public question.

Personally, she would willingly forgive even this latest crime. Indeed, she would be happy to die, if her death could ensure England got a better monarch: 'for your sakes it is I desire to live: to keep you from a worse.' She was not afraid of death:

I have had good experience and trial of this world. I know what it is to be a subject, what to be a sovereign, what to have good neighbours and sometimes meet evil-willers. I have found treason in trust, and seen great benefits little regarded ... These former remembrances have ... taught me to bear with a better mind these treasons, than is common to my sex – yea, with a better heart perhaps than is in some men.

As for Mary, 'In this late Act of Parliament you have laid a hard hand upon me – that I must give directions for her death.' But 'we princes are set on stages, in the sight and view of all the world duly observed ... It behoveth us to be careful that our proceedings be just and honourable.' She must take time to consider; she would pray for guidance; delay was necessary, but 'you shall have with all conveniency our resolution delivered by our message'. The speech had a great effect. Bromley said it was so remarkable that he 'would not take upon him to report it as it was uttered by her Majesty'; Burghley claimed it 'drew tears from many eyes'.[116]

But of course it did not solve anything. After the week-end, Elizabeth sent the Commons, through Hatton, a message asking them to suggest possible alternatives to beheading Mary. The question was put to MPs again, a week later; no one answered. In the Lords, every peer, beginning with the most junior, was asked his opinion if the execution should proceed: 'they all answered (not one gainsaying) that they could find none other way of safety for her Majesty and the Realm.' On 24 November, the parliamentarians went to Richmond to give Elizabeth their unanimous opinion. According to her account, she had debated anxiously whether to say anything on this occasion. But she decided in the end to speak, and produced one of her most passionate outpourings. It reflects her extraordinary obsession for her reputation as a woman of clemency. To some extent it was aimed – as were all her actions at this time – at reconciling international opinion to Mary's death. Indeed, it later became the basis of a propaganda tract, written by Robert Cecil. At the same time it is clear that she was genuinely, almost desperately, anxious to appear on the stage of Europe, and on the stage of history, as a woman who never willingly dipped her hands in blood. It was as though she wished to reverse the memory of her father. She admitted that the advice she received was unanimously in favour of Mary's death. If she hesitated, and looked for an alternative to execution, it was not to win some spurious reputation for kindness. She was serious: if 'other means might be found out', she would be more glad 'than in any other thing under the sun'. Evidently her safety could not be guaranteed 'without a princess's head'. Was it not monstrously unjust that

> I, who have in my time pardoned so many rebels, winked at so many treasons, and either not produced them or altogether slipped them over with silence, should now be forced to this proceeding, against such a person? I have besides, during my reign, seen or heard many opprobrious books and pamphlets against me, my realm and my state, accusing me to be a tyrant. I thank them for their alms. I believe therein their meaning was to tell me news: and news it is to me indeed ... What will they not now say, when it shall be spread that, for the safety of her life, a maiden queen could be content to spill the blood even of her own kinswoman?

She was not cruel: on the contrary, 'I am so far from it that for mine own life I would not touch her.' Her object throughout had been not so much to preserve her own life from Mary, but to save the lives of both of them, 'which I am right sorry is made so hard, yes, so impossible'. She was grateful for their concern, and asked leave 'to say somewhat for myself'. She had thought a good deal about 'those things that best fitted a king – justice, temper, magnanimity, judgment'. She made no claim to the last two, but

> among my subjects I never knew a difference of person, where right was one; nor never to my knowledge preferred for favour what I thought not fit for worth; nor bent mine ears to credit a tale that first was told me; nor was so

rash to corrupt my judgment with my censure, ere I heard the cause ... this dare I boldly affirm: my verdict went with the truth of my knowledge.

They would all agree, she hoped, that she had never been over-hasty in deciding great matters of state. She had heard their advice; she knew it to be 'wise, honest and consciable'. But she had yet to make up her mind, and in the meantime, she asked them to 'accept my thankfulness, excuse my doubtfulness, and take in good-part my answer-answerless'.

Reading this remarkable speech, perhaps the most personal she ever made, one feels that Elizabeth, as the moment for decision approached, saw the fate of Mary as in some way epitomizing all the agonizing responsibilities of kingship. Here, in the clearest possible manner, could be seen the conflict between personal inclination and state duty. She had tried to avoid the issue; it had been forced upon her. She had looked for an alternative; there was none. She had sought to pass the burden of choice to others; it had been firmly handed back to her. She was alone, with her conscience, her feelings, and her task. Here was the divine right of kings stripped of its tinsel and glamour, and revealed in all its naked truth. In an increasingly complex world, where wealth, population and firepower were growing fast, where wars now ranged over oceans and continents, and affected the lives and fortunes of multitudes, was it not too much to ask a solitary individual to wear Jupiter's mantle? Could not a better form of government be found?

Two things were required of this lonely woman, by the unanimous and grim-faced men who surrounded her. First, she had to authorize the formal proclamation of Mary's sentence, as required by the statute; second, she had to sign the actual warrant for execution. Both must be done before parliament dispersed – it had been brought to London for no other object – or else, as Burghley put it, 'the realm may call this a vain parliament, or otherwise nick-name it a parliament of words'. On the evening of 24 November, the Queen sent her instructions to Chancellor Bromley to read the proclamation to parliament before it was prorogued. It was in her own hand, and almost illegible. Burghley, more experienced, had to read it to him. During the night – clearly a sleepless one – Elizabeth changed her mind, and issued an order, which arrived only minutes before Bromley set out for Westminster, to adjourn parliament for a week. During that week she steeled herself to authorize the proclamation – which she wrote, and re-wrote, with Burghley at Richmond – and it was finally published on 2 December. Parliament was then adjourned until 15 February 1587, giving Elizabeth a little over ten weeks in which to bring herself to sign the death order. If she failed to do so, the parliament would have to be dissolved, for even she could not meet it again, having done nothing and, in effect, revealed herself an irresolute coward, unfit for her position.

The sentence of death was publicly proclaimed throughout the country on 4 December, and Walsingham immediately drafted the terms of the death-warrant itself. Burghley drew up the letter-patent directing Sir Amyas Paulet and his fellow-gaoler Sir Dru Drury to hand over the person of Mary to the commissioners for her execution, the Earls of Shrewsbury and Kent. The court moved to Greenwich just before Christmas, and there Elizabeth authorized Burghley to have the warrant prepared in final form.[117] Both the French and the Scottish ambassadors asked for, and received, audiences of the Queen, and went through the motions of demanding clemency. This was pressure on one side – though not of a very formidable kind. On the other, there were reports and rumours of plots to release Mary, which both ministers, and the men who held her in custody, took very seriously. Walsingham was ill, and the secretary in attendance at the palace was Davison, a man of much experience as an official and diplomat – Burghley said he was capable of any post in the realm – but unused to Elizabeth's ways. Burghley, who was also in poor health after a fall from his horse, realized by now that Elizabeth wanted her hand to be forced; and it has often been suggested – some believed it at the time – that Davison was deliberately picked by his colleagues, as an expendable person of little conse-quence, to do the forcing and receive the subsequent blame. But I do not believe this. It seems to me that his role in the business is accidental, though unhappily his inexperience led the Queen to confuse the reality of events in her own mind. According to his account, he had the death-warrant in his possession, ready for her signature, for from five to six weeks, that is from the last part of December until the end of January. On 1 February Elizabeth sent for him, told him that she was disturbed by reports that an attempt would be made to release Mary, and that she would therefore sign the warrant at once. She did so, and in-structed him to have it passed under the Great Seal, and then show it to the sick Walsingham – adding, ironically, 'the grief thereof would go near to kill him outright'. Davison (still according to his account) told Burghley immediately, but next day, when the warrant had been sealed, the Queen again spoke to Davison, and asked why he was in such a hurry. This was the danger signal, and he should then have asked for Elizabeth's written instruction to him per-sonally to allow the machinery to proceed. He was, however, sufficiently apprehensive to consult Hatton; the two of them went to Burghley, and all the councillors then available held an emergency meeting and assumed responsi-bility, swearing an oath to each other not to consult the Queen further, until Mary was dead. They took the warrant, wrote the necessary letters to accompany it, and sent the batch off to Fotheringay by Robert Beale, secretary to the Council.

Elizabeth had a different version. According to her, after she had signed the warrant, she told Davison to keep it secret. Learning it had passed the Great Seal, she charged him on his life not to let it go out of his hands until she had so directed. There may be some truth in this, and it is possible that the nervous and frightened Davison misunderstood something she said, but this is unlikely, and his own account is clear and straightforward enough. A more probable explanation of the conflict of evidence is that she wanted Davison to organize the dispatch of Mary under the Oath of Association. Both the Scottish and the French ambassadors indicated that they would prefer Mary to die that way. At the time when she signed the warrant – directing that the execution should be as secret as possible and take place in the Great Hall at Fotheringay – she complained to Davison that others might have eased her of the burden, and suggested that he write to Paulet and Drury reminding them of their oath, and hinting that they should dispose of Mary without warrant. When Davison objected strongly, she said that wiser persons than himself had thought of the scheme. He did as he was asked, and wrote to Fotheringay. Then, after the warrant had passed out of his hands, and was already with Beale on the way to the castle, Elizabeth saw Davison again. She said she had had a bad dream about Mary. Did she then, Davison asked, wish to go through with the execution? 'Her answer was yes, confirmed with a solemn oath in some vehemency.' But she again raised the Oath of Association, and asked if he had heard from Paulet. He said no, but a letter from Paulet arrived later that day, and Davison showed it to the Queen the following morning. It was, from her point of view, highly unsatisfactory:

> My good livings and life are at her Majesty's disposition and I am ready to so leave them this next morrow if it shall so please her . . . But God forbid that I should make so foul a shipwreck of my conscience or leave so great a blot to my poor posterity as to shed blood without law or warrant.[118]

Elizabeth angrily complained of the letter's 'daintiness'. Why, then, had Paulet and Drury signed the oath? She was disgusted by the 'niceness of those precise fellows [as she termed them] who in words would do great things but in deed perform nothing'. She said she believed 'one Wingfield' and some others would do it. But she did not press the point. As a matter of fact, when Beale arrived at Fotheringay, there was a discussion (according to Beale's account) with Paulet and Drury, and probably with the two commissioner-earls also, of Elizabeth's suggestion. They debated the cases of Edward II and Richard II, but 'it was not thought convenient or safe to proceed covertly, but openly according to statute'. Mary was executed on the morning of 8 February. How deeply Elizabeth was attached to the murder-proposal it is impossible to say. She seems, in the end, to have rejected it. In his last talk about Mary with her, Davison records that she said firmly 'it were time the matter were dispatched', and swore a great oath that it should have been done long since, since she, as Queen, had 'done all that law or reason could require of her' to save Mary's life. By this time, of course, Mary was already dead, and the news reached court the next morning.

If Elizabeth had at last seen reason, when the matter had been taken out of her hands, the news that the deed was irrevocable almost deprived her of her senses. It has often been suggested that the indignation she displayed at Mary's death was deliberately feigned to impress foreign courts, and shuffle off responsibility from her own shoulders. Of course she was indeed capable of such a performance. But those close to her at the time would not have used such a word. Davison was immediately arrested and taken to the Tower. She refused to listen to his explanations or answer his letters. John Wooley, the Latin Secretary, wrote to Leicester on 11 February: 'It pleased her Majesty yesternight to call the lords and others of her Council before her into her withdrawing chamber where she rebuked us all exceedingly ... But her indignation particularly lighteth most upon my Lord Treasurer and Mr Davison.'[119]

She was evidently neither sleeping nor eating. A joint letter from her senior councillors the next day urged her 'to give yourself to your natural food and sleep, to maintain your health'. She would see neither Hatton nor Walsingham, and Burghley was in deep disgrace. Letters he wrote to her, offering to resign all his offices, were endorsed 'not received'.[120] Having excluded herself rigorously from the company and advice of her most senior ministers – the men who were actually directing the state on all major issues – she seems to have turned, instead, to the judges, and to have wildly discussed all sorts of proposals to use her prerogative to punish the offenders. It was as though all her experience in managing a carefully-balanced form of government, under the statutory and Common law, and conducted according to the traditional procedures of advice, was to be recklessly cast aside. Angered by the execution of a Stuart Queen, she seemed poised, for a time, to behave like one. A cypher from Burghley survives in the Lansdowne manuscripts, fortunately accompanied by a set of clues inserted by his secretary;[121] it reveals the Lord Treasurer as a badly frightened man, suddenly deprived of all the constitutional certitudes which thirty years of working with Elizabeth had made to seem so solid. It was addressed, almost certainly, to his neighbour and closest colleague in the government, Sir Walter Mildmay:

Her Majesty, I know not how, is informed that by her prerogative she may cause Mr Davison to be hanged and that we may all be so convicted as we shall require pardon. Hereupon yesterday she, having Mr Justice Anderson with her, and demanding whether her prerogatives were not absolute, he answered, as I hear, yea. And so, charging my Lord of Buckhurst with his assertion that she could not hang the Secretary against the law, she rebuked him bitterly and avouched Mr Anderson's answer for the same ... She since hath declared the judgment of Mr Anderson to serve her purpose and as I think, she, being led by this fearful or ill-advised judge, will have the minds of the rest of the judges understood ... I would be loath to live to see a woman of such wisdom as she is to be wrongly advised, from fear or other infirmity. And I think it as hard time if men for doing well before God and man shall be otherwise punished than law may warrant, with an opinion that her prerogative is above the law – nay, as the case is intended, it may be extended against the laws ... and I am only fearful of the harm may grow to her reputation if it should be known.

He begged his correspondent to see four of the leading judges, including the Chancellor, and get them to disavow Anderson's advice. He was plainly scared that Elizabeth, in her anger and distress, was about to drive a coach and horses violently through the centre of England's legal and constitutional system, and in doing so wreck her government, and destroy the Protestant consensus of the nation, at a time of growing crisis when it most needed to be preserved and strengthened. All the constitutional achievements of the reign would be destroyed, the nation would be divided, and Elizabeth herself would be revealed as a foolish and frightened woman, seeking to quench her hysteria in tyranny.

Mildmay, if it was he, was able to carry out Burghley's request. Evidently he saw all the leading members of the legal profession, and he was later able to tell Davison (in the Tower), that both the Attorney and the Solicitor-General, who would have to prosecute, insisted they would resign their offices rather than deal with Davison except in Star Chamber, which could not touch life or property. The government, in fact, was in revolt, and there can be little doubt that there would have been mass-resignations from the Council if Elizabeth had persisted in her apparent desire to have Davison executed. At the time, some believed Leicester was behind the Queen's insensate behaviour, and indeed Leicester himself, surrounded by the mess he had contrived in the Low Countries, was in a mood verging on paranoia. But men were always too quick to blame Leicester for anything unpleasant. He stood to lose as much as any if Burghley, Walsingham and the rest forfeited power. There is no evidence he was urging Elizabeth to folly, and such evidence as does exist points in exactly the opposite direction. It was the Queen herself, assisted by a craven judge, who was bent on self-destruction.

Nor was her mood exactly transitory. More than a month later, on 27 March, she ordered the councillors who had directed Mary's execution to appear before the Lord Chancellor, the two chief justices, and the Archbishop of Canterbury, to explain and justify their actions. Burghley submitted written answers to the questions put to him, insisting that the Queen had made it quite clear to Davison that Mary was to be executed, and that he and his colleagues had acted swiftly simply to ensure Elizabeth's safety. It was not mentioned then, or at the subsequent trial of Davison in Star Chamber, that the inner group of councillors had sworn not to reveal their deliberations, or their actions, to Elizabeth until Mary was dead. By this time, the English political establishment was closing ranks and recovering its nerve after the shock of their Queen's anger. Many matters were hushed up. It was now conceded that there had to be a victim, of sorts. James, who had received the news of his mother's death calmly – it was scarcely unexpected – had demanded no less; indeed he had asked for more. In reply to Elizabeth's letter of explanation, he had said he accepted it, but cynically added: 'to confirm it to be true – I speak plain language – *necesse est unum mori pro populo.*'[122] Robert Beale's account says the suggestion was mooted that Burghley should be imprisoned temporarily; but 'her Majesty thought that to commit him to the Tower would kill him'. 'Mr Secretary Walsingham', he adds, 'was thought too stout and would utter all. Therefore, Mr Davison must bear the burden.' But Elizabeth's desire to execute Davison – if it had ever been serious – soon evaporated. The Star Chamber sentenced him to a fine of 10,000 marks (£6,666), and imprisonment during the Queen's pleasure. Eighteen months later, when the Armada had been disposed of, he was released into private custody, and excused the fee normally paid by prisoners to Tower officials. In summer 1589, his fine was remitted. He kept his fees as Secretary, and in 1594 was granted lands worth £200, which he capitalized for £5,000. Elizabeth never again gave him employment, though she was often urged to do so. She continued to believe that he had behaved with less discretion than she expected of her key servants. But as a sacrificial victim he escaped lightly.[123]

The storm slowly subsided. The reactions of French and Scottish opinion were much as Walsingham had expected – negligible – and as the weeks went by Elizabeth realized that the heavens were not going to open on her head. The life of an executed queen was, it seemed, of less account to the world than she had been brought up to believe. The execution of Mary not only did Elizabeth no damage; it ended, once and for all, any real threat of internal subversion, and it made possible a much more businesslike understanding with Scotland and France. Yet Elizabeth continued to harbour resentment against the inner group. Burghley was removed from the commission which dissolved parliament. On 3 April Walsingham reported to Leicester:

> Our sharp humours continue here still . . . The Lord Treasurer remaineth still in disgrace and behind my back her Majesty giveth out very hard speeches of myself, which I the easier credit for that I find in dealing with her I am nothing gracious. And if her Majesty could be otherwise served I know I should not be used.[124]

Some time in May Burghley was allowed back at court, though it was reported:

> Not many days past, her Majesty entered into marvellous cruel speeches with the Lord Treasurer, calling him traitor, false dissembler and wicked wretch, commending him to avoid her presence, and all about the death of the Scottish queen.[125]

Elizabeth saw, rightly, that Burghley had been the master-spirit in Mary's execution, and she wished to signalize that she resented his infringement of her rights on such an issue. He took his continued disgrace philosophically, knowing by now that Elizabeth had returned to her senses, and that the old order would soon be resumed again. He, and in the end she, too, had taken a look at the pit which would open in English public life if she overrode law and custom, and both had decided they disliked it exceedingly. Elizabeth was always willing to learn from her mistakes, even if she would not confess them. She never apologized to Burghley for her behaviour, or even mentioned the episode thereafter. That was not her way. But she had taken the point, and never again was she tempted to play the tyrant – that was left to her successors. It could be said that her quarrel with her councillors after Mary's death adumbrated many of the great issues of legal and constitutional principle which convulsed England in the seventeenth century. The difference between Elizabeth, and James I and Charles I, was that she could smell political danger, and knew when to draw back before her prestige and dignity were irrevocably committed. It was this capacity which made her such a remarkable, and durable, sovereign, so well equipped to run a political system based on ambiguity and dependent on a consensus.

Moreover, she had magnanimity. If she did not apologize to Burghley, she made her feelings clear. In mid-June she agreed to pay him a visit at Theobalds. She went there towards the end of the month, and was still there on 16 July, nearly three weeks later. We know little of this visit, the longest she ever spent at any of his houses, and we may interpret the silence as a good sign. At all events, both emerged from it once again firm friends and close associates. All the other planets of the court slowly fell back into their accustomed orbits. The Elizabethan system of government was restored – and not before time. Mary's death might have been received with indifference in Paris and Edinburgh, but in Madrid it was seen to remove the last possibility of bringing England to heel by any means short of direct invasion. The threat of the Spanish fury was now a reality, and a united nation was needed to meet it.

9

The Dice is Thrown

One of the reasons why Elizabeth was so affable during her long visit to Burghley at Theobalds in June and July 1587 was that there she received the news that Drake had returned to Plymouth on 26 June with enormous booty. The primary object of Drake's expedition, which we will examine later in its military context, had been to interrupt – or 'distress', as it was termed – Spanish naval preparations for the invasion of England. But while standing off the coast of Spain, having raided the harbour of Cadiz, he learned that a great Spanish cargo-ship or carrack from the East Indies was approaching home waters, and he hastened to the Azores to intercept it. The *San Felipe*, which was the personal property of King Philip, as well as bearing his name, was taken without difficulty, and brought back with its cargo intact: the goods alone were valued at £114,000. Of this Elizabeth's share, in cash, was £40,000, well over half an annual parliamentary subsidy.[1] To give an idea of the use to which such a sum could be put, in military terms, a flagship galleon could be built for £2,600 or hired for £28 a month; its crew could be paid and fed for a further £175. Such a windfall, almost alone, could tip the balance of strategy for a season, and, of course, what the Queen gained, Philip lost.

There could be no doubt that Elizabeth was increasingly worried about money. The £300,000 'war chest' she had accumulated up to 1585 was being rapidly emptied by the cost of the Low Countries campaign, and though losses could be made up by subsidies, the effect of regular parliamentary taxation, with its unequal incidence, was to weaken the economy as a whole, which was already under strain as a result of hostilities in Flanders and elsewhere.[2] In May 1587, Burghley was so worried by the decline in English cloth exports that he called an emergency meeting of the Council, revoked the monopoly of the Merchant Adventurers, and authorized a limited experiment in free trade – not to much purpose, since it was abandoned after a year.[3] Elizabeth took a close interest in these matters. As always, she regarded money as the key to military strategy, as indeed to every other aspect of government: her ability to pay cash, and maintain her credit, was to her the ultimate war-winning weapon and, at the same time, the best deterrent to Philip's invasion schemes. The harvest of

1586 had been bad, and by summer 1587 had had the effect of slowing down the flow of money into the Treasury from the crown's regular sources. At the same time, the demands on her cash reserves were increasing. She was now acting as paymaster not only in the Low Countries, but in France, where her Protestant ally, the King of Navarre, was battening her for money to pay his German mercenaries. She was being forced to turn increasingly to such money-raisers as Sir Horatio Palavicino, who operated both in the City and the Continental markets.[4] In September 1587, in a letter to Walsingham, Burghley gave a vivid picture of Elizabeth's anxieties and her methods. He said he had just succeeded, after a long argument, in persuading Elizabeth to send more money for Navarre's Swiss and German troops. He was about to leave her, in search of Palavicino, to arrange the transfer of funds across the exchanges, when a packet of letters from Walsingham, addressed to Burghley, arrived. Elizabeth was no respecter of other people's correspondence; indeed she believed that all letters sent to her ministers were state papers, and therefore hers (this was one reason why they sometimes communicated with each other in code). She snatched the packet 'and would needs see all the writing'. Pouncing on an intelligence report forwarded by Stafford from Paris, she read out one sentence – not, as Burghley noted, in context – and concluded from this that the mercenaries were 'well contented, desirous of nothing but bread and not to be naked . . . So she framed a conclusion that there was no need of money, and to confirm this she said that Palavicino had reported to her the like.' Burghley hotly denied this, but the moment he left the room to go to a Council meeting, she sent for Palavicino and tried to bully him 'to remember such a speech, but he answered her that in part it was true' (clearly, it was a case of 'up to a point, Lord Copper'). Burghley ended his letter, after a harassing day, by asserting that he intended to send the money all the same: 'What may follow tomorrow, I know not, but I hope well, for I see she seeth the danger. And so I take my leave, being almost asleep.'[5]

One may take a sardonic view of this characteristically feline behaviour of Elizabeth's. But behind its apparent irrationality there was a strong force of reason. She was resisting an attempt to be cajoled into a series of overseas commitments which, in the past, had always proved disastrously beyond England's resources. She knew it was not possible to defeat the Spanish armies in the Low Countries decisively. The Dutch could not produce a field army of more than 2,000. The French could raise ten times as many, but not for long enough to be of much use. In the late sixteenth century, the fortunes of war rested heavily with the defensive. There was no likelihood whatever of forcing a series of quick and decisive battles in the field. Infantry units were huge, and cavalry unable to deploy, especially in the Netherlands. As musketeers replaced pikemen, the infantry itself became less manœuvrable. Fortresses were immensely strong, and encouraged the tactics of blockade rather than assault. Contemporary strategists saw the science of war as essentially one of manœuvre, and condemned open battle as the last resort of an incompetent general. So, as one military historian has put it, 'Strategic thinking withered away, and war eternalized itself.'[6] In the Low Countries, endurance was all; and endurance meant money. It cost Elizabeth £21 a year to keep a man there; to achieve anything like success she would have needed to provide 50,000 men over three years – this allowing for the normal wastage rate. In the opinion of one of her advisers, the idea of a campaign stretching into years was itself unthinkable. As Dr Bartholomew Clerk minuted: 'These hundred years and more never any king of this land was able to continue wars beyond sea above one year.'[7] In fact, Elizabeth did provide 50,000, but over a period of twelve years, from 1585 to 1597. This imposed a huge strain on the Exchequer, and of course it was not enough to achieve decisive victory. But it had the merit of containing Parma, and in particular of robbing the Spanish of the one deep-water port, Flushing, that they needed to ensure success for their Armada campaign. To this extent, Elizabeth's intervention in the Low Countries was successful, and she was content that it should have such a limited bearing on the overall strategy. No wonder, then, that she resented further encroachments on her treasure, to set up anti-Spanish fronts elsewhere, for such expenditure had to be made at the cost of England's home and naval defences.[8]

Her one consolation, as always, was that Philip's financial difficulties were greater than her own. She could usually borrow money at 8 per cent (rising on occasion to 10 per cent during the Armada period); Philip, who had already defaulted, and was to do so again, had to pay up to 18 per cent, and sometimes more in emergencies. In September 1585, following Philip's seizure of English shipping, Elizabeth had unleashed Drake with a fleet of thirty ships against the West Indies. He had captured and ransomed San Domingo and Cartagena, and though the loot was in some respects disappointing (Elizabeth did not recover all her investment), the damage to Spanish military and naval prestige was immense, and when the news of Drake's exploits reached Europe early in April 1586, the effect on the money-markets was immediate. Walsingham noted (11 April): 'The Genoese merchants that were wont to furnish [Philip] with money in time of necessity, for that they fear a revolt of the Indians, begin to draw back.'[9] Unfortunately, for both Spain and England, Philip was less impressed by financial factors than Elizabeth. His disregard of them, indeed, was in the long run to ruin his empire. But for the moment economic pressure, paradoxically, had the effect of persuading him to press ahead with plans for 'the enterprise of England'. He feared English barbarism, as he put it, 'as the burned child fears the fire'. But unless the fire were extinguished, and quickly, it would spread to all his dominions. Lack of money, in fact, strengthened the ideological character of his self-imposed mission, for it drew him into closer alliance with the Pope who controlled the only solvent state in Europe, apart from England. From the summer of 1585 Philip began to negotiate secretly with Sixtus v to obtain papal finance for an invasion which was to restore England to the Catholic faith.[10] Sixtus proved an even harder paymaster than Elizabeth. Although, in December 1586, he finally agreed to a contract under which he was to provide a million crowns for a Spanish invasion, the first instalment (500,000 crowns) was not to be paid over until after Spanish troops had landed, and the remainder in sums of 100,000 spread over two years. Thus Philip was to carry the entire burden if the expedition failed. On the other hand, if the invasion succeeded, he would be in a strong position to dictate the political settlement of England, on which he and the Pope were unable to agree in advance. So long as Mary of Scotland lived, she was the obvious candidate for the throne. After her death, Philip's Catholic allies in France wished James to succeed, under the impression that a Spanish occupying army could persuade him to embrace Catholicism. This was also the Pope's preferred solution. But Philip had his own claim to the English throne through his Lancaster descent, and there can be little doubt that his object throughout was to add England and Ireland to his dominions.

Detailed Spanish military planning for the invasion of England went back to 1582, immediately after the Spanish Admiral Santa Cruz had defeated the French fleet at Terceira. This cleared the way for a possible assault on the English coast, and Santa Cruz envisaged a direct invasion from Spain, by a force of 556 ships, escorting 85,000 troops in 200 flat-bottomed boats. But the cost alone made it impracticable. At the end of 1586 Mendoza, from Paris, proposed a much cheaper alternative: a comparatively small military force to be landed in Scotland. If the expedition were a success, and led to Catholic risings in England itself, then more Spanish troops could be sent, and the Spanish fleet brought into play. The merit of the plan, in Mendoza's opinion, was that 'It will be no small advantage to your Majesty that the game should be played out on the English table, just as [Elizabeth] has tried to make Flanders and France the arena.'[11] Of course Mendoza exaggerated the strength of pro-Catholic feeling in both Scotland and England – as far back as 1580 he had prophesied that Elizabeth's régime was on the verge of collapse. On the other hand there can be little doubt that, if Spanish troops could have been landed in the Forth, Philip would have achieved a remarkable military advantage at comparatively modest cost. But he himself was determined to strike at England, and to use Parma's troops from the Low Countries as his decisive instrument. The naval escort was to come from Spain, the troops from Flanders. This was always his view of how the thing should be done, and it was the plan eventually adopted. His insistence that Parma's army – the best he had – should be used, indicated that he put little faith in the claims of Cardinal Allen and Father Parsons that half England would rise to welcome the liberating Spanish. But the weakness of the plan was that the two forces would have to rendezvous at sea, since Philip did not possess a deep-water port on the Flanders coast, nor did he have any realistic hope of securing one in England, before Parma's troops embarked. Ralegh's judgment on Philip's plan was scathing: 'for to invade by sea upon a perilous coast, being neither in possession of any port, nor succoured by any party, may better fit a prince presuming on his fortune than enriched by understanding.'[12] Parma, indeed, never had any enthusiasm for the Armada scheme, which he saw as a diversion from Spain's real strategy, which was to complete the conquest of the Netherlands. He demanded a deep-water port on the Continent as a *sine-qua-non* for the expedition setting out at all, since the warships of the Armada would not be able to stand inshore to escort his shallow-draft barges, and his troops would therefore be mercilessly exposed to the fury of English and Dutch coastal vessels, heavily armed with cannon and grapeshot. But Parma was overruled; his advice was always suspect in Philip's eyes, who regarded him – not without reason – as an over-mighty subject.[13] Instead, Santa Cruz was induced by Philip to re-cast his original scheme, and he eventually produced a plan for an invasion fleet of 77,000 tons, manned by 30,000 mariners, and capable of transporting 60,000 men, including Parma's contingents.[14] Nothing approaching this force was ever assembled. Drake returned from the West Indies with 240 captured Spanish guns, and this loss was never made good. Spain did not make her own naval artillery, and ships due to sail in the Armada were stripped of guns to refurbish the West Indies forts and squadrons. Moreover, in spring 1587, Drake succeeded in penetrating the defences of Cadiz harbour, where a large section of the Spanish fleet was assembling. He destroyed Santa Cruz's own flagship, a vessel of 1,500 tons, a huge Biscayan warship of 1,200 tons, and 22 other warships, great and small (this was the official Spanish estimate; Drake claimed 37 ships sunk, burned or captured).[15] He also succeeded in intercepting a group of coastal vessels carrying cooper's stores, 'hoops and pipe-staves and such like'. The stores were, he reported to Walsingham,

above 16 or 17 hundred tons in weight, which cannot be less than 25 or 30 thousand tons, if it had been made into cask, ready for liquor, all which I commanded to be consumed into smoke and ashes by fire, which will be unto the King no small waste of his provisions . . .[16]

These losses, too, could not be, or were not, made good. Lack of matured barrels limited the size of the Armada, and the supplies of food and water it could carry, and much of what was put on board was wasted because of green barrel staves. Nor was there any possibility of Philip landing as many as 60,000 troops, even assuming the English fleet was defeated. By the spring of 1588, Parma's effective troops in the Low Countries were down to 17,000, and he was strongly opposed to sending any of them. He warned Philip that it made sense to carry on peace talks with Elizabeth, at least for the time being, to 'escape the danger of some disaster, causing you to fail to conquer England, while losing your hold here'.

But with all these reservations, Philip's invasion plans were formidable. Drake reported, on the basis of eye-witness accounts, 'the like preparation was never heard of, nor known, as the King of Spain hath and daily maketh to invade England'.[17] In February 1588, the great Santa Cruz died, and was succeeded by a landsman, the Duke of Medina Sidonia, who described himself as possessing 'neither aptitude, ability, health, nor fortune for the expedition'. In fact in some ways the change was to Spain's advantage. Santa Cruz had been in desperately poor health for the last year of his life. In equipping the fleet he had lacked the strength to insist on many necessary supplies, and accounts of how the ships were loaded while he was still in command show that he was losing his grip.[18] Sidonia was a soldier, but then the object of the expedition was military rather than naval, and Drake always referred to the Armada as the 'Spanish Army'. Moreover, the Duke, if pessimistic and reluctant, was a man of high determination and skill in organizing large bodies of men and supplies. He greatly improved on the chaos of Santa Cruz's supply arrangements, raised the number of guns in the fleet, and, equally important, their ammunition quotas (to fifty rounds of shot per gun; Santa Cruz had been willing to settle for thirty), and he reloaded the ships in an orderly manner. By the time he was ready to set sail in May 1588, he had 130 ships, including a first line strength of 20 galleons, 4 galleases, and 4 gigantic armed merchant ships, a second line of 40 armed merchantment, many of them bigger than any of the ships in Elizabeth's service (except her two largest, the *Triumph* and the *White Bear*), and 70 troopships, hulks and scouts. His fleet was nearly twice as big as the Armada with which Santa Cruz was preparing to set sail at the time of his death, and was roughly equivalent, in tonnage and manpower, to Elizabeth's entire navy. The list of the fleet, its complement and equipment was not only drawn up in the greatest detail by Sidonia, but actually published at the time: it contained 8,350 sailors plus 2,080 galley slaves, 19,290 soldiers, and 2,630 large guns, provided with 123,790 cannon balls. No such expedition had ever put to sea before in history.[19]

At no stage, so far as I have been able to discover, did Elizabeth ever express an opinion on the likely outcome of a conflict with such a war-machine. She seems to have been satisfied that, when it came to the point, England could defend herself. But right to the last she made strenuous, persistent and, among most of her ministers, highly unpopular efforts to avoid a showdown. Walsingham assisted, or rather controlled, her peace-efforts because he thought that, if he did not do so, Elizabeth would use her own secret channels of communication without his knowledge. In November 1585, using Dr Hector Nunez, a Portuguese physician, he established contact with a former Portuguese ambassador to England, Antonio de Castello. By this means messages between the English and Spanish governments were exchanged on four occasions up to April 1587. He also encouraged, with Elizabeth's knowledge, the peace-making efforts of old Sir James Crofts, her Comptroller, who had graduated from Protestant activism to pro-Catholic conservatism, and was now in receipt of a Spanish pension. Crofts had his own channel to Parma, though the Prince thought him 'a weak old man of seventy with very little brains'. Burghley, too, had his personal line to the Spanish headquarters in the Low Countries, and at one time there were five different sets of contacts in operation. Walsingham had no illusions about the Spanish desire to make peace. He thought it non-existent, and he was right. Even Parma, while doubting the wisdom of the invasion scheme, regarded peace-talks as simply a means to gain time for more promising military plans. Philip was still more hostile.

Elizabeth, however, was kept well informed about Spain's real intentions. As Walsingham reported to Leicester on 9 October 1587:

> Sir Edward Stafford hath advertised here that the French king hath specially sent to his agent in Spain, to learn there whether the King of Spain meant soundly to proceed in this treaty of peace with the Queen, from whom he hath received undoubted answer that the King doth it only to win time and to abuse the Queen of England. This notwithstanding ... is offensively taken here, so much do we [Elizabeth] mislike anything which may hinder the said treaty of peace.[20]

Croft's contact was one Andrea de Loo, an Italian banker with direct access to Parma. While Elizabeth was staying with Burghley in July 1587, she got through this route what purported to be Parma's peace-terms, and showed a degree of interest which led Burghley to wail to Walsingham: 'I am unfit to be executor of these sudden directions, especially where the effects are so large and dangerous. But lords and ladies command and servants obey.'[21] What became cynically known as 'Mr Comptroller's Peace' was taken up officially in December 1587, immediately after Leicester's final return from the Low Countries. Elizabeth appointed peace commissioners: the Earl of Derby, Lord Cobham (Warden of the Cinque Ports), Crofts himself, Dr Valentine Dale, an expert on international law, and Dr John Rogers, who spoke fluent Italian. None of the big men in the government expressed any interest in forming part of it, though they perversely criticized its composition as lightweight, as indeed it was. The party set off in mid-February 1588, but did not reach Ostend until mid-March, and then spent two months on procedural argument. In April Crofts paid a personal visit to Parma at his HQ, but this merely led to misunderstandings, as Crofts spoke nothing but English. Walsingham, who knew Crofts to be a fool, encouraged his venture, hoping the old man would destroy himself in Elizabeth's eyes, and so discredit the peace-party.[22] This is more or less what happened, as Crofts was imprisoned in the Tower immediately he got back, and kept there for a year. All the same, the talks were not finally abandoned until the Armada was actually sighted off the Lizard. Elizabeth may not have believed that the peace moves held out any real hope, but she was determined to preserve her reputation as a woman who would do almost anything, short of surrender, to avoid bloodshed. As, from the accounts of Camden and others, it is clear that peace-mongers were roundly denounced by majority opinion as cowards if not crypto-Catholics, what she did was highly unpopular and demanded, in its own way, a species of heroic courage. Moreover, it is relevant to add that her practice has since been followed by virtually all British governments placed in similar circumstances.

In any case, defensive preparations went ahead without interruption. They had been in hand, indeed, ever since her accession. Elizabeth had never neglected her navy. One of her first acts had been to authorize Burghley to look into the state of the fleet. In January 1559, he had commissioned an analysis called the *Book of Sea Causes*, completed two months later.[23] It reported the present state of the fleet as 22 sail of all classes, 45 convertible merchant ships, and 20 supply ships; 10,600 sailors were needed to man them, and mobilization would take two months. The report recommended a 50 per cent increase in ships, with the emphasis on medium-sized vessels of 400–500 tons, highly manœuvrable and with heavy fire-power. Broadly speaking, these recommendations were adopted, and after Elizabeth appointed Sir John Hawkins as Treasurer of the Navy in 1578, England slowly acquired the most modern and formidable fleet in the world.[24] His appointment was bitterly resented by the Winter family, which had hitherto exercised a near-monopoly of naval administration. Though Sir William Winter himself was not above peculation – two of his ships, the *Edward* and the *Mary Fortune*, had been built from the Queen's seasoned timbers – he did not hesitate to accuse Hawkins of corruption, and to assert, right up to the end of 1587, that the Queen's ships were in a thoroughly unprepared and rotten state. Elizabeth never believed these charges, and a departmental inquiry set up by Burghley completely vindicated Hawkins's tenure of office. In his dealings with the Queen he seems to have been scrupulously honest, and as a superintendant of naval construction he had genius. Only two of Elizabeth's ships – both of them small – were wrecked during her reign, though the older craft were gradually replaced by thirty-seven new vessels.[25] Ralegh, an articulate expert, testified:

> . . . in my own time, the shape of our English ships has been greatly bettered. It is not long since that the striking of the topmast (a wonderful ease to great ships, both at sea and in harbour) hath been devised, together with the chain-pump, which takes up twice as much water as the ordinary did.[26]

Hawkins introduced capstans to weigh anchor, longer cables, and new ranges of sails. Above all, unlike the Spanish, he resisted the temptation to build ever-bigger ships, and concentrated on medium-sized vessels with low-profiles, vast quantities of guns, and huge crews to man them. As Ralegh said:

> We find by experience that the greatest ships are least serviceable, go very deep to water and of marvellous charge [expense] . . . they are less nimble, less mainable and very seldom employed . . . a ship of 600 tons will carry as good ordnance as a ship of 1,200 tons and . . . the lesser will turn her broadsides twice before the greater one can wind once.

A typical such ship was Grenville's *Revenge*, which proved itself one of the stoutest vessels ever to carry the royal ensign. Ralegh knew what he was talking about, since he built the *Ark Ralegh* in 1587, and handed her over to Elizabeth (re-christened the *Ark Royal*) in time to serve in the Armada fight as Effingham's flagship. 'I think her', said Effingham, 'the good ship in the world for all conditions, and truly I think there can be no great ship to make me change and go out of her.' We can fairly assume that Ralegh often talked to Elizabeth about naval matters. What she valued in him was a capacity rare among men of action: the skill to explain military and naval technology in terms ordinary people could understand. Ralegh's advocacy kept the Queen solidly behind Hawkins. But she had plenty of other sources of information. When at Greenwich, she was at the centre of naval activity and could watch her ships exercising from her bedroom window. One of her best friends, Lady Clinton, wife of the old Admiral, was immensely knowledgeable in naval affairs; indeed the court and government ladies made flags and bunting for the Queen's ships: green and white (Tudor colours) for the *Revenge* and *Scout*, red for the *White Bear*, black and white for the *Bonaventure*, 'timber colours' for the *Lion*.

Any intrinsic advantage which England possessed in the coming naval confrontation was very much increased by the excellence of Walsingham's intelligence service. He knew, early in 1586, that Philip was actively preparing an invasion force of great strength.[27] The close watch kept on English ports prevented the Spanish from obtaining comparable information about Elizabeth's naval strength and dispositions. Nevertheless, Walsingham was not satisfied with his efforts, and in spring 1587 he presented Elizabeth with a paper, 'A Plot for Intelligence out of Spain', which laid down lines on which the system could be improved. Elizabeth's support for his ideas is underlined by her authorization of a huge increase in his secret fund – between March 1587 and June 1588, £3,300 was paid over to him, the most he ever got for this purpose.[28] A member of Santa Cruz's personal staff at his Lisbon HQ was suborned, and sent to Walsingham a copy of the Admiral's detailed report to Philip on his ships, stores and men. It was dated 22 March 1587, and reached the English a few weeks later. Elizabeth thus knew as much about the Armada preparations as did Philip himself. In Madrid, the view seems to have been taken that reports of the size of the Armada would cause despondency in England. But Parma, who after all was engaged in active warfare, deplored the laxity of Spanish security. 'The affair is so public', he lamented to Philip in January 1588, 'that I can assure your Majesty that there is not a soldier but has something to say about it, and the details of it.'[29] Walsingham's most effective agent was Anthony Standen, who worked under the code-name of Pompey Pellegrini, from the Italian courts. Standen put Walsingham in touch with the Tuscan Ambassador in Madrid, who reported to the English authorities, and early in 1588 Standen moved to Madrid himself, sending information to London, via Italy, by fast courier. Another English agent in Spain, Nicholas Ousley, was by now on the run, but managed to get letters through, and Walsingham had a third agent in Parma's camp. So good was the English system that Walsingham was able to take risks: in July 1587, he advised Elizabeth that the Armada could not reach England for another twelve months, and she gratefully ordered a stand-down. Most of the fleet was decommissioned, though a squadron under Sir Henry Palmer continued to blockade the Flemish coast. The saving in money was considerable, since her fleet-in-being cost £12,000 a month. From the beginning of 1588, the flow of information to England became a flood, and Elizabeth could study the detailed Spanish order of battle long before the Armada was sighted.[30] By contrast, Walsingham was highly successful in concealing information of English naval movements. Early in 1586 he discovered that Sir Edward Stafford, English ambassador in Paris, was unreliable. Stafford was well-connected: his father's first wife had been Mary Boleyn, Elizabeth's aunt, and his own mother was Mistress of the Robes, and one of the Queen's favourite ladies. But Stafford had married a crypto-Catholic, Lady Douglas Howard, and was a desperate and unsuccessful gambler. The Duke of Guise paid his gambling debts, and in return Stafford passed intelligence to Mendoza. Knowing this, Walsingham controlled letters to Stafford, and held them up completely when Drake was about to raid Cadiz; relying on the Stafford link, the Spanish were taken unawares, and the first they knew of the expedition was when Drake turned up, guns blazing, in Cadiz harbour. Walsingham was adept at turning treason to advantage, and Elizabeth relished this aspect of his work: was not her own motto *Video, Taceo* – I see all, but say nothing?[31] She found Stafford, properly controlled, a useful extra channel to Spain.

By the beginning of 1588, in strictly naval terms, the balance of advantage rested with England. It was a different matter on land. Elizabeth was always reasonably confident that her navy could deal with the Armada in a fleet action, but if the Spanish slipped through and landed troops, the balance would swing to them. It was partly a matter of organization. Since 1546, the navy had been controlled by a central body, later the Navy Board; there was no comparable structure for the army.[32] What Elizabeth did was to develop the system of lords lieutenancies, placing counties, or groups of counties, under her principal ministers for defensive purposes. Thus, in 1588, Burghley had Lincolnshire, Hertfordshire and Essex; Hatton, Northamptonshire; Hunsdon, Norfolk and Suffolk; Ralegh, Cornwall; Pembroke, Somerset, Wiltshire and most of Wales; and the Earl of Derby Lancashire and Cheshire. Thus the ruling circle, in addition to their collective national responsibilities, also had direct regional duties in the areas where their power chiefly lay. The bulk of the actual work – holding musters, and organizing arms depots and training – was carried out by deputy-lieutenants, of whom there were several for each county, chosen from the best of the JPs. It was thoroughly characteristic of Elizabeth to prefer, and develop, this system, rather than set up a central organization. It was not entirely dissimilar to the methods used in the old Anglo-Saxon state, found so lamentably wanting at the time of Hastings, the last successful invasion of England by a foreign power. Fortunately on this occasion it was not put to the test. But it is a curious fact, and an illustration of the tenacious continuity of English history, that when William Pitt the Younger was confronted with the prospect of invasion in the 1790s, over 200 years later, he ordered an inquiry into the preparations made by Elizabeth.[33] As a result of Pitt's action, we know a good deal about what Elizabeth planned, though the details are not always reliable. A sub-committee of the Council was formed in February 1588 to take charge of home defences: Hatton, Leicester, Wooley, Walsingham and Burghley. The last, as usual, produced a detailed memo, which costed the defence, assuming a stand-to of three months, at £250,000.[34] In July, when the invasion became imminent, Leicester was appointed commander-in-chief, in charge of the main repellent force. This was grouped in Essex, to command both banks of the Thames Estuary. It was known the Spanish hoped to effect a landing 'in the neighbourhood of the Cape of Margate', but the Essex deployment covered the possibility of a descent on East Anglia also. Lord Hunsdon, with another large force, was charged with Elizabeth's personal safety.

How many troops were actually raised and deployed is difficult to discover. On 2 December 1587, Walsingham calculated that there was a force in being of 26,000 foot to repel the Spanish landing force, and another of 24,000 foot to protect the Queen. But these were estimates, based largely on optimistic guess-work, and Walsingham had to leave the figures for cavalry blank.[35] In the event, the best troops were raised not so much by the national musters, as by the methods of feudalism, or rather the 'Bastard Feudalism' that prevailed in the fourteenth and fifteenth centuries. In June 1588, Elizabeth solemnly called upon her nobility and gentry 'to attend upon her with such a convenient number of lances and light horse as might stand with their ability'. The response was impressive, considering that the notables had to pay the bills themselves. Burghley provided 50 lances and 50 light horse; Hatton 100 horse and 300 foot; Warwick 150 horse and 200 foot; Essex 244 horse and 50 foot. Walsingham, not normally a 'swordsman', raised 50 lances, 10 petronels (carabineers) and 200 foot; he planned to dress himself in complete armour – he ordered a new suit for the occasion – and lead his men personally. In all, 1,610 horse and 1,448 foot were raised in this manner, and they formed the hard core of both the English armies. Leicester's army in Essex, assembled in camp at Tilbury, never numbered more than 11,500 all told, and Hunsdon's bodyguard for the Queen – at any rate during the critical period – was only 1,200 foot and 87 horse. Altogether, about 50,000 foot and 10,000 horse were stood to arms in July and August 1588, but the great majority of these were locally mustered in the maritime counties, from Cornwall up to Yorkshire.[36] All the same, bearing in mind the enormous demands of the navy, and Elizabeth's existing commitments in Ireland and the Netherlands, this was the largest military effort England had ever made, and testifies both to the organizational ability of Walsingham and Burghley (the two ministers chiefly responsible), and to the loyalty of the nation to their Queen. Elizabeth had always believed that the people would stand by her in unanimity. She had never accepted the possibility that a Catholic faction would rise against her, and events justified her confidence. Although the Council insisted, against her wishes, on precautionary measures against known recusants, most of the Catholic gentry insisted on their right to provide troops, and hotly resented aspersions on their loyalty.[37] The supposedly recalcitrant Northerners were particularly anxious to provide family and estate units for the armies, though they characteristically insisted – it was an old grievance of the Northerners going back to Magna Carta – that they should not be sent 'beyond the seas'.

How far the enthusiasm of the nobility and gentry reflected the national mood is, in the light of the evidence, a matter of opinion. That old and recurrent theme of English history, now known as the 'Dunkirk Spirit', always tends to dissolve when subjected to detailed examination. Elizabeth received an invaluable access of popular support when, on 12 June, she got the text of an extraordinary attack on her by Cardinal Allen, followed ten days later by a papal Bull, calling on her subjects to rise and depose her. Allen and Parsons were, of course, wholly out of touch with English opinion, otherwise they would have remained silent. Burghley prevented these documents from circulating, but he referred to them with great effect when, early in July, he addressed a meeting of justices and JPs who were about to return to their counties to take up station. Allen, he emphasized, was not even a gentleman, but 'a base companion', who had the impudence to claim 'Luciferian authority' to dispose of the crown of England on anyone Philip and the Pope should select. The Spanish might not fight at all; if they did, the English navy was the strongest in the world. It was Elizabeth's policy to pursue peace, but in the meantime, 'every man should provide to serve his Queen and his country, men of peace with looking to the peace, men of arms with addressing themselves to arms'.[38] This address has the stamp of Elizabeth's composition. Actually, she herself was less worried by political disaffection – of which there was no sign – than by the possibility of common-or-garden resentment at the financial burdens she was driven to impose. The money was running out, and as it was inexpedient to summon parliament, whose members were all at their military stations, she had to resort to temporary expedients which, in other circumstances, would have been hotly resented. In January 1588, she called on a defence loan from 2,415 of her wealthier subjects: this raised £75,000. In March she borrowed £30,000 from the City. In April, she imposed a primitive form of

Ship Money, levied on the coast towns. In August she got another £25,970 from the London merchants. The longer the armies and fleets stood to, the more likely it was that the Treasury would have to default. Early in July, Burghley wrote anxiously to Walsingham: 'A man could wish, if peace cannot be had, that the enemy would no longer delay but prove (as I trust) his evil fortune.'[39] He was afraid, as he admitted, that the financial demands of the government might produce popular tumult, especially in the coast areas. Elizabeth could reflect that, had she followed the advice of Burghley and Walsingham earlier, and provided more money for the Continental campaigns, the situation would have been far worse. Her relative parsimony in 1586-7 saved the nation from bankruptcy in 1588. Hence, Burghley's fears were not realized. The coast towns, especially the smaller ones, protested at the Council's orders to produce ships for naval service – but they provided them all the same. Afterwards, Elizabeth (using Burghley as draftsman) was able to publish a pamphlet praising the English people for their unprecedented voluntary response in the defence 'of their religion and liberties'. They had shown 'a most vehement and unaccustomed affection and devotion in the cities and port towns, such as they showed themselves therein ready to fight, as it had been, *pro aris et focis*'.[40]

The Queen's own mood was confident and composed. In the early summer of 1588, under her direction, a gentleman of her Chapel, Anthony Martin, wrote a magnificent prayer, for use at services of intercession. Its felicitous language reflects and combines her theory of kingship, her view of religion, her desire for peace, and her calm assurance of victory if peace failed:

O Lord God, heavenly Father, the *Lord of Hosts*, without whose providence nothing proceedeth, and without whose mercy nothing is saved; in whose power lie the hearts of princes, and the end of all their actions; have mercy upon thine afflicted Church, and especially regard thy servant Elizabeth, our most excellent Queen, to whom thy dispersed flock do fly, in the anguish of their souls, and in the zeal of thy truth. Behold! how the princes of the nations do band themselves against her, because she laboureth to purge thy sanctuary ... Consider, O Lord, how long thy servant hath laboured to them for peace: but how proudly they prepare themselves unto battle. Arise, therefore, maintain thine own cause, and judge thou between her and her enemies. She seeketh not her own honour, but thine; not the dominion of others, but a just defence of herself; not the shedding of Christian blood, but the saving of poor afflicted souls. Come down, therefore, come down, and deliver thy people by her ... O! possess the hearts of our enemies with a fear of thy servants. The cause is thine, the enemies thine, the afflicted thine;

the honour, victory and triumph shall be thine ... Bless thou all her forces by sea and land. Grant all her people one heart, one mind, and one strength, to defend her person, her kingdom, and thy true religion. Give unto all her councils and captains wisdom, wariness, and courage; that they may speedily prevent the devices, and valiantly withstand the forces of all our enemies: that the fame of the gospel may be spread unto the ends of the world.[41]

The imminence of danger brought to an end, for the time at least, any hint of faction-fighting at court. Burghley and Walsingham, who had differed greatly in the past, moved closer together, and Walsingham sealed their firm friendship by the gift of 'a new-fangled coach'. Elizabeth had made it clear that all personal differences were to be submerged in the coming struggle, and there was remarkably little bickering about appointments. She met no opposition when she gave the command of the fleet to Lord Howard of Effingham, 'of whose fortunate conduct', wrote Camden, 'she had a very great persuasion, and whom she knew by his moderate and noble carriage to be skilful in sea matters, wary and provident, valiant and courageous, industrious and active, of great authority and esteem amongst the seamen of her navy'. These adjectives were, for the most part, well-merited: Elizabeth had chosen him well, for though he possessed the authority of a great aristocrat, he was singularly lacking in arrogance, and always willing to listen to expert advice. He deprecated his own naval experience, but in fact it was considerable. His father, the 1st Lord Howard of Effingham, and a younger son of the 2nd Duke of Norfolk, had been Lord Admiral under Mary and had taken his heir with him on active naval operations when the lad was only seventeen. Effingham had since served as a general of horse under Warwick during the 1569 rising, but the following year he had successfully commanded the Channel squadron, when, says Hakluyt, he forced all foreign ships 'to stoop gallants and to veil their bonnets for the Queen of England'. He was married to Catherine, daughter of Elizabeth's cousin, Lord Hunsdon, and one of her closest women friends, but this connection does not seem to have determined Effingham's appointment, which rested on his varied military experience, his tact, and his unusual lack of enemies among the professional sea-commanders. Later, in his *History of the World*, Ralegh was to pay Effingham a notable tribute in his handling of the Armada campaign. He thought the Admiral

better advised than a great many malignant fools were, that found fault with his demeanour. The Spaniards had an army aboard them, and he had none; they had more ships than he had, and of higher building and charging;

so that had he entangled himself with those great and powerful vessels, he had greatly endangered this kingdom of England.

It was a mark of Effingham's calm self-confidence and lack of professional envy that he did not hesitate to pick all the best captains to serve under him. With the exception of Ralegh, who was busy with the land defences of the West, all the leading seamen were employed, and offered no objections to Effingham's leadership, though they sometimes ignored his orders on points of detail. Elizabeth picked her Admiral for his character and for his personal and political loyalty as much as for his skill, because she knew that, as the time of the Armada approached, events would pass out of her control.

Volumes have been written on English strategy in 1588.[42] Was the Royal Navy to take the offensive, and try to destroy the Armada in its own waters? Effingham reported:

> The opinion of Sir Francis Drake, Mr Hawkins, Mr Frobisher and others that be men of greatest judgment and experience is that the surest way to meet with the Spanish fleet is upon their coast, or in any harbour of their own, and there to defeat them ... I confess my error at that time, which was otherwise; but I did and will yield ever unto them of greater experience.[43]

The Council hesitated to authorize this strategy, because it was feared the fleets might miss each other at sea, and the Armada arrive on an unprotected English coast, as indeed nearly happened later in the reign. But on 17 April Elizabeth bowed to the weight of naval opinion, and Effingham was ordered to take the main royal squadrons to Plymouth, to join Drake's ships. 'There is here', he wrote to Burghley

> the gallantest company of captains, soldiers and mariners that I think ever was seen in England ... I do thank God that [the ships] be in the estate that they be in; and there is never a one of them that knows what a leak means ... Myself and my company do continually tarry and lie abroad in all the storm, where we may compare that we have dances as lustily as the gallantest dancers at the court.[44]

This was a metaphor Elizabeth appreciated. On 10 May, following a long Council meeting, she authorized Effingham to take the offensive, and on 17 June she gave him full discretion to conduct the naval war as he and his vice-admirals thought fit. It was a signal mark of her confidence in her naval officers, showing Elizabeth was willing to delegate completely in matters she felt beyond her competence. The contrast with Philip II, who tied down Medina Sidonia to a detailed and inflexible set of orders, was both striking and fortunate. In fact, the weather, which turned stormy and westerly in April, made any English offensive out of the question. Apart from a few days early in July, when Effingham put briefly to sea, the winds tied down the fleet to defensive tactics throughout the summer: 'Such summer season', wrote Seymour, the Admiral of the Downs squadron, 'saw I never the like, what for storms and variable unsettled winds.' The same westerlies brought the Spanish out of Lisbon on 18–20 May (thus wholly confirming Walsingham's intelligence report that the Armada would set out in mid-May), forced them to shelter in Corunna, then set them on a fair course for England in the second week of July.

Drake, in Plymouth, got the news of the sighting of the Armada at 3.00 p.m. 19 July. It seems to have reached court that night or the following morning. Elizabeth was at Richmond: it is evidence of her confidence that she had not moved to Windsor, her normal station in times of military danger. From 20 July, the Council met daily in the palace, until on the 30th she moved to St James's, the London palace where security was most easily maintained (the Tower, of course, was an operational ordinance and supply headquarters). There, too, the Council sat daily until the danger receded in the second week of August. From Elizabeth's actions and movements, it is clear that the arrival of the Armada came as no shock. A generation later, the Spaniards claimed to have achieved tactical surprise: 'Did we not in 1588 carry our business for England so cunningly and secretly . . . as in bringing our navy to their shores, while their commanders and captains were at bowls upon the hoe of Plymouth?'[45] This is the origin of the most famous of all Drake stories. Very likely Drake was playing bowls, and when he heard of the sighting finished his game because he knew he had only the weak last ninety minutes of the ebb tide to warp out, and that therefore there was no point in hurrying.[46] In the prevailing weather conditions, the English always knew they would face a disadvantage in taking station at the outset. They were prepared for it, and worked their way to wind-ward of the Armada without difficulty. As Sidonia put it in his official account, 'the enemy recovered the wind, their ships being very nimble and of such good steerage as they did with them whatever they desired'.[47]

At the opening of the action, the Spanish had the advantage of more large warships than the combined fleets of Drake and Effingham. But they had many vulnerable lesser vessels to protect, and, granted the limitations of Spanish marine architecture and seamanship, Sidonia did well to keep his forces in the tight crescent formation he had decided to adopt. The Armada thus moved up the Channel with the English squadrons hanging on to its tails. Assuming the rendezvous with Parma was to take place, this was the right tactic for the Spanish. But it led to a war of attrition which was profoundly demoralizing for Sidonia's soldiers and seamen. The English ships were manœuvrable enough to engage at long range, with their heavier artillery, and in the knowledge that they were in sight of their home ports for fresh supplies of powder and shot, and repairs. The Spaniards could not grapple, and use the advantage of the vast number of armoured men they carried; and in artillery duels they were bound to suffer damage and losses which could not be made good. On Sunday, 21 July, the first contacts were made. Almost immediately, the Armada's treasure-ship, the *San Salvador*, was damaged by an explosion and fell behind, and another big galleon, the *Rosario*, collided in the close formation and also dropped back. Both ships surrendered the next morning. On 23 July, in a general engagement off Portland Bill, severe damage was inflicted on a number of the biggest Spanish warships. There was no fighting on the 24th, but on the Thursday, a big Portuguese galleon was badly mauled, and the Vice-Admiral's flagship, the *Santa Anna*, was demasted and wrecked on the French coast. The following day, Effingham was confident enough to confer knighthoods on his cousin, Thomas Howard, Lord Sheffield, Frobisher and Hawkins.

On the 27th, the Armada put into the Calais roads, to await the rendezvous with Parma. Though it had suffered losses, and was short of ammunition and supplies, the great fleet was still a formidable instrument, fully capable of providing a naval screen for Parma's barges, in addition to landing the 10,000 or more troops it carried on board. By the Calais stage, the invasion of England was by no means a lost venture; indeed, in some ways time was on the side of Spain. Effingham had now been reinforced by Seymour's Downs squadron, levelling the odds in terms of warships. But his own ships were low on supplies and ammunition, and there could be no question of his standing-to outside Calais, and waiting for the Spanish to emerge. Within a week or less he would have to seek harbour, and thus leave the barring of the invasion route entirely to Seymour. It was imperative that he force the Armada out quickly, and this meant using fire-ships. The Administration had foreseen the possibility that they would be needed. Walsingham had ordered seventy-two barrels of pitch to Dover, and authorized the preparation of fire-ships there. But Effingham rightly decided not to lose time and tide by sending for them. Instead he called a council of admirals and captains, ordered a fireship attack that night, Sunday, and called on his colleagues to prepare the means immediately. Drake promptly offered to sacrifice a ship of his own, the 200-ton *Thomas*; Hawkins produced one of his, and the other commanders volunteered six more, from 90 to 200 tons. Then the captains dispersed to get the ships ready. Crews and stores were evacuated, and combustibles hurried aboard. The guns were left behind, and filled with powder and double-shot, which would automatically detonate when the fire grew hot enough. It was a work of dazzling improvisation, for the use of fire-ships on this scale had never before been attempted. Manœuvring them into position, and releasing them, ignited, at the precise moment, required prodigies of exact seamanship and courage on the part of the skeleton crews, and the crucial moves had to be carried out in darkness.

Sidonia was well aware fire-ships might be used. During Sunday afternoon, he warned the Armada to prepare, and ordered out a protective screen of pinnaces and ships' boats, equipped with grapnels. Their instructions were to grapple the fire-ships and tow them ashore. But such orders were more easily given than carried out. Just before midnight, the Spaniards saw fires approaching them, eight in all – not small boats, loaded with tar, but full-masted ships, with all sails set, bearing down on them with wind and tide, and blazing like giant balls of fire. The Spaniards were so amazed by the tight formation the fireships kept that they imagined men were still aboard to control them. Moreover, the English warships had moved close behind, to keep the intercepting pinnaces within shot. Under these circumstances, grappling the fire-ships and towing them out of the danger area required even more skill and fortitude than launching them accurately in the first place – more, evidently, than the pinnace-crews possessed. They managed to deflect two of the fire-ships, which were found burnt up on the coast the next morning. But then the pre-loaded guns began to go off, splattering the men on board the pinnaces with white-hot shot. The screen pulled back in surprise and terror, and during those few vital seconds the six remaining fireballs swept through and bore down straight on the anchorage. For the first time, discipline on board the Armada, hitherto admirable, broke down completely. The captains simply ordered the cables to be cut, and ran before the wind. In the darkness and the confusion, they were as frightened of colliding with each other as with the fire-ships, and the Armada dispersed over a wide area, with only vague orders to rendezvous off Dunkirk. The Admiral of the galleasses ran his ship aground, and it proved impossible to resume the crescent formation effectively. The fire-ship attack thus proved fatal both to the morale and the tactical efficiency of Sidonia's command.

The following day, Monday, the English fleet moved in closer, though still well outside boarding distance. The action off Gravelines was the end of the Armada as an offensive expedition. Many of its warships had now run out of heavy ammunition. One galleon was sunk outright; two more, the *San Mateo* and the new *San Felipe*, were driven ashore and later taken captive to Flushing. Many smaller ships were sunk or holed, and the fleet as a whole had lost its will, and for the most part its capacity, to fight. Sidonia had no harbour in which to seek refuge, take on supplies, or effect repairs. That evening, Effingham reported to Walsingham: 'I will not write unto her Majesty until more be done. Their force is wonderful great and strong; and yet we pluck their feathers little by little.'[48] The next day Sidonia took the only practicable course open to him: to head for the North Sea and bring his fleet back to Spain by circumnavigating the British Isles. Drake wrote to Walsingham on 31 July: 'There was never anything pleased me better than the seeing the enemy flying with a southerly wind northward. I doubt not, ere it be long, so to handle the matter with the Duke of Sidonia as he shall wish himself at St Mary Port among his orange trees.' In fact, hot pursuit was impossible, as most of Effingham's and Drake's ships had run out of ammunition too by this stage. Leaving Seymour behind to watch Parma, they escorted the fleeing Spaniard as far north as the Firth of Forth, and then broke off the action. No doubt they knew by now that wind and weather would do their work for them. The English had lost not a single ship, and barely 100 men in action; but, while Hawkins had performed prodigies in equipping the fleet, he had not been able to solve the problem of fresh food supplies, and the ships were stricken with scurvy: over 10,000 of the sailors were sick, and many died. The Armada had come just in time, and had been driven north just in time. By the beginning of August the English fleet was deteriorating rapidly, and there was no alternative but to de-commission most of it, though a squadron under Grenville was detached to guard the western approaches. Meanwhile, the Armada disintegrated on the high seas, the remnants reaching Spanish ports in September and October. Some 31 great ships, 10 pinnaces, 2 galleasses and 1 galley had been lost – a total of 44 out of an original fleet of 128; most of the surviving ships were so badly damaged as to be unfit for further service. About two-thirds of the men had died at sea, or were to die ashore from wounds and disease.[49]

Elizabeth had followed the Channel fight from St James's. 'It is a comfort', wrote Burghley's son, Robert Cecil, 'to see how great magnanimity her Majesty shows, who is not a whit dismayed.' After the fleets had broken off direct contact, and it was still unclear whether the Armada would return or, indeed, whether Parma would take advantage of the exhaustion of the English fleet to make a cross-Channel dash to invade, Elizabeth decided to visit her troops. She would have gone before, but the main camp at Tilbury was in such a state of confusion that Leicester would not hear of it. On 8 August, she got into her big state barge at Whitehall Steps, and went down river, escorted by the Yeomen of the Guard. She disembarked at the river-front of the Tilbury Fort, where Leicester met her, his troops drawn up by regiment of foot, and with an impressive cavalry escort. Elizabeth had chosen white as her theme: a big white gelding to ride, a white velvet dress, and, on her breast, a silver cuirass, which she wore 'like some Amazonian empress'. She was bareheaded, one of two pages carrying her silver helmet before her on a white cushion, the other holding the reins of her horse. She dismissed her escort, which remained lined up before the fort, and inspected the militia accompanied only by Leicester, Sir John Norris, her young Master of the Horse, the Earl of Essex, and the Earl of Ormonde, who carried the Sword of State.[50] The Queen herself held in her right hand a small silver truncheon, chased in gold. There was a service of intercession at which, one presumes, her personal prayer was read; the men knelt down in their ranks. Elizabeth spent the night of the 8th at the house of Lord Rich's son, a few miles away, and she returned to the camp the next day to address the troops. What she said was taken down by one of her chaplains, Dr Lionel Sharp, and later read out to those of the army who were unable to hear her.[51]

My loving people, we have been persuaded by some that are careful of our safety, to take heed how we commit ourselves to armed multitudes, for fear of treachery. But I assure you, I do not desire to live in distrust of my faithful and loving people. Let tyrants fear! I have always so behaved myself that, under God, I have placed my chiefest strength and safeguard in the loyal hearts and good will of my subjects; and therefore am come amongst you, as you see, at this time, not for my recreation and disport, but being resolved, in the midst and heat of the battle, to live or die amongst you all, and to lay down for God, for my kingdom and for my people, my honour and my blood, even in the dust. I know I have the body of a weak and feeble woman, but I have the heart and stomach of a king, and of a king of England too; and I think foul scorn that Parma or Spain, or any prince of Europe, should dare to invade the borders of my realm; to which, rather that any dishonour should grow by me, I myself will take up arms, I myself will be your general, judge and rewarder of every one of your virtues in the field. I know already for your forwardness you deserve rewards and crowns; and we do assure you, on the word of a prince, they shall be duly paid you. In the meantime, my Lieutenant-General shall be in my stead, than whom never prince commanded a more noble or more worthy subject; not doubting but that by your obedience to my general, by your concord in the camp and by your valour in the field, we shall shortly have a famous victory over these enemies of my God, my kingdom and of my people.

That day, at dinner, a rumour was circulating that Parma was already embarking his troops, and that the Spanish fleet planned to return. Walsingham, who was with her at the camp, wrote to Burghley that Elizabeth first decided that she would remain with the army

> a conceit her Majesty had that, in honour, she could not return [to court] in case there were any likelihood that the enemy would attempt anything. But she presently changed her mind. Thus your Lordship seeth that this place breedeth courage.[52]

Elizabeth remained in Essex for a week, by which time it was clear the crisis was past. There was no immediate rejoicing. Indeed, the one thing on Elizabeth's (and Burghley's) mind was to get the troops stood-down as rapidly as possible, and back into the fields where the harvest was waiting. Already, three days before Elizabeth arrived at Tilbury, Leicester had been sent instructions to discharge one-third of his infantry, selected from nearby counties so that they could be easily recalled. On 9 August, Burghley was discussing plans to de-commission part of the navy. He got this in train towards the middle of the month, and by 4 September only 34 ships out of 197, with crews of 4,453 out of a grand total of 15,925, were still on the Queen's payroll. One evil the Elizabethans did not suffer was delay in demobilization! The fleet was costing £13,033 16s. a month, and Burghley was desperately anxious to staunch the flow from the Treasury.[53] Hawkins had the wearisome business of carrying through this operation as rapidly as possible, and he found it far more disagreeable than fighting the Armada: 'I would to God', he wrote to Walsingham, 'I were delivered of the dealing for money . . . for there is no other hell.'[54] But at least the English sailors were paid: those of the Spanish who were lucky enough to survive got nothing, for Philip had nothing to give them. The Pope publicly deplored the English victory, privately exulted in Elizabeth's behaviour, and kept his cash firmly locked up, according to his hard bargain.

There was one final casualty of the Armada campaign. On 17 August Leicester broke up his Tilbury camp, and left it a sick man: he was probably dying of cancer of the stomach. He made his way, by slow stages, to Buxton, or 'Buckstones' as it was then called, to take the waters. *En route*, he sent the Queen a letter, dated 29 August:

> I most humbly beseech your Majesty to pardon your old servant to be thus bold in sending to know how my gracious lady doth, and what ease of pain she finds, being the chiefest thing in the world I do pray for, for her to have good health and long life. For my own poor case, I continue still your medicine and it amends much better than any other thing that hath been given me . . . I humbly kiss your foot, from your old lodging at Rycott this

Thursday morning, by your Majesty's most faithful and obedient servant, R. Leicester.[55]

A week later he was dead. The note survives in the state papers, endorsed in Elizabeth's hand: 'His last letter'. She kept it, until her death, in a jewel-box in her bedroom. There is no indication from anyone close to her how she took the news. If her ministers were relieved, as very likely they were, to see the last of Leicester, they kept their feelings to themselves. He went virtually unlamented, even by poets he had patronized generously. As Spenser, for a time one of his secretaries, put it:

> *He now is dead and all his glories gone*
> *And all his greatness vapoured to naught*
> *That as a glass upon the water shone*
> *Which vanished quite, as soon as it was sought*
> *His name is worn already out of thought.*
> *Ne any poet seeks him to revive*
> *Yet many poets honoured him alive.*[56]

Spenser says he was present when Leicester was dying, and that the Earl – he was fifty-five, stout, white-haired, red-faced and unloved – was virtually alone: 'scarce any left to close his eyelids near'. Elizabeth seems to have taken no part in arranging his funeral. Perhaps she was too busy – the writs were going out for a new parliament, and emergency measures were being taken to reinforce the garrison at Bergen-ap-Zoom. Or perhaps she was too distressed. A Spanish agent, who may have been reporting mere rumour, wrote on 17 September:

> The Queen is sorry for his death, but no other person in the country. She was so grieved that for some days she shut herself in her chamber alone, and refused to speak to anyone, until the Treasurer and other counsellors had the doors broken open and entered to see her.[57]

But this sounds more like Queen Victoria than the 'Amazonian Empress'. Other records indicate she was busy on state affairs. Nor did sentiment cloud her attitude to Leicester's estate. He had left her a diamond pendant set in emeralds and a rope of 600 fine pearls.[58] But she was interested in more substantial assets. Though a letter from Walsingham indicates that Elizabeth missed the Earl, she soon took steps to secure his property against his debts to the crown, and on 23 October she seized Kenilworth Castle and all his lands in Warwickshire.[59]

Leicester, no doubt, would have taken charge of the celebrations which followed the confirmation of the Armada's ruin. But others were there to take his place: Hatton (now Lord Chancellor), Sir Henry Lee, the Queen's master of ceremonies, and Leicester's stepson, the Earl of Essex. It was an autumn of profound relief, especially for the citizens of London. The year 1588 had been widely expected to prove a climacteric. The second edition of Holinshed's *Chronicles*, published in 1587 (it was the one Shakespeare used), had alluded to an ancient prophecy that 1588 would be 'a year of wonders ... either a final dissolution or a wonderful, horrible alteration of the world is then to be expected'.[60] Like most prophecies, it tried to hedge its bets; the English were glad to see events had turned out 'wonderful' for them, and 'horrible' for Spain. No similar victory had been acclaimed in London since the days of Agincourt. On 12 November, the Queen moved her court to Somerset House, to be in the thick of things. She had announced that St Elizabeth's Day, 19 November, was to be added to her accession day as a public holiday to mark the victory, and there were three days of tilting, bear-baiting and cock-fighting. At the end of the week, on Sunday, 24th, she went to St Paul's Cathedral for a special service of thanksgiving. Her train was described as 'enormous', and she travelled in a chariot supported by four pillars, and drawn by two white horses. At the West Door she got out, fell on her knees, and prayed aloud before a vast crowd. Dr Pearce, the eloquent Bishop of Salisbury, preached the sermon, and after it, it seems, Elizabeth herself addressed the congregation, exhorting them to be grateful for their deliverance: would that we had the text of what she said! Then she dined with the Bishop of London in his palace, and returned to Somerset House by torchlight. It is, indeed, by the flickering light of torches, in the long, foggy evenings of winter, that we should see Elizabeth at the end of this remarkable year. Many years later, Bishop Goodman of Gloucester, who had been a boy of five in 1588, recalled the excitement of the times:

I did then live at the upper end of the Strand near St Clement's Church, when suddenly there came a report to us (it was in December, much about 5 o'clock at night, very dark) that the Queen was gone to Council, and if you will see the Queen you must come quickly. Then we all ran; when the court gates were set open and no man did hinder us from coming in ... when we had stayed there an hour and a half, and that the yard was full, there being a number of torches, the Queen came out in great state. Then we cried: 'God save your Majesty! God save your Majesty!' Then the Queen turned to us and said: 'God bless you all my good people!' Then we cried again: 'God save your Majesty!' Then the Queen said again unto us: 'You may well have a greater prince, but you shall never have a more loving prince.' And so, looking one upon another a while, the Queen departed. This wrought such an impression upon us, for shows and pageants are ever best seen by torch-light, that all the way long we did nothing but talk what an admirable Queen she was, and how we would adventure our lives to do her service.[61]

This was all very well, but Elizabeth did not want adventure: she wanted peace, tranquillity, a return to old times. She was fifty-five on 7 September 1588, and had now to reconcile herself – the passing of her contemporary Leicester symbolized it – to 'creeping time' and the coming of old age. She was never, as Ralegh put it, 'a lady whom time had surprised': on the contrary, she was continually and bitterly aware of its ravages and disappointments. But she had hoped, she still hoped, to achieve serenity in her final years, and serenity she equated with a world at peace. Instead, the conflict was to deepen and the burden she carried to increase. The defeat of the Armada was not the culmination but the overture to a war, fought at mounting cost in men and money, which was to follow the pacifist Queen to her grave, and beyond.

❦ 10 ❦

Holding the Balance

In later years, surveying the last decade and a half of Elizabeth's reign, Ralegh made a fundamental criticism of the Queen's post-Armada strategy towards Spain:

> If the late Queen would have believed her men of war as she did her scribes, we had in her time beaten that great empire in pieces and made their kings kings of figs and oranges as in old times. But her Majesty did all by halves and by petty invasions taught the Spaniard how to defend himself, and to see his own weakness which, till our attempts taught him, was hardly known to himself.[1]

Of all Elizabeth's great statesmen, Ralegh was the most resolutely hostile to Spain, but there can be no doubt that many of his contemporaries would have agreed with his analysis, as have most historians since. But it is open to a number of objections, political, military and, indeed, factual. In the first place, Elizabeth never showed any desire to 'beat that great empire in pieces'. Her war aims were defensive, not acquisitive; conservative, not revolutionary. She wished to preserve the Protestant settlement in north-west Europe, and to prevent the Netherlands from being wholly absorbed into the Spanish system. She wanted to destroy Spain's military capacity to invade England. But she had no desire to reduce Spain to the status of a second-rate power, and so re-create the 'French problem'; or, for that matter, to eliminate Spanish influence altogether from the Catholic provinces of Belgium. An unrestrained English assault on Spain's American empire and lines of communication, and so on her sources of wealth, would have achieved these objects. But Elizabeth was fighting a limited war, in order to force Spain to accept a compromise peace, which would have restored the *status quo* of the early 1560s. A reduction in Spanish naval power; the removal of her army from England's flank; the relinquishment of Spanish authority in Portugal; an English share in the riches and commerce of the Americas – these were the limits of her ambitions. If these could be secured, it would then be possible to prohibit the use of force in settling Europe's religious divisions, and indeed to rebuild the old Anglo-Habsburg amity. Nothing was more abhorrent to her than the concept of unrestricted warfare and 'unconditional surrender'. She longed for the ancient international order (as she conceived it) which had been disturbed by the thrust of the Counter-Reformation and Philip II's authoritarian definition of sovereignty. She wished to use her military and naval power solely to restore the old balance, and to hold it. In this sense, she might be defined as a very old-fashioned stateswoman – or, equally, as a very modern one. Her tragedy is that she was a moderate, living in immoderate times.

Nevertheless, within the limits she had set herself – limits defined by financial as well as political factors – she pursued her war aims with energy, if never with enthusiasm. But she naturally had to take the advice of her 'men of war', and – *pace* Ralegh – this was not always unanimous, or consistent. Nor, indeed, having had it accepted, did they always follow it themselves. As early as mid-August 1588, when the battered Armada was still on its way home, Elizabeth was evidently keen to take retaliatory action against Spain: an assault on the treasure-fleet, due to reach Spain early in September, was suggested.[2] Drake came to court to discuss the matter with her personally, but he had to report that many of the English ships were in need of repair, and that it was too late to organize a high-seas expedition. As the weeks went by, news came that a portion of the Armada had regained Spain, and was now lying exposed to attack in northern harbours. Elizabeth seized on this point: her salient object was to destroy the offensive capacity of Spanish naval power. In some ways she had a better strategic grasp than any of her commanders, and she never moved from her view that the prime aim of the navy must be to sink Spanish ships. For a raid of this type, Drake was the obvious man, and he got the command. But Drake was ambitious. If the expedition were postponed until the spring, it could encompass other objectives: the seizure of the plate-fleet at the Azores, and the landing of men in Portugal to place the Pretender, Don Antonio, on the throne. This, of course, meant not only a confusion of objects, but a much larger force: 20,000 men were to be recruited under the military command of Sir John Norris. There were ample objections to such a scheme: Drake was a small-force naval commander, excelling at cutting-out forays and harbour-raiding, and with some experience of leading men on shore when surprise could be guaranteed. He was not the man to fight an ambitious land-campaign. Nor could the preparation of such a large force be kept secret. There were other objections. Who was to take the final decisions, Drake or Norris? And, since a great portion of England's armed forces were to be committed, why was Effingham excluded? When he learnt of the nature of the expedition, he was understandably angry: 'I think he liveth not that in any age that any man was seen in this realm where any landing of men was, but it did ever belong to the Admiral of England . . .'³ His history was faulty, but his reasoning was sound. He had proved himself superbly competent as a supreme commander, able by the authority of his high birth, and by his natural tact and modesty, to manage brilliant subordinates. If the expedition was to be on a grand scale, he was the man to run it. Here we have a classic military case of a campaign changing its objects and size in the course of its preparation, and therefore outstripping its command structure and the capacity of its original leaders. Moreover, as the scheme grew, no comparable steps were taken to master the technical difficulties of supplying 20,000 sea-borne troops.⁴

Elizabeth watched the plan get out of hand with growing misgivings. As always, she knew that, once the 'men of war' got to work, her control over events would diminish and eventually disappear completely. She was worried by the evidence that Drake and Norris did not set a sufficiently high priority on the destruction of Philip's ships, to her the be-all and end-all of the plan. Walsingham voiced her fears on 23 December, when Drake's eagerness to chase after treasure on the high seas, and booty in Portugal, became plain: 'while we attempt an uncertainty, we shall lose a certainty, and so seek for a bird in a bush and lose what we have in a cage'.⁵ To guard against the expedition losing sight of its prime object, Elizabeth did her best: she appointed Anthony Ashley, clerk of the Council, to accompany the fleet, and briefed him personally in the presence of the Council; Marmaduke Darrell, a senior dockyard officer, and one of her muster-masters, Ralph Lane, were also sent as her personal representatives. The commanders did not like this: 'We have never received', grumbled Norris to Burghley, 'any favourable answer [from Elizabeth] to any matter moved by us, but only contrary threatenings and chidings.'⁶ What Elizabeth wanted to do was to tie them down to their orders, and they had no intention of surrendering their operational freedom.

Her suspicions were abundantly confirmed when, on 4 April 1589, ten days before the expedition sailed, the young Earl of Essex secretly left court and joined it on the *Swiftsure*. The Earl was already established in her favour, and she did not want to part with him. But her reasons were not entirely personal. She had a well-grounded dislike for the unmilitary practice of high-born young men taking unofficial employment on such ventures: they disturbed the normal hierarchy of command and provoked indiscipline and rows over precedence. Besides, Essex had disobeyed her explicit orders, and had done so with the connivance of Drake and Norris, and with the active assistance of Sir Roger Williams – the type of low-born unscrupulous captain whom she most distrusted. She sent angry signals to the fleet, and followed them, on

4 May, with a majestic letter of rebuke to the joint-commanders. Williams's offence was 'in so high a degree that the same deserveth by all laws to be punished by death'. If he had not already been hanged, under their authority as generals, then

> we will and command you sequester him from all charge and service, and cause him to be safely kept, so as he slip not away until you shall know our further pleasure therein, as you will answer to the contrary at your perils, for as we have authority to rule, so we look to be obeyed, and to have obedience directly and surely continued unto us, and so look to be answered herein at your hands.[7]

But the incident merely served to emphasize the practical limits of Elizabeth's authority in a war-situation. Weather and communications were rapidly wheeled forward as excuses for ignoring her instructions. Essex was not sent back, as she had commanded. Williams was not hanged, or even imprisoned; indeed, he was later promoted. And Drake and Norris proceeded to conduct the expedition according to their own ideas, as they had all along intended.

On 20 April, the English landed at Corunna, sacked the town, burnt a galleon, and seized sixty pieces of ordinance. The rest of the Spanish ships were abandoned by their crews, but Drake argued that he could not take and destroy them until the guns of the Upper Fort, which the Spanish still manned, were silenced. Norris replied that he could not do this without a siege-train, which he did not possess. In any case, he was anxious to get on to Lisbon, where the prospects of military glory were greater. Drake complied, because he believed there was more booty to be had in Portugal. Thus the prime object of the expedition was abandoned, half-completed. But the invasion of Portugal could not succeed because the Portuguese did not rise in response to Don Antonio's summons: his supporters had all been hanged or terrorized by the savage Cardinal-Archduke Albert, Philip's deputy. Moreover, instead of making straight for Lisbon, via the Tagus, Norris landed his men nearly fifty miles away, and marched overland: they never got further than the Lisbon suburbs (which, in deference to Don Antonio's claims, they were not allowed to pillage), and were soon decimated by sickness and heat. Drake and Norris then quarrelled on whether, and if so how, to take Lisbon or not, and inter-service rivalry and recrimination did the rest. The remainder of the troops were re-embarked, and Drake sacked Vigo. But weather prevented him from sailing to the Azores, and his only prizes were eighty grain-ships, carrying supplies from Poland to Spanish and Portuguese harbours. Their cargoes realized £30,000, and though technically the property of Hansa merchants, their seizure was justified by Burghley on the grounds that they were munitions of war, part of the preparations for a new Armada. Even so, the expedition did not pay for itself, and Drake's action aroused hostility in the Baltic states. He and Norris claimed, with some justice, that they had put off any possibility of a further Spanish invasion of England for at least a year: among other things, they had taken a total of 150 guns. This was evidently Philip's view, for all news of the campaign was suppressed in Madrid. As Norris complained to Walsingham: 'If the enemy had done so much upon us, his party would have made bonfires in most parts of Christendom.'[8] But the fact is they had failed to destroy the Spanish warships in Santander, San Sebastian or even in Corunna, and this was what Elizabeth had commanded them to do. As she wrote:

> before your departure hence you did, at sundry times, so far forth promise
> as with oaths to assure us and some of our Council that your first and prin-
> cipal action should be to take and distress the King of Spain's navy and ships
> where they lay; which if you did not, you affirmed that you were content
> to be reputed as traitors.[9]

They had no answer to this point. Elizabeth showed herself very well-informed about the details of the expedition, the weather conditions, and other factors brought up as excuses. They had 'gone to places more for profit than for service' and allowed themselves 'to be transported with an haviour of vainglory' which had 'obfuscated' their 'judgment'.[10] Moreover, the losses in manpower had been enormous: some thousands, though the total figure is unknown. Two colonels and thirty captains were killed or died of disease. Of 1,100 gentlemen who set out, only 350 returned, according to one contemporary.[11] The soldiers who survived were promptly disbanded as soon as they reached home, but could not be paid in full. As Elizabeth expected, they made nuisances of themselves. Over 500 gathered neared Westminster, and threatened to pillage Bartholomew Fair; four were hanged, one complaining on his way to the gallows that this was a fine reward to soldiers for going to the wars. Despite a series of proclamations, disorders continued until the end of the year. In October, Elizabeth ordered Drake and Norris to answer a series of questions put to them by the Council – in effect, a Court of Inquiry. Drake seems to have got most of the blame, and probably deserved it: he received a land post in 1590, but no more active employment at sea until the last year of his life, 1595.

More important, the affair swung the Queen heavily against major offensive operations. Publicly, she expressed gratitude: 'We cannot but acknowledge ourselves infinitely bound unto Almighty God in that it hath pleased him in his great goodness and mercy to bless your attempt.' She told Norris and Drake that 'we do most thankfully accept of your service and do acknowledge that there hath been as much performed by you as true valour and good conduction could yield'.[12] But the expedition was not repeated. Elizabeth switched instead to a systematic policy of commerce-raiding. A Council decree ordered all ships passing through the Channel to be stopped and searched unless they had a pass from the Lord Admiral.[13] Her policy was set out in characteristic manner, appealing to law and precedent, and all the reflexes of conservatism:

> Her Majesty thinketh and knoweth it by the rules of the law as well of nature as of men, and specially by the law civil, that whenever any doth directly help her enemy with succours of any victual, armour or any kind of munition to enable his ships to maintain themselves, she may lawfully interrupt the same; and this agreeth with the law of God, the law of nature, the law of nations, and hath been at all times practised and in all countries betwixt prince and prince, and country and country.[14]

In fact, no nation hitherto had conducted anything approaching such operations, in scale, intensity and thoroughness. Once again, Elizabeth was establishing a new procedure – which was to become an axiom of British naval policy in wartime for 350 years – under the guise of following time-honoured practice.

In strategic terms, such a policy made more sense than a direct assault on Spain, which in any case conflicted with Elizabeth's political aims. Faced with a permanent threat to his sea-communications – to the New World as well as to the Netherlands – Philip was obliged to order an ambitious new programme of naval construction. By 1592 he had forty galleons laid down.[15] He developed fast frigates, or cruisers, called *gallezabras*, to carry his treasure, and even faster pinnaces, or *avisos*, to carry intelligence of English naval movements. Ports in the West Indies and the Azores were heavily fortified: it was calculated that any fleet would be safe under the batteries of Terceira, a proposition not to be falsified until the days of the Commonwealth and Admiral Blake. But this maritime programme inevitably diverted scarce resources from the principal theatre of his war effort in the Low Countries, where Parma, despite all his efforts, was progressively starved of men and money. And this, in turn, allowed Elizabeth to cut back on her enormously costly military effort there. It was a sign of her increasing dissatisfaction with the Dutch that Leicester was replaced not by another grandee, but by a much more modest professional, Peregrine Bertie, Lord Willoughby: 'He was none of the reptilia,' said Naunton, 'and could not brook the obsequiousness and assiduity of the court.'[16] Willoughby successfully defended Bergen-ap-Zoom, and brought to an end Parma's last serious effort to break Dutch military resistance. When the Dutch showed themselves ungrateful, and disinclined to fulfil their financial commitments, Elizabeth pulled him out in March 1589, and sent out instead a still humbler professional, Sir Francis Vere, who was invested merely with the title of Sergeant-Major-General.

Others, besides Elizabeth, were losing confidence in the Dutch. Walsingham, once their most enthusiastic advocate, came to see the new leader of the States, John Van Barneveldt, as essentially anti-English. Sir Thomas Bodley, whom he sent over to negotiate, reported: 'I could never find in him but a rude and intractible nature, delighting continuously to oppose himself against the English government, for so it pleaseth him and some others to term her Majesty's directions.'[17] Walsingham replied: 'They grow very proud . . . I wish that our fortune and theirs were not so straightly tied as it is.' When the Dutch issued anti-English propaganda after the capitulation of Gertruidenberg in April 1589 – the English garrison handed over the town to Parma when the Dutch refused to pay their wages – Walsingham thought that 'with the loss of the town they have also lost their wits'. Burghley, too, was disillusioned by repeated Dutch demands for loans which they had, on past practice, no intention of repaying: 'I see the intention of the sending of the Deputies hither from the States is, as I at first did conjecture, to borrow money of her Majesty, which in a paraphrase is, to carry away money, and to leave writings under seals, whereof her Majesty hath a great plenty.'[18] Ralegh went further, and openly accused the Dutch of assisting Spanish military power by selling contraband munitions direct to Spain:

> The nature of the Dutchman is to fly to no man but for his profit, and they will obey no man long . . . The Dutchman by his policy hath gotten trading with all the world into his hands . . . They are the people who maintain the King of Spain in his greatness. Were it not for them, he were never able to make out such armies and navies by sea; it cost her Majesty £160,000 a year the maintaining of these countries, and yet for all this they arm her enemies against her.[19]

There were times when Elizabeth herself 'swore by the living God' she would have 'nothing more to do with such people'. Her government had now come round to her way of thinking: English policy in the Low Countries must be confined to ensuring that the Dutch had just enough military support to prevent conquest. Vere was an admirable instrument for this purpose: he was a thorough soldier, loathed display, was cost-conscious, completely non-political, and, at a personal level, thoroughly acceptable to the Dutch commanders. Under his régime, English costs were scaled down, expenditure reduced, and the Low Countries moved away from the centre of Elizabeth's war effort.

Instead, the focus of attention switched to France. In December 1588, Henri III had had the Duke of Guise and his brother the Cardinal murdered. Elizabeth, not normally a supporter of such ruthless tactics, was delighted: she saw the act as a judicial process, conducted by exceptional means, in exceptional circumstances, against rebellious subjects. 'She is minded to send a gentleman over', wrote Walsingham to Stafford, 'to comfort and encourage the king to proceed thoroughly.'[20] The stroke completed the cleavage of France into religious camps, one looking to Spain, the other to England; in July 1589, Henri was murdered in turn, and when Navarre assumed the crown as Henri IV, the Catholic League, backed by Philip II, elected the Cardinal of Bourbon anti-King. Paris had to be evacuated to the Catholic party, and Henri himself pulled back towards the Normandy coast and sent urgent demands for Elizabeth's assistance. She responded with, by her standards, unparalleled alacrity. Early in September Burghley paid over to French envoys, at his house in the Strand, £20,000 in chests, an impressive demonstration of England's continued solvency. When he got the treasure, Henri said he had never seen so much money in cash in his life: he did not believe any other sovereign in the world capable of such a feat.[21] Within a year, the loan had been raised to £60,000. Moreover, Elizabeth sent troops as well. By the end of September 1589, Willoughby was in Dieppe with an army of 4,000, for a three-month campaign; Elizabeth was to find its wages for the first month, and thereafter Henri was to pay. Of course he was able to do no such thing, and in the final stages the army was ill-fed and half-naked. But it fought with conspicuous gallantry, provoking a spirited letter from the Queen to its commander: 'My good Peregrine, I bless God that your old prosperous success followeth your valiant acts, and joy not a little that safety accompanieth your luck. Your loving sovereign, Eliz. R.'[22]

Thus the diplomatic revolution was finally completed. While Elizabeth was assisting the King of France to establish himself in his kingdom, she was providing £3,000 to James of Scotland to put down Catholic rebels under the Earl of Huntly, and financing him to the tune of another £3,000, in cash and plate, to set up house for a Protestant bride, Anne of Denmark, whom he married in November 1589. Burghley underlined the changed international situation in a letter to the Earl of Shrewsbury:

My lord, the state of the world is marvellously changed when we true Englishmen have cause, for our own quietness, to wish good success to a French king and a King of Scots . . . for which the Queen and all of us are more deeply bound to acknowledge His miraculous goodness, for no wit of man could otherwise have wrought it.[23]

It might be argued that, in switching England's main effort in the war from the Netherlands to France, Elizabeth had merely exchanged one undependable ally for another, or rather accepted the financial obligation of supporting both. But this was not exactly how she saw it. She had always been unhappy about encouraging Dutch rebels against Philip, whom she had continued to recognize as their legitimate sovereign. In France the roles were reversed, for it was Philip who was promoting rebellion and she herself who was upholding the man who, by every precept of law and international justice, had the best title to the throne. The French intervention, as it were, squared her royalist conscience. Moreover, Henri, unlike the Dutch, was an ally with whom she could deal personally. Elizabeth had hitherto been uneasily aware that, among the ranks of the monarchs' trades union, the great majority had swung behind Rome, leaving her in almost solitary isolation. Since James of Scotland had reached his maturity, she had gratified herself by corresponding with him, as her 'royal brother', distilling the wisdom of an elder sister, and conscious that their links reflected the solidarity of Protestant sovereigns. But James was merely the pensioner-king of a bankrupt dependency on the periphery of civilization: her new 'brother' was the legitimate tenant of the most majestic throne in the world. She enjoyed writing to him, and conducting international affairs at the sovereign-to-sovereign level she felt proper. Henri was her 'dearest brother', and she 'your very assured good sister and cousin'.[24] During 1590 she wrote six times to him, four of the letters being in her own hand (and, of course, in French). She sent him a pretty scarf she had made, and an emerald; and, at Oatlands, she personally shot a deer for his ambassador: 'I was myself where the beast fell dead', he reported to King Henri, 'and took first essay of it.'[25] She also gave Henri pungent advice on military tactics and statecraft.

From Elizabeth's point of view, the change was an improvement at more than the level of monarchical decorum. Philip's intervention in French affairs meant the end of his attempt to subjugate all the Low Countries. He could keep up the struggle there, but it was no longer an offensive one. In 1590, a reluctant Parma turned his troops south and moved into France. Henceforth, Philip's main fighting-force was engaged on two fronts, without much prospect of success on either. It was the end of the first phase of the Counter-Reformation. As the axis of Philip's strategy shifted to France, pressure on the English forces in the Low Countries was relaxed; Vere was able to detach troops from his garrisons and build up a field army. In 1591 he helped to take Zutphen, Deventer and

Nymegen, and later beat the Spanish *tercios* in open combat.[26] Philip created
a second French front by landing troops in Brittany; Elizabeth responded by
negotiating a further agreement with Henri, under which Norris joined the
Breton campaign with an English force, and occupied cautionary towns.
Paimpol remained an English possession for some years. In theory, of course,
Philip stood a chance of securing the conjunction Elizabeth most feared – the
spectre that had haunted her father – an alliance of the Spanish and French
crowns in a Catholic crusade. In Brittany, and later in Calais, he held toeholds
on the southern side of the Channel, for a prospective invasion. But his hopes of
crushing a legitimate French king assisted by England were never strong; and
the English also could now operate from southern Channel ports.

The campaigns were inconclusive, as might have been expected. Henri could
not fulfil his bargain to provide two French soldiers for every Englishman,
and Norris's troops accomplished little other than holding down valuable
Spanish resources.[27] Essex, after begging Elizabeth on his knees for over two
hours, on three different occasions (as he claimed), was allowed to take over
another force into Normandy, to occupy Dieppe and capture Rouen. 'I am
commanded in France', he exulted, 'for the establishment of the brave king in
quiet possession of Normandy.'[28] He angered the Queen by failing to write to
her often enough, and by ignoring her sound advice to concentrate everything
on taking Rouen – she always seems to have driven to the heart of a military
problem. His troops suffered badly from malaria, and greatly resented having
the bankrupt Henri as paymaster: 'Much more contented would we be', complained one of the captains, 'to be in the pay of the blessed Queen' – an answer
to those who claim Elizabeth never paid her men.[29] After six months, Elizabeth
pulled Essex back, replacing him by the hated, but brave and efficient, Roger
Williams. There were two more campaigns, in 1592 and 1593: they had the
merit of frustrating Philip's vision of a Leaguist France – Parma was now dead
and his army in tatters – but they brought Henri no nearer to the possession of
Paris. He was, wrote Elizabeth's new ambassador at the French court, Sir
Henry Unton, 'a king without a crown, who maketh wars without money'.[30]
On 15 July 1593, Henri reluctantly decided that Paris was worth a Mass, and
was received as a Catholic at St Denis. Elizabeth was dutifully horrified:

Ah, what griefs, what regret, what groanings I feel in my soul at the sound
of such news … Can we reasonably even expect a good issue from an act
so iniquitous? … Ah, it is dangerous to do ill that good may come of it. Yet
I hope that sounder inspiration shall come to you. In the meantime I shall
not cease to set you in the foremost rank of my devotions, that the hands of

Esau undo not the blessing of Jacob ... Your very assured sister, if it be after the old manner; with the new, I have nothing to do. E.R.[31]

In fact she was not so much worried by Henri's change of religion as by the possibility, happily remote, that he would form an alliance with Spain, and the much more likely possibility that he would repudiate his debts to her. As it turned out, Henri's conversion helped Elizabeth's overall strategy. The Catholic League promptly collapsed, leaving Philip to struggle on alone. The Queen and Henri continued to work together, and in 1594 the English sent a successful naval expedition to dislodge the Spanish from their positions near Brest, though Frobisher, who led it, was killed. The French theatre continued to hold down the bulk of Philip's striking forces, but without any prospect of depriving Henri of his crown. In 1595, the English were able to disengage, leaving France and Spain still locked in combat: not a bad outcome from Elizabeth's standpoint. The French campaigns had cost her £200,000, which remained an unpaid debt, but they had cost Philip a great deal more, in men and prestige as well as cash, and they had achieved their political object of keeping the two greatest powers in Europe in conflict.

This analysis suggests that, even after Elizabeth abandoned the 'big expedition' strategy, she was considerably more active, and intelligent, in pursuing the struggle with Spain than Ralegh's criticism will allow. Like modern strategists, she tended to see war in terms of the total deployment of resources, with ultimately an economic basis. By using her available resources judiciously, she consistently forced Philip into over-deploying his, and so moved towards not an annihilating victory (which she did not want) but a compromise peace forced on Spain by exhaustion, her real object. Philip was losing the land war on the Continent because he was overstretched, partly at least because of his naval efforts to keep his Atlantic communications open. But even in this theatre, where his warships in the 1590s heavily outnumbered Elizabeth's, he suffered some terrible blows. In the 1590s, Hawkins and Frobisher were in action off the Spanish sea-lanes. Two vessels of the Spanish treasure-fleet were taken in the West Indies, which forced Philip to turn again to his Italian bankers, whom he eventually put out of business. A further attempt to seize the *flota* was made in 1591, when Lord Thomas Howard and Sir Richard Grenville were dispatched with six royal galleon to wait off the Azores. After being at sea for over three months, they anchored off Flores to take on supplies and allow their men, many of whom were sick, to recover on land. There they were surprised by Philip's main fleet of more than twenty galleons, which had come up from the east to cover the *flota*. Howard managed to get away with five ships, but Grenville, on the *Revenge*, was slow at re-embarking his crew – he had only about a hundred on board when the action began – and faced the entire Spanish squadron alone, partly, perhaps, because he had no alternative, partly also out of sheer bravado. He attempted to cut right through the Spanish ships and nearly succeeded. But the *Revenge* lost the wind under the huge side of the *San Felipe*, Philip's largest warship, and was promptly grappled. The fight went on through the night, and during it two of the Spanish ships were sunk. At dawn, Grenville, who was dying of his wounds, wanted to blow his ship up, but was forced by the remains of his crew to surrender. He died on board the *Felipe*, but he won a posthumous victory. In a week, a terrible storm swept down on the Azores. By now, both the incoming and the outgoing *flotas* had been concentrated in the area, but they were unable to move off because of the damaged condition of the Spanish naval squadron, all of whose ships had been hit by *Revenge*'s gunfire. Of about 120 Spanish vessels in the area, most of them at anchor, 70 were reported lost in the storm. In some ways it was a more substantial defeat than Spain suffered during the 1588 Armada campaign; and Ralegh, recording the death of Grenville, his friend and kinsman, was able to write with bitter satisfaction: 'So it pleased them to honour the burial of that renowned ship, the *Revenge*, not suffering her to perish alone, for the great honour she achieved in her lifetime.'

In 1592, an expedition organized by Ralegh (he was in disgrace for his marriage to Elizabeth Throckmorton, and was not allowed to lead it), took the great East India carrack, the *Madre de Dios*. She had on board a cargo of jewels, spices, drugs, silks, calicoes, carpets and scent – everything from elephants' teeth and Chinese porcelain to oriental bedsteads – and the value was computed at £150,000.[32] When the prize was brought into Plymouth, the crew got out of hand and began to pillage the cargo. London jewellers, alerted, had hurried down to the quayside and bought up treasures dirt-cheap. Young Robert Cecil was appointed commissioner for the prize, and sent down to stop the plunder. He got back £13,505 out of £28,500-worth that had been stolen; the rest, he said, was irrecoverable. 'Everyone I met within seven miles of Exeter that either had anything in a cloak, bag or malle which did but smell of the prizes . . . (for I could well smell them also, such had been the spoils of musk and ambergris among them) I did (though he had little about him) return him with me to the town of Exeter.' 'By my rough dealing', he added, 'I have left an impression . . . my sending-down hath made many stagger.'[33] Ralegh was sent down too, released on parole, 'still the Queen's poor prisoner' as he put it, to help recover the loot. He stormed: '. . . if I meet any of them coming up, if it be upon the wildest heath in all the way, I mean to strip them as naked as ever they were born, for it is infamous that her Majesty hath been robbed, and that of the most rare things.'[34] Of course, he had been robbed too, which explains his fury. The evidence about the total value of the cargo is confused. But, even allowing for the spoilage, it was enormous: £141,200 was realized at Leadenhall Market from part of it. The Earl of Cumberland, one of the investors, and Ralegh got £36,000 each. Elizabeth appropriated the most easily realizable part of the prize, 750,000 lbs of pepper, which was taken over by a syndicate which paid her £90,000 in yearly instalments.

The *Madre de Dios* affair gave a tremendous impetus to privateering. Cumberland, now a southern courtier rather than a northern border-baron – his change of role was a sign of the times – became a professional, and invested £100,000 in voyages.[35] The Queen encouraged him. In 1597 Robert Cecil noted archly: 'Lord Cumberland is a suitor to go a royal journey in October. The plot is very secret between her Majesty and him.'[36] Elizabeth evidently relished the idea of collaborating with a noble pirate, writing to Cumberland:

> It may seem strange to you that we should once vouchsafe to trouble our thoughts with any care for any person of a roguish condition, being always disposed rather to command others to chasten men of that profession. But such is our pleasure at this time ... as we are well content to take occasion by our letters to express our great desire to hear of your well-doing ... hoping well of good success in the action you now have in hand.

The letter has the signature: 'Your very loving sovereign, Elizabeth R.'[37] Not all these ventures against Spanish commerce succeeded: sometimes the *flota* got home safely, and sometimes rich Spanish cargoes were sunk rather than captured. But what the sea claimed, Philip lost. In 1594, Cumberland caught an even richer prize than the *Madre de Dios*, a giant carrack called the *Cinque Lagos*, or 'Five Wounds'. She burned to the waterline, and most of her wretched crew and passengers were drowned:

> In which burning and sinking of this carrack as also drowning of many hundreds of the passengers, soldiers and sailors, also very many of their bravest Spanish gallants, men and women, goodly personages gorgeously apparelled, yea and decked with rich chains of gold, jewels, pearls and precious stones of great price, stripping themselves of all this ... all naked upon a sudden desperately cast themselves into the sea.[38]

How far commerce-raiding benefited the English economy is difficult to compute. It raises the same problems as the calculation of overall English losses and gains in the Hundred Years War. Some men made fortunes; others lost their investment and their lives. Among the more enterprising and far-sighted, the attempts to establish colonies absorbed much of the profits of privateering, for until the English learned to produce tobacco as a cash-crop, colonization was a loss-making business. Elizabeth showed some keenness for the early efforts to colonize North America, because like others she believed gold could be mined there. She gave her blessing to Frobisher's voyages, and before he set out on the third she herself placed a gold chain round his neck.[39] She gave a charter to Dee, John Davis and Ralegh to set up a 'Fellowship for the Discovery of the Northwest Passage',[40] and another to Ralegh to establish his colony at Roanoke Island in Virginia, a territory called after her. But once the gold theory was exploded, she was not prepared to put up money. Private men found, by bitter experience, that the investment was prohibitively high. Ralegh lost £40,000 on his colonizing ventures, 'learning too late', as Camden put it, '. . . that it is a difficulter thing to carry over colonies into remote countries upon private men's purses than he and others in an erronious credulity had persuaded themselves'.[41] 'Private purses', Ralegh added himself, 'are cold comfort to adventurers.' Elizabeth, being a realist, switched her interest from colonizing the West to trading with the East. She backed ventures to Archangel and Russia, to the Baltic states, to Persia, and above all to the eastern Mediterranean and Turkey, where her ambassador in Constantinople led the thrust: 'Mercurial-breasted Mr Harborne', as Thomas Nash called him, 'who hath noised the name of our Island and of Yarmouth so tritonly that not an infant of the cur-tailed skin-clipping pagans but talk of London as frequently as of their prophet's tomb at Mecca'.[42] On the basis of Harborne's work, the Levant Company was organized in 1600, and during the 1590s England became a major trading nation, fighting for routes and concessions all around Europe. Together, then, commerce-raiding and trading added enormously to individual fortunes in the last decade of Elizabeth. The net economic effect of the war with Spain was clearly positive, though this cannot be demonstrated on a statistical basis. But it was the unanimous opinion of contemporaries. 'It is incredible', wrote Thomas Wilson in 1600, 'what treasure hath been brought into England, by prize and from the Indies, within this 12 or 16 years'. He attributed this to the mercantile laws, and thus explained 'the desire to continue in wars with Spain and enmity with some other countries'.[43]

But for Elizabeth, the arithmetic was less satisfactory. In his analysis, Ralegh ignores altogether the financial factor in her strategy; but it was the one uppermost in her mind. Fighting a war of attrition against the Spanish empire, with the object of securing a compromise peace, she aimed to destroy Philip's financial power, while conserving her own. The latter became increasingly difficult.

Normal pre-war expenditure had been about £150,000 a year. It rose to £367,000 in 1587 and £420,000 in 1588, and by the end of the latter year Elizabeth had spent £245,000 of her £300,000 war-chest.[44] Huge and increasing subsidies were passed by parliament, but they were slow in coming in, and though double, and eventually treble, subsidies were voted, the actual receipts fell off. The Exchequer reported to Burghley on 4 December 1591 that only 20 per cent of the third tranche (slice) of the taxes voted in 1589 had been received.[45] Elizabeth was forced repeatedly to call in loans under the Privy Seal, a form of borrowing she disliked intensely. Although the loans were all eventually repaid, they had the appearance of a forced capital levy – an appearance which, under the Stuarts, became a reality.[46] Thomas Windebank, Clerk of the Signet, has left a touching description of Elizabeth's hesitations in signing the documents for these loans, on 8 November 1590. Was the money, she asked, really necessary? Might not Philip forebear from another attack? On the other hand, it was only a loan; she could repay it. Or she could keep it as a stand-by. Or something unexpected might turn up. She would speak to the Chancellor of the Exchequer before deciding to sign. 'Howbeit,' Windebank adds, 'I do mean to engross the warrant this day to be read at any sudden calling for it, for I think her Majesty will sign it at length.' When he did get such papers signed, he swept them off immediately, for on one occasion, a few hours after she had signed, 'her Majesty, in the midst of the sermon, sent a message unto me . . . that I should stay those things that her Majesty had signed'.[47] It was not the moral of the sermon that made her change her mind; she hated sermons and rarely listened to what was being said. She used them as quiet intervals to compose her thoughts.

This, and many other incidents, indicate that Elizabeth intensely disliked direct taxation. It was not a method of raising money she exploited but rather, to her mind, a monarchical privilege which was to be used sparingly. Direct taxation cost her popularity, and employing it had therefore to be balanced against the necessity to furnish the Exchequer. She was just as reluctant to raise money as to spend it. Whenever possible, she turned to other methods. She sold £125,000-worth of crown lands in 1590, for instance. In 1591 there was a more bizarre effort: negotiations with Edward Kelly, a medium with whom John Dee had been experimenting in the transmutation of base metal into gold, and who was now at the Emperor's court at Prague. Elizabeth was sceptical of Kelly's powers, but determined, if they existed, that they should be used in the service of England. Burghley wrote to Kelly in May 1591, saying he was

expressly commanded of her Majesty to require you to have regard for her honour ... I do conjure you not to keep God's gifts from your natural country, but rather to help to make her Majesty a glorious and victorious prince against the malice of her enemies ... Let no other country bereave us of this felicity that only, yea only, by you, I say, is to be expected.[48]

And the Treasurer asked Sir Edward Dyer, who was visiting Bohemia, to try to get hold of Kelly's alleged 'magic powder': 'I wish he would, in some secret box, send to her Majesty for a token some such portion as might be to her a sum reasonable to defray her charges for this summer for her navy which is now preparing to the sea.'[49] Of course Kelly's claims were fraudulent (the Emperor had him defenestrated).

There was no short-cut to solvency. Intervention in France cost Elizabeth £200,000; her Low Countries expenditure ran around £150,000 a year. On 1 March 1593 Burghley reported to a conference of both Houses that the double subsidy granted in 1589 had yielded only £280,000 so far, and that since that date her actual expenditure had been £1,040,000 – the first time a seven-figure sum obtruded itself into English public finance.[50] As the decade progressed, the raising of comparatively trivial sums for urgent current expenditure sometimes presented grave difficulties. In 1598, Robert Cecil, about to leave for France on embassy, deplored 'the scarcity of money'. 'I have been all day reckoning with the Receiver of the Wards,' he told Windebank, 'I think I can wring from him £3,000 ... By getting this I shall be the Lord Treasurer's *filius albus*, for there are payments that must be made in four days.'[51] Elizabeth might have avoided these troubles by a more ruthless policy of direct taxation; but this would have upset the political and economic balance she was determined to hold. And, on the whole, she did hold it. If sometimes, as Ralegh complained, she under-financed her war policies, she maintained political solidarity and economic expansion by keeping the English the lowest-taxed nation in Europe, a fact to which Bacon paid tribute: 'He that shall look into other countries and consider the taxes, and tallages, and impositions, and assizes and the like that are everywhere in use, will find that the Englishman is most master of his own valuation, and the least bitten in purse of any nation in Europe.'[52]

There was another form of internal balance which Elizabeth had to maintain in conducting the war against Spain: the delicate equipoise of her religious settlement, now being assaulted by Catholicism from without, and by Protestant sectarianism from within. In some ways it was the most difficult problem which faced her throughout her reign, for it was continuous, and it affected large numbers of people, high and low, in an age when men and women were increasingly making up their own minds about religion, and were accordingly less responsive to royal authority.

For the first twenty years of her reign, Elizabeth refrained from virtually any form of state action against those who declined to accept the form of religion laid down by parliament. Even those who made no secret of their religious beliefs, and felt unable to take the oath to the Queen, were left unmolested, provided they expressed no ostensible disloyalty to the régime. In his propaganda pamphlet, first published in 1583, *The Execution of Justice in England*, Burghley was able to cite the case of Archbishop Heath who

> showing himself a faithful and quiet subject . . . [and] leaving willingly both his offices, lived in his own house very discretely and enjoyed all his purchased lands during his natural life, until by very age he departed this world and then left his house and living to his friends, an example of gentleness never matched in Queen Mary's time.[53]

This policy of toleration towards Catholics was undoubtedly the Queen's own. She 'would not have any of the consciences unnecessarily sifted, to know what affection they had towards the old religion'.[54] In some parts of the country, particularly in the North, even the 1559 Acts were barely enforced. Scarcely a dozen clergymen were deprived of their livings in the Northern Province, which included the strongly conservative and Catholic Lancashire, where only three were deprived.[55] Most of the northern magistrates leaned towards Catholicism, at any rate in the earlier decades; the Earl of Derby, the lord lieutenant, had a Catholic wife and many Catholic relations. If he had joined the Northern rebels in 1569, the story might have been different, for then a strongly Protestant régime would have been established. His very loyalty to Elizabeth paradoxically led to a lax enforcement of the law. Even after 1569, northern magistrates were reluctant to act against neighbours and friends. Earnest Protestants were happy to do so, but there were few of them in the North, and imported strangers made themselves thoroughly unpopular. Fines were evaded, or remained unpaid; the worst offenders were often women, who had no property to be seized. Some of the gentry sired priests and, later, sent their sons to be educated in English colleges established in the Spanish-controlled Low Countries. Even at the end of the reign, there were 2,500 declared Catholics in Yorkshire, out of a total population of 300,000; the proportion in Lancashire was higher especially north of the Ribble.[56]

Elizabeth was not unduly disturbed by these Catholic survivals, so long as they centred round the gentry. In some ways she assisted the process. By her desire, Catholic peers were excused the oath. She did not, on the whole, give them public employment, but she liked to have them at court. In some ways she regarded Catholic peers as supports of her throne, a balancing factor against the aggressive Protestantism of men like Huntingdon, Bedford and Warwick. At various times, Catholics or crypto-Catholics like Arundel, Oxford and Southampton, the Berkeleys, the Vaux, the Monteagles, the Pagets, the Brownes and the Arundell, enjoyed her favour. This was maintained well after the period of acute religious crisis began. She made the Earl of Worcester her Master of Horse. Sometimes she visited the houses of known Catholics. Thus, on 15 August 1591, she came to stay with Anthony Browne, Lord Montague, at his splendid house at Cowdray, near Farnham. She stayed there a week, and this was not a hole-and-corner visit but one celebrated with feasting, hunting and spectacular theatricals.[57] The fact is that Montague, like many Catholic grandees, was almost fanatically loyal to the Queen: it was precisely because they were Catholics that they made a point of their devotion to her. Montague bitterly resented not receiving a personal summons to war during Armada year, and he was one of the first to bring his troops to the Tilbury Camp. Camden says that Elizabeth 'having experienced his loyalty, had a great esteem for him, 'tho a stiff Romanist'. She even forgave him for the fact that his youngest son, William, became a Jesuit. In a sense she liked large Catholic households: they radiated conservative links with the past which she found both emotionally satisfying and politically attractive. One is not surprised to hear that, in 1782, when Dr Johnson visited Cowdray (it was burned down eleven years later), he remarked: 'Sir, I should like to stay here 24 hours. We see here how our ancestors lived.' The remark was true even in 1591.

Indeed, by virtually excluding the Catholic gentry from the operations of her anti-Catholic legislation, Elizabeth effectively tamed Catholicism, at least for a time. Catholicism as a religious structure collapsed when state institutions withdrew their support in 1559. It survived in remote areas where private institutions, above all the landowning gentry, were the mainstay of society. Only large households could maintain the cyclical apparatus of Catholicism, the fasts and great feasts, the elaborate ceremonials of the liturgy. Lord Vaux, charged in May 1581 with not coming to the parish church, 'did claim his house to be a parish by itself', as indeed it was.[58] The lords and squires thus became the effective government of English Catholicism, and the clergy merely household servants: it was a return to the old proprietory church of the Dark Ages.[59] Since the gentry were in charge, Elizabeth could hold them responsible: and they repaid her toleration by their loyalty. She was quite happy with this situation, and so were the Catholic landowners and their tenants. Indeed, the tenants were particularly well off, since the Catholic gentry, to avoid unpopularity, tended to be unenterprising in their estate policies.[60] They believed in an ancient, hierarchical world, in which loyalty to the sovereign was the central point of their social philosophy. Hence their declaration of support for the Queen at the time of the Armada.[61]

The Counter-Reformation in England, as Elizabeth always insisted, was not therefore indigenous, but a foreign importation. The Catholic gentry deplored the papal Bull of 1570, and still more the violent manifesto of Cardinal Allen in 1588. They realized that the training of priests on the Continent was, in some ways, aimed at their status – a reassertion of the independence of the clerical order. The new priests, and especially the Jesuits, were not prepared to be treated as household servants. Moreover, since their seminary efforts needed finance, they accepted help and subsidies from the Catholic powers, above all Spain, and thus became involved in national and international politics. This, too, the Catholic gentry hated, for it upset the *status quo* and imperilled their lives and property. We get echoes of these tensions in the controversy between Lord Montague's chaplain and Father Parsons. Charles Paget said he did not understand why Allen 'and other priests and religious men should meddle in public matters in our country and not ... gentlemen'.[62]

But the gentry could not stop the operations of the Counter-Reformation (at least until Henri IV dismantled the Catholic League and so deprived the emigrés of their base), and so Elizabeth was forced, progressively and reluctantly, to act. In the 1570s and 1580s, she fought a number of bitter rearguard actions in parliament to stem the enthusiasm of Protestant MPs for severely repressive legislation.[63] Thus, in 1581, she personally intervened to scale down the penalties provided for in the 'Act to retain the Queen's Majesty's subjects in their due obedience'.[64] In some cases death was replaced by a 200-mark fine; hearing Mass was punished by a 100-mark fine, instead of six months' imprisonment; and non-attendance by a £20 fine instead of a rising scale – this saved the Catholic gentry from financial ruin. Nevertheless, the penal legislation mounted. As always happens in such situations, the witch-hunt intensified as the real threat became more remote. The events of 1569–70 had shown that England was impervious to a Catholic *coup*; 1588 confirmed that the Queen could deal with external invasion also. Elizabeth herself, as always, was against special legislation. She possessed a well-grounded confidence in the ability of the Common Law and existing statutes to deal with almost any threat to the state. The Jesuit incursions of 1580–1, which alarmed her government, were in fact crushed by using the old treason laws. But there was a point beyond which she did not think it politic to resist parliament. In 1585 she allowed through an anti-Jesuit Act, which ordered Jesuits and priests to leave the country forthwith.

Thereafter, any who entered were *ipso facto* guilty of high treason, and those who maintained them of felony. In 1593, recusants were placed under restrictions, in effect a five-mile Act.[65] The parliamentary pressure against Catholics was only relaxed later in the decade of the 1590s, when Puritan MPs realized that anti-Catholic legislation could be turned against themselves. In practice, Elizabeth preferred to act by using royal proclamations to define, and if necessary extend, the law of treason. She did this on 15 July 1580, for instance, and again on 10 January 1581 (the latter was used against Philip Howard, Earl of Arundel). This placed the control of law-enforcement more firmly in her own hands; she could be strict, or lenient, as she felt the occasion required.[66]

Nevertheless, it is clear her hand was often forced, particularly over the more petty aspects of persecution. After the religious legislation of 1559 there was a terrific outburst of iconoclasm, which she was powerless to stop. She was forced to sanction the removal of chalices, rood-lofts, and stone altars, and to allow wall-paintings to be whitewashed. Many old service books and vestments were destroyed. She tried to keep stained glass, fonts, lecterns and some vestments, and fought hard for church-tombs: a Proclamation of 1561 forbade 'defacing monuments of antiquity set up in the churches for memory, not superstition'. But many of her earlier prelates were notorious iconoclasts. Between them, Dean Horne and Bishop Pilkington gutted Durham Cathedral, whose internal decorations were among the most splendid in Christendom. It is a miracle that Canterbury was not pillaged also. Where iconoclasm was brought to the Queen's attention, she did her best to get the damage repaired. She commanded local authorities 'for such [monuments] as be already spoiled in any church or chapel, now standing, to employ . . . such sums (as any wise may be spared) upon the speedy repair and re-edification of such monuments so defaced or spoilt, as agreeable to the original as the same conveniently may be.' In 1573 she herself restored the tombs of the Dukes of York in Fotheringay Church.[67] Often, where she succeeded in getting statues set up again, the broken heads were replaced on the wrong shoulders. But perhaps she did not mind: when controversy arose over what to do with the bones of rival Catholic and Protestant martyrs at Christ Church, Oxford, tradition has it that the Queen said: 'Mix them.' Hence a canon of the church rhymed:

> *Papists and Protestants should now in peace abide,*
> *As here religion true and false lie side by side.*

But often Elizabeth's efforts to stem iconoclasm were defeated. Stow records the painful story of Cheapside Cross, smashed up by Puritan vandals on Midsummer Night, 1581. Elizabeth offered a reward for the detection of the offenders, but there were no takers. On at least two occasions she ordered the cross to be set up again, the Lord Mayor being told, in 1599, it was her express wish, 'respecting especially the antiquity and continuance of that monument, an ancient ensign of Christianity'. But when this was finally done, vandals struck again twelve nights later, and Elizabeth gave up in disgust.[68]

Of course London was a notorious centre of iconoclasm. But sometimes, on progress, Elizabeth was forced to countenance the spiteful persecution of perfectly loyal provincial Catholics. In 1578, during her progress through East Anglia, she seems to have been the victim of a squalid plot, organized by Protestant court officials and local zealots. She was deliberately put up at the house of a known Catholic, Mr Rookwood. When Rookwood, who had been told to vacate his house, Euston Hall, during the visit, appeared to pay his respects and kiss the Queen's hand, he was bawled out by the Lord Chamberlain, who 'said he was fitter for a pair of stocks; commanded him out of court, but yet to attend her Council's pleasure; and at Norwich he was committed'.[69] Seven other local Catholic gentlemen were locked up on the same occasion. Richard Topcliffe, the most violent of the Catholic-hunters, had contrived to be present, and produced his own spiteful little drama, which he gleefully recorded:

A piece of plate being missed from the Court, and searched for in [Rookwood's] hay-house, in the hayrick such an image of Our Lady was there found, as for greatness, for gayness and workmanship, I never did see a match. And after a sort of country dances ended, in her Majesty's sight the idol was set behind the people, who avoided: she rather seemed a beast, raised upon a sudden from Hell by conjuring, than the picture for whom it had been so often and so long abused. Her Majesty commanded it to the fire, which in her sight by the country folk was quickly done to her content, and the unspeakable joy of everyone, but some one or two who had sucked of the idol's poisoned milk.[70]

This must have been a painful occasion for Elizabeth; presumably she put up with it to avoid giving public scandal. Where life and death were at stake, however, she tried to keep a firm grip on the execution of the law, not always successfully. As a rule, she flatly refused to put Catholic laymen to death. Instead, she preferred to milk them, to help pay for the prosecution of the war. Bishops were instructed to return details of all recusants, and to value their lands and goods 'as you think they are indeed, and not as they be valued in the subsidy books' – Catholics, in short, were not to share the scandalous privilege of under-assessment enjoyed by other landowners.[71] The milking policy was probably suggested by Walsingham, as a compromise between the

Queen, who wanted to do little or nothing, and the Council – solidly Protestant since the death of Arundel in 1580 – who wanted to execute the laws.[72] From time to time, Catholics were rounded up, and held in such centres as Wisbech and Framlingham. Walsingham, as head of security, also favoured a lenient policy towards laymen; in 1582 he even favoured a plan, conceived by some of the Catholic gentry, to set up a colony in North America – thus adumbrating the nonconformist settlements of the next generation.[73]

Both Walsingham and the Queen thought a more severe attitude was necessary to the seminary-trained priests, all of whom were sworn to subvert the régime, though some, like Campion, had obtained dispensations to repudiate their vows when being examined. Here again, Walsingham and Elizabeth were anxious to avoid the ultimate confrontation under the law. They tried, by a close watch on the ports, to keep the priests out, and to use banishment rather than execution. Walsingham set out this policy, with the Queen's approval, in a memo of December 1586.[74] But port officials were often corrupt, and for a variety of complex reasons connected with the farming of the customs, Walsingham was not always able to exert an effective grip on the port authorities. So many priests got through, and from time to time they were executed. The figures rose as the war-tension mounted: there were two executions in 1583, fifteen in the next year, as many as thirty-four in 1588 – altogether nearly a hundred in the troubled 1580s. Thereafter, executions tended to rise during war-scares, and fall in periods of relative calm, but they never reached more than ten a year; in Elizabeth's last year only one was put to death. In all, during the thirty years when active Catholics went in peril of their lives, something under 300 were executed, approximately the same as in the three-year Marian persecution.[75] Elizabeth was never happy about these executions. She thought they were counter-productive, and tended to produce martyrs who could be exploited by Catholic and Spanish propaganda. She was not a student of John Foxe for nothing, for Foxe had shown conclusively how the blood of martyrs fostered faith, and he himself advocated the maximum tolerance.[76] She particularly regretted the execution of Campion, whom she had met and admired as a young man. Oddly enough, Walsingham agreed with her view, and so, in the end, did Burghley.[77] But the machinery of religious warfare and the frenetic atmosphere of the times proved too powerful for Elizabeth, and for the wiser heads in her government. And, of course, most members of the Council felt that she executed not too many, but too few – an attitude shared by the overwhelming majority of MPs. Indeed, it was the prevailing opinion in parliament, put by Thomas Norton in 1571, that Catholics should be arrested, questioned, convicted and punished, not only for political offences, but for their beliefs: 'not only the external and outward show is to be sought, but the very secret of the heart in God's cause ... must come to a reckoning, and the good seed so sifted from the cockle that the one may be known from the other.'[78] This was the very antithesis of Elizabeth's view, and she rejected it absolutely. Throughout the last thirty years of her reign, she dealt with the Catholic problem entirely on a political basis. In all capital cases where Catholics were dealt with, the offence was not heresy or nonconformity, but treason.

There was, however, a drawback to this approach, sensible though it was as a general policy. By dealing with Catholic priests as traitors, Elizabeth necessarily exposed them to the full ferocity of Tudor judicial and penal methods. This helps to explain the appalling cruelty with which, in some cases, the priests were treated. But it must be remembered that everyone in Tudor society, from the Queen to the poorest, lived in the shadow of corporal, indeed capital, punishment. Half-a-dozen of Elizabeth's relatives had been executed. If her régime had collapsed, she would have been the first victim: she might well have been burned alive. Even on the throne, she was in constant danger of assassination, though she made light of the possibility. Her ministers knew they would be hanged if Catholicism triumphed; they often spoke of the possibility. MPs stood in the same danger, as they frequently reminded the House in debates. The rope, the block, above all the whip were the ubiquitous instruments of discipline in sixteenth-century England. Parents flogged their children, boys and girls alike, without mercy, well into their teens and beyond. Masters flogged their servants. Magistrates ordered public floggings of men, women and children for the most trivial offences. Recorder Fleetwood's gossipy letters to Burghley tell a sickening tale of his harsh efforts to maintain law and order in the capital – and Fleetwood claimed to be a lenient official, always anxious to err on the side of mercy.[79] William Harrison, in his *Description of England*, gives a gruesome list of the physical punishments authorized by law. In addition to cases of high treason, wilful murder and felony, where the normal punishment was hanging, drawing and quartering, 'notable' thieves were hanged alive in chains at the spot where the felony was committed, and so starved to death. Often a thief had his right hand struck off before being led to execution. Then:

If a woman poison her husband she is burned alive; if the servant kill his master, he is to be executed for petty treason; he that poisoneth a man is to be boiled to death in water or lead, although the party die not of the practice. In cases of murder all the accessories are to suffer pains of death accordingly. Perjury is to be punished by the pillory, burning in the forehead with the letter P . . . and loss of all his moveables. Many trespasses also are punished by the cutting of one or both ears from the head of the offender . . . Rogues are burned through the ears; carriers of sheep out of the land by the loss of their hands.[80]

These details are confirmed by the *Eirenarcha*, the learned handbook written for the guidance of JPs by the Kent antiquary, William Lambarde.[81] The evidence seems to suggest that various forms of corporal punishment, especially whipping, became more common as the reign progressed. Members of the judiciary were constantly thinking up new ones: Burghley, for instance, suggested in 1595 that forgers be indelibly tattooed, as well as branded, as the brand-mark tended to fade.[82] There was some disagreement among public men as to whether the penal code was sufficiently severe. Sir Thomas Smith thought there were fewer drastic punishments in England than elsewhere:

> Heading, tormenting, demembering, either arm or leg, breaking upon the wheel, impaling and such cruel torments as be used in other nations by the order of their law, we have not: and yet as few murders committed as anywhere.[83]

But Sir Edward Coke, not in most respects a tender-hearted man, thought there were too many hangings:

> What a lamentable case it is to see so many Christian men and women strangled on that cursed tree of the gallows; in so much as if in a *large field* a man might see together all the Christians that, but in one year throughout England, came to that untimely and ignominious death, if there were any spark of grace or charity in him, it would make his heart bleed for pity and compassion.[84]

In fact there is a good deal of evidence that death-sentences were often commuted, not as a result of any judicial process, but through bribery and influence. Fleetwood identified the court as the chief offender: 'It is growen for a trade now in the court to make means for reprieves; twenty pounds for a reprieve is nothing, although it be but for a bare ten days.' He quoted the old Marquess of Winchester: 'When the court is furthest from London, then is there the best justice done in all England.'[85] Sometimes the Controlment Rolls were falsified to conceal the fact that executions had not been carried out. Elizabeth knew perfectly well that such things went on, and did nothing to stop them. On the whole she disliked executions, and was very fond of issuing reprieves herself. This was why she hated summary justice. When Sir John Carey summarily executed John Dagleish for Border offences, Burghley wrote to him that the

Queen was angry. She thought his action 'very barbarous and seldom used [even] among the Turks'.[86] But she threw the whole weight of her authority behind law enforcement as such: that is, she wanted offenders brought to justice and convicted. Only afterwards did she lean to clemency, 'a very merciful lady', as Burghley called her. She took enormous trouble in selecting her judges. They were, as a rule, honest, efficient but severe men. She also took a hand in picking JPs, and claimed, probably with some exaggeration, that she knew them all by name and sight. In 1595, the Lord Keeper recorded that, since there were

> many insufficient, unlearned, negligent and undiscreet [magistrates], her Majesty therefore, like a good housewife looking unto all her household stuff, took the book in her own hands and in the sight of us, the Lord Treasurer and the Lord Keeper, went through and noted those justices she would have continued in commission, and whom she thought not meet, and willed us to consider of the rest.[87]

We know from many instances that she took a direct and detailed interest in all trials which affected the security of the state, or the public attitude to religion, made her feelings plain, and interfered if she thought it necessary. For these reasons we must assume that she authorized the execution of Catholic priests, both as a general policy and in particular instances, because she had concluded there was no other way of dealing with the problem.

To what extent did she acquiesce in the use of torture during their interrogation? Catholic apologists, at the time and since, have given the impression that torture was used as a routine procedure in dealing with Catholics. Thus Cardinal Allen, in his most famous propaganda tract, accused Elizabeth of using torture in mere cases of conscience:

> See whether a portable altar be a sufficient cause to give the torture to a grave, worshipful person, not so much suspected of treason or any disobedience, other than in cases of conscience. Whether books of prayers and meditation spiritual, or the printing and spreading of them, be a rack matter in any commonwealth Christian ... Let the world see what one confession of treasonable matter you have wrested out by the so often tormenting of so many ... No, no, nothing was there in those religious hearts but innocency and true religion. It is that which you punished, tormented and deadly hated in them.[88]

Allen's accusation (if true) was all the more serious in that in the view of most English legal authorities – Fortescue in the fifteenth century, for instance –

torture was not, and never had been, legal under English common law. A man might be pressed to death for obstinately refusing to plead at all, as this was taken to be a rejection of the whole judicial process; but torture was not to be used to extract information or confession of guilt.[89] The practice had been strongly condemned by Cicero, Seneca, Justinian and other classical jurists. It had been authorized by canon law in the thirteenth century, and had in fact first been used in England, under royal warrant, to extract confessions from the Knights Templar in 1310. In the fifteenth century, when its use became widespread in France, Italy, Spain and Germany, it had made some penetration into England, but under judicial disapproval. In Elizabeth's reign, the government was equipped to torture, at the Tower and the Bridewell, but many of its members hotly opposed the practice, and said so privately and publicly. Ralegh thought the use of the rack particularly arbitrary and capricious: 'The rack is used nowhere as in England; they take a man and rack him I know not why or when.' Robert Beale, a strong and energetic Protestant, and a hammer of treason, protested against the use of torture in any circumstances, and declined absolutely to deal in cases where it was authorized. Sir Thomas Smith thought the jury system quite adequate to find out the fact of guilt: 'without racking, wresting and tormenting the deed may be found'. Torture, he said, was contrary to the spirit of the laws and the national character:

> For what can he serve the commonwealth after as a free man, who hath his body so hailed and tormented, if he be not found guilty, and what amends can be made him? . . . The nature of Englishmen is to neglect death, to abide no torment . . . In no place shall you see malefactors go more constantly, more assuredly and with less lamentation to their death than in England . . . The nature of our nation is free, stout, haughty, prodigal of life and blood: but contumely, beatings, servitude and servile torment and punishment it will not abide.[90]

All the same, torture was used, though a special warrant of the Council was necessary to authorize it. There are many references in the state papers to such authorizations, though the step was rarely taken without a good deal of argument and heart-searching.[91] Torture was used against Northamptonshire gypsies, who were believed to form a secret revolutionary society, to discover their supposed objects and ringleaders.[92] It was used against Oxfordshire rioters, suspected of organizing rebellion.[93] It was used against pirates, and in 1597 against a man charged with attempting to burn the fleet.[94] Elizabeth, of course, was well aware of the practice. Indeed, on two occasions she specifically authorized it. Thus, she directed that Norfolk's two secretaries. Higford and Barker, be racked, to get them to reveal details of the 1571 Ridolfi conspiracy.[95] And, in April 1583, during the Throckmorton plot, when Father William Holt, SJ, was seized at Leith, Walsingham wrote to Sir Thomas Bowes, at Berwick: 'Her Majesty doth earnestly desire that Holt might be substantially examined and forced by torture to deliver what he knoweth.'[96] In neither case, as it happened, was torture actually used, and I have been unable to discover any other instances in which the Queen was personally involved. Her government was throughout shamefaced in the use of torture, particularly in the cases of Catholic priests, where the practice was exposed to international propaganda. Thomas Norton MP, who personally supervised the examination of prisoners in the Tower, defended his methods in a letter to Walsingham, who was disturbed by public criticism:

> None was put to the rack that was not first by manifest evidence known to the Council to be guilty of treason, so it was well assured beforehand that there was no innocent tormented. Also none was tormented to know whether he was guilty or no: but for the Queen's safety, to know the manner of the treason and the accomplices . . . Nor was any man tormented for matter of religion, nor asked what he believed in any point of religion, but only to understand of particular practices against the Queen for setting up their religion by treason or force. If any one of them did say that he would truly answer to such things as he was demanded on the Queen's behalf, or would by oath, or without oath, seriously and upon his allegiance say that he did know or believe his answers to be true, he was never racked. Neither was any of them racked that had not both obstinately said, and did persist in that obstinacy, that he would not tell truth though the Queen commanded him.[97]

This was the line of defence taken by Burghley in two pamphlets, *A Declaration of Favourable Dealing by Her Majesty's Commissioners Appointed for the Examination of Certain Traitors*, and his more famous *Execution of Justice in England*, both published in 1583, presumably with Elizabeth's approval (Norton wrote the text of the first).[98] Burghley claimed that Campion 'was never so racked that he was able to walk', and that the torturers had been ordered to rack 'in as charitable manner as such a thing might be'.[99]

The assertion that the Council kept a tight control over the torturers (a councillor was usually present) may have been true in the cases of most of the twenty or so priests we know to have been brutalized. But it was not always true. Winslade, an English deserter captured in one of the Armada ships, was handed over to the Lieutenant of the Tower and four magistrates, 'for the examination of the said Winslade on the rack, using torture to him at their pleasure'. As he was later discharged as innocent, Burghley's claim that only the guilty were tortured is likewise refuted. One or two of the agents used by the Council were monsters. Topcliffe would be classed, by modern clinical standards, as a pathological sadist, as the curious comments and gallows-illustrations he made in his copy of a history of the English Reformation seem to indicate.[100] A Catholic correspondent of Father Parsons claimed that 'because the often exercise of the rack in the Tower was so odious, and so much spoken of by the people, Topcliffe had authority to torment priests in his own house in such sort as he shall think good'.[101] The source of this statement makes it highly suspect, and, if the claim is true, the Council must have been in flagrant breach of its own definite rules. But even under supervision in the Tower, one or two priests were dreadfully handled. Robert Cecil is supposed to have visited Robert Southwell SJ while he was being questioned, and to have said: 'We have a new torture which it is not possible for a man to bear. And yet I have seen Robert Southwell hanging by it, still as a tree-trunk, and no one able to drag one word out of his mouth.' Again the source is suspect,[102] but there can be no doubt of Southwell's sufferings.

The Queen knew Topcliffe and Norton quite well, and there can be little doubt that she was aware of their activities. Indeed, in 1597, when Thomas Travers was arrested for stealing the Queen's standish (inkwell), it was Topcliffe who put him to the manacles. But such men were in danger of Elizabeth's wrath. Norton was himself imprisoned in the Tower in 1581–2 (where he found time to draft the *Declaration*), and Topcliffe was twice gaoled for exceeding his warrant and contempt of court. Elizabeth seems to have accepted the use of torture where she was advised that information about proposed acts of high treason could be obtained by no other means. She regarded the horrible business, and the executions, as among the inevitable consequences of the religious fanaticism she hated and strove against. But she did, or said, or wrote, nothing to indicate that she had any animus against Catholics. On the contrary, where they were loyal, she saw them as supports of her state. They not only did not oppose, but enthusiastically defended, her concept of monarchical authority, and therefore they were a valuable balancing factor against the fundamentalist criticism of the Puritans.

Indeed, it was against the left-wing of Christianity (if it can be so termed) that Elizabeth acted not merely out of necessity, but from genuine conviction. She did not share the Puritan view that religious and secular life were all one. She thought it the duty of the clergy to inculcate obedience and the practice of outward decorum, and to leave public affairs to laymen. Her bishops were mainly middle-class men, whom she kept busy in their dioceses. She rarely gave them public employment or a share in the spoils of state.[103] Often she kept their sees vacant for long periods. The worst example was Ely, which had no bishop between July 1581 and February 1600 (for a time part of its revenues were diverted to keep the bankrupt Earl of Oxford from indigence). But Bath and Wells was vacant a total of six years, Bristol fourteen, Chichester seven, Gloucester five, Salisbury five, and Oxford she barely filled at all, though this was a special case, having only been brought into existence in 1542.[104] Moreover, owing to frequent translations, and the Queen's entitlement to first fruits, the bishops were usually in debt to her, and with few exceptions were no richer than the lowest ranks of the nobility. Most of them did as she told them. They wore, as Bishop Aylmer put it, 'the Queen's livery'.[105]

It was a different matter with the more active elements among the lower clergy, some of whom were Calvinists. They believed in a theocracy, in a clerical caste close to the people, indeed, and by virtue of this authorized to interfere in every aspect of life. They had no patience with the unadventurous Church Elizabeth had established, resting comfortably but ambiguously halfway between Rome and Geneva. It was, they said, a sanctuary of 'dumb dogs, unskilfully sacrificing priests, destroying drones, or rather caterpillars of the world'. Cathedrals were 'dens of lazy, loitering lubbards', the Prayer Book 'a thing picked out of that popish dunghill, the Mass-book, full of abominations'. They wanted an industrious, learned, above all vociferous clergy, 'zealous preachers of the Gospel', what Sir Francis Knollys, for many years the leading Puritan layman at the court, called 'diligent barkers against the popish wolf'.[106] The image of the clergy as ubiquitous and noisy watchdogs was a favourite one among the elect. William Turner, Dean of Wells (evicted during the Vestment purges of 1566) trained his pet dog to leap up and snatch the caps off the heads of conformist clergymen.[107] The row between Puritan clergymen and the established Church first centred on vestments, an issue which had been left unresolved by the 1559 legislation. But it soon broadened to the key topic of sermons, and the right, indeed the duty, of clergymen to preach constantly on any topic whatever. Elizabeth's hatred of sermons was an abiding passion, which grew stronger with age. She rationalized her dislike: she told the bishops in 1577 that as a result of sermons, and especially their more apocalyptic form known as prophesyings, 'great numbers of our people, especially of the vulgar sort, meet to be otherwise occupied with honest labour for their living, are brought to idleness and seduced: and in manner schismatically divided among themselves into a variety of dangerous opinions'.[108] But her objections were emotional too. From long and bitter experience, she loathed listening, for an hour or more, to foolish and arrogant clergymen – most of whom emphatically believed no woman should ever occupy a position of responsibility – instructing her on her duties. Sermons in the Abbey and St Margaret's at the opening of parliament she particularly resented. The preachers almost invariably made gratuitous comments on political matters. Sometimes their remarks were directly addressed to her, as she sat bridling in the face of the congregation. Thus, Edward Dering, after denouncing the Church she had established root and branch, added: 'And yet you, in the meanwhile that all these whoredoms are committed, you at whose hands God will require it, let men do as they list. It toucheth not, belike, your commonwealth, and therefore you are so well contented to let all alone.'[109] Sometimes she interrupted offensive preachers ('To your text, Mr Dean, to your text!'), or sent angry messages up to the pulpit. She cut down court sermons to the minimum. Goodman recalls: 'Queen Elizabeth was wont to say she had rather speak to God herself, than to hear another speaking of God; she seldom heard sermons, but only in Lent.'[110] She listened to them from her closet, opening into the chapel, and sometimes kept the lattice closed. Once, says Harington, she was caught out, for after the sermon, which contained matter she did not like, she congratulated the preacher.[111] The amazing thing is that so many preachers, knowing her views, continued to offend her, but Puritans were notoriously insensitive, particularly to female opinion.

Wherever possible, she controlled sermons, especially in London. Several times she vetoed men proposed for St Paul's Cross.[112] In 1579 she ordered preachers

> that in their sermons and preachings they do not intermeddle with any such matters of state, being in very deed not incident or appertaining to their profession ... but rather teach the people to be thankful towards Almighty God for the great benefits both of liberty of conscience, peace and wealth which they have hitherto enjoyed by her Majesty's good means.[113]

She called such instructions 'tuning her pulpits'.[114] But, in general, she thought the less sermons the public heard, the better. She wanted, indeed, Sunday 'homilies', delivered by rote from texts approved by the bishops – this was the Catholic practice. In the 1570s, the first generation of Elizabethan bishops – many of them from Geneva and Frankfurt – began to die off, to be replaced by more placid brethren, and the Puritan leadership passed to men from the rank and file. They began to organize themselves, in parliament, and in the country, using the *classis* system developed by the Huguenots in France. Sermons and prophesying meetings (where clergymen and leading laymen met from a whole neighbourhood) were their chief activity, and Elizabeth determined to curb it. In 1577 she instructed Edmund Grindall, who had succeeded Parker as Archbishop of Canterbury, to cut down on all Puritan activities, but especially preaching. All preaching-meetings, prophesyings or similar exercises were to be specifically licensed by the bishops; no laymen were to speak at them; and there were to be no reflections on matters of state or Church government. Three or four licensed preachers were quite enough for each county, and homilies would do for the rest.[115] But Grindal was no Erastian: he flatly refused to carry out her orders. Sermons, he told Elizabeth, were 'the only means and instrument of the salvation of mankind'. Moreover, he challenged the Queen not merely over the specific issue of sermons, but on her right to regulate the Church in general:

> when you deal in matters of faith and religion, or matters that touch the Church of Christ . . . you would not use to pronounce so resolutely and peremptorily, *quasi ex auctoritate*, as ye may do in civil and extern matters . . . God hath blessed you with great felicity in your reign, now many years; beware you do not impute the same to your own deserts and policy, but give God the glory.[116]

Elizabeth was not standing for this. She knew very well that her 'felicity' was the direct result, if not of her 'deserts', at least of her 'policy', and she intended to keep things that way. She sequestered Grindal from exercising his offices, and for six months confined him to his house. But, being a realist, she did not actually deprive him; that would have upset the balance. As Knollys wrote (January 1578), using a terrifying analogy of which Elizabeth was always aware:

> If the Bishop of Canterbury shall be deprived, then up starts the pride and practice of the papists, and down declineth the comfort and strength of her Majesty's safety; and then King Richard the Second's men will flock into court apace, and will show themselves in their colours.[117]

Instead, she allowed Grindal to crumble into old age and blindness, and then replaced him by Whitgift, her personal choice, or 'little black husband' as she called him. Whitgift was a Calvinist, too, but a disciplinarian and a man who believed in hierarchy. He had already shown his ruthlessness, as Vice-Chancellor of Cambridge University, by dismissing the Professor of Divinity, Thomas Cartwright, who was the leading exponent of Puritan doctrines. Whitgift was learned, harsh, inflexible, narrow-minded, impervious to argument and obstinately brave. He was also a hard-working and capable administrator, and not merely in clerical matters. During the invasion scares of the 1590s he proved himself exceptionally assiduous in marshalling the resources of the Church for the defence of the realm.[118] Where Parker had wavered on exercising discipline, and Grindal resisted, Whitgift acted, on Elizabeth's explicit and detailed instructions: 'Her Majesty moveth and earnestly exhorteth me thereunto with straight charge as I shall answer the contrary.'[119] And in the Court of High Commission, set up by the 1559 statute, he had a judicial instrument, whose potentialities, for the first time, he began to exploit. Thus another element in the approaching confrontation of the seventeenth century emerged. In using Whitgift thus, Elizabeth acted without the agreement, indeed against the strongly-argued advice, of her ministers. Many of them had individual contacts and friendships with clergymen whom Whitgift brought before his court. On 1 July 1584, for instance, Burghley protested strongly to the Archbishop over the case of two preachers. He found the charges against them, he wrote

> so curiously penned, so full of branches and circumstances, as I think the Inquisitors of Spain use not so many questions to comprehend and to trap their prey ... this kind of proceeding is too much savouring of the Roman inquisition, and is rather a device to seek for offenders than to reform any.

Three weeks later the Council wrote Whitgift a formal letter, signed by Burghley, Leicester, Warwick, Howard, Hatton, Croftes and Walsingham, protesting about his activities. It was as near to a direct command to desist as they dared go without Elizabeth's authority. Whitgift was unmoved: 'I am determined', he told Burghley, 'to do my duty and conscience without fear'.[120] He knew he had the Queen's support (on the only occasion when he angered her, on a Calvinistic point of doctrine, he immediately complied with her wishes).

Elizabeth acted against Puritans with an uncharacteristic lack of tolerance because she undoubtedly saw them as a threat to monarchical government. By imposing the authority of the bishops, and their ecclesiastical court, on dissenting ministers, Whitgift was upholding the hierarchical structure in which she believed. She fully accepted his point: 'In the end your Majesty will find that those which now impugn the ecclesiastical jurisdiction [will] endeavour also to impair the temporal, and to bring even kings and princes under their censure.'[121] This was quite correct: the beginning of the 'No bishop, no king' argument. The Puritans, under their brilliant young general secretary, John Field, were organizing a party within the state.[122] He was a new kind of figure on the English political scene: doctrinaire, committed, personally unambitious and uninterested in money and place, blazing with zeal to transform society, and travelling the country to organize the means. When Puritan leaders were brought before Star Chamber in 1591, the depositions of the renegade John Johnson (the former Vicar of All Saints in Northampton, a hotbed of the sect) showed that a *classis* structure had been developed, on the basis of county surveys of sympathetic ministers and laymen; representatives were being appointed to go to London when parliament sat, acting as almost a parallel assembly; Puritans were influencing elections and lobbying MPs. And, of course, in parliament itself, men like the Wentworths and Morice were openly using the popular issue of freedom of speech to debate religious matters, and try to pass Acts, against Elizabeth's express injunction. When Elizabeth used her authority to frustrate their activities in the parliamentary sphere, some were prepared to go further, and to talk of a mass-movement, orchestrated by tightly-disciplined cadres (the modern party system, in fact). Thus Edmund Sharpe, minister at St Peter's, Northampton, was alleged to have told some of his flock: 'How say you if we devise a way whereby to shake off all the anti-Christian yoke and government of bishops and ... jointly together erect the discipline and government [of presbyterianism] all in one day; and that in such a way as they that be against it shall never be able to prevail to the contrary.'[123] Or, as Field put it: 'Seeing that we cannot compass these things by suit nor dispute, it is the multitude and people that must bring the discipline to pass which we desire.'[124]

By 'suit or dispute', of course, Field meant parliament. Elizabeth had fought a battle with Puritan MPs in every parliament since 1563, though the issue had varied: sometimes it had been the succession, sometimes her marriage, sometimes Mary Queen of Scots, sometimes purely religious matters. On the last point, at least, she had always won, in the sense that she had prevented the Puritans from re-opening the whole question of the basic religious settlement of 1559, which they now bitterly regretted. She conceded that further reform of abuses was needed, but only within the framework of the 1559 legislation, which placed the initiative entirely in her hands and those of the bishops.[125] There was no doubt about the scandals, and the Puritans found it easy to compile lists of examples. The great and the powerful, led by the Queen herself, practised simony. In 1584, Thomas Godwin was made Bishop of Bath and Wells only after he made over a favourable ninety-nine year lease to Elizabeth, in Ralegh's favour. Richard Fletcher got London after Aylmer's death by handing over leases and £2,100. Bishop Scambler of Peterborough and, later, Norwich, rose by granting leases to such ministers as Burghley and Heneage. Bishop Hughes of St Asaph held an archdeaconry and sixteen benefices in plurality, and distributed valuable leases to his wife, children, sisters and cousins. Despite cutbacks in episcopal incomes, such bishops as Aylmer, Berkeley and Still (the latter two both of Bath and Wells) died rich by impoverishing their sees. Many unsuitable clergymen got benefices through political patronage and bribery.[126] But the powerful patrons of the Puritans were also involved in the racket. Such families as the Richs, the Russells, the Knightleys, the Bacons, the Hastings, the Petres and the Fiennes appointed clergymen by the score, and Leicester's grip on a wide range of Church activities was notorious. With some justice, Bancroft attacked Cartwright and his followers: 'They care not for religion, so they may get the spoil.' One leading Puritan, John Penry, made no secret of his aim to strip the bishoprics, as Henry VIII had stripped the monasteries and Edward VI's ministers the chantries. There was, he said, 'an infinite mass of wealth, even the very greenest of the land, which these locusts now unprofitably devour', waiting to be, as he put it, 'spiled'.[127]

Elizabeth had no intention of confiscating the episcopal estates: she wanted to go on milking them. The most she would promise was to see to it that 'more worthy' persons were appointed. But, granted the system, this was a slow business, and one, moreover, that aroused the opposition of the bishops on trades union grounds. As Robert Beale wrote to Hatton: 'Her Majesty once promised her poor Commons that such abuses should be reformed, and commanded the bishops to see it done. But your Lordship can, I think, remember what angry words [Whitgift] used to your Lordship and Sir Walter Mildmay.'[128] A document which fortunately has survived gives a verbatim record of a discussion, on 27 February 1585, between the Queen, a group of bishops led by Whitgift, and several councillors, including Burghley, when the whole question of Church abuses was raised.[129] This account provides a clear indication of how Elizabeth saw the problem of Church reform. She said to the bishops that she understood some Puritans MPs were attacking them, 'which we will not suffer'; and that they were meddling with religious matters 'above their capacity'; for that, 'we will call some of them to accompt'. She had also heard that such MPs had tacit backing among certain councillors (she meant Mildmay and Knollys), 'which we will redress or else uncouncil some of them'. The bishops were to blame, she said, both for appointing corrupt and 'lewd' ministers, and also for allowing Puritan ministers 'to preach what they list ... to the breach of unity'. She had been told 'there be six preachers in one diocese the which do preach six sundry ways'. Such men were to be 'brought to conformity and unity'. It was no use going gently with them, 'hoping for their conformity, and inclining to noblemen's letters and gentlemen's letters, for they will be hanged before they will be reformed'. They should be made simply to read out homilies, 'for there is more learning in one of those than in twenty of some of their sermons'. The Puritans were 'curious and busy fellows' and their preaching 'tendeth only to popularity' – the worst fault of all in the Queen's eyes: only she was allowed to seek 'popularity'. Whitgift then promised to look into the Queen's criticisms, and meet them. At this point, Burghley interjected, and turned on Whitgift: 'Truly, my Lord, her Majesty hath declared unto you a marvellous fault, in that you make, in this time of light, so many lewd and unlearned ministers.' But Elizabeth came to Whitgift's defence: 'My Lord of Canterbury said well. Draw articles and charge them with it that have offended.' Burghley countered: he was not attacking the bishops present, but the Bishop of Lichfield (the notorious Overton), 'who made seventy ministers in one day for money: some tailors, some shoemakers, and other craftsmen. I am sure the greatest part of them are not worthy to keep horses.' Whitgift replied that it was impossible to find learned ministers for 13,000 parishes. The actual figure was about 9,000. 'Jesus!' said Elizabeth, '13,000! It is not to be looked for.' Then she summed up: 'My meaning is not [that] you should make choice of learned ministers only, for they are not to be found, but of honest, sober and wise men, and such as can read the scriptures and homilies well unto the people.' This being her position there could of course be no compromise with the Puritans.

Between 1588 and 1593 Elizabeth, therefore, had to break the Puritan movement, or rather push it underground. Such action became possible owing to radical changes in the composition of her government, which took place about this time. The Council of the 1580s had become increasingly homogeneous under the stress of war, and though its members disagreed among each other, and with the Queen, on many aspects of policy, they had learned to work together and to respect each other. They were, to some extent at least, a band of brothers, with the Queen as an arbitrary but much-loved elder sister. Though she often abused them to their faces (and behind their backs), she never thought seriously of dismissing any of them, nor they of leaving her service (Davison, the exception, was never admitted to the brotherhood). Elizabeth was extraordinarily loyal to her ministers: she expected them to die in office, and pooh-poohed any idea of resignations on grounds of ill-health, though all of them were seriously ill from time to time. But she could not hold back *Anno Domini*. Bacon, the first of her great servants to go, had died in 1579. Leicester had followed in 1588. Walsingham was increasingly ill: he was out of action for most of 1589, and died in April 1590. This brought a great change, for much of his security network went with him. It had been heavily biased in an anti-Catholic, and pro-Puritan direction (most of his agents were Puritans), and Elizabeth seemed reluctant to replace it. As things stood, a new, efficient system would be pro-Puritan too, and as she was much less disturbed by the possibility either of invasion, or assassination and internal uprising, after 1588, she let things slide. Walsingham was not formally replaced until 1595, and only slowly did Robert Cecil (who did his work), and later Essex build up their own intelligence systems. During this period of hiatus, Whitgift operated his clerical system, under Bancroft, and there was no countervailing Puritan network to frustrate it. Of the remaining chief councillors prepared to protect the ultra-Protestant element, Mildmay died in 1589, and both Burghley and Knollys were very old men. Knollys was hotly opposed to Whitgift: he told him he was 'treading the highway to the Pope', and he 'marvelled', in January 1591, that 'her Majesty can be persuaded that she is in as much danger of such as are called Puritans as she is of the Papists'.[130] But though he lived on until 1596, he spent less and less time at court. Much the same could be said of Burghley. At intervals, he got through mountains of business in the 1590s, but he was disinclined to argue with the Queen on salient issues. There was a further loss in 1591, when Hatton died. Elizabeth had specifically pushed him forward as anti-Puritan. But he had always behaved with moderation, tact and restraint, and worked in close harmony with Burghley and Walsingham. He had been strongly opposed to Whitgift's inquisitorial methods, and had signed the Council's letter of protes against them. His departure meant that, on the right wing of the politico-religious spectrum, Whitgift now had a monopoly of influence over the Queen.

The Puritan activists themselves suffered a heavy blow with the death, early in 1588, of John Field. He was not only a brilliant organizer but a man who, despite his extreme views, had a clear view of what was politically possible. No one dominant figure replaced him, and the leadership of the *classis* passed into the hands of hotheads. Late in 1588, the first of the Marprelate tracts appeared.[131] They rightly caused a sensation, and were read by all the establishment from the Queen down, for they were written in a highly popular manner, full of fire and wit, and reflecting the explosion of literary skill which was now enveloping the London theatre. Their authorship is still disputed, but the most likely candidate is Job Throckmorton MP – a Puritan member of that very lively, if divided, clan – who had already been in trouble with the Queen for his exhilarating speeches in parliament. Whitgift trundled up Bishop Cooper to reply to the early tracts, but his lame riposte was demolished by Marprelate himself, in *Hay any Worke for Cooper?*

There is no doubt that, in terms of literary controversy, Marprelate got by far the best of the argument. Tactically, the operation was a scintillating success. But strategically, it was a gross error of judgment. Even the strongest protectors of the Puritans among the government were shocked at the racy attacks on the episcopate, and the flippant handling of religious problems. Walsingham, though himself (as Naunton put it), 'one of the great allays of the austerian embracement',[132] deplored this degradation of high issues, and the empty-headed lack of prudence it revealed. He had always said, on the Puritan question, that 'policy carrieth more sway than zeal'. Burghley was outraged, and henceforth would have nothing to do with the extremists. The removal of his protection opened the way for penal measures. Francis Bacon, in his *On the Controversie of the Church*, makes it clear that the success of Marprelate was counter-productive, since the powerful of all shades of opinion objected to 'this immodest and deformed manner of writing lately entertained, whereby matters of religion are handled in the style of the stage'. Moreover, Bancroft, acting under Whitgift's orders, managed to track down the printing-presses which had been used, and the printers were tried under the Act of 1581 against the use of seditious words.

Indeed, Elizabeth, as with the Catholics, was able to get Puritan offenders on political charges, thus by-passing the much more tricky religious issues. Her proclamation against them on 13 February 1589 treated them as subversives: they had attempted 'to dissolve the estate of the prelacy, being one of the three ancient estates of this realm'. Legend says that, when Elizabeth was discussing this proclamation with Essex, the young man suddenly took a copy of the latest Marprelate tract from his pocket, and asked: 'What, then, is to become of me?' But the fact is that the nobility liked the tracts little more than the bishops. As the Earl of Hertford put it, 'As they shoot at bishops now, so will they do at the nobility also, if they be suffered.' Even Robert Beale, and Cartwright himself, made it plain they disapproved of Marprelate, and in the consequent revulsion from Puritan extremists, Whitgift was able to get three leading sectarians, Barrow, Greenwood and Penry, executed. It is impossible to discover whether Elizabeth herself wanted such drastic action. But the trouble was that Puritanism tended to topple over into religious mania. In 1591, the year Barrow and his colleagues went to the scaffold, a man called William Hacket had appeared in London, claiming to be Jesus Christ and, in front of multitudes, had made violent attacks on Elizabeth herself as well as Whitgift. The executions had the effect of stopping a movement of religious fervour which was threatening to lead to rioting and pillage – reinforced by the thousands of unemployed soldiers now hanging about the capital.

By the time the parliament of 1593 assembled, the Puritans had lost their foothold in the power-establishment. Beale commented to Burghley on the small number of Puritan-inclined MPs returned, and though Peter Wentworth has made this parliament famous by his courageous advocacy of free speech, he was essentially a lonely figure in his campaign to get the Queen to establish a firm Protestant succession. He seems to have believed that, if only Elizabeth could be induced to read the various documents he had prepared – including his *Pithie Exhortation to her Majestie for Establishing her Successor to the Crowne* – she would immediately fall in with his views. In fact she almost certainly had read it (it was far from pithy), and was unlikely to be moved from the firm convictions she had formed over thirty-five years, by the meandering and offensive arguments deployed by a sectarian she regarded as a near-crackpot. She put Wentworth in the Tower, and refused to release him until he made some form of apology. Wentworth, despite the urgings of Burghley and others, would do no such thing. He preferred to die in the Tower, though the Queen mitigated his hardships by giving him a free run of the building and by allowing his wife to stay there with him.[133] Wiser heads among the Puritan MPs refused to work with Wentworth. James Morice, a senior attorney at the Court of Wards, in conjunction with Robert Beale, fought the religious battle in this parliament on the much more popular and productive grounds of anti-clericalism and the hatred of the Common Lawyers for the civil lawyers of the Court of High Commission. But these tactics, though they elicited some support among MPs, did not succeed either. Morice, too, was put in custody for a time, and Burghley apathetically advised him that, if he had any complaints about the way the Church was being run, it was his duty to make them to the Queen alone: 'If it pleased her to reform it, it was well; if not, we were to pray to God to move her heart thereunto, and to leave the matter to God and her Majesty.'[134] Altogether, in this parliament, Elizabeth took disciplinary action (mostly short-lived) against seven MPs, and there was no effective protest in any case. Puritanism, for the time being at least, was retiring from the parliamentary scene, and concentrating on grassroots activities, above all on the creation of endowed lectureships, chiefly in London and the big boroughs. These continued to proliferate, and in the next generation would produce a host of problems for Church and King.[135] But in the meantime the Queen had driven the movement underground, and, to all appearances, had maintained a firm religious balance between popery and Calvinism.

We must not suppose that, in acting as she did, Elizabeth was going against the mainstream of popular opinion. On the contrary, the evidence suggests that she had widespread public support in curbing Puritan policies. The idea of a 'preaching ministry' had a strong appeal to lower-middle class and middle-class townsmen, especially in the larger cities. But the bulk of the people did not want it. Nor did they welcome Puritan attempts to curb their pleasures. In

1585, Elizabeth had vetoed a bill to create 'the English Sunday', which would have banned cock-fighting, bear-baiting and all profane sports, wakes, markets and fairs, hawking, hunting and rowing – in short, any Sunday activity except worship and 'works of mercy'.[136] This use of the veto – taken against the advice of her Council – was made in the interests of ordinary people who were not effectively represented in the Commons. Elizabeth thought the poor had a right to enjoy themselves on their one day of rest. She was also, and again with popular support, hotly opposed to the use of criminal sanctions in the field of private morals. Cartwright, for instance, wanted a statutory death penalty for adultery, blasphemy and heretical opinion: 'If this be bloody and extreme, I am content to be counted with the Holy Ghost.'[137] Elizabeth would have none of it.

Nor was she prepared to tolerate Puritan assaults on the arts. Indeed, the maintenance of the arts, and of popular pastimes, was closely related; often it was impossible to draw a distinction between the two. The Puritans disliked public performances of any kind, because they drew the rabble away from their sermons, and, since Elizabeth hated sermonizing, this was an additional reason for allowing people their pleasures. The battle was fought in virtually every town and city in the country, with Elizabeth strongly on the side of freedom. In 1575, for instance, at Coventry, she found that the famous cycle of plays had been put down by the Puritan clergy, 'too sour in preaching away their pastimes'. She had them revived. Many games were forbidden within town limits – Shrewsbury would not allow football, or Leicester maypoles – but such practices came to life again when Elizabeth went on progress. In London itself, she successfully kept the theatre going, despite Puritan objections that it spread the plague (those who attended sermons, presumably, were immune). Players had had to be licensed by local authorities since 1531, but from the late 1570s, the Puritan Corporation of London began to use this licensing power to suppress plays altogether. In January 1583, the issue came to a head, when eight people were killed by the collapse of a scaffold at the bear-pit in Paris Garden. This was seen as a judgment, and brought forth John Field's tract, *A Godly Exhortation*. Two months later, in a defensive move, Elizabeth formed the 'Queen's Men', to overawe the City by the use of her name. This was, henceforth, to be the favoured method of circumventing the City, for companies of players, attached to great men like Leicester, Pembroke or Hunsdon, being licensed by the Master of the Revels by the issue of patents under the Council, escaped the control of the London authorities. By attempting to convert their licensing power into the power of suppression, the City, in effect, handed over control of the theatre to central government.[138] Elizabeth underlined the new system by appointing Hunsdon Lord Chamberlain in 1585. He was not only keen on theatricals, but soon acquired a mistress from the fringes of show business, Emilia Lanier.[139]

When Hunsdon died in 1596, and was replaced by Lord Cobham, the City staged a counter-offensive. In 1597 they got a court order to pull down theatres in and about the City limits, and, thanks to a play by Thomas Nashe, *The Isle of Dogs*, which criticized the government, the Council was persuaded to ban all plays for a time. The City fathers, with the odious Topcliffe leading the hunt, began to campaign against theatres anywhere in Middlesex. Nashe had to flee, and Ben Jonson was arrested. But Elizabeth got the Council to rescind the order, and when Cobham himself died, she put Hunsdon's son in his place. The theatre, in fact, was only suppressed for a few months, and thereafter it flourished on the South Bank: the Globe was built in 1598.[140] When Thomas Platter travelled through England in 1599, and saw *Julius Caesar* at the Globe, he found that two, and sometimes three, plays were performed in London every day, 'very marvellously and gracefully'.[141] The fact is, the plays in which Elizabeth delighted at court could not be maintained without the existence of a popular theatre, or vice-versa. Over a wide range of issues, she had a common interest with ordinary people, and she saw to it that those interests were fully upheld. It was another aspect of her theory and practice of balance in the state.

But could she continue to hold the balance in the central machinery of government, the system of allocating jobs, privileges and spoils, and harmonizing policy, on which her own personal authority rested? This was a problem which, by its nature, could never be finally solved, and containing it became progressively more difficult as Elizabeth grew older, the war continued, and her financial outgoings multiplied. Although we tend to see Elizabeth's reign as dominated by the great struggle with Spain, to contemporaries its most marked characteristic – and the feature on which she herself dwelt most proudly – was the long continuance of internal peace. It was, in fact, unprecedented. Never before had the English ruling class contrived to resolve its disagreements for so many years without resorting to the arbitration of force. Welcome as this new phenomenon might be, it produced strains of its own, as politics grew more sophisticated, and men sought power increasingly through institutions – and the ideas that shaped them – rather than through an ancient hierarchy whose origins were military. Then, too, the spread of education, and the rapid diffusion of novel and complex secular notions, led to a willingness to challenge received opinions over the whole spectrum of conduct. What had been taken for granted was now probed, and found wanting. Arguments hitherto accepted as circular were seen to be open-ended.

We get a glimpse of such forces at work in a conversation between Ralegh and his brother Carew, and a group of country friends who included the Rector of Winterbotham, the Reverend Ralph Ironside. Carew was reproved by Sir Ralph Horsey for 'some loose speeches' on the subject of religion: 'Evil words', said Sir Ralph, 'corrupt good morals'. Here was the old world speaking. What danger, therefore, would he incur, asked Carew. 'The wages of sin is death,' said the clergyman. But death was common to all, said Carew. Not the death of the soul, he was told. ' "Soul," quoth Mr Carew Ralegh, "what is that?" ' Better, said the clergyman, to be 'careful how the souls might be saved, than to be curious in finding out their essence' – the old world speaking again. At this point Ralegh interjected, and said in all his studies at Oxford he had never found anyone to define 'soul' satisfactorily. The Rector supplied him with a text from Aristotle. 'Obscure and intricate', said Ralegh; 'try again.' The Rector then produced the definition: 'a spiritual and immortal substance breathed into man by God, whereby he lives and moves and understandeth, and so is distinguished from all other creatures.' 'Yes,' said Sir Walter, 'but what is that spiritual and immortal substance?' 'The soul,' said the Rector, baffled. 'You answer not like a scholar,' said Sir Walter. The exchange was later reported to the authorities.[142] Elizabeth quashed the subsequent investigation into Ralegh's alleged 'atheism'. This was the kind of argument she enjoyed herself, and permitted to the favoured few. She also was 'curious'. But, beyond a very limited circle, she applied 'curious' as a term of reproval, especially to MPs and clergymen. As she grew older, she increasingly denounced what she termed 'the wit of the fox' making its appearance in political life. She felt in her bones the clash of the generations. With each parliament, the MPs looked, indeed were, younger, their ideas and attitudes more alien.

In the 1590s, she had to come to terms with the younger generation. The old guard of her intimates had largely disappeared: only Burghley, Knollys, Hunsdon, all elderly and often away from court, survived, and they dropped off one by one. Elizabeth would not, or perhaps could not, change her methods of running the government. *Semper eadem* was one of her favourite mottoes. She wanted, on the one hand, hard-working professional administrators, with the Burghley stamp about them: the 'scribes'. On the other hand, she wanted to draw to herself clever and adventurous young men of the old blood, to give glitter and glamour to her court, and emphasize the close links of the Tudors with the ancient nobility. There was no problem about the first category. Burghley had written off his elder son Thomas, by his first wife, as a fool, fit for dignified, but not for demanding, employment. But Robert, the clever child of his second wife, Mildred Cooke, he had trained to succeed him. Robert had a twisted spine, the result of a fall from his nurse's arms, and so his upbringing had been heavily concentrated on study and affairs of state, rather than field-sports and arms.[143] He probably sat in parliament for the first time in 1581, when he was only eighteen; and his political mentor was his father's secretary for domestic affairs, Michael Hicks. He was not a religious man, like his father, and altogether more sprightly in his approach to life. His private letters were witty, irreverent and highly readable, in marked contrast to Burghley's solemn expositions of dry fact. He enjoyed poetry, speculation, the theatre, gossip. Though cast, in many respects, in the same political mould as the old Treasurer, he was emphatically a man of the new generation, with fewer principles, a greater love for money, and less scruple in getting it. Robert Cecil has been portrayed as cold, remorseless, vindictive and calculating. But the contemporary evidence gives a different portrait: of an enthusiastic and sometimes rash young man, who married for love the penniless Elizabeth Brooke, daughter of Lord Cobham, and who enjoyed gambling and noisy dinner-parties. Though handsome, he was desperately conscious of his twisted body. He hesitated to propose to Miss Brooke, fearing 'the risk of mislike of my person'; but she took him, and made him a good, though talkative, wife. She was not, he wrote to Hicks, 'to let anybody know that she paid under £3.10 a yard for her cloth of silver. I marvel she is so simple as to tell everybody what she pays for everything.'[144]

The Queen had no particular affection for Cecil, though she occasionally wrote him teasing letters. Like her father, she gave all her chief men nicknames: Leicester was 'eyes', Hatton 'lids', 'mutton' and 'Bellweather', Walsingham her 'moor', Burghley her 'spirit', Essex her 'wild horse'. Sometimes, in a good mood, she called Robert Cecil her 'elf'; usually he was 'pigmy', and the tone was condescending. 'I mislike not the name only because she gives it,' said Cecil with feeling. Obviously he resented it very much.[145] But she recognized his great capacity for work, and a valuable trait he shared with his father: an anxiety to avoid quarrels, or to make them up when they occurred. His first important public service was to act as *rapporteur* at the meetings between Elizabeth and MPs over Mary Queen of Scots in 1586. He took shorthand, and later drafted an account of the transactions for publication, which the Queen edited. When Walsingham died, he automatically took over the bulk of the secretarial work, though he did not get the title (or the pay) until six years later. Eighteen months after taking on the duties, in August 1591, Elizabeth swore him of the Council, 'after a princely, prudent admonition', as he put it. In 1592, he was on the high-powered Commission which tried Sir John Perrot, who claimed to be the Queen's bastard half-brother, and was therefore hated by her relatives, the Careys and the Knollys. The only real evidence against Perrot was his habit of abusing the Queen in his cups: 'Ah, silly woman, now she shall not curb me, she shall not rule me . . . God's wounds! This is to serve a base, bastard, pissing kitchen woman; if I had served any prince in Christendom, I had not been so dealt withal.'[146] She had 'pissed herself with fear' at the time of the Armada. Oddly enough, the Queen did not resent this language, and was grateful to the Cecils, father and son, for trying to save Perrot from the death sentence. When he was condemned, she refused to sign his warrant, and he died in the Tower. In the early 1590s, she allowed Robert to take over more and more of his father's work, and to insinuate himself into the interstices of her government. By February 1594, he was described by an eye-witness as marching through the Presence Chamber on his way to the Queen 'like a blind man, his hands full of papers and head full of matter'.[147] Three years later, by which time he was Secretary in name as well as fact, he was 'the greatest councillor of England . . . without whose favour little good is done here . . . in greatest credit, the Queen passing the most of the day in private and secret conference with him'.[148] He was now, too, the principal manager of government business when parliament met.

Finding a noble 'swordsman' to balance Cecil's emergence as her principal 'scribe' proved beyond Elizabeth's power. The natural choice was Leicester's stepson, the Earl of Essex. He had the ancient blood of the Devereux and the Bourchiers; his mother, Lettice, was a Knollys, and therefore, as Leicester put it, 'of the tribe of Dan' – the untouchable relatives of the Queen. In fact Elizabeth hated Lettice for marrying Leicester in 1578, but she did not hold this against the son. Indeed, she had strong personal grounds to advance his interests. Essex's father, the first Earl, had served the Queen valiantly in Ireland, not indeed to much purpose, but to the best of his abilities and to the limits of his purse. Ireland, then as now, was a highly unpopular assignment, usually unrewarding and often ruinous. It cost the first Earl the bulk of his fortune – he had had to sell estates in Staffordshire, Cornwall, Essex, Wiltshire and Yorkshire – and eventually his life. He died of dysentery in Dublin Castle, in 1576, leaving his heir, then nine, in the care of the Queen and Burghley, who brought him up.[149] Elizabeth met Essex for the first time the same year, at Cecil House in the Strand. He was educated in Burghley's household, alongside the other noble wards, and of course Robert Cecil. But Robert was four years older, and the two boys went to different colleges at Cambridge, Essex to the now-fashionable Trinity, under Whitgift, Robert to his father's old college, St John's. The two were never close, though the assumption that the twisted Robert envied Essex's physique and omni-competence in sports and war-games is pure speculation. After Cambridge, Essex was brought to court by his stepfather in 1584, when he was sixteen, and the next year he was taken campaigning in the Low Countries. By early 1587 he was a regular attender at court, and within a few months he was spending a great deal of time in the Queen's company. His servant, Anthony Bagot, reported in May:

> When she is abroad, nobody near her but my Lord of Essex, and at night, my Lord is at cards, or one game or another with her, that he cometh not to his own lodging till birds sing in the morning ... he told me with his own mouth that he looked to be Master of the Horse within these ten days.[150]

This letter should be taken with some reserve. No doubt Elizabeth welcomed Essex as a palliative to her insomnia. But she did not make him Master of Horse for another six months, and then only after many entreaties from Leicester, who saw his stepson (as Burghley saw Robert Cecil) as his heir to his role in the state. This was Elizabeth's view also, but there is no real evidence she ever felt any physical infatuation for the young Earl. He was to be a state instrument.

Unhappily, there were two powerful reasons why this was not possible. To be the leader of the swordsmen, the principal grandee at court, and in the country the dazzling embodiment of the Queen's favour, Essex needed a great deal of money. This he never possessed. In a strict sense, he was bankrupt from first to last. Leicester, too, had possessed no money when Elizabeth first decided to make him her instrument, but she was able to endow him from his father's confiscated lands, and also to give him a wide range of financial privileges which were then at her command. Even so, Leicester barely remained solvent, and if he had lived he must have come crashing down in ruin. In his will he stated: 'I have always lived above any living I had (for which I am heartily sorry).' He died owing over £50,000, half of it to the Queen, and all he could leave Essex, apart from his town house, was 'the best armour I have, one my Lord Chancellor gave me, two of my best horses, with a George and Garter, in hope he will wear it shortly'. Essex, aged sixteen, was already in debt to the Queen for £10,000, plus £25,475 on his mortgaged lands. His affairs were not in competent hands, for as a boy he formed a close relationship with Gelly Meyrick, the rascally son of a bishop of Bangor, and as soon as he was able he made Meyrick his steward. Meyrick had military and knightly ambitions, and encouraged the Earl to take a full and expensive share in the war: Essex spent £4,000 in the Low Countries, £3,500 during the Armada scare, £7,000 on the Lisbon expedition and £14,000 on the 1591 campaign in Normandy. By this time, all his unmortgaged lands had been sold, and a further £5,000 raised, and spent, by fining tenants in return for long, favourable leases. To balance this expenditure, and the drain on capital, he had only the Queen to look to.

Elizabeth did her best. She paid Essex £1,500 a year as Master of the Horse, plus the perks of the stables; she made over to him £300 a year from the vacant see of Oxford, forwent the interests on his debts, and lent him an additional £3,000 in cash; another £300 a year came from a shady deal in Church property, and in 1590 Elizabeth made over to him Leicester's farm of the sweet wines customs, worth £2,500 a year.[151] She had no more to give him. Her own finances were increasingly strained, and all other major offices of profit were filled. Off to the Lisbon expedition, Essex left a letter outlining his problem:

> My revenue [is] no greater than when I [ceased to be a ward]; my debts at the least two or three and twenty thousand pounds; her Majesty's goodness hath been so great as I could not ask more of her; no way left to repair myself but mine own adventure, which I had much rather undertake than to offend her Majesty with suits, as I have done heretofore. If I should speed well, I will adventure to be rich; if not, I will never live to see the end of my poverty.[152]

But this letter was merely the prelude to fresh expenditure, both military and civil. Essex was congenitally extravagant, not least in generosity to his friends. By 'adventure to be rich', he meant the plundering of Spain. But Essex never made a killing like the *Madre de Dios*, and he was incapable of placing his expeditions on a businesslike basis. Thus he was, after all, forced to 'offend her Majesty with suits', and his relations with her, almost from the start, were poisoned by his importunities for money. In the meantime, he ran a crazy financial empire, whose foundations were wholly insubstantial, and whose very existence depended on his creditors' belief that he had unique access to the Queen, and was head of a powerful party in the state.

This might not have been fatal if Essex's personal characteristics had been cast in the Leicester mould. But the two were very different. Leicester, at least in the Queen's company, always subjected himself to her imperious will, and accepted his role as her instrument. He saw himself as a creature elevated by Tudor power, as his father and grandfather had been, and dependent on that power for mere existence. He knew when to grovel, and his courtesy to his mistress was always excessive, and to some extent absolutely genuine. He did not dispute that Elizabeth was in every respect, morally, intellectually and socially, his superior. And his friendlessness underwrote his submission to the one person who seemed to value him for his own sake. By contrast, Essex was a proud man, whose family had been great when the Tudors were small. He was also an attractive man, who radiated friendship, open-heartedness, and an astonishing frankness which make his letters among the most readable of any written in the reign. While Leicester's monolithic unpopularity remains an enigma, it is easy to see why so many loved Essex. He had no emotional need for Elizabeth, who was in any case a woman in her sixties, and therefore felt no moral duty to return her the obedience and respect which Leicester, in his gratitude, always provided. Essex thought her old-fashioned and narrow-minded, and he greatly underestimated both her intellect and her strength of character. If her relations with him were tinged by affection, they were controlled by a bedrock of common sense and a determination to do her duty to the state. Essex was to be used, if indeed he showed his value to the Commonwealth, but she was not to be bullied, or persuaded, into allowing him more influence than he merited. Essex never grasped this. He felt that her regard for him was an inexhaustible seam to be ruthlessly exploited. We get a hint of his obtuseness in a letter he wrote to Francis Bacon at a time when he was pressing the Queen to make Bacon Solicitor-General. He had, he said, driven Elizabeth into a 'passion' by his repeated refusal to take no for an answer. She 'bade me go to bed if I could talk of nothing else ... In passion I went away ... Tomorrow I will go to her ... On Thursday I will write an expostulating letter.'[153]

The folly of Essex's handling of the Queen was compounded by his belief that her refusal to do what he wanted sprang, not from her own will and judgment, but from the machinations of others. This was a common mistake at her court. Burghley constantly insisted, because he knew it to be true, that Elizabeth always made up her own mind, and that even his powers were limited to access and the chance to deploy convincing arguments. Not only did Essex reject this view; his suspicious nature discerned enmities where none existed. Thus, after unsuccessfully demanding the Chancellorship of Oxford University, he wrote angrily to Robert Cecil:

> Sir R. I have been with the Queen and have had my answer. How it agrees with your letter you can judge, after you have spoken with the Queen. Whether you have mistaken the Queen, or used cunning with me, I know not. I will not condemn you, but leave you to think if it were your own case, whether you would not be jealous. Your friend, if I have cause, R. Essex.[154]

In fact, Cecil's correspondence shows that at no point did he intrigue against Essex. And he did his best to disarm suspicion. While away from court, in 1594, he suggested to Essex:

> My good Lord, you shall not need to make ceremony with me for opening

of any letters, public or private. If public, they be matters where your lord-ship hath a great portage [share]. Of private, I dare trust you, seeing I am no lover.[155]

Essex's suspicions were coloured by the fact that Cecil was steadily promoted by the Queen, and by the coincidence that such promotions were made when he himself was away from court on active service. But the promotions were made on merit, and they occurred in Essex's absence because Elizabeth wanted to avoid prolonged and tiresome scenes with him.

In 1594 the relations between the two men deteriorated over Essex's unsuc-cessful attempt to get his friend Francis Bacon appointed Attorney-General. The obstacle was not, as Essex supposed, Cecil, but the Queen herself. She had been angered by a foolish speech Bacon had made in the Commons, criticizing her tax-policies; she deeply distrusted his character – no doubt she thought he was a homosexual – and was uncertain of his moral capacity to hold high legal office. The dispute was envenomed by Essex's ruthless determination to indict one of Elizabeth's doctors, a Portuguese Jew called Lopez, on a charge of attempting to poison the Queen.[156] Elizabeth doubted Lopez's guilt, and so did Cecil, but both eventually fell in with the prevailing mood of anti-semitism Essex had engineered. On 30 January 1594, returning from interrogating the suspect, Essex and Cecil shared a coach, and the question of the Attorney-Generalship was raised. Cecil said that Bacon had no chance, as he was too young. Essex offensively pointed out that Cecil himself had been raised to high office at a much younger age, and with far less experience, than Bacon. Cecil replied that he had been trained up to the Secretaryship since childhood. Why didn't Bacon aim to be Solicitor-General, for which he had a much better chance – 'of easier digestion to her Majesty', as he put it. Then Essex exploded:

Digest me no digestions. For the Attorneyship for Francis is that I must have; and in that will I spend all my power, might, authority and amity, and with tooth and nail defend and procure the same for him against whom what-soever; and that whosoever getteth this office out of my hands for any other, before he have it, it shall cost him the coming by. And this be assured of, Sir Robert, for now do I fully declare myself.[157]

Essex's words betrayed a curious ignorance of how Elizabeth operated. As Burghley said, the Earl's best friend was the Queen, and he had no enemies; but his behaviour threatened to lose the first, and make multitudes of the second. In the event, he got neither job for Bacon, even though he eventually took Cecil's advice and asked for the Solicitorship. He was always pressing in-temperately for places for his friends. If he gained his point, he boasted of his power over the Queen; if he failed, as he usually did, he accused her of treachery and others of intrigue. His friend Bacon offered good advice, notably in his essay 'On Faction', published in January 1597: 'Mean men must adhere, but great men that have strength in themselves were better to maintain themselves indifferent and neutral.' Essex was incapable of following such counsel. He always invested the whole of his credit in any cause he urged with the Queen, however insignificant the object. And he would not permit indifference in others, either. Those who were not wholeheartedly with him, he marked as enemies. As one of his staff noted: 'He can conceal nothing: he carries his love and his hatred on his forehead.'

It is surprising the Queen put up with Essex for so long. She is alleged to have said: 'I shall break him of his will and pull down his great heart.' This accords with her constant desire to master men of character, but does not explain her persistence in giving him opportunities to do service. The truth, rather, is that she respected his undoubted talents, admired his extraordinary energy and enthusiasm, and believed, at least until 1598, in her well-tried capacity to harness them to the state. But in what role? Here again, Bacon proffered good advice. He told Essex that the Queen was not impressed, but rather alarmed, by his military obsessions. Let him display his ability in the civil sphere. Leicester had always been assiduous in attending Council meetings, he had been a minister in the full sense. Essex, a councillor since 1593, was often absent from the board; he did not pull his weight in the business of government. Instead, he adopted the posture of a soldier, seeking 'popularity'. There was nothing, said Bacon, the Queen hated more: 'I demand whether there can be a more dangerous image that this represented to any monarch living, much more to a lady, and of her Majesty's apprehension.'[158] Essex did not take this advice either. He asked for, and got, first the Mastership of the Ordinance, then the post of Earl Marshal. Both were military jobs.

Essex undoubtedly had some military talent; indeed he had a talent for almost everything. It has been argued that he alone of Elizabeth's commanders recognized that the only way to win a decisive victory over Spanish naval power was to maintain an all-season, all-weather inshore guard on Spanish ports, from a base on Spanish territory – a Gibraltar policy, as it were.[159] But this was probably beyond England's physical capacity, and certainly Elizabeth's willingness to finance it. No other naval man shared the view. His own naval campaigns were flawed. In the summer of 1596, sharing a joint command with Effingham, he took a large amphibious force to Cadiz, broke into the harbour – largely through the enterprise of Ralegh – burnt two of Philip's great 'Apostle' galleons, and captured two more. The destruction impressed even the most case-hardened men in the fleet. Ralegh wrote: 'If any man had a desire to see Hell itself, it was then most lively figured.' The young poet John Donne, serving with the fleet, put it in verse:

> *So all were lost which in the ship were found:*
> *They in the sea being burnt, they in the burnt ship drowned.*[160]

The English destroyed Cadiz, after looting it. The loss of the town, and the evidence of English naval power, added enormously to the war-weariness of Spain. But Essex failed to negotiate the ransom of the Spanish merchant fleet, worth twenty million ducats, lying helpless in the inner harbour, and it was put to the flames. Returning to England, he missed the Spanish plate-fleet, and the booty already acquired slipped through the Queen's hands. Her agent reported: 'All or most of the goods landed in this place was given by the Generals to men of desert and is by them sold to others, and the money received, which will hardly be gotten from them.' The Queen lost most of her £50,000 investment, and blamed Essex, probably with justice. She was angered, too, by his wholesale creations of knights.[161]

Essex's next expedition, the 'Islands Voyage' in 1597, was a failure. Its object was to disperse or destroy a new Armada Philip was gathering in Ferrol. Essex was chief commander, subject to majority decisions of his council of war. His instructions, drafted under Elizabeth's supervision, were clear and made sound strategic sense. He was to go to Ferrol, and if he found the Armada, destroy it and blow up the port. If the Armada had already left, he was to fall back to defend the English and Irish coast. Only if the threat of the Armada was found to be spurious, or removed, was he given discretion to go to the Azores and search for the plate-fleet. Elizabeth put winning the war before plunder. But Essex disregarded her orders. His sailing was delayed by atrocious weather, and by the time he reached Spain he calculated his assault troops were too weak to take Ferrol. He then sailed for the Azores, with a complicated plan which led to the dispersal of his forces, and violent quarrels among the commanders. He missed the plate-fleet, which got safely under the Terceira guns, and arrived back at Plymouth in October to find that only bad weather had prevented Philip's Armada from reaching the English coast.[162] Upbraided by Elizabeth, he boycotted the court, refused to attend the parliament, and protested loudly when Effingham, his co-commander at Cadiz, was made Earl of Nottingham. The Queen felt obliged to forgive him this, and more, for Henri IV was moving towards peace with Spain, and she wanted to present a united front in the complex three-cornered negotiations. But Essex did not make for harmony at the Council table, even when he was willing to attend it. In May 1598, hotly advocating the rigorous pursuit of the war, he drew from Burghley, now seventy-seven, almost deaf, and soon to die, a solemn warning. According to Camden, the old Treasurer told Essex that he breathed nothing but war, slaughter and blood. He passed his open psalter across the board, pointing silently to the 23rd verse of the 55th psalm: 'The bloody and deceitful men shall not live out half their days.'[163]

The point was lost on Essex, but not on Elizabeth. He compounded his folly by making his support for all-out war public, in the form of a letter to Anthony Bacon, which he circulated. It was a breach of his councillor's oath, as well as a palpable bid to win 'popularity'. The Queen's anger smouldered, and finally burst into flame during a painful scene in her Privy Chamber on 1 July. The two of them became involved in a fierce argument, and Essex turned his back in contempt. Elizabeth struck him hard in the face. In nearly forty years, she had never used physical violence against a Councillor. Essex was not a man to accept a blow, especially from a woman, and put his hand on his sword. He said he would not have taken such a thing even from her father. Nottingham, who was listening in horror, placed himself between them, and Essex was got out of the room, still voicing threats. He followed them by a letter, defiant and insolent: 'The intolerable wrong you have done both me and yourself, not only broke all laws of affection, but done against the honour of your sex . . . I cannot think your mind so dishonourable but that you punish yourself for it, how little so ever you care for me.'[164]

Thus, by the summer of 1598, the problem of Essex was getting beyond Elizabeth's capacity to contain it. She was growing old. She still worked extremely hard at her papers, and she could put on a good show for the public, especially at her Accession Day tilts, which she thoroughly enjoyed.[165] A Dutch ambassador, Noel de Caron (whom she knew as Charon, because he was always demanding the bodies of more Englishmen for the wars) left a vignette of her at one of these tilts, in 1595. She spent most of the time chatting to him about politics – economic conditions in the Low Countries, developments in Ireland, Henri IV's reconciliation with Rome and so forth – but occasionally she called out to encourage the knights, and smiled at and bowed to the people, mingling business, pleasure and public relations, as she liked to do.[166] But her appearance, on close inspection, seemed increasingly bizarre. Another ambassador, the Frenchman, Sieur de Maisse, who came to discuss the Franco-Spanish peace talks, sent back a verbal portrait:

She was strangely attired in a dress of silver cloth, white and crimson, or silver 'gauze' as they call it. This dress had slashed sleeves lined with red taffeta, and was girt about with other little sleeves that hung down to the ground, which she was for ever twisting and untwisting. She kept the front of her dress open, and one could see the whole of her bosom, and passing low, and often she would open the front of this robe with her hands, as if she was too hot . . . On her head she wore a garland (of rubies and pearls), and beneath it a great reddish-coloured wig, with a great number of pearls, not of great worth. On either side of her ears hung two great curls of hair, almost down to her shoulders and within the collar of her robe, spangled like the top of her head. Her bosom is somewhat wrinkled . . . As for her face, it is and appears to be very aged. It is long and thin, and her teeth are very yellow and irregular . . . and on the left side less than on the right. Many of them are missing, so that one cannot understand her easily when she speaks.[167]

Decorated like a Christmas-tree to keep up the image of regality in public, in private she often did not bother at all, and hardly concealed from her ministers that she was an old lady, still very much in control, but increasingly inclined to dwell in the past. When Lord Keeper Puckering died in 1597, she quickly appointed Sir Thomas Egerton in his place. He was a friend of Essex's, but his selection was entirely her doing. She had once heard him plead against the crown, admired his lucidity and panache, had promptly brought him into her service and promoted him rapidly. A crown clerk, Stephen Powle, wrote down an eye-witness account of what followed Egerton's reception of his seals. She brought him into her Privy Chamber, together with Burghley, and said to him: 'I began first with a Lord Keeper [Nicholas Bacon], and he was a wise man, I tell you, and I will end with a Lord Keeper.' Burghley: 'God forbid, madam, I hope you will bury four or five more.' Elizabeth: 'No. This is the last.' Then she burst into tears. Egerton, upset, mumbled that Bacon had, indeed, been a wise man, and this brought a fresh outburst of tears. She had both admired and often quarrelled with the witty Bacon, and made jokes about his weight: 'His soul lodgeth well,' she used to say. She covered her confusion by moving towards her bedroom, saying: 'None of the Lord Treasurer's men will come to fetch him away so long as I am here' – Burghley was lame and had to be carried – 'and therefore I will be gone.' But at the door, still in tears, she turned: 'He will never be an honest man until he be sworn. Swear him! Swear him!'[168] There is something almost Shakespearean in this odd little scene, of an ageing monarch conscious of the new generations rolling past her.

On 4 August 1598, Burghley died. Elizabeth had been constant at his bedside – she always, if possible, visited her great servants when they were sick – and had fed him his gruel, as he put it, 'with her own princely hand, as a careful nurse'.

He added, in this last letter to his son Robert, 'And if I may not be weaned to feed myself I shall be more ready to serve her on the earth. If not, I hope to be in heaven a servitor for her and God's Church.' Then a postscript: 'Serve God by serving the Queen, for all other service is indeed bondage to the devil.'[169] Thus a central pillar of the state was removed, and Elizabeth lost someone she had known better and longer than anyone else still living – the end of a unique relationship which had lasted more than half a century. A fortnight later, the English forces in Ireland were annihilated at the Battle of the Yellow Ford. After decades of neglect and improvisation, the Irish spectre, which had haunted English statesmen for centuries, emerged once more, huge and hideous, to confront an exhausted Queen, and a government enfeebled by faction.

᭦᭦.11 ᭦᭦

The Public Burden of a Nation's Care

Throughout Elizabeth's reign, the Irish problem constituted what was potentially the greatest single threat to her régime – more serious than a Scottish intervention, or a direct invasion from Spain, or an internal uprising among English discontents. In the late 1590s the potential threat became actual, and urgent.[1] Mastering it absorbed the bulk of Elizabeth's energies, political intelligence and sense of strategy in the final years of her life. It was her last great effort on behalf of the state she ruled, and in some ways her finest. Never in her reign did she feel so strongly 'the public burden of a nation's care'.[2] Never did she rise so resolutely and stoutly to shoulder it. The effort drained her remaining physical resources, and encompassed her death.

The magnitude of the Irish crisis which confronted her after the disaster of the Yellow Ford was in part her own responsibility. Like other great English statesmen, before and since, she had allowed Ireland to fester through neglect and parsimony. She shared the distaste of almost all Englishmen for the affairs of that unhappy island: she 'grew weary with reading the Irish dispatches'.[3] Her Secretary, Sir Thomas Smith, noted that her tendency to procrastinate was most marked when Ireland was on the agenda.[4] Nor is this surprising. Ireland was the despair of the English. Its poverty and savagery were notorious, closer to the barbarism of the Americas than anything the Elizabethans experienced in their own country, or even in Wales and Scotland. Ireland, wrote Bacon, was 'the last of the daughters of Europe', waiting 'to be reclaimed from desolation and a desert (in many parts) to population and plantation; and from savage and barbarous customs to humanity and civility'.[5] Spenser, who knew the country from personal and bitter experience, compared it to Britain in the Dark Ages, 'at what time England was very like to Ireland as it now stands'. There was, it seemed to him and others, something mysterious and baffling about the insuperability of the Irish 'disease':

Marry, so there have been divers good plots devised, and wise counsels cast already about reformation of that realm; but they say, it is the fatal destiny of that land, that no purposes, whatsoever are meant for her good, will prosper or take effect, which, whether it proceed from the very genius of the soil, or influence of the stars, or that Almighty God hath not yet appointed the time of her reformation, or that he reserveth her in this unquiet state still for some secret scourge, which shall by her come into England, it is hard to be known, yet much to be feared.[6]

Spenser said he had seen an old hag, after the execution of a traitor at Limerick, 'take up his head while he was quartered and suck up all the blood that ran thereout, saying that the earth was not worthy to drink it, and therewith also steeped her face and breast'. The Elizabethans found the savagery of Irish customs hair-raising, more particularly since they corrupted and debased Englishmen sent to deal with the place, as they had already ruined successive waves of Anglo-Irish. The Earl of Connaught boasted in the 1570s that 'I did within one twelve-month hang my own son, my brother's son, and one of the captains of my gallowglass, besides 50 of my own followers.'[7] There the young Ralegh had hanged scores without trial, and it was the usual practice, when a fortified place was taken, to put all the garrison to the sword. The Queen was disgusted, in 1597, to receive a present of the severed head of a leading Irish rebel, Fiach McHugh, sent to her in an access of zeal by one of her more ruffianly captains, Thomas Lee. The Council was ordered to 'send the head back again by the same messenger' to be 'bestowed away with other like fragments of the heads and carcasses of such rebels'.[8]

A few more sensitive souls, like Sir John Harington, had an occasional good word to say for the Irish. 'I was often well entertained,' he wrote, 'and in some sort got ill-will for speaking in praise of their civil usage among our commanders'. But most Englishmen treated the Irish as savages, on a level with the American Indians; men dressed as 'wild Irish' staged mock fights at the royal tilts, as the epitome of barbarous warfare. Irish native dress caused particular offence to the English. Their mantle, wrote Spenser, 'is a fit house for an outlaw, a meet bed for a rebel, and an apt cloak for a thief'. Since the time of the Statutes of Kilkenny under Edward III, a system of legislative *apartheid* had been imposed to keep the English and Anglo-Irish of the Pale from being infected by the barbarous customs of the natives. They might not sell horses to the Irish, or armour or weapons, or consort with them, or intermarry, or wear Irish dress. These laws were constantly being extended and reinforced. Sir John Perrot, Deputy in 1571, laid down:

The inhabitants of cities and corporate towns shall wear no mantles, shorts, Irish coats or great shirts, nor suffer their hair to grow long ... but to wear gowns, jerkins and some civil garments; and no maid or single woman shall put on any great roll or kirchen of linen cloth upon their heads, neither any great smock with great sleeves, but to put on hats, caps, French hoods, tippets or some other civil attire ... All carroughs, bards, rhymers and common idle men or women within this province making rhymes ... to be spoiled of all their goods and chattels and to be put in the next stocks, there to remain till they shall find sufficient surety to leave that wicked 'thrade' of life ...[9]

Even Sir Henry Sidney, a notably sympathetic administrator of backward peoples, who found the Welsh 'among the most easily governable peoples in Christendom', formed a low opinion of the Irish during his spells as Deputy:

Surely there was never people that lived in more misery than they do, nor as it should seem of worse minds, for matrimony among them is no more regarded in effect than conjunction between unreasonable beasts. Perjury, robbery and murder counted allowable. Finally, I cannot find that they make any conscience of sin, and I doubt whether they Christen their children or no; for neither find I a place where it should be done, nor any person able to instruct them in the rules of a Christian ...[10]

The Reformation had left Ireland virtually untouched. Henry VIII's breach with Rome had provoked trouble in the mid-1530s, which had been put down mercilessly, and he had followed this with a declaration turning his 'lordship' of Ireland into a kingdom. But the administrative grip which Cromwell had established on England had never been extended across the Irish Channel. Reformers were few, even in the Pale. Under Edward VI, a rudimentary Protestant hierarchy was set up in Dublin, but this was overthrown under Mary, who extended the settled area to the south-west of the Pale with the first 'plantations', creating two new counties, King's County and Queen's County, named after Philip and herself. The Irish parliament confirmed Elizabeth's religious legislation, but little effort was made to enforce it. Protestant bishops were appointed, but rank and file clergymen did not want to go to Ireland, where benefices were miserable or non-existent. Thus there was an unbridgeable divide between a tiny Protestant ruling class and a mass of semi-paganized Irish. Beyond the Pale, civil disorder was endemic, occasionally erupting into a more general revolt, when the natives gathered round the leader of some ancient Irish or Anglo-Irish clan. Thus, the O'Neills of Ulster rose in 1559–66, the Fitzmaurices of Munster in 1569–72, the Desmonds of Munster in 1579–83. These disturbances became more serious as the religious cold war penetrated to Ireland, and as the hot war with Spain provided the rebels with active Spanish assistance. In the 1580s, the Jesuits moved into Ireland in some strength, filling

what was in effect a religious vacuum, and in no way matched by a corresponding zeal among the Protestant clergy. A parallel Catholic hierarchy was established, and its members subjected to persecution when they were caught. The
Catholic Archbishop O'Hurley was seized and tortured by the Protestant
Primate Archbishop Loftus: there was no rack in Dublin Castle, so his feet
were roasted in hot boots.[11] The Queen was strongly opposed to these methods;
so were the civil commanders. In any case, they were ineffective. The mass of
the Irish remained Catholic, and as the reign progressed became increasingly
militant in their religion, which began to underpin their hostility to England.
'It is incredible', wrote one observer, 'to see how our nation and religion are
maligned, and the awful obedience that all the nation stands in to the Romish
priests, whose excommunications are of greater terror unto them than any
earthly horror whatsoever'.[12] Even in many towns and cities, mayors and
aldermen were Catholic and disloyal, and juries refused to convict in crown
cases.

The English were fundamentally divided on how Ireland was to be ruled.
Elizabeth, characteristically, preferred the minimum of English interference.
She wanted the country loosely administered by the traditional Irish and Anglo-
Irish chieftains, responsible directly to her – especially her Boleyn relatives, the
Butler Earls of Ormond. This policy was not so imprudent as it might seem,
provided the right men could be chosen, educated in 'civility' at the English
court, and then sent as emissaries of English culture among their tribesmen. It
testified to Elizabeth's profound belief in the ancient class-system, and her
confidence in the power of education. And of course it was cheap. At the beginning of Elizabeth's reign, crown revenues in Ireland were barely £5,000 a
year – not enough to meet the cost of the 500-strong garrison in Dublin, let
alone the civil administration. Anything else had to be paid for out of the
Queen's pocket. But this method of indirect rule came in conflict with the
'plantation' system, for the old Anglo-Irish chiefs resented English settlers. If
the plantation policy was pushed, their loyalty collapsed. Then, too, it forbade
any attempt to implant Protestantism, even in the towns. The Irish parliament
would vote subsidies only in return for the non-application of the penal laws,
and this anomaly became more marked as Elizabeth's conflict with the Counter-
Reformation deepened. The men through whom Elizabeth wished to govern
became increasingly committed to the Catholic cause, and sent their children
to be educated in Spain and Flanders.[13]

There were two alternatives to the Queen's policy. Ralegh, as always ingenious and far-sighted, wanted to build up the lesser chieftains and landowners
against their great feudal lords, whom he regarded as incompetent, treacherous

and authoritarian. He despised Ormond and the men through whom Elizabeth worked. Instead, he wanted a gentry class, generating a class of yeomen, both of which would have common economic and political interests with English settlers. But this view was hotly rejected by the English governing establishment in Dublin. Lord Grey, the Deputy, objected strongly to a memo by Ralegh on these lines, as being contrary 'to the judgments of those which, with grounded experience and approved reason, look into the conditions of things'.[14] They – the governors and military men – wanted an outright policy of conquest and plantation. They called for the creation of administrative structures in Connaught, Munster and Ulster, under 'Presidents' or deputy-governors, the replacement of the Celtic land-system by English feudal tenures (which would allow the lands of traitors to be forfeited), and the imposition of English dress, counties, sheriffs, JPs, regular assizes and juries. Sidney, a strong supporter of this approach, told Elizabeth that the Irish wanted direct rule:

> The gentlemen of Cork was begging for it, with open mouth and held up hands to heaven, crying out for justice, and that it might please your Majesty to cause your name to be known amongst them, with reverence, and your laws obeyed, offering to submit themselves, life, lands and goods, to the same.[15]

The 'experts', and especially the lawyers and generals, were pretty well unanimous in agreeing with Sidney. They believed, as did Oliver Cromwell when he came to tackle Ireland, that the English legal system, once fully established and honestly administered, would produce a revolution in Irish attitudes to English rule. Ireland's woes, they argued, were the result of the failure to do this in the past. Thus, the Attorney-General of Ireland, Sir John Davies, commented at the end of the Elizabethan period:

> I note as a great defect in the civil policy of this kingdom, in that for the space of 350 years at least after the conquest first attempted, the English laws were not communicated to the Irish, nor the benefit and protection thereof allowed unto them . . . if the English would neither in peace govern them by the law, nor could in war root them out by the sword, must they not needs be pricks in their eyes and thorns in their sides till the world's end, and so the conquest never be brought to perfection?[16]

The trouble with this policy was that it involved large expenditure: the payment of troops and administrators, the building of forts and towns, and the regular supply of necessities which Ireland did not produce. This was why Elizabeth called the loyal and hardworking Sidney 'a very expensive servant';

his proposals always involved spending cash. Nevertheless, with great reluctance, she began to adopt this approach. Presidencies were created in Connaught and Munster, and settlement followed. But the policy was underwritten by a very inadequate military presence, and the troops were of abysmally low quality: 'the men are such poor and miserable creatures', wrote Ralegh, 'as their captains dare not lead them to serve'. The English settlements were thus precarious. They were, moreover, tiny. By the time Elizabeth came to the throne, little remained of the plantation settlements Queen Mary had tried to create in the new counties carved out of the O'More and O'Connor lands in Leix and Offaly. By trying to implant an English system of land tenure on the tribal system which covered most of Ireland, the authorities merely created legal confusion, in which no one's title was safe, and an 'English' title was in some respects the most vulnerable of all. Settlers found they had to defend their properties by force. Most lacked the means to do so, and the authorities could not supply the troops (there were no police) to enforce the verdicts of the courts. The 'wild' Irish then infiltrated the plantations, which had to be abandoned after a few seasons, and the land reverted to pasture. English experts were unanimous that planting, to be successful, had to be carried out on a considerable scale, backed by private armies, and with sufficient finance to be maintained until they became self-supporting. Several such ventures were organized. In 1572, Sir Thomas Smith, Secretary of State, planned a colony on the borders of Ulster, to be led by his son Thomas. Some 700 colonists were assembled in Liverpool but only 100 actually reached their destination, to find the Irish had destroyed all stone buildings which would have given them shelter throughout the winter. Next spring, Thomas Smith was murdered by his Irish household servants, and the colonists dispersed. Walter Devereux, 1st Earl of Essex, promptly organized a more ambitious plantation, in the nearby territory of Antrim. He and the Queen jointly were to provide 400 horse and 800 foot to protect it, and many leading gentlemen took a share. But this scheme, too, failed as a result of disease, and a shortage of supplies. Again, in 1583–5, after the suppression of the Desmond rebellion, leading courtiers, among them Hatton and Ralegh, organized a plantation to settle the forfeited lands in Munster. The members undertook to farm large blocks of land at a nominal rent to the crown. Among the undertakers was Spenser, who secured 3,000 acres near Cork, at an initial rent of £8 13s. 9d.; Ralegh himself got 12,000 acres near Youghal – the nucleus of the later territorial empire of the Boyles, Earls of Cork. But Ralegh's disgrace ended his active participation in the venture. By 1592, it was found that, of fifty-eight undertakers, only thirteen were resident, and no more than 245 English families had actually settled on the land.

The problem was not so much absentee landlords – for a man who was not physically present and active in Ireland had little hope of collecting any revenue – as the almost total lack of security. Farmhouses, or bawns, had to be fortified, protected by high walls and strong gates locked at night-time. But such places were proof only against small bands of marauders. In the *Faerie Queene*, Spenser gives a picture of the more serious risings the settlers had to expect:

> . . . *with outrageous cry*
> *A thousand villeins rownd about them swarmed*
> *Out of the rocks and caves adjoining nye;*
> *Vile caitive wretches, ragged, rude, deformed,*
> *All threatening death, all in straunge manner armed;*
> *Some with uneldy clubs, some with long speares,*
> *Some rusty knives, some staves in fier warmed . . .*

The men who planned the colonies might boast to prospective settlers: 'You may keep a better house in Ireland for £50 a year than in England for £200 a year,' but experience showed that such houses were liable to be burned down without warning, and their inhabitants massacred. 'There is no land in the world', wrote one observer, 'of so continual war within himself, nor of so great shedding of Christian blood, nor of so great robbing, spoiling, preying and burning, nor of so great wrongful extortion continually, as Ireland.'

Moreover, in Ulster, the wildest of the Irish provinces, no administration was imposed at all. The Queen's writ did not run beyond the fort on the Blackwater, which guarded the approach to Dublin and the south. Beyond it, the O'Neills held sway, like barbarous medieval princes, raising mercenary armies from the wild Scots of the Highlands and Islands, who were constantly settling in the Ulster glens. When Shane O'Neill, paramount chief of Ulster, came to court to do homage to Elizabeth in 1562, he brought with him a bodyguard of 'gallow-glasses', with long hair over their eyes, 'surplices' of saffron, and mantles made of the skins of wild beasts. The London mob gazed at them as 'they do to them of China or America'. Shane could speak no English, not even the mixture of English and Irish used in the southern towns and known as gallimaufry. He made his homage in Erse, which to the court sounded like 'howling'.

It was, perhaps, only a matter of time before some Ulster chieftain of above-average intelligence arose to challenge the fragility of English rule, and exploit the enmity of Spain. Hugh O'Neill, made Earl of Tyrone in 1585, illustrated the weakness of Elizabeth's policy of indirect rule: her inability to ensure the continuing loyalty of her instruments. He was the ablest Irishman of his generation. Camden gives a little vignette of him:

A strong body he had, able to endure labour, watching and hunger; his industry was great, his mind great and able to the greatest business; much knowledge he had of military skills and a mind most profound to dissemble, in so much as some did then foretell that he was born to the very great good or hurt of Ireland.[17]

Tyrone had spent a good deal of time at the English court. He could assume at will the manners and appearance either of an English gentleman or of an Irish warlord. He had helped to put down the Desmond rebellion in the early 1580s – indeed, it was for that reason he was given his earldom. But he was subtle and disingenuous, a born diplomat whose word could not be trusted, and whose intentions were always difficult to fathom. For the first time, the Irish had a leader versed in modern military technology and with a grasp of the political scene beyond Ireland, who knew how to exploit Elizabeth's relations with Scotland, the factions at her court, the religious issue, and the war with Spain. Hitherto, Irish rebel chieftains had never commanded regular troops, or organized commissariats. They had been disposed of comparatively easily by small English armies. On average, there were only 1,000–5,000 English soldiers to keep order, and even during the Desmond rebellion the number had never risen above 9,000. For the first time, Tyrone equipped his men with modern arms. He had 300 of them drilled and dressed in red coats, 'like English soldiers', and even some cavalry.[18] He used the customary Irish guerrilla tactics, and his army normally lived off the land. As a force it was virtually confined to summer campaigning, for in the winter his Celtic peasant troops worked the land. But he could, in the right conditions, summon and deploy regular formations, able to meet the limited English forces in open combat, and storm forts normally garrisoned only by twenty to thirty men.

In 1595 Tyrone took the forbidden title of 'The O'Neill' and made contact with the Spaniards, who got money and supplies to him the following year. The Spanish military and naval effort was now increasingly geared to the Irish theatre, the real weakness in Elizabeth's armour. The Armada Philip prepared in 1595–6, and which was wrecked by the Cadiz expedition, and the Spanish invasion fleets of 1597 and 1599, were primarily designed to open up an Irish front. Spanish commanders did not like fighting in Ireland any more than the English did. As one of them remarked in disgust, 'This land seems destined especially for the Princes of Hell.' But if the Spanish had been able to land a sizeable force, with naval support, it is hard to see how Elizabeth's slender grip on the country could have been maintained, and the loss of Ireland would have changed the whole strategy of the war. As it was, Tyrone inflicted more damage on English interests than any other opponent Elizabeth had to face. His victory at the Yellow Ford was the greatest military disaster the English ever suffered in Ireland. The defeat sprang from the determination of Sir Henry Bagenal, the Marshal of the Army, to relieve the key fort on the Blackwater. Tyrone had attempted to storm it in 1597, but had been bloodily repulsed by the garrison, under a determined Welshman, Captain Thomas Williams. The next year, he blockaded the fort, in an attempt to starve it out. Bagenal went north with 4,000 foot-soldiers, against the advice of Ormonde, the Lieutenant-General and his nominal superior, who thought the fort would have to be abandoned. But Bagenal had a personal grievance against Tyrone, who had abducted his sister, married her under duress, and then ill-treated her. He took with him only 300 cavalry – all he could gather in the time, and not enough for the task. At the Yellow Ford on the Blackwater, which he had to force to relieve the fort, he found Tyrone's army, on the left flank, drawn up behind a bog, supported by the troops of the O'Donnells, the other leading Ulster chieftains, entrenched beside a wood on the right. Bagenal advanced in column of regiments, two in the van, commanded by himself, two in the main body, and two in the rearguard. He was, in fact, moving straight into a trap, relying on superior firepower. But many of the Irish had firearms, and knew how to use them. The van, caught by fire from both sides, broke in disorder, and fell back on the main body. The confusion was increased by desperate efforts to extricate a cannon, which had stuck in the mud, and by the explosion of a powder-barrel. The Irish mercenaries in the English army promptly deserted, as did many of the raw English recruits. With the van and the main body mixed up, the Irish took the opportunity to charge. This was the moment, of course, for the English to deploy cavalry, the one arm the Irish really feared. But none was available. The two regiments of the rearguard attacked again and again to provide a protective screen for the frightened mass of the two forward bodies, but they were not enough to prevent a general retreat, and the inevitable heavy losses which followed. Bagenal was killed, and 1,300 of his men were reported lost or missing; about 700 more seem to have deserted. The destruction of his army led to a virtual collapse of English administration through most of Ireland. Settlers, like Spenser, had to abandon everything and run to the towns – or England. The authorities in Dublin panicked, and the Lords Justices wrote to Tyrone in grovelling terms, asking for an armistice.

Elizabeth always hated war. Her instincts were pacifist. But it must be said she was never unnerved by reverses. Her reaction to the Yellow Ford defeat was angry and defiant. How monstrous it was, she fumed, 'that it must be the Queen of England's fortune (who hath held down the greatest enemy she had) to make a base Irish kerne to be accounted so famous a rebel'.[19] She was shocked by the pusillanimity of the Dublin government, and instantly repudiated their request for terms. She wrote them a blazing letter:

> We may not pass over this foul error to our dishonour, when you of our Council framed such a letter to the traitor, after the defeat, as never was read the like, either in form or substance, for baseness, being such as we persuade ourself, if you shall peruse it again, when you are yourselves, that you will be ashamed of your own absurdities, and grieved that any fear or rashness should ever make you authors of an action so much to your sovereign's dishonour and to the increasing of the traitor's insolency.[20]

There was never the slightest doubt in her mind that the rebellion had to be crushed by military force, whatever the cost. Yet she knew very well that the Yellow Ford disaster came at a bad time. During the mid-1590s, the English economy was undergoing the worst recession of her reign. The days of rapid mercantile expansion, which characterized the decades 1570–90, were over. The war with Spain, which paradoxically had enormously increased the prosperity of the Dutch, had hit the English maritime counties hard, and they were the main source of direct taxation. Parliamentary subsidies, granted without too much murmuring by the Commons, raised over £2 million over the 1590s decade, but each subsidy brought in less than the last, and it was evident that direct taxation was having a depressing effect on at least some forms of economic activity. Even so, revenue did not meet expenditure, now averaging well over £300,000 a year, and the gap was filled by sales of crown lands and forced loans. Elizabeth was painfully aware of the crushing burden of emergency war-taxation. In one of her Irish letters, almost a cry from the heart, she speaks of it as something

> which our crown of England cannot endure, without the extreme diminution of the greatness and felicity thereof, and alienation of our people's minds from us, considering that for these only rebellions in Ireland, we have been forced to part with many of our ancient possessions, which are part of the flowers of our crown, and to draw from our subjects (a thing contrary to our nature) those great payments . . . they would not so willingly have borne, nor we so justly could have imposed upon them.[21]

Cecil's letters betray an equal anxiety that the Exchequer might not be able to meet regular demands on it: 'the receipts are so short of the issue that my hair stands upright to think of it.'[22]

The fear of popular unrest as a result of the government's financial impositions was not entirely a figment of the Queen's imagination. Hitherto, her reign had been singularly free of rural disorder provoked by food-shortages. It was one of the great features of her rule, in which she took understandable pride, and in which both her ministers and the people themselves rejoiced. No such prolonged period of calm had been known before in English history, and it contrasted strikingly with reports of peasant riots in other parts of Europe. Much of the credit can be assigned to her government. Both she and her Council kept a close watch on food prices and supplies, and reacted speedily to reports of shortages.[23] But such success depended to a great extent on luck. A sixteenth-century economy, with its overwhelming reliance on agriculture, could survive one bad harvest without difficulty; two in succession posed serious problems; a third meant crisis. In the period 1594–7 there were no less than four disastrously wet harvests.[24] In 1595, average wheat prices rose to 7s. a bushel, twice the average of 1592; in London it was 10s., in Bristol up to 15s., in Shrewsbury 18s.; rye rose correspondingly, and oatmeal even more.[25] Even at sky-high prices, food was not always available, especially in the north and west. Camden reports that, in the north, the poor sometimes had to travel sixty miles to buy bread.

The government and local authorities took vigorous action. Thus Shrewsbury, after negotiations with the Council, bought 3,200 bushels of rye from Denmark and Danzig, and sold it at 4s. below the market-price. Some was baked into small loaves for sale to the poor. Bristol bought 24,000 bushels of Danish rye. Elizabeth took a direct hand in curbing profiteers, especially engrossers (those who cornered supplies until the market-price rose) and forestallers (those who speculated in 'futures'). The Council was told:

> Her Highness doth verily think the fault thereof, in part, to be the covetous disposition of such as be farmers and corn-masters, that not acknowledging God's goodness, do seek immoderate gain by enhancing the prices of corn and grain, to the great oppression of the poorer sort.[26]

She allowed grain to be imported free of duty, and after December 1595 threw open the ports until further notice. She urged the Council to impose heavy fines and imprisonment on profiteers, and the gentry to live on their estates and dispense 'hospitality'. Well-to-do people were to do without suppers on Wednesdays, Fridays and fast-days, and give the money saved to the poor; Whitgift was told that his clergy were to preach sermons insisting that 'gain is most ungodly that is gotten by pinching and starving of poor people'; rectors and vicars were to send lists of defaulters to the Archbishop, and he was to report personally to the Queen.

These efforts were not very effective, and any system of direct rationing was, of course, beyond the capacity of a Tudor government. Moreover, efforts to control prices conflicted with the Council's own attempts to amass food supplies for military purposes. This was one additional reason why the extension of the fighting in Ireland, and the consequent need for a huge expeditionary force, was so unwelcome. For practical purposes, Ireland was barren. Food supplies for the English army had to be shipped over. This was the rock on which Richard II's Irish wars had foundered (always his shade seemed to haunt the Queen!). But there was another reason, too. With the risk of peasant discontent, it was doubly important to keep to a minimum the numbers of footloose and penniless soldiers and ex-soldiers wandering around the countryside. Experience showed that these bands supplied the focus for local rioting, and of course the expertise to make riots formidable. And, often, protests against high prices blended with protests against overseas service, especially as the draft fell most heavily on the poorest elements. Service in France and the Low Countries was increasingly unpopular, but service in Ireland was the most hated of all, and with good reason. As a matter of fact, the government had no legal basis for exacting overseas service at all. On the contrary, a number of statutes provided specifically against it.[27] The government did not want to take the risk of asking parliament for statutory powers. It sought, instead, to give the impression that the old statutes had lapsed, and, from time to time, punished savagely those who reminded the public of their existence. Thus, in 1596, at Colchester, Sir John Smythe, who fancied himself as a military expert, appeared at the musters and made a speech saying that parliamentary authority was needed before mustered men could be sent abroad. He was brought before the Star Chamber, and his excuse that he was drunk at the time brushed aside. He was made to sign a statement that 'the Queen's Majesty both by the common law and by statute laws of this realm may lawfully compel and enforce her subjects to serve her beyond the seas in any parts where and whensover it shall please her Highness, and that the experience of all times hath been so'. Despite this, he was kept in the Tower for two years.[28] The thoroughness with which the Council investigated this affair betrayed their sensitivity on the issue, as did their conviction that peasant discontent and hatred of military service were combining to create secret societies in the countryside. This was why gypsies, and other vagrants, were sometimes tortured to elicit information.[29]

In the light of all these factors, it took courage and determination on Elizabeth's part to send a major expedition to Ireland. Campaigning in Ireland posed special problems. It was possible to fill the ranks with locally-recruited Irish troops, who were willing to serve for low pay. But the English captains did not like them, and recommended that they should never constitute more than 6 per cent in any unit. They deserted at the first opportunity, and often took their arms with them, for sale to the rebels. Though Tyrone got weapons from both Glasgow and Spain, his chief source of supply (as in so many guerrilla movements in our own times) was the occupying forces. 'There is no soldier with a good sword', wrote Sir John Dowdall, 'but some Irish merchant or townsman will buy it from him.' Then, at a profit, it was passed on to the rebels: they would pay up to £4 for a sword sold by a deserter for 12s. and 3s. for a pound of powder sold for 12d.[30] In default of reliable Irish troops, men had to be drafted from Wales, Cheshire, Shropshire and other western areas. They hated the very thought of Ireland, where malaria, or marsh-fever as they called it, was endemic. All united to curse the incessant Irish rain, which destroyed the grain supplies shipped from England, rusted weapons and equipment, and rotted their clothes. The whole island, wrote Moryson, was 'uneven, mountainous, soft, watery, woody and open to winds and floods of rain, and so fenned that it hath bogs upon the very tops of mountains, not bearing man or beast but dangerous to pass'.[31] The English general, Mountjoy, complained: 'Our tents are often blown down, and at this instant it doth rain into mine, so that I can scant write.'[32] The wet weather of the 1590s, so destructive in England, was still worse in Ireland, 'which maketh me to think', wrote Sir Geoffrey Fenton, 'that if God hath given liberty to the witches of that country (which aboundeth with witches), they are all set on work to cross the service by extraordinarily unseasonable weather.'[33] The more sensible men – Mountjoy was one – abandoned their campaign finery and concentrated on keeping warm and dry. Mountjoy wore an extra pair of woollen stockings, three waistcoats, and a specially thick ruff; for good measure, he wound a 'russet scarf' three times round his neck.[34] But many of the troops had no such resources, and had only the clothes they stood in.

Getting disciplined bodies of troops to Ireland thus posed extraordinary problems. Unless heavily escorted, the drafted men tended to slip away on the march to Chester, the embarkation point. In October 1598, a large body of men mutinied before they reached the town, and scattered all over the countryside. The Cheshire justices were ordered by the Council to round them up and, when captured, put them in the pillory with paper caps on their heads.[35] But of course many of the men never reached Chester, and there, at the port, there was an organized racket, run by the captains, to falsify musters. On the whole, good captains preferred to serve in the Low Countries rather than in Ireland. One of the muster officials, Maurice Kyffin, told the Treasury that the captains, and the muster-men they corrupted, had 'irrecuperably damnified the state'. Private soldiers who informed on their captain's frauds risked being hanged as mutineers once the officials' backs were turned, and Elizabeth was sardonically informed that she would be better off paying £1,000 a year to certain captains to keep them from ruining her army.[36] The Irish wars brought to a head her long-smouldering resentment against the whole crooked tribe of captains. No wonder she enjoyed the character of Falstaff, in which Shakespeare personified all the vices of the caste. 'A captain!' exclaimed Doll Tearsheet. 'God's light, these villains will make the word as odious as the word "occupy", which was an excellent good word before it was ill-sorted.'[37] ('Occupy' was a polite expression for sexual intercourse.) Elizabeth could say 'amen' to that, as also to Falstaff's description on his recruiting methods:

I have misused the King's press damnably. I have got, in exchange of a hundred and fifty soldiers, three hundred and odd pounds . . . I press'd me none but such toasts-and-butter, with hearts in their bellies no bigger than pin's heads, and they have bought out their services; and now my whole charge consists of . . . slaves as ragged as Lazarus in the painted cloth, where the Glutton's dogs licked his sores; and such as indeed were never soldiers, but discarded, unjust serving-men, younger sons to younger brothers, revolted tapsters, and ostlers trade-fall'n . . . No eye hath seen such scarecrows. I'll not march through Coventry with them, that's flat.[38]

But at least Falstaff turned up on the battlefield. Many actual captains, as Elizabeth well knew, were absentees, pocketing the cash and serving by deputy. Very occasionally, a captain was brought to book. Thus, John Chamberlain reports on 11 June 1597: 'This term, here was one Long, a captain of Somersetshire, condemned in the Star Chamber in 500 marks and to stand in the pillory, for chopping and making portsale of his soldiers.'[39] Long was unlucky. Probably he lacked high-up contacts. Most captains attached themselves to great men, and thus secured immunity from inquiry or punishment.

There was even larger-scale fraud in the commissariat. From Sir George Carew, the Irish Treasurer-at-War, downwards, virtually everyone in this department swindled the Queen, though the facts did not emerge until twenty years later. The biggest frauds were over clothing, so important in the Irish wars. In the winter of 1598–9, the merchants, who were in league with both the commissariat and the captains, were paid for supplying suits of clothes to all the troops. In fact they delivered only 2,500 and some of these were rotten. The situation got so desperate that the captains won a victory that had been denied them in the Low Countries – the right to handle clothing supplies themselves – and this made matters infinitely worse; it was soon revoked.[40]

Thus in Ireland Elizabeth had to cope with problems which had baffled her in the Netherlands ten years earlier, but in a more acute form, and on a much bigger scale.

She also had to find a commander-in-chief. There is evidence that, by the summer of 1598, Elizabeth had come to a parting of the ways with Essex. She was tired of his scenes and tearful reconciliations. She was not yet prepared to break him, she still admired his gifts, and was still anxious to employ them in her service. But henceforth he must behave within the accepted disciplines of her court and government. She undoubtedly made this clear to him at the time. After Essex's death, the French ambassador, the Count de Beaumont, reported a conversation he had had with her on the subject of the Earl. She

> touched upon the subject of the Earl's death, and said, that having been apprehensive from the impetuosity of his temper, and his ambition, that he would precipitate himself into destruction by some ill design, she had advised him above two years before to content himself with pleasing her on all occasions, and not to show such an insolent contempt for her, as he did; but to take care not to touch her sceptre, lest she should be obliged to punish him according to the laws of England, and not according to her own, which he had found too mild and favourable for him to fear any suffering from them; but that her advices, however salutory and affectionate, could not prevent his ruin.[41]

Word of this advice got around. Thus John Chamberlain saw Essex at Burghley's funeral in August 1598, and reported: 'Methought [he] carried the heaviest countenance of the company . . . the Queen says he hath played long enough upon her, and that she means to play a while upon him, and to stand as much upon her greatness as he hath done upon stomach.'[42] Francis Bacon, too, noted that a turning point had been reached: 'I did as plainly see his over-throw chained, as it were, by destiny to that journey as it is possible for any man to ground a judgment upon future contingents.'[43]

This being so, why did Elizabeth give Essex the key command in Ireland? There is no easy answer to this question. We can rule out the suggestion that Elizabeth sent him to Ireland with the deliberate intention of encompassing his ruin, knowing that the task was beyond him. Having given her warning, she was on comparatively friendly terms with Essex in the autumn and winter of 1598-9. She did not give him the Mastership of the Wards (vacated by Burghley's death), as he had hoped, but she is recorded as dancing with him in January 1599, the last occasion, so far as is known, when their contact was warm and intimate.[44] The truth is, the Irish command posed almost as many difficulties as the army itself. No man of high status wanted it. Ralegh, who was now back in the Queen's high favour, could have had the job for the asking. But he was busy rebuilding Sherborne Abbey to his taste, and showed no interest. His solution was to have Tyrone murdered: 'It can be no disgrace', he wrote to Cecil, 'if it were known that the killing of a rebel were practiced; for you see that the lives of annointed princes are daily sought, and we have always in Ireland given head-money for the killing of rebels.'[45] The Queen would not hear of it. Her own choice as commander was Sir Charles Blount, Lord Mountjoy – the man who eventually carried out the operation successfully. But Essex, according to Camden, objected strongly: Blount, he argued, was a man of little experience of war, of small estate, and 'too much drowned in book-learning'. Another possibility, Sir William Russell, an Irish 'expert', turned it down: 'Sir William Russell hath absolutely refused to go.'[46] Sir Richard Bingham, the most experienced Irish commander, was an obvious choice: but he was ill, and early in 1599 he died.

Since the Yellow Ford disaster, Essex had been showing an increasing interest in Irish affairs, apparently on Francis Bacon's advice.[47] He took a leading part in the Council debates about Ireland in the winter of 1598-9, objecting to various men put forward, and laying down that the man to be sent should be 'some prime man of the nobility, strong in power, honour and wealth, in favour with military men, who had been before general of an army'. Essex, said Camden, 'seemed to point the finger at himself'. Apart from wealth, he had all these qualifications. The Queen probably picked him, in the end, because he had the undoubted capacity to attract able men to his service, even in such an unpopular theatre as Ireland. If a big army was needed, and she was now convinced that it was, Essex had real claims to lead it. But she cannot have taken the decision without the gravest misgivings, and Essex, too, was in two minds. He recognized that he had been given a last opportunity to distinguish himself, in the biggest and most difficult appointment the Queen had to bestow. He knew the risks, but the rewards of success would be, in political terms, enormous. Pride won the battle. This, I think, is the correct interpretation to be placed on the curious letter he wrote to his friend the Earl of Southampton on 4 January 1599:

Unto Ireland I go. The Queen hath irrevocably decreed it; the Council do passionately urge it, and I am tied to my reputation to use no tergiversation. And as it were *indecorum* to slip the collar now, so were it *minime tutum*, for Ireland would be lost, and although it perished by destiny, yet should I be accused of it, because I saw the fire burn, was called to quench it, and yet gave no help.[48]

He claimed to be the greatest man in the state: he could not decline to shoulder its greatest task.

Essex reached Ireland early in April 1599, and was almost immediately in difficulties. He claimed, then and later, that his expedition had been sabotaged by his enemies at home. 'Is it not known', he wrote to Elizabeth, 'that from England I receive nothing but discomforts and soul's wounds? Is it not lamented of your Majesty's faithfullest subjects, both there and here, that a Cobham and a Ralegh – I will forebear others, for their places' sake – should have such credit and favour with your Majesty when they wish the ill-success of your Majesty's most important action?'[49] But this was merely Essex's growing paranoia. Ralegh had the best of reasons for wishing all success to the venture – the safety of his own estates in Ireland. He had, by this stage, become disgusted with Essex's relentless faction-fighting, his sheer divisiveness, but nothing in the surviving documents indicates any anxiety, on his part, that Essex should fail. Cecil, too, did his best. He performed prodigies to finance the expedition, in the end being forced to go to the City to raise a loan at 10 per cent, more than the Queen usually paid.[50] Essex's army was easily the largest, and on the whole the best equipped, England had ever sent to Ireland. The only possible evidence of sabotage is the failure to supply enough horses.[51] But it is inconclusive and circumstantial. Most likely the fault, even here, lay with Essex himself: he seems to have paid virtually no attention to commissariat and supply problems, though he was well aware of their importance. And if horses were one of his chief problems, as he claimed, why did he appoint as commander of his cavalry the inexperienced and unreliable Earl of Southampton, purely on grounds of personal friendship? All his decisions, in organizing his army, seem to have been based on factional and political considerations.

The cavalry appointment brought his first clash with Elizabeth. She had many reasons for disapproving of Southampton. He had married against her wishes, indeed in flagrant and open defiance of them.[52] Her grievance on this score was in no way mitigated – it was increased – by the fact that she suspected him of homosexuality, a characteristic of a number of members of the Essex circle, including Francis Bacon.[53] (Indeed, in Ireland, though Elizabeth was not to know of it, Southampton shared a tent with one Captain Piers Edmonds, and 'would cull and hug him in his arms, and play wantonly with him'.[54]) The sort of wild behaviour in which Southampton indulged had been illustrated the year before, when he had made a scene in the Presence Chamber after Elizabeth had gone to bed. The Earl, Ralegh and a Mr Parker had been playing primero. Ambrose Willoughby, the Squire of the Body on duty, following standing court orders required them to give over. Soon after, he spake to them again that, if they would not leave, he would call on the guard to put down the board: which Sir Walter seeing, put up his money and went his ways [he was presumably winning]. But my Lord of Southampton took exceptions at this, and told him he would remember it. And so, finding him between the Tennis Court wall and the garden, struck him, and Willoughby pulled off some of his locks. The Queen gave Willoughby thanks for what he did in the Presence, and told him he had done better if he had sent him to the Porter's Lodge to see who durst have fetched him out.[55]

Elizabeth had explicitly to ban a duel Southampton planned to fight with Lord Grey of Wilton. They should, she said, 'reserve yourself for [her] service, and not to hazard them on private quarrels.'[56] The Earl not only had rows himself, he encouraged others. One of his protegés, Sir Charles Danvers, picked a quarrel with a Hampshire neighbour, Henry Long. Long told him that 'wheresoever he met him, he would untie his points and whip his etc with a rod: calling him ass, puppy, fool and boy.' Danvers killed Long, not even in a fair fight, and Southampton smuggled him out of the country. This had been in 1594, but it still rankled with Elizabeth five years later.[57] The idea that Southampton should be made Lord-General of Horse was preposterous. Indeed, before Essex set out, Elizabeth had explicitly forbidden him to give Southampton any particular office. The cavalry command added insult to disobedience, for the Queen, with her usual sound grasp of the realities of strategy, recognized that the cavalry was England's war-winning weapon if, as she hoped, it came to an open battle with Tyrone. It was the one arm in which England held a decisive advantage, properly used. Lord Grey, Southampton's senior in experience and everything else, was the obvious man to command. Instead, he was placed under the Earl, his bitter enemy, and they promptly had another fight. This provoked the first in Elizabeth's series of angry letters to Essex:

For the matter of Southampton, it is strange to us that his continuance or displacing should work so great an alteration either in yourself (valuing our commandments as you ought) or in the disposition of the army, where all the commanders cannot be ignorant that we not only not allowed of your desire for him, but did expressly forbid it, and being such a one whose counsel can be of little, and experience of less, use. Yea, such a one as, were he not lately fastened to yourself by an accident . . . you would have used many of your old lively arguments against him for any such ability or commandment. It is therefore strange to us, knowing his worth by your report, will dare thus to value your own pleasing in things unnecessary, and think by your own private arguments to carry for your own glory a matter wherein our pleasure to the contrary is made notorious.[58]

There were other arguments between the Queen and her Deputy over marginal points, notably his reckless creation of knights. He might argue that the chance of getting a knighthood was one chief factor why so many were anxious to serve under him: his prodigality in this respect was notorious. But Elizabeth knew that a man who went soldiering for an Essex knighthood was usually a rascal. In any case, some of the creations took place before Essex's men had heard a shot fired in anger. Not only the Queen, but the whole court was shocked by their numbers, as Chamberlain reported:

It is much marvelled that this humour should so possess [Essex] that, not content with his first dozens and scores, he should thus fall to huddle them up by half-hundreds, and it is noted as a strange thing that a subject in the space of six or seven years (not having been six months together in any one action) should, upon so little service and small desert, make more knights than are in all the realm besides, and it is doubted that if he continue this course he will shortly bring in tag and rag, cut and long tail, and so draw the order into contempt.[59]

But the Queen's chief grievance was the central one, that Essex was mismanaging the campaign, and flying in the face of her own carefully-considered and unambiguous orders. She knew very well that a large army like Essex's would rapidly deteriorate, both in numbers and morale, during an Irish campaigning season, unless it fought a general action at the earliest opportunity. The rebellion was widespread, but the heart of Tyrone's power was in Ulster. There lay his main army, and there, since he had now abandoned the role of mere guerrilla chieftain and was aspiring to rule the island by open conflict, he would be obliged to give battle if the English army made an appearance in strength north of the Blackwater Fort. Essex's first and essential task, therefore, as soon as his army was assembled in Dublin, was to force his way north. Once Tyrone's main army was defeated and scattered, the pacification of the rest of the country could be undertaken at leisure.

This was obvious to the Queen. It is obvious to us. It is extraordinary that it was not equally obvious to Essex. Yet in fact, from the moment he landed in Dublin, he seems to have decided to set about the campaign in precisely the reverse order. His reasoning is difficult to fathom.[60] He arrived in Dublin in a mood of pessimism, even defeatism, as his letters testify. His feelings were confirmed by the advice he received from the Council at Dublin Castle, still shocked and bewildered by the Yellow Ford disaster, and the consequent erosion of English power throughout the country. Many of them were more anxious about the safety of their properties in the south and west, and in the Pale itself, than by the core of the threat in Ulster, where they held no land. At all events, from self-interest, fear or genuine conviction, they unanimously accepted Essex's decision to move, not to Ulster, but through Leinster and Munster. This occupied him from May until July 1599. He met little opposition, but by the time he returned to Dublin his army had dwindled to half its theoretical size – the cavalry was particularly badly hit by losses and sickness – and he was short of supplies. He was already stressing, in his reports to the Queen, that 'the war of force will be great, costly and long', implying that negotiations with Tyrone were a permissible, and possibly even a desirable, alternative to the policy of unconditional surrender of the rebels, on which the Queen had constantly and vociferously insisted. All he had to show, so far, was the taking of Cashel Castle, which the Queen, rightly, dismissed as seizing 'an Irish hold from a rabble of rogues'.

Meanwhile, Sir Henry Harrington, with a separate detachment, had been badly beaten in Wicklow, and on 4 August Sir Conyers Clifford, with another, had been routed and killed in the Curlew Hills, in the north-west. By 21 August, when Essex held a Council of War in Dublin, his effective forces were little more than 3,500 foot and 300 horse.[61] 'Every town and place of garrison is a hospital', he wrote to the Council, 'where our degenerate countrymen are glad to entertain sickness as *supersedas* for their going to the field . . . and we can never make account what numbers we have of them.'[62] To Elizabeth, excusing his failure, he placed the blame on individual subordinates and, still more basely, on his men:

> your army, which never yet abandoned the body of any principal commander being dead, doth now run away from their chief commander, being alone and in fight [he meant Clifford] . . . your people had rather be hanged for cowardice, than killed or hurt in service.[63]

Elizabeth was always at her most tense when committed to an active war situation, especially one involving great and unrepeatable expense, where time was of the essence, and strict adherence to carefully-considered orders imperative. It was on such occasions that she felt most powerfully and painfully the limitations of her sex, which debarred her from the physical control of events in person, and which forced her to commit her reputation and her nation's security into the frail hands of subordinates, who lacked both her intellectual capacity to drive to the heart of the matter, and her moral resolution to pursue it to the end. What a miserable creature was Essex when put to the test! Since reaching Dublin his conduct had been in the highest degree insubordinate, imprudent and pusillanimous. He had wasted an army, the raising of which had placed almost intolerable burdens on her resources. Thus he risked imperilling not merely the English position in Ireland but the financial solvency of the state which was the engine of her war-effort against Spain and the key to her world strategy. He had done this not in the face of unforseeable misfortunes – for they had all been calculated in advance – but by recklessly defying her commands. Confronted by the results of his folly, he sought refuge in blaming his officers, in conjuring up mythical enemies at home, and, most contemptible of all, in blackguarding his troops, whose sufferings sprang in large part from his own incompetence. Those at court caught only faint echoes of Elizabeth's anger: 'The Queen is nothing satisfied with the Earl of Essex's manner of proceeding', noted Chamberlain, 'nor likes anything that is done; but says she allows him £1,000 a day to go on progress.'[64] Her real fury and apprehension she reserved for her closest councillors and her communications with the Earl. She could not sear him with her tongue, but into her letters to him she poured all her authority, intellect and passion. They are her finest compositions. Controlled rage expelled all her literary affectations. They are stripped to the bare bones of argument, and their invective and rhetoric are not superimposed but consist of the sledge-hammer force of the reasoning itself.

What, she wrote on 19 July, had he accomplished by his two-months' journey? The 'eyes of foreign princes' were on his actions; so were those of the English people, 'who groan under the burden of continual levies and impositions'. So far, he had brought in 'never a capital rebel, against whom it would have been worthy to have adventured one thousand men'. Such 'successes' as he claimed were purely due to the use of artillery, which always made any Irish fort untenable. A provincial governor could have done as much, with far less fuss. Meanwhile, the whole point of the enterprise – the expedition to Ulster – had been neglected. The waste of money and men was deplorable. But what displeased her most of all was

> that it must be the Queen of England's fortune (who hath held down the greatest enemy she had) to make a base bush kern to be accounted so famous a rebel, as to be a person against whom so many thousands of foot and horse, besides all the force of the nobility of that kingdom, must be thought too little to be employed.

When Essex had arrived, she went on, the rebels were not in possession of any important town or port whatsoever. Nor had they since been 'strengthened by foreign armies, but only by such of his offal as he was content to spare and let slip from himself'. All over Europe Tyrone was 'blazing' his victories, 'the defeat of regiments, the death of captains, and loss of men of quality in every corner'. When the safety of a kingdom was at stake, and one where long experience of war was vital, Essex had handed over commands to 'young gentlemen that rather desire to do well than know how to perform it'. His letters claimed victories, but 'your pen flatters you with phrases'. This was not how his actions were seen in London and Europe: 'here, you are defeated'. Why had he not gone north? That was the whole object of his campaign: 'we must now plainly charge, according to the duty you owe us . . . with all speed to pass thither in such order, as the axe may be put to the root of that tree, which hath been the treasonable stock from whence so many poisoned grafts and plants have been devised.'[65]

As the full magnitude of Essex's disobedience and inactivity unfolded, Elizabeth's letters became more peremptory. She was alarmed by reports that, far from moving into Ulster, he was planning to return to England for undisclosed purposes. He had, indeed, a licence to do so, provided he appointed a deputy. On 30 July she revoked it, telling him to 'adventure not to come out of that kingdom by virtue of any former licence whatever . . . until the Northern action be tried.'[66] In the meantime, according to Camden, precautions were taken to put the realm of England into a state of defensive readiness. The ostensible reason was the assembly of yet another Armada in Spanish ports, but Camden says the Council feared Essex might be intending to ship the remains of his army back to Chester to settle political scores at home.

On 21 August, in conference with his senior officers, Essex decided to bow to the Queen's wishes, and move north. He sent his secretary, Henry Cuffe, back to court with this news; but it was a defeatist report, stressing the weakness of his force, and the impossibility of accomplishing Tyrone's defeat. He was preparing Elizabeth's mind for negotiations. Her reaction, in a letter she dispatched to Essex on 14 September, was scornful. She rehearsed in detail the whole object and strategy of the expedition, the vast preparations made for it, the huge sums of money spent, the Earl's own repeated demands for reinforcements, and her own strenuous attempts to meet them. All these activities had been directed, by unanimous agreement, to one end: the seizure of Ulster. 'Before your departure, no man's counsel was held sound, which persuaded not presently the main prosecution in Ulster; all was nothing without that; and nothing was too much for that.' But instead of doing this, Essex had done nothing but produce reasons for delaying the northern venture, and, now he at last said he was willing to go, nothing but reasons for prophesying the venture must fail:

> If sickness in the army be the reason, why was not the action undertaken when the army was in better state? If winter's approach, why were the summer months of July and August lost? If the spring were too soon, and the summer that followed otherwise spent, if the harvest that succeeded were so neglected as nothing hath been done, then surely we must conclude that none of the four quarters of the year will be in season for you . . . [67]

Two days after this letter was dispatched from Nonsuch, another Essex messenger, Captain Lawson, arrived at the palace with news that Essex had broken a further commandment of the Queen, and entered into a parley with Tyrone. It may be that by this stage he had little other alternative. He had made contact with Tyrone's forces on 3 September, at Ardee in Louth, when the two armies paraded out of musket range. Essex was outnumbered, by his own calculation, more than two to one. Tyrone declined to engage him in personal combat (he was twenty years older than Essex), or to bring his men down from the carefully-chosen positions they occupied. Essex felt he could not attack. Messages were exchanged between the two camps, and on 7 September, the earls met, totally unaccompanied, at a ford in the River Lagan. They talked for half an hour, and there is no record of their conversation. Afterwards, a truce was arranged, renewable at six-weekly intervals. The rebels were to remain in possession of everything they held on the date of agreement, 8 September, and the English undertook not to establish new forts. Essex appears to have believed he had received Tyrone's submission. At all events, that was his story, and he sought to represent the parley, without much conviction, as a triumph of political skill as an alternative to military ruin. But of course Tyrone had given undertakings before, and broken them at his pleasure – it was the most notorious fact about him. And there were many at the English court who suspected, not without some cause, that he and Essex had discussed other matters, including the political balance in London, the claims of James of Scotland to the English throne, and the chances of his establishing them 'before his time'.

When Elizabeth got the news of the parley, on 17 September, she sent an immediate reply by the same messenger. Where was the triumph in getting Tyrone to negotiate? He had always offered to do so, 'instantly', whenever he saw an English force approaching. So he and Essex had spoken for half an hour together. What had been said? Essex had not told her 'what passed on either side'. Nor had he let her know his instructions to the truce commissioners. Was she expected to learn them 'by divination'? Personally she trusted Essex;

others did not. Why had he taken no witnesses with him? Or secured the consent of his advisers, his invariable practice before? His handling of the military side of the campaign did not inspire confidence in his ability to make a satisfactory treaty. Unless the truce terms secured all the political and military objects of the expedition, then the whole campaign had been 'dishonourable and wasteful', and the future outcome 'like to prove perilous and contemptible'. What were the terms? And what guarantee had he they would be kept? 'To trust this traitor upon oath is to trust a devil upon his religion.' As for pledges, that was mere illusion. Unless Tyrone agreed to have garrisons established throughout his territory, and to come over to make his peace in person, and unarmed, at her court, the treaty was worthless, 'and so the end prove worse than the beginning'. She noted that Essex, by his own account, had not yet committed her to anything: 'We absolutely command you to continue and perform that resolution.' No pardon was to be granted, and nothing to be concluded, until the terms had been explained to her in full, and her express authority secured.[68]

Elizabeth might have saved her energy. Her letter was sent but never delivered. Before it reached Dublin, on 24 September, Essex had decided to stake all on a personal interview with her, had handed over the sword of state to Archbishop Loftus and Sir George Carew, and had taken ship with Southampton, Danvers and a few of his intimates, on a desperate dash back to court. He could not have chosen a set of companions, swordsmen and wastrels all, less likely to impress the Queen, or convince her he had acted wisely, or even loyally. At one point, according to later depositions, he had thought of taking a thousand picked men with him, but the plan was abandoned as impracticable. Everything had to be sacrificed to speed, to enable him to reach court, and tell his tale to the Queen, before his enemies in the army got there first with a different version. He made the journey in four days, but Grey, who had set out to overtake him, was only ten minutes behind at Nonsuch, and went straight to Cecil's quarters. Essex had been weakened by repeated bouts of dysentery; his sense of political realism, rarely pronounced, had vanished. There was never any possibility of his convincing Elizabeth that he had acted prudently in reversing her policy of unconditional surrender. And to attempt to do so in person involved a breach of her emphatic command not to return without leave. Moreover, his multiple offences were compounded by his rudeness in breaking into her apartments without warning. Lord Talbot's correspondent, Rowland Whyte, was at court that day, 28 September, and described what happened:

Nonsuch, Michaelmas Day, 1599.
On Michaelmas Eve, about 10 o'clock in the morning, Lord Essex lighted

at Court Gate Post, made all haste up to the Presence, and so to the Privy Chamber, and stayed not till he came to the Queen's Bedchamber, where he found the Queen, newly up, her hair about her face; he kneeled unto her, kissed her hands, and had some private speech with her, which seemed to give him great contentment; for coming from her Majesty to go shift himself in his chamber, he was very pleasant, and thanked God that, though he had suffered much troubles and storms abroad, he found a sweet calm at home. 'Tis much wondered at here that he went so boldly to her Majesty's presence, she not being ready, and he so full of dirt and mire, that his very face was full of it. When ready he went up again for half an hour after twelve. As yet all was well, and her usage very gracious towards him.[69]

In fact, Elizabeth's reception of the Earl, bursting into her bedroom with mud all over his face, was not so much mild as non-committal. For all she knew, he had arrived with a section of his army, and had surrounded the palace with his troops – no great guard was kept at Nonsuch. It must be doubted whether she paid much attention to his explanation. She played for time until she could find out exactly how secure the palace, and the kingdom, was. Between noon and two or three in the afternoon, she gathered all the necessary information, no doubt from Cecil, and then Essex began to realize the truth of his predicament. Whyte continues:

But when, after dinner, he again went into her presence, he found her much changed, for she began to call him to question for his return, and was not satisfied in the manner of his coming away and leaving all things at so great hazard. She appointed the lords to hear him, and so they went to Council in the afternoon. It is mistrustful that for his disobedience he shall be committed. On the same evening a commandment came from the Queen to my Lord of Essex, that he should keep his chamber.

There were only four Privy Councillors at Nonsuch that day: Cecil, Hunsdon, North and Sir William Knollys. More were hastily summoned, and they debated the issue, without Essex, the whole of the following morning, 29 September. Whyte gives a picture of the uneasy atmosphere in the palace that day, with the two factions dining separately. Cecil ate with the Earls of Shrewsbury and Nottingham, Lord Thomas Howard, Cobham and Ralegh. Meanwhile, up in Essex's quarters, were

the Earl of Worcester, Rutland, Mountjoy, Rich, Lord Harry [Howard] (but the last is held a ranter and, I pray you, take you heed of him, not to trust him, if you have not already gone too far), Dier, Lord Lumley, Mr Controller, with many knights.[70]

After dinner, Essex was summoned before the Council, and ordered to remain standing bareheaded, at the end of the board. The clerks were sent out of the room. Cecil read out a list of six charges, which he had drawn up in consultation with Elizabeth. The councillors cross-questioned Essex for five hours, then dismissed him, and took only fifteen minutes to decide to recommend to the Queen that he should be kept under arrest. She thought this over all the next day, Sunday, 30 September, and the following morning committed him to the custody of Lord Keeper Egerton, at his official residence, York House. He was bundled off there in Worcester's coach, with only two servants, and told he must receive no visitors, even his wife. Permission to walk in the garden of York House was refused.

It was the end of Essex as a power in the state. He had lost Elizabeth's regard a year before. Now, progressively, he lost everything else, including all his Establishment supporters. The Queen was not vindictive. When, on 10 December, she heard he was still ill with dysentery, she sent him her doctors and a quantity of her special broth – her sovereign remedy. But after that last meeting with him, after dinner on 28 September, she showed not the slightest disposition to see him again. She had no wish to smash him to atoms at a public trial; merely to expose him for what she now knew him to be. In March 1600 he was allowed to return to Essex House, but without his household and in the custody of Sir Richard Berkeley, who held all the keys and presided over a tiny staff. On 5 June, he was brought back to York House, to appear before a special commission of seventeen, mainly councillors and judges, presided over by Egerton. Some 200 eminent persons were summoned to hear the complaints against him. There was no trial as such. No witnesses were examined. Four crown lawyers, including Francis Bacon, whose desertion symbolized the end of the Essex party, presented the facts of his behaviour, drawn from government dossiers. Some of the material was new, and damaging. It included a letter written to Egerton two years before, after the painful scene in the Privy Chamber, when the Queen had boxed Essex's ears. The Lord Keeper had advised apology and submission, but Essex had hotly declined. The fault, he wrote, lay with the Queen: he was the injured party:

> When the vilest of all indignities are done unto me, doth religion enforce me to sue, or doth God require it? Is it impiety not to do it? What, cannot princes err? Cannot subjects receive wrong? Is an earthly power or authority infinite? Pardon me, pardon me, my good Lord, I can never subscribe to these principles.[71]

Such eloquent words might later serve as a text for the subjects of King James.

In the context of Elizabeth's use of her authority, which was conservative or liberal as the occasion demanded, they were curiously inept, and must have seemed so to the well-informed audience who heard them read out. Far from abasing Essex, she had accorded him a freedom not merely beyond custom, but almost beyond reason. She had acted to curb his pride not too soon, but too late, and the state had suffered accordingly, as events in Ireland proved. If the letter to Egerton meant anything, it signified that Essex was not a man with whom a sovereign could do reasonable business, or employ with profit. The legal proceedings thus served Elizabeth's purpose. They finally separated Essex from the company of all those of his supporters who carried any authority or weight in society, and left him isolated among his noble hotheads and upstart knights. Nearly three months later, on 26 August 1600, he was told he was at liberty, but banned from court or any public employment.

In settling for this compromise, which broke Essex's political power, but left him at large, Elizabeth allowed her sympathies to guide her head. Of course she had her reasons, too. Essex could be held in reserve, if the Cecil faction, now triumphant, became difficult to manage, and needed to be balanced by a countervailing force. But Essex was not a man who could be safely placed in suspended animation. For one thing, his debts did not permit it. His ten-year lease on the sweet-wines customs farm, his biggest single source of income and the only one on which he could now raise cash, expired in the autumn of 1600, and unless it were renewed, he was ruined, and his creditors would take all he had. Some £5,000 was due for immediate repayment. He wrote Elizabeth a desperate letter:

> This day se'night, the lease which I hold by your Majesty's beneficence expireth, and that farm is both my chiefest maintenance and mine only means of compounding with the merchants to whom I am indebted. . . . If my creditors will take for payment as many ounces of my blood, or the taking away of this farm would only for want finish me of this body, your Majesty should never hear of this suit. For in myself I can find no boldness to importune, and from myself I can draw no argument to solicit.[72]

But this was a bad argument, for Elizabeth knew that Essex wanted to keep up his credit mainly to sustain his faction of penniless knights and captains who swarmed about his house. All of those soon to be associated with the Essex conspiracy, in varying degrees, were near the edge of bankruptcy, or over it. The Earl of Rutland owed £5,000, and many of his lands were already mortgaged. Southampton had sold a third of his inheritance for £20,000, but was still in debt for £8,000. Lord Mounteagle's estate was impoverished, and

Lord Cromwell had got hopelessly in debt in the Low Countries and Ireland. Bedford, though potentially rich, also owed money, and was legally barred from mortgaging his lands. Lord Sandys had sold much of his property. So had Sussex, though he still owed the Queen £5,000, as well as debts to others. The Essex knights were in even worse state. One or two held positions: Sir Fernando Gorges was Governor of Plymouth, but he was never there, and spent his time in London trying to compound with his creditors. Others, Sir William Constable, Sir Edward Littleton, Sir George Devereux, Sir Robert Cross and Sir Griffin Markham, were unsuccessful courtiers, now on their uppers (Littleton was actually arrested for debt on the day of the rising).[73]

Impoverishment, indeed, was the great – almost the sole – unifying force of the Essex rising. It in no way adumbrated the constitutional struggles of the seventeenth century. The Earl had no programme beyond seizing the person of the Queen, and obtaining a monopoly of court offices for his adherents. He had been, it is true, one of the first magnates to attempt systematically to secure seats in the House of Commons for his men. But his object seems to have been more to reward their services than to use a block of MPs to effect his political purposes in the Commons. After his most successful electioneering effort, in 1597, he in fact declined to attend the parliament, in protest against Elizabeth's promotion of Effingham to an earldom.[74] Parliament, to Essex, was merely another sphere in which to exercise patronage. His instincts were not modern, but late medieval: in sixteenth-century terms he was in the tradition of Buckingham, Surrey and the 4th Duke of Norfolk. There was no consistency in his political views, which reflected the ephemeral demands of the power-struggle. Like his stepfather, Leicester, he had no deep religious convictions, though he exhibited a noisy piety in times of despair. Some of those closest to him were Catholics: Sir Charles Danvers, for instance, and Sir Christopher Blount, Mountjoy's brother, who had married Essex's mother. Blount afterwards stated that the Earl had promised a 'toleration of religion' if the plot succeeded. He 'was wont to say that he did not like any man to be troubled for his religion'. This attitude may have attracted such Catholic militants as Robert Catesby and Francis Tresham who, with at least five other Essex conspirators, were later involved in the 1605 'Gunpowder Plot'.[75] On the other hand, a number of Puritan ministers were prominent in the Essex faction. Reports of their sermons, preached in the courtyard of Essex House, first drew official attention to the riotous situation which was brewing there. But most of Essex's followers had no interest in religion. There was a group of Welsh swordsmen, recruited by the reckless Gelly Meyrick; disreputable captains like Thomas Lee; cashiered officers like John Selby, Piers Edmonds and William Green – the last with convictions for theft, lock-picking and purse-cutting – and family retainers from the Devereux estates in Staffordshire. Their motives were crudely but accurately summarized by the war-cry attributed to one of them: 'Seize the Queen and be our own Carvers!'

'I was ever sorry', wrote Francis Bacon to Essex in September 1600, 'that your lordship should fly with waxen wings, doubting Icarus's fortune.' So long as the issue of the wine-licence was unresolved, Essex might hope for a reconciliation with Elizabeth. But, despite his pressing communications, she delayed a decision: 'The licence of sweet wines', wrote Chamberlain, 'lies at anchor aloof, and will not come in.' At the end of October she announced that she was not renewing the licence, but would administer the sweet-wine customs herself. This was another way of marking time, but Essex seems to have interpreted it as a final slap in the face, and evidence that the Queen was now wholly in the hands of the Cecil faction. His mind appears to have become clouded in the last three months of his life, leading to the suspicion that he was suffering from tertiary syphilis, though there is no direct evidence of this. His belief that he was the victim of a systematic persecution by his enemies became more pronounced. Elizabeth's mind, he said, was 'as crooked as her body'; she was in the plot. But he believed there was another plot, being organized by Cecil. The claims of the Spanish Infanta to the succession were to be advanced, as part of a peace-treaty with Spain. If Elizabeth demurred, she was to be arrested, and replaced by the Infanta forthwith. Essex himself was to be murdered. It is difficult to say how far the Earl was really convinced by these fantasies; perhaps he needed them to justify in his own mind his drift towards rebellion. But on 9 January 1601, his closest associate, Southampton, met Lord Grey in the street near Durham House, and in the scrimmage that followed, Southampton's page lost a hand. Elizabeth duly had Grey arrested, and confined in the Fleet. Few people liked Grey, who was morose and vile-tempered. But he had received a great deal of provocation from Southampton, and Elizabeth did not believe he was responsible for perpetuating the feud. On 2 February she ordered his release. The fight outside Durham House had convinced Essex that his enemies were now preparing to kill him and his friends. He took Grey's release as proof that such murderous schemes had the sanction of the Queen.

Plans for a rising were discussed by Essex's leading followers at a meeting held on the evening of Grey's release, and again the following day. Essex was present at neither, presumably from the same motives which led Norfolk to decline to see the letters, written in his name, given to Ridolfi. But there were many irrational aspects to the rising. One of the plotters, Sir John Davies, a professional Welsh soldier whom Essex had made his deputy at the Ordinance, at least produced a coherent scenario: they were to infiltrate Whitehall Palace, occupy the guardhouse (many of the guards had been appointed by Essex), shut the gates and arrest any members of the Cecil faction within. Essex was then to arrive in state with a number of peers, and proceed to Elizabeth's presence. Heralds would proclaim the news to the City, and a parliament would be summoned to try and execute the 'traitors'. Essex had supplied Davies with a list of 120 peers, knights and gentlemen who would support him. This list was certainly fantasy at least in part. In any case the plan was not adopted. Gorges, a very reluctant supporter, opposed it· 'I utterly disliked that course as, besides the horror I felt at it, I saw it was impossible to be accomplished.' They 'broke up resolved upon nothing, and referred all to the Earl of Essex himself'.[76] In fact no final plan was ever determined. But some of the plotters made a public gesture by persuading the Lord Chamberlain's men at the Globe to put on a special performance (in return for an extra fee of 40s.) of Shakespeare's *Richard II*, from which the abdication scene had hitherto been omitted. This was a deliberate act of defiance. Only a few weeks before, the Council had again examined John Hayward, who was in the Tower, about the dedication of his *History of Henry IV*, in which he compared Essex to Bolingbroke. The play was performed after dinner on Saturday, 7 February, and the same evening the Queen instructed the Council to take action. A meeting was held at Lord Buckhurst's house, where reports were presented that large numbers of military men were gathering at Essex House. Welsh swordsmen, it was said, were sleeping in the cellars and attics, and it was feared there were plans to rouse the City apprentices, who would not be working the next day. John Herbert, the Secretary, was instructed to go to Essex and command him and his principal followers to attend the Council and explain their activities. This was the same procedure that had been followed in 1569. It forced suspected plotters either to submit or to show their hands. Herbert returned with the news that Essex claimed he feared for his life and refused to leave his house.[77]

The effect of the Council intervention was to precipitate the rising. At dawn on Sunday, 8 February, Ralegh had himself rowed down the Thames to a spot near Essex House, where he had a rendezvous with Gorges, his Devon friend and colleague. Gorges made it plain he did not like the drift of events, but could tell Ralegh nothing specific about Essex's intentions, for there was no plan of action. All he could say was that 'you are like to have a bloody day of it'. From the bank, one of the Essex House plotters, Thomas Blount, took a number of pot-shots at Ralegh, and he hurried back to Whitehall to sound the alarm and get the Queen up.[78] By all accounts, Elizabeth behaved with exemplary coolness throughout the day. She gave her orders to Cecil, who executed them promptly. The Lord Keeper Egerton, accompanied by Sir William Knollys, Chief Justice Popham, and the Earl of Worcester, were to proceed immediately to Essex House and to order him and his men to lay down their arms and disperse. She picked this group deliberately from among Essex's friends (Knollys was also his uncle), in the hope that they could persuade him that his cause was already lost, and that at all cost bloodshed must be avoided. Meanwhile, a large number of peers and courtiers – Cumberland, Nottingham, Lincoln, Lord Thomas Howard, Lord Burghley, Lord Grey, Lord Compton, Sir Robert Sidney and Sir John Leveson – were ordered to collect troops and to converge on Essex House. In the City, the Mayor and aldermen were warned of the Essex plot before they gathered for the first sermon of the day at St Paul's Cross at eight o'clock. At no point does Elizabeth seem to have doubted the outcome, or allowed herself to betray any sign of anxiety. She carried on with her routine, and ate her dinner as though all was normal. Cecil recorded two days later: 'even when a false alarm was brought to the Queen, that the City was revolted with them, she never was more amazed than she would have been to have heard of a fray in Fleet Street.'[79]

Her confidence was abundantly justified. When the Lord Keeper and his colleagues arrived at Essex House, just after ten o'clock they were let in through the side, or 'wicket', entrance, but their followers were refused admittance. In the courtyard, Essex complained that 'his life was sought, and that he should have been murdered in his bed'. Egerton, who had the Great Seal with him, thereupon put his hat on, and read the sixteenth-century equivalent of the Riot Act: 'I command you all upon your allegiance to lay down your weapons and to depart, which you all ought to do being thus commanded, if you be good subjects and owe that duty to the Queen which you possess.' Essex's response was to order the councillors to be locked up. He then left the house, accompanied by about 200 men, many of them armed. As he knew the court was now alerted, and guarded, he did not march to Westminster but instead turned east, to the City. He had once been popular there, especially after his return from the Cadiz expedition, and he presumably hoped to rouse an impressive mob. This hope was doubtless illusory. In any case Essex had mis-timed his move, since he arrived at St Paul's too late to address the crowd at the main sermon. Instead, he went to Fenchurch Street, to the house of a friend, Sheriff Smythe, the rich son of old 'Customer' Smythe. He seems to have believed that Smythe would be able to supply him with the City's trained bands. But Smythe said he had no troops, and wanted to have nothing to do with the affair. He made an excuse to get out of his own house, and went straight to the Mayor. It says a good deal for Essex's general incompetence and irresolution that, after this setback, he remained in Smythe's house for three hours, eating dinner, and when he emerged government troops were already converging on the City. Lord Burghley, Cecil's half-brother, indeed rode as far as Fenchurch Street itself, and there read a royal proclamation declaring Essex a traitor, and promising pardon to those who deserted him immediately. This had its effect: two of Essex's leading supporters, Cromwell and Bedford, crept off.

With a rapidly dwindling band, Essex decided to return to his house, but found Ludgate firmly barred to him by Leveson's men. Here, Christopher Blount was wounded and knocked unconscious. Essex retreated to St Paul's, then made his way down to the river, where he seized boats. In the hurry and confusion Lord Monteagle fell in the water and was nearly drowned, and it was a very depressed and meagre group of rebels who returned to Essex House by the river entrance. There, Essex found that Gorges had released the councillors, and that the house was surrounded by large bodies of government soldiers, commanded by virtually all the members of the Elizabethan establishment. Once Essex got inside, the troops penetrated the garden and cut him off from the river. Cannons from the Tower were on the way, and it was a question whether Essex and his friends were to perish in the house, or surrender. He burned his papers, letters and diary, and then negotiated a surrender, in return for promises of civil treatment, a fair trial, and the attendance of the Reverend Mr Ashton, his favourite chaplain. Essex and Southampton were hustled across the river to Lambeth Palace; then, at three o'clock in the morning, as soon as the tide was high enough, they were taken secretly and swiftly to the Tower. These were Elizabeth's express orders, and she did not go to bed until she was informed they had been carried out. It had been a long and painful day, but it had demonstrated with absolute conclusiveness that she still held the realm in her hand, and that no rebel, however much he might seek, or even possess, 'popularity', could hope to raise any significant proportion of her subjects against her. When the moment of decision came, Bolingbroke-Essex had been left with only his hard core of 'desperates'. It was not a rising, but a fiasco.

For this reason, Elizabeth felt able to act with a good deal of forbearance, though she took all the needful precautions. Nearly 2,000 men levied from the Home Counties were brought to London and encamped in strategic places. On Thursday, 12 February, Captain Thomas Lee was discovered and arrested near Elizabeth's private apartments. He admitted that he was going to break in upon her at supper, and force her to sign a warrant for Essex's release. She had him tried at Newgate two days later, and executed the next morning (she had not forgotten the affair of the head). On 13 February, the Council had made a public statement in Star Chamber on the facts of the conspiracy, and six days later its two chief agents, Essex and Southampton, were tried in Westminster Hall before twenty-five peers, Buckhurst, as High Steward, presiding.[80] The Queen, of course, was not present, the only member of the cast of characters who dominated the last years of her reign to miss what was undoubtedly a dramatic performance. Essex laughed, and tugged at Southampton's sleeve, when he saw that the hated Grey was to be one of their judges; and he sneered when Ralegh was sworn to give evidence: 'What booteth it to swear the fox?' Chamberlain reported that when he 'came first to the bar his countenance was unsettled; but once in, he showed the greatest resolution and contempt of death, real or assumed.'[81] Yelverton, Coke and Bacon prosecuted, the last anxious both to ingratiate himself with the Queen by the vehemence of his *requisitoire*, and to refute allegations that he was turning treacherously on his former friend and patron. 'I confess', he told the court,

> I loved my Lord of Essex as long as he continued a dutiful subject, and I have spent more hours to make him a good subject to her Majesty than ever I did about my own business ... [to Essex:] I did but perform the part of an honest man, and ever laboured to have done you good, if it might have been.

Bacon and the other prosecutors were, no doubt, briefed by the Queen on how to handle the case. She always paid the closest attention to the ground covered in important treason trials, and in this case she was anxious to narrow it to the undisputed facts of the rising, where evidence of guilt was overwhelming. Nothing was to be said about the Richard II analogy, or the possibility of a deposition of the Queen, or the succession issue. But it proved impossible to keep the last subject out of the trial, for in attempting to refute part of the evidence, Essex said:

> as for that I spake in London that the crown of England was sold to the Spaniard, I speak it not of myself, for it was told me that Mr Secretary should say to one of his fellow-councillors, that the Infanta's title comparatively was as good in succession as any other.

This was a serious charge to make against Cecil; since, as Thomas Wilson put it, 'to determine thereof [the succession] is to all English capitally forbidden'.[82] Moreover, the charge was coloured slightly by the fact that Cecil, with the Queen's agreement, was putting out peace-feelers to Spain. The Secretary was attending the trial concealed behind a curtain. He now emerged and, on his knees, asked Buckhurst's permission to answer Essex's statement. He was anxious, too, publicly to disprove Essex's reiterated claim that he had organized a ferocious and remorseless campaign against him and his friends.

My Lord of Essex, the difference between you and me is great. For wit, I give you pre-eminence: you have it abundantly. For nobility also I give you place: I am not noble, yet a gentleman. I am no swordsman: there also you have the odds. But I have innocence, conscience, truth and honesty to defend me against the scandal and sting of slanderous tongues, and in this court I stand as an upright man, and your Lordship as a delinquent. I protest before God I have loved your person and justified your virtues; and I appeal to God and the Queen that I told your Majesty your afflictions would make you a fit servant for her, attending but a fit time to move her Majesty to call you to the court again.

He challenged Essex to name who it was who had told him of Cecil's preference for the Infanta's claim. Essex replied that it was Sir William Knollys, and messengers were promptly sent to bring Knollys to the stand. Knollys was able to explain that Cecil, far from favouring the Spanish claim, had said it was 'strange impudence' for a Catholic writer, Doleman, to give it equal right with any other claim. This was the only time he had heard Cecil mention the point, and 'Hereupon was grounded the slanders upon Mr Secretary, whereof he is as clear as any man present'. Tudor treason trials were carefully stage-managed: but this episode was clearly unpremeditated, and therefore all the more impressive in discrediting Essex and vindicating Cecil. The Secretary drove the point home:

I stand for loyalty, which I never lost; you stand for treachery, wherewith your heart is possessed; and you charge me with high things, wherein I defy you to the uttermost. You, my good lords, counsellors of state, have had many conferences, and I do confess I have said that the King of Scots is a competitor, and the King of Spain is a competitor, and you [to Essex] I have said, are a competitor; you would depose the Queen, you would be King of England, and call a parliament. Ah, my Lord, were it but your own case, the loss had been the less: but you have drawn a number of noble persons and gentlemen of birth and quality into your net of rebellion, and their bloods will cry vengeance against you.[83]

This completed the demolition of Essex, and at six o'clock (the trial had begun at nine that morning), the peers, after retiring for half an hour, judged Essex and Southampton guilty on all charges. Two days later, Essex not only made a full confession, but showed himself willing to betray all his friends, 'to lay open the plot, and impeach some persons not yet called in question'.[84] He was particularly savage against his secretary, Henry Cuffe, whom he accused of being his chief instigator.[85] He also denounced his sister. Essex was not a noble man.

Many must have agreed with Lady Sandys who, lamenting her husband's involvement, wrote that he 'was drawn into that clay by that wild Earl's craft, who hath been and [is] unlucky to many but never good to any. I would he had never been born'.[86]

Cecil's statement, to which he asked Elizabeth to bear witness, that he had wanted Essex brought back to favour in due course, is almost certainly true. Like his father, he did not believe in faction-fighting, nor did he welcome being regarded as the sole depository of power:

> *Little Cecil trips up and down,*
> *He rules both court and crown.*[87]

Such ditties, circulating at the time, were dangerous, threatening both to envenom the public against him, and poison his relationship with the Queen. The evidence suggests that Elizabeth herself prevented Essex's return from the shadows. Far from being the tool of the Cecil faction, she was a disillusioned woman who had reached the reluctant, but settled, conclusion that her 'wild horse' was untamable, and useless to the public service. She might eventually have allowed him back to court, but never again, I feel, to high office. And, once he had shown his treasonable face, and been convicted, she did not flinch from executing him. To most of the other rebels she showed mercy. Of eighty-five listed as arrested, thirty-two were promptly discharged without bonds or penalty, and only six went to the scaffold. She denied Meyrick, an 'Essex knight', the privilege of knighthood, and had him hanged and quartered. Otherwise she was not vindictive. Considering her animus against the captain-class, this is surprising, but she preferred them to be mocked by Shakespeare rather than get what she felt to be their true deserts. Even Southampton was spared, thanks partly to the intervention of his mother and Cecil, but chiefly to Elizabeth's lifelong reluctance to kill anyone, if it could be avoided.

Being the person she was, Elizabeth made some fuss about signing Essex's death warrant (perhaps to give him time to make a full confession), and revoked it once. But her superscribed signature on the document is as firm and fine as ever. She cannot have had any doubt that Essex had to die. He had added enormously to her burdens, and his continued existence, even in prison, would have demonstrated her lack of resolve to govern firmly to the end, and might have threatened a disputed succession. On 24 February, only five days after Essex was sentenced, she authorized the Council to have the necessary preparations made at the Tower: 'We would first have these two persons [executioners] secretly conveyed within the Tower; if one faint, the other may perform it to him on whose soul God have mercy.'[88] The next day, Ash Wednesday, at eight in the morning, Essex was beheaded, his head being severed at the first stroke. Later, a story was told that Elizabeth had given Essex a ring, to be sent back to her if ever he stood in need of her forgiveness. From the Tower, the story continues, Essex sent the ring to Lady Scrope, with instructions to hand it to the Queen, but his messenger made a mistake, and instead of handing the ring to Lady Scrope, gave it to Lady Nottingham, wife of his enemy the Admiral. Lady Nottingham kept it, and did not reveal the fact to Elizabeth until she herself was on her deathbed two years later. 'May God forgive you madam,' said Elizabeth, 'but I never can.' But the story is a fiction, dating from a generation later; it is first heard of in 1620, and was printed in 1695.[89] Far from quarrelling with Lady Nottingham on her deathbed, Elizabeth attended her last hours with her customary fortitude and kindness, and grieved bitterly over the loss of her last remaining old friend. On several occasions after Essex's death, Elizabeth is reported to have mentioned his name sorrowfully – and she wore a ring he had given her until she died. But she gave no sign that she regretted his execution: merely the circumstances which made it necessary.

Indeed, it would be a mistake to assume that the Essex crisis had any profound emotional effect on Elizabeth, or that his death marked, as it were, the beginning of the coda to her life. Her last years were, in fact, ones of considerable accomplishment, of recovery from the dark period of economic distress which lasted from the mid-1590s until the end of the decade. Essex's death removed a serious obstacle to the smooth workings of government. Nor did it mean that all effective power slipped into the hands of Cecil and his associates. She was still, and she remained to the end, very much his authoritarian mistress, as Cecil himself testified. 'But myself,' he wrote, 'I know not one man in this kingdom that will bestow six words of argument to reply, if she deny it.'[90] 'She could put forth such altercations when obedience was lacking,' said Harington of these years, 'as left no doubtings whose daughter she was.'[91]

Cecil's position was exceptionally difficult, for he had to take steps to ensure a peaceful succession, without involving Elizabeth, who would not have the subject discussed, and without – ostensibly at least – letting her know that he was handling the matter. It is clear from her own correspondence with James, in which she adopted the role of a worldly-wise and experienced sovereign advising a neophite, that she regarded him as her natural, indeed inevitable, successor.[92] But she was not prepared to acknowledge the fact openly, or even covertly, for fear that this would diminish her personal authority, and turn the eyes of powerful men at court to the north. Even as things stood, Harington noted the focus of attention was shifting to James: 'I find some less mindful of what they are soon to lose, than of what they may perchance hereafter get.'[93]

Cecil's great service to Elizabeth was to persuade James to await her death in patience, rather than risk the stability of the kingdom by a precipitous move. The Scots King acknowledged that he accepted Cecil's advice to 'enjoy the fruits at my pleasure, in the time of their greatest maturity', rather than 'hazard my honour, state and person, in entering the kingdom by violence as an usurper'.[94] In the meantime, James agreed to 'deal with the Queen of England fair and pleasantly for my title to the Crown of England after her decease'.[95] For the purposes of their secret correspondence, the two men agreed on a code: Cecil himself was '10', Elizabeth '24', James '30', and so forth. Lord Henry Howard, at James's request, was the only man privy to the code and the contents of the letters.[96] To ensure secrecy, Cecil dismissed one of his secretaries, Simon Willis, because he could not absolutely rely on his discretion: 'I was loath that he should have come to some discovery of that correspondency which I had with the King our sovereign, which without great difficulty I could not have avoided ... [Willis] might have raised some such inferences thereof as might have bred some jealousy in the Queen's mind.'[97] He was clear that this element of concealment was in Elizabeth's own interests: 'If her Majesty had known all I did ... her age and orbity, joined to the jealousy of her sex, might have moved her to think ill of that which helped to preserve her.'[98] But the accent here should be placed on 'all'. It is clear that Elizabeth knew Cecil was in contact with James, and relied on his good sense to ensure that the negotiations were in her interests, as well as those of the state. *Video, taceo* – her motto was very apt here.

But while Elizabeth was content, in the special circumstances of the succession issue, to allow Cecil the initiative, in every other area of policy she kept all the threads in her hands. She was unquestionably the dominant figure in her last parliament, in the autumn of 1601. Parliament should have met in the spring of the year, when the last of the subsidies from the previous parliament were collected. But the Essex rising made a postponement inevitable, and its ripples were still being felt when Members assembled on 27 October. The state was moving slowly, but inexorably, towards bankruptcy, and there were many grievances. Considerable efforts were made to ensure that government was well represented. Cecil secured nominations to a score or more boroughs, and six of his personal staff sat in the Commons. Egerton had four MPs (including John Donne), and Buckhurst three; Whitgift had a block of his own members, and it is probable that more government MPs sat than in any previous parliament.[99]

We have a comparatively full record of this parliament because a young lawyer-MP, Hayward Townshend, kept a day-by-day record during the sittings of the House.[100] The details provided by this diary illustrate the difficulty of managing any Elizabethan parliament, and give the erroneous impression that this one was particularly turbulent. Elizabeth herself did not appear to think so, to judge by her comments. She had met worse before, and her mood remained benign, though always watchful. But some incompetence was shown in the arrangements, and in the handling of the Lower House. Cecil, no doubt, was anxious to dispel any impression that he was sole minister, and sometimes declined to give a lead when it was his duty to do so. He was poorly supported by other councillors and officials. Knollys, Essex's uncle, was unhelpful; Ralegh, resentful at the continuing failure to make him a Privy Councillor, played an individualist role; other government members, like Herbert, seem to have carried little weight. Many MPs were annoyed, on the opening day, to find themselves excluded from the Upper House, and so missed Egerton's speech. It was a mistake by an official, but it rankled, and two days later, when the Speaker made his customary plea for freedom of speech, and received the Queen's reply through Egerton – it was a generous one, which suggests Elizabeth did not anticipate trouble – there was an uneasy scene when she passed out of the Upper House through the crowd of Commoners. Once again, the arrangements were ill-planned, and the occasion lacked dignity. Townshend reports that the Queen looked silent and preoccupied, and few greeted her:

And the throng being great, and little room to pass, she moved her hand to have more room; whereupon one of the gentlemen ushers said openly: 'Back, masters, make room.' And one answered stoutly behind: 'If you will hang us, we can make no more room.' Which the Queen seemed not to hear, though she heaved up her head, and looked that way towards him that spake.[101]

The strains of the war, and heavy taxation, were beginning to tell: MPs were obsessed by finance, as was the Queen herself. Complaints covered virtually the whole spectrum of government operations in the raising and spending of money. In his last year, Burghley had completed his long-promised arrangements to reform the system of purveyance for the royal household – it was his final service to Elizabeth – and this issue was pushed into the background.[102] But the reform of Exchequer abuses, which had been raised as long ago as 1571, and which Elizabeth had promised to carry out herself in 1589, was still a grievance. Evidently the changes she had introduced had been ineffective, and a Bill was brought forward and passed both Houses, with the support of Privy Councillors, judges, and even such extreme prerogative men as Bacon. Elizabeth vetoed it without hesitation, and apparently entirely on her own initiative. The management of central finance was still, in her eyes, the exclusive concern of the executive. She also killed Bills to control the export of bullion and armaments, believing that their purposes could be effected more conveniently by government, than by statute.[103] Here again, the Queen acted alone. 'It was much marvelled and grutched at,' wrote Dudley Carleton, 'that the bills touching the abuses of the Exchequer and the transportation of ordnance were put by.'

Nevertheless, Elizabeth, as always in handling her parliaments, blended firmness with concession. On one issue she had to give way: monopolies. She had never liked them herself. A generation before, Sir Nicholas Bacon had warned her that they were against all the principles of English law, and she had agreed with him. But they were a convenience to a government perpetually short of money, and to a Queen increasingly at a loss to find means of rewarding ministers and servants. The issue had been raised in the 1597–8 parliament, and she had promised to curb them. According to Bacon, fifteen or sixteen patents had been revoked on her express command, and others sent to the Common Pleas and the Exchequer Court to be tested as to their legal validity. But new ones had been created. Early in 1601 she had asked Buckhurst and Cecil to carry out an inquiry, and they reported to her that the situation was very bad indeed. She appointed a commission of four Councillors, plus the Chief Justice, to take action. But by August nothing, evidently, had been done, since Buckhurst wrote to Cecil: 'The sooner we take action, the better.'[104] No action, however, had been taken by the time parliament met, and monopolies became the dominant theme for MPs. It was raised on 4 November and again on the 18th and, despite attempts by Cecil and the Speaker to suppress discussion on the subject, a Bill was presented two days later, in an atmosphere which showed MPs were determined on a decision. Many speakers cited individual, and shocking, cases affecting their own constituents. William Spicer, MP for Warwick, said the worst offender in his town was an obstinate recusant. Dr Bennett, MP for York, cited a long list of monopolies, including playing-cards, 'whereat Sir Walter Ralegh blushed' (he held the monopoly). When Ralegh rose to defend the practice, 'a great silence' fell. Richard Martin called monopolists 'bloodsuckers of the Commonwealth'. Francis Moore, MP for Reading, maintained: 'There is no act [of the Queen's] that hath been or is more derogatory to her own majesty or more odious to the subject or more dangerous to the Commonwealth than the granting of these monopolies.' Richard Wingfield said that, in the previous parliament, Elizabeth had promised redress: 'If not, she would give us free liberty to proceed in making a law the next parliament.'[105]

Pressure was being brought to bear from outside the House. Lists of monopolies were being circulated in London, giving names and cases, and petitions were presented to the Queen and MPs. On 23 November, there was an unruly lobby at the doors of the House. Sir Edward Hoby reported 'a multitude of people ... who said they were Commonwealth men, and desired [the House] to take compassion on their griefs, they being spoiled, imprisoned and robbed by monopolists'. Cecil, who was fighting an angry rearguard-action on Elizabeth's instructions, deplored the manner in which public opinion was being used to influence MPs: 'What meaneth this? Shall we suffer it?' He added: 'I fear we are not secret among ourselves ... Why! Parliament matters are ordinarily talked of in the street. I have heard myself, being in my coach, these words spoken aloud: "God prosper those that further the overthrow of these monopolies. God send the prerogative touch not our liberty!"' He protested, too, when government MPs, rising to defend the practice, were virtually shouted down:

> Order is attended by these two handmaids, gravity and zeal, but zeal with discretion. I have been, though unworthy, a Member of this House in six or seven parliaments, yet never did I see the House in so great confusion. I believe there was never in any parliament a more tender point handled than the liberty of the subject and the prerogative royal of the prince. What an indignity there is to the prince, and injury to the subject, that when any is discussing this point he should be cried and coughed down. This is more fit for a grammar school than a Court of Parliament.[106]

But this was an occasion when the Commons were not prepared to be lectured into compliance. The government claim that action was about to be taken when the Essex rebellion had intervened was brushed aside. Sir Robert Wroth replied: 'Why not before? ... There was time enough ever since the last parliament. I speak it, and I speak it boldly: these patents are worse than ever they were.' He read out a list of them. A young lawyer, William Hakewill, asked: 'Is not bread there?' ' "Bread?" quoth one; "Bread?" quoth another. "This voice seems strange", quoth a third. "No," quoth Mr Hakewill, "but if order be not taken for these, bread will be there before the next parliament".[107] One MP suggested that the House should 'do generously and bravely like parliament-men' – simply summon the patent-holders, cancel their patents before their faces, arraign them at the bar, and clap them in the Tower. This got a laugh, but the next day, 24 November, the House made it clear it was serious by refusing to discuss the Subsidy Bill until the monopoly issue was settled.

That evening, Cecil had to report to the Queen that the government had lost control of the House, and she took the matter into her own hands. She sent a message to the Speaker, informing MPs that she would issue a proclamation, revoking a large number of monopolies, which she listed. The proclamation was in print three days later, and a copy was sent to each MP. Elizabeth always believed that, if a concession had to be made, it should be made generously, fully, and with a certain amount of theatricals. She had been perturbed by the mess her officials had made of the opening of parliament, and now that she had felt obliged to give way to MPs on an important issue, she wanted to make a virtue of necessity, and win back their customary enthusiasm by a display of her talents. She said she would be delighted to see a delegation of MPs at Whitehall Palace. This led to a cry, from 'the lower end of the House', where the younger and less important MPs sat: 'No. All, all, all!' So she invited them all to come, if the room would hold them, and at 3.00 p.m. on 30 November, in the Council Chamber, she delivered what later became known as her 'Golden Speech'.[108] Her official version of this speech, which she elaborated in her customary way, was promptly published by the royal printer, but, as always, her actual words were more simple, direct and telling. Fortunately, she handed her rough notes, from which she spoke extempore, to the Provost of Eton, Henry Saville, and this got into print in an unofficial version, which coincides almost exactly with the record Townshend made at the time, and therefore constitutes the speech as delivered.

She understood, she said, that the MPs had come to see her to give their thanks for her concession over monopolies: 'I accept with no less joy than your loves can have desire to offer such a present.' It was sign of their affection: she reciprocated it.

There is no jewel, be it of never so rich a price, which I set before this jewel: I mean your love. For I do esteem it more than any treasure or riches; for that we know how to prize, but love and thanks I count unvaluable. And, though God hath raised me high, yet this I count the glory of my crown, that I have reigned with your loves. This makes me that I do not so much rejoice that God hath made me to be a Queen, as to be a Queen over so thankful a people . . . Neither do I desire to live longer days than I may see your prosperity; and that is my only desire . . . Of myself I must say this: I never was any greedy, scraping grasper, nor a strait, fast-holding prince, nor yet a waster. My heart was never set on any worldly goods, but only for my subjects' good. What you bestow on me, I will not hoard it up, but receive it to bestow on you again. Yea, mine own properties I account yours, to be expended for your good.

At this point, she told MPs, who had been kneeling, to rise up, with a gesture 'of honourable and princely demeanour'. She said she was grateful to them for bringing her attention to abuses. She had known they existed, and had fought against them, but had not realized they were so serious: 'Yes, when I heard it, I could give no rest unto my thoughts until I had reformed it.' She now knew the full extent of 'these errors, troubles, vexations and oppressions'. Those responsible, 'these varlets and lewd persons, not worthy of the name of subjects', had 'dealt with me like physicians who, ministering a drug, make it more acceptable by giving it a good aromatical savour'. But now she would root them out: 'I have ever used to set the last judgment-day before mine eyes, and so to rule that I shall be judged to answer before a higher judge.' To be a King was a 'glorious title': but

> To be a King and wear a crown is a thing more glorious to them that see it, than it is pleasant to them that bear it. For myself, I was never so much enticed with the glorious name of a King, or royal authority of a Queen, as delighted that God hath made me His instrument to maintain His truth, and glory, and to defend this Kingdom (as I said) from peril, dishonour, tyranny and oppression. There will never Queen sit in my seat with more zeal to my country, care for my subjects, and that will sooner with willingness venture her life for your good and safety, than myself. For it is my desire to live nor reign no longer than my life and reign shall be for your good. And though you have had, and may have, many princes more mighty and wise sitting in this seat, yet you never had, nor shall have, any that will be more careful and loving.

She knew she was only a woman, and an unworthy one. But God had given her strength, and 'a heart that yet never feared any foreign or home enemy'. She did not 'attribute anything to myself'. It was the doing of Providence: 'For I, oh Lord, what am I, whom practices and perils past should not fear? Or what can I do? That I should speak for any glory, God forbid!' She spoke these words, said Townshend, 'with a great emphasis'. It was an emotional moment: a woman nearing seventy, looking back on more than four decades of successful personal government, and identifying and humbling herself as the mere handmaid of the Almighty. This was the Virgin touch, a form of personal and secular *magnificat anima mea*. After she had finished, Elizabeth told the councillors present that they were to be sure to bring to see her all those Members of Parliament who wished to kiss her hand, before they departed to their neighbourhoods.

She seems to have enjoyed this parliament, perhaps recognizing that it was to be her last. She was not to know that her 'Golden Speech' was to be printed, and reprinted, in the next two generations, as a testament to her political virtue, and an admonition to her successors, so that James I, and his hapless son, were to come to regard her as possessing some mystical mortmain on the affections of the English people, the key to which they never discovered. Among other things, the 1601 parliament summarized and codified the social legislation, on poverty and employment, which had been one of her abiding interests, and which had been begun in 1563, with her great Statute of Artificers. This legislation, like her religious settlement, had been carried through jointly, by herself, by her ministers, and by Members of Parliament themselves.[109] It embodied the experience of local communities, like London and Norwich, in tackling the problems of economic dislocation, homelessness and population growth, and translated them into a country-wide scheme – part of the nation-building process of unification and anti-parochialism which she had done so much to promote.[110] It looked back to the first, tentative efforts of her father's great minister, Thomas Cromwell, and forward to the creation of a welfare state.[111] It testified to the political resources and resiliency of Elizabethan government, and of the Queen herself, in facing the challenge of fundamental social issues, during a period when war was straining the energies of the nation.

Elizabeth's last parliament was critical, active and vigorous in viewing the shortcomings of society. But it still had a strong sense of partnership with the monarchy, and gratitude to the remarkable woman who had made this possible. At the dissolution, on 19 December, the Speaker, John Croke, drew attention to the fact that England, alone in Europe, had known nothing but internal stability throughout her reign. He expressed thanks for 'the happy and quiet and most sweet and comfortable peace . . . we have long enjoyed and, blessed be God and your Majesty, do still enjoy'.[112] Elizabeth responded with one of her rare discourses on foreign policy. She reviewed the long course of her relations with Spain. She had never shown any hostility to Philip II, 'whose soul, I trust, be now in heaven', still less to his son, 'whom I never did in my life offend'. She had been obliged to intervene in the Low Countries only at the urgent request of the States, and while still doing everything in her power to make peace by persuading the Spanish crown to restore their ancient liberties. In response, Spain had first tried to stir up rebellion in England; this failing, had sent its fleet to invade; and, having been defeated at sea, was now trying to suborn her authority in Ireland. She had always sought peace. She had gone to war with reluctance. Her conscience was clear. Peace would be made, or the war would continue, entirely in accordance with the rights and just interests of the nation.

This was the message MPs were to carry back to their constituents: 'that your Sovereign is more careful of your conservation than of herself, and will daily crave of God that they who wish you best may never wish in vain.'[113] Toby Matthew, Bishop of Durham, told Dudley Carleton he had never heard Elizabeth 'in better vein'. She had spoken her last will and testament as a national leader.

Yet the reference to Ireland in the speech was significant. This last great problem of state was still unresolved at the end of 1601. She was determined, before she died, to see her authority there fully established. Fortunately, for once in her military ventures, she was admirably served. Lord Mountjoy, though a member of the Essex faction – he was in love with Essex's sister, Penelope Rich – was conspicuous for his loyalty, his lack of political and court ambition, and his absolute concentration on the practicalities of soldiering – all the virtues Essex lacked.[114] He concentrated, first, on rebuilding the morale of the army, which Essex had left in ruins: 'the hearts of the English common soldiers, broken with a current of disastrous successes, he heartened and encouraged by leading them warily, especially in his first action: he was more careful that our men should not be foiled, than that the rebels should be attempted with boldness'.[115] His strategy was to secure pacified areas by the erection of strongpoints and blockhouses, thus limiting Tyrone's mobility and narrowing the field in which he could operate. This process was expensive. Ireland was costing, Cecil calculated, £300,000 a year.[116] But Mountjoy was ably assisted by Sir George Carew, now President of Munster, who succeeded in rapidly pacifying the province, while building up supplies for a final confrontation with Tyrone, assisted (as was expected) by a Spanish expeditionary force. Carew was a Cecilian, but he worked in harmony with the Deputy, and there was no hint of faction in the Irish command. Elizabeth kept the closest watch on events, and encouraged her generals with frequent personal letters, blending shrewdness with warmth. To Carew she wrote:

> My faithful George, If ever more service of worth were performed in shorter space than you have done, we are deceived among many eye-witnesses: we have received the fruit thereof, and bid you faithfully credit that whatso wit, courage and care may do, we truly find they have all been thoroughly acted in all your charge. And for the same believe that it shall be neither unremembered nor unrewarded, and in meanwhile believe my help nor prayers shall never fail you. Your Sovereign that best regards you, E.R.[117]

The Spanish finally arrived in September 1601, and fortified Kinsale with about 5,300 men and some artillery. Tyrone marched south to join them, so the Irish problem was now concentrated in one area, outside Tyrone's natural territory. This was fortunate for Elizabeth, but she made strenuous practical efforts to enable Mountjoy to seize the opportunity. Altogether, 5,000 men were sent as reinforcements, and Sir Richard Leveson, her ablest admiral, was ordered to the Munster coast: 'there never was such a fleet of the Queen's ships so suddenly sent out by any admiral before', said Nottingham.[118] The supplies Carew had organized in Munster enabled Mountjoy to march west immediately, and thus prevent the Irish and the Spaniards from uniting. Kinsale was invested before Tyrone could get there. Mountjoy reported to London that the hour of decision had come: 'If we beat them, let it not trouble you though you hear all Ireland doth revolt, for (by the grace of God) you shall have them all return presently with halters about their necks: if we do not, all providence bestowed on any other place is vain.'[119] Cecil replied that Elizabeth had had his letter 'read to all of us in Council', and expressed her view that he would make Munster 'serve for a sepulchre to these new conquerors'. To Mountjoy himself she wrote, in her own hand:

> Tell our army from us, that they may make a full account, that every hundred of them will beat a thousand, and every thousand theirs doubled. I am the bolder to pronounce it in His name, that hath ever protected my righteous cause, in which I bless them all. And putting you in the first place, I end, scribbled in haste, Your loving sovereign, E.R.[120]

The issue was still in doubt when Elizabeth's last parliament met, and indeed when it dispersed. But a week later, on Christmas Eve, the Irish army, which had finally arrived to raise the siege, deployed itself in open country, and Mountjoy leapt joyfully at the chance to use his cavalry. As Elizabeth had always predicted, cavalry properly used was the decisive arm in the Irish theatre. In less than an hour, the Tyrone forces were beaten, and the Spanish in Kinsale promptly made overtures for surrender. Their commander, Aguila, said he found 'the Irish not only weak and barbarous but (as he feared) perfidious friends'. Mountjoy, reporting the Spanish surrender, noted with satisfaction: 'The contempt and scorn in which the Spaniards hold the Irish, and the distaste which the Irish have of them ... [mean] it will be a difficult thing for the Irish hereafter to procure aids out of Spain.'[121]

The remains of Tyrone's army melted away as he made his way back north. His offensive power had been broken, but Ireland still remained a problem while he was at large, and Elizabeth was unwilling to offer him any kind of terms to induce him to surrender. She wanted him hanged. Even granted her general dislike of capital punishment, this is not entirely surprising. This man, whom she had once favoured, had come nearer to overthrowing her authority than any other of her enemies. Both Mountjoy and Cecil advised that it would save money to grant him his life, if he surrendered himself into her custody. But Cecil reported to the Deputy that she was adamant: 'as her Majesty (in these cases) may well (out of experience of government) assume more to her royal prudence than any of her Council: so (God in Heaven doth know) that even in these great causes, she is pleased to proceed more absolutely than ever, by the rules of her own princely judgment.' But the year 1602 passed without Tyrone's capture, and financial factors began to weigh more heavily in the scales than Elizabeth's desire for revenge. In December Tyrone offered to submit, simply and absolutely, to Elizabeth's mercy, on the understanding that his life would not be forfeit. Mountjoy, forwarding the letter in which this offer was made, begged the Queen to accept. This was also the unanimous view of her Council. She was now in her last weeks, and perhaps realized it (had Tyrone possessed the same knowledge he would undoubtedly have waited for her to die in the certainty of getting better terms from James). On 16 February she wrote Mountjoy a letter authorizing him to accept Tyrone's submission, but laying down strict conditions about how it was to be carried out. She wanted the Irish problem to be resolved before her reign ended, but she was anxious there should be no mistake or treachery. The next day, she sent Mountjoy a further letter, setting out the conditions for the surrender in more detail, and followed this, after the two letters had been sent, by further instructions forwarded by Cecil. He accompanied these by a private and secret letter of his own to Mountjoy, making it clear that, in his view, not all the provisions laid down by the Queen could be met, that Mountjoy was to do his best, but that at all costs nothing was to be written in his dispatches which might offend the Queen, or give her the impression that her orders were being flouted. Cecil's secret letter is an extraordinary testimony to the authority Elizabeth still exercised, on the threshold of eternity:

Now, Sir, know I pray you hereby, that this is her own, and neither our propositions nor conceit; but rather suffered *pro tempore* than we would lose the former warrant [authorizing Mountjoy to accept the surrender], by contesting too long against that which will die as soon as she is satisfied from you that we have obeyed her, and that you find the impossibility of these things which she would be glad of, but so as not to prevent the rest; and, therefore, now I have done and said all, I know in these last I have said nothing, and yet in obeying I have done much. And so hoping, by your next dispatch, you will write that which is fit to be showed her Majesty, and that which is fit for me to know (*a parte*), in which kinds all honest servants must strain a little when they will serve princes, I end.

He might have added: 'when they serve princes like Queen Elizabeth'. Instead, he wrote a postscript asking Mountjoy to return this private letter. Such was his fear of his mistress.[122]

The defeat and surrender of Tyrone brought to an end the old Gaelic state, which Elizabeth, in her traditionalist manner, had wished to preserve against the irresistible forces of change. It gave birth to the modern Irish problem, which is with us yet. It was also the last great public act of her life and reign. This, too, was moving to its close.

In Our Blessed Queen's Time

In her last years, many people throughout Christendom regarded Elizabeth as the most remarkable living phenomenon in the world. Her virginity, her wit and intelligence, her political and military triumphs, her sheer endurance, her renowned skill as a stateswoman – all these made her unique. She had reigned longer than any other European monarch of her time. She had outlived all her enemies: popes, kings, rivals, generals, conspirators. She had, alas, also outlived virtually all her friends. She was older than any of her predecessors on the throne of England. At her splendid palaces, a traditional form of state ceremonial was kept up which had vanished elsewhere, and those who came from abroad to see and admire it did so in the knowledge that she alone of her fellow-sovereigns could pay her bills. It was already apparent that she had changed the course of history, broken the thrust of the Counter-Reformation, and established England as a great power in Europe and on the oceans. Yet here she still was, a living memorial to momentous changes and events, absolute mistress of a thrusting and dynamic people, presiding regally over the high flowering of a new culture, in a capital city which was now the largest on earth, and in a country which had ceased to be a backwater and was now regarded as a centre of the world's motions. She was, as the ballad singers called her, 'the great lioness'.[1]

But all monarchs must die. Elizabeth never feared death. She said so, often, and she meant it. She showed no curiosity about what would happen to her when she ceased to live. She regarded herself as a great functionary of an inscrutable but just deity. When the audit and the judgment came, she would be content to rest on her record. She was equally calm about the prospects for her country after she was gone. She had played her part, discharged her responsibilities in full. Others must then shoulder her burdens. It was not for her to offer advice (which would doubtless be disregarded) on how to do it. In the meantime, she ruled and lived, and waited for the end with equanimity.

She led a healthy life. Right to the end, she followed Robert Dudley's advice, given to her at her accession, to take frequent and vigorous exercise. She was proud of her health, and with reason. Her absences from work or ceremonial through illness were far less frequent, and less prolonged, than those of any of her leading ministers. If she was sick, or in pain, she tried to conceal it if possible. Apart from her major bout of smallpox, her one serious malady had been an ulcer in her leg, first reported in July 1569. Nearly a year later Ambassador Fénelon saw her 'in her private chamber, dressed like an invalid, having her leg in repose'. De Silva described the trouble as 'an open ulcer [*una llaga*] above the ankle, which prevents her from walking'.[2] During her summer progress of 1570, therefore, she had travelled by coach. The sore seems to have healed the following year, but it left her with a slight limp: hence Essex's angry reference, much resented by the Queen, to her mind being 'as crooked as her body'. She deplored any suggestion she was ill. On 23 July 1577, at her request, Leicester wrote to Burghley, who was in Buxton, asking him to send the Queen a tun of the local water. The tun duly arrived, but it led to the rumour that her leg was inflamed again, and she refused to drink the water. Indeed, she blamed Leicester for getting it sent.[3] Though she had excellent doctors, by the standards of the day, she made little use of them. Throughout her life she disliked taking medicine in almost any form. She had seen enough of the ravages of Tudor medicine, especially in the case of her half-brother, King Edward, to know that it was more likely to kill than cure.[4] She tried to prevent her ministers and servants from taking drastic remedies. Thus, in May 1593, Burghley wrote to Robert Cecil that the doctors had recommended him to take 'quicksilver' and 'tincture of gold', but that he did not dare do so 'with fear for offending her Majesty, if I should thereby impair my health, contrary to her careful advice'. He thought that her instructions to take nothing, and allow nature to work the cure, might have 'some secret impulse from God, her head and my director'.[5] Elizabeth particularly objected to purges, both because they were harmful and because they were the most frequent excuse for her employees to be absent from work. The maids were forbidden purgatives. Elizabeth Bridges and Elizabeth Russell were slapped and 'put out of the Coffer Chamber' for three days in April 1597, 'The cause of this displeasure said to be their taking of physic, and one day going privately through the Privy Gallery to see the playing at ballon.'[6] Elizabeth had her own private cures, chiefly 'cordial broths', which she sent to friends, ministers and servants when they were sick, often spooning in the mixture herself. She had ancient recipes – very likely more effective than fashionable or professional treatment – for almost any ailment. In this, as in many other ways, she was a very old-fashioned woman. One of her cures, for deafness, which she sent to Lord North, has survived: 'Bake a little loaf of bean flower, and being hot, rive it in halves, and into each half pour in three or four spoonfuls of bitter almonds; then clap both halves to both ears before going to bed, keep them close, and keep your head warm.'[7]

When physical action had to be taken, Elizabeth always resisted till the last moment. In 1578, the saga of her tooth-ache lasted nine months. She first felt 'grievous pangs and pains' in April, but refused extraction. Instead, Dee was sent abroad to consult with learned physicians. He and the Council produced one John Anthony Fenotus, 'an out-landish physician of some note', who advised that the tooth could be filled with poppy-juice and stopped with wax. Then it would become loose and she could pull it out with her fingers. But he, too, recommended extraction, if she would 'submit to such chirurgical instruments' (which it seems he had heard something of the Queen's abhorrence of). Thanks to Hatton's careful tact and stage-management, Bishop Aylmer heroically offered to have a tooth, 'perhaps a decayed one', pulled out in the Queen's presence, to show there was nothing to it. This was done, in December, and Elizabeth then underwent the pincers.[8] Like many people who suffer from bad teeth, she was highly sensitive on the subject. On the whole, she preferred to keep them, and suffer, than have them all out like Philip II, and live on slops. But her teeth caused neuralgic pains in her face and neck, from which she is often reported as suffering. Sometimes she had swellings in her cheek, forehead, chest and shoulders, perhaps from the same cause, and she had many headaches. But she would not stop eating sweet things. Indeed, towards the end of her life cakes, sweets, custards and puddings became her chief source of nourishment. Elizabeth also suffered from occasional bouts of rheumatism, sometimes severe ones, and these, too, she preferred to bear in silence. Robert Cecil wrote to Essex on August 1597: 'The Queen hath a desperate ache in her right thumb, but will not be known of it, nor the gout it *cannot* be, nor *dare* not be, but to sign [letters] will not be endured.'[9]

Like her father, Elizabeth had extraordinary resilience. Periods of lassitude and exhaustion would be followed by determined efforts at furious activity. From 1599 onwards, it was plain that the Queen's general strength was progressively declining. She was aware of this, and her efforts to conceal it became more systematic. She was the last of the omni-competent monarchs of England, running a personal system of authority. She knew that to admit openly that her physique was fading must erode her ability to get herself obeyed. In the summer of 1599, it was noted: '. . . when she rideth a mile or two in the park, which now she seldom doth, she always complaineth of the uneasy going of her horse; and when she is taken down, her legs are so benumbed that she is unable to stand'.[10] This summer was one of particular anxiety for her. She was desperately worried by Essex's mismanagement of affairs in Ireland. Many men of birth, especially the young, were with the Earl on campaign, and her retinue had shrunk. Lord Hunsdon, the Lord Chamberlain, complained to Cecil: 'She ... will go more privately than is fitting for the time, or beseeming her estate; yet she will ride through Kingston in state, proportioning very unsuitably her lodgings at Hampton Court unto it, making the Lady Scudamore's lodgings her Presence Chamber, and Mrs Ratcliffe's her Privy Chamber.'[11] But the word evidently got around that she was ailing, and the Queen immediately fought back. Rowland White reported to Sir Robert Sidney: 'Her Majesty, God be thanked, is in good health, and likes very well Nonsuch air. Here hath many rumours been bruted of her, very strange, without any reason, which troubled her a little; for she would say, *mortua sed non sepulta*.'[12] Indeed, she deliberately lengthened her summer progress, 'by reason of an intercepted letter, wherein the giving over of long voyages was noted to be a sign of age'. The next month, the Scots ambassador, Beltreis, reported she had been furious with Hunsdon when the latter imprudently protested that it was unwise for 'one of her years' to ride horseback all the way from Hampton Court to Nonsuch. 'My years?' she replied. 'Maids! To your horses quickly.'[13] She refused to speak to Hunsdon for the next two days. Of course many of her courtiers were now elderly themselves, and found both the range and the speed of her progresses excessive. But the Queen was obdurate. White reported from Nonsuch: 'The lords are sorry for it, but her Majesty bids the old stay behind, and the young and able to go with her.'[14]

With the dismissal of Essex, and the placing of Ireland in more competent hands, Elizabeth seems to have recovered her spirits almost completely. She was very active in the year 1600, hunting regularly and engaging in the full round of court entertainments. Nor was her sport confined to the butts. She was reported to be 'excellently disposed to hunting, for every second day she is on horseback and continues the sport long'.[15] In May, she was 'very well. This day she appoints to see a Frenchman do feats upon a rope in the Conduit Court. Tomorrow, she hath commanded the bears, the bull, and the ape, to be baited in the Tiltyard. Upon Wednesday she will have solemn dancing.'[16] Right to the end, she remained addicted to the baiting of animals. She hated cockfighting, which she regarded as a purely masculine pastime, but bear-baiting was a royal sport. The pit at Paris Garden on the South Bank was her personal property, and her bears – Harry Hunks, Great Ned and Sackerson, who figures in Shakespeare – were famous and venerable beasts. She had a Master of the Bears, and another official in charge of her mastiffs, which came from Lyme, and were huge, pale yellow in colour, with black ears and muzzles and soft brown eyes: three were regarded as a match for a bear, four for a lion.[17] She watched her bears on several occasions in 1600, and rode often on her two favourite horses, Pool (a grey) and Black Wilford. At the end of the year, during the theatre season, she saw eleven plays performed, the greatest number recorded in her reign.[18]

During this final period, we have a number of intimate glimpses of the Queen, many from her godson, Harington, and his friends. Harington had a talent to amuse, and he did his best to keep the old lady happy. In 1596, he had published an illustrated pamphlet on water-closets, *The Metamorphosis of Ajax*, designed to improve the sanitation of the great palaces and country houses, and, among other things, to reduce the infamous smells which pervaded them. As such, he expected it to appeal strongly to the Queen, who hated smells. She disliked particularly the smell of new leather, and a variety of stories were told about her protests when men came for an audience in new boots (Burghley, when discussing with Cambridge University officials the presentation of a book to her, warned them that the leather must be old and odourless). She complained about the breath of one French ambassador (he presumably indulged in garlic), and said she could smell it an hour after he had left her Privy Chamber. Harington's plan to reduce the stink of sewage at court – especially in the 'close-stools' in the Privy Chamber – went adrift, because his *Ajax* included a disparaging reference to the dead Leicester, which Elizabeth resented, but the author's cousin was soon able to report: 'And though her Highness signified displeasure in outward sort, yet did she like the marrow of your book.' Harington's relations with his godmother had their ups and downs. He had gone with Essex to Ireland, and foolishly accepted a knighthood from the Earl. When he got back after the débâcle, she gave him a roasting, and he fled from court 'as though all the rebels in Ireland were at my heels'. He sent his wife on a flattering mission, and told her to tell the Queen that she kept his love by showing she loved him. The tactical analogy worked, for Elizabeth replied: 'Go to, go to, mistress, you are wisely bent, I find: after such sort do I keep the goodwill of all my husbands, my good people; for if they did not rest assured of some special love towards them, they would not readily yield me such good obedience.'[19] Harington eventually had the nerve to show his face at court again during Essex's disgrace. The trouble was, the moment the Queen saw him, she was reminded of his knighthood. To Sir Anthony Standen, he recounted what happened:

I came to court in the very heat and height of all displeasures. After I had been there but an hour, I was threatened with the Fleet. I answered poetically that, coming so late into the land-service, I hoped that I should not be pressed to serve in her Majesty's fleet, in Fleet Street. After three days, every man wondered to see me at liberty ... But I had this good fortune that, after four or five days, the Queen had talked of me and twice talked to me, though very briefly. At last she gave me a full and gracious audience in the Withdrawing Chamber at Whitehall, where her self being accuser, judge and witness, I was cleared, and graciously dismissed. What should I say? I seemed to myself for the time like St Paul, rapt into the third heaven, where he heard words not to be uttered by men; for neither must I utter what I then heard; until I come to heaven I shall never come before a statelier judge again, nor one that can temper majesty, wisdom, learning, choler and favour, better than her Highness did at that time.[20]

The Queen was undoubtedly distressed in spirit during 1601, in the aftermath of the Essex rising, and his execution. But her moods came and went. In August, staying with Sir William Clark, she had a long conversation with Sir William Browne, one of her generals, who had just returned from the Low Countries. He left a full account of it. 'I had no sooner kissed her sacred hands but that she presently made me stand up and spake somewhat loud and said, "Come hither, Browne!" and pronounced that she held me for an old faithful servant of hers, and said "I must give content to Browne." ' She told her train of courtiers to stand back, so they could talk in private. She called for a stool, and sat on it, and when Browne attempted to speak to her kneeling, she told him to get up, and be comfortable, and said she would not speak to him if he continued to kneel. Not that he had much chance to say anything. Their talk ranged over all the complex military and political affairs of the Low Countries, but when he attempted to defend the conduct of the Dutch she interjected: 'Tush, Browne! I know more than thou dost.' She also criticized the French, and brushed aside Browne's attempt to explain their motives with another 'Tush, Browne!' As for the argument that English soldiers had not received enough backing from her government, she pointed to Cecil, who was nearby: 'Dost thou see that little fellow that kneels there? It hath been told you that he hath been an enemy to soldiers. On my faith, Browne, he is the best friend that soldiers have.' This was true, as Cecil's activities in parliament show, but the Secretary was quick to add: 'it was from her Majesty alone from whom floweth all soldiers' good'. Elizabeth, indeed, was conducting an essentially political conversation with an important military personality, and skilfully blending graciousness and flattery with her own propaganda. She made a very deep impression: Browne rushed off delighted to record the talk verbatim, and says he got such joy from meeting the Queen 'as that I shall think of it during life'.[21]

But the same month, we have a record of a more melancholy conversation she had at Greenwich with William Lambarde, her archivist, who had produced a volume of state records, which he presented to her. Again she was gracious and warm, as only she knew how to be, but in looking through the book 'her Majesty fell upon the reign of King Richard II, saying: "I am Richard II, know ye not that?" ' Thus the spectre of the deposed and murdered king appeared again. Lambarde expressed his horror at the Essex rising: 'Such a wicked imagination,' he commented, 'determined and attempted by a most unkind gentleman, the most adorned creature that ever your Majesty made.' Elizabeth said: 'He that will forget God, will also forget his benefactors; this tragedy was played forty times in open streets and houses.' She sighed, as she looked over the medieval records in the book, commenting: 'In those days force and arms did prevail; but now the wit of the fox is everywhere on foot, so hardly a faithful or virtuous man may be found.'[22]

It may be that, in the light of the Essex revolt, Elizabeth was worried by the approaching parliament in the autumn of 1601. Sir Robert Sidney reported to Harington that she had been very pleased with some presents he had conveyed to her: verses, a prose pamphlet, and sweets: 'The Queen hath tasted your dainties, and saith, you have marvellous skill in cooking of good fruits.' But he added: 'She doth wax weak since the late troubles, and Burghley's death doth often draw tears from her goodly cheeks; she walketh out but little, meditates much alone, and sometimes writes in private to her best friends.' Shortly afterwards, she visited Sidney's house and 'did vouchsafe to eat two morsels of rich comfit cake, and drank a small cordial from a gold cup'. She was finely dressed in 'a marvellous suit of velvet' borne by four ladies; but 'at going upstairs she called for a staff, and was much wearied in walking about the house, and said she wished to come another day'.[23] Harington was able to see her state for himself only a fortnight before parliament met in October 1601:

She was quite disfavoured, and unattired, and these troubles waste her much. She disregardeth every costly cover that cometh to the table, and taketh little but manchet and succory potage. Every new message from the City doth disturb her, and she frowns on all the ladies. I had a sharp message from her brought by my Lord Buckhurst, namely thus: 'Go tell that witty fellow, my godson, to get home; it is no season now to fool it here.' I liked this as little as she doth my knighthood, so took to my boots and returned to the plough in bad weather ... the many evil plots and designs hath overcome all her Highness's sweet temper. She walks much in her Privy Chamber, and stamps with her feet at ill news, and thrust her rusty sword at times into the arras in great rage. My Lord Buckhurst is much with her, and few else since the City business; but the dangers are over, and yet she always keeps a sword by her table.[24]

When Harington wrote this letter to Hugh Portman, the writs for parliament were out and the elections were taking place. Elizabeth was plainly apprehensive about the composition of the House, and its likely mood. She was also hag-ridden by the news from Ireland, where the Spaniards had at last landed. Marshal Biron, envoy of Henri IV, was in town, and according to Ralegh, no proper preparations had been made for his reception. The Queen's mind was elsewhere. 'I never saw so great a person so neglected', said Ralegh, and put on some enter-tainments himself. Then the Queen stirred herself, and took Biron down to Hampshire, where he was put up in great state at Lord Sandys's house, The Vyne, which was decked out with hangings and plate from the Tower and Hampton Court. Satisfied, she boasted 'she had done that in Hampshire, that none of her ancestors ever did, neither that any prince in Christendom could do: that was, she had in her progresses at her subjects's houses, entertained a royal ambassador, and had royally entertained him'.[25] Back in London, she met parliament, and after the initial mismanagement of the opening, her success in coming to terms with what might have been a difficult assembly completely restored her self-confidence. She was particularly delighted with the reception of her 'Golden Speech', and her parting with her parliamentarians – for the last time – could not have been more mellow.

Thus 1602, the final full year of her life, was one of reasonable content and, it seems, tolerable health. The New Year brought excellent news from Ireland: the crushing of Tyrone's forces and the surrender of the Spanish. In June, Sir Richard Leveson, the ablest of her second generation of naval commanders, attacked a Spanish convoy under the guns of Coimbra Castle. He had only five ships, but he destroyed two galleys, and captured nine more and a carrack – a smashing victory which ensured English naval supremacy during the final months of the reign. And the harvest in England was good: 'I never knew a later, nor withall a better or more plentiful harvest', wrote Chamberlain.[26] The Queen had good reason to enjoy herself and, within limits, she did. She kept up her dancing. The days when 'six or seven galliards of a morning' were her 'ordinary exercise', and when a Spaniard could write that 'the head of the Church of England and Ireland was to be seen in her old age dancing three or four galliards', were drawing to their close.[27] But she was seen at one wedding dancing '*gayement et de belle disposition*' and at another there was 'singing, dancing and playing wenches'.[28] Early in 1602, when he was sixty-eight, she entertained the Orsini Duke of Bracchiano, 'very graciously; and, to show she is not so old as some would have her, danced both measures and galliards in his presence'. This was Chamberlain reporting; and again, in April 1602, he noted during the visit of the Duke de Nevers: 'The Queen graced him very much, and did him the favour to dance with him.'[29] As a rule, however, she no longer danced herself, but watched instead. Ambassador de Maisse sat next to her on one of these occasions, and said she

> took great pleasure in the ball and music . . . [and remarked] that in her youth she danced very well . . . when her maids are dancing she follows the time with her head, hand and foot. She rebukes them if they do not dance to her pleasure, and without doubt she is an expert. She says she used to dance very well when young; after the Italian manner of dancing high.[30]

Sometimes, however, she could not resist dancing, when she thought she was alone. She was seen thus at Hampton Court, doing a 'Spanish panic', to the music of a fife and tambour, in her private quarters. She still took exercise. As late as August 1602, she rode ten miles and then went out hunting on the same day. On 26 September, the Duke of Stettin saw her walking in the garden at Oatlands, 'as briskly as though she were 18 years old' – this was her old promenade habit, 'to get up a heat'. The same month, Fulke Greville was able to inform Lady Shrewsbury: 'The best news I can yet write your ladyship is of the Queen's health and disposition of body, which I assure you is excellent good, and I have not seen her every way better disposed these many years.'[31]

So far as the public could observe, Elizabeth was still capable of enjoying herself, right up to the end of 1602. On Accession Day, 17 November, Chamberlain reported to Carleton that the court fool, Garret, 'made as fair a show as the proudest of them [at the tilt], and was as well disguised, marry not altogether so well-mounted, for his horse was no bigger than a good ban-dog; but he delivered his scutcheon with his *impressa* himself, and had good audience of her Majesty and made her very merry'.[32] Her leading ministers made valiant efforts to entertain Elizabeth at their houses, partly to keep up her spirits, partly to keep her in London, and so avoid the travelling which they knew was beginning to tire her. On 6 December she dined at Cecil's new house in the Strand – it was a house-warming party – and was 'marvellously well-contented, but at her departure she strained her foot'.[33] Then followed a dinner-party given by Lord Hunsdon, and, on 22 December, a big party at the Earl of Nottingham's. He had been expected to present Elizabeth, on this occasion, with his 'rich hanging for all the fights with the Spanish armada in eighty-eight', but he proved unwilling, at the last moment, to part with such a treasure, and gave her a new dress instead. As a result of these feastings, Elizabeth kept the court in Whitehall for Christmas, and Chamberlain was glad to record that the holidays were much gayer than anyone expected. The new Comptroller, Sir Edward Wotton, 'hath put new life into it by his example (being always freshly attired, and for the most part all in white, *cap-à-pied*)'. There was, he said, 'much dancing, bear-baiting, and many plays', and also a good deal of gambling, with Cecil losing £800 in a single evening.

But despite this gaiety, it became evident, in the autumn of 1602, that the Queen's powers were failing, though not dramatically. On 12 October, she had to be reminded what were the duties of various courtiers who came to pay their respects to her. She could remember their faces, and names, but not always their offices.[34] Her authority was in no way declining, but she was becoming more difficult to manage, and less inclined to attend to business. The same month, Cecil discussed with Hunsdon how to deal with her over a transfer of property. Cecil was to determine the time of presentation of the document, so he could be in the room at the reading of it, and explain it, but Greville (of whom she was very fond) was actually to hand it to her.[35] We get another hint, shortly afterwards, in a letter written by Cecil, who was absent sick for a few days, to Windebank, Clerk of the Council:

> Upon some intelligence received, I have directed a longer letter to the Queen than is fit for her fair eyes to read. Pray deliver it, and crave liberty to read it to her [her eyesight was failing]; but read it to yourself first, to be perfect, and then seal it up with my seal, which I send you. PS: Do not show the Queen this letter, but tell her I willed you to desire leave to read mine to her, rather than to trouble her. If she asks you how I do, say my man told you I could go with a little stick very well, and say no more, nor that but by accident of her question . . . If she should say it is not my hand, do not in any way say but that it is, for when I take leisure I write legibly.[36]

The Queen was still handling Irish affairs with great attention, but very little else, at least in detail. And she had longer, and more frequent, periods of melancholy. A correspondent of one of James's friends wrote to Scotland: 'Our Queen is troubled with a rheum in her arm, which vexeth her very much . . . She sleepeth not so much by day as she used, neither taketh rest by night. Her delight is to sit in the dark, and sometimes with shedding tears to bewail Essex.'[37]

On 1 and 6 January 1603 Elizabeth saw plays performed at Whitehall. On the 17th she dined with Lord Thomas Howard, in the lodgings at the Charterhouse she had lent him. Four days later, she set out for Richmond, 'her warm winter box', but broke her journey at Putney to dine with her old cloth-merchant friend, John Lacy. The court was established at Richmond by the last week of the month, 'in very foul and wet weather'. Then the wind moved round to the north-east, and brought great cold. The Queen was now definitely ailing, suffering from a combination of insomnia, cold, rheumatism and sadness, to which it is impossible to assign any particular cause. She was simply an old, tired woman in mid-winter, trying to attend to business and keep the court routine going, but feeling the weight of her years and the physical exhaustion of decades. On 2 February, Giovanni Scaramelli, the first Venetian ambassador to be appointed since her accession, arrived in London and went straight to Richmond. She received him in audience, fully and magnificently dressed, and apparently in good spirits. His coming, after such a long boycott by the Doge, was something of a success for her diplomacy, and evidence of the papacy's waning powers. So she put on a brave show, and gently rebuked the Venetian Republic for waiting until the forty-fifth year of her reign to acknowledge her existence by sending a diplomatic representative. There was a last, tiny flash of vanity at the end of the audience: 'I do not know if I have spoken Italian well; still, I think so, for I learnt it when a child and believe I have not forgotten it.'[38] The following week she was busy with final negotiations for Tyrone's surrender. The reign was ending in triumph, but it was ending none the less. That month, the swelling in her fingers made it necessary for her to have her coronation ring, a plain gold band which she wore on her wedding finger, cut off. She was no longer symbolically married to her people.[39] Bishop Goodman later wrote that at Richmond she 'was very much neglected, which was an occasion of her melancholy . . . I was an eye-witness.'[40] But there is no supporting evidence for this statement. Most of the great men of the régime were at, or near, court.

The beginning of the end seems to have come in the last days of February. De Beaumont, the French ambassador, stated that, when he asked her for an audience on 26 February, she begged to be excused for a few days, on account of the death of Lady Nottingham, 'for which she has wept extremely, and shown an uncommon concern'.[41] 'She has suddenly withdrawn into herself,' wrote Scaramelli, 'she who was wont to live so gaily, especially in these last years of her life.' The beginning of her last illness is described by Sir Robert Carey, of whom she was fond. He was brother of the Lord Chamberlain, and youngest son of her old warrior-cousin, Hunsdon. When he reached court, he found the Queen

> in one of her withdrawing chambers, sitting low upon her cushions. She called me to her; I kissed her hand and told her it was my chiefest happiness to see her in safety and in health, which I wished might long continue. She

took me by the hand and wrung it hard, and said: 'No, Robin, I am not well', and then discoursed with me of her indisposition, and that her heart had been sad and heavy for ten or twelve days, and in her discourse she fetched not so few as forty or fifty great sighs. I was grieved at the first to see her in such plight; for in all my lifetime before I never knew her fetch a sigh but when the Queen of Scots was beheaded. . . . This was upon a Saturday night, and she gave command that the great closet should be prepared for her to go to chapel the next morning. The next day, all things being in readiness, we long expected her coming. After eleven o'clock, one of the grooms came out and bade make ready for the private closet; she would not go to the great. There we stayed long for her coming; but, at last, she had cushions laid for her in the Privy Chamber, hard by the closet door, and there she heard service. From that day forwards she grew worse and worse.[42]

On 9 March, De Beaumont reported that she had been ill for the best part of a fortnight

being seized with such a restlessness, that though she has no formed fever, she felt a great heat in her stomach, and a continual thirst, which obliged her every moment to take something to abate it, and to prevent the hard and dry phlegm, with which she is sometimes oppressed, from choking her . . . she has been obstinate in refusing everything prescribed by her physicians during her sickness.

On 12 March, De Beaumont noted that she had been better on the previous day, but was now worse, 'and so full of chagrin, and so weary of life, that notwithstanding all the importunities of her counsellors and physicians to consent to the use of proper remedies for her relief, she would not take one'. He describes her saying to Cecil and Whitgift 'that she knew her own strength and constitution better than they, and that she was not in such danger as they imagine'. To the end, she held Tudor medicine at bay. Snatches of her remarks are recorded. When Cecil tried to insist she went to bed, there was a flash of old fire: 'The word *must* is not to be used to Princes.' To Nottingham, she said: 'My Lord, I am tied with a chain of iron about my neck . . . I am tied, I am tied, and the case is altered with me.'[43] She complained of 'a heat in her breasts, and a dryness in her mouth, which kept her from sleep frequently, to her disgust'. There were a series of crises, recoveries, and relapses. Evidently a form of bronchitis, or pneumonia, was setting in. On 18 March, De Beaumont wrote that she was much worse, 'and appeared already in a manner insensible, not speaking sometimes for two or three hours, and within the last two days for above four-and-twenty, holding her finger continually in her mouth, with her eyes open and fixed to the ground, where she sat upon cushions without rising or resting herself, and was greatly emaciated by her long watching and fasting'. She had been lying on these cushions for ten days, in her day clothes, almost motionless. On 21 March she was finally persuaded to undress and go to bed. There, for a time, she felt better, and called for broth, 'but soon after she began to lose her speech, and from that time ate nothing, but lay on one side, without speaking or looking upon any person, though she directed some meditations to be read to her'.

It was now clear that the Queen would not survive. A contemporary note, written possibly by a secretary of Cecil's, describes how, on 22 March, with Nottingham on her right, Egerton on her left, and Cecil at the foot of the bed, Elizabeth indicated that James of Scotland should succeed her: 'Who should succeed me but a king . . . who, quoth she, but our cousin of Scotland?' The next day, her last, being unable to talk, she made the sign of a crown to emphasize the point.[44] But this was too neat, and too convenient from Cecil's point of view, and not in Elizabeth's character. The story seems to have been cooked up by Cecil and his leading colleagues after her death. Not until eleven days later was it reported by the punctilious and accurate De Beaumont. The likelihood is that she said absolutely nothing on the subject. She had been without speech for at least thirty-six hours before she died, and she had been sleeping peacefully for five hours before she ceased to breathe. Her final preoccupations seem to have been exclusively religious, and all the objective eye-witness accounts agree that her last days were edifying, with Whitgift and other clergy in constant attendance. John Manningham reached Richmond on 23 March, and there heard Dr Parry, one of her favourite chaplains, hold service in the chapel. The Queen was still alive, but in her last pangs. Whitgift, Egerton, Nottingham, Shrewsbury, Worcester, Grey, Sir William Knollys and Sir Edward Wotton attended the service, and heard Parry preach 'a very learned, eloquent, religious and moving sermon', on the subject of vows: 'his prayer, both in the beginning and conclusion, was so fervent and effectual for her Majesty that he left few dry eyes.'[45] Afterwards, waiting for the end, Manningham dined in the Privy Chamber with Parry and three other senior clerics. They told him

> that her Majesty hath been by fits troubled with melancholy some three or four months, but for this fortnight extreme oppressed with it, in so much that she refused to eat anything, to receive any physic, or admit any rest in bed, till within these two or three days. She hath been in a manner speechless for two days, very pensive and silent; since Shrovetide sitting sometimes with her

eye fixed upon one object many hours together, yet she always had her perfect sense and memory, and yesterday signified by the lifting of her hand and eyes to heaven, a sign which Dr Parry entreated of her, that she believed that faith which she hath caused to be professed, and looked faithfully to be saved by Christ's merits and mercy only, and by no other means. She took great delight in hearing prayers, would often at the name of Jesus lift up her hands and eyes to heaven. She would not hear the Archbishop [Whitgift] speak of hope of her longer life, but when he prayed or spoke of heaven, and those joys, she would hug his hand, etc. It seems she might have lived if she would have used means; but she would not be persuaded, and princes must not be forced. Her physicians said she had the body of a firm and perfect constitution, likely to have lived many years.[46]

Early the next day, 24 March, Elizabeth died. It was a Thursday, the death-day of her father, and of his other children. 'This morning, about three o'clock,' wrote Manningham, 'her Majesty departed this life, mildly like a lamb, easily like a ripe apple from the tree . . . Dr Parry told me he was present, and sent his prayers before her soul; and I doubt not but she is amongst the royal saints in heaven in eternal joys.'[47]

The more malicious papist propagandists immediately began to spread rumours that the Queen's last days had been terrifying, and her end grotesquely marked by evil portents. Only six days later, on 30 March, Chamberlain wrote to Carleton: 'Even here, the papists do tell strange stories, as utterly void of truth, as of all civil honesty and humanity.' The stories took many forms: that Elizabeth had always been provided with a false mirror, and only in her last days saw her face as it was, and unadorned; that she had seen her own body in the light of a fire, and died in despair of hell-flames; that after her death her body had swollen monstrously, and burst its coffin. The reports gained some credence through the publication of part of a manuscript drawn up by Elizabeth Southwell, the granddaughter of Lady Nottingham, and Elizabeth's own goddaughter, who had attended as a maid during the Queen's last days. This account, in manuscript, preserved at Stonyhurst, is endorsed in the hand of Father Parsons: 'The relation of the Lady Southwell, *primo aprilis*, 1607', and he later used it in writing his propaganda tract, *Discussion of an Answer*, in 1612. Elizabeth Southwell, however, was a compromised figure. In 1605 she eloped, disguised as a page, with Sir Robert Dudley, the illegitimate son of Leicester. Dudley was already married, but he left his wife behind, and fled with Elizabeth to the Continent. After some bargaining, the Pope granted Dudley an annulment, and the pair were married according to Catholic rites. The Southwell manuscript was the *quid pro quo*. By the time that Robert Carey came to write his memoirs, in 1627, the Southwell inventions, and other scurrilous stories, had reached their mature form. He denounced them all as 'false lies'. Carey's account is the fullest we have of the Queen's death; he was present at court, and his sister, Lady Scrope, was at the Queen's side virtually throughout the last weeks, and attended her when she died. His witness is thus of great value. In any case, none of the ugly rumours is corroborated by any of the strictly contemporary accounts: Chamberlain's, Manningham's, Clapham's, or the French and Venetian ambassadors, to list only five. In particular, there is no mention of the bursting coffin, which, had it occurred, must surely have caused a sensation.[48]

It rained heavily the night Elizabeth died. John Clapham, Burghley's former servant, who wrote an account of the Queen shortly afterwards, inserted a marginal note in his first draft: 'The Queen's body left in a manner alone a day or two after her death, and mean persons had access to it.'[49] The great ministers and officials at court were busy in London, ensuring a peaceful succession; and for a time the Queen's body was left to her ladies. Scaramelli reported: 'The body of the late Queen, by her own orders, has neither been opened, nor indeed seen by any living soul, save by three of her ladies.' A thirteen-year-old girl, Anne Clifford, later Countess of Pembroke, was present at Richmond during these days, sleeping on a pallet in the chamber of Lady Warwick, who was in charge of the arrangements. She later recorded that, a few days after the death, the body was taken at night by barge to Whitehall, where it stood in the drawing chamber, with various lords and ladies watching by day and night. Then it was taken to Westminster where, said Scaramelli, 'it lies in the palace, all hung with mournings . . . and so, in accordance with ancient custom, will it continue until the King gives orders for her funeral.'

Cecil and the other chief ministers, who had long ago concluded that James must succeed, had taken precautions to ensure that the transfer of power was swift and orderly. On 5 November 1602, Cecil, with Elizabeth's permission, had issued a proclamation against both the regular and the secular factions among the Catholic clergy, insisting there could be no question of 'toleration of two religions within her realm'. All priests must leave the realm by 1 January 1603, but those who submitted to Elizabeth's mercy could remain. Some of the seculars did so, and thus Cecil split the Catholics, and defused the papist threat, weeks before the Queen died.[50] Even so, further precautions were taken. Writing to Sir Robert Cotton, William Camden states that on 11 March, when it was still possible that the Queen might recover, the Council nevertheless ordered the arrest of certain 'vagrants' and shipped them to the Low Countries.

They brought munitions to the court, set a special guard on the Exchequer, ordered out the fleet to the Narrow Seas, and committed to house arrest 'some gentlemen hunger-starved for innovations'. These included old associates of Essex, notorious recusants, and men, such as Catesby and Tresham, who later became conspirators under James.[51]

On the morning of 24 March, immediately after they were satisfied that Elizabeth was dead, Cecil, Buckhurst and Nottingham went straight to Whitehall for a Council meeting, where Cecil, in his own hand, drafted the proclamation announcing the Queen's death and James's succession. He read it out aloud, first on the green at Whitehall, opposite the Tiltyard, and virtually on the spot where Downing Street now stands. Then the official party rode down the Strand to Ludgate, which was locked. To prove their *bona fides*, Buckhurst pushed his gold SS collar, plus the proclamation, through a lattice in the gate. Then they were admitted, and Cecil read the proclamation a second time, in front of St Paul's and again at Cheapside cross. Then the councillors formally claimed entrance to the Tower, in the name of King James I. There was no trouble whatever. Elizabeth's maids and ladies, according to Anne Clifford, had been anxiously waiting for news in the Coffer Room at Richmond; Lady Warwick had sent a message that there was likely to be some 'commotion'. But nothing happened: 'This peaceable coming in of the King was unexpected of all sorts of people.' Manningham, back in London, described the reception of the news there:

> There was a diligent watch and ward kept at every gate and street day and night, by householders, to prevent garboils; which God be thanked were more feared than perceived. The proclamation was heard with great expectation and silent joy, no great shouting. I think the sorrow for her Majesty's departure was so deep in many hearts they could not so suddenly show any great joy, though it could not be less than exceeding great for the succession of so worthy a king. And at night they showed it by bonfires and ringing. No tumult, no contradiction, no disorder in the City; every man went about his business as readily, and as peaceably, as securely, as though there had been no change, nor any news ever heard of competitors.

Three days later, on 27 March, James received the news of his accession, and promptly wrote to Cecil authorizing members of the Council to retain their offices, and to discharge their functions until his arrival in London. The transfer of power from the Tudors to the Stuarts was complete, and it had been done without bloodshed or dispute, in a manner of which the old Queen would have approved. Indeed, she would doubtless have claimed that it was precisely her prudent, but much-criticized, handling of the succession issue which had made the tranquil accession of James possible.

Her funeral on 28 April, five weeks after her death, was impressive in concept and execution, and was long remembered by those who witnessed it as fitting the solemnity of her departure. More than a thousand persons, all dressed in hoods and suits of black, composed the procession. First came bell-ringers and marshal's men to clear a way through the crowd. They were followed by 260 poor women, and 16 poor men, marching four abreast. Then came artisans, servants and messengers from the royal laundry, buttery, scullery, woodyard and stable, driving the carts, now empty, used by the household. The next phalanx was composed of the menial servants of the gentry and nobility of the court. Then, riderless, two of the Queen's horses, one covered in black cloth, the other in black velvet. The procession was kept in order by trumpeters blowing periodic blasts, and by sergeants-at-arms with maces, who paced along the line. The main part of the cortège began with the pursuivants and hereditary standard-bearers, carrying the Dragon, the Greyhound, the Lion, the Portcullis, and other ancient emblems of the crown. Then came the principal royal clerks, the musicians, the apothecaries, physicians and marshals of the court, the Cofferer leading the clerks of the Council, the Signet, the Privy Seal and parliament, the chaplains and vergers, and the gentlemen and children of the Chapel Royal, 'all singing a mournful tune'. Lord Zouche carried the banner of Cheshire, and Lord Herbert the banner of Cornwall. Next came the Mayor, Recorder and aldermen of London, the principal law officers and the crown judges, followed by the gentlemen-pensioners, holding their axes downwards. Lord Bindon carried the banner of Wales, and the Earl of Clanricard the banner of Ireland. Cecil himself walked with the Lord Chief Justice, followed by the principal officers of the household and the resident Dutch agent. Then came Egerton and Whitgift, with the French ambassador, whose train, carried by pages, was six yards long. The great banner of England was held by Nottingham and Pembroke, surrounded by the heralds. Immediately behind the banner was the hearse itself, surmounted by a waxen image of the Queen, 'the lively picture of her Majesty's whole body in her parliament robes, with a crown on her head, and a sceptre in her hands, lying on top of the corpse enshrined in lead and embalmed, covered with purple velvet, borne in a chariot drawn by four horses trapp'd in black velvet'. Over the hearse was a canopy, carried by six earls, with twelve lesser nobles carrying six banners alongside. Then the Earl of Worcester, Master of the Horse, followed, leading Elizabeth's favourite palfrey, with the Garter and Clarencieux heralds behind it. Lady Northampton, as the senior lady-member of the nobility, acted as chief mourner, her train held by two countesses. The Treasurer, Buckhurst, and the rest of the nobility, male and female, marched in ranks as assistant mourners; and Ralegh, with the guard in ranks of five, halberds downwards, brought up the rear.[52]

Many thousands, perhaps hundreds of thousands, watched the funeral. Stow says:

> Westminster was surcharged with multitudes of all sorts of people in their streets, houses, windows, leads, and gutters, that came to see the obseqy, and when they beheld her statue or picture lying upon the coffin set forth in royal robes, having a crown upon the head thereof, and a ball and sceptre in either hand, there was such a general sighing, groaning and weeping as the like hath not been seen or known in the memory of man . . . [53]

In the Abbey, after the coffin was lowered into its space, the chief household officers ceremonially broke their white staves across their knees, and threw the pieces into the grave. Then the tomb was closed. Three years later, in 1606 Elizabeth's monument, which had been ordered by James I, was completed. It is not so sumptuous as the one he had made for his mother, and cost a good deal less: £765. But the recumbent figure of Elizabeth, in full-length marble, is fine and accurate, so far as we can judge. The sculptor, Maximilian Colt, was paid £150 for his work. The realism of the features suggests that he used a death-mask as his source for the portrait. At the time, the effigy was coloured by Nicholas Hilliard, and gilded by John de Critz I. Colouring and gilt have long since vanished, as have the crown on the monument, and other accessories. Otherwise, little has changed in nearly 370 years. The Latin inscription calls Elizabeth 'the mother of this her country, the nurse of religion and learning; for perfect skill of very many languages, for glorious endowments, as well of mind as of body, a prince incomparable'.[54]

It was not long before the English people, who had wept at the Queen's passing, but had hailed her successor, began to regret her departure in earnest. Cecil himself, who flourished mightily under the new régime, none the less wrote to Harington:

> You know all my former steps: good knight, rest content, and give heed to one that hath sorrowed in the bright lustre of a court, and gone heavily even on the best-seeming fair ground. Tis a great task to prove one's honesty, and yet not spoil one's fortune. You have tasted a little hereof in our blessed Queen's time, who was more than a man and, in troth, sometimes less than a woman. I wish I waited now in her Presence Chamber, with ease at my foot,

and rest in my bed. I am pushed from the shore of comfort, and know not where the winds and waves of a court may bear me.[55]

Humbler people were soon even more sharply aware of what they had lost. 'After a few years', wrote Goodman

> when we had experience of a Scottish government, the Queen did seem to revive; then was her memory much magnified: such ringing of bells, such public joy and sermons in commemoration of her, the picture of her tomb painted in many churches, and in effect more solemnity and joy in memory of her coronation than was for the coming-in of King James.[56]

The romantic memory of the Queen, the posthumous longing for the balance and harmony of her rule, gave an emotional dynamic to the leaders of the Long Parliament, when they set about the dismantling of the Stuart tyranny in 1640. Since those days, Elizabeth's memory has ceased to be potent as a political slogan, but it lingers in the imagination of all English men and women who care about their country and its history.

It is superfluous to summarize her achievements. I have set out the record, in so far as it is possible in her own words, and those of her contemporaries. Her failings were and are self-evident. Few of those who knew her well, and who worked with her, were in any doubt that she was a creature of unusual intelligence, energy, determination and wisdom. They were conscious that they served a remarkable sovereign, fully worthy of her station. She had a genuine affection for her subjects; a high sense of natural justice; loyalty to her friends and ministers; a profound awareness of her responsibilities; a devotion to duty. She was avid for peace, courageous in war. These are kingly qualities.

But Elizabeth also had a gift, part rational, part instinctive, which may have been directly related to the fact that she was a woman: an accurate perception of the weakness, as well as the strength, of her country. It was this unsentimental realism, this unwillingness to become intoxicated by the rhetoric of force, which made her such a formidable figure of the international stage. She never overplayed her hand. She always operated well within the limits of her resources. She did not seek to impose upon the nation more than it could carry; and it was therefore always able to respond to the demands she felt obliged to make. Such an unemotional approach to the use of power sprang from a cool and pragmatic view of power itself. Elizabeth had a healthy regard for the possession of power: she did not allow power to possess her. She never shrank from sharing or delegating it, when prudent. Her self-confidence allowed her to select an extraordinary range of talents for employment in the public service;

and most of her leading ministers were not only able, but men of strong convictions, tenaciously held and frequently expressed, often in opposition to her own. No woman in history, before or since, has been invested with such a degree of personal authority over so long a period, and has remained so acutely aware of its limitations and dangers. In this sense she was incorruptible, and so kept her balance and judgment to the end. Behind a meretricious façade of vanity, she imposed upon herself an internal discipline, fortified indeed by a fine and flexible intellect, but whose roots were essentially moral. All monarchs of her day believed themselves to be trustees of the deity; Elizabeth accepted the practical implications of her position, and treated her public as well as her private actions as morally accountable.

The sophistication and complexities of her statesmanship enshrined a simple purpose. She held that the greatest benefit the tenant of a personal monarchy could confer upon her people was the maintenance of stability and order within the traditional framework of law and custom. Every other consideration was subordinated to this salient object. Such singlemindedness won the recognition and approval of contemporaries. In her time, wrote Holinshed, 'it pleased God to send England a calm and quiet season, a clear and lovely sunshine, a quittance from former broils of a turbulent estate, and a world of blessings by good Queen Elizabeth.' After her death, Camden endorsed this judgment:

Though beset by divers nations her mortal enemies, she held the most stout and warlike nation of the English four and forty years and upwards, not only in awe and duty, but even in peace also. Insomuch as, in all England, for so many years, never any mortal man heard the trumpet sound the charge to battle.

In our age, when the state and its leaders are universally expected to discharge much wider and deeper responsibilities on the popular behalf, such an accolade seems negative and meagre. But this was not the view of Elizabethan England. Those who inhabited it recognized both the truth and the value of the achievement Camden saluted, and were grateful. The function of the monarch was to hold the peace, without infringing the rights and liberties of the subject; and this Elizabeth had done. Of course, the personal monarchy which she inherited, and preserved for nearly half a century, was ultimately doomed. By her death it had largely served its historic purpose; a change to more complex forms of government was not only inevitable, but desirable, even essential. Elizabeth's state was merely one phase in a continuous process of national development. The point was gracefully made by her old tutor, Roger Ascham, in a passage which might have served as a comment on her life-work:

No perfection is durable. Increase hath a time, and decay likewise, but all perfect ripeness remaineth but a moment: as is plainly seen in fruits, plums, and cherries; but more sensibly in flowers, as roses and suchlike, and yet as truly in all great matters.[57]

Elizabeth herself would have put it more prosaically. She had a high sense of regal responsibilities; but she also loved the political game for its own sake. Its function was sublime; but the playing itself was pleasurable. She had no illusions about her life and career, and parted from both without regret. But she enjoyed them also. She was glad to be Elizabeth; proud to be Queen of England. Ralegh's parting words will serve just as well for his mistress:

I have had my part in this world, and now must give place to fresh gamesters. Farewell. All is vanity and weariness, yet such a weariness and vanity that we shall ever complain of it and love it for all that.[58]

Notes

CHAPTER I: HER FATHER'S DAUGHTER

1. Stephen Gardiner, *De vera obedientia oratio* (London 1535); quoted by
   D.M.Loades, *Two Tudor Conspiracies* (Cambridge 1965). Gardiner had
   (illegitimate) Tudor blood on his mother's side.
2. *Letters and Papers, Foreign and Domestic, of the Reign of Henry VIII*
   (1509–47), IV (3), 6179.
3. For the text see *Rotuli parliamentarum*, VI, 268–70; S.B.Chrimes, *Henry
   VII* (London 1972), pp. 61–2.
4. See genealogical table in Chrimes, *op. cit.*, p. 338.
5. T.Artemus Jones, 'Owen Tudor's Marriage', *Bulletin of the Board of Celtic
   Studies*, XI (1943); Chrimes, *op. cit.*, pp. 5–7; O.Williams, 'The Family of
   Henry VII', *History Today*, IV (1954).
6. Chrimes, *op. cit.*, p. 13.
7. R.P., VI, 288–9; *Calendar of Papal Registers*, XIV (1960), 1–2; Chrimes,
   op. cit., p. 66 and Appendix D.
8. See genealogical tables I, II and III in J.B.Black, *The Reign of Elizabeth*
   (Oxford, 2nd ed. 1969); Mortimer Levine: *Tudor Dynastic Problems,
   1460–1571* (London 1973), who prints relevant documents.
9. Garrett Mattingly, *Catherine of Aragon* (London 1950), p. 123;
   J.J.Scarisbrick, *Henry VIII* (London 1968), p. 147.
10. Lacey Baldwin Smith, *Henry VIII: the Mask of Royalty* (London 1971),
    p. 231; A.S.MacNalty, *Henry VIII: a Difficult Patient* (London 1952),
    pp. 180, 199; Ove Brinch, 'The Medical Problems of Henry VIII',
    Centaurus V (1958), 3, p. 367.
11. By Dr A.S.Currie, 'Notes on the Obstetric Histories of Catherine of
    Aragon and Anne Boleyn', *Edinburgh Medical Journal*, I (1888), pp. 1–34.
12. Baldwin Smith, *op. cit.*, pp. 65–6; Jean Kaulek (ed.), *Correspondence
    politique de MM. de Castillon et de Marillac 1537–42* (Paris 1885), 99,
    pp. 80–1.
13. Scarisbrick, *op. cit.*, p. 5.
14. G.R.Elton, *Policy and Police: the Enforcement of the Reformation in the Age
    of Thomas Cromwell* (Cambridge 1972), p. 177, n. 2.
15. Listed in British Museum, Additional MSS., 4729.
16. Scarisbrick, *op. cit.*, pp. 8–9; Chrimes, *op. cit.*, p. 285.
17. Baldwin Smith, *op. cit.*, pp. 109ff.

18. For a discussion of this impediment, Scarisbrick, *op. cit.*, p. 194; Chrimes, *op. cit.*, p. 286, n.1, gives reasons why Catherine's word may be doubted; see also Mattingly, *op. cit.*, pp. 48–52.

19. By Scarisbrick; but see Baldwin Smith, *op. cit.*, pp. 113–4; a glossary of both Leviticus and Deuteronomy is listed in Henry's library.

20. Full discussion in Scarisbrick, *op. cit.*, Chapter VII.

21. Baldwin Smith, *op. cit.*, p. 111; A.E.Pollard, *Henry VIII* (London 1913), pp. 184, 286.

22. Paul Friedmann, *Anne Boleyn, a Chapter of English History, 1527–36* (2 vols, London 1884), Appendix B.

23. Scarisbrick, *op. cit.*, p. 148.

24. George Cavendish, *The Life and Death of Cardinal Wolsey* (Early English Texts Society 1959), pp. 29ff.

25. P.Thomson, *Sir Thomas Wyatt and his Background* (London 1964), p. 28.

26. 'Green grow'th the Holly'; recorded, arranged Sothcott/Grub, and performed by the St George's Canzona, on EMI CFP 177, stereo.

27. For examples, see Elton, *op. cit.*, pp. 11, 24, 58, 60, 107, 137, 277–9, 282, 300, 331, 347, 354, 357, 384.

28. Scarisbrick, *op. cit.*, pp. 349–50; the only one of her 'lovers' to confess, Smeaton, did so under threat of torture.

29. Even Elizabeth Blount was endowed by parliament, at Henry's request: Mattingly, *op. cit.*, p. 123.

30. Cavendish, *op. cit.*, p. 117.

31. Baldwin Smith, *op. cit.*, p. 112 and n.

32. Elton, *op. cit.*, pp. 175ff.

33. The generally accepted date given in John Stow's *Chronicle*; see n. 2 in Neville Williams, *Elizabeth I, Queen of England* (London 1971 edn), p. 356.

34. Printed in full in F.A.Mumby, *The Girlhood of Queen Elizabeth* (London 1909), pp. 2–3; *L & P Henry VIII*, VI, no. 1089.

35. *L & P Henry VIII*, VI, no. 1112.

36. *Ibid.*, no. 1125.

37. For source material for these complex events see *L & P Henry VIII*, X, especially 282, 351, 495, 752, 864, 915; M.A.S.Hume (ed. and trans.), *Chronicle of King Henry VIII of England* (London 1889); Thomson, *op. cit.*, pp. 28ff.

38. *Calendar of State Papers, Spanish*, V, pt 2.

39. Scarisbrick, *op. cit.*, p. 349.

40. H.F.M.Prescott, *Spanish Tudor: the Life of Bloody Mary* (London 1940), p. 254; Henry Clifford, *Life of Jane Dormer* (ed. J. Stevenson, London 1887), pp. 78–80.

41. *CSP Venetian*, VI, 3, 1274.

42. 1 Mary, st. 2, c. 1 (*Statutes of the Realm*, IV, i, 200–1).

43. The two Acts are 1 Eliz., caps 3, 23 (*Statutes*, IV, i, 358–9, 397); see J.E. Neale, *Elizabeth I and her Parliaments*, Vol. I, 1559–89 (London 1969 edn), pp. 44–5.

44. PRO SP 12/31, no. 25.

45. Roy Strong, *Portraits of Queen Elizabeth I* (Oxford 1963), p. 5.

46. C.A.Patrides (ed.), *Sir Walter Ralegh: the History of the World* (London 1971), p. 59.

47. E.Auerbach, *Tudor Artists* (London 1954), p. 147.

48. Strong, *op. cit.*, p. 7.

49. *CSP Venetian*, 1556–7, 1058.

50. *Ibid.*, 1592–1603, 239.

51. G.B.Harrison and R.A.Jones (eds), *De Maisse's Journal* (London 1931), pp. 25–6.

52. Quoted in W.B.Rye, *England as Seen by Foreigners in the Days of Elizabeth and James I* (London 1865), p. 104.

53. Sir James Melville, *Memoirs of His Own Life 1549–93* (ed. A.F.Steuart, London 1929).

54. *Felicitie of Queen Elizabeth*, p. 18, in Francis Bacon, *Collected Works* (London 1857–74), vol. 2.

55. Baker, *Chronicle*, pp. 420, 422; quoted in John Nichols, *Progresses and Public Processions of Queen Elizabeth* (London 1823), vol. I.

56. See Elizabeth Jenkins, *Elizabeth the Great* (London 1958 edn), Preface; various authorities are examined.

57. Chrimes, *op. cit.*, pp. 302, 335.

58. R.P.Howgrave-Graham, 'The Earlier Royal Funeral Effigies', *Archaeologia*, XCVIII (1961).

59. According to Polydore Vergil; quoted in Chrimes, *op. cit.*, p. 299.

60. For Henry VII's financial reputation, see Chrimes, *op. cit.*, pp. 209 and n. 1, 214–15.

61. 18 April 1534; Mumby, *op. cit.*, p. 14.

62. *L & P Henry VIII*, IX, no. 568.

63. *Ibid.*, no. 132.

64. 28 Henry VIII, c. 7 (*Statutes*, III, 655ff.); Elton, *op. cit.*, p. 277.

65. Printed in full in Mumby, *op. cit.*, p. 14.

66. Thomas Hearne, *Syllogue Epistolarum* (London 1716), pp. 149–51.

67. Foster Watson, *Vives and the Renaissance Education of Women*, p. 41; quoted in Prescott, *op. cit.*, p. 11.

68. Text in Mumby, *op. cit.*, pp. 27–8.

69. J.A.Muller, *Stephen Gardiner and the Tudor Reaction* (New York 1926), p. 121; articles in *Dictionary of National Biography* on Sir John Cheke and Sir Thomas Wilson.

70. Full text of speech in Neale, *op. cit.*, vol. II, 1584–1601, pp. 99–101.

71. Anthony Wood, *Annals* (London 1796), pp. 248–53.
72. Nichols, *op. cit.*, III, pp. 416–19; Thomas Wright, *Queen Elizabeth and her Times* (London 1838), II, p. 479.
73. Francis Peck, *Desiderata Curiosa* (London 1779), I, p. 259.
74. A.L.Rowse, *The Elizabethan Renaissance* (vol. I, London 1971), pp. 17ff.
75. For a discussion of this problem see Garrett Mattingly, *Renaissance Diplomacy* (London 1955), Chapter 24.
76. Nichols, *op. cit.*, I, quoting *Bayle's Dictionary*, under 'Elizabeth'.
77. Best edition in W.A.Wright (ed.), *The English Works of Roger Ascham* (Cambridge 1904).
78. Neale, *op. cit.*, II, 1584–1601, p. 132; for Elizabeth's influence on hand-writing see Giles E.Dawson and Laetitia Kennedy-Skipton, *Elizabethan Handwriting: a Guide to the Reading of Documents and MSS.* (London 1968).
79. The first two are printed in Hearne, *op. cit.*, pp. 164–5, 161–3; the third is BM, Royal MSS., 7D.X. See Margaret H. Swain: 'A New Year's Gift from the Princess Elizabeth', *The Connoisseur*, Vol. 183, August 1973.
80. *Hamlet*, Act V, sc. ii.
81. *L & P Henry VIII*, XXI, ii, 347.
82. For a discussion of the chronology of these events, and the doubt about the Will's sealing, Scarisbrick, *op. cit.*, pp. 488ff.
83. W.K.Jordan, *Edward VI: the Young King: the Protectorship of the Duke of Somerset* (London 1968), pp. 55–65. Hertford was made a duke on 17 February.

CHAPTER 2: CHASTE AND UNEXPRESSIVE SHE

1. W.K.Jordan, *Edward VI: the Young King* (London 1968), p. 32.
2. N.Williams, *Henry VIII and his Court* (London 1971), p. 233.
3. Evelyn Read, *My Lady Suffolk* (New York 1963), pp. 51–2.
4. J.K.McConica, *English Humanists and Reformation Politics under Henry VIII and Edward VI* (Oxford 1965), p. 229.
5. John Foxe, *Acts and Monuments* (London 1870 edn), V, pp. 559–61.
6. Charles Whibley (ed.), *Edward Hall: Chronicle* (2 vols, London 1904), pp. 865–6.
7. A.G.Dickens, *The English Reformation* (London 1970 edn), p. 262.
8. Jordan, *op. cit.*, Chapter 1, 'The Henrician Background'.
9. *SP Dom. Edward VI*, VI, pp. 19–22.
10. Jordan, *op. cit.*, p. 370; no official documentation has ever been found.
11. See the Table in *ibid.*, p. 116.
12. *HMC Salisbury MSS.*, I, pp. 61, 62, 64, 67, 69, 70; *SP Dom. Edward VI*, VI, pp. 6, 19, 20, 21, 22.

13. Printed in full in G.B.Harrison (ed.), *Letters of Queen Elizabeth* (London 1968 edn), p. 7.
14. *Ibid.*, p. 8.
15. *Ibid.*, pp. 9–13, letters dated 28 January and 6 February 1549.
16. Jordan, *op. cit.*, p. 373; *SP Dom. Edward VI*, VI, p. 6.
17. Conyers Read, *Mr Secretary Cecil and Queen Elizabeth* (London 1955).
18. John Maclean, *Life of Sir Thomas Seymour* (London 1869), *passim*.
19. *HMC Salisbury MSS.*, I, 1, 65; Samuel Haynes and William Murdin, *State Papers etc.* (London 1740–57), I, pp. 84–6.
20. For the Sharington fraud, see Jordan, *op. cit.*, pp. 382ff.
21. For the debasement, see S.T.Bindoff, *Tudor England* (London 1969 edn), pp. 118ff.
22. *CSP Spanish*, IX, pp. 332–3.
23. Ellis, *Original Letters*, Series 2, II, pp. 256–7.
24. Jordan, *op. cit.*, p. 377.
25. *L & P Henry VIII*, XIX, ii, 726.
26. Haynes, *op. cit.*, p. 69.
27. *Ibid.*, pp. 70–1. Also printed in Mumby, *op. cit.*, pp. 39–43.
28. Dated 28 January 1549; Harrison, *op. cit.*, pp. 9–11.
29. 21 February; Harrison, *op. cit.*, pp. 12–13.
30. 7 March; *ibid.*, pp. 13–14.
31. Lord Strangford, *Household Expenses of the Princess Elizabeth* (Camden Society. Miscellany ii, 1853).
32. *Acts of the Privy Council*, II, p. 260.
33. Leti was described, as long ago as 1823 by Nichols, *op. cit.*, I, p. xxxii, as 'a scandalous Novelist, and not a faithful Historian'.
34. E.P. and Conyers Read (eds), *John Clapham: Elizabeth of England* (Philadelphia 1951), p. 68.
35. *As You Like It*, III, ii, 9.
36. *SP Dom. Edward VI*, VII, p. 5.
37. Jordan, *op. cit.*, pp. 496–7.
38. For Somerset's policies, see Jordan, *ibid.*, especially Chapter VI and pp. 386ff.; Dickens, *op. cit.*, pp. 279–83; Bindoff, *op. cit.*, pp. 127ff.
39. *Victoria County History*, Herts, III, p. 92.
40. Ian Dunlop, *Palaces and Progresses of Elizabeth I* (London 1962), under 'Hatfield'.
41. Conyers Read, *Mr Secretary Cecil*, p. 64.
42. For Elizabeth's letters to Edward, see Harrison, *op. cit.*, pp. 15, 16; Mumby, *op. cit.*, pp. 64–9.
43. In J.G.Nichols (ed.), *Literary Remains of King Edward VI* (2 vols, London 1857).
44. Jordan, *op. cit.*, p. 44.

45. J.G.Nichols (ed.), *The Diary of Henry Machyn, 1550–63* (Camden Society, 1848).
46. Nichols, *Progresses*, I.
47. W.K.Jordan: *Edward VI: The Threshold of Power* (London 1970), p. 510.
48. For the emergence of the boy-king as a factor in the power struggle, see *ibid.*, 402ff., and 515ff.
49. Mumby, *op. cit.*, p. 81.
50. Williams, *op. cit.*, p. 23, quoting the French ambassador, Antoine de Noailles.
51. *BM Add. MSS.*, 58541, fol. 137v; quoted in Dickens, *op. cit.*, p. 353.
52. W.D.Hamilton (ed.), *Charles Wriothesley: a Chronicle of England* (Camden Soc., 1875–7), II, pp. 90–1.
53. Neale, *op. cit.*, I, p. 149.

CHAPTER 3: IN TRUST I HAVE FOUND TREASON

1. On 22 August 1553.
2. A.F.Pollard, *Political History of England 1547–1603* (London 1910), p. 172.
3. For the evolution of the Tudor Council, see G.R.Elton, *The Tudor Constitution* (Cambridge 1968), pp. 87ff.
4. Council minute in Gilbert Burnett, *History of the Reformation* (Oxford 1865 edn), V, pp. 117–20; extracts printed in Elton, *op. cit.*, pp. 96–7.
5. Prescott, *op. cit.*, p. 333; Tytler, *op. cit.*, II, pp. 371–8.
6. For extracts, see Elton, *op. cit.*, pp. 99–100.
7. 1 Mary, st. 2, c. 2; 1 Mary, st. 1, c. 2.
8. *CSP Spanish*, XI, pp. 363–6.
9. F.Madden, *Privy Purse Expenses of the Princess Mary* (London 1831), pp. 85, 88.
10. *Ibid.*, p. 194.
11. Roy Strong and Julia Trevelyan Oman, *Elizabeth R.* (London 1971), p. 8.
12. Prescott, *op. cit.*, p. 253.
13. Williams, *op. cit.*, p. 25; Ambassador Noailles to Henri II, 9 August.
14. *CSP Spanish*, 1553, p. 188.
15. For the indictment of the conspirators, see KB 27/1174 Rex V.
16. E.H.Harbison, *Rival Ambassadors at the Court of Queen Mary* (Princeton 1940), p. 112.
17. For a full analysis of the plan, see D.M.Loades, *Two Tudor Conspiracies* (Cambridge 1965).
18. J.G.Nichols (ed.), *The Chronicle of Queen Jane* (Camden Soc., xlviii, 1850), p. 69.
19. Neale, *op. cit.*, I, p. 148.
20. *HMC Second Report*, Appendix 154.

21. *SP Dom. Mary*, III, no. 21.

22. Machyn, *op. cit.*, p. 57; P.R.Tytler, *England under Edward VI and Mary* (London 1856), pp. 306–12.

23. *Chron. Queen Jane*, p. 54.

24. *CSP Spanish*, XII, p. 162.

25. *SP Dom. Mary*, III, no. 13.

26. Printed in Ellis, *Original Letters*, 2nd Series, II, p. 255; original in PRO, SP 11/4, fols. 3, 3d.

27. For Elizabeth's stay in the Tower, see Foxe, *Acts and Monuments etc.* (London 1870); *Chron. of Queen Jane*; Raphael Holinshed, *Chronicles etc.* (London 1807–8); John Strype, *Ecclesiastical Memorials etc.* (3 vols, London 1721). For a plan of the Tower, see *Tower of London* (HMSO 1971), pp. 14–15.

28. For an analysis of the convictions and executions, see Loades, *op. cit.*

29. *CSP Spanish*, XII, p. 168.

30. For Throckmorton's defence, see William Cobbett, etc, *State Trials* (London 1816–98), pp. 870ff.; A.L.Rowse, *Ralegh and the Throckmortons* (London 1962), pp. 18–25.

31. *Chron. of Queen Jane*, p. 74.

32. *CSP Spanish*, XII, p. 201.

33. Foxe, *op. cit.*, VIII, ii, p. 614.

34. *State Papers Relating to the Custody of Princess Elizabeth at Woodstock in 1554* (Norfolk Archaeological Soc., IV, 1855); also referred to as *Bedingfeld Papers*; see also *HMC Third Report*, XVI and Appendix, pp. 237–40.

35. K.B.McFarlane, *The Nobility of Late Medieval England* (Oxford 1973), pp. 47ff.

36. *Bedingfeld* (see n. 34), p. 208.

37. Contemporary references to Elizabeth's health at this time are collected in Frederick Chamberlain, *Private Character of Queen Elizabeth* (London 1922); his interpretations are unreliable.

38. Holinshed, IV, p. 133.

39. Tytler, *op. cit.*, II, pp. 392–8; Prescott, *op. cit.*, pp. 337–8.

40. Prescott, *op. cit.*, pp. 11, 351.

41. *Ibid.*, p. 354; Martin Hume, 'The Visit of Philip II', *EHR*, VII (1892), pp. 253ff.

42. J.A.Froude, *History of England from the Fall of Wolsey to the Defeat of the Spanish Armada* (London 1909 edn), V, pp. 529–30.

43. *CSP Venetian*, VI, i, 42.

44. Prescott, *op. cit.*, p. 397.

45. *Ibid.*, p. 329.

46. Renaud to Charles V, 27 March 1554.

47. *CSP Spanish*, 1554–8, p. 145.

48. Strype, *op. cit.*, III, pp. 554–6, lists 282; Foxe, *op. cit.*, lists 275; a number of others, included in neither list, were recorded.

49. William Haller, *Foxe's Book of Martyrs and the Elect Nation* (London 1963).

50. Dickens, *op. cit.*, pp. 364–5; J.H.Blunt, *The Reformation of the Church of England* (London 1878–82), II, pp. 220ff.

51. Blunt, *op. cit.*, II, p. 245n.

52. Foxe, *op. cit.*, VI, p. 86.

53. *CSP Venetian*, VI, 3, Appendix 136; Jeremy Collier, *Ecclesiastical History of Great Britain* (London 1708–14), II, p. 371.

54. Dickens, *op. cit.*, pp. 363–4.

55. Prescott, *op. cit.*, pp. 391–2.

56. Agnes Strickland, *Queens of England* (London 1873 edn), III, pp. 89–90.

57. *CSP Venetian*, VI, 126.

58. For the Dudley conspiracy, see Loades, *op. cit.*, pp. 176ff.

59. *CSP Dom. Mary*, VIII, nos. 80, 54.

60. *Calendar of Patent Rolls*, III, 396.

61. *CSP Venetian*, VI, 474.

62. *CSP Dom. Mary*, VIII, no. 46.

63. Nichols, *Progresses of Queen Elizabeth*, I, pp. 16–18.

64. For details of the Stafford rising, see Loades, *op. cit.*

65. *CSP Spanish*, XIII, 372.

66. Printed in Mumby, *op. cit.*, pp. 236–8.

67. BM Cotton MSS., Vespasian FIII, fol. 27; quoted by J.E.Neale, 'The Accession of Queen Elizabeth', *History Today*, May 1953.

68. Prescott, *op. cit.*, p. 496.

69. Thynne Papers, vol. III, fols 21, 23, 24; quoted in Neale, *op. cit.* The Thynnes were leading landowners in Wiltshire.

CHAPTER 4: THE DEEP CONSENT OF ALL GREAT MEN

1. John Strype, *The Life of the Learned Sir T. Smith* (Oxford 1820 edn), pp. 249–50.

2. Printed by J.E.Neale in *EHR* (July 1950), p. 305.

3. Text in Henry Gee, *The Elizabethan Prayer Book and Ornaments* (London 1902).

4. J.E.Neale, 'Sir Nicholas Throckmorton's Advice to Queen Elizabeth', *EHR*, LXV (1950), pp. 91–8.

5. Feria to Philip II, 14 November 1558.

6. The old Cecil family tombs are at St Mary's, Welsh Newton; see Nicholas Pevsner, *The Buildings of England: Herefordshire*.

7. For the origins of the Cecil family, see Conyers Read, *Mr Secretary Cecil and Queen Elizabeth*, Chapter I.

8. PRO SP, XII, I, 7.
9. A.G.R.Smith, *The Government of Elizabethan England* (London 1967), pp. 47ff.
10. R.Cecil, 'The State and Dignity of a Secretary's Place', *Harleian Miscellany*, II (1809), pp. 281–2.
11. Memo on foreign policy, 1567, quoted in B.W.Beckinsale, *Burghley: Tudor Statesman* (London 1967).
12. Nichols, *Progresses*, I.
13. Peter J.French, *John Dee* (London 1972), p. 6.
14. For Pole's unorthodox beliefs, see Dermot Fenlon, *Heresy and Obedience in Tridentine Italy* (Cambridge 1973).
15. Neale, *History Today*, May 1953.
16. G.E.Phillips, *The Extinction of the Ancient Hierarchy* (London 1905).
17. Williams, *Elizabeth, Queen of England*, p. 55.
18. Roy Strong, *Portraits of Elizabeth I*, pp. 55–6 and Plate 7; now in Warwick Castle. For description, see Nichols, *Progresses*, III, p. 502.
19. Williams, *op. cit.*, pp. 53–4.
20. Extracts in Nichols, *op. cit.*
21. Williams, *op. cit.*, p. 57.
22. For the coronation, see N.Williams, 'The Coronation of Queen Elizabeth', *Quarterly Review*, 597 (1953), pp. 397–411; A.L.Rowse, 'Elizabeth's Coronation', *History Today*, III (1953), pp. 301–10.
23. For Elizabeth's government-making, see Wallace MacCaffrey, *The Making of the Elizabethan Regime* (London 1969), Chapter I.
24. PRO SP 12/1/7,8, printed in MacCaffrey, *op. cit.*
25. Rowse, *Ralegh and the Throckmortons*, pp. 25–6.
26. See John Aubrey, *Brief Lives* (ed. Oliver Lawson Dick, London 1962), pp. 221ff.
27. F.C.Dietz, *English Government Finance 1485–1558* (Illinois 1920), and *English Public Finance 1558–1641* (New York 1932).
28. For details see MacCaffrey, *op. cit.*
29. John Ruskin, *The Two Paths*, lecture II.
30. Sir Fulke Greville, *Life of the Renowned Sir Philip Sidney* (London 1652).
31. Sir Robert Naunton, *Fragmenta Regalia* (London 1653; ed. Edward Arber, London 1870).
32. Sir John Harington, *Nugae Antiquae* (London 1769–79 edn), II, pp. 215ff.
33. H.M.Colvin, 'Castles and Government in Tudor England', *EHR*, 83 (April 1968).
34. Patent Roll c. 66/972, m. 31d; quoted in Colvin, *op. cit.*
35. H.M.Colvin, *History of the King's Works*, I–III, *passim*.

36. R.R.Tighe and J.E.Davis, *Annals of Windsor* (London 1858), I, pp. 639ff.
37. See endpaper maps.
38. E.K.Chambers, *The Elizabethan Stage* (Oxford 1923), IV, pp. 75ff.
39. Ian Dunlop, *Palaces and Progresses of Elizabeth I* (London 1962), 'Newhall'.
40. *Ibid.*, 'Richmond'.
41. Clare Williams (ed.), *Thomas Platter's Travels in England 1599* (London 1937); Ernest Law, *History of Hampton Court Palace* (London 1890), I.
42. Letters of Rowland White in *Sidney Papers*, ed. Arthur Collins (2 vols, London 1746); John Summerson, *Architecture in Britain 1530–1830* (London 1953); John Dent, *The Quest for Nonsuch* (London 1962).
43. Quoted in Dunlop, *op. cit.*, 'Greenwich'.
44. F.Chapman, *Ancient Royal Palaces in or Near London* (London 1902).
45. E.K.Chambers, 'The Court', in *Shakespeare's England* (Oxford 1925), I.
46. W.F.Taylor, *The Charterhouse of London* (London 1912).
47. T.N.Brushfield, *The History of Durham House* (Trans. Devon. Assoc., XXXV), pp. 538ff.
48. R.Needham and A.Webster, *Somerset House Past and Present* (London 1905).
49. W.J.Loftie, *Memorials of the Savoy* (London 1878).
50. Chapman, *op. cit.*, p. 36.
51. E.Sheppart, *Memorials of St James's Palace* (London 1894).
52. Instructions by Lord Hunsdon, Lord Chamberlain, in 1601, quoted in Dunlop, *op. cit.*, 'Whitehall'.
53. Quoted in Dunlop, *op. cit.*
54. The painting was destroyed in the fire of 1698; a smaller copy is at Hampton Court, and the original cartoon in the National Portrait Gallery.
55. Machyn's *Diary*.
56. Quoted in Dunlop, *op. cit.*, 'Whitehall'.
57. For Mildmay, see S.E.Lehmberg, *Sir Walter Mildmay and Tudor Government* (Texas 1964); for Winchester, see W.C.Richardson, *Tudor Chamber Administration* (Baton Rouge 1952) and *History of the Court of Augmentations* (Baton Rouge 1961).
58. Christopher Hill, *The Economic Problems of the Church* (Oxford 1956), Chapter II; Phyllis M.Hembry, *The Bishops of Bath and Wells 1540–1640* (Athlone 1967).
59. Joan Thirsk (ed.), *The Agrarian History of England and Wales, IV, 1500–1640* (Cambridge 1967), Chapter V.
60. H.E.Bell, *Introduction to the History and Records of the Court of Wards and Liveries* (Cambridge 1953).
61. Y.S.Brenner, 'The Inflation of Prices in England 1551–1650', *Economic History Review*, 2nd Series, XV (1962).
62. Thirsk, *op. cit.*

63. See McFarlane, *op. cit.*
64. Thirsk, *op. cit.*
65. For Gresham, see J.W.Burgon, *Life and Times of Sir Thomas Gresham* (London 1839). Gresham had begun a restoration of the coinage under the Duke of Northumberland: see Jordan: *Edward VI: The Threshold of Power*, pp. 464–6.
66. Burgon, *op. cit.*, pp. 234, 356, 485.
67. Nichols, *Progresses*, I.
68. Conyers Read, *Mr Secretary Cecil*, Chapter IX, 'The Restoration of the Coinage'.
69. Burgon, *op. cit.*, pp. 344–5.
70. On efforts to create a domestic arms industry, A.L.Rowse, *The England of Elizabeth* (London 1964 edn), pp. 124ff.
71. E.g., Lawrence Stone, 'State Control in 16th Century England', *Econ. H.R.*, 12 (1947), pp. 103–20; and G.R.Elton, 'State Planning in Early Tudor England', *Econ. H.R.*, 13 (1960–1), pp. 433–9.
72. William Cunningham, *The Growth of English Industry and Commerce* (Cambridge 1907–10), II, p. 71.
73. Rowse, *op. cit.*, pp. 128ff.
74. J.U.Nef, *The Rise of the British Coal Industry* (London 1932).
75. William Cunningham, *Alien Immigrants to England* (London 1897).
76. R.B.Wernham, *Before the Armada: the Growth of English Foreign Policy, 1485–1588* (London 1966).
77. Earl of Hardwicke (ed.), *Hardwicke State Papers* (London 1778), I, p. 167.
78. MacCaffrey, *op. cit.*
79. L.Pastor, *History of the Popes* (London 1891–1933), XIV, pp. 69–70.
80. James Spedding, *Life and Letters of Bacon*, I, pp. 97–8.
81. 31 Henry VIII, c. 14.
82. Neale, *Elizabeth I and her Parliaments*, I, p. 42.
83. Text in Gee, *op. cit.*
84. Neale, 'Sayings of Queen Elizabeth', *History*, X, October 1925.
85. R.Crawfurd, *The King's Evil*, pp. 64ff.; Marc Bloch, *Les Rois Thaumaturges* (Paris 1924), p. 339; English version *The Royal Touch* (London 1973).
86. F.W.Maitland, 'The Anglican Settlement and the Scottish Reformation', *Cambridge Modern History*, II; *CSP Spanish*, 1558–67, p. 105.
87. MacCaffrey, *op. cit.*; Neale, *op. cit.*, I, Chapter I.
88. *CSP Venetian*, VII, 22–3.
89. Neale, *op. cit.*, I, pp. 40, 45–6.
90. Cecil to Throckmorton, 15 July 1561, PRO SP 71, 28; quoted in Read, *Mr Secretary Cecil.*
91. A.G.Dickens, *The English Reformation*, pp. 409ff.; *Zurich Letters* (Parker Society, 1842), II.

Notes

92. For details of the parliamentary battles, Neale, *op. cit.*, I, Chapters 2–3; Dickens, *op. cit.*, pp. 408ff.

93. *CSP Spanish*, Elizabeth, I, 61–2.

94. Neale, *op. cit.*, I, p. 81.

95. Black, *The Reign of Elizabeth*, pp. 19ff.

96. Dickens, *op. cit.*, Chapter 12.

97. J.Bruce and T.T.Perrowne, *Correspondence of Matthew Parker 1535–75* (Parker Soc., 1853), p. 391.

98. *Ibid.*, pp. 279–80, 311.

99. Harington, *Nugae Antiquae*, I, p. 4; Neale, 'Sayings of Queen Elizabeth'.

100. Quoted in Rowse, *England of Elizabeth*, p. 402.

101. *CSP Dom. Addenda*, 1566–79, 59.

102. Harington, *op. cit.*, I, p. 31.

103. John Knox, *History of the Reformation in Scotland* (vols. I–II of the *Collected Works*, ed. D.Laing 1846–54); P.F.Tytler, *History of Scotland* (Edinburgh 1866), VI, pp. 97–115.

104. Quoted in Read, *op. cit.*, pp. 137–8.

105. *CSP Foreign*, 1558–9, 523.

106. For Sadler, see A.J.Slavin, *Politics and Profit: A Study of Sir Ralph Sadler 1507–47* (Cambridge 1966).

107. Arthur Clifford (ed.), *Sadler Papers* (Edinburgh 1809), II, p. 207.

108. For Scottish policy 1559–60, Read, *op. cit.*, Chapter VII, and MacCaffrey, *op. cit.*

109. N.M.Sutherland, 'Elizabeth and the Conspiracy of Amboise', *EHR* (1966), and 'The Origins of Queen Elizabeth's Relations with the Huguenots', *Proc. of the Huguenot Soc. of London* (1966); Amos C.Miller, *Sir Henry Killigrew* (Leicester 1963).

110. Cecil to Sadler, 23 March 1560, *Sadler Papers*, II, p. 248.

111. C.G.Cruickshank, *Elizabeth's Army* (Oxford 1966 edn), pp. 207–35.

112. Read, *op. cit.*, p. 178.

113. Tytler, *op. cit.*, VI, pp. 211ff.

114. *Ibid.*, VI, pp. 231ff.

115. J.H.Pollen, *Letters of Mary to the Duke of Guise, etc.* (Scottish Hist. Soc., XLIII, 1904, p. 38).

116. Read, *op. cit.*, Chapter XI, 'Scotland 1560–2'.

117. *Ibid.*, Chapter XII, 'War with France'.

118. MacCaffrey, *op. cit.*, 'The Newhaven Adventure'; Read, *op. cit.*, 'War with France'.

CHAPTER 5: THE BEST MATCH IN HER PARISH

1. The most comprehensive list is in Frederick Chamberlain, *Private Character*

456

of Queen Elizabeth (London 1922 edn); see also A.S.MacNalty, *Elizabeth Tudor: the Lonely Queen* (London 1954), pp. 220–46.

2. Lacey Baldwin Smith, *The Elizabethan Epic* (London 1969 edn), p. 181.

3. For Elizabeth's medical men, see R.R.James, 'William Goodorus: Sergeant-Surgeon to Queen Elizabeth', *Lancet*, 231 (1936); L.G.H. Horton-Smith, *Dr William Baily, physician to Queen Elizabeth* (London 1952); F.E.Halliday, 'Queen Elizabeth and Dr Burcot', *History Today*, V (1955); C.A.Bradford, *Hugh Morgan, Queen Elizabeth's Apothecary* (London 1939); Arthur S.MacNalty, 'Medicine in the Time of Queen Elizabeth', *British Medical Journal*, 30 May 1953.

4. Cecil Papers, 148/25; quoted in Read, *Lord Burghley and Queen Elizabeth* (London 1960), pp. 210–11.

5. Ben Jonson, *Conversations with William Drummond* (Shakespeare Soc. 1842), pp. 484–5.

6. They are summarized in Pollard, *op. cit.*, p. 181, n. 2.

7. *CSP Venetian*, VII, 330.

8. Thomas Thomson (ed.), *Sir James Melville: the Memoirs of his Own Life* (Bannatyne Club 1829).

9. Read, *Mr Secretary Cecil*, p. 350, n. 52.

10. Neale, 'Sayings of Queen Elizabeth', *History*, October 1925.

11. A.L.Rowse, *The Elizabethan Renaissance: the Life of the Society* (London 1971), pp. 142–3.

12. Letter dated 20 September 1572; quoted in Black, *op. cit.*, pp. 152–3.

13. Nichols, *Progresses*.

14. See the correspondence in *The Times*, March 1973.

15. *CSP Dom.*, 1598–1601, 97; A.L.Rowse, *Shakespeare's Southampton* (London 1965), pp. 123ff.

16. See Lawrence Stone, *The Crisis of the Aristocracy* (Oxford 1965), Chapter XI, 'Marriage and the Family'.

17. *CSP Scottish*, 1589–93, 51.

18. Stone, *op. cit.*

19. *HMC Bath MSS.*, IV, 158.

20. Text in Thomas Wright, *Queen Elizabeth and her Times* (London 1838), II, pp. 193–4.

21. Eric St John Brooks, *Sir Christopher Hatton* (London 1946), p. 170; original in Bath MSS.

22. Quoted in Chambers, *The Elizabethan Stage*, I, p. 107.

23. Antonia Fraser, *Mary Queen of Scots* (London 1971 edn), pp. 548–9; the letter (in French) is printed in Murdin, *op. cit.*, and Prince Labanoff, *Lettres, Instructions et Mémoires de Marie, Reine d'Ecosse* (7 vols, Paris 1844); English text in Chamberlain, *op. cit.*, pp. 166–9.

24. Brooks, *op. cit.*, p. 87; Harleian MSS., 787, fol. 88.
25. Brooks prints many of these letters in *op. cit.*, Chapter IX.
26. Quoted in Chamberlain, *op. cit.*; *Anglica Legatum N. Gyldenstiernas*, 1561–2 (Stockholm), p. 18.
27. Chamberlain, *op. cit.*, pp. 266–7.
28. La Mothe-Fénelon, *Correspondence Diplomatique* (Paris and London 1838–40), III, p. 456; IV, p. 11.
29. Michel de Castelnau, Seigneur de la Mauvissière, *Mémoires* (Paris 1731), I, p. 62.
30. Bodleian, Ashmoleian MSS., 226; quoted in Rowse, *Elizabethan Renaissance*, p. 144.
31. There are unreliable biographies by, e.g., Samuel Jebb (1727) and Aubrey Richardson (1907); and a study by Milton Waldman, *Elizabeth and Leicester* (Boston 1945); for his letters, see Conyers Read, *Bibliography of British History 1485–1603* (Oxford 1959 edn), items 901–2, 907.
32. See *EHR*, 87 (1972), pp. 82–99; Chrimes, *Henry VII*, pp. 311–12.
33. F.J.Burgoyne (ed.), *Leycester's Commonwealth* (London 1904).
34. Sidney's defence is in A.Feuillerat (ed.), *Works of Sir Philip Sidney* (4 vols, Cambridge 1922–6).
35. The best portrait of Dudley as a young man is in the Wallace Collection.
36. BM Cotton MSS., Titus B XIII, fol. 15; quoted in Read, *Mr Secretary Cecil*, p. 199.
37. Neale, *Essays in Elizabethan History* (London 1958), pp. 72–3, quoting *The Secret Memoirs of Robert Dudley*, p. 52.
38. Naunton, *Fragmenta Regalia* (under Leicester).
39. Read, *op. cit.*, pp. 191–2.
40. e.g., MacCaffrey, *op. cit.*, 'The Emergence of Dudley'.
41. Professor Ian Aird, 'The Death of Amy Robsart', *EHR* (1956), pp. 69ff.
42. Read, *op. cit.*, p. 199.
43. *Ibid.*, pp. 199–200, quoting Froude's version of this dispatch; *CSP Spanish*, 1556–67, 174–5.
44. Hardwicke, *State Papers*, I, p. 167.
45. Read, *op. cit.*, p. 211.
46. *Cal. Patent Rolls*, Eliz., I, 44, 165.
47. *CSP Foreign*, 1560–1, 467.
48. Quoted by MacCaffrey, *op. cit.*
49. For the way the system operated, see Wallace T.MacCaffrey, 'Place and Patronage in Elizabethan Politics', in *Elizabethan Government and Society* (London 1961); and Stone, *op. cit.*, Chapter VIII.
50. See MacCaffrey, *Making of the Elizabethan Regime*, 'The Newhaven Adventure'.

51. Read, *op. cit.*, pp. 252ff.
52. Neale, *The Elizabethan House of Commons* (London 1963 edn), p. 78.
53. *Ibid.*, p. 156.
54. For Elizabeth's creations, see *ibid.*, p. 134, n. 1 and 2.
55. Sir James Harrington, *Oceana* (London 1656).
56. Neale, *op. cit.*, pp. 283–4.
57. F.J.Fisher, 'The Development of London as a Centre of Conspicuous Consumption in the 16th and 17th Centuries', in Ian R.Christie (ed.), *Essays in Modern History* (London 1968).
58. Neale, *Elizabeth I and her Parliaments*, I, p. 44.
59. *Ibid.*, I, p. 189.
60. *Ibid.*, II, pp. 249–50.
61. *Ibid.*, I, p. 134.
62. Neale, *Eliz. House of Commons*, pp. 348–9.
63. *Lords Journals* (London 1846), II, p. 225; Neale, *Eliz. House of Commons*, p. 409.
64. *Ibid.*, p. 408.
65. Sir Simonds D'Ewes, *Journals* (London 1693), p. 46.
66. *Ibid.*, p. 46; text also in Neale, *Parliaments*, I, pp. 48–50.
67. *CSP Spanish*, 1558–67, 262ff.; Read, *op. cit.*, pp. 265–6; Neale, *Parliaments*, I, pp. 87ff.
68. *CSP Spanish*, 1558–67, 265, 271, 273.
69. Dietz, *English Public Finance, 1558–1641*, p. 16.
70. The manuscript is in the Cambridge University Library, fols v. 14; analysed in Neale, *op. cit.*, I, pp. 91ff.
71. Wright, *op. cit.*, I, p. 126.
72. Text in *SP Dom. Eliz.*, 27/36; Neale, *op. cit.*, I, pp. 107ff.
73. *Ibid.*, pp. 126ff.
74. Wright, *op. cit.*, I, pp. 173–4; Haynes, *Burghley Papers*, pp. 411ff.
75. Murdin, *Burghley Papers*, p. 762; Neale, *op. cit.*, I, pp. 132–3.
76. *CSP Spanish*, Eliz., I, 589ff.
77. Neale, *op. cit.*, I, pp. 142–3.
78. *Sadler Papers*, II, pp. 553–5.
79. Neale, *op. cit.*, I, pp. 145–6.
80. In the Cambridge University Library; printed extracts in Neale, *op. cit.*, I, pp. 146ff.
81. *CSP Spanish*, Eliz., I, 595.
82. *Commons Journals* (London 1803), I, pp. 76–7.
83. *Ibid.*, I, p. 78.
84. Neale, *op. cit.*, I, pp. 160ff.
85. *Ibid.*, I, p. 170.
86. *Ibid.*, I, pp. 174ff., for full text of speech.

CHAPTER 6: MONSTROUS DRAGONS AND ROARING LIONS

1. R.B.Wernham, *Before the Armada: the Growth of English Foreign Policy, 1485–1588* (London 1966), Chapter 18.

2. Black, *Reign of Elizabeth*, pp. 120–1; Kervyn de Lettenhove, *Rélations Politiques des Pays-Bas et l'Angleterre 1555–79* (11 vols, Bruxelles 1882–1900); P.Geyl, *The Revolt of the Netherlands* (London 1932).

3. J.L.Motley, *The Rise of the Dutch Republic* (London 1903 edn), I, Chapter VII.

4. *Ibid.*, II, Chapter VIII.

5. W.Scott (ed.), *Somers Tracts* (London 1809), I, p. 169; Wernham, *op. cit.*

6. Haynes, *op. cit.*, p. 444; Read, *Mr Secretary Cecil*, pp. 336–7.

7. Dudley Digges (ed.), *The Compleat Ambassador* (London 1655), pp. 120–1.

8. Letter to Sir Henry Sidney, PRO SP 63/25/63; Read, *op. cit.*, pp. 424–5.

9. Black, *op. cit.*, pp. 126–7.

10. *CSP Foreign*, 1563, 303, 608; Lettenhove, *op. cit.*, III, p. 556.

11. A.L.Rowse, *The England of Elizabeth*, Chapter 2; E.G.R.Taylor, *Tudor Geography 1485–1583* (London 1930).

12. Garret Mattingly, 'No Peace Beyond What Line?', *TRHS* (5th series), XIII, pp. 145–62.

13. For Hawkins, see James A.Williamson, *Hawkins of Plymouth* (Oxford 1969 edn); Michael Lewis, *The Hawkins Dynasty* (London 1970); Gordon Connell Smith, *Forerunners of Drake* (London 1954).

14. C.R.Markham (ed.), *The Hawkins Voyages* (Hakluyt Soc.), p. 38.

15. *CSP Spanish*, 1558–67, 588.

16. Read, *op. cit.*, pp. 427–8.

17. For this voyage, see Rayner Unwin, *The Defeat of John Hawkins* (London 1960); Michael Lewis, 'The Guns of the *Jesus* of Lubeck', *Mariner's Mirror* (July 1936), pp. 324–45; John Hampden (ed.), *Francis Drake Privateer: Contemporary Narratives and Documents* (London 1972), Chapter 2.

18. Lettenhove, *op. cit.*, V, pp. 253ff.

19. For details, see Read, 'Queen Elizabeth's Seizure of the Duke of Alva's Pay-Ships', *Journal of Modern History*, V (1933), pp. 443–64.

20. Black, *op. cit.*, p. 129.

21. Read, *Mr Secretary Cecil*, pp. 432ff.

22. Haynes, *op. cit.*, pp. 579ff.

23. 31 Henry VIII, c. 8; Elton, *The Tudor Constitution*, pp. 27–30.

24. F.L.Van Baumer, *The Early Tudor Theory of Kingship* (New Haven 1940), pp. 220–1; but see also Joel Hurstfield, 'Was There a Tudor Despotism After All?', *TRHS* (5th series), 1967.

25. P.Williams, *The Council of the Marches of Wales under Elizabeth I* (Cardiff 1958).

26. R.R.Reid, *The King's Council in the North* (London 1921); for Huntingdon, see Claire Cross, *The Puritan Earl* (London 1966); for Sidney see *Sidney Papers*.

27. Sir Walter Ralegh, *History of the World* (London 1614), Preface.

28. Mary Bateson (ed.), 'A Collection of Original Letters from the Bishops to the Privy Council', *Camden Miscellany*, IX (London 1895).

29. A.G.R.Smith, *The Government of Elizabethan England* (London 1967), pp. 13ff.

30. Stone, *Crisis of the Aristocracy* (Oxford 1967 edn), p. 115.

31. SP 12/36/66; Stone, *op. cit.* (1965 edn), pp. 232–3.

32. Stone, *op. cit.*, p. 113.

33. *Ibid.*, Part V, Chapters 2–3, *passim*.

34. T.D.Whitaker, *History and Antiquities of the Deanery of Craven* (London 1878); Stone, *op. cit.*, p. 220.

35. *Life of Sir Philip Sidney* (1907 edn), p. 189.

36. For a diagrammatical analysis of Elizabeth's creations (contrasted with the Stuarts), see Fig. 5 in Stone, *op. cit.*

37. Naunton, *Fragmenta Regalia*, p. 148.

38. Read, *Lord Burghley and Queen Elizabeth*, p. 437.

39. *HMC De Lisle and Dudley MSS.*, II, pp. 294–488, *passim*; Stone, *op. cit.*, p. 100.

40. *De Republica Anglorum* (London 1583).

41. I.H.Jeayes (ed.), *Letters of Philip Gawdy 1579–1616* (Roxburghe Club 1906).

42. *HMC Salisbury MSS.*, II, p. 446.

43. Arthur Collins (ed.), *Sidney Papers* (London 1746), I, p. 285.

44. MacCaffrey, 'Place and Patronage', pp. 98–9.

45. *Ibid.*, pp. 104ff.

46. A.G.R.Smith, 'The Secretariats of the Cecils, 1580–1612', *EHR*, July 1968.

47. St John Brooks, *Hatton*, pp. 359–60.

48. L.Stone, 'Anatomy of the Elizabethan Aristocracy', *EHR* (1948); Rowse, *England of Elizabeth*, p. 254.

49. Stone, *Crisis of the Aristocracy*, p. 199.

50. Neale, *Parliaments*, I, p. 219.

51. See examples in E.F.Jacob, *The Fifteenth Century* (Oxford 1961), pp. 333ff.

52. Rowse, *Ralegh and the Throckmortons*, p. 224.

53. Neville Williams, *Thomas Howard, 4th Duke of Norfolk* (London 1964); *APC*, XVII, pp. 413–14; Read, *Burghley and Queen Elizabeth*, pp. 458–9.

54. Read, *op. cit.*, p. 378.

55. *Ibid.*, p. 308.

56. *Ibid.*, p. 345.

57. Tytler, *op. cit.*, VII, p. 19.

58. Labanoff, *op. cit.*, I, p. 351.

59. D.Hay Fleming, *Mary Queen of Scots* (Edinburgh 1897), pp. 138–40.
60. *CSP Scottish*, 1563–9, 316.
61. Read, *op. cit.*, pp. 378–9.
62. *Ibid.*, p. 385.
63. *CSP Spanish*, 1558–67, 35–6.
64. James Anderson, *Collections Relating to Mary* (Edinburgh 1727–8), IV, pp. 34–44.
65. *CSP Scottish*, 1563–9, 465.
66. Full text of all the letters is in M.H.Armstrong Davison, *The Casket Letters* (London 1965).
67. See for instance, Antonia Fraser, *op. cit.*, Chapter 20, for a full analysis.
68. *CSP Scottish*, 1563–9, 587–90.
69. Williams, *4th Duke of Norfolk*, p. 105.
70. *Ibid*, p. 113.
71. Haynes, *op. cit.*, p. 574.
72. Peck, *op. cit.*, I, pp. 15–16.
73. Williams, *op. cit.*, pp. 74–5.
74. Fénelon, *op. cit.*, I, pp. 233ff.; Camden (1635 edn), p. 104; Clapham, pp. 75–6; Read, pp. 442–3.
75. PRO SP 12/85/21; quoted in Read, *op. cit.*
76. Williams, *op. cit.*
77. Read, *Mr Secretary Walsingham* (Oxford 1925), I, Chapter I, Appendix I.
78. Camden, *op. cit.*, p. 130.
79. Williams, *op. cit.*
80. Lettenhove, *op. cit.*, V, p. 458.
81. Williams, *op. cit.*, pp. 161ff.
82. *CSP Scottish*, 1563–9, 684.
83. Read, *op. cit.*, pp. 455–6.
84. *CSP Domestic*, Addenda 1566–79, 95.
85. *Sadler Papers*, II, p. 325.
86. R.R.Reid, 'The Rebellion of the Earls, 1569', *TRHS* (2nd Series), XX (1906), pp. 171–203.
87. Harrison, *Letters of Queen Elizabeth I*, pp. 82–3.
88. Stone, *Crisis of the Aristocracy*, pp. 121–3.
89. Read, *op. cit.*, pp. 463–4.
90. Williams, *op. cit.*
91. *CSP Domestic*, Addenda, 1566–79, 195.
92. Stone, *op. cit.*
93. Haynes, *op. cit.*, p. 589; Read, *op. cit.*, pp. 465–6.
94. See Northumberland's confession in Cuthbert Sharp, *Memorials of the Rebellion of 1569* (London 1840), p. 189.
95. Fénelon, *op. cit.*, III, p. 123.

96. *Ibid.*, III, pp. 187, 199.
97. Black, *op. cit.*, pp. 167–70.
98. Neale, *Parliaments*, I, pp. 177–8.
99. *Ibid.*, pp. 237–8.
100. Read, *Mr Secretary Walsingham*; Cecil's memo on the origins of the Ridolfi Plot is in PRO SP 12/85/11; Read, *Lord Burghley*, Chapter III.
101. For Norfolk's involvement in the plot, see Williams, *op. cit.*
102. Murdin, *op. cit.*, p. 67.
103. *Ibid.*, p. 148.
104. *Ibid.*, p. 57; *HMC Hatfield*, I, p. 564.
105. For an analysis of charges and Norfolk's guilt, see Williams, *op. cit.*
106. Digges, *op. cit.*, pp. 164, 166.
107. Read, *Burghley*, p. 48.
108. Neale, *Parliaments*, I, p. 260.
109. *Ibid.*, p. 280.
110. SP 12/88/2; quoted in Williams, *op. cit.*
111. T.B.Howell, *State Trials*, I, p. 1035.
112. Read, *op. cit.*, p. 50; Digges, *op. cit.*, p. 219.
113. Often printed, e.g. in Lucy Aikin, *Court and Times of Queen Elizabeth* (London 1818), Chapter 17.
114. For his early career, see Read, *Walsingham*, I, Chapter I.
115. *Ibid.*, I, pp. 153–4.
116. Read, *Burghley*, p. 59.
117. Digges, *op. cit.*, p. 253.
118. Fénelon, *op. cit.*, IV, p. 370.
119. Digges, *op. cit.*, p. 253.
120. Fénelon, *op. cit.*, V, pp. 120–33; Digges, *op. cit.*, p. 246.
121. Read, *Burghley*, pp. 97ff.
122. Black, *op. cit.*, pp. 164–5.
123. Quoted in Neale, 'November 17th', in *Studies in Elizabethan History* (London 1958).
124. Text not from King James Version, but from the one actually used in Elizabeth's time.

CHAPTER 7: GOD'S VIRGIN

1. *HMC Bath MSS.*, IV, p. 158.
2. Neale, *Parliaments*, II, p. 132.
3. *Ibid.*, II, p. 152.
4. *Sidney Papers*, II, p. 64.
5. *HMC Salisbury MSS.*, VII, p. 41; *ibid.*, VII, p. 55.
6. *Annals of Windsor*, I, p. 641.

7. Edmund Lodge, *Illustrations of British History* (London 1838 edn), II, p. 98.
8. Tenison, *Baconiana* (London 1679).
9. Nichols, *Progresses*, I.
10. John Norden, *Speculum Brittaniae: Description of Middlesex and Hertfordshire* (London 1723 edn), quoted in Rowse, *England of Elizabeth*, pp. 72–3.
11. Fynes Morrison, *Itinerary* (London 1619 edn), 3 III, p. 197.
12. Ashmolean MSS., 38/113; quoted by Sir W.Ralegh in *Shakespeare's England*, Introduction.
13. Clapham, *op. cit.*, p. 89.
14. Strong and Oman, *Elizabeth R*, pp. 6ff.; F.W.Fairholt, *Costume in England* (2 vols, London 1896 edn); I.Brooke, *English Costume in the Age of Elizabeth* (London 1950 edn).
15. Rowse, *Elizabethan Renaissance: the Life of the Society*, pp. 46ff.; C.C.Stopes, *Shakespeare's Environment*, pp. 269ff.
16. G.Babst, *Histoire des Joyaux de la Couronne de France* (Paris 1889), p. 61.
17. Nichols, *Progresses*, II, p. 412.
18. G.C.Williamson, *Catalogue of the Collection of Watches, the Property of J. Pierpont Morgan* (New York 1912).
19. Joan Evans, *A History of Jewellery, 1100–1870* (London 1953), pp. 126ff.
20. *Ibid.*, plate 85; see also Joan Evans, *English Jewellery from the 5th Century AD to 1800* (London 1921), plate 19.
21. Harington, *op. cit.*, II, p. 135.
22. Nichols, *Progresses*, I, p. ix.
23. A.G.R.Smith, *The Government of Elizabethan England.*
24. Printed in Read, *Walsingham*, I, pp. 423–43.
25. Harington, *op. cit.*, II, pp. 215ff.
26. 6 March 1574; Wright, *Queen Elizabeth and her Times*, II.
27. *SP Domestic*, Eliz., 174, 40; quoted by E.P.Cheyney, *History of England from the Defeat of the Armada to the Death of Elizabeth* (London 1914), I.
28. Read, *Burghley*, p. 528.
29. *HMC De L'Isle MSS.*, II, 254.
30. *HMC Salisbury MSS.*, X, 172–3.
31. Chambers, *Elizabethan Stage*, I, p. 69, n. 2.
32. *Ibid.*, I, pp. 47–8.
33. Wright, *op. cit.*, II, pp. 156–61.
34. The incident occurred on 17 July 1579; Stow, *Annals.*
35. Harington, *op. cit.*, I, pp. 75–7.
36. Chambers, *op. cit.*, I, Chapter 2; C.C.Stopes, 'Elizabeth's Fools and Dwarfs', in *Shakespeare's Environment*; Rowse, *op. cit.*, Chapter 2.
37. A.Peel (ed.), *The Seconde Parte of a Register* (Cambridge 1915), I, pp. 49ff.
38. Quoted by Rowse, *The England of Elizabeth*, pp. 478–9.
39. Quoted by Dunlop, *op. cit.*, 'Greenwich'.

40. Wright, *op. cit.*, II, pp. 173–4.
41. *TRHS*, New Series, IX (1895), pp. 250–1.
42. Quoted by Dunlop, *op. cit.*
43. Quoted by John Buxton, *Elizabethan Taste* (London 1965 edn), p. 195.
44. *Ibid.*, p. 180.
45. *Ibid.*, p. 172.
46. Dunlop, *op. cit.*, 'Whitehall'.
47. *Ibid.*
48. Recorded by the Purcell Chorus of Voices on *Argo ZRG 643* (stereo).
49. Buxton, *op. cit.*, Chapter 5, *passim*; W.L.Woodfill, *Musicians in English Society from Elizabeth to Charles I* (Princeton 1953); P.C.Buck, etc., *Tudor Church Music* (10 vols, London 1923–30); Greville Cooke, 'Queen Elizabeth and her Court Musicians', *Musical Times*, 79 (1938), pp. 419–21.
50. Baldwin Smith, *Henry VIII: the Mask of Royalty*, pp. 81ff.
51. *A Collection of Ordinances and Regulations for the Government of the Royal Household, made in Diverse Reigns* (London, Society of Antiquaries, 1790), pp. 153–4.
52. A.Woodworth, 'Purveyance for the Royal Household under Queen Elizabeth', *Transactions of the American Philosophical Society*, 35 (1945–6), pp. 55, 57, 62, 65–6.
53. Nichols, *Progresses*, I.
54. *Annals of Windsor*, I, p. 646.
55. 'The Late Queen Majesty's Speeches Oftentimes to R.Brown, for Household Causes', printed in Nichols, *Progresses*, I.
56. *Ibid.*
57. Rowse, *England of Elizabeth*, p. 327; E.Hughes, *Studies in Administration and Finance* (Manchester 1934), p. 80.
58. *Journal of Sir Roger Wilbraham*, Camden Society Miscellany, X, pp. 57–8.
59. *Calendar of Patent Rolls, Elizabeth*, IV, 1566–9 (1964).
60. *CSP Domestic*, 1585 (184), 22, 23; W.K.Jordan, *Philanthropy in England, 1480–1660* (London 1959).
61. D.Ewes, *Journals*, p. 473.
62. Extracts printed in Nichols, *Progresses*, I.
63. *Complaints, Mother Hubbard's Tale*, I, p. 895.
64. 'Instructions to his Son', Ralegh, *Works* (ed. Oldys and Birch, 8 vols, London 1829), VIII, pp. 557ff.
65. *HMC Salisbury MSS.*, I, 163.
66. Quoted by Rowse, *England of Elizabeth*, p. 259.
67. Rowse, *op. cit.*
68. Quoted by Rowse, *op. cit.*, p. 256.
69. *HMC Salisbury MSS.*, I, 482–3.
70. *Ibid.*, VII, 270.

71. *De Republica Anglorum*, pp. 39–41.
72. St John Brooks, *Hatton*, p. 66; Henry Bradley in *Shakespeare's England*, II, p. 541.
73. Minutes of the Court of the Merchant Taylor's Company, 16 August 1562; E.J.Dobson, *English Pronunciation, 1500–1700* (2 vols, Oxford 1957), I, pp. 45, 106, 116, 125.
74. Aubrey, *Brief Lives* (ed. Oliver Lawson Dick), pp. 316ff.
75. Naunton, *Fragmenta Regalia*, 'Hatton'.
76. Brooks, *Hatton*, Chapter IV.
77. Barnaby Rich, *Riche, his Farewell to Military Profession* (London 1581).
78. Brooks, *op. cit.*, Chapter V.
79. For Hatton as a Commons operator, see Neale, *Parliaments*, I, pp. 283, 330, 338–43, 379–82, 386–7, 396–7; II, pp. 114–15, 165–6, 243–4; Brooks, *op. cit.*, Chapter VI.
80. Brooks, *op. cit.*, p. 156.
81. e.g. in Harrison, *Letters of Queen Elizabeth I* (1968 edn), p. 121.
82. *HMC Salisbury MSS.*, II, 120.
83. For Hatton's spoliation of the Church, see Brooks, *op. cit.*, Chapter 15.
84. Ronald A.Rebholz, *Life of Fulke Greville* (Oxford 1971), pp. 22–3; *Sidney Papers*, I, ii, p. 293.
85. For Ralegh's connections, see Rowse, *Ralegh and the Throckmortons*, Chapter 8.
86. *Fragmenta Regalia*, p. 47.
87. *Ibid.*
88. Neale, 'Sayings of Queen Elizabeth', *History*, October 1925.
89. D.B.Quinn, *Ralegh and the British Empire* (London 1947); Willard M. Wallace, *Sir Walter Ralegh* (Princeton 1959).
90. Edward Edwards, *Life of Sir Walter Ralegh* (London 1868), II, pp. 41–2.
91. *HMC Appendix, 4th Report*, p. 338.
92. F.A.Yates, *The Theatre of the World* (London 1969).
93. Eleanor Rosenberg, *Leicester, Patron of Letters* (New York 1955).
94. The best recent survey of Dee's work is Peter J.Finch, *John Dee: the World of an Elizabethan Magus* (London 1972).
95. Geoffrey Shepherd (ed.), *Sidney's An Apology for Poetry* (London 1965), p. 104.
96. *The Compendious Rehearsal* (Chetham Society, XXIV, Manchester 1851), p. 21.
97. *Ibid.*, pp. 19, 17.
98. Walter I.Trattner, 'God and Expansion in Elizabethan England: John Dee, 1527–83', *Journal of the Historical Institute*, XXV (1964).
99. Harington, *op. cit.*, II, pp. 37–8.
100. Dante Gabriel Rossetti, *Mary's Girlhood*.

101. Keith Thomas, *Religion and the Decline of Magic* (London 1971), p. 405.
102. 23 Eliz., c. 2; Coke, *Institutes*, III, Chapter 1.
103. Thomas, *op. cit.*, pp. 189, 232.
104. Roy Strong, *Portraits of Queen Elizabeth*, p. 40.
105. Thomas, *op. cit.*, p. 299.
106. The portrait has since vanished.
107. H.Peacham, *The Complete Gentleman*.
108. Chambers, *Elizabethan Stage*, I, pp. 17-20; Rowse, *Elizabethan Renaissance*, pp. 90-6.
109. Nichols, *Progresses*, I, pp. li-lv.
110. William Harrison, *Description of England* (London 1908 edn).
111. Nichols, *Progresses*, I, pp. 315-16.
112. *Ibid.*, II, p. 12.
113. For details, see Dunlop, *op. cit.*, 'The Queen in Progress'.
114. Edward Arber (ed.), *Puttenham's Arte of Poesie*, p. 301.
115. Chambers, *op. cit.*, I, Chapter 4.
116. A case came before Star Chamber in 1606; Wright, *op. cit.*, I, p. 370.
117. Ellis, *op. cit.*, II, p. 271.
118. *Sussex Archaeological Collections*, V, p. 194.
119. Quoted by Chambers, *op. cit.*
120. Read, *Burghley*, Chapter IX, n. 10 (p. 556).
121. Egerton Papers, 340, quoted by Chambers, *op. cit.*
122. *Household Ordinances*, p. 145. For the background to the Berkeley castle affair, see Lawrence Stone: *Family and Fortune: Studies in Aristocratic Finance in the Sixteenth and Seventeenth Centuries* (Oxford 1973), pp. 247-8, and H.P.R.Finberg: *Gloucestershire Studies* (Leicester 1957), pp. 153-4.
123. F.J.Furnivall (ed.), *Kenilworth Festivities* (New Shakespeare Society 1890).
124. Fénelon, *op. cit.*, VI, p. 478.
125. John Summerson, 'The Building of Theobalds', *Archaeologia*, CVII, 1954.
126. Quoted by Dunlop, *op. cit.*, 'Theobalds'.
127. Read, *Burghley*, p. 216; Brooks, *Hatton*, Chapter 16.
128. Nichols, *Progresses*, I, pp. 233-58.
129. Glynn Wickham, *Early English Stages, I: 1300-1576* (London 1959), pp. 248ff.; F.S.Boas, *University Drama in the Tudor Age* (London 1913), pp. 89-108.
130. Wickham, *op. cit.*, I, Appendix H.
131. *Ibid.*, I, p. 225.
132. BM, Lansdowne MSS, 64/145, quoted by Howell A.Lloyd, 'Camden, Carmarthen and the Customs', *EHR*, LXXXV (1970), pp. 776-87.
133. Camden, *Elizabeth* (1688 edn), pp. 439-40.
134. Ralegh, *Works*, VIII, pp. 14, 187.

CHAPTER 8: DAUGHTERS OF DEBATE

1. *CSP Holland and Flanders*, 23, no. 28.
2. D'Ewes, *Journals*, pp. 285–8.
3. John Strype, *Annals of the Reformation* (Oxford 1820–40), I, p. 150.
4. Camden, *Elizabeth*, p. 223.
5. *Nugae Antiquae* (1804 edn, edited T.Park), I, p. 127; Harrison, *Letters of Elizabeth*, p. 123.
6. Garrett Mattingly, *Renaissance Diplomacy*, Chapter 28.
7. H.Robinson, *The British Post Office* (Princeton 1948); E.Vaille, *Histoire Générale des Postes Française* (Paris 1947–9); Henry Kamen, *The Iron Century* (London 1971), prints a communications speed map (fig. 1), based on F.Braudel, *La Mediterranée et le monde mediterranéan* (Paris 1966), pp. 333–6.
8. J.Stevenson (ed.), *Henry Clifford's Life of Jane Dormer* (London 1887).
9. Mattingly, *op. cit.*, pp. 194–5.
10. Ernle Bradford, *The Great Siege of Malta* (London 1961), p. 225; H.G. Rawlinson, 'The Embassy of Sir William Harborne to Constantinople', *TRHS*, V (1922).
11. *HMC Salisbury MSS*, XIV, Addenda, 249.
12. PRO SP 12/203/34 and 132, quoted by B.W.Beckinsale, *Burghley: Tudor Statesman* (London 1967).
13. *Harleian Miscellany*, II, p. 278; F.Raab, *The English Face of Machiavelli* (Toronto 1964).
14. Quoted in Wernham, *Before the Armada*.
15. *CSP Spanish*, 1580–6, 607 n.
16. A.O.Meyer, *England and the Catholic Church under Elizabeth* (trans. J.R. McKee, London 1916), pp. 269–71, 489–91; this work carries the *imprimatur* of the Roman Catholic authorities.
17. BM Cotton MSS., Gaba C, XI, 79, quoted by Beckinsale, *op. cit.*
18. Baldwin Smith, *The Elizabethan Epic*, p. 168.
19. For narratives of and commentary on this voyage, see John Hampden (ed.), *Francis Drake Privateer* (London 1972), pp. 45–106.
20. K.R.Andrews, 'The Aims of Drake's Expedition of 1577–80', *American Historical Review*, LXXIII, 3 February 1968.
21. Preface to *Sir Francis Drake Revived* (London 1626).
22. William Haller, *Foxe's Book of Martyrs and the Elect Nation* (London 1963).
23. See E.G.R.Taylor, *Geographical Journal*, January 1930, and *Mariner's Mirror*, April 1930; the texts of the draft and report are in Hampden, *op. cit.*, pp. 107–22.
24. *HMC Salisbury MSS.*, IV, 72.
25. Hampden, *op. cit.*, p. 230.

26. *CSP Spanish*, 1580–6, 95, 101.

27. Zelia Nuttall (ed.), *New Light on Drake* (Hakluyt Society, 2nd Series, XXXIV 1914), p. 303n. The authority for the account of the huge profits made on the voyage is Lewes Roberts, *The Merchant's Map of Commerce* (London 1638). Roberts said he had seen the final accounts 'subscribed under [Drake's] own hand, £47 for one pound . . . so that he who invested . . . £100 had £4,700 for the same.'

28. F.C.Prideaux Naish in the *Mariner's Mirror*, January 1948 and April 1950.

29. Hampden, *op. cit.*, pp. 209–10.

30. *Ibid.*, p. 237.

31. Quoted by Rowse, *Ralegh and the Throckmortons*, p. 270; Ralegh, *History of the World*, Preface (preface pages unnumbered in early editions); this passage is surprisingly omitted from the most recent (somewhat shortened) edition of the *History*, edited by C.A.Patrides (London 1971).

32. R.B.Wernham, 'Elizabethan War Aims and Strategy', in *Elizabethan Government and Society*, pp. 340–2.

33. Read, *Burghley*, pp. 73–4.

34. C.G.Cruikshank, *Elizabeth's Army* (Oxford 1966 edn), p. 192; Sir Clement Edmondes, *The Manner of Our Modern Training* (London 1600).

35. Sir Roger Williams, *The Action in the Low Countries* (London 1618), p. 56; J.W.Fortescue, *History of the British Army* (13 vols, London 1899–1930), I, p. 134; Rowse, *Expansion of Elizabethan England* (London 1955), pp. 339ff.

36. Lettenhove, *op. cit.*, VIII, p. 157.

37. *Ibid.*, VIII, p. 227.

38. BM Harleian MSS., 6991/216, quoted in Read, *Walsingham*, II.

39. SP Foreign, Elizabeth, CXL, fol. 869, quoted in *ibid*.

40. Read, *Walsingham*, II, p. 199.

41. *CSP Foreign*, 1578–9, 86.

42. Strype, *Annals*, IV, p. 641.

43. London 1579; Froude, *op. cit.*, X (1968 edn), Chapter 61, pp. 495ff.

44. I & II, Philip and Mary, c. 2.

45. Camden, *Elizabeth*, III, p. 10.

46. *CSP Spanish*, 1568–79, 704.

47. Read, *Burghley*, pp. 219–20.

48. Digges, *op. cit.*, pp. 396, 408.

49. *Ibid.*, p. 424.

50. *CSP Spanish*, 1580–6, 206.

51. *Holinshed* (1587 edn), III, p. 1315; Read, *Burghley*, p. 258.

52. C.T.Martin (ed.), *Journal of Sir Francis Walsingham 1570–83* (Camden Soc., Misc., IV, 1871), p. 44.

53. Read, *Burghley*, p. 271.

54. *CSP Spanish*, 1580–6, 226.
55. Camden, *Elizabeth*, II, p. 376.
56. *CSP Foreign*, 1581–2, 409.
57. *CSP Spanish*, 1580–6, 310–12.
58. *Ibid.*, p. 243.
59. *CSP Scotland*, 35, no. 14.
60. John Bruce (ed.), *Leicester Correspondence* (Camden Soc., 1844).
61. For Walsingham's paper, see Read, *Walsingham*, III, pp. 73–5; *CSP Domestic*, 171, n. 80.
62. *CSP Foreign*, 1583–4, 622.
63. Read, *Burghley*, pp. 307ff.
64. Camden, *Elizabeth* (1635 edn), p. 282.
65. *CSP Foreign*, 1584–5, 424.
66. Motley, *The United Netherlands* (1904 edn), I, p. 362 (trans. from Dutch).
67. *CSP Foreign*, 1584–5, 618.
68. *A Declaration of the Causes moving the Queen of England to give aid to the Defence of the People Afflicted and Oppressed in the Low Countries* (London 1585).
69. For the full list see Roy Strong and J. A. Van Dorsten, *Leicester's Triumph* (Leiden 1964), Appendix III.
70. For details of Leicester's progress, see Strong and Van Dorsten, *op. cit.*; Bruce, *Leicester Correspondence*, p. 263.
71. *Ibid.*, p. 110.
72. *Ibid.*, p. 243.
73. *History of the British Army*, I, p. 146.
74. *CSP Foreign*, 22, 166–7; Cruikshank, *Elizabeth's Army*, p. 169.
75. Cruikshank, *op. cit.*, Chapter 9.
76. Quoted by Neale, 'Elizabeth's War Finances and Expenditure: the Netherlands, 1586–7', *EHR*, XLV (1930).
77. *CSP Foreign*, XXI, iii, 441.
78. *Ibid.*, p. 396.
79. *Ibid.*, pp. 369, 447.
80. Karl Stahlin, *Der Kampf um Schottland und die Gesandtschaftsreise Sir Francis Walsingham im Jahre 1583* (Leipzig 1902), pp. 158–9; quoted by Read, *Walsingham*, III.
81. James Howell, *Cottoni Posthuma* (London 1679 edn), pp. 337–8; quoted by Read, *Walsingham*, III.
82. *CSP Domestic*, 232, no. 12. Financial details of Walsingham's services in Read, *op. cit.*, III.
83. *CSP Foreign*, 1572–4, 93.
84. *CSP Mary Queen of Scots*, XII, no. 83.
85. *Ibid.*, X, no. 2.

86. Lettenhove, *op. cit.*, X, p. 405.
87. *CSP Domestic*, 163, no. 65.
88. Labanoff, *op. cit.*, V, p. 424.
89. John Morris (ed.), *The Letter Books of Sir Amias Paulet* (London 1874), *passim*.
90. *Ibid.*, p. 49.
91. Neale, *Parliaments*, II, pp. 16ff.
92. *Ibid.*, p. 28.
93. *Ibid.*, pp. 36–7.
94. *Ibid.*, pp. 45–8.
95. 27 Eliz. I, c. 1; printed in Elton, *Tudor Constitutions*, pp. 76ff.; Neale, *op. cit.*, II, pp. 51–3.
96. Morris, *op. cit.*, p. 151.
97. *CSP Scottish*, 1585–6, 390, 389.
98. *CSP Mary Queen of Scots*, 19, no. 68.
99. Morris, *op. cit.*, p. 234.
100. J.H.Pollen, 'Mary Queen of Scots and the Babington Plot', *Scottish Historical Society*, 3rd series, III (1922); Read, *Burghley*, p. 347.
101. Read, *Burghley*, Chapter 18, n. 28 (p. 572).
102. e.g., Fraser, *op. cit.*, p. 575.
103. Pollen, *op. cit.*, p. 41.
104. Read, *Burghley*, p. 344.
105. Harrison, *Letters of Queen Elizabeth*, p. 180.
106. Fraser, *op. cit.*, p. 585.
107. Conyers Read (ed.), *The Bardon Papers: Documents Relating to the Imprisonment and Trial of Mary, Queen of Scots* (Camden Soc., 3rd series, XVII, 1909), p. 45.
108. Froude, *op. cit.*, XII, p. 175.
109. Read, *Burghley*, p. 347.
110. Neale, *Parliaments*, II, p. 104.
111. Read, *Burghley*, p. 351.
112. Wright, *op. cit.*, II, p. 320.
113. Keith Thomas, *Religion and the Decline of Magic*, p. 407.
114. Neale, *Parliaments*, II, p. 106.
115. *Ibid.*, p. 116.
116. Speech in Neale, *Parliaments*, II, pp. 116–20.
117. For the narrative of these events, see Neale, *op. cit.*, pp. 134ff.; Read, *Burghley*, pp. 356ff.; J.Morris, *Paulet*, pp. 359–62; N.H.Nicholas, *Life of William Davison* (London 1823), pp. 86–7, 100–1, 211ff., 245.
118. Morris, *op. cit.*, p. 361.
119. Wright, *op. cit.*, II, p. 332.
120. Read, *Burghley*, pp. 371ff.

121. Lansdowne MSS., 108/90, printed in Read, *Burghley*, pp. 373–4.
122. *CSP Scottish*, IX, 285.
123. Neale, *Parliaments*, II, p. 138; *EHR*, XLIV, pp. 104–6; XLVI, pp. 632–6.
124. Wright, *op. cit.*, II, p. 335.
125. Read, *Burghley*, p. 378.

CHAPTER 9: THE DICE IS THROWN

1. Garrett Mattingly, *The Defeat of the Spanish Armada* (London 1962 edn), pp. 142ff. For the Cadiz voyage, see J.S.Corbett, *Drake and the Tudor Navy* (2 vols, London 1898–9), II; J.Hampden, *op. cit.*, pp. 249–50.
2. J.D.Gould, 'The Crisis in the Export Trade', *EHR*, LXXII (1956).
3. Read, *Burghley*, pp. 379ff.
4. Lawrence Stone, *An Elizabethan: Sir Horatio Palavicino* (London 1956).
5. Read, *Burghley*, p. 385.
6. Michael Roberts, *The Military Revolution, 1560–1660*, pp. 6–7; Cruikshank, *op. cit.*, pp. 198–9.
7. *CSP Foreign*, 1586–7, 248.
8. Wernham, in *Elizabethan Government and Society*, pp. 347–50.
9. Bruce, *Leicester Correspondence*, p. 223.
10. Black, *op. cit.*, pp. 389ff.; for Philip's political strategy, see J.H.Elliot, *Imperial Spain, 1469–1716* (London 1963); J.Lynch, *Spain under the Habsburgs* (Oxford 1964), I.
11. For Spanish documentation during the pre-Armada period, see *CSP Spanish*, IV; bibliographical notes in Mattingly, *op. cit.*, pp. 429–30; Black, *op. cit.*, pp. 504–5; *Coleccion de Documentos ineditos para la Historia de España* (Madrid 1842–95), vols 90–2.
12. Ralegh, *History of the World* (1677 edn), p. 427.
13. Parma's correspondence with Philip II is printed in L.P.Gasherd (ed.), *Correspondence de Alexandre Farnese, Prince de Parme, avec Philippe II, 1578–81* (Brussels 1853), and in the appendices to E.Poullet and Charles Piot (eds), *Correspondence de Cardinal Granvelle* (Brussels 1878–96), vol. 12.
14. C.F.Duro, *La Armada invencible*, I, pp. 244ff.
15. Mattingly, *op. cit.*, p. 125.
16. *Ibid.*, p. 138.
17. Quoted by Rowse, *Expansion of Elizabethan England*, p. 264; SP 12/200/46.
18. Mattingly, *op. cit.*, pp. 221ff.
19. Duro, *op. cit.*, p. 410; Mattingly, *op. cit.*, pp. 263–5.
20. Wright, *op. cit.*, II, pp. 354–5.
21. Read, *Burghley*, p. 398.
22. Read, *Walsingham*, III, p. 274.
23. Corbett, *op. cit.*, I, pp. 133ff.

24. J.A.Williamson, *Sir John Hawkins* (Oxford 1949 edn), and *The Age of Drake* (London 1952 edn).
25. N.Oppenheim, *History of the Administration of the Royal Navy, 1509–1660* (London 1896), p. 123.
26. Ralegh, 'A Discourse on the Invention of Ships', *Works*, VIII.
27. Bruce, *Leicester Correspondence*, p. 53; *CSP Irish*, 1586–8, 37; J.H. Laughton (ed.), *State Papers Relating to the Defeat of the Spanish Armada* (Naval Records Society, 1894), pp. 52–64.
28. Read, *Walsingham*, III, pp. 286–7.
29. Black, *op. cit.*, p. 395.
30. Mattingly, *op. cit.*, pp. 264–5.
31. For Stafford, see Read, *Burghley*, pp. 386–90; Read, 'The Fame of Sir Edward Stafford', *American Historical Review*, 20 (1915), and *AHR*, 35 (1930); Neale, *EHR*, 44 (1929).
32. Smith, *Government of Elizabethan England*, pp. 48–50.
33. John Bruce (ed.), *Report on the Arrangements when Spain Projected the Invasion and Conquest of England, 1798*.
34. Read, *Burghley*, pp. 420ff.
35. Read, *Walsingham*, III, p. 270, n. 1.
36. For evidence of the number of troops raised in 1588, see Read, *Burghley*, p. 579, n. 37, where contemporary calculations are cited and analysed.
37. *Ibid.*, pp. 421–2.
38. *Ibid.*, p. 427.
39. *Ibid.*, p. 425; PRO SP 12/212/66.
40. John Malham (ed.), *Harleian Miscellany* (London 1808–13), II, p. 68.
41. Printed in full, Read, *Burghley*, pp. 428–9.
42. For an excellent summary, see Rowse, *Expansion of Elizabethan England*, Chapter 8.
43. Laughton, *op. cit.*, I, p. 205.
44. *Ibid.*, I, p. 201.
45. *Mariner's Mirror*, 57 (November 1971), pp. 447ff.
46. Robert Birley, *The Undergrowth of History* (Historical Association Pamphlet 1955).
47. Laughton, *op. cit.*, I, p. 357.
48. *Ibid.*, I, p. 341.
49. For a detailed discussion of the Armada's losses in ships and men, see Mattingly, *op. cit.*, pp. 442–4.
50. Miller Christy, 'Queen Elizabeth's Visit to Tilbury', *EHR*, 34 (1919), pp. 43–61; Nichols, *Progresses*, II, pp. 536ff.; Thomas Deloney, 'The Queen at Tilbury', in Edward Arber (ed.), *An English Garland* (London 1877–96), VII.
51. Printed in the *Cabala: Mysteries of State and Government in Letters of*

Illustrious Persons (London 1654); for the authenticity of the text, see Neale, 'Sayings of Queen Elizabeth', *History*, 10 (October 1925).

52. Read, *Burghley*, p. 430; Laughton, *op. cit.*, II, p. 82.
53. Read, *Burghley*, pp. 430–1.
54. Laughton, *op. cit.*, II, p. 213.
55. PRO SP 12/215/65.
56. 'The Ruines of Time', *Complaints* (London 1591), lines 218–24.
57. *CSP Spanish*, 1587–1603, 431.
58. Nichols, *Progresses*, II.
59. Read, *Burghley*, p. 581, n. 104.
60. *Chronicles*, III (1592), pp. 1356–7.
61. J.S.Brewer (ed.), *The Court of King James I by Dr Godfrey Goodman* (London 1839), I, p. 163; Geoffrey Soden, *Godfrey Goodman, Bishop of Gloucester, 1583–1656* (London 1953), pp. 26–7; the incident must have taken place in November, not December as Goodman stated, since Elizabeth left Somerset House for Greenwich on 30 November 1588.

CHAPTER 10: HOLDING THE BALANCE

1. E.Edwards, *Life and Letters of Sir Walter Ralegh*, I, p. 245.
2. Laughton, *op. cit.*, II, p. 167.
3. Corbett, *Drake and the Tudor Navy*, II, p. 296.
4. Rowse, *Expansion of Elizabethan England*, pp. 282–4; R.B.Wernham, 'Queen Elizabeth and the Portuguese Expedition of 1589', *EHR* (April 1951).
5. *CSP Dom.*, Elizabeth, pp. 219, 37.
6. *Ibid.*, pp. 223, 71.
7. Harrison, *Letters of Queen Elizabeth*, pp. 197–8.
8. Rowse, *op. cit.*, p. 288; SP 12/225/5.
9. Quoted by Wernham, *op. cit.*, p. 202.
10. Rowse, *op. cit.*, p. 288; SP 12/224/53.
11. M.Oppenheim, *Monson's Naval Tracts* (Naval Records Society, 1902–14), I, p. 216.
12. Quoted Rowse, *op. cit.*, p. 288.
13. E.P.Cheyney, 'International Law under Queen Elizabeth', *EHR*, XX (1905).
14. *Ibid.*, p. 664.
15. Corbett, *op. cit.*, II, pp. 336–40.
16. *Fragmenta Regalia*, pp. 42–3.
17. Read, *Walsingham*, III, 'After the Armada'.
18. To R.Cecil, 7 December 1593; Wright, *op. cit.*, II, pp. 429–30.
19. D'Ewes, *Journals*, pp. 508–9.

20. Read, *Burghley*, p. 455.
21. Cheyney, *History of England from the Armada to the Death of Elizabeth*, I, p. 216; Wright, *op. cit.*, II, p. 402; Read, *Burghley*, p. 459.
22. Read, *Burghley*, pp. 459–60.
23. Lodge, *Illustrations*, II, pp. 372–3.
24. Letter of 27 July 1591; Harrison, *Letters of Queen Elizabeth*, pp. 209–10.
25. J.B. de Xivrcy and J.Guardet, *Henri IV: Recueil des Lettres Missives* (Paris 1843–76), III, pp. 190–1, 279, 282–3, 333n.; *CSP France*, 21, 308.
26. C.R.Markham, *The Fighting Veres* (London 1888), pp. 148–58; Vere, *Commentaries*, reprinted in *An English Garner* (London 1877–96), VIII, pp. 57–184.
27. Thomas Churchyard, *Service of Sir John Norris in Brittany in 1591*.
28. W.B.Devereux, *Lives and Letters of the Devereux, Earls of Essex* (2 vols, London 1853), I, pp. 213–15.
29. J.G.Nichols (ed.), *Thomas Coningsby's Journal of the Siege of Rouen, 1591* (Camden Society Misc., I, 1847), pp. 29–31.
30. Joseph Stevenson (ed.), *Unton Correspondence* (Roxburgh Club, 1847), pp. 128, 237.
31. Harrison, *Letters of Queen Elizabeth*, p. 225; *Henri IV: Lettres Missives*, IV, pp. 13–14.
32. Oppenheim, *Monson Tracts*, I, pp. 280–96.
33. Rowse, *Expansion*, quoting SP 12/243/16; P.M.Handover, *The Second Cecil: the Rise to Power, 1563–1604, of Sir Robert Cecil* (London 1959), quoting SP 12/246/40–1.
34. Edwards, *Ralegh*, II, pp. 69, 70–1.
35. G.C.Williamson, *George, Third Earl of Cumberland, 1558–1604* (Cambridge 1920).
36. *Ibid.*, p. 174.
37. *Ibid.*, pp. 78–9.
38. *Ibid.*, pp. 128–36.
39. Richard Collinson (ed.), *The Three Voyages of Martin Frobisher* (Hakluyt Society, 37, 1867).
40. *CSP Colonisation*, 1513–1616, 234–6.
41. Camden, *Elizabeth* (1688 edn), p. 287.
42. A.C.Wood, *A History of the Levant Company* (London 1935).
43. *The State of England in Anno Domini 1600*.
44. Read, *Burghley*, p. 439; Wernham, *EHR*, 1951, p. 6.
45. Read, *Burghley*, p. 584, n. 42.
46. Dietz, *op. cit.*, p. 64.
47. Read, *Burghley*, p. 584, n. 43; Rowse, *England of Elizabeth*, p. 328; Edward Hughes, *Studies in Administration and Finance 1558–1825* (Manchester 1934), p. 80.

48. Read, *Burghley*, pp. 475–6; see also R.J.W.Evans, *Rudolf II and his World* (Oxford 1973).

49. Strype, *Annals of the Reformation*, III, Part 2, pp. 617ff.

50. Read, *Burghley*, pp. 492–3.

51. Handover, *op. cit.*, p. 165; SP Dom., 12/266/36.

52. Quoted by Stephen Dowell, *A History of Taxation and Taxes in England* (4 vols, London 1884–8), I, p. 158.

53. R.M.Kingdon (ed.), in the Folger Shakespeare Library edition (Ithaca 1965), pp. 9–10.

54. Meyer, *England and the Catholic Church under Queen Elizabeth*, p. 128.

55. J.S.Leatherbarrow, *The Lancashire Elizabethan Recusants* (Chetham Society, 1947), p. 19; *Victoria County History: Lancashire*, II, p. 50.

56. A.G.Dickens, 'The First Stage of Romanist Recusancy in Yorkshire', *Yorkshire Archaeological Journal*, 35 (1941); 'The Extent and Character of Recusancy in Yorkshire in 1604', *ibid.*, 37 (1948).

57. For Cowdray and the visit, see Dunlop, *Palaces and Progresses*.

58. G.Anstruther, *Vaux of Harrowden* (Newport 1953).

59. John Bossy, 'The Character of Elizabethan Catholicism', *Past and Present* (April 1962), pp. 39ff.

60. J.E.Monsley, 'The Fortunes of Some Gentry Families of Elizabethan Sussex', *EHR*, 2nd Series, 10 (1959), pp. 478–9.

61. Printed in *HMC 5th Report*, Appendix, p. 406.

62. Philip Hughes, *The Reformation in England* (London 1954), III, *passim*.

63. For the details, see Neale, *Parliaments*, especially I, pp. 378–92; II, pp. 280–97.

64. 23 Eliz. I, c. 1; Elton, *Tudor Constitution*, pp. 422ff.

65. 27 Eliz. I, c. 2; 35 Eliz. I, c. 2; Elton, *Tudor Constitution*, pp. 424ff., 427ff.

66. Frederick A.Young Jr, 'The Definition of Treason in Elizabethan Proclamations', *Historical Journal*, 14, 4 (1971).

67. Buxton, *Elizabethan Taste*, pp. 145–6.

68. Stow, *Annals*, I, pp. 266–7; Rowse, *England of Elizabeth*, p. 195.

69. Nichols, *Progresses*, I.

70. Augustus Jessopp, *One Generation of a Norfolk House* (London 1913), pp. 67ff.

71. Read, *Walsingham*, II, p. 304.

72. *CSP Dom.*, 116, 15.

73. R.B.Merriman, *AHR*, 13, pp. 480ff.

74. *CSP Dom.*, 157, no. 89.

75. *Catholic Record Society*, vol. 5.

76. W.K.Jordan, *The Development of Religious Toleration in England* (Cambridge, Mass. 1932); A.G.Dickens, *The English Reformation* (London

1967 edn), pp. 438ff., quoting V.N.Olsen, 'John Foxe the Martyrologist and Toleration' (unpub.).

77. For Walsingham's views, see Read, *Walsingham*, II, pp. 322–9; for Burghley's, see Read, *Burghley*, pp. 250ff.

78. Neale, *Parliaments*, I, p. 215.

79. For example, Wright, *op. cit.*, II, pp. 156–61, 164–7.

80. F.J.Furnivall (ed.); 1877 edition, I, pp. 222–5.

81. 1599 edition, pp. 60–3.

82. W.P.Baildon (ed.), *John Hawarde: Les Reportes del Cases in Camera Stellata, 1593–1609* (London 1894), p. 64.

83. Smith, *op. cit.*, pp. 104–6.

84. Quoted in *Shakespeare's England*, I, p. 398.

85. Fleetwood to Burghley, 7 July 1585, printed in Wright, *op. cit.*

86. *CSP Border Papers*, II, 167.

87. Rowse, *England of Elizabeth*, p. 342.

88. *A True, Sincere and Modest Defence of English Catholics* (Ithaca 1965), pp. 73–4.

89. David Jardine, *A Reading on the Use of Torture in the Criminal Laws of England* (London 1837).

90. *De Republica Anglorum*, 106.

91. For instance, *CSP Dom.*, 1581–90, 646; 1591–4, 297; *Acts of the Privy Council*, VII, p. 373; X, p. 373; XIII, pp. 37, 172, 249; XVI, p. 273; XVII, p. 310; XVIII, pp. 62, 387; XIX, p. 70; XXI, p. 300; XXII, pp. 40, 42, 512; XXIII, p. 340; XXIV, p. 222; XXVI, pp. 10, 325, 373, 457.

92. Strype, *Annals*, IV, pp. 404–12.

93. *APC*, XXVI, p. 548.

94. R.G.Marsden, *Select Pleas in the Court of Admiralty* (Selden Society, 1892–7), II, LXXVII.

95. *CSP Scottish*, 1569–71, 691, 701.

96. *Ibid.*, 31, 99.

97. 27 March 1582; Read, *Burghley*, pp. 251ff.

98. For details of their publication, see Read, *Burghley*, p. 566, nn. 75, 76.

99. *Harleian Miscellany* (1808), I, p. 513.

100. Neale, *Parliaments*, II, p. 153.

101. *DNB* under 'Topcliffe'.

102. Letter from Fr. Garnett SJ to unknown correspondent; transcript at Farm Street.

103. F.O.White, *Lives of the Elizabethan Bishops* (London 1898).

104. For dates of appointments to bishoprics, see Maurice Powicke and E.B.Fryde, *Handbook of British Chronology* (London 1961 edn).

105. William Pierce, *A Historical Introduction to the Marprelate Tracts* (London 1908).

106. M.M.Knappen, *Tudor Puritanism* (Chicago 1939), p. 275.
107. Patrick Collinson, *The Elizabethan Puritan Movement* (London 1967), p. 73.
108. Strype, *Life of Grindal* (London 1821), p. 574.
109. Knappen, *op. cit.*, p. 235.
110. *Court of King James I.*
111. *Nugae Antiquae*, I, pp. 217–20.
112. M.Maclure, *The Paul's Cross Sermons, 1534–1642* (Toronto 1958), pp. 13–14.
113. Quoted by Christopher Hill, *Society and Puritanism in pre-Revolutionary England* (London 1964).
114. P.Heylyn, *Cyprianus Anglicus* (1671).
115. W.Nicholson, *The Remains of Edmund Grindal* (Parker Society, 1843), pp. 372–5.
116. *Ibid.*, pp. 381–90.
117. Quoted Collinson, *op. cit.*, p. 200.
118. Cruickshank, *op. cit.*, pp. 71–3.
119. *HMC Bath MSS*, II, p. 26.
120. Read, *Burghley*, pp. 294ff.
121. Neale, *Parliaments*, II, pp. 273–4.
122. Patrick Collinson, 'John Field and Elizabethan Puritanism', in *Elizabethan Government and Society*, pp. 127–62.
123. Neale, *Parliaments*, II, p. 218.
124. Collinson in *Elizabethan Government*.
125. For the parliamentary struggles, see Neale, *Parliaments*, I, pp. 165–9, 191–217, 291–304, 349–52, 398–406; II, pp. 58–71, 145–65, 216–32.
126. Christopher Hill, *Economic Problems of the Church* (London 1968 edn), pp. 14ff.
127. A.Peel (ed.), *The Notebooks of John Penry* (Camden Society, 1944), pp. 85ff.
128. Quoted Collinson, *Elizabethan Puritan Movement*, p. 206.
129. SP Dom., Eliz., 176/68; quoted extensively in Neale, *Parliaments*, II, pp. 251–66.
130. Wright, *op. cit.*, II, p. 417.
131. Chief texts printed in Edward Arber, *An Introductory Sketch to the Martin Marprelate Controversy* (London 1895) and in William Pierce, *Historical Introduction to the Marprelate Tracts* (London 1909).
132. *Fragmenta Regalia*, p. 37.
133. For the Wentworth affair, see Neale, *Parliaments*, II, pp. 251–66, and 'Peter Wentworth', *EHR*, 39 (1924).
134. Neale, *Parliaments*, II, p. 276.
135. Paul E. Seaver, *The Puritan Lectureships: the Politics of Religious Dissent, 1560–1662* (Oxford 1970).
136. Neale, *Parliaments*, II, pp. 58–9.

137. A.F.S. Pearson, *Thomas Cartwright and Elizabethan Puritanism* (Cambridge 1925), pp. 90ff.

138. Chambers, *Elizabethan Stage*, I, pp. 269–307.

139. Rowse, *Shakespeare the Man* (London 1973), pp. 106–7.

140. Wickham, *Early English Stages*, III, pp. 9ff.

141. Clare Williams (trans), *Thomas Platter's Travels in England 1599* (London 1937), pp. 166–7.

142. N. Williams, *Sir Walter Ralegh* (London 1965 edn), pp. 133–4.

143. Ellis, *Original Letters*, 2nd Series, III, p. 246; Handover, *op. cit.*, Chapter 2.

144. Quoted Handover, *op. cit.*, p. 69.

145. *CSP Dom.*, Addenda, 1586–1625, 241.

146. Handover, *op. cit.*, p. 83.

147. Anthony Standen to Anthony Bacon: Thomas Birch, *Memoirs of the Reign of Queen Elizabeth* (2 vols, London 1754).

148. Rowland Whyte to Sir Robert Sidney; *Sidney Papers*, II, p. 25.

149. For Essex and his father, see Devereux, *op. cit.*; the most recent life of the 2nd Earl is Robert Lacey, *Robert, Earl of Essex: an Elizabethan Icarus* (London 1971).

150. Devereux, *op. cit.*, I, p. 185.

151. For Essex's finances, see Lacey, *op. cit.*, Chapter 10.

152. Devereux, *op. cit.*, I, p. 206.

153. Spedding, *Letters and Life of Francis Bacon*, I, p. 289.

154. July 1592; Murdin, *op. cit.*, II, p. 655.

155. SP Dom. 12/249/3; quoted in Handover, *op. cit.*

156. For the Lopez Case, see *CSP Dom.*, 1591–4, 390–1, 394, 411–14, 422; Birch, *op. cit.*, I, pp. 150–60.

157. Birch, *op. cit.*, I, pp. 152–3.

158. Lacey, *op. cit.*, pp. 171–2.

159. L.W. Henry, 'The Earl of Essex as Strategist', *EHR*, 68 (July 1958).

160. Donne, 'A Burnt Ship'; Sir Herbert Grierson (ed.), *The Poems of John Donne* (Oxford 1951 edn), p. 67.

161. For the Cadiz expedition, see W. Ralegh (ed.), *Hakluyt's Principal Navigations* (London 1903–5); W. Harrison, *A Historical Description etc.* (London 1908 edn); Rowse, *Expansion*, pp. 304–12; Cruikshank, *op. cit.*, pp. 251–79.

162. For the Islands Voyage, Hakluyt, *op. cit.*; Rowse, *Expansion*, pp. 313–18.

163. Read, *Burghley*, pp. 544–5; Birch, *op. cit.*, II, p. 384; Camden, *Elizabeth*, pp. 711–17.

164. Devereux, *op. cit.*, I, p. 493; Camden, *Elizabeth*, p. 718.

165. Roy Strong, 'The Popular Celebration of the Accession Day of Queen Elizabeth I', *Journal of the Courtauld and Warburg Institutes*, XXI, and Frances A. Yates, 'Elizabethan Chivalry: the Romance of the Accession Day Tilts', *ibid.*, XX (1947).

166. *HMC De L'Isle MSS.*, II, p. 187.
167. G.B.Harrison and R.A.Jones (trans.), *André Herault, Sieur de Maisse: Journal 1597* (London 1931).
168. Read, *Burghley*, p. 522.
169. *Ibid.*, p. 545.

CHAPTER II: THE PUBLIC BURDEN OF A NATION'S CARE

1. For Elizabethan Ireland, see Fynes Moryson, *An Itinerary concerning his Ten years' travel, etc.* (Glasgow 1907-8 edn); Richard Bagwell, *Ireland Under the Tudors* (3 vols, London 1885-90); Rowse, *Expansion of Elizabethan England*, Chapters 3, 4 and 11.
2. Matthew Prior (1664-1721), *Solomon*, Book III, line 276.
3. Quoted by Rowse, *op. cit.*
4. Smith to Burghley, 6 March 1574; Wright, *op. cit.*, II.
5. Spedding, *Life and Times of Sir Francis Bacon*, VI, p. 207.
6. Edmund Spenser, *A View of the State of Ireland in 1596*, printed in W.L.Renwick (ed.), *Complete Works of Spenser* (London 1934), IV.
7. *HMC Salisbury MSS.*, X, 18.
8. Edwards, *Ralegh*, I, p. 105.
9. Quoted by Black, *op. cit.*, pp. 473-4.
10. Collins, *Sidney Papers*, I, pp. 24-5.
11. Rowse, *op. cit.*, p. 121.
12. Quoted by Black, *op. cit.*, p. 487.
13. See R.Dudley Edwards, 'Ireland, Elizabeth and the Counter-Reformation', in *Elizabethan Government and Society*, pp. 315-39.
14. Edwards, *Ralegh*, II, pp. 4-5.
15. Collins, *Sidney Papers*, I, p. 23.
16. Sir John Davies, *Discovery of the True Causes why Ireland was never Entirely Subdued*, printed in H.Morley (ed.), *Ireland under Elizabeth and James I* (London 1890).
17. Quoted by Rowse, *op. cit.*, p. 147.
18. For Tyrone's military organization, see Cyril Falls, *Elizabeth's Irish Wars* (London 1950).
19. J.S.Brewer and William Bullen (eds), *Calendar of the Carew MSS.* (London 1867-73), 1589-1600, p. 315.
20. Quoted by Falls, *op. cit.*, p. 222.
21. Moryson, *op. cit.*, III, p. 225.
22. J.Maclean (ed.), *Letters from Sir Robert Cecil to Sir George Carew* (Camden Society, 88, 1864), p. 148.
23. R.H.Tawney and Eileen Power, *Tudor Economic Documents* (3 vols, London 1924).

24. For the agricultural crisis of the 1590s, see Cheyney, *op. cit.*, II, Chapter 1; Peter H.Ramsey, *Tudor Economic Problems* (London 1963), pp. 27–47; R.B.Outhwaite, *Inflation in Tudor and Early Stuart England* (London 1969); Joan Thirsk, *Agrarian History of England and Wales* (Cambridge 1967), IV, 1500–1640; W.G.Hoskins, 'Harvest Fluctuations and English Economic History, 1480–1619', *AHR*, XII (1965), pp. 28–46.

25. *APC*, XXV, pp. 153, 206; XXVI, pp. 81, 113, 380.

26. *Ibid.*, XXV, p. 8.

27. e.g. I Edward III, st. 2, c. 5; 4 Henry IV, c. 13.

28. For the Smythe affair, see Cruikshank, *op. cit.*, pp. 10–15.

29. Strype, *Annals*, IV, pp. 404–12.

30. *CSP Ireland*, 1600–1, ix.

31. Moryson, *op. cit.*, IV, p. 191; Cyril Falls, 'The Elizabethan Soldier in Ireland', *History Today* (1951).

32. *Carew MSS.*, 1589–1600, p. 466.

33. *CSP Ireland*, 1600–1, ix.

34. Moryson, *op. cit.*, II, pp. 262ff.; Moryson was Mountjoy's secretary.

35. *APC*, 1598–9, p. 215.

36. *CSP Ireland*, 1596–7, 172.

37. *Henry IV, Part Two*, Act II, scene iv.

38. *Henry IV, Part One*, Act IV, scene ii.

39. Sarah Williams (ed.), *Letters of John Chamberlain* (Camden Society, 79, 1861).

40. For the commissariat scandals, see Cruickshank, *op. cit.*, pp. 98–101.

41. Birch, *op. cit.*, II, p. 506.

42. *Chamberlain*, 30 August 1598.

43. Spedding, *op. cit.*, III, p. 146.

44. *Chamberlain*; the occasion was Twelfth Night.

45. Edwards, *op. cit.*, II, pp. 198–9.

46. Collins, *Sidney Papers*, II, pp. 94, 96.

47. Devereux, *op. cit.*, II, pp. 3–5.

48. *HMC Salisbury MSS.*, IX, 6.

49. Devereux, *op. cit.*, II, pp. 40–1.

50. Handover, *op. cit.*, p. 183.

51. Black makes great play with this in *op. cit.*, p. 430 and n. 1.

52. Rowse, *Shakespeare's Southampton*, Chapter 7.

53. Birch, *op. cit.*, I, p. 143.

54. *HMC Salisbury MSS.*, XI, 94; Rowse, *Elizabethan Renaissance*, I, p. 162.

55. *Sidney Papers*, II, p. 82.

56. *HMC Salisbury MSS.*, X, 262.

57. G.P.V.Akrigg, *Shakespeare and the Earl of Southampton* (London 1968).

58. *CSP Ireland*, 1599–1600, pp. 100–1.

59. *Chamberlain*, 23 August 1599.
60. For a defence of Essex's strategy, see Black, *op. cit.*, pp. 431ff.
61. *CSP Ireland*, 1599–1600, pp. 129–31.
62. *Ibid.*, p. 124.
63. Quoted by Black, *op. cit.*, p. 435.
64. *Chamberlain*, 28 June 1599.
65. Harrison, *Letters of Queen Elizabeth I*, pp. 264–8.
66. Black, *op. cit.*, pp. 433–4.
67. Harrison, *Letters*, pp. 270–4.
68. *Ibid.*, pp. 274–6.
69. *Sidney Papers*; *CSP Ireland*, IV, 150; G.B.Harrison, *Robert Devereux, Earl of Essex* (London 1937), pp. 227–50.
70. Whyte to Robert Sidney, *Sidney Papers*, II, p. 129.
71. Essex to Egerton, 18 October 1598, printed in Birch, *op. cit.*, II, pp. 386–8.
72. Quoted by Lacey, *op. cit.*, p. 259.
73. For the financial position of the rebels, see Lacey, *op. cit.*, Chapter 28.
74. Neale, *The Elizabethan House of Commons*, pp. 229–31.
75. H.H.Spink, *The Gunpowder Plot and Lord Monteagle's Letter* (London 1902).
76. Lacey, *op. cit.*, p. 282.
77. Handover, *op. cit.*, p. 221.
78. Rowse, *Ralegh and the Throckmortons*, p. 220.
79. Cecil to Sir George Carew, 10 February 1601; Birch, *op. cit.*, II, pp. 468–9.
80. For the proceedings, see David Jardine, *Criminal Trials* (London 1832).
81. Chamberlain to Dudley Carleton, 24 February 1601; *CSP Domestic*, 1598–1601, 590.
82. *The State of England, Anno Domini 1600*.
83. Jardine, *op. cit.*
84. Chamberlain to Carleton, 24 February 1601.
85. *CSP Domestic*, 1598–1601, 588.
86. *HMC Salisbury MSS.*, XIV, 193.
87. Ballad, written in 1601; PRO SP Dom., 12/278/23.
88. *CSP Domestic*, 1598–1601, 591.
89. *The Secret History of the Most Renowned Queen Elizabeth and the Earl of Essex*. By a Person of Quality (London 1695).
90. *Letters of Cecil to Carew*, p. 139.
91. *Nugae Antiquae*, II, p. 215.
92. Harrison, *Letters*, pp. 221–4, 226–30, 329–40, 257–9, 278–9, 287–8, 292, 295–6; see also John Bruce (ed.), *Letters of Queen Elizabeth and James VI of Scotland* (Camden Society, 46, 1849).

93. *Nugae Antiquae*, I, p. 321.
94. Lord Hales (ed.), *Secret Correspondence of Sir Robert Cecil and James I* (Edinburgh 1766), p. 62; Joel Hurstfield, 'The Succession Struggle in late Elizabethan England', in *Elizabethan Government and Society.*
95. D.H.Willson, *King James VI and I* (New York 1956), p. 111.
96. Handover, *op. cit.*, pp. 238–9.
97. A.G.R.Smith, 'The Secretariats of the Cecils, 1580–1612', *EHR*, July 1968.
98. *Sidney Papers*, II, p. 362.
99. Neale, *Parliaments*, II, pp. 370–1.
100. Hayward Townshend, *Historical Collections* (London 1680); A.F.Pollard, 'Hayward Townshend's Journals', *BIHR*, XIII (1935), pp. 9–34, and *ibid.*, XIV (1937), pp. 149–65, XV (1937), pp. 1–18.
101. *Townshend*, p. 179.
102. Read, *Burghley*, p. 527; Woodward, *op. cit.*, pp. 40ff.
103. Neale, *Parliaments*, II, pp. 417ff.
104. *HMC Salisbury MSS.*, XI, 234–5.
105. For the monopolies debates, see Neale, *Parliaments*, II, pp. 376–93.
106. *Ibid.*, p. 384.
107. *Ibid.*, p. 380.
108. *Ibid.*, pp. 388–91.
109. For co-operation between government and MPs over the 1563 statute, see S.T.Bindoff, 'The Making of the Statute of Artificers', in *Elizabethan Government and Society*, pp. 56–94.
110. W.K.Jordan, *Philanthropy in England, 1480–1660* (London 1959).
111. For Cromwell's social welfare policy, see G.R.Elton, *Reform and Renewal: Thomas Cromwell and the Common Weal* (Cambridge 1973), pp. 98ff. For late-Elizabethan social legislation, see Neale, Parliaments, II, pp. 333–51.
112. Neale, *Parliaments*, II, p. 424.
113. *Ibid.*, pp. 428–31.
114. For Mountjoy, see Cyril Falls, *Mountjoy: Elizabethan General* (London 1955).
115. *Moryson*, II, p. 268.
116. *Letters of Cecil to Carew*, p. 148.
117. *Moryson*, II, p. 449.
118. Falls, *Elizabeth's Irish Wars*, p. 298.
119. *Moryson*, II, p. 454.
120. Harrison, *Letters*, p. 288.
121. *Moryson*, III, pp. 189–90.
122. For Elizabeth's two letters to Mountjoy, and Cecil's letters, see Harrison, *Letters*, pp. 296–301.

CHAPTER 12: IN OUR BLESSED QUEEN'S TIME

1. C.H.Firth, 'The Ballad History of the Late Tudors', *TRHS*, 3rd Series, III (1909).
2. Fénelon, 27 July 1569 and 29 June 1570; De Spes, 1 July 1570; references in Chamberlain, *Private Character of Queen Elizabeth*.
3. Read, *Burghley*, p. 182; *HMC Salisbury MSS.*, II, 157, 159.
4. For an example of the drastic treatment prescribed, see the case of Lady Throckmorton, wife of Sir Arthur Throckmorton, quoted by Baldwin Smith, *Elizabethan Epic*, pp. 235–6.
5. Burghley to Cecil, 21 May 1593; Wright, *op. cit.*, II, p. 426.
6. *HMC De L'Isle MSS.*, II, 265, 322.
7. Lady Frances Buckley, *Three Men of the Tudor Time*, quoted by Dunlop, *Palaces and Progresses*.
8. John Strype, *Historical Collections of . . . John Aylmer* (Oxford 1829); Brooks, *Hatton*, pp. 131–2.
9. Quoted Chamberlain, *op. cit.*
10. *CSP Domestic*, 1598–1601, 252.
11. *Ibid.*, 94.
12. *Sidney Papers*, 29 August 1599.
13. Quoted Chamberlain, *op. cit.*
14. *Sidney Papers*, II, p. 211.
15. P.Chambers, *The History of Hunting*, p. 287.
16. *Sidney Papers*, II, p. 194.
17. C.L.Kingsford, 'Paris Garden and the Bear-Baiting', *Archaeologia*, pp. 70, 155ff.
18. Chambers, *Elizabethan Stage*, I, p. 214.
19. Nichols, *Progresses*, III.
20. *Nugae Antiquae*, I, pp. 40–1.
21. *HMC De L'Isle MSS.*, III, pp. 531–4.
22. Nichols, *Progresses*, III, pp. 552–4.
23. *Ibid.*, I, xxxvii.
24. 9 October 1601; *Nugae Antiquae*, I, pp. 46–7.
25. Nichols, *Progresses*, I, p. xxxii.
26. *Letters of John Chamberlain*, 2 October 1602.
27. Lodge, *op. cit.*, II, p. 368.
28. Laffleur de Kermaingant, *L'Ambassade de France en Angleterre sous Henri IV* (4 vols, Paris 1886–95), I, p. 415; Chambers, 'The Court', in *Shakespeare's England*.
29. Nichols, *Progresses*, III, p. 577.
30. Quoted by Chamberlain in *Private Character*.
31. Lodge, *op. cit.*, II, p. 582.

32. *Letters of John Chamberlain*, 19 November 1602.

33. *Manningham's Diary*, 6 December.

34. *HMC Salisbury MSS.*, XII, 438 (Greville to Cecil, 12 October); 445 (Sidney to Cecil, 16 October).

35. *Ibid.*, XII, 448.

36. *CSP Domestic, 1601–3*, 154–5.

37. Birch, *op. cit.*, II, p. 506.

38. *CSP Venetian, 1592–1603*, 531–3, 565.

39. *Manningham's Diary*, 3 April 1603.

40. Goodman, *Court of King James I*, pp. 16–17.

41. De Beaumont's letters on the last days of Elizabeth are quoted in Birch, *op. cit.*, II, and printed in De Kermaingant, *L'Ambassade de France*.

42. Sir W.Scott (ed.), *Memoirs of the Life of Robert Carey, Written by Himself* (Edinburgh 1808).

43. *HMC 7th Report*, 528; *HMC Salisbury MSS.*, XII, 667.

44. BM Cotton MSS., Titus C vii, 57; Handover, *op. cit.*, pp. 295–6.

45. *Manningham's Diary*, 23 March.

46. *Ibid.*

47. *Ibid.*, 24 March.

48. Sir John Neale analyses, and dismisses, the rumours in 'Sayings of Queen Elizabeth', *History* (October 1925).

49. *Clapham*, p. 110.

50. Handover, *op. cit.*, pp. 291–2.

51. Wright, *op. cit.*, II, p. 494.

52. Henry Chettle, *The Order and Proceeding at the Funerale of . . . Elizabeth* (London 1603), reprinted in *Somers Tracts*, I, pp. 248–50; Nichols, *Progresses*, III, pp. 621–6.

53. Stow, *Chronicle*.

54. Strong, *Portraits of Queen Elizabeth I*, pp. 153–4; *Westminster Abbey Official Guide* (1971 edn), p. 74.

55. *Nugae Antiquae*, II, pp. 263–5.

56. Goodman, *Court of King James I*.

57. *English Works of Roger Ascham* (London 1904), p. 286.

58. Ralegh, *Works*, VIII, 'Instructions to His Son', pp. 557ff.

Select Bibliography

Place of publication is London unless otherwise indicated.

PRINTED SOURCES

For home affairs, *Calendar of State Papers, Domestic*, ed. Robert Lemon and
M.A.E.Green (12 vols, 1856–72). For foreign affairs, *Calendar of State Papers,
Foreign*, ed. W.B.Turnbull, etc. (23 vols, 1863–1950); *State Papers, Foreign Series,
Elizabeth I, 1589–90*, ed. R.B.Wernham (1964); *Calendar of State Papers, Ireland*,
ed. H.C.Hamilton and R.P.Mahaffy (11 vols, 1860–1912); *Calendar of State
Papers, Scotland*, ed. Joseph Bain, etc. (12 vols, Edinburgh and Glasgow 1898–
1952); *Calendar of State Papers, Spanish, Elizabethan*, ed. M.A.S.Hume (4 vols,
1892–9); *Relations politique des Pays-Bas et de l'Angleterre sous le règne de
Philippe II*, ed. Kervyn de Lettenhove, etc. (11 vols, Brussels, 1882–1900). Of the
Historical Manuscripts Commission reports, the most important is *Calendar of
the MSS. of the Marquess of Salisbury ... preserved at Hatfield House* (18 vols,
1883–1940), referred to as *IIMC Salisbury MSS.*, or *HMC Hatfield MSS.*;
see also *Collection of State Papers ... left by William Cecil, Lord Burghley*, ed.
Samuel Haynes and William Murdin (2 vols, 1740–59). Other state, and private,
papers are published in Henry Ellis (ed.), *Original Letters* (11 vols, in 3 series,
1824–46); the *Cabala, sive scrinia sacra* (2 parts, 1691); Thomas Wright (ed),
Queen Elizabeth and Her Times (2 vols, 1838); Francis Peck (ed.), *Desiderata
Curiosa* (2 vols, 1732–5); Dudley Digges (ed.), *The Compleat Ambassador*
(1655), which includes some of Walsingham's correspondence; Arthur
Collins (ed.), *Letters and Memorials of State* (2 vols, 1746), usually known as the
Sidney Papers; Thomas Birch (ed.), *Memoirs of the Reign of Queen Elizabeth*
(2 vols, 1754); E.Lodge (ed.), *Illustrations of British History* (3 vols, 1838); John
Strype (ed.), *Annals of the Reformation* (4 vols, Oxford 1820–40); Philip Yorke
(ed.), *Miscellaneous State Papers* (2 vols, 1778), usually known as the *Hardwicke
Papers*; and Henry Harington (ed.), *Nugae Antiquae* (3 vols, 1779), which contains Sir John Harington's papers. Some of Elizabeth's letters (including palpable
forgeries) are printed in G.B.Harrison (ed.), *Letters of Queen Elizabeth* (new
edition, 1968), and in F.A.Mumby (ed.), *The Girlhood of Queen Elizabeth* (1909).
A great deal of material concerning Elizabeth is published in John Nichols (ed.),
The Progresses and Public Processions of Queen Elizabeth (3 vols, 1823). Other
valuable material is in John Boyle (ed.), *Memoirs of the Life of Robert Carey*
(1759); N.E.McClure (ed.), *Letters of John Chamberlain* (Philadelphia 1939);
J.P.Collier (ed.), *The Egerton Papers* (Camden Society, 1840); John Bruce (ed.),

The Diary of John Manningham (Camden Society, 1868); and in the *Bedingfeld Papers* (Norfolk Archaeological Society, iv, 1855); Of the early biographical accounts of Queen Elizabeth, the most useful are: William Camden, *The historie of the most renowned and virtuous Princess Elizabeth, late queen of England* (1630); Francis Bacon's sketch in Vol. 11 of his *Collected Works*, ed. J.Spedding, R.L.Ellis and D.D.Heath (14 vols, 1857–74); E.P.Read and Conyers Read (eds.), *John Clapham's Elizabeth of England* (Philadelphia 1951); and in Edward Arber (ed.), *Sir Robert Naunton's Fragmenta Regalia* (1895). The most useful chronicles, besides William Camden, are Raphael Holinshed, *Chronicles* (ed. Henry Ellis, 6 vols, 1807–8); John Stow, *Chronicles* (1605); and John Hayward, *Annals of the first four years of the reign of Elizabeth* (ed. John Bruce, Camden Society, 1840). General descriptions of Elizabeth's England include: William Harrison, *An historical description etc.* (part-edition in 4 vols, 1908); and Thomas Wilson, *The State of England Anno Domino 1600* (ed. F.J.Fisher, Camden Miscellany 1936). Constitutional documents are published in G.R.Elton (ed.), *The Tudor Constitution: Documents and Commentary* (Cambridge 1968); economic documents in R.H.Tawney and Eileen Powers (eds), *Tudor Economic Documents* (3 vols, 1924); and state proclamations in P.L.Hughes and J.F.Larkin (eds.), *Tudor Royal Proclamations* (3 vols, Yale 1964–9). For a short but excellent general collection of extracts, see Joel Hurstfield and A.G.R.Smith, *Elizabethan People, State and Society* (1972).

SECONDARY WORKS

GENERAL. J.B.Black's *Reign of Elizabeth 1558–1603* (Oxford 1959, 2nd edn) is still useful, and particularly good on Anglo-Scottish relations; also still useful are A.F.Pollard, *Political History of England, 1547–1603* (3rd impr. 1915); J.A.Froude, *History of England from the Fall of Wolsey to the Defeat of the Spanish Armada* (12 vols, 1904), and its continuation, E.P.Cheyney, *History of England from the defeat of the Armada to the death of Elizabeth* (2 vols, New York 1914–26). Good modern surveys include: G.R.Elton, *England Under the Tudors* (Cambridge 1969 impr.), and S.T.Bindoff, *Tudor England* (Penguin 1969 impr.), which is excellent on the economic side.

BIOGRAPHIES OF ELIZABETH. The standard work is J.E.Neale, *Queen Elizabeth*, first published in 1934; but it does not give references and should be supplemented by B.W.Beckinsale, *Elizabeth I* (1963). Of recent biographies, Joel Hurstfield, *Elizabeth I and the Unity of England* (1960) is brief but excellent on politics and foreign policy; Neville Williams, *Elizabeth, Queen of England* (1967) is good on the personal side. Of the older biographies, the best is Mandell Creighton, *Queen Elizabeth*, first published in 1896, but it has no references or index. Roy Strong, *Portraits of Queen Elizabeth I* (Oxford 1963) is the standard work on her iconography, and A.S.MacNulty, *Elizabeth Tudor* (1954) on her health.

THE POLITICAL SCENE. For parliament, J.E.Neale, *Elizabeth I and her Parliaments*, *Vol. I 1559–81*, *Vol. II 1584–1601* (1949–57), and *The Elizabethan House of Commons* (1949) are indispensable. Neale's more important monographs are reprinted in *Essays in Elizabethan History* (1959), and there are a number of valuable studies in S.T.Bindoff, J.Hurstfield and C.H.Williams (eds.), *Essays Presented to Sir John Neale* (1961). The Queen's early years as monarch are covered in detail in Wallace T.MacCaffrey, *The Shaping of the Elizabethan Regime* (Princeton 1968); and in Mortimer Levine, *The Early Elizabethan Succession Question, 1558–68* (Stanford 1966). The later succession question is dealt with in Helen G.Stafford, *James VI of Scotland and the Throne of England* (New York 1940), and J.Hurstfield's essay, 'The Succession Struggle in Late Elizabethan England' in *Neale Essays*. The best short introduction to Elizabethan government is A.G.R.Smith, *The Government of Elizabethan England* (1967); more detailed studies include, J.Hurstfield, *The Queen's Wards* (1958); W.J. Jones, *The Elizabethan Court of Chancery* (Oxford 1967); F.C.Dietz, *English Public Finance, 1558–1641* (New York 1932), and *The Exchequer in Elizabeth's Reign* (Smith College Studies, viii, 2, 1923); Rachel R.Reid, *The King's Council in the North* (1921); F.W.Brooks, *The Council of the North* (1953); Penry H. Williams, *The Council in the Marches of Wales under Elizabeth I* (Cardiff 1958); and J.H.Gleason, *The Justices of the Peace in England, 1558–1640* (Oxford 1969). For the struggle for place and patronage, see W.T.MacCaffrey's account in *Neale Essays*; Lawrence Stone, *The Crisis of the Aristocracy* (Oxford 1965), supplemented by his *Family and Fortune: Studies in Aristocratic Finance in the 16th and 17th Centuries* (Oxford 1973); some of the contributions to the controversy Stone's work aroused are reprinted in *Social Change and Revolution in England 1540–1640* (1970) and others listed in G.R.Elton, *Modern Historians on British History 1485–1945* (1970), p. 44, n. 259; A.G.R.Smith, 'The Secretariats of the Cecils', *EHR*, 83 (1968); and various essays reprinted in J.Hurstfield, *Freedom, Corruption and Government in Elizabethan England* (1973).

DIPLOMACY AND WAR. A useful introduction is R.B.Wernham, *Before the Armada: the Growth of English Foreign Policy 1485–1588* (1966); there is valuable background material in Garrett Mattingly, *Renaissance Diplomacy* (1955), and a good general survey of Elizabeth's Europe in L.Baldwin Smith, *Elizabethan Epic* (1966). The diplomatic history of the reign (up to 1598) is exhaustively covered in the work of Conyers Read, especially his *Mr Secretary Walsingham and the Policy of Queen Elizabeth* (3 vols, Oxford 1925), *Mr Secretary Cecil and Queen Elizabeth* (1955), and *Lord Burghley and Queen Elizabeth* (1960). Read's notes, as well as his texts, are extremely valuable. Other diplomatic studies include: C.Wilson, *Queen Elizabeth and the Revolt in the Netherlands* (1970) and A.C.Miller, *Sir Henry Killigrew: Elizabethan Soldier and Diplomat* (Leicester 1963). For war policy, R.B.Wernham, 'Elizabethan War Aims and Strategy', in *Neale Essays*. The best account of the Armada episode is Garrett Mattingly, *The Defeat of the Spanish Armada* (1959). For the navy: M.Oppenheim, *A History of the Administration of the Royal Navy, 1509–1660* (1896); J.S.Corbett, *Drake and the Tudor Navy* (2 vols, 1898–9) and *The Successors of Drake, 1596–1603* (1900); for freelance naval activities, K.R.Andrews, *Elizabethan Privateering ... during the Spanish War, 1585–1603* (Cambridge 1964). See also Michael Lewis, *Armada Guns* (1961). For the army: C.G.Cruikshank, *Elizabeth's Army* (2nd edn, Oxford 1966), and Cyril Falls, *Elizabeth's Irish Wars* (1950). The best general survey of exploration and warfare under Elizabeth is A.L.Rowse, *The Expansion of Elizabethan England* (1955), which also deals with Scotland, Wales and Ireland. For military organization and theory: H.J.Webb, *Elizabethan Military Science* (Wisconsin 1965), and Lindsay Boynton, *The Elizabethan Militia* (1967).

RELIGION. The best account of the 1559 settlement is in Neale, *Parliaments*, I, Part One (see above); see also: C.S.Meyer, *Elizabeth I and the Religious Settlement of 1559* (St Louis 1960). For vestments, see J.H.Primus, *The Vestments Controversy* (Kampen 1960); for sermons, Millar Maclure, *The St Paul's Cross Sermons, 1534–1642* (Toronto 1958); for social-religious problems, Christopher Hill, *Economic Problems of the Church* (Oxford 1956) and *Society and Puritanism in pre-Revolutionary England* (1964). For the Anglican position: R.G.Usher, *The Reconstruction of the English Church* (2 vols, New York 1910) and *The Rise and Fall of the High Commission* (Oxford 1913); E.T.Davies, *Episcopacy and the Royal Supremacy;* Claire Cross, *The Royal Supremacy in the Elizabethan Church* (1969); J.E.Booty, *John Jewel as Apologist of the Church of England* (1963); W.M.Southgate, *John Jewel and the Problem of Doctrinal Authority* (Harvard 1962); P.M.Dawley, *John Whitgift and the English Reformation* (New York 1954); and L.Baldwin Smith, *Tudor Prelates and Politics* (Princeton 1953). For Catholicism under Elizabeth, the standard work is A.O. Mayer, *England and the Catholic Church under Queen Elizabeth* (trans. 1916); Philip Hughes, *The Reformation in England* (3 vols, 1951–4) gives a general history from a Catholic viewpoint; W.R.Trimble, *The Catholic Laity in Elizabethan England* (Cambridge, Mass. 1964); J.A.Bossy, 'The Character of Elizabethan Catholicism', *Past and Present*, 21 (1962) is the most penetrating recent study of the subject. Patrick McGrath, *Papists and Puritans under Elizabeth I* (1967) deals with both extremes of the religious spectrum. On Puritanism the standard work is Patrick Collinson, *The Elizabethan Puritan Movement* (1967), supplemented by his study of John Field in *Neale Essays*. See also: J.H.F.New, *Anglican and Puritan: the Basis of their Opposition, 1558–1640* (Stanford 1964);

D.J.McGinn, *John Penry and the Marprelate Controversy* (New Jersey 1966); H.C.Porter, *Reformation and Reaction in Tudor Cambridge* (Cambridge 1958); and Irvonwy Morgan, *The Godly Preachers of the Elizabethan Church* (1965). For the influence of Foxe, see W.Haller, *Foxe's 'Book of Martyrs' and the Elect Nation* (1963), and for toleration, W.K.Jordan, *The Development of Religious Toleration in England* (Cambridge, Mass. 1932).

SOCIAL AND ECONOMIC. The best general survey is A.L.Rowse, *The England of Elizabeth* (1950), supplemented by his *The Elizabethan Renaissance: the Life of the Society* (1971). See also: A.H.Dodd, *Life in Elizabethan England* (1961) and Penry Williams, *Life in Tudor England* (1964). Studies of special subjects include: Mildred Camden, *The English Yeoman under Elizabeth and the Early Stuarts* (New Haven 1942); Carroll Camden, *The Elizabethan Woman* (1952); L.E. Pearson, *Elizabethans at Home* (Stanford 1957); W.K.Jordan, *Philanthropy in England, 1480–1660* (New York 1959); and Frank Aydelotte, *Elizabethan Rogues and Vagabonds* (Oxford 1913). On the economy: E.Lipson, *Economic History of England*, Vol. 3 (1956 edn); Eric Kerridge, *Agrarian Problems in the 16th Century and After* (1969); Joan Thirsk, *Tudor Enclosures* (1959), and the volume edited by her in the *Agrarian History of England and Wales: IV 1500–1640* (Cambridge 1967); P.H.Ramsey, *Tudor Economic Problems* (1963); R.B.Outhwaite, *Inflation in Tudor and Early Stuart England* (1969); and M.B.Donald, *Elizabethan Monopolies* (1961). There is distressingly little material on Elizabeth's crown lands, apart from references in the *Agrarian History* (above), but B.P.Wolfe, *The Crown Lands: an Aspect of Yorkist and Early Tudor Government* (1970) is helpful.

INTELLECTUAL AND CULTURAL. On scientific subjects: E.G.R.Taylor, *The Mathematical Practitioners of Tudor and Stuart England* (Cambridge 1954); W.P.D.Wightman, *Science and the Renaissance* (Vol. 1, 1962); A.R.Hall, *The Scientific Revolution, 1500–1800* (Boston 1956, 2nd edn); P.H.Kocher, *Science and Religion in Elizabethan England* (San Marino 1953); and Miss Taylor's two studies, *Tudor Geography, 1485–1583* (1930) and *Later Tudor and Early Stuart Geography, 1583–1650* (1934). On learning: Joan Simon, *Education and Society in Tudor England* (Cambridge 1966); H.S.Bennett, *English Books and Readers, 1475–1603* (2 vols, Cambridge 1952–65); G.E.Dawson and Laetitia Kennedy-Skipton, *Elizabethan Handwriting* (1968); and E.J.Dobson, *English Pronunciation, 1500–1700* (2 vols, Oxford 1957). On the drama: E.K.Chambers, *The Elizabethan Stage* (4 vols, Oxford 1923) is the standard work, and also contains much information about the court; but must be supplemented by Glynn Wickham, *Early English Stages* (2 vols, 1959–63) and by D.Berrington, *Tudor Drama and Politics* (Harvard 1968). Non-dramatic literature is surveyed by C.S.Lewis in *Oxford History of English Literature*, Vol. III (1954), supplemented by Emile Legouis and Louis Cazamian, *History of English Literature* (1948), important for initial dates of publication. See also, John Buxton, *Sir Philip Sidney and the English Renaissance* (1954) and his admirable *Elizabethan Taste* (1963). On the fine arts, John Summerson, *Architecture in Britain, 1530–1830* (1953); Thomas Garner and Arthur Stratton, *The Domestic Architecture of England during the Tudor Period* (2 vols, 1929); Ellis Waterhouse, *Painting in Britain, 1530–1790* (1953); Erna Auerbach, *Tudor Artists* (1954); Margaret Whinney, *Sculpture in Britain, 1530–1830* (1964); W.L.Woodfill, *Musicians in English Society from Elizabeth to Charles I* (Princeton 1953); M.C.Boyd, *Elizabethan Music and Music Criticism* (Philadelphia 1962, 2nd edn); and E.H.Fellowes, *The English Madrigal Composers* (1921).

BIOGRAPHIES. Among the most useful biographies of prominent Elizabethans are: S.E.Lehmberg, *Sir Walter Mildmay and Tudor Government* (Texas 1964); W.Dunkel, *William Lambarde, Elizabethan Jurist* (New Jersey 1965); E.St-J. Brooks, *Sir Christopher Hatton* (1946); Neville Williams, *Thomas Howard, 4th Duke of Norfolk* (1964); Mary Dewar, *Sir Thomas Smith* (1964); N.H. Nicolas, *Life of William Davison* (1823); Claire Cross, *The Puritan Earl: Life of Henry Hastings, 3rd Earl of Huntingdon* (1966); Cyril Falls, *Mountjoy, Elizabeth's General* (1955); Lawrence Stone, *An Elizabethan: Sir Horatio Pallavicino* (Oxford 1956); P.J.French, *John Dee* (1972); L.V.Ryan, *Roger Ascham* (Stanford 1963); R.A.Rebholz, *The Life of Fulke Greville* (Oxford 1971); F.S.Boas, *Sir Philip Sidney* (1955). P.M.Handover, *The Second Cecil 1563–1604* (1959) is the best study of the younger Cecil; and B.W.Beckinsale, *Burghley, Tudor Statesman* (1967) supplements the volumes of Read (above). The best account of Bacon's career under Elizabeth is C.D.Bowen, *Francis Bacon: the temper of a man* (Boston 1963). For Essex, W.B.Devereux, *Lives and Letters of the Devereux, 1540–1646* (2 vols, 1853) and Robert Lacey, *Robert, Earl of Essex* (1971). For Ralegh, A.L.Rowse, *Ralegh and the Throckmortons* (1962); W.M. Wallace, *Sir Walter Ralegh* (Princeton 1959); N.L.Williams, *Sir Walter Ralegh* (1962); there is a valuable introduction to C.A.Patrides's edition of the *History of the World* (1971).

BIBLIOGRAPHIES. The most comprehensive is Conyers Read (ed.), *Bibliography of British History: Tudor Period 1485–1603* (Oxford 1959, 2nd edn), which lists 6,543 annotated items; this should be supplemented by Mortimer Levine, *Bibliographical Handbooks: Tudor England* (Cambridge 1968), and by Chapter 5 of G.R.Elton, *Modern Historians on British History 1485–1945* (1970). See also the chapters by L.Baldwin Smith and Perez Zagorin in E.C.Furber (ed.), *Changing Views on British History: essays in historical writing since 1939* (Cambridge, Mass. 1966), and the *Annual Bulletin of Historical Literature*.

Index